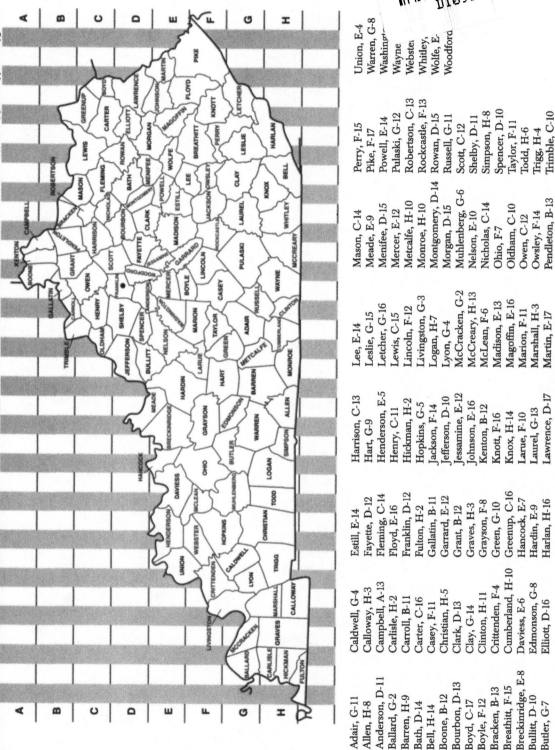

Adair, G-11
Allen, H-8
Anderson, D-11
Ballard, G-2
Barren, H-9
Bath, D-14
Bell, H-14
Boone, B-12
Bourbon, D-13
Boyd, C-17
Boyle, F-12
Bracken, B-13
Breathitt, F-15
Breckinridge, E-8
Bullitt, D-10
Butler, G-7

Caldwell, G-4
Calloway, H-3
Campbell, A-13
Carlisle, H-2
Carroll, B-11
Carter, C-16
Casey, F-11
Christian, H-5
Clark, D-13
Clay, G-14
Clinton, H-11
Crittenden, F-4
Cumberland, H-10
Daviess, E-6
Edmonson, G-8
Elliott, D-16

Estill, E-14
Fayette, D-12
Fleming, C-14
Floyd, E-16
Franklin, D-12
Fulton, H-2
Gallatin, B-11
Garrard, E-12
Grant, B-12
Graves, H-3
Grayson, F-8
Green, G-10
Greenup, C-16
Hancock, E-7
Hardin, E-9
Harlan, H-16

Harrison, C-13
Hart, G-9
Henderson, E-5
Henry, C-11
Hickman, H-2
Hopkins, G-5
Jackson, F-14
Jefferson, D-10
Jessamine, E-12
Johnson, E-16
Kenton, B-12
Knott, F-16
Knox, H-14
Larue, F-10
Laurel, G-13
Lawrence, D-17

Lee, E-14
Leslie, G-15
Letcher, G-16
Lewis, C-15
Lincoln, F-12
Livingston, G-3
Logan, H-7
Lyon, G-4
McCracken, G-2
McCreary, H-13
McLean, F-6
Madison, E-13
Magoffin, E-16
Marion, F-11
Marshall, H-3
Martin, E-17

Mason, C-14
Meade, E-9
Menifee, D-15
Mercer, E-12
Metcalfe, H-10
Monroe, H-10
Montgomery, D-14
Morgan, D-15
Muhlenberg, G-6
Nelson, E-10
Nicholas, C-14
Ohio, F-7
Oldham, C-10
Owen, C-12
Owsley, F-14
Pendleton, B-13

Perry, F-15
Pike, F-17
Powell, E-14
Pulaski, G-12
Robertson, C-13
Rockcastle, F-13
Rowan, D-15
Russell, G-11
Scott, C-12
Shelby, D-11
Simpson, H-8
Spencer, D-10
Taylor, F-11
Todd, H-6
Trigg, H-4
Trimble, C-10

Union, E-4
Warren, G-8
Washington
Wayne
Webster
Whitley,
Wolfe, E-
Woodford

Roadside History

Roadside History
A Guide to Kentucky Highway Markers

Dianne Wells, Compiler

Edited by
Melba Porter Hay &
Thomas H. Appleton Jr.

The Kentucky Historical Society
Frankfort

Copyright © 2002 by The Kentucky Historical Society

Library of Congress Cataloging-in-Publication Data

Wells, Dianne.
  Roadside history : a guide to Kentucky highway markers / Dianne
Wells, compiler; edited by Melba Porter Hay and Thomas H.
Appleton Jr.
      p. cm.
Includes indexes.
  ISBN 0-916968-28-6 (hardbound : alk. paper) – ISBN
0-916968-29-4 (pbk. : alk. paper)
  1. Historical markers–Kentucky–Guidebooks. 2. Automobile
travel–Kentucky–Guidebooks. 3. Kentucky–Guidebooks. 4.
Kentucky–History, Local. I. Hay, Melba Porter, 1949- II.
Appleton, Thomas H., 1950- III. Title.
  F452 .W44 2002
  917.6904'44–dc21

2001006218

Contents

Kentucky Historical Highway Marker Program   ix

Procedures for Obtaining a New Historical Marker xi

Highway Marker Text 1

County Index 273

Subject Index 277

Acknowledgments

Many people aided in the preparation of this publication. The Historical Highway Marker Program wishes especially to thank Gretchen M. Haney of the Kentucky Historical Society for her work in design and layout of the book; Mary Lou Madigan for assisting with the index; and the KHS photographic services for providing most of the illustrations for the volume. In addition, support from the following Kentucky Historical Society staff has been essential: J. Kevin Graffagnino, executive director; Kim Lady Smith, division manager for the Oral History and Educational Outreach division; and Karla Nicholson, Community Services branch manager.

The Kentucky Historical Highway Marker Program is dedicated to commemorating the commonwealth's history through roadside markers that recognize Kentucky historical sites, events, and personalities. Since 1949, the program has erected more than 1,800 markers that highlight the rich diversity of Kentucky's local and regional history as well as topics of statewide importance.

Between 1949 and 1962, 175 markers were installed through the efforts of the Kentucky Historical Highway Marker Committee in cooperation with the Kentucky Highway Department. In 1962 responsibility was assigned to the Kentucky Historical Society, which continues to administer the program in partnership with the Kentucky Transportation Cabinet.

The process of taking a marker from an idea to a finished product requires the assistance of many people. It involves the guidance of 120 county chairmen, an advisory committee, an in-house editing committee, a program manager, and Transportation employees who install the markers. It also requires the support of countless Kentuckians who care deeply about the heritage of their local communities, regions, and state.

All highway markers have been privately funded since 1992. Prior to that, funding was both state and private. Over 10 percent of the present markers have been sponsored through the generosity of local groups or individuals.

The markers one sees along Kentucky roadways are of three different formats. Markers numbered up to 250 are in the original format–white letters on a black background–and were cast at the University of Kentucky's Metallurgical Laboratory. Those numbered from 501 are in the more familiar design–gold leaf letters on a dark green background. A third, smaller style was recently developed as a distinct category of markers to recognize sites on state university campuses. Each marker has an identifying number located on its post.

Roadside History: A Guide to Kentucky Highway Markers combines the first Guide (1969), Supplement (1973), *Update: Guide to Kentucky Historical Highway Markers* (1983 and 1985), and additional texts through June 2001. The book enables travelers to experience Kentucky history without stopping to read each marker they pass. There are two indexes arranged by subject and county.

In this publication, some numbers are omitted, indicating an early marker that has been abandoned or one that has been damaged and not replaced. The gap in numbering from the original style (1–250) to the present design (501–2071) explains the discrepancy between the last marker number in this book (2071) and the actual number of markers (as of June 2001 approximately 1,800).

Three markers are located out-of-state. They are the Kentucky Historical Monument/Marker at Soldiers' National Cemetery in Gettysburg, Pennsylvania; "Kentucky Troops in the Battle of Shiloh" historical marker at Shiloh, Tennessee; and the USS *O'Bannon* marker.

The marker text contained in this book is identical to that on the marker. Text is either continued from one side of a marker to the other or repeated on both sides. You will note that some of the earlier marker texts include "see over" or an arrow that indicates the text continues on the opposite side. *Bear in mind that the information on a marker was judged to be accurate based on the resources available at the time the marker was approved.*

It must also be noted that the specific location of a marker may be different from that described in this book. Road construction and other property development often result in a marker's having to be relocated. Working with our county committee members, we made every effort to ascertain current locations, but we cannot guarantee that each location offered here is correct.

The Highway Marker Program encourages you to report any discrepancies in location and also any markers that are damaged. We are actively working to repair the many markers that have fallen victim to age, vandalism, or traffic accidents. We need your help to identify those in need of maintenance. To report a problem with a marker, contact the Highway Marker Program, 100 West Broadway, Frankfort, Kentucky 40601 or call (502) 564-1792.

Travelers on Kentucky highways can learn much about the state's rich and colorful past through these roadside history lessons. This book not only enhances that experience, it provides all readers with an enjoyable and entertaining glimpse into the tremendous diversity of Kentucky's heritage.

PROCEDURES FOR OBTAINING A NEW HISTORICAL MARKER

Kentucky's Historical Highway Marker Program erects markers throughout the state that commemorate sites, buildings, people, and organizations that have been significant in local, state, or national history. Before a subject can be considered for a historical marker, the request goes through a lengthy process that can take up to a year. However, this process is required in order to ensure that each marker is significant and that the text is accurate and reflects the best scholarship available. Procedural steps involved in selecting new markers to install include researching and documenting the historical facts, writing the text, and soliciting approval of the subject by the marker advisory committee.

Requests for highway markers must be made in writing to the Kentucky Historical Society's Historical Highway Marker Program and submitted on a standard form obtained from KHS. The initial request must also be approved by the marker chairman for the county in which the marker is planned. With the application, the organization or community submitting the request is responsible for providing initial documentation with references that verify all facts included. The request then goes to the marker advisory committee, made up of citizens and historians from around the state. The committee reviews the documentation and makes a decision whether the subject merits a historical marker. If approved, KHS researchers independently verify all statements and facts concerning the subject.

Next, the text for the marker is written and sent to the submitting organization or community as well as the county marker chairman for approval. Once approved by all parties, the marker itself is ordered from the manufacturer. Since 1992, KHS has had no state funding to erect markers. Therefore, the cost for manufacturing the marker must be provided by the sponsoring organization or community.

During the process, the KHS staff works with representatives of the Kentucky Transportation Cabinet to select the most appropriate site for the marker. The marker must be placed near a road or highway where it will not obstruct the view of traffic. Additionally, the staff tries to place markers where there is enough room for an automobile to pull off the road safely to read the text.

Once the marker is received from the manufacturer, staff of the Kentucky Department of Highways installs the marker at the selected site. Finally, a dedication ceremony for the newly installed marker is held.

Requests for the following subjects are not accepted for historical highway markers:

1. A marker for an individual who is living.
2. A marker of a purely genealogical or family interest.
3. A marker that promotes or may work to the financial benefit of an individual or business.
4. A marker for a cemetery, unless someone significant to Kentucky's history is buried there or there was an event of outstanding historical importance connected with it.
5. A marker for a church, unless it meets one of the following criteria:

A. The church is connected with a significant historical event or individual.
B. The church congregation has existed, uninterrupted, for at least 150 years.
C. The church building itself was constructed over 100 years ago and has been used continuously by the same congregation.
D. The building has significance due to unique architectural features.

6. No marker will be erected where it will create a traffic hazard or in any location not agreeable to the property owner or the governmental agency that has jurisdiction over the site.

"Ashland," the estate of Henry Clay, Lexington. Kentucky Historical Society Collection.

1 "ASHLAND"

(120 Sycamore Rd., Lexington, Fayette Co.)

Historic home of Henry Clay. Orator–Statesman–Patriot. Kentucky's favorite son. Born–1777. Died–1852.

2 KEENELAND

(Lexington, US 60, Fayette Co.)

Here on May 14, 1825, General LaFayette was entertained by Major John Keene who had served as his Aide-De-Camp during the Revolutionary War.

3 MORGAN HOUSE

(201 N. Mill St., Lexington, Fayette Co.)

Home of John Hunt Morgan, "Thunderbolt of the Confederacy." Born Huntsville, Alabama, June 1, 1825. Killed Greeneville, Tennessee, September 4, 1864. Lieutenant, Kentucky Volunteers in Mexican War 1846–1847. Major General, C.S.A., 1861–1864.

4 JEFFERSON DAVIS

(Limestone & High Sts., Lexington, Fayette Co.)

For three years (1821–1824) while a student at Transylvania University Jefferson Davis (afterwards President of Southern Confederacy) lived here with Joseph Ficklin then Postmaster of Lexington.

6 FIRST RACE COURSE

(343 South Broadway, Lexington, Fayette Co.)

Near this spot pioneers in 1780 established the starting point of the first race path in Kentucky, extending southward one quarter mile.

9 FORT CLAY

(West end of viaduct, Lexington, US 60, Fayette Co.)

Extensive earthworks with ditch, drawbridges and magazine were constructed here by Federal forces after the Battle of "Ashland," May 1862.

10 MASTERSON'S STATION

(Masterson Station Park, US 421, Fayette Co.)

Near here stood two-story log house built by Richard Masterson. This station was site of first Methodist church in Ky. In Masterson home, May 1790, Bishop Francis Asbury held the first Methodist Conference west of the Alleghenies. When Richard and Sarah Masterson moved to Port William (present-day Carrollton), they continued to lead Methodist activities.

11 TODD HOUSE

(578 W. Main St., Lexington, Fayette Co.)

Home of Mary Todd Lincoln from 1832 to 1839. To this house in after years she brought Abraham Lincoln and their children.

12 MARY TODD LINCOLN
(511 W. Short St., Lexington, Fayette Co.)

On this site Mary Todd, wife of Abraham Lincoln, was born Dec. 13, 1818, and here spent her childhood.

14 BECK HOUSE
(209 E. High St., Lexington, Fayette Co.)

Residence of James Burnie Beck. Born Dumfriesshire, Scot., 1822, died Washington, D.C., 1890. Law partner John C. Breckinridge. Congressman from Ky., 1867–75. U.S. Senator from Ky. 1876–90.

16 MT. ZION PRESBYTERIAN CHURCH
(Short St., Lexington, Fayette Co.)

Here stood the pioneer church of Lexington, organized 1784. About 1795, the property passed to "Associate Reformed" Church. The Rev. Adam Rankin was minister from 1784 until his death in 1827.

17 BOONE'S STATION
(Athens-Boonesboro Rd., Fayette Co.)

Stood about one-half mile east. Established in 1779 by Daniel Boone who, with his family, resided there for several years.

18 BLUE LICKS BATTLEFIELD
(US 68, approx. 200 ft. W. of Jct. with KY 165, Robertson Co.)

On Aug. 19, 1782, between this hill-top and Licking River a bloody battle was fought by Kentucky pioneers against a superior force of Indians and British-Canadians.

19 MAIN STREET CHRISTIAN CHURCH
(162 E. Main St., Lexington, Fayette Co.)

Built on this site in 1842. The 12-day Campbell-Rice debate on Christian Baptism, etc., was held here Nov. 1843, Hon. Henry Clay presiding.

20 OHIO COMPANY OF VIRGINIA
(5 mi. N. of Lexington, Russell Cave Pk., Fayette Co.)

Southerly line of survey of 800,000 acres (nominally 200,000) made by Capt. Hancock Lee in 1775 for company formed in 1748 to acquire lands in Ohio Valley. A corner is S 70° E about 1 mile.

21 BRYAN'S STATION
(5 mi. N. of Lexington, Bryan Station Pk., Fayette Co.)

Camping place in 1775–76 of the brothers Morgan, James, William and Joseph Bryan. In 1779 was fortified as a station which in Aug. 1782 repelled a siege of Indians and Canadians under Capt. William Caldwell and Simon Girty.

22 THE DISCOVERY OF THE OHIO RIVER
(S. end of George Rogers Clark Mem. Bridge at north end of 2nd St., Louisville, Jefferson Co.)

In A.D. 1669 Robert Cavelier, Sieur de LaSalle, commissioned by the French officials of Louis XIV at Quebec, seeking a water route to China and Japan, guided by an Indian and accompanied by a party in canoes, descended this river, called by the Iroquois Indians the Ohio, meaning the beautiful river. *Sponsored by The National Society of the Colonial Dames of America.*

23 DR. EPHRAIM McDOWELL, 1771–1830
(125 S. 2nd St., Danville, Boyle Co.)

Eminent American physician and surgeon. The father of American surgery. Lived and performed the first laparotomy operation in this house in 1809. *Erected by the Danville Chamber of Commerce.*

24 POET, LAWYER AND SOLDIER
(Danville, Courthouse lawn, Main St., US 127, 150, Boyle Co.)

Theodore O'Hara was born in this city, Feb. 11, 1820. He read law with Judge Wm. Owsley. Newspaper work included editing *Frankfort Yeoman* and *Louisville Times*. He served in Mexican War, Cuban rebellion and Civil War; on staffs of Generals J. C. Breckinridge and A. S. Johnston, CSA. Died 1867; reinterred with military honors, 1874, in Frankfort Cemetery.
(Reverse)
THEODORE O'HARA

O'Hara's memorable poem, "The Bivouac of the Dead," was written to commemorate the burial of Kentucky soldiers who fell at Battle of Buena Vista. By act of legislature O'Hara was reinterred beside his Mexican comrades. "On Fame's eternal camping ground Their silent tents are spread, And Glory guards with solemn round The bivouac of the dead."

25 THE TRAVELING CHURCH, 1781
(SE of Lancaster, KY 39, Garrard Co.)

In search of religious freedom, the Reverend Lewis Craig led his entire congregation of 200 Baptists and 400 other settlers from Spotsylvania County, Virginia, and established them here on Gilbert's Creek. This expedition, guided through the wilderness by Captain William Ellis, was the largest group of pioneers ever to enter the District of Kentucky in a single body. *Erected by the National Society of the Colonial Dames of America.*

26 SPRING FORT
Built Before 1782
(McCready Ave. & Trinity, Louisville, Jefferson Co.)

The rock spring on Beal's Branch 800 feet south marks Spring Fort. One of the pioneer "Beargrass settlements" contemporary with the founding of Louisville. When its commander, Richard Steele, was wounded in an Indian attack at Floyd's first fort, his wife seized her baby and, riding through the night amid shots from the red men, sped up what is now Story Avenue across Beargrass Creek and Lexington Road and through the fort's hastily opened gateway to the succor of her husband.

28 SQUIRE BOONE'S STATION, 1779
(Shelbyville, 5th & Main Sts., US 60, Shelby Co.)

"Painted Stone" 2½ miles north on Eminence Road, thence, ½ mile west to site on Clear Creek. For nearly 2 years only large station on the Wilderness Road between Harrodstown and the Falls of the Ohio River. Ground plan found among papers of Gen. George Rogers Clark. Disastrous attack by Indians 1781—re-occupied by the whites. First improved 1775—called "Painted Stone Tract" 1776.

31 SHANNOAH
(South Portsmouth, KY 10, Greenup Co.)

First village in Kentucky built by Shawnee Indians and French traders. Was visited January 1751 by Christopher Gist, George Croghan, Andrew Montour, Robert Kallendar and a servant. Located on the site of an earlier Fort Ancient settlement, it stood 500 yards Northwest of these

Adena earthworks. *Erected by the National Society of Colonial Dames of America in the Commonwealth of Kentucky, June 1946.*

32 BIG BONE LICK, THREE MILES
(Big Bone Lick State Park, KY 338, Boone Co.)

Discovered in 1739 by French Capt. Charles Lemoyne de Longueil. Early explorers found countless bones and teeth of extinct Pleistocene elephants, the mammoth and the mastodon. This saline-sulphur spring was popular for salt making until 1812; also a health resort from 1815–30. Its waters were noted for mildly curative qualities.
(Reverse)
BIG BONE LICK

Robert Smith, an Indian trader, recognized the significance of the large bones. From 1751–80, Big Bone Lick had many visitors, including Christopher Gist, John Finley, Mary Ingles, John Floyd and the McAfee brothers. Thomas Jefferson sent expedition headed by William Clark to collect bones; the next largest collector was N. S. Shaler. Some tusks measured 8–10 feet long.

34 BIRD'S WAR ROAD; JUNE, 1780
(Shelby & Main, Falmouth, KY 22, Pendleton Co.)

Acting under orders from the British commandant at Detroit, Col. Henry Bird landed near here with 200 Canadian rangers and 600 Indians—Shawnees, Ottawas, Hurons, Chippewas, Delawares, Mingoes and 'Taways—to attack the frontier forts of Kentucky. News of George Rogers Clark's approach caused their hasty retreat with 400 captives from Kentucky forts.

36 BIRNEY HOME
(Danville, US 150, Boyle Co.)

Birthplace of James G. Birney, abolitionist leader, candidate for President 1840 and '44. His 1844 votes caused Henry Clay's defeat. Birney's father built home, 1800. One son was Gov. of Mich., 1861–63, and Min. to the Hague; two were Maj. Gens. and two Colonels, USA.

43 HART COUNTY
(Munfordville, Courthouse lawn, US 31W, KY 88, Hart Co.)

Created January 19, 1819, named for Cap-

Daniel Carter Beard (left) introduced the Boy Scout movement in the United States. Kentucky Historical Society Collection.

tain Nathaniel G. T. Hart. Born 1784. Died 1813.Brought in childhood from Hagerstown, Md. to Lexington, Ky. Successful in both law and mercantile business. In 1812 raised and commanded Lexington Light Infantry; with his company went to Northwest Territory; severely wounded at Battle of Raisin; taken prisoner by the British. Promised safe escort home he was betrayed by British officer he had once befriended: brutally murdered by Indian escort. *Erected by schoolchildren of Hart Co. under auspices of National Society United States Daughters of 1812.*

46 THE PRINCE OF THE FRENCH EXPLORERS
(Wickliffe Mounds Research Center, Wickliffe, US 51, 60, Ballard Co.)

Commissioned by Louis XIV of France, the Sieur Robert de LaSalle, sweeping down the Mississippi with his flotilla of canoes, stopped in 1682 at this place, in his quest for the mouth of the Mississippi and an outlet for the French fur trade. This river, called Ohio by the Iroquois and Quabache (Wabash) by the Algonquins, was proclaimed by LaSalle, April 9, 1682, to be the northern watershed of the New Province of Louisiana of the French Colonial Empire.
(Reverse)

FRENCH EXPLORERS AT THE CONFLUENCE OF THE OHIO AND MISSISSIPPI RIVERS

Accompanied by Pere Jacques Marquette, the Sieur Louis Joliet, commissioned by the French Government at Quebec to explore the Mississippi River, stopped on this bank in 1673, according to the "Jesuit Relations" by Thevenot. They were feasted by the Indians on buffalo meat, bear's grease and white plums.

49 SITE OF LOG COURTHOUSE
(134 S. 2nd St., Constitution Square, Danville, Boyle Co.)

Kentucky District Court sessions held here March 14, 1785, until Court of Appeals set up in 1792. Created by Virginia statute on May 6, 1782, the court first met in Harrodsburg on March 3, 1783. Later meetings at Low Dutch Station and John Crow's Station before moved here. Samuel McDowell, John Floyd, George Muter, first judges; Walker Daniel, prosecutor; John May, clerk.

50 DANIEL CARTER BEARD, 1850–1941
(322 E. Third St., Covington, Kenton Co.)

Boyhood home of "Uncle Dan," youth leader, outdoorsman, artist and author. Born in Cincinnati and later came to Covington to live. Inaugurated Boy Scout movement in America, 1905, and was one of the first National Commissioners of the Boy Scouts of America. He was awarded the first medal for outstanding citizenship of state of Kentucky.

51 CANE RIDGE MEETING HOUSE
(6 mi. E. of Paris, KY 537, Bourbon Co.)

Built by Presbyterians, 1791. Here Barton W. Stone began his ministry, 1796. Famous revival attended by pioneers of many faiths, 1801. Springfield Presbytery dissolved and "Christian Church" launched June 28, 1804.

52 JAMES A. GARFIELD
(Pikeville City Park, US 119, 460, Pike Co.)

Here Col. Garfield was commissioned Brigadier General in the Union Army. The man who later became President was sworn in as General by Squire Charles of Pike County, January 1862.

53 THE HAZEL PATCH
(7 mi. N. of London, KY 490, Laurel Co.)

Half mile east. Crossroads of wilderness. Skaggs Trace, 1769, Boone Trace, 1775. Here Logan disapproved Colonel Henderson's settlement plans and parted company. Site of Wood's Blockhouse, 1793. Earliest permanent building in wilderness.

54 THE WILDERNESS ROAD
(South of Pineville, US 25-E, Bell Co.)

Opened Kentucky and the West to rapid settlement and major development. First wagon road built by Kentucky (1796), Crab Orchard to Cumberland Gap. A principal highway, maintained as turnpike (toll road) for 80 years.

55 THE WILDERNESS ROAD
(London, US 25, Laurel Co.)

Opened Kentucky and the West to rapid settlement and major development. First wagon road built by Kentucky (1796), Crab Orchard to Cumberland Gap. A principal highway, maintained as a turnpike "toll road" for 80 years.

56 LOGAN'S STATION
(Waterworks & Danville Sts., Stanford, US 150, Lincoln Co.)

Or St. Asaph. Colonel Benjamin Logan settled here after leaving party of Colonel Henderson at Hazel Patch because of settlement plans. Scene of courageous rescue of fallen companion by Logan in Indian attack (1777).

57 JEFFERSON DAVIS BIRTHPLACE
(Fairview, US 68, Todd Co.)

Here the only President of the Confederate States of America was born June 3, 1808, the son of Samuel and Jane Cook Davis. The family moved to Mississippi during his infancy.

58 BATTLE OF PERRYVILLE
(Perryville Battlefield State Historic Site, KY 1920, Boyle Co.)

October 8, 1862. Here 16,000 Confederates under General Braxton Bragg fought 22,000 Federals under General Don Carlos Buell. Bragg, facing superior forces, withdrew. Union casualties, 4211; Confederate, 3396.

60 IRON BANKS
(Columbus, KY 58, 80, Hickman Co.)

So named by early French explorers. Columbus was proposed as the Nation's Capital after the War of 1812. The area was fortified by the Confederate Army during the War Between the States.

61 KELLY FURNACE
(Kuttawa, just behind furnace, US 62 & 641, Lyon Co.)

Here William Kelly (1811–1888) discovered a steel making method, later known as the Bessemer Process, which made it possible for civilization to pass from the Iron Age to the Steel Age.

63 ROYAL SPRING
(Georgetown, Big Spring Park, Water St., Scott Co.)

One of the finest in Kentucky discovered July 9, 1774, by Colonel John Floyd and party. Georgetown's source of water supply since earliest settlement. Site of McClelland's Station, 1775.

64 FORT JEFFERSON
(1 mi. S. of Wickliffe, US 51, 60, Ballard Co.)

Erected here in 1780 by General George Rogers Clark to protect claim of infant United States to a western boundary on the

Mississippi River.

65 TRANSYLVANIA UNIVERSITY
(W. 3rd St., Lexington, Fayette Co.)

Pioneer in higher education in Kentucky and west. Founded by The Commonwealth of Virginia, 1780. Located in Lexington since 1789.

66 TRANSYLVANIA COMPANY
(Henderson, KY 351, at jct. with old US 41, Henderson Co.)

The company founded Henderson in 1797. John James Audubon made his home here. The town established the first municipal park west of the Alleghenies.

67 CONFEDERATE STATE CAPITAL OF KENTUCKY
(Bowling Green, Ky. Mus., US 68, Western Ky. Univ. Campus, Warren Co.)

Bowling Green was named State Capital at the convention in Russellville, November 20, 1861. First Governor: George W. Johnson. Commissioners to the Confederate Congress: William Preston, W. E. Simms, and Henry Burnett.

68 LIMESTONE
(Maysville, Courthouse lawn, US 62, 68, Mason Co.)

Settled in 1784 by Edward and John Waller and George Lewis. Named Maysville 1787. Pioneer river gateway to the new west. Located on lands owned by John May and Simon Kenton.

69 LEXINGTON & OHIO R.R.
(Frankfort, Near Industrial Park, US 421, Franklin Co.)

Site of first railroad west of the Alleghenies. Built 1833–34. Flat iron rails were pinned to quarried limestone blocks. The 23-mile run between Lexington and Frankfort required four hours.

71 RED RIVER MEETING HOUSE
(10 mi. S. of Russellville, US 431, Logan Co.)

Three miles east is site of early pioneer church. Organized by "A Society of Presbyterians" in 1789. Here The Great Revival of 1800 was conducted by Reverend James McGready. First Camp Meeting held here.

72 FIRST CABIN IN KENTUCKY
(Barbourville, US 25 & Knox St. [Cumberland Gap Parkway], Knox Co.)

Near here is site of first structure built April 1750 by a white man in Kentucky. Erected by Dr. Thomas Walker's party while exploring in the interest of the Loyal Land Company.

73 LINCOLN FAMILY TRAIL
(Cloverport, US 60, Breckinridge Co.)

Abraham Lincoln, then a lad of 7, with other members of the Thomas Lincoln family crossed the Ohio River on a log raft ferry near here in 1816. The Lincolns were moving to Indiana.

74 CONFEDERATE STATE CONVENTION
(Russellville, US 68, 431, Logan Co.)

Here November 20, 1861, Confederate leaders from 64 Kentucky counties seceded from the Union. The state was admitted as the 13th into the Confederate States of America Dec. 10, 1861.

75 MILL SPRINGS
(E. of Mill Springs, KY 90 [old], Wayne Co.)

Near here, January 19, 1862, 4,000 Confederate troops were engaged and defeated by 12,000 Federalists. The southern leader, General Felix Zollicoffer, was killed in the action. The historic old mill was built in 1840.

77 TWITTY'S OR LITTLE FORT
Three quarter-miles west (S. of Richmond, US 25, 421, Madison Co.)

Site of the first fort in Kentucky. Built March 1775 by Daniel Boone and party. Named for William Twitty, killed by Indians and buried by his slave Sam, near the fort.

78 CAPTAIN JACK JOUETT HOME
(4 mi. SW of Versailles, Craigs Creek Pike, Woodford Co.)

Here lived the Revolutionary War hero who made the historic ride from Cuckoo Tavern to Charlottesville in 1781 to warn Jefferson of the approach of the British. Father of famous artist, Matthew Harris Jouett.

79 CHRISTOPHER (KIT) CARSON
(Richmond, Tate's Creek Rd. [KY 169], Madison Co.)

Famous hunter, soldier and scout born near here. Carson (1809–1868) grew up in Mo.; began scouting career in Taos, N.M., at age 17. Won renown in piloting Fremont's Western expeditions; served in Mexican War. Appointed Indian agent, 1853, he was peacemaker and counselor. In Civil War, breveted brig. gen., U.S.A. Buried in Taos. Carson City, Nev., named for him.

81 HOUSE ON THE HILL
1,000 ft.
(Washington, 1 block south, US 62, 68, Mason Co.)

Built in 1800 by Col. Thomas Marshall 1730–1802, staff officer for Washington at Monmouth and Brandywine. Married Mary Keith. Father of John Marshall, Chief Justice, U.S. Supreme Court, 1801–1835.

82 SITE OF FAIRFIELD
(4 mi. NW of Paris, US 27, Bourbon Co.)

One mile northeast. Built by James Garrard, second Governor of Kentucky, 1796–1800; reelected 1800–04. Bourbon County's first court held here, 1786. Near here, Mt. Lebanon, Kentucky's earliest Governor's mansion.

83 ALANANT-O-WAMIOWEE
(Approx. 1 ½ mi. NE of New Circle Rd. & Paris Pike, US 27, Fayette Co.)

Ancient buffalo trace carved in the wilderness by prehistoric animals seeking salt. Trace was later used by buffaloes, mound builders, Indians and pioneer settlers. Also known as Warrior's Trace.

84 ALANANT-O-WAMIOWEE
(4th & Market, Maysville, Mason Co.)

Ancient buffalo trace carved in the wilderness by prehistoric animals seeking salt. Trace was later used by buffaloes, mound builders, Indians and pioneer settlers. Also known as Warrior's Trace.

85 BATTLE OF MIDDLE CREEK
(1 mi. W. of Prestonsburg, KY 114, Floyd Co.)

Deciding factor in control of Big Sandy Valley. On Jan. 10, 1862, Gen. Humphrey Marshall, leading Confederates, was defeated here by Union forces under Col.

James A. Garfield, later President of the U.S.

86 PISGAH CHURCH
¾ Mile →
(3½ mi. E. of Versailles, US 60, Woodford Co.)

Pioneer Presbyterian Church, organized in 1784. Here Kentucky Academy opened in 1797. The school united with Transylvania University in 1798.

87 STUBBLEFIELD BIRTHPLACE
(Murray State Univ., US 641 & KY 94, Calloway Co.)

Nathan Bowman Stubblefield was born near here in 1860. He successfully demonstrated wireless voice transmission as early as 1892. His early patents were granted in that year.

88 BANK OF LOUISVILLE
(Main St., Louisville, Jefferson Co.)

Designed and built by Gideon Shryock, father of Greek Revival architecture in Kentucky. Bank was chartered by General Assembly in 1832 and building completed in 1837.

89 BATTLE OF GREEN RIVER BRIDGE
(9 mi. S. of Campbellsville, Bypass on Old KY 55, Taylor Co.)

Here on July 4, 1863, Confederates of Morgan's Brigade under Colonel A. R. Johnson attacked entrenched position of Federal forces under Colonel O. H. Moore. They were repulsed eight times.

91 JOHNSTON BIRTHPLACE
→
(Main St., Washington, Mason Co.)

Near here on February 3, 1803, General Albert Sidney Johnston, Confederate leader, was born. He resigned from the U.S. Army in 1861 to join the South. Killed at Shiloh, April 6, 1862.

92 MEFFORD'S FORT
(Main St., Washington, Mason Co.)

Built of boards of the flatboat on which George Mefford, his wife, & thirteen children, of Maryland, descended the Ohio in 1787. Many such houses were built along the river prior to 1800.

93 Duncan Tavern
(323 High St., Paris, US 68, 460, Bourbon Co.)

Built in 1788. Gathering place of pioneers. Shrine, Museum, Library. Restored by Kentucky Daughters of the American Revolution.

94 Augusta College 1822–1849
(Augusta College Grounds, KY 8, 19, Bracken Co.)

In 1822 the trustees of Bracken Academy with conferences of the Methodist Church of Kentucky and Ohio merged to found Augusta College, the first established Methodist College in the world.

95 Traveler's Rest
(Shelby City, US 127, Lincoln Co.)

← 2 mi. Site of home of Isaac Shelby (1750–1826), Kentucky's first and fifth governor, soldier of three decisive American battles. He and his wife, Susannah Hart Shelby (1764–1833), are buried here.

96 Sportsman's Hill
(2 mi. NW of Crab Orchard, US 150, Lincoln Co.)

2 mi. → Whitley House. Built at Whitley's Station by Col. William Whitley, noted pioneer and Indian fighter who was born in Virginia in 1749, came to Kentucky in 1775, and was killed at the Battle of the Thames in 1813.

97 Stockton's Station
← ½ Mile
(Flemingsburg, W. of city limits, KY 11, Fleming Co.)

Site of station built in 1787 by Major George Stockton, who raised a crop here in 1786, while living at Strode's Station. This was the first of three forts in the area becoming Fleming County in 1798.

100 Jackson-Dickinson Duel
(Adairville, Town Square, US 431, Logan Co.)

On the Jeff Burr farm in second "Poplar Bottom" is the site of the duel fought May 30, 1806. Andrew Jackson was wounded. Half mile west of site is Will Tyler farm where Charles Dickinson died. Miller's "Buttermilk Spring" is south on highway 75 two miles, on Old Burr farm.

101 Abraham Lincoln
(1 mi. E. of Eastwood, US 60, 460, Jefferson Co.)

Two miles northeast of here Abraham Lincoln, grandfather of the president, was massacred by Indians in May 1786. Long Run Baptist Church, standing on the Lincoln land grant, marks the traditional site of the pioneer's grave. *The original marker was erected by The Filson Club 1937.*

102 Defeated Camp
McNitt's Defeat (2 mi. S. of London, Levi Jackson State Park, near McHargue's Mill, US 25, Laurel Co.)

Here in 1786 pioneers encamped for the night were attacked by Indians and nearly all were slain or captured.

103 Leestown
(Entrance to Buffalo Trace Distillery, Wilkinson Blvd., Franklin Co.)

In 1773 McAfee Company and Hancock Taylor came here and surveyed area, an early pioneer stopping place. By 1775 Leestown settled and named by Hancock and Willis Lee; established by Va. Assembly, 1776. Temporarily abandoned in 1777 because of Indian attack, it was reestablished and became well-known shipping port for tobacco, hemp, corn and whiskey to New Orleans market. Over.
(Reverse)
Leestown
Va. General Assembly had tobacco inspection warehouse erected in Leestown, 1783. A hemp factory was here for many years. At one time Leestown was a commercial center and contender for the state capital. During the War of 1812 it served as supply base against Indians. In 1827 the stones for the Old State House were quarried from river bank near here. Over.

105 & 106 Frankfort
(Near cemetery, E. Main St., Franklin Co.)
(Frankfort, Scenic Overlook, US 60, Franklin Co.)

Site surveyed July 16, 1773. Founded by General James Wilkinson. Chartered by Virginia Legislature, October 1786. Chosen Capital of Kentucky, December 1792.

107 Ruddle's Station
(4 mi. S. of Cynthiana, US 27, Harrison Co.)

Settled by John Hinkston, 1775. Aban-

ROADSIDE HISTORY: A GUIDE TO KENTUCKY HIGHWAY MARKERS

doned 1776. Rebuilt by Isaac Ruddle 1779. Destroyed by British and Indians under Captain Henry Bird 1780. Hinkston later settled opposite this site.

109 BATTLE OF CYNTHIANA
(300-400 ft. S. of US 27, 62, bridge, Harrison Co.)
Here Colonel John Hunt Morgan defeated Federal forces and captured the town July 18, 1862. On June 12, 1864, Morgan, as Brigadier General, was defeated here by Federal General Stephen Burbridge.

111 ZACHARY TAYLOR HOME
(Louisville, Blankenbaker Ln., N. of US 42, at Apache St., Jefferson Co.)
Zachary Taylor (November 24, 1784–July 9, 1850), soldier and twelfth president of the United States, lived here between 1785–1808.

112 GEN. JOHN BELL HOOD HOME
(4 mi. W. of Mt. Sterling, US 60, Montgomery Co.)
Home of Hood family, 1835–1857. From here John Bell Hood (1831–1879) went to West Point, 1849. Resigned commission in 1861, joined Confederate Army, served with Texas Brigade throughout war. Hood wounded at Gettysburg; lost leg at Chickamauga.

113 DANIEL BOONE'S GRAVE
(Frankfort Cemetery, E. Main St., Franklin Co.)
Born 1734, died 1820. Entered Eastern Kentucky, 1767; explored Bluegrass Region, 1769–71; guided Transylvania Company, blazed Wilderness Trail, built Fort Boonesborough in 1775; directed defense of the fort, 1778; emigrated to Missouri, 1799; reinterred, with wife Rebecca, in Frankfort Cemetery, 1845.

114 BUCK POND
1¼ miles →
(1½ mi. E. of Versailles, Woodford Co.)
Built about 1783 by Colonel Thomas Marshall 1730–1802, staff officer under Washington, Surveyor General of bounty lands for Revolutionary soldiers. Father of John Marshall, Chief Justice of the United States.

115 MORGAN'S STATION
6 Miles →
(2 mi. E. of Mt. Sterling, Montgomery Co.)
Settled in 1789. Attacked by Indians April 1, 1793. 19 women and children captured while men worked in fields. One woman hid in spring house and gave the alarm. 12 of the prisoners were massacred.

116 CANEWOOD
1¼ miles →
(6½ mi. N. of Winchester, KY 627, Clark Co.)
Home of two Revolutionary War officers: built about 1793 by Col. Nathaniel Gist 1735–1796 and Gen. Charles Scott 1739–1813, Governor of Kentucky 1808–1812 who married the widow Gist, 1807.

117 LEITCH'S STATION, 1789
(Station Tract at entrance to Knepfle's & Port Hosea, KY 9, Campbell Co.)
Site of first white settlement in Campbell County. Established by Major David Leitch (1753–1794), aide-de-camp to General Lawson during the Revolutionary War.

119 BATTLE OF MUNFORDVILLE
(2 mi. S. of Munfordville, US 31-W, Hart Co.)
Union forces commanded by Colonel Wilder surrendered to Mississippi regiments of General Bragg's army on September 17, 1862, following battle on the 14th. 50 killed and 307 wounded. Bragg evacuated Munfordville on 20th before General Buell's forces arrived. Confederates destroyed railroad bridge. Site of Fort Craig and monument to Colonel R. A. Smith 1500 ft. west.

120 LINCOLN KNOB CREEK FARM
(6 mi. NE of Hodgenville, US 31-E, Larue Co.)
Abraham Lincoln (1809–1865) lived on this 228 acre farm, 1811–1816. He wrote in 1860: "My earliest recollection is of the Knob Creek place." A younger brother was born here.

121 GENERAL JAMES TAYLOR HOME
(E. 3rd & Overton St., Newport, Campbell Co.)
Underground railroad station. Mansion built by Gen. Taylor, pioneer, banker, statesman, general in the War of 1812.

Original house designed by Benjamin H. Latrobe. Present house built, 1837.

122 DRENNON SPRINGS
← 9 miles
(1 mi. N. of New Castle, US 421, Henry Co.)

Discovered and used by Indians for medicinal properties. Claimed by Jacob Drennon and Matthew Bracken, July 26, 1773. On April 1, 1785, Patrick Henry, Governor of Virginia, issued to George Rogers Clark a patent for 400 acres including the springs. Site of the famous Drennon Springs Hotel and the Western Military Academy 1851.

123 CORNER IN CELEBRITIES
(Wapping & Washington Sts., Frankfort, Franklin Co.)

Homes of Thomas S. Todd, John M. Harlan, George M. Bibb, John J. Crittenden, John Brown, James Brown, Thomas Metcalfe, Robert P. Letcher, George G. Vest, Benjamin G. Brown, James Harlan, Charles Slaughter Morehead, Thomas S. Crittenden, John C. Watson, Hugh Rodman.

124 CHARLES YOUNG BIRTHPLACE, 1864–1922
(2 mi. W. of Wedonia, KY 24, Mason Co.)

Third Negro to graduate from West Point Military Academy. Colonel, United States Army. Distinguished for his service in Haiti and Liberia as a military organizer, map maker and road builder.

125 COLONEL GEORGE NICHOLAS
(Episcopal Cemetery, E. 3rd, Lexington, Fayette Co.)

Grave of George Nicholas 1754–1799. Revolutionary soldier, Virginia House of Delegates, Father of Kentucky Constitution, First Kentucky Attorney General, Professor of Law at Transylvania University.

127 GOVERNOR JAMES CLARK
(Colby Rd., Winchester, KY 627, Clark Co.)

Home and monument of James Clark 1779–1839. Governor of Kentucky, 1836–1839. Member of Congress; Judge, Court of Appeals. As Circuit Judge he rendered his famous decision which set off the old and the new court fight in 1821.

Jane L. Clemens (left), age 79, mother of Mark Twain. Kentucky Historical Society Collection.

128 JANE LAMPTON HOME
(Opposite Courthouse yard, Columbia, KY 55, 80, Adair Co.)

Girlhood home of Jane Lampton (1803–1891). Wife of John Marshall Clemens. Mother of "Mark Twain." Granddaughter of Colonel William Casey, original Adair County settler.

129 COLONEL ARTHUR CAMPBELL
(Middlesboro, US 25-E, Bell Co.)

Grave of Colonel Arthur Campbell (1734–1811). Statesman, Revolutionary soldier, justice, legislator, County Lieutenant. Sons, James and John, killed in War of 1812.

130 MATTHEW LYON GRAVE
(At Cemetery, Overlook Dr., .6 mi. off KY 730, Lyon Co.)

Grave of Matthew Lyon (1750–1833). Soldier, politician, pioneer. Protested Sedition Acts. Moved to Eddyville 1801. Kentucky Representative 1802; Congressman 1803–1811. Died Spadra Bluff, Arkansas. Reinterred Eddyville Cemetery 1833.

131 YELLOW FEVER EPIDEMIC
(Hickman Cemetery, KY 94, Fulton Co.)

August–November 1878. 462 cases, 150

deaths. Dr. Luke P. Blackburn, Governor of Kentucky, 1879–83, together with local and visiting doctors, rendered heroic services.

132 PILOT KNOB
(4 mi. W. of Stanton, KY 11, 15, Powell Co.)

Daniel Boone and party first viewed "The Beautiful Level of Kentucky," June 7, 1769, from bench atop this knob.

133 BULLITT'S LICK
(3 mi. NW of Shepherdsville, KY 44, Bullitt Co.)

Located by Captain Thomas Bullitt, 1773. Site of early commercial production of salt in Kentucky. This lick provided salt for Kentucky settlements and the Illinois country.

134 WILLIAM (INDIAN BILL) HARDIN, 1747–1821
(Hardinsburg, US 60, Breckinridge Co.)

Founder of Hardinsburg. Virginia Revolutionary soldier, third continental line. Built Hardin's Fort here in 1780.

135 CHOCTAW INDIAN ACADEMY 1825–1843
2 Miles →

(Georgetown, US 460, near Jct. US 227, Scott Co.)

The U.S. Government established at Blue Springs Farm, home of Vice President R. M. Johnson, its first Indian school for sons of Indian Chiefs. Future leaders of many tribes were educated here.

136 LEXINGTON
(In front of Cardinal Hill Hospital, Versailles Rd., Lexington, Fayette Co. Duplicate markers in front of Zandale Shopping Center, Nicholasville Rd., US 27, and approximately 1½ mi. NE of New Circle Rd. & Paris Pike, US 27, Fayette Co.)

Named in honor of first Battle of the American Revolution. William McConnell was among the party of hunters who came to site from Harrodsburg in 1775. Built cabin to obtain land title but driven off by Indians. Lexington later settled by Robert Patterson and companions, 1779. Major frontier town. Home of Henry Clay, Mary Todd Lincoln and John C. Breckinridge.

137 LULBEGRUD CREEK
(Clark-Powell Co. line, KY 15, Clark Co.)

Near site of winter camp of Daniel and Squire Boone, Alexander Neeley, and John Stuart, 1769–70. Creek named by these pioneers after "Lorbrulgrud" of *Gulliver's Travels*, first known book brought to Kentucky. Corrupted to Lulbegrud.

138 SIMON KENTON'S STATION
(Maysville, AA Highway, Mason Co.)

About ½ mile west is site of camp made by Simon Kenton and Thomas Williams in the spring of 1775. They left this camp in the fall and visited stations in area. Kenton returned to camp in 1784, and brought with him a group of his family and friends. During 1784 and 1785, they fortified the station, which became a major stronghold north of Kentucky River.

139 HENRY CLAY'S LAW OFFICE
(176 N. Mill St., Lexington, Fayette Co.)

Erected 1803–04, this is the only office standing used by Clay; he occupied it from 1804 until circa 1810. During these significant years in his career, Clay was elected to successive terms in legislature and to unexpired terms in the United States Senate. Builders Stephens and Winslow used their characteristic brick basement. Original floorboards remain.

140 STEUBEN'S LICK
(3½ mi. N. of Madisonville at Manitou, US 41-A, Hopkins Co.)

Named for the Prussian soldier Friedrich Wilhelm Ludolf Gerhard Augustin, Baron von Steuben. Born in 1730, he came to America in 1777 to aid the cause of the Revolution. Steuben instructed Washington's army at Valley Forge and was first Inspector General of the Army. Came here to inspect his military grants and visited the Lick. Died in New York, 1794.

141 OLD MUD MEETING HOUSE
(Dry Branch Pike, off US 68, Mercer Co.)

First Dutch Reformed Chuch west of the Allegheny Mountains, established by fifty heads of families who came to Mercer County from Pennsylvania in 1781. Organized in 1796, the church was built on land purchased in 1800. In the church cemetery is the grave of Dominie Thomas Kyle, first pastor.

142 TRAIL OF TEARS
(Big Springs Park, E. Washington St., Princeton, Caldwell Co.)

At this point on the "Varmintrace" Road from Princeton toward Cumberland River the Cherokee Indians in 1838 camped on the 1200-mile "Trail of Tears." The enforced trek began in the Great Smoky Mountains and led westward to Indian Territory, costing the Cherokees nearly one-third of their population.

143 CABIN CREEK
(Tollesboro, KY 10, 57, Lewis Co.)

Early point of entry into Kentucky for explorers and pioneers. From it marauding Indians forded across the Ohio River. War roads, marked with drawings of animals, the sun, and the moon, led from its mouth to Upper Blue Licks.

144 MAYSVILLE ROAD
(Maysville, top of Maysville Hill near Country Club, US 68, Mason Co.)

Built by "Maysville and Washington Turnpike Company," incorporated January 29, 1829. First four-mile stretch, Maysville to Washington, was earliest macadamized road in Kentucky and country west of the Alleghenies. Completed November 7, 1830. The road, Lexington to Maysville, was opened to travel in 1835 with thirteen tollhouses and six covered bridges.

145 BLACK PATCH WAR
(Princeton, US 62, Caldwell Co.)

Here on December 1, 1906, began Black Patch War, which lasted to the end of 1908. "Night Riders" fought against non-cooperative farmers and businessmen who opposed the dark tobacco pool.

146 JOHN FLOYD'S GRAVE
(Breckinridge Ln. at Hillsboro Ave., Louisville, Jefferson Co.)

Grave of John Floyd, near here. Pioneer and surveyor. Born Amherst County, Virginia, 1750. Killed when ambushed by Indians in Jefferson County, District of Kentucky, 1783. Colonel of Militia and County Lieutenant of Jefferson County.

147 FORT HEIMAN
(Near state line, KY 121, Ft. Heiman Rd., Calloway Co.)

Confederate fort erected in 1861. Federals occupied 1862. Seized by CSA Gen. Forrest in fall 1864. With field cannon his cavalrymen sank 2 Union river transports, captured another and a gunboat, and commandeered them. Due east, this side of Kentucky Lake.

148 LONG HUNTER CAMP
(8 mi. S. of Greensburg, off KY 61, Green Co.)

Long Hunter collection camp. In 1771, a small party of Long Hunters surprised Daniel Boone. He was alone and singing when found.

150 MARTIN'S STATION
One mile →
(3 mi. NW of Paris, US 27, Bourbon Co.)

Revolutionary fort built in 1779, destroyed by British and Indians commanded by Captain Henry Bird, June 18, 1780.

151 BOONE SALT SPRINGS
(David, KY 404, Floyd Co.)

Discovered by Daniel Boone and one or two companions while exploring Eastern Kentucky, winter 1767–68. Later called Young's Salt Works. These springs provided salt for pioneers in the valley and for troops on both sides during the Civil War.

152 CRAB ORCHARD SPRINGS
(Crab Orchard, US 150, Lincoln Co.)

Site of popular watering place, 1827 until early 1930's. Famed for number and excellence of mineral springs. Crab Orchard salts, medical remedy, produced here by evaporation.

153 ESTILL'S DEFEAT
(Mt. Sterling, US 60, Montgomery Co.)

Here on March 22, 1782, in Battle of Little Mountain, Captain James Estill and 7 of his force of 25 pioneers were killed in desperate hand-to-hand fighting with a band of 25 marauding Wyandots.

155 GLEN LILY
(Munfordville, US 31-W, Hart Co.)

Built 1819–1822 by Colonel Aylette Hartswell Buckner. Birthplace of his son,

General Simon Bolivar Buckner (1823–1914), Confederate States Army Commander, Governor of Kentucky, 1887–1891, nominee for Vice-Presidency, 1896.

157 SITE OF FIRST KENTUCKY LEGISLATURE
(Lexington, US 421, Fayette Co.)

Site of the first meeting of the General Assembly for the Commonwealth, the two sessions begun and held on Monday, June 4, and Monday, November 5, 1792. Isaac Shelby, Governor; James Brown, Secretary of State; John Logan, treasurer.

158 CHAUMIERE DES PRAIRIES
(Catnip Rd., 3½ mi. N. of Nicholasville, US 27, Jessamine Co.)

Estate of Colonel David Meade III, who lived here, 1796–1832, and who spent three fortunes on its development. House originally a cluster of small buildings connected by stone and brick arcades surrounded by a 100-acre park and garden.

161 JEPTHA'S KNOB
(Clayvillage at Jeptha Knob Rd., US 60, Shelby Co.)

A cryptovolcanic structure. Crustal forces which caused this feature failed to reach eruptive stage. Top elevation 1,163 feet above sea level.

162 LOWER BLUE LICKS
(N. of Licking River, US 68, Nicholas Co.)

Famous salt lick. Bones of large prehistoric animals dating from late glacial and early post-glacial epochs recovered here. In February, 1778, Daniel Boone and thirty companions, while making salt at this lick, were captured by Indians.

163 MARY INGLES
(Silver Grove, KY 8 at Oak St., Campbell Co.)

Said to have been first white woman in Kentucky. Captured by Indians in Virginia, July 1755, and taken to Ohio. Later she escaped a salt-making party at Big Bone Lick and made her way across the Kentucky wilderness back to Virginia.

164 BATTLE OF IVY MOUNTAIN
(S. of Prestonsburg, US 23, 460, Floyd Co.)

Site of first important Civil War engagement in Big Sandy Valley, November 8, 1861,

Gen. Simon Bolivar Buckner. Kentucky Historical Society Collection.

when Confederate forces led by Captain Andrew Jackson May were defeated by Federal troops under General William Nelson.

165 GREENSBURG COURTHOUSE
(Greensburg, US 68, Green Co.)

One of the oldest public buildings still standing in Kentucky. Built between 1802–1804 by Robert Ball, Edward Bullock, Thomas Metcalfe, Walter Bullock and Daniel Lisle. Used as courthouse for 135 years. Jane Todd Crawford Library on second floor.

166 COLDSTREAM FARM
(Newtown Pike, 1 mi. N. of New Circle Rd., Fayette Co.)

Famous Kentucky horse farm. Known earlier as McGrathiana. The home of Aristides, the first winner of the Kentucky Derby.

167 JOHN G. CARLISLE/COVINGTON
(Covington, John G. Carlisle Elem. School, Pike St. & Holman Ave., Kenton Co.)

Home of John Griffin Carlisle, born Kenton County 1835, died New York City 1910. U.S. Representative 1877–90, Speaker 1883–89, Senator 1890–93, Secretary of the Treasury 1893–97. Buried Linden Grove Cemetery, Covington.

168 GETHSEMANI
(E. of New Haven, KY 247, Nelson Co.)

Abbey of Our Lady of Gethsemani. Founded–1848–by the Order of Trappist-Cistercians. Founded–1098–in France. Noted for prayer, labor and silence.

169 JACKSON PURCHASE
(State Line Rd. [KY 166] & Highland Dr., Fulton, US 45 Bypass, Fulton Co.; Paducah, US 60, W. end of Tenn. River Bridge, McCracken Co.; Kentucky Lake, US 68, Marshall Co.).

8,500 sq. mi. area, former tribal lands of Chickasaw Indians. U.S. paid $300,000 for tract in 1818 after negotiations by Gen. Andrew Jackson and Gov. Isaac Shelby. Bordered by Tenn., Ohio and Miss. Rivers. Now comprises Ky.'s 8 and Tenn.'s 20 westernmost counties.

170 GASPER RIVER MEETING HOUSE
(Jct. of US 68, & KY 73, Logan Co.)

One of three churches of Reverend James McGready, a Presbyterian minister, in Logan County-Gasper River, Muddy River, and Red River–around which the great frontier revival of 1797 to 1805 began.

172 GARFIELD PLACE
1 block west →
(Prestonsburg, US 23, 460, Floyd Co.)

Used by Colonel, later President, James A. Garfield as his headquarters following Battle of Middle Creek, January 10, 1862.

173 JAMES J. ANDREWS
(Flemingsburg, Courthouse lawn, KY 11 & 32, Fleming Co.)

Andrews lived here 1859–62. In 1862 he led 22 Union soldiers into Georgia to cut the railway between Marietta and Chattanooga. Their capture of the locomotive "The General" and their pursuit by Confederates was a dramatic incident of the Civil War.

174 FARMINGTON
←
(Jct. Bardstown Rd. & Wendell St., US 31-E, Louisville, Jefferson Co.)

Historic residence completed by John Speed in 1810 from designs by Thomas Jefferson. Abraham Lincoln was a guest here of his close friend Joshua Speed in 1841. Open to the public.

175 HAZEL GREEN ACADEMY
(Hazel Green, KY 191, 203, Wolfe Co.)

Organized 1880 by J. Taylor Day, William O. Mize and Green Berry Swango. Only college preparatory school serving this area for years. Many of its graduates have gone on to prominence.

177 BATTLE OF MT. STERLING
(Mt. Sterling, Courthouse lawn, US 60, Montgomery Co.)

On March 22, 1863, about 300 Confederate cavalrymen under Colonel R. S. Cluke captured this city, taking 438 prisoners, 222 wagon loads of military stores, 500 mules, and 1000 stand of arms. Confederate losses: 8 killed, 13 wounded. Union losses: 4 killed, 10 wounded.

178 WILLIAM HOLMES McGUFFEY
(High St., Paris, Bourbon Co.)

Born September 23, 1800–Died May 4, 1873. Famous for his eclectic readers which introduced thousands of children to the treasures of literature. At this site he taught from 1823 to 1826 before joining the faculty of Miami University.

179 SHAKER COLONY
(Near Warren Co. line, US 68, Logan Co.)

Organized in 1807 as the Gasper Society of United Believers in Christ's Second Appearing. Last western colony to disband, 1922. Enrollment reached 349; acreage, 6000. Noted for silk and woolen cloth, furniture, tools, seeds, preserves and purebred stock.

180 CAMP BEAUREGARD
(North edge of Water Valley, US 45, Graves Co.)

On hill one mile east of this point stood Camp Beauregard. Training base for Confederate troops from six states 1861–1862. Severe epidemics caused heavy mortality rate here.

182 CSA CEMETERY
(Maple Ave., Pewee Valley, KY 146, Oldham Co.)

In burying ground 1 mile south, marked

by granite obelisk, lie remains of 313 soldiers who died while residents of the Kentucky Confederate home. The home was located on the high ground just northwest of here. It was used for CSA veterans, 1902 to 1934.

183 JANE TODD CRAWFORD
(7½ mi. S. of Greensburg, KY 61, Green Co.)

This pioneer woman rode a horse from this home sixty-four miles to Danville. On Christmas Day 1809 was operated on by Ephraim McDowell, M.D., for an ovarian tumor. Four weeks later she came back after recuperating from the world's first ovariotomy.

185 MORGAN ROW—1807
(Chiles St., Harrodsburg, US 68, 127, Mercer Co.)

First row-house in Kentucky. Built by Squire Joseph Morgan. English traditional plan. Early Harrodsburg noted tavern, social, business center. Vice President Richard M. Johnson, hero Battle of the Thames, was guest here at reunion of survivors, Oct. 5, 1836.

187 CIVIL WAR ACTION
(Old Caseyville, KY 130, Union Co.)

Every inhabitant of this pro-southern town was taken prisoner by the crew of a Union gunboat, July 26, 1862. All were released except 19 men who were taken to Evansville, Indiana, as hostages to guarantee payment of $35,000 damages done by rebel guerrillas.

188 WILLIAMSTOWN RAID
(Williamstown, Courthouse lawn, US 25, Grant Co.)

On November 1, 1864, planning to seize reported large sum of USA money, a Confederate force of 32 under Colonel R. J. Breckinridge, Jr., and Maj. Theophilus Steele raided the city. Finding money removed, they plundered Tunis' store, taking 30 USA muskets.

189 MURDER BRANCH MASSACRE
(10 mi. E. of Frenchburg, KY 1274, Menifee Co.)

April 1793, Indians captured 19 women and children of Morgan's Station in Montgomery County. Overtaken north of here by posse. Indians massacred some captives, taking others across Ohio River. Last Indian raid into Kentucky.

190 WALKER DANIEL
(2nd & Main St., Danville, Boyle Co.)

Founded Danville, 1781. First Atty. Gen. of Ky. District, 1783. As a member of Commission went to Falls of Ohio to allot lands in Clark's grant to members of Ill. Regt. Daniel was killed by Indians, Aug. 1784, on way to visit brother at Bullitt's Lick.

191 MOTHER'S DAY
(Henderson schoolyard, Center St., Henderson Co.)

Here, Mary Towles Sasseen Wilson in 1887 first observed Mother's Day. Started with her pupils. In 1893, she obtained national observance. Kentucky Legislature recognized her as "originator of idea." Congress adopted second Sunday of May as holiday in 1914.

192 BOTTOM HOUSE
(Perryville Battlefield, US 68 & 150, Boyle Co.)

Owned by Squire H. P. Bottom, it was a key position in Battle of Perryville, Oct. 8, 1862. At the beginning of battle, held by USA troops. After a massed attack, Confederates took the house and held it. The battle over, Bottom identified and buried CSA dead.

193 CRAWFORD HOUSE
(Perryville Battlefield, US 68 & 150, Boyle Co.)

Used by Confederate General Braxton Bragg as headquarters during the Battle of Perryville, October 8, 1862. Crawford Spring back of the house furnished vital water supply to CSA troops on the drought-stricken battlefield.

194 RUSSELL HOUSE
(Perryville Battlefield, US 68 & 150, Boyle Co.)

On the knoll, it was a key position on the Union left flank under Maj. Gen. McCook in Battle of Perryville, Oct. 8, 1862. The scene of desperate fighting, it changed hands twice and was hit many times. After the battle it was used as a hospital.

195 DORSEY HOUSE
(Perryville Battlefield, US 68 & 150, Boyle Co.)

Union General Don Carlos Buell used the house located a few yards from the road as headquarters during the Battle of Perryville, October 8, 1862. Centrally located, the house was near roads leading to the center left and right of Union lines.

196 BOONE'S STATION
(Booneville, Courthouse lawn, KY 11, 30, Owsley Co.)

Near this spot, Daniel Boone and party camped in 1780–1781. Camp called Boone's Station until Owsley County was organized in 1843, then named Booneville. Records in Clay County show that Boone's family owned land here until it moved to Missouri.

197 SCHOOL FOR THE DEAF
(4th & Main Sts., Danville, Boyle Co.)

On this corner, in 1823, Kentucky founded the first state-supported school in the United States for the instruction of deaf children. Classes met in an old inn that was known as the Yellow House. Reverend and Mrs. John R. Kerr served as first Superintendent and Matron from 1823 until 1833. School was moved to present campus on South Second Street in 1827.

198 JOSHUA FRY BELL
(Pineville, Courthouse lawn, US 25-E, Bell Co.)

Bell County formed from Harlan and Knox counties, 1867. Named for Joshua Fry Bell, 1811–70, Congressman, Ky. Sec. of State. Comr. to Peace Conference in 1861 and state legislator. He was great-grandson of Dr. Thomas Walker, explorer of Kentucky wilderness, 1750.

199 IRVINE
(Irvine, Courthouse lawn, KY 52, 89, Estill Co.)

Named, 1812, for Col. Wm. Irvine. Member from Madison Co. of 1787 and 1788 conventions that sought separation from Va. and statehood for Ky.; member of Constitutional Convention, 1799. "He had strong hold on affection of people. Few have gone to grave more lamented."

200 WADESBORO
(Dexter, Jct. US 641 & KY 1346, Calloway Co.)

Two miles west was District seat of Jackson Purchase area 1818, now being Kentucky's eight and Tennessee's twenty westernmost counties. Settled in 1821 and U.S. Public Land Office opened. Calloway County Seat, 1822–1842. Then it was moved to Murray.

201 FIRST CELEBRATION
(Jct. Clear Creek Rd., US 68, Jessamine Co.)

July 4, 1794, Col. William Price, veteran of the Revolutionary War, held the first celebration of Independence Day west of the Alleghenies. At his plantation, near here, forty veterans dined to commemorate the "glorious birthday of our freedom."

202 FIRST SETTLEMENT
(Near Salyersville city limits, KY 7 & US 460, Magoffin Co.)

Archibald Prater, John Williams, Ebenezer Hanna, Clayton Cook and others attempted to settle here in 1794 but were driven out by Indians. They returned in 1800 and settled Licking Station on hill in horse shoe bend of river, a good defense against Indians.

203 SHAKER MUSEUM →
(Auburn, US 68, Logan Co.)

Handicrafts, furniture, books, and inspirational drawings of the Shakers, 1807 to 1922. It is located on land that formerly was Shakers' sugar maple farm, a part of 6000 acre holdings. Headquarters of colony at South Union. Top enrollment was 349.

204 OLD MUNFORD INN
(lst & Main, Munfordville, US 31-W, Hart Co.)

One block west stands a log inn built on a pioneer trail in 1810 by Thomas Munford, brother of founder of Munfordville. Among the many distinguished guests was General Andrew Jackson in 1829 enroute to his inauguration as seventh President of USA.

205 ROUTE FOR HORSES AND CATTLE
(W. of Vanceburg, KY 8, 3037, Lewis Co.)

In 1775, Col. Robert Patterson, Wm.

McConnell, David Perry and Stephen Lowry brought the first horses (9) and cattle (14) into northern Kentucky. Animals were brought by boat from Ft. Pitt and driven overland from here to the early inland settlements.

206 LORETTO SISTERS
(St. Mary, KY 84, 327, Marion Co.)

In a log cabin, on this site, Rev. Charles Nerinckx, a pioneer missionary, founded the Sisters of Loretto at the Foot of the Cross, April, 1812. Since that time, their educational work has expanded to many parts of the United States and South America.

207 LORETTO
(Entrance to Loretto Academy, KY 49, 152, Marion Co.)

Motherhouse and Novitiate of the Sisters of Loretto, an American congregation founded in 1812 by Reverend Charles Nerinckx, dedicated to education of youth. Located on the site of home of Rev. Stephen T. Badin, the first priest ordained in U.S. (1793).

208 PEWEE VALLEY
(Old L & N Depot, Pewee Valley, Oldham Co.)

Formerly "Smith's Station"
Setting of famous "Little Colonel" and other fictional portrayals of life in Pewee Valley by Annie Fellows Johnston. Her stately home, "The Beeches," ½ mi. N.W. Most prominent town founder was Henry S. Smith, 1802–83. A trustee of town, he owned property, surveyed roads, and helped establish girls' college and Pewee Valley Cemetery.

209 SALTPETER CAVE
(Carter Caves State Park, KY 182, Carter Co.)

Saltpeter mined here from which gunpowder was made that was used by Kentucky riflemen during the War of 1812. There are remains of those works in cave. Reputed rendezvous for counterfeiters in early years. Artifacts and Indian graves found in cavern.

211 U.S. TREASURER
(N. of Sturgis, near Jct. KY 109 & 130, Union Co.)

Samuel Casey, 1788–1859, Treasurer of U.S., 1853–59, under Presidents Pierce and Buchanan. He resided 1811–59 in Caseyville, three miles west. Elected clerk of Circuit and County Courts; later, 1830–32, member of the State Senate.

212 WASHINGTON'S LAND
(W. of Yeaman Church of Christ, KY 54, Grayson Co.)

Filson's 1784 map of "Kentucke" showed "abundance of iron ore" here. General A. Spotswood visited area in 1797 and reported to George Washington, who purchased tract of 5,000 acres, Nov., 1798. His death, 1799, came before he could visit or develop the land.

213 LESLIE COUNTY
(Hyden, Courthouse lawn, US 421, Leslie Co.)

Created 1878, from Clay, Harlan, and Perry counties. Named for Preston H. Leslie, Governor of Kentucky, 1871–75. Montana Territorial Governor, 1887–89, U.S. District Attorney, 1894–98, appointed by President Cleveland. Died 1907, buried in Montana.

214 A FIRST IN STEEL
(Boyd Co. line, US 23, Greenup Co.)

World's first continuous steel sheet rolling mill put into operation here, 1923. Conceived by John B. Titus and built by Armco, process rated as one of the great inventions in human history. In 1953 hot-strip mill replaced first continuous mill.

215 UNION MEMORIAL
(Vanceburg, Courthouse lawn, KY 59, 3037, Lewis Co.)

The only Union monument south of the Mason-Dixon line erected by public subscription except those in cemeteries. This unique memorial was dedicated in 1884 to the 107 Lewis County soldiers who gave their lives for the Union during the Civil War.

216 CARROLLTON
(NE city limits of Carrollton, US 42, Carroll Co.)

First settled 1792, incorporated as Port William 1794. Carroll County formed and name of town changed to Carrollton by the Kentucky Legislature, 1838, both honoring "Charles Carroll of Carrollton" of Maryland, bold signer of the Declaration of Independence.

217 STAMPING GROUND
(Stamping Ground, Woodlake Pk., KY 1688, Scott Co.)

This area first explored April 1775 by William McConnell, Charles Lecompte and party from Penn. Buffalo herds had stamped down undergrowth and ground around the spring—origin of town's name. McConnell and Lecompte in Battle of Blue Licks, Ky., 1782.

218 LINDSAY'S STATION
(1 mi. N. of Stamping Ground, Jct. KY 227 & 368, Cedar Pk., Scott Co.)

Anthony Lindsay chose this site for his station, built about 1790. It was located near Lecompte's Run, a branch of the Elkhorn named for Charles Lecompte, who was here with William McConnell and others in 1775. The station was on old buffalo trace, leading north to Ohio River, and was a regular stop for travelers and traders. Lindsay's grave is 100 yds. north.

219 WILDERNESS ROAD
(Okolona, KY 61, 1065, Jefferson Co.)

Trail of thousands of pioneers through here, 1775 to 1811. Made into wagon road by Act of the Legislature 1796. Lifeline for Gen. George Rogers Clark's army at Falls of Ohio, Louisville, 1778–83. Road abandoned 1840. It followed ancient buffalo path.

221 CIVIL WAR REUNION
(Ky. Christian College Campus, Old US 60, Grayson, Carter Co.)

In their blue and gray uniforms, for over forty years, Civil War veterans gathered here annually. Around campfires, with song and story, friends and former foes revived war memories, and always a pilgrimage to graves of their comrades in cemetery on the hill.

222 FIRST EXPLORED
(2nd & Highland Ave., Carrollton, US 42, Carroll Co.)

In 1754 James McBride canoed down the Ohio to the mouth of this river—now Kentucky. Here, as first explorer, he carved his initials and the date on tree, a landmark for 30 years. Cited for part in defense of Bryan Station and Battle of Blue Licks, 1782.

250 DEDICATED TO THE MEMORY OF GENERAL CHRISTOPHER RIFFE 1764–1850. SITE OF HIS CABIN AND GRAVE
(Middleburg Cemetery, Lynn St., Middleburg, Casey Co.)

Christopher Riffe accompanied Col. William Casey (Great-Grandfather of Mark Twain) to Kentucky in 1784. Riffe lived at Bryan's Station, Boonesborough, Logan's Station and Carpenter's Station. He bought 800 acres of land from the Grandfather of Abraham Lincoln. Riffe became the first white settler of Casey County in 1793. He was the first State Representative from Casey County, served seven terms. He fought in the Battle of the Thames (in which Tecumseh was killed) in the Kentucky Sixth Regiment. He was Lieutenant-General of the Kentucky State Militia.

501 AUGUSTA IN CIVIL WAR
(Augusta, KY 8, Bracken Co.)

By Sept. 1862, 6,000 Union troops had gone from this district. Only 100 Home Guards left, under Col. Bradford. On Sept. 27, Col. Duke with 350 Morgan Raiders attacked. Guards secreted in houses fought until Raiders penetrated area, burned and cannonaded houses. CSA losses of men and ammunition forced return to Falmouth and abandonment of raid into Ohio.

503 OCTAGON HALL
(N. of Franklin, US 31-W, Simpson Co.)

An antebellum landmark built by Andrew Jackson Caldwell, an ardent advocate of the southern cause. Many Confederate soldiers found shelter here. Bricks were made, wood cut and finished, stone quarried on the place. The house erected by Caldwell and his men. Three floors, with four large rooms, hall and stairway. Large basement provided hiding place.

504 A CIVIL WAR REPRISAL
(New Capitol Grounds, Frankfort, Franklin Co.)

Near here on Nov. 2, 1864 four innocent Confederate prisoners were executed in reprisal for the murder of Union supporter,

Robert Graham of Peaks Mill, Franklin Co. All Kentuckians: Elijah Horton of Carter, Thomas Hunt and John Long of Mason, Thornton Lafferty of Pendleton counties. Hunt's body reburied at Maysville, others in the Frankfort Cemetery.

505 GUERRILLA QUANTRILL
(5 mi. S. of Taylorsville, KY 55, Spencer Co.)

William Quantrill, alias Captain Clarke, 4th Mo. Cav., taken here on May 10, 1865, ending four months Central Kentucky guerrilla raids. Surrounded in Wakefield's barn by Captain Terrill's 30 Kentuckians. Quantrill tried escape, mortally wounded and moved to Louisville Military Prison Hospital. He died June 6th, ending career as outlaw, then guerrilla for southern cause.

506 CAMP CHARITY
(7 mi. E. of Bardstown, US 62, Nelson Co.)

Named by Lexington Rifles, under John Hunt Morgan, who camped here Sept. 1861. Friendly people took no pay for food. With additional recruits, horses and supplies they joined Confederates at Green River September 30. The Rifles were mustered in as Second Cavalry Regiment, Ky. Volunteers, CSA, which developed into a Division, renowned as "Morgan's Raiders."

507 NEWPORT—WAR OF 1812
(Newport, Courthouse lawn, KY 8, Campbell Co.)

Kentuckians crossed here August 1812 marching to relieve Gen. Hull at Detroit. Took Frenchtown (Monroe) on January 18, 1813. Four days later all but 30 were killed or captured. Other Kentuckians gathered here Aug. 31, 1813. Led by Governor Shelby these men defeated British and Indians in Battle of Thames in Canada Oct. 5, 1813. This ended fighting in the Old Northwest.

508 REMEMBER THE RAISIN
(Georgetown, Courthouse lawn, US 25, 460, Scott Co.)

Rendezvous of Kentucky Volunteers, Aug. 15, 1812, ordered to relieve Gen. Hull at Detroit. Kentuckians took Frenchtown (Monroe) on Raisin River Jan. 18, 1813. Four days later enemy attacked–killed, massacred, wounded, or captured all but

30. Of 1050 men not half reached home. Ky. counties named for officers: Allen, Ballard, Graves, Hart, Hickman, Edmonson, McCracken, Meade, Simpson.

509 EDDYVILLE
(Eddyville, Overlook Dr., just off KY 730, Lyon Co.)

Several brisk skirmishes took place in this area because of the importance of Cumberland River navigation. Oct. 17, 1864, General H. B. Lyon with small CSA force attacked Union garrison, which surrendered and was taken from town. Union gunboat "Silver Lake" shelled town, took Lyon's wife hostage. Lyon then released Capt. Hugh M. Hiett and 8 USA officers.

510 POUND GAP
(Jenkins, US 23, 119, Letcher Co.)

Route through here discovered by Christopher Gist, April 1, 1751. Brig. Gen. Garfield and 700 Union troops forced 500 CSA men from here Mar. 16, 1862 and burned CSA supplies. On last raid in Kentucky, Morgan's Raiders dislodged Union forces here June 1, 1864 and moved on to Mt. Sterling, Lexington and Cynthiana. They then returned to Virginia.

512 WEST LIBERTY—CIVIL WAR
(West Liberty, Main St., US 460, Morgan Co.)

The first important engagement in eastern Kentucky occurred here on Oct. 23, 1861. USA forces led by Brig. Gen. Wm. Nelson surprised enemy under Capt. Andrew J. May. Civilian secessionists were captured and jailed Unionists released. Confederate losses 21 dead, 40 wounded, 34 captured. One Union soldier wounded. On Nov. 4, 1861 Gen. Nelson captured Prestonsburg.

513 SCOTT'S RAID
(Williamsburg, Courthouse lawn, US 25-W, Whitley Co.)

Col. John S. Scott with 1,600 of 2nd Cav. Brig. CSA came up from Eastern Tenn. on raid to destroy USA communications and obtain cattle, horses, mules and arms. At Williamsburg on July 25, 1863 he was met by 100 pickets of 44th Ohio Inf. After a skirmish, he drove then toward London. Scott went on to Winchester, retreating then to Tenn. with heavy losses.

514 CIVIL WAR ACTION
(Big Hill, US 421, Madison Co.)

Aug. 23, 1862, Col. Scott's La. cavalry, of Gen. Kirby Smith's invading army from Tenn., routed Col. Metcalfe and Union troops. Approaching Richmond as USA army arrived, Scott went back to Camp Wildcat, then joined Smith in Richmond victory, Aug. 30, 1862. Mar. 1864, Gen. Grant on way to take command of all US armies stopped at house south of here.

515 MORGAN—ON TO OHIO
(Burkesville, Courthouse lawn, KY 61, 90, Cumberland Co.)

July 2, 1863, CSA Gen. John Hunt Morgan crossed Cumberland River near here, brushing aside Union patrols on north bank. Morgan placed some troops in ambush one mile from here and drove Union forces back to camp at Marrowbone. Morgan crossed Kentucky, invading Indiana and on into Northeastern Ohio, where he surrendered July 26. He was imprisoned at Columbus, Ohio.

516 MORGAN AT MIDWAY
(Midway, US 62 at railroad, Woodford Co.)

Taking 300 abandoned USA horses and mules at Versailles, Morgan's Raiders came here July 15, 1862. Advised of troop train approach from Frankfort he had tracks torn up and howitzers set. Train warned and returned to Frankfort. Morgan took telegraph line and coaxed train at Lexington to come on but it turned back. He and his men reached Georgetown that evening.

517 FORREST'S RAID
(Beltline near 21st & Old Mayfield Rd., Paducah, McCracken Co.)

General N. B. Forrest with Thompson's Ky. and Bell's Tenn. Brigades raided Paducah on March 25, 1864. Union's Fort Anderson held with aid of gunboats. Guards at USA warehouse captured. Part of town burned. Supplies of food taken by withdrawing CSA forces. Boast in Union newspaper prompted Forrest to send Gen. Abe Buford back to capture some overlooked horses.

518 CIVIL WAR ACTIONS
(Near city limits of Barbourville, US 25-E, Knox Co.)

First skirmish in eastern Ky. On Sept. 19, 1861, Zollicoffer's CSA troops approached Barbourville. Home guard obstructed bridge. CSA took another route, were repulsed twice before guards retreated. Considerable property destroyed in town. CSA Gen. Kirby Smith's hdqrs. here Aug. 18 to 25, 1862 while preparing invasion of Central Ky.

519 A CONFEDERATE THRUST
(Ft. Mitchell Country Club, off US 25, 42, Kenton Co.)

In the Confederate effort to gain control of Central Ky., Gen. Heth and troops reached outskirts of Covington Sept. 6, 1862 as threat to the North. Object was to hold USA troops here and prevent their moving to resist Bragg's forces nearing Louisville. Large Union forces crossed river for defense. Heth withdrew Sept. 12, obtaining recruits, food and supplies.

520 A MASTERFUL RETREAT
(Greenup, Courthouse lawn, US 23, Greenup Co.)

USA Brig. Gen. George W. Morgan with 8000 men reached here Oct. 3, 1862 on way to Camp Dennison, Ohio, after retreating over 200 miles from Cumberland Gap in sixteen days, harassed by CSA Morgan's Raiders. USA forces had held Gap but Confederate operations based in Barbourville, 24 miles north of Gap, had cut off Union supplies and made retreat necessary.

521 A MASTERFUL RETREAT
(Cumberland Gap, US 25-E, Bell Co.)

During the Civil War, Cumberland Gap was held alternately by Union and CSA armies. USA forces under Gen. George W. Morgan occupied it June 18 to Sept. 17, 1862. Cut off from supplies and surrounded, Morgan with 9,000 men retreated successfully to Greenup on Ohio River, 200 miles in 16 days over mountain roads, and despite the harassment of CSA Morgan's Raiders.

522 CONFEDERATES HERE
(Old Capitol Grounds, Frankfort, Franklin Co.)

The Kentucky State Government moved to Louisville before CSA entered Lexington Sept. 2, 1862. Confederate cavalry moved through Sept. 3 on way toward Louisville. Richard Hawes was inaugurated second Confederate Governor October 4. Generals Bragg and Kirby Smith with large CSA force were present. They withdrew and Union forces occupied Frankfort, Oct. 7, 1862.

523 SURPRISE ATTACK HERE
(Sacramento, KY 81, 85, McLean Co.)

CSA cavalry from Hopkinsville under Colonel Nathan Bedford Forrest surprised Union forces under Major Eli H. Murray December 18, 1861. Forrest sent dismounted men to attack both enemy flanks, and, with the remainder mounted, he bore down road upon Union center, which broke and fled. Forrest pursued 4 miles, dispersed USA troops, returned to Hopkinsville.

524 MORGAN'S FIRST RAID
(Tompkinsville, KY 63, 100, Monroe Co.)

July 9, 1862, Morgan's Raiders, coming from Tenn. on first raid into Ky., attacked force of 9th Pa. Cav. at USA garrison. Raiders captured 30 of retreating enemy and destroyed tents and stores. They took 20 wagons, 50 mules, 40 horses, sugar and coffee supplies. At Glasgow they burned supplies, then went north, raiding 16 other towns before returning to Tenn.

525 MORGAN'S SECOND RAID
(Elizabethtown at Cemetery, US 31-W, Hardin Co.)

North of here Morgan's Raiders destroyed two of the most important L&N R.R. trestles Dec. 28, 1862, rendering line impassable for two months. Circling this area, they returned to Tenn. on Jan. 2, 1863. In eleven days they destroyed $2,000,000 of U.S. property, wrecked L&N line from Munfordville to Shepherdsville, and captured, then paroled, 1,877 prisoners.

526 LINCOLN HOMESTEAD
(Springfield, Courthouse lawn, US 150, KY 55, Washington Co.)

The certified marriage bond of Thomas Lincoln to Nancy Hanks, parents of Abraham Lincoln, is on file here in Washington Co. Courthouse. Here also preserved is full account of the wedding. Lincoln Homestead State Park, seven miles north, now marks the site of log house where marriage was performed June 12, 1806 by the Reverend Jesse Head, Methodist pastor.

527 A CIVIL WAR ACTION
(Henderson, Courthouse lawn, Old US 41, KY 54, Henderson Co.)

Brig. General A. R. Johnson and 30 CSA raiders took city, capturing 50 guns, hospital supplies, and commissary stores July 17, 1862, then raided Newburg, Ind., and returned to Henderson. Threat of Morgan's Raiders prevented USA Hdqrs. at Louisville from sending relief. July 22 troops arrived here from Evansville, Ind., but CSA troops had abandoned area.

528 "GIBRALTAR OF THE WEST"
(Columbus, Columbus-Belmont State Park, Hickman Co.)

Troops under Gen. Leonidas Polk fortified strategic line of bluffs here Sept. 3, 1861, marking CSA's first move in Ky. To prevent passage of Union gunboats, a huge chain was stretched across the Mississippi River. After Union success in Tenn., CSA evacuated on Mar. 2, 1862. Union troops moved in the next day and held position throughout the war.

529 MORGAN—ON TO OHIO
(Main St. at river, Brandenburg, KY 228, Meade Co.)

July 7, 1863, Morgan's CSA Cavalry arrived here, captured steamers *John B. McCombs* and *Alice Dean*. Next day they began crossing river. Indiana militia fired on them but fled under return fire. *Alice Dean* burned after crossing. Morgan went on to northeastern Ohio, where he surrendered July 26. Imprisoned at Columbus, Ohio, he escaped Nov. 24, returned south.

530 BACON CREEK BRIDGE
(Bonnieville, US 31-W, Hart Co.)

The L&N R.R. bridge near here, a main USA supply line between Louisville and Bowling Green, was destroyed by Confederate troops in late 1861. Before repairs were complete, Morgan's Raiders burned it Dec. 5, 1861. This act brought Morgan's daring to public eye. A year later Morgan again burned the trestle and stockade, taking 93 prisoners of 91st Ill. Vol.

531 GOOSE CREEK SALT WORKS
(2½ mi. S. of Manchester, KY 11, Clay Co.)

On Oct. 23, 1862, 22nd USA Brig. including lst, 2nd, and 20th Ky. Infantry moved here in wake of retreating CSA forces. 500 men worked 36 hours to destroy salt works mainly owned by unionists but used by Confederates. Loyal USA citizens allowed to remove salt enough for their own needs on taking oath none of it would be used to benefit Confederacy.

532 YOUNGLAND
(Shively, US 31-W, Jefferson Co.)

Home of Bennett H. Young (1843–1919). Member of famed CSA unit, Morgan's Raiders, Lt. B. H. Young led 21 soldiers in raid October 19, 1864 on St. Albans, Vermont, Civil War's northernmost action. Robbed three banks of over $200,000 and attempted to burn town. Captured in Canada, they were released. After war, he became a business and civic leader in Louisville.

533 "LION OF WHITE HALL"
(7 mi. N. of Richmond, Jct. US 25 & KY 627, Madison Co.)

West of here is White Hall, home of Cassius M. Clay (1810–1903). For a half century, Clay was a "firebrand" in American life. Fearless abolitionist, publisher of anti-slavery paper, *The True American*, captain in the Mexican War, legislator and Minister to Russia. When Ft. Sumter fell, he organized civilian guard for U.S. Capitol until army could protect.

534 SOLDIER'S RETREAT
(E. of St. Matthews, US 60, 460, Jefferson Co.)

Home of Richard Clough Anderson, Revolutionary hero, built before 1785 half-mile south. Anderson, who served on staff of Lafayette, is buried in cemetery near home, which burned 1842. The birthplace, in 1805, of Robert Anderson who, as commander of Fort Sumter in April, 1861, was first Union hero of Civil War. Commander Dept. of Ky. Sept., 1861.

Cassius M. Clay, "Lion of White Hall." Kentucky Historical Society Collection.

535 THE GALT HOUSE
(Second & Main Sts., Louisville, Jefferson Co.)

A world-famed inn operated here from 1835 until it burned in 1865. Host to notables, such as author Charles Dickens, it was scene of assassination of USA Gen. Wm. Nelson, Sept. 1862, by USA Gen. J. C. Davis. Sherman and Grant met here March 1864, to plan invasion that led to the "March to the Sea." Traditions carried on at new Galt House at lst and Main, 1869–1921.

536 "SUE MUNDY CAPTURED"
(2 mi. E. of Breckinridge Co. line, US 60, Meade Co.)

At age of 17, in 1861, Jerome Clarke, called Sue Mundy, joined Confederate Army. He was with Morgan's Raiders from 1862 until Morgan's death in 1864. He then became notorious as a guerrilla. On March 12, 1865 Union soldiers captured him here with two other leaders of guerrilla bands. Clarke, then only 20, was executed three days later in Louisville.

537 "SUE MUNDY" HERE
(Midway, US 62, Woodford Co.)

Jerome Clarke, called Sue Mundy, one of Morgan's Raiders, formed his own guerrilla band on Morgan's death Sept. 1864. Clarke and band raided here November

1, 1864, killing Adam Harper. Four Confederate prisoners executed in reprisal by Union forces. On Feb. 2, 1865, Clarke returned with William Quantrill, another guerrilla leader, burned depot here and stole 15 horses.

538 A CIVIL WAR DEFENSE LINE
(2nd & High Sts., Bowling Green, US 31-W, 68, Warren Co.)

Troops under Generals S. B. Buckner and A. S. Johnston, CSA, took up this key position in the Southern defense line on September 18, 1861. After Fort Henry fell and Fort Donelson was threatened, they evacuated Feb. 11–13, 1862. Gen. O. M. Mitchell and Federal troops entered Feb. 14, 1862, occupying the evacuated fort and securing the defense line for the North.

539 A GENERAL'S PRAYER
(Chiles St., St. Philips Epis. Church, Harrodsburg, Mercer Co.)

"Peace to the land and blessings on friend and foe alike." Prayer by Gen. Leonidas K. Polk, CSA, an Episcopal Bishop, offered on October 9, 1862 following the Battle of Perryville. Shaken by the horrors of war, just witnessed, Polk entered this church asking that bell be tolled. Soldiers' and civilians' tears mingled with prayers in one great supplication.

540 JEROME CLARKE ("SUE MUNDY")
(18th & Broadway, Louisville, Jefferson Co.)

Born in Franklin, Kentucky, 1844, Jerome Clarke enlisted in Company B, Fourth Regiment, Kentucky Confederate Orphan Brigade, 1861. Captured at Fort Donelson, he escaped from Camp Morton. Clarke saw action at Chickamauga and then became one of "Morgan's men." After Morgan's death, this Confederate raider became notorious as woman marauder "Sue Mundy." Over.
(Reverse)

"SUE MUNDY" EXECUTED

Jerome Clarke, 20, was captured in March 1865, and tried and convicted for guerrilla activities as Sue Mundy. He claimed to have been operating as a Confederate soldier rather than a lawless guerrilla. In the block bounded by Broadway, Magazine, 17th and 18th streets, Clarke was hanged

on March 15, 1865. A crowd of several thousand witnessed his death. See over.

541 BELKNAP CAMPUS
(University of Louisville Campus, Louisville, Jefferson Co.)

Originally this was site of the old Industrial School of Reform and House of Refuge, established 1860. During Civil War, institution used by Union troops as barracks and parade grounds. The property, with several original buildings, taken over by Univ. of Louisville in 1923 and called the University campus. Renamed in 1927 in honor of benefactor William R. Belknap.

542 PRENTICE SCHOOL
(525 S. 6th St., Louisville, Jefferson Co.)

On this site stood the George D. Prentice School, which was one of nineteen in Louisville that were commandeered for use as hospitals during Civil War. Worden Pope, an early Louisville civic and political leader, built his home here ca. 1830. It housed the Kentucky School of Medicine from 1887–1914 and later the Stevens School for Retarded Children.

543 DEATH OF A MORGAN
(Lebanon, US 68, Marion Co.)

Lt. Thomas Morgan, 19, one of four brothers then in Morgan's Raiders under another brother, Gen. John Hunt Morgan, was killed near here July 5, 1863 as he led an attack on Union forces in the depot at Lebanon. He died in his brother Calvin's arms as the Union troops surrendered. He was reinterred in the Lexington Cemetery in 1868 where this Morgan family rests.

544 CHRISTMAS MISHAP
(Glasgow, Courthouse lawn, US 31-E, 68, Barren Co.)

On Dec. 24, 1862, main body of Morgan's Raiders made camp south of here. Capt. Quirk and scouts entered town although USA troops patrolled area. CSA scouts wished to celebrate Christmas Eve, and dismounted at tavern. A patrol of 2nd Michigan Cavalry, USA, rode up with same desire. After skirmish, with slight losses, both parties stampeded without a celebration.

545 CIVIL WAR ACTION
(Benton, US 641, Marshall Co.)

On March 23, 1864, two days before the Battle of Paducah, detached forces of Confederate General Nathan B. Forrest's cavalry coming up from Columbus, Miss., and Union troops, both searching for horses, met by accident near here. In two skirmishes which took place, three were killed in first engagement and four in the second. Burial was in the old Gilbert cemetery.

546 FORT MITCHEL
(Dixie Highway, Ft. Mitchell, Kenton Co.)

Near here stood old Ft. Mitchel, erected Oct. 1861. Scene of several skirmishes between CSA forces under Gen. Henry Heth and USA troops under Gen. Lew Wallace September, 1862. Major anchor in a line of seven forts defending Cincinnati. They ran along hills around Covington about 10 miles, from Bromley, on river to west, east to river near Ft. Thomas.

547 LOUISA IN CIVIL WAR
(Louisa, Courthouse lawn, US 23, Lawrence Co.)

River traffic caused Union forces under Gen. James A. Garfield, 20th U.S. President, to occupy Louisa Dec. 1861. CSA troops attempted capture March 12 and 25–26, 1863. Southern partisans raided area Nov. 5, 1864, burning houses and 2 steamers, and looting stores. Fort Bishop, USA, completed here just as war ended in 1865. Also called Fort Gallup and Fort Hill.

548 PERRYVILLE PRELUDE
(W. of Middletown, US 60, 460, Jefferson Co.)

Two largest skirmishes of Civil War in Jefferson County occurred here Sept. 27 and 30, 1862. CSA forces, already in control of the State Capital, were threatening Louisville. In first clash the Confederates were driven back to Floyds Fork. Three days later CSA again halted at Union line. Both were preliminary to Battle of Perryville on Oct. 8, 1862.

549 CIVIL WAR ACTIONS
(1 mi. N. of New Castle, US 421, Henry Co.)

On Sept. 21, 1862 cavalry men under Maj. George M. Jessee, a native here, attacked provost marshal Robert Morris' home guard. Guards surrendered men, horses, and 300 stand of arms. Dec. 13, 1864, Maj. Jessee and Confederate forces were defeated here after a spirited skirmish with state troops and home guards led by Capt. Jas. H. Bridgewater.

550 SKIRMISH AT FLORENCE
(Florence, US 25, 127, Boone Co.)

Union troops had built forts around Covington to repel expected attack from CSA troops under General Heth. Detachment of 101 CSA troops camped at Snow's Pond, attacked here by scouting party of 53 USA cavalrymen Sept. 17, 1862. In the skirmish 1 Union, 5 Confederates killed and 1 Union, 7 Confederates were wounded. Larkin Vaughn, a civilian, killed by a stray shot.

551 HARRODSBURG SPRINGS
(Moreland Ave., E. of US 127, Harrodsburg, Mercer Co.)

An exclusive spa was located here from 1820–1853, then sold to U.S. Government as Western Military Asylum for aged veterans. After main building burned, veterans were moved in 1859 to Washington, D.C. Ballroom and cottages were opened Oct. 8, 1862 to care for thousands of CSA and USA wounded from Battle of Perryville. Last of buildings had burned by 1885.

552 JOSEPH HOLT
(4 mi. E. of Cloverport, US 60 & KY 144, Breckinridge Co.)

Six miles north are birthplace and grave of Joseph Holt, 1807–1896. He was Commissioner of Patents, Postmaster General and Secretary of War in President Buchanan's Administration, 1857–1861. Lincoln named him Judge Advocate General of the Union army in 1862. Holt prosecuted conspirators in the assassination of Lincoln, 1865. He retired as Judge Advocate in 1875.

553 BATTLE OF PERRYVILLE, OCT. 8, 1862
(Perryville, US 68, 150, Boyle Co.)

The battle was brought on by Confederate Lieut. Gen. Braxton Bragg as a delaying action to insure safe withdrawal of a huge wagon train of supplies and to enable him to effect a junction with the army of Maj.

Gen. E. Kirby Smith in the vicinity of Versailles.

In overall command of the Union Army (Army of the Ohio) was Maj. Gen. Don Carlos Buell, with Maj. General George H. Thomas second in command. Buell had three corps. First: Maj. Gen. Alexander McDowell McCook. Second: Maj. Gen. Thomas L. Crittenden. Third: Maj. Gen. Charles C. Gilbert.

In overall command of the Confederate Army (Army of the Mississippi) was Gen. Bragg, with Maj. Gen. Leonidas Polk commander of the Right Wing and Maj. Gen. William J. Hardee of the Left Wing. Bragg had three divisions: Maj. Gen. Benjamin F. Cheatham's; Brig. Gen. J. Patton Anderson's; and Maj. Gen. Simon Bolivar Buckner's.

The main action began at 2:00 p.m. with a fierce charge by Brig. Gen. John A. Wharton's cavalry, on the extreme Confederate right, followed immediately by a rapid advance of Cheatham's entire line. Simultaneously, Buckner's and Anderson's moved forward, amid heavy cannonading from numerous batteries on both sides.

Cheatham's charge caught a large number of McCook's men (many fresh enlistees) unaware and off guard, far in advance of their lines, seeking water in the vicinity of Doctor's Creek. Both Cheatham's and Buckner's divisions drove McCook's men back to their former ill-formed positions and, after heavy, often desperate, hand-to-hand fighting, dislodged his entire corps, pushing him back a distance of approximately a mile west of the Creek. On the Confederate left, however, Anderson was unable to dislodge the division of Brig. Gen. Philip H. Sheridan, timely enforced by Brig. Gen. Albin Schoepf's division.

Late afternoon, Anderson's advancing left was struck by a determined charge of Col. William P. Carlin's brigade (R. B. Mitchell's division, Gilbert's Corps) between the Springfield and Lebanon roads, the charge carrying through Perryville and out on the Danville and Harrodsburg roads. Toward dusk, desperate staying actions by brigades of Col. John C. Starkweather (Rousseau's division) and Col.

Michael Gooding (Mitchell's division) enabled McCook to stabilize his battered corps along a line immediately beyond the Russell house and Benton road. In his favor too were the coming of darkness and near exhaustion of the Confederates.

General Buell, headquarters at the Dorsey house on Springfield road, was not aware that the battle was in progress until 4:00 p.m., too late to have Crittenden's corps, along Lebanon road, pivot around in an attempt to envelop the enemy forces.

After nightfall, Bragg finally realized that his small force faced practically Buell's entire army. This knowledge caused him to order withdrawal at midnight toward Harrodsburg. On the whole, the Confederate troops were better handled and used than these of the Union. The battle ended as a tactical victory for Bragg; a strategic victory for Buell, who held the field.

The Confederate commander employed only 16,000 men and sustained 3,396 casualties; 510 killed, 2,635 wounded, and 251 missing. Buell used between 22,000 and 28,000; sustained 4,421 casualties; 845 killed, 2,851 wounded and 515 captured or missing. The battle was one of the fiercest and bloodiest of modern times.

Had Buell and Bragg been better informed and more aggressive, the battle of Perryville might have been the decisive engagement of the Civil War in the West. After this battle, the Confederates never returned to Kentucky in great force; the state remained firmly in the Union.

554 LEXINGTON NAMED
(Entrance to McConnell Springs Dr. & Old Frankfort Pk., Lexington, Fayette Co.)

In early June of 1775, a party of frontiersmen, led by William McConnell, camped near here on a branch of Elkhorn Creek. Upon hearing of the colonists' victory at Lexington, Mass., on April 19, 1775, they named their campsite Lexington to commemorate the first battle of the American Revolution. Impressed with the area, they hoped to see a town here some day.
(Reverse)

LEXINGTON SETTLED
Due to danger of Indian attacks, perma-

nent settlement was delayed for four years. In 1779 Colonel Robert Patterson and 25 companions came from Fort Harrod and erected a blockhouse at present Main and Mill streets. Cabins and stockade were soon built, making fort a place of importance. The town of Lexington was established on May 6, 1782, by act of Va. Gen. Assembly.

555 ESTILL SPRINGS
(½ mi. N. of Irvine, KY 89, Estill Co.)

Mineral springs visited by Boone, Boyle, McAfee and other pioneers. Early camp of Shawnee Indians. First school of early settlers located here. Operated as resort, 1814 until hotel burned 1924. In 1861, owner Col. Sidney M. Barnes organized 8th Ky. Inf. Vol., USA. Used as recruiting station and camp. Morgan's men held several reunions here, including the last.

556 MISSION ACCOMPLISHED
(Paintsville, US 23, 460, Johnson Co.)

On mission to clear area of CSA forces, Colonel G. W. Gallup with USA troops was attacked here April 13, 1864 by CSA force under Lt. Colonel E. F. Clay. Union troops repulsed Confederates. Next day USA attacked CSA at Half Mountain, south of Salyersville. 60 CSA killed or wounded; 60 men, 200 horses, 400 saddles, 300 small arms captured. USA losses were slight.

557 FIRST COAL OIL
(3 mi. E. of Cloverport, US 60, Breckinridge Co.)

Coal oil first produced here 1851. Plant built 1857, reputed first of kind in world. Mine known for extensive veins of cannel coal. Coal loaded here, exported to England via New Orleans for gas manufacture. English-owned with Prince of Wales (King Edward VII) an investor. Disastrous fire, the discovery of petroleum, and Civil War caused cessation of operation.

558 FRONTIER NURSING
(Hyden, Courthouse lawn, US 421, Leslie Co.)

Mary Breckinridge founded the Frontier Nursing Service, 1925. Midwives from England helped to bring medical service that saved hundreds of mothers and babies of "remote hollows and hills of Clay,

Leslie and Perry counties." 1928, a 28-bed hospital opened in Hyden and in 1939 Frontier Graduate School of Midwifery founded, one of three such schools in U.S.

559 SWIFT'S SILVER CAMP
(Campton, Courthouse lawn, KY 15, Wolfe Co.)

John Swift's fabulous journals report silver operations in East Kentucky. References to ships on the Spanish Seas and to coinage of silver in this area with six trips from Atlantic Coast to this region, 1761 to 1769, is an unsolved mystery. Intrepid searchers have found no trace of cache or mine. One Swift camp reputed to have been on site of this Court House.

560 BATTLE OF LONDON
(London, Courthouse lawn, Main St., US 25, Laurel Co.)

500 CSA cavalry led by Colonel J. S. Scott attacked 200 USA troops and 98 convalescents under Colonel L. C. Houk here Aug. 17, 1862; killed 13, wounded 17, captured 111 men and 40 wagons. CSA lost 2 killed, 4 wounded. Houk forced back to Gen. George W. Morgan's main USA force at Cumberland Gap. Cut off from supplies, Morgan began his retreat to Ohio thirty days later.

561 CIVIL WAR ACTIONS (BOONEVILLE)
(Booneville, Courthouse lawn, KY 11, 30, Owsley Co.)

Retreating to Ohio from Cumberland Gap, part of USA Brig. Gen. George W. Morgan's command passed by here obtaining supplies, Sept. 21, 1862. Force of 40 local citizens drove off 75 Southern partisan guerrillas, April 14, 1864. Col. C. H. Hanson and 300 USA troops pursuing Morgan's Raiders stopped here to obtain guides and information, June 17, 1864.

562 "SUE MUNDY'S" GRAVE
(Franklin, North Main & Finn Sts., Simpson Co.)

Marcellus Jerome Clarke enlisted in the Confederate Army, 1861, at age 17. Attached to Morgan's Cavalry in 1863. Captured on March 12, 1865, taken to Louisville, hanged three days later, courtmartialed as guerrilla "Sue Mundy." His last words: "I believe in and die for the Confederate cause." In 1865 body brought here, reburied 1914 two blocks east by CSA veterans.

563 DEMONSTRATION—1862
(Bardwell, US 51, 62, Carlisle Co.)

Jan. 1862, Brig. Gen. Ulysses S. Grant sent 5,000 USA troops from Cairo as demonstration against Columbus, a Confederate stronghold on the Miss. River. Combined forces led by Brig. Gen. J. S. McClernand from Ft. Jefferson at Wickliffe through here to Milburn and back to Cairo. It acquainted U.S. Army with the area. It "inspired hope" among many loyal Federal citizens.

564 CIVIL WAR RECRUITING
(Owenton, KY 227, Owen Co.)

Two Confederate recruiting camps were located in Owen Co. in the Civil War. Camp Marshall, at Lusby's Mill 7 miles east of here, was organized in 1861 by Gen. Humphrey Marshall of Kentucky. The other was in Vallandingham's Barn near here. Hundreds enlisted from this county to protect their homes, but were sent to various parts of Kentucky and Tennessee.

565 ALMAHURST FARM
(In front of the Old Coach Stop, Jct. of US 68 & KY 169, Jessamine Co.)

Part of original land granted to James Knight, 1750–1831, for his services in the Revolutionary War. A portion owned by heirs, 1962. Among the famous horses bred, foaled, and raised on this farm were: Greyhound, world's champion trotter of all times; Peter Volo, founder of one of the great trotting families; Exterminator, known wherever thoroughbreds are raced.

566 CIVI WAR ACTION
(3 mi. S. of Royalton, KY 7 at mouth of Puncheon Cr., Magoffin Co.)

On mission to clear area of CSA forces, Col. Geo. W. Gallup with USA troops repulsed Confederate attack led by Lt. Colonel E. F. Clay at Paintsville April 13, 1864, and pursued enemy to this point. Union men attacked next day. Clay was mortally wounded: CSA suffered 60 casualties and 60 men, 200 horses, 400 saddles, 300 small-arms taken. USA sustained only slight losses.

567 MORGAN RAIDERS' CAMP
(1 mi. E. of Licking River, Farmers, US 60, Rowan Co.)

On last tragic raid, the fourth into Kentucky, Morgan's Raiders took Mt. Sterling, then lost it, took Lexington and June 11, 1864 took Cynthiana. Next day USA men under Brig. General S. G. Burbridge dispersed raiders. Morgan then retreated through Flemingsburg and camped here June 12. He and his men returned to Virginia, but never recovered from this reverse.

568 A MASTERFUL RETREAT
(2½ mi. S. of Manchester, KY 11, Clay Co.)

Gen. George W. Morgan's Union forces occupied Cumberland Gap, June 18 to Sept. 17, 1862. Cut off from supplies and surrounded, Morgan with 9,000 men withdrew. They camped here Sept. 19–21, to perfect organization for march. Made fruitless supply search. Entire retreat to Ohio River, 200 miles, made in 16 days, despite harassment by CSA Morgan's Raiders.

569 CIVIL WAR ACTION
(Morgantown, US 79, 231, Butler Co.)

Oct. 1861, Col. J. H. McHenry, Jr., USA, at Hartford warned of threat of CSA attack. Col. S. G. Burbridge brought USA force from Owensboro and joined in move to Morgantown. Advance cavalry routed CSA scouts here. Burbridge then moved on to attack and destroy Confederate camp at Woodbury. Report of CSA re-enforcement caused Union Army to withdraw to Cromwell's Ferry.

570 CIVIL WAR ROUTES
(4 mi. S. of Cawood, US 421, Harlan Co.)

This area important passageway for Union and Confederate forces. USA moved along Poor Fork and CSA along Clover Fork of Cumberland River; each route reflected local sentiment. February 1862 USA forces under Brig. Gen. T. T. Garrard, grandson of Ky.'s second governor, camped here. Later CSA troops under Gen. H. Marshall camped here.

571 JENNIE'S CREEK
(Paintsville, ½ mi. W. of Jct. US 23 & 460, Johnson Co.)

Under orders to dislodge CSA from this area Col. James A. Garfield's troops reached Paintsville on Jan. 6, 1862. The next day he sent Col. Wm. Bolles to clear out CSA cavalry at mouth of Jennie's Creek. After Confederate defeat here, Gen. Humphrey Marshall withdrew to Middle Creek. After a heavy engagement there on Jan. 10, Marshall returned to Virginia.

572 DAY OF PERRYVILLE
(5 mi. W. of Lawrenceburg, US 62, Anderson Co.)

Oct. 8, 1862, during Battle of Perryville, Gen. James Withers' troops of Gen. Kirby Smith's CSA army attacked USA force of Gen. J. W. Sill near Fox Creek while Smith skirmished with Sill's rear guard. Many Union prisoners and 20 wagons captured. A Confederate shot seven Federals but later was killed. He with four others are buried in Lawrenceburg Cemetery.

573 BARKLEY'S BIRTHPLACE
(NW of Mayfield, Jct. KY 339 & 121, Graves Co.)

Alben W. Barkley, U.S. Senator and Vice President, was born near here, November 24, 1877. A life-long leader in Democratic party. Elected Prosecuting Attorney for McCracken Co. 1905, County Judge 1909, Congressman 1912, and U.S. Senator 1926. Majority Leader of Senate longer than any other man. Vice President, 1949–53. Elected Senator 1954. Death on Apr. 30, 1956.

574 GRAVE OF LUCY VIRGIN DOWNS, 1769–1847
1,000 feet west
(Oldtown, KY 1, Greenup Co.)

The first white child born of American parents, west of the Allegheny Mountains– Mrs. Lucy Virgin Downs–was a resident of Oldtown, Greenup County, from 1807 until her death in 1847. She was the daughter of Jeremiah and Lucy Virgin, born September 17, 1769, in what is now Fayette County, Pennsylvania, near Uniontown, which was then called Beesontown. In 1790, with her parents and brother, Brice, she came to Limestone, now Maysville, Kentucky. In 1792, she and her brother moved to Cincinnati. She was married

there to John Downs September 20, 1800 under a marriage license issued by General Arthur St. Clair, as Governor of the Northwest Territory. In June, 1845, at a family gathering, she related that General George Washington visited her father and a neighbor in 1773, when he was surveying a tract in Pennsylvania that was afterwards called Washington Bottoms. Many of her descendants are still living in this part of Kentucky. This marker erected under the terms of the will of the late Jennie Scott Osenton, great-granddaughter of Lucy Virgin Downs.

575 GEN. GEORGE ROGERS CLARK
(Riverfront, Broadway & Ky. Ave., Paducah, McCracken Co.)

visited this spot, 1778.

GEN. ULYSSES S. GRANT

landed here Sept. 6, 1861 to occupy Paducah for Federal Union.

CAPT. JACK B. SLEETH

laid first successful submarine cable, 1847. It reached from foot of Campbell St. to Illinois shore. *Presented 1963 by Woodmen of the World.*

576 DANIEL BOONE—PIONEER
(Frankfort Cem., E. Main St., US 60, Franklin Co.)

Born, Pa., 1734. Died, Mo., 1820. Married Rebecca Boone, 1756, N.C. First trip to Kentucky, 1767. Set up Fort Boonesborough, 1775, blazed Wilderness Trail and settled. Frontiersman, surveyor, settler, legislator and sheriff. Defender against Indians and British. His claim to 100,000 acres lost, 1784. Emigrated to Missouri in 1799. See other side.
(Reverse)

GRAVE OF DANIEL BOONE

In the cemetery stands a monument to Daniel and Rebecca Boone, done by a grateful Commonwealth in 1860. Their remains had been brought back from Missouri and reburied, on September 13, 1845. A tribute to that outstanding frontiersman and his wife, who pioneered in carving out a wilderness empire–now Kentucky. See other side. *Presented by Rotary Club, District 671.*

577 COURTHOUSE BURNED
(Hopkinsville, Courthouse lawn, US 41, 68, Christian Co.)

Gen. Hylan B. Lyon with 800 men invaded Ky., Dec. 1864, to enforce CSA draft law and divert USA from Nashville. In 23 days he burned seven courthouses used by Union forces. (See map on reverse side.) Courthouse at Hopkinsville burned Dec. 12. All county records saved. Commandeered clothing and went on. Returned on 16th, skirmished with US force and moved to Madisonville.

578 COURTHOUSE BURNED
(Cadiz, Courthouse lawn, US 68, Trigg Co.)

Gen. Hylan B. Lyon with 800 men invaded Ky., Dec. 1864, to enforce CSA draft law and divert USA from Nashville. In 23 days he burned seven courthouses used by Union forces. (See map on reverse side.) Lyon came to Cadiz, December 13. US force fled courthouse, leaving man with smallpox. Lyon burned "contaminated" building, moved to Eddyville. County records saved.

579 COURTHOUSE BURNED
(Princeton, Courthouse lawn, US 62, Caldwell Co.)

Gen. Hylan B. Lyon with 800 men invaded Ky., Dec. 1864, to enforce CSA draft law and divert USA from Nashville. In 23 days he burned seven courthouses used by Union forces. (See map on reverse side.) US troops fled Princeton as Lyon came from Eddyville. Courthouse burned on December 15. Records saved. Next day, Lyon stopped US force, then moved toward Madisonville.

580 COURTHOUSE BURNED
(Madisonville, Courthouse lawn, US 41-A, Hopkins Co.)

Gen. Hylan B. Lyon with 800 men invaded Ky., Dec. 1864, to enforce CSA draft law and divert USA from Nashville. In 23 days he burned seven courthouses used by Union forces. (See map on reverse side.) Courthouse at Madisonville burned December 17. All county records saved. All able-bodied men conscripted, took oath to meet Lyon, Jan. 20, released, but oath not fulfilled.

581 COURTHOUSE BURNED
(Hartford, Courthouse lawn, US 231, Ohio Co.)

Gen. Hylan B. Lyon with 800 men invaded Ky., Dec. 1864, to enforce CSA draft law and divert USA from Nashville. In 23 days he burned seven courthouses used by Union forces. (See map on reverse side.) At Hartford, garrison captured by Lyon, Dec. 20–later paroled–and courthouse burned. Records, in other building, saved on plea by Samuel O. Peyton, local doctor.

582 COURTHOUSE BURNED
(Campbellsville, Courthouse lawn, US 68, Taylor Co.)

Gen. Hylan B. Lyon with 800 men invaded Ky., Dec. 1864, to enforce CSA draft law and divert USA from Nashville. In 23 days he burned seven courthouses used by Union forces. (See map on reverse side.) The courthouse at Campbellsville was burned December 25. Some records saved. Desertions had reduced ranks to 250 and Lyon moved out of state via Burkesville, Jan. 3.

583 COURTHOUSE BURNED
(Burkesville, Courthouse lawn, KY 61, 90, Cumberland Co.)

Gen. Hylan B. Lyon with 800 men invaded Ky., Dec. 1864, to enforce CSA draft law and divert USA from Nashville. In 23 days he burned seven courthouses used by Union forces. (See map on reverse side.) Raid ended at Burkesville with robbery of stores, impressment of horses and burning of courthouse, Jan. 3. All county records saved. Lyon then moved south to Alabama.

584 COURTHOUSE BURNED
(Hardinsburg, Courthouse lawn, US 60, Breckinridge Co.)

Twenty-two Kentucky courthouses were burned during Civil War, nineteen in last fifteen months: twelve by Confederates, eight by guerrillas, two by Union accident. See map on reverse side. Dec. 28, 1864, guerrillas set fire to courthouse at Hardinsburg but citizens saved building and records. CSA came in and allowed public to keep arms for defense.

585 COURTHOUSE BURNED
(Lebanon, Courthouse lawn, US 68, Marion Co.)

Twenty-two Kentucky courthouses were

burned during Civil War, nineteen in last fifteen months; twelve by Confederates, eight by guerrillas, two by Union accicdent. See map on reverse side. July 5, 1863, clerk's office at Lebanon was burned by Morgan to destroy treason indictments against some of his men. All the county records were destroyed.

586 COURTHOUSE BURNED
(Mt. Sterling, Courthouse lawn, US 60, Montgomery Co.)

Twenty-two Kentucky courthouses were burned during Civil War, nineteen in last fifteen months: twelve by Confederates, eight by guerrillas, two by Union accident. See map on reverse side. Dec. 2, 1863, CSA cavalry burned courthouse at Mt. Sterling to stop its use as a USA garrison. Clerk's records, in rear, saved. Circuit court records destroyed.

587 COURTHOUSE BURNED
(Stanton, Courthouse lawn, KY 11, 15, Powell Co.)

Twenty-two Kentucky courthouses were burned during Civil War, nineteen in last fifteen months: twelve by Confederates, eight by guerrillas, two by Union accident. See map on reverse side. Courthouse and records at Stanton and other buildings were burned by guerrillas, spring of 1863. Buildings rebuilt. June 1, 1864, jail and records again burned.

588 COURTHOUSE BURNED
(Harlan, Courthouse lawn, US 119, 421, Harlan Co.)

Twenty-two Kentucky courthouses were burned during Civil War, nineteen in last fifteen months: twelve by Confederates, eight by guerrillas, two by Union accident. See map on reverse side. The courthouse at Harlan was burned in reprisal for burning of Lee County, Va., courthouse, October, 1863. County records in clerk's office nearby were saved.

589 COURTHOUSE BURNED
(Leitchfield, Courthouse lawn, US 62, Grayson Co.)

Twenty-two Kentucky courthouses were burned during Civil War, nineteen in last fifteen months: twelve by Confederates, eight by guerrillas, two by Union accident. See map on reverse side. Dec. 24, 1864, a contingent of CSA Gen. Lyon's force, ordered to harass and delay pursuing Union troops, burned courthouse at Leitchfield. Records destroyed.

590 COURTHOUSE BURNED
(Owensboro, Courthouse lawn, US 60, Daviess Co.)

Twenty-two Kentucky courthouses were burned during Civil War, nineteen in last fifteen months: twelve by Confederates, eight by guerrillas, two by Union accident. See map on reverse side. Jan. 4, 1865, the courthouse at Owensboro, occupied by Union troops, was burned by guerrillas. The records of all county offices saved by the respective officers.

591 COURTHOUSE BURNED
(Hodgenville, Courthouse lawn, US 31-E, Larue Co.)

Twenty-two Kentucky courthouses were burned during Civil War, nineteen in last fifteen months: twelve by Confederates, eight by guerrillas, two by Union accident. See map on reverse side. The courthouse at Hodgenville was burned by guerrillas Feb. 21, 1865. It had been used by Union soldiers as barracks. All of the county records were saved.

592 COURTHOUSE BURNED
(Owingsville, Courthouse lawn, S. Court St., US 60, Bath Co.)

Twenty-two Kentucky courthouses were burned during Civil War, nineteen in last fifteen months: twelve by Confederates, eight by guerrillas, two by Union accident. See map on the reverse side. March 21, 1864, Union troops fled courthouse here as CSA force came up. Overheated stove started fire, burning building. Guerrillas burned many county records December 4.

593 COURTHOUSE BURNED
(Tompkinsville, Courthouse lawn, KY 63, 100, Monroe Co.)

Twenty-two Kentucky courthouses were burned during Civil War, nineteen in last fifteen months: twelve by Confederates, eight by guerrillas, two by Union accident. See map on reverse side. Courthouse and other buildings in Tompkinsville burned by CSA force, April 22, 1863, in reprisal for Federals burning Celina, Tenn. Monroe County records were lost.

594 COURTHOUSE BURNED
(Taylorsville, Courthouse lawn, KY 44, 55, Spencer Co.)

Twenty-two Kentucky courthouses were burned during Civil War, nineteen in last fifteen months: twelve by Confederates, eight by guerrillas, two by Union accident. See map on the reverse side. Courthouse at Taylorsville was burned by guerrillas in January, 1865. Federal scouts caught them at Mt. Eden, killing one; captured and executed one. Records saved.

595 UPPER BENSON CHURCH
(Near Anderson-Franklin Co. line, US 127, Franklin Co.)

The earliest Presbyterian Church in Franklin County was built in 1795 on a site one mile to the east; organized by Thomas Paxton and located on land owned by him. Services held in it until 1848. Rev. Samuel Shannon was its first Minister. Mr. Paxton and others from Upper Benson Church aided in founding The First Presbyterian Church of Frankfort in 1815. *Presented by First Presbyterian Church, Frankfort.*

596 COURTHOUSE BURNED
(Marion, Courthouse lawn, US 60, 641, Crittenden Co.)

Twenty-two Kentucky courthouses were burned during Civil War, nineteen in last fifteen months: twelve by Confederates, eight by guerrillas, two by Union accident. See map on reverse side. The courthouse at Marion was burned by guerrillas in January, 1865. Building a total loss, though walls stood. County records lost. Courthouse again burned in 1870.

597 COURTHOUSE BURNED
(Albany, Courthouse lawn, US 127, Clinton Co.)

Twenty-two Kentucky courthouses were burned during Civil War, nineteen in last fifteen months: twelve by Confederates, eight by guerrillas, two by Union accident. See map on reverse side. The courthouse at Albany was burned by guerrillas late in 1864 and all county records destroyed.

598 FORREST FORAGED
(Gold City, KY 265, Simpson Co.)

In September 1862, Gen. N. B. Forrest's CSA cavalry camped for three days on the farm of Union sympathizer, Stephen T. Barnes, near here. The famished men and horses consumed all food, feed and water in sight. Assigned to harass the Union army moving north to the west of here, Forrest's force was part of CSA invasion under Gen. Braxton Bragg ending at Perryville Oct. 8, 1862.

599 NEWPORT BARRACKS
(Newport, Riverfront Park, Campbell Co.)

An early army post, built in 1804, at junction of Licking and Ohio Rivers. In War of 1812 used as a military prison. Kentucky troops assembled here for the Canadian invasion, 1813. Used for training volunteers during Mexican War. Headquarters of Southern District, US Army, until Civil War, then Union recruiting depot. Granted to city by United States Congress, 1894.

600 BATTLE OF LEBANON
(At R.R. Station, off US 68, Lebanon, Marion Co.)

Morgan's 2,400 Raiders, on way to Ohio, met by Colonel C. S. Hanson's 380 Union men here, July 5, 1863. During battle Hanson barricaded in railroad depot. Raiders fired buildings but rain prevented wide destruction. After 7-hour battle, Union troops, almost encircled, gave up. Forced at double-quick to Springfield, then paroled. Raiders crossed Ohio River at Brandenburg.

601 RAIDERS ENTERED HERE
(Burkesville, Courthouse lawn, KY 61, 90, Cumberland Co.)

CSA Morgan's Raiders entered Kentucky here July 2, 1863. Union forces skirmished at Burkesville that day, followed by battles at Tebb's Bend July 4 and Lebanon on the 5th. At Brandenburg crossed Ohio River July 8 into Indiana. In northeastern Ohio, ammunition used up, they surrendered on July 26. Imprisoned at Columbus, Ohio, Morgan escaped Nov. 24, returned south.

602 MORGAN'S HEADQUARTERS
(Brandenburg, KY 228, Meade Co.)

This house, built 1832, owned in 1863 by Col. Robert Buckner, War of 1812 veteran, was headquarters, July 7–8, of CSA General J. H. Morgan. Raiders crossing river on captured steamers interrupted as US gunboat *Elk* arrived. They exchanged fire and then *Elk* retired, ammunition exhausted. After crossing river, CSA burned steamer *Alice Dean*. Hulk at river bottom to the west.

603 CIVIL WAR GENERALS
(Greensburg, Courthouse lawn, KY 61, Green Co.)

Union Generals from Greensburg. Major General William T. Ward, 1808–1878. U. S. Congressman 1851–53. He recruited three regiments in this area. On Sept. 2, 1864 Atlanta surrendered to him. In Sherman's March to Sea. Brig. Gen. E. H. Hobson, 1825–1901, leader of 13th Ky. Inf., engaged at Shiloh, Corinth, Perryville. July 1863, pursued Morgan across Ky. to his capture in N.E. Ohio.

604 COL. FRANK L. WOLFORD
(Columbia, Courthouse lawn, KY 80, Adair Co.)

A foremost champion of the Union, a staunch friend of the stricken South, defender of constitutional freedom. Born Columbia 1817, died 1895 and buried in city cemetery. Veteran Mexican War, leader famed First Kentucky Union Cavalry, hero of many battles, eight times wounded. Bold warrior, chivalrous foe. Renowned lawyer and orator. Member Legislature and Congress.

605 INDEPENDENCE DAY—1863
(9 mi. S. of Campbellsville, Bypass on old KY 55, Taylor Co.)

Morgan's Raiders, on way to Ohio, July 4, 1863, approached 200 USA Mich. Inf. under Col. O. H. Moore intrenched here. Morgan demanded surrender. Moore replied Fourth of July no day to entertain such a proposition. Eight CSA assaults repulsed in 3-hour battle, 36 CSA killed, 45 wounded. 6 USA killed, 23 wounded. Morgan bypassed and moved on after significant delay.

606 GENERAL CUSTER HERE
(Elizabethtown, Courthouse lawn, US 31-W, 62, Hardin Co.)

Cavalry and infantry battalions under Gen. George Custer assigned here, 1871 to 1873, to suppress Ku Klux Klan and carpetbaggers, to break up illicit distilleries. Those gangs becoming inactive, he was sent to Chicago to maintain order after big fire. Returning, he led an active social life. In 1873 ordered to Dakota, ending in "Custer's Last Stand," June, 1876.

607 CIVIL WAR SKIRMISH
(Near Green River Bridge, Brownsville, KY 259, Edmonson Co.)

Brig. Gen. T. C. Hindman's force, reconnoitering to protect Bowling Green portion of CSA defense line, approached Brownsville on Nov. 20, 1861. They skirmished here with the Union cavalry regiment of Colonel James S. Jackson, posted at Leitchfield. The Union loss was 7 killed, 5 wounded; CSA, one wounded. Confederates succeeded in obtaining vital medical supplies.

608 WAR ON THE BIG SANDY
(Hager Hill, US 23, 460, Johnson Co.)

On mission to dislodge CSA from area, Colonel James A. Garfield's troops reached Paintsville on Jan. 6, 1862. Under threat of USA flank movement on left and rear, Gen. Humphrey Marshall abandoned his strong breastworks here at Hager Hill. Moving to Middle Creek he was overtaken on Jan. 10 by large USA force. After engagement Marshall retreated to Virginia.

609 HOME OF GOV. LESLIE
(Glasgow, US 31-E, 68, Barren Co.)

Preston H. Leslie, born Ky., 1819. Died Montana, 1907. Completed term of Gov. John Stevenson from Feb. to Sept., 1871, when elected 27th Governor of Kentucky. Known for his sound judgment of State affairs and meeting the needs of growing population and business. Territorial Governor of Montana, 1887–89, US District Attorney, 1894–98. Appointed by Pres. Cleveland.

610 CONFEDERATE GOVERNOR
(4 mi. SW of Georgetown, US 62, Scott Co.)

Home of George W. Johnson, born 1811 in Scott Co. Named first Confederate Governor of Ky. in Nov. 1861, he followed CSA army's withdrawal to Tenn. from Bowling Green in Feb., 1862. He became aide to General John C. Breckinridge but fought as private in Battle of Shiloh and mortally wounded, Apr. 7, 1862 – still as CSA

Governor. Burial was in cemetery here.

611 NOTED DUELING GROUND
(Near Tennessee State Line, US 31-W South, Simpson Co.)

1819–27, known as Linkumpinch. Tennesseans fought two famous duels here. General Sam Houston, in September 1826, severely wounded General William White. Houston later Gov. of Tenn., U.S. Sen., and Gov. of Texas. March 1827, attorneys R. M. Brank and C. M. Smith dueled. Brank was killed. Smith disbarred by Tenn. court action which brought end of dueling here. See other side.

(Reverse)

SANFORD DUNCAN INN

Built about 1819, as stage coach inn, by Sanford Duncan, a large land owner and leader in forming Simpson County. Most of original structure remains. Linkumpinch, a famous dueling ground on Duncan's land, one mile south. Tennessee had outlawed dueling and during 1819–27 Inn was frequently host to notable antagonists, including General Sam Houston. See other side.

612 FORREST RECONNOITERED
(Morganfield, US 60, 641, Union Co.)

CSA General Nathan Bedford Forrest, on reconnaissance and foraging mission toward the Ohio River Nov. 24 to Dec. 5, 1861, passed here with 300 cavalry on way to Caseyville. There he found large supply of hogs and took some along. After he left, USA picked up remainder. While returning to Hopkinsville Forrest captured horses, cattle and more hogs. Map on other side.

613 FORREST RECONNOITERED
(US 41-A & Hanson St., Madisonville, Hopkins Co.)

CSA General Nathan Bedford Forrest, on reconnaissance and foraging mission toward the Ohio River Nov. 24 to Dec. 5, 1861, passed here with 300 cavalry on way to Caseyville. There he found large supply of hogs and took some along. After he left, USA picked up remainder. While returning to Hopkinsville Forrest captured horses, cattle and more hogs. Map on other side.

614 FORREST RECONNOITERED
(Greenville, Courthouse lawn, US 62, Muhlenberg Co.)

CSA General Nathan Bedford Forrest and cavalry came here 3 times on reconnaissance missions from Hopkinsville. Captured USA arms and equipment here, Nov. 24, 1861. Moved through here Dec. 28 on way to victory over larger USA force at Sacramento and returned for camp here that night. Jan. 1862, here to burn Pond River bridges, delay Union army. See the other side.

615 FORREST RECONNOITERED
(1 mi. NE of Marion, US 60, Crittenden Co.)

Returning from reconnaissance and foraging mission to Ohio River, CSA Gen. Nathan Bedford Forrest with cavalry here Dec. 1, 1861, learned of threats to and arrests of Southern sympathizers. While capturing a few instigators, regimental Surgeon S. M. VanWyck was killed. Forrest stayed here another day before returning to Hopkinsville. See map other side.

616 FORREST RECONNOITERED
(Sturgis, US 60, 641, Union Co.)

CSA Gen. Nathan Bedford Forrest and 300 cavalry sent on foraging and reconnaissance mission from Hopkinsville reached Ohio River at Caseyville, Nov. 30, 1861. See map on other side. He found large supply of hogs, taking some along. After he left, USA got the rest and much whiskey. While returning to Hopkinsville Forrest captured horses, cattle and more hogs.

617 FORREST RECONNOITERED
(Providence, US 41, KY 120-A, Webster Co.)

CSA General Nathan Bedford Forrest, on reconnaissance and foraging mission toward the Ohio River Nov. 24 to Dec. 5, 1861, passed here with 300 cavalry on way to Caseyville. There he found large supply of hogs and took some along. After he left, USA picked up remainder. While returning to Hopkinsville Forrest captured horses, cattle and more hogs. Map on other side.

618 FORREST RECONNOITERED
(Hopkinsville Stone Company, US 41, Christian Co.)

CSA General Nathan Bedford Forrest with 6 cavalry companies joined Gen. Charles Clark here November 15, 1861. Forrest made reconnaissance and foraging expeditions out of here. See map on other side. When on one he defeated USA forces in Battle of Sacramento on December 28. After occupation of Hopkinsville for almost three months CSA evacuated. They withdrew into Tennessee.

619 CAVALRY VS. GUNBOAT
(Canton, US 68, Trigg Co.)

CSA General Nathan Bedford Forrest with 6 cavalry companies joined Gen. Charles Clark, Nov. 15, 1861, at Hopkinsville. On reconnaissance learned of USA gunboat *Conestoga*'s intent to destroy CSA supplies at Canton. They met here November 20 in 7 hours of ship-to-shore combat. *Conestoga* left. Forrest's command had stood ground well, first time under fire. See map other side.

621 MORGAN'S LAST RAID
(W. of Flemingsburg, KY 11, Fleming Co.)

On tragic last Kentucky raid, CSA Gen. John H. Morgan and Raiders entered state June 1, 1864, took Mt. Sterling June 8, lost it on 9th, took Lexington on 10th, and Cynthiana on 11th. USA under General S. G. Burbridge defeated CSA next day. Morgan retreated through here, reaching Virginia June 20. See map on other side. Raiders never recovered from this reverse.

622 MORGAN'S LAST RAID
(4 mi. S. of US 460, US 119, Pike Co.)

On tragic last Kentucky raid, CSA Gen. John H. Morgan and Raiders entered state June 1, 1864, took Mt. Sterling June 8, lost it on 9th, took Lexington on 10th, and Cynthiana on 11th. USA under General S. G. Burbridge defeated CSA next day. Morgan retreated through here, reaching Virginia June 20. See map on other side. Raiders never recovered from this reverse.

623 MORGAN'S LAST RAID
(Prestonsburg, W. of Bridge, KY 114, Floyd Co.)

On tragic last Kentucky raid, CSA Gen. John H. Morgan and Raiders entered state June 1, 1864, took Mt. Sterling June 8, lost it on 9th, took Lexington on 10th, and Cynthiana on 11th. USA under General S. G. Burbridge defeated CSA next day. Morgan retreated through here, reaching Virginia June 20. See map on other side. Raiders never recovered from this reverse.

624 MORGAN'S LAST RAID
(Hindman, KY 80, Knott Co.)

On tragic last Kentucky raid, CSA Gen. John H. Morgan and Raiders entered state June 1, 1864. Moved through here. Took Mt. Sterling June 8, lost it on 9th, then took Lexington on 10th, and Cynthiana on the 11th. Next day USA under General S. G. Burbridge defeated CSA. Morgan retreated, reaching Virginia June 20. See map other side. Raiders never recovered from this reverse.

625 "MORGAN'S MEN" HERE
(Winchester, Courthouse lawn, US 60 & KY 627, Clark Co.)

CSA Gen. John H. Morgan's cavalry first raided Kentucky July, 1862. Took Cynthiana but, faced by large USA forces, withdrew. Destroyed arms here on 19th and went to Richmond. On last raid, June 1864, after two battles at Mt. Sterling, they moved by here to Lexington and to Cynthiana where they met defeat on 12th and retreated to Virginia. See map on other side.

626 MORGAN'S FIRST RAID
(Monticello, N. of city limits, KY 90, 92, Wayne Co.)

On first Kentucky raid CSA Gen. John H. Morgan with 900 cavalry went as far north as Cynthiana. Returned via Paris, Winchester, Richmond, Somerset, then here on July 22, 1862. See map other side. Next day moved toward Livingston, Tenn. Morgan was gone 24 days on this raid, traveling 1,000 miles, raiding 17 towns and destroying USA supplies and arms found there.

627 "MORGAN'S MEN" HERE
(Shakertown at Pleasant Hill, US 68, Mercer Co.)

Shakers hid their horses as CSA Gen. J. H. Morgan's cavalry came this way July 13, 1862. But he forbade command to trespass or molest Shakers out of respect for their religion. Grateful for this good treatment

Shakers fed Morgan and his men magnificently as they retreated through here on Oct. 11, 1862 after Battle of Perryville. See map on other side.

628 BATTLE—JUNE 8, 1864
(Mt. Sterling, US 460, Montgomery Co.)

Early this day CSA forces under Gen. John H. Morgan on his tragic last raid attacked Union camp here under Capt. Edward Barlow. CSA took 380 prisoners and material. $59,000 taken from Farmers' Bank. Leaving a force here under Col. H. L. Giltner, Morgan moved west with 2nd Brigade. Next morning CSA driven out. Joined by Morgan, took Lexington next day. See map.

629 BATTLE—JUNE 9, 1864
(Mt. Sterling, W. on US 60, Montgomery Co.)

CSA took Mt. Sterling on previous day. Early on 9th US forces under General S. G. Burbridge attacked CSA under Col. R. M. Martin camped on Camargo Pike. Col. H. L. Giltner brought CSA force from Levee Road, but both driven through city. CSA counterattacked, but was repulsed. Heavy loss on both sides. Morgan joined them and took Lexington next day. See map other side.

630 1862 IN LAWRENCEBURG
(Woodford St., Lawrenceburg, US 62, Anderson Co.)

CSA General J. H. Morgan's cavalry, on first Kentucky raid, here July 14, 1862; as threat to Frankfort. Went instead to Georgetown, took Cynthiana and Paris, returned to Tennessee. Raid covered 1000 miles, 17 towns taken, US stores destroyed. October 8, 1862, during Perryville battle, CSA Gen. E. Kirby Smith's men defeated US under Gen. J. W. Sill west of here. Map other side.
(Reverse)
Map showing Confederate Raids and Invasions and a Federal Retreat, in Kentucky.

631 SGT. WILLIE SANDLIN
(Hyden, Courthouse lawn, US 421, Leslie Co.)

Only Kentuckian to receive the Congressional Medal of Honor in World War I. Born in Kentucky on Jan. 1, 1891. He en-

Sgt. Willie Sandlin, World War I Medal of Honor winner. Kentucky Historical Society Collection.

listed 1917, serving as sergeant in 132d Inf., 33d Div. Medal was awarded for bravery, coolness in putting three machine-gun nests out of action, Sept. 26, 1918 at Bois de Forges, France. Residing in this county after War, he died May 29, 1949.

632 FORT BISHOP
(Louisa, Bypass, Lawrence Co.)

USA Ft. Bishop, 100 yards west, was built to protect against CSA raids. It was named for Captain William Bishop, 100th Ohio Inf., killed in action at Dallas, Ga., May 1864. USA engineers, using detail from 109th Col. Inf., began fort, September 23, 1864. At end of war, April 1865, work was almost complete. Fort had seven field guns. Also called Ft. Gallup and Ft. Hill.

633 BELL MINES
(Sturgis, US 60, Union Co.)

John Bell, 1797–1869, of Tenn. owned mines two miles south of here. In 1860 he was nominated as candidate for President by the Constitutional Union Party. He campaigned to preserve the Union and carried Kentucky, Tennessee, and Virginia against Abraham Lincoln. Later Bell advocated secession. He was Congressman, 1827–41, and member U.S. Senate, 1847–59, from Tenn.

634 HOME OF GEN. BUTLER
(Carrollton, Courthouse lawn, US 42, Carroll Co.)

Gen. William O. Butler, born Kentucky 1791, died here, 1880. War of 1812: River Raisin, Pensacola, and New Orleans. Gen. Andrew Jackson's staff 1816–17. Cited for heroism in Mexican War 1846–48. Practiced law here. Congressman 1839–43. Defeated as candidate for Governor 1844, Vice President 1848 and US Senate 1851. A Kentucky Commissioner to Peace Conference in Feb. 1861.

635 LONG HUNTERS' CAMP
(.5 mi. N. Jct. with KY 90, US 31-E, Barren Co.)

Henry Skaggs and two companions trapping beaver, winter 1770–71, were probably first white men in the area. Named Long Hunters due to long period away from home in the East. Came through Cumberland Gap, 1769, in party led by James Knox. Skaggs' group left the main party to spend the winter here. Friendly with the Indians, Skaggs brought many pioneers here later.

636 FREDERICK M. VINSON
(Louisa, Bypass, Lawrence Co.)

"A great jurist, a distinguished Secretary of the Treasury, and a noted Congressman." Born in Louisa Jan. 22, 1890. City Atty.; Comm. Atty.; Congressman, 1923–29, 31–38. D.C. Court of Appeals, 1938–43. Director Economic Stabilization, Federal Loan Admin., Director War Mobilization. Secretary of Treasury, 1945. United States Chief Justice 1946 until his death, Sept. 8, 1953.

637 A MASTERFUL RETREAT
(6 mi. S. of Grayson, KY 7, Carter Co.)

Retreating from Cumberland Gap, General George W. Morgan's Union force of 8,000 men camped here September 1862. CSA Morgan's Raiders harassed USA, 30 miles along here; skirmishing, felling trees across roads and preempting food and sup-

plies. Covering 200 miles in 16 days, USA reached Greenup on Ohio River Oct. 3, on way to Camp Dennison, Ohio. Map on other side.

638 A MASTERFUL RETREAT
(Beattyville, KY 11, 52, Lee Co.)

Gen. George W. Morgan's 9,000 USA force occupied Cumberland Gap June 18 to Sept. 17, 1862. Cut off from supplies, Morgan began 200-mile retreat. Searching for supplies the command came this way. CSA had burned flour mill night before. Retreat from Gap to Greenup on Ohio River, made in 16 days despite harassment by CSA Morgan's Raiders. Map other side.

639 LOOKOUT MOUNTAIN HERO
(West Irvine, KY 52, Estill Co.)

In that crucial battle of the Chattanooga campaign, Nov. 25, 1863, Capt. John C. Wilson and 5 others from Estill Co., of 8th Ky. Inf., answered call for volunteers to plant U.S. flag on Lookout Mtn. Reaching summit in sight of both armies, they planted their colors, made by Estill County women. Regiment followed, taking mountain. His grave in Station Camp Cemetery, 4 miles S.W.

640 HOME OF GOV. FIELDS
(1 mi. E. of Olive Hill, US 60, Carter Co.)

"Honest Bill from Olive Hill." Home of Gov. William Jason Fields, 34th Governor of Kentucky, 1923–27. He promoted Kentucky's first grant of Federal aid for road construction, consolidation of schools, teacher-training colleges at Murray and Morehead. Member U.S. Congress, 1911–23, Commonwealth Attorney, 1932–33. Born 1874 and died 1954 in Carter County. Buried Olive Hill.

642 A MASTERFUL RETREAT
(Grayson, US 60, Carter Co.)

As Gen. George W. Morgan's Union force, 8,000 when here, retreated from Cumberland Gap, they were harassed from West Liberty by CSA General John H. Morgan's Raiders. Failure of reinforcements to reach here caused Confederates to leave October 1, 1862 and rejoin main CSA force in

Lexington. Union forces reached Greenup Oct. 3, 200 miles in 16 days. See map other side.

643 CIVIL WAR ARMY BASE
(Catlettsburg, 26th & Louisa, US 23, 60, Boyd Co.)

USA post located here to protect Ohio River traffic. Became supply base and communication center for Union forces in the Big Sandy region. In winter 1861–62, troops under Col. J. A. Garfield, later 20th President U.S., drove CSA from area by victory at Middle Creek. Area cleared of CSA again in 1864 by USA Kentucky forces under Col. George W. Gallup.

644 A MASTERFUL RETREAT
(Sandy Hook, Courthouse lawn, KY 7, 32, Elliott Co.)

General George W. Morgan's 9,000 USA force occupied Cumberland Gap June 18 to Sept. 17, 1862. Cut off from supplies, Morgan began 200-mile retreat. On way through here USA harassed by CSA Morgan's Raiders. Failure of reinforcements caused CSA withdrawal at Grayson, Oct. 1. Union retreat, from Gap to Greenup on Ohio River, made in 16 days. See map other side.

645 A MASTERFUL RETREAT
(Booneville, Courthouse lawn, KY 11, 30, Owsley Co.)

General George W. Morgan's 9,000 USA force occupied Cumberland Gap June 18 to Sept. 17, 1862. Cut off from supplies, Morgan began 200-mile retreat. From Manchester they moved in two columns, both seeking supplies, through here on to Proctor. Retreat from Gap to Greenup on Ohio River made in 16 days despite harassment by CSA Morgan's Raiders. Map other side.

646 USA GENS. MORGAN CSA
(Hazel Green, KY 191, 203, Wolfe Co.)

General George W. Morgan's 9,000 USA force, cut off from supplies at Cumberland Gap, retreated 200 mi. in 16 days to Greenup on Ohio River. It camped here Sept. 23, 1862. Gen. John Hunt Morgan's CSA men, on tragic last raid into Kentucky, moved by here. After two battles in Mt. Sterling, they met defeat at Cynthiana, June

12, 1864, and retreated to Va. Map other side.

647 USA GENS. MORGAN CSA
(Campton, Courthouse lawn, KY 191, 203, Wolfe Co.)

General George W. Morgan's 9,000 USA force, cut off from supplies at Cumberland Gap, retreated 200 mi. in 16 days to Greenup on Ohio River. Passed near here Sept. 23, 1862. Gen. John H. Morgan's CSA men, on tragic last raid into Kentucky, moved by here. After two battles at Mt. Sterling, they met defeat in Cynthiana, June 12, 1864, and retreated to Va. Map other side.

648 CSA GENS. MORGAN USA
(West Liberty, Main St., US 460, Morgan Co.)

General George W. Morgan's 9,000 USA force, cut off from supplies at Cumberland Gap, retreated 200 mi. in 16 days to Greenup on Ohio River. Camped here Sept. 24–25, 1862. Gen. John H. Morgan's CSA men, on tragic last raid into Kentucky, after two battles in Mt. Sterling met defeat at Cynthiana June 12, 1864. They moved through here on retreat to Va. Map on other side.

649 WOODFORD COUNTY'S CIVIL WAR GENERALS
(Versailles, US 62, Woodford Co.)

Major General Charles William Field, 1828–1892, soldier, engineer; West Point, 1849. Frontier service in southwest to 1855, instructor in cavalry tactics West Point to 1861. Colonel 6th Virginia Cav. 1861. Brig. gen. infantry brigade 1862. Opened battle at Mechanicsville; fought at Cedar Mt., 2nd Bull Run, in latter seriously wounded, never fully recovering. 1864, maj. gen. in command Hood's Texas div. Bore heavy part in battles at Cold Harbor and Petersburg. His division half of Lee's army and only effective fighting unit intact left to surrender at Appomattox.

Brig. General James S. Jackson, 1823–1862, Union soldier, lawyer, Congressman, veteran Mexican War. Authorized by Lincoln, he recruited 3rd Ky. Cav. in fall 1861. For a time commanded Buell's entire cavalry. Commissioned brig. gen., assigned to command 10th Div. of Buell's army, July 1862. Leading troops at Perryville, he was killed Oct. 8, 1862. Forney wrote: "To die such a death, and for such a cause, was the highest ambition of a man like James S. Jackson. . . . He was a Union man for the sake of the Union; and now with his heart's blood, he has sealed his devotion to the flag."

Maj. General Eli Long, 1837–1903, Union soldier, graduated from Kentucky Military Institute, 1855. Frontier service against Indians until 1861. Organized 4th Ohio Cavalry as colonel, 1862. Commissioned brig. general, 1864. Commanded brigade during Atlanta campaign, 1864. He led an assault at Selma, Alabama, March 1865, where his bravery inspired the troops in Union's greatest cavalry victory and for which he was breveted maj. gen. During the Civil War he was wounded five times and cited for gallantry five times. After war lived at Plainfield, New Jersey, and is buried there in Hillsdale Cemetery.
(Reverse)

WOODFORD COUNTY'S CIVIL WAR GENERALS

Brigadier General Abraham Buford, 1820–1874; Confederate cavalryman; cousin of John and N. B. Buford. Graduate West Point, 1841; frontier service Kansas and Indiana terr., 1842–1846; brev. capt. Mexican War; raised, equipped a Kentucky Brig. for CSA, commissioned brig. general, 1862. Covered Bragg's retreat from Ky.; in Vicksburg campaign; twice raided Western Ky. and Paducah, capturing horses and vast supplies, spring 1864; led brigade in CSA victory, Brice's Cross Roads, Miss., June 1864; covered Hood's retreat after defeat at Nashville December 1864; defeated at Selma, Ala., March 1865. He lived at Bosque Bonita in Woodford Co., owning famous race horses Nellie Gray, Inquirer, Crossland, and Versailles.

Maj. Gen. Napoleon Bonaparte Buford, 1807–1883, Union soldier, graduate West Point 1827. Artillery school, 1827–1828; professor philosophy, West Point, 1834–1835; engineer Licking River improvement, 1835–1842; businessman, banker, Rock Island, Illinois, colonel Illinois Reg., 1861; brig. gen. 1862; commander District

of East Arkansas; breveted maj. gen. 1865; U.S. Comm. to inspect Union Pacific R.R., 1867–1869.

Maj. Gen. John Buford, 1826–1863, Union cavalryman, graduate West Point 1848. Scouting, fighting Indians in west and southwest, 1848–61. Great endurance, fine disciplinarian, brig. gen. cav., 1862, and chief of cavalry, Army of Potomac. He fought at 2nd Bull Run, Fredericksburg, Antietam, Chancellorsville; scouted Lee's move into Penn., selected strategic defense positions at Gettysburg and held CSA advance until Union infantry arrived. He died of overexertion and wounds, at age 37, Dec. 16, 1863, holding a major general commission signed by Abraham Lincoln.

650 DAVID WARK GRIFFITH, 1875-1948
(Crestwood, KY 22, 146, Oldham Co.)

Oldham County native buried here. Renowned as director-producer of *The Birth of a Nation*, film drama of Civil War and post-bellum era, and also *Intolerance, Orphans of the Storm, Broken Blossoms*. He created dramatic and photographic effects, close-up and fade-out. He brought out Mary Pickford, Lillian and Dorothy Gish and other stars.

651 A RENOWNED PISCATOR
(Cynthiana, S. of bridge, US 27, Harrison Co.)

Dr. James A. Henshall, 1836–1925, author *Book of the Black Bass* and others, brought fame to Kentucky's South Licking, Elkhorn, and Stoner streams. He came here to practice medicine. During Civil War healed wounds for men in Blue and Gray. Left, regained health, returned in 1880, wrote book. With U.S. Bureau of Fisheries, 1896–1917, he found new method for fish propagation.

652 RAILROAD WRECKED 1862
(Jordan, KY 116, 239, Fulton Co.)

Brig. General N. B. Forrest's troops took Union City, Tenn., and moved thru here into Kentucky. They wrecked rails, bridges, trestles north to Moscow, December 24–25, 1862, preventing use of tracks between Columbus, Ky. and Jackson, Tennessee, until after the war. Union army forced to ship supplies by river. Gen. Grant's Vicksburg campaign seriously delayed. Map other side.

653 ALICE LLOYD COLLEGE
(Garner, KY 80, Knott Co.)

Renowned mountain school located eight miles east. Alice Lloyd came from Boston, 1916, dedicating her life to education of youth in area. The Caney Creek Community Center was organized, 1917, and Caney Junior College, 1923. After her death, 1962, college renamed honoring founder, who inspired graduates to serve this region. It is supported by friends throughout U.S.

654 TWO SUCCESSFUL RAIDS
(Mayfield, US 45, KY 80, Graves Co.)

CSA General Nathan B. Forrest with main body of cavalry passed thru Mayfield to and from destructive raid on Paducah, March 25, 1864. Gen. Abraham Buford's division camped here. Kentucky regiments given leave to visit homes, enlist recruits. All returned. News item led Forrest to send Buford from Tenn. thru here again, April 14, to capture horses missed before.

655 TWO SUCCESSFUL RAIDS
(Dukedom, KY 116, 129, Graves Co.)

CSA Gen. N. B. Forrest with main body of cavalry passed this way before and after destructive raid on Paducah, March 25, 1864. Returning, Kentucky regiments, camping near here, given leave to seek food, horses, get recruits, visit families. Not one deserted. News item led Forrest to send men back thru here again, April 14, to capture horses missed before.

656 ROWLETT'S STATION
(1,000 ft. N. of Rowletts on US 31-W, Hart Co.)

In fall of 1861, Federals planned move into Tennessee by the Cumberland River and, under General D. C. Buell, by land through here. CSA wrecked important bridge over Green River Dec. 10, to block USA move. Union force under Col. A. Willich sent to repair, defend bridge. CSA led by Gen. T. C. Hindman came here to wreck tracks, December 17, 1861. After sharp battle CSA

withdrew south.

657 GOVERNOR'S CORNER
(Russellville, 113 W. 9th St., Logan Co.)

John J. Crittenden, 1787–1863, lived here, 1811–18. War of 1812, State Legislator, 15th Kentucky Governor. U.S. Atty. Gen. under three Presidents. Five times U.S. Senator. Noted for Crittenden Compromise, 1860, futile effort to avert Civil War and preserve the Union. His last words: "Let all the ends thou aimest at be thy country's, thy God's and truth's."

658 GOVERNOR'S CORNER
(Russellville, 145 E. 5th St., Logan Co.)

Home of Governor John Breathitt, born 1787, Virginia. Came here, 1800. Lawyer, legislator. Elected Lieut. Governor, 1828, and Governor, 1832. He was advocate of need for preserving Kentucky's valuable documents. He wrote: "There is a laudable solicitude to know everything in respect to our history." Breathitt died in office, 1834. Monument in Maple Grove Cem. by Kentucky.

659 JEROME BONAPARTE ROBERTSON, 1815–1891
(Versailles, US 60, Woodford Co.)

Confederate brigadier general. Born in Woodford County. Transylvania University, medicine, 1835. Moved to Texas, 1836. Practiced medicine, Indian fighter, member legislature and Texas secession convention. Wounded at Second Manassas and Gettysburg. Fought at Chickamauga, Knoxville, and in Texas. Father of CSA Brig. Gen. Felix H. Robertson.
(Reverse)

RANDALL LEE GIBSON, 1832–1892

Confederate brigadier general. Born in Woodford, home of his grandfather. Parents lived Louisiana. Graduate Yale Univ., 1853. Distinguished for leadership at Shiloh, in 1862 Kentucky campaign, Chickamauga, Atlanta, and Hood's later invasion of Tennessee. U.S. House 1875–83, and Senate 1883–92, from Louisiana. Buried Lexington, Ky., Cemetery.

660 FOREST RETREAT
(4 mi. NW of Carlisle, US 68, KY 32, Nicholas Co.)

Built in 1820 by Thomas Metcalfe, born Va. 1780, died 1855, buried here. Capt., War of 1812; member Congress 1819–28; Governor 1828–32; Ky. Senate 1834–38; U.S. Senate 1848–49, completing Crittenden's term. "Old Stone Hammer" laid the foundation, 1797, of Governor's Mansion, now used by Lieutenant Governor, and built Green County Courthouse, 1806, in use, 1964.

661 LAUREL SEMINARY
(London Elem. School, N. Main St., US 25, Laurel Co.)

In 1826, the legislature granted land to Laurel and some other counties for educational purposes. Land sold; Seminary opened, 1858. Used for hospital in Civil War. Gov. W. S. Taylor called special session of legislature here, 1900. Common school, 1870–84; private school, 1884–93; common school, 1893–1906; then public school. Original building replaced, 1954.

662 OLD MEETING HOUSE
(6 mi. N. of Bowling Green, KY 263, near Jct. KY 185, Warren Co.)

Green River Union Meeting House, part of Great Frontier Revival of early 1800's, and burial ground are three miles northwest. Huguenots came 1806 and 1814, organized and built log church, then about 1845 present meeting house. Methodists, Baptists, Presbyterians met there before building own churches in area. Many leading ministers of those days were trained there.

663 CIVIL WAR BASE
(Smithland, US 60, Livingston Co.)

September 1861, Union forces occupied strategic Smithland. The junction of the Ohio and Cumberland Rivers became a rendezvous and staging area for troops and supplies in support of Gen. Grant's campaign against Fort Donelson. Two forts, on hills south, commanded the two rivers. Smithland continued thru the war as a supply base for USA river transports and gunboats.

664 JAMES BETHEL GRESHAM
(Beech Grove, Jct. KY 56 & 136, McLean Co.)

First American killed in action, World War I. Born Beech Grove, 1893, moved to Indiana, 1901, and enlisted there, 1914. Served under Gen. Pershing on Mexican border, 1916. Sent overseas June 14, 1917. Pfc. Gresham killed, Nov. 3, 1917, in the battle of Sommerviller, Lorraine. French honored him with monument there. Buried in Indiana. Silver Star citation, Jan. 1920.

665 FORREST RECONNOITERED
(Calhoun, KY 81, McLean Co.)

On reconnaissance and search for supplies, late Nov. 1861, CSA Gen. Nathan B. Forrest's cavalry scouted area. Reported USA forces of Gen. T. C. Crittenden gathered here. Forrest moved on to west. Again in area, Dec. 28, 1861, Forrest met and defeated Union scouting force in battle at Sacramento. CSA escaped capture by USA troops sent from Calhoun. See map over.

666 4-H CRAFT CENTER
(4 mi. W. of Cumberland Falls Park, KY 90, McCreary Co.)

Established 1963 by 4-H Clubs of McCreary County, the first such center in the U.S. developed by 4-H Clubs. The original log cabin built on this site in a 200-acre land grant to John Abbott, 1842. Abbott and Indian wife, Oocella, lived in cabin until 1863. The cabin used continuously as a home by five generations until rebuilt as "Falls 4-H Craft Center."

667 LINCOLN ACQUITTED
(3 mi. W. of Hawesville, KY 334, Hancock Co.)

Abraham Lincoln, 16th president of United States, won his first law case here, 1827. Charged by the Commonwealth of Kentucky with operating ferry without license; Lincoln pleaded his own case in trial at the home of presiding Justice of the Peace, Samuel Pate. Pate encouraged Lincoln to study law and loaned him books. Lincoln often visited here on "law days."

668 A RENOWNED SENATOR
(4 mi. W. of Marion, US 60, KY 297, Crittenden Co.)

Ollie M. James born 1871, three miles N.W. United States Representative, 1903–13, and

Senator, 1913 until death, 1918. Chairman, Democratic National Conventions that nominated Woodrow Wilson for President, 1912 and 1916. Last speech, in Senate Feb. 1918, upheld Wilson's conduct of World War I. "Liberty will be safe and Americanism secure." Monument in Marion Cemetery.

670 SANDUSKY STATION, 1776
(6 mi. NE of Lebanon, 4 mi. N. of US 68 on KY 1195, Marion Co.)

James and Jacob Sadowski (later Sandusky) came from Virginia in 1774 with Hite's surveying party and helped lay out Harrodstown. James chose site at Pleasant Run Spring, 150 feet S.E. of here for settlement. Harrod's men helped him erect fort in 1776. He and Jacob moved, 1785, to present Jessamine County; James' son, Anthony, stayed. Family long identified with area.

671 A SKIRMISH IN 1861
(Cromwell, US 231, Ohio Co.)

Sept. 1861, General S. B. Buckner with 5,000 CSA occupied Bowling Green, part of Confederate defense line along Ky.-Tennessee border. Purpose: to prevent USA moves south, provide base for future CSA moves north. Scouting in this area, October 31, CSA attacked home guard and small Union force here. After skirmish, CSA retired "with three buggy loads of killed and wounded."

672 "AUNT JULIA" MARCUM
(Williamsburg, Courthouse lawn, US 25-W, Whitley Co.)

Only woman, as a fighter, to receive a U.S. pension: special Act of Congress, 1884. Marcum home in Tenn., a depot for southerners going north to Union army. She lost eye; badly wounded defending home against marauders; then the family came here. Unionist father killed in action. Her life devoted to patriotic, religious work. Died in 1936, age 91, military funeral.

673 THE CONFEDERATES HERE
(N. of Viaduct, Cynthiana, US 27, Harrison Co.)

CSA Gen. John H. Morgan's Cavalry on first Kentucky raid defeated USA here, July 17, 1862. Burned railroad depot and Union stores. June 11, 1864, Morgan again took

area. Next day reinforced USA defeated CSA who retreated to Virginia. Gen. Henry Heth's forces held Cynthiana, Sept. 6–17, 1862, in Confederate threat to Covington. See map on other side.

674 CONFEDERATES HERE
(Bardstown, Courthouse lawn, US 62, 150, Nelson Co.)

On CSA invasion, Bragg's army of 28,000 camped here, September 20 to October 3, 1862. Moved to Harrodsburg, then met Buell's Union army in Battle of Perryville, Oct. 8. CSA Gen. John H. Morgan, on raid, camped here, Dec. 29, 1862. On a later raid, July 6, 1863, Morgan delayed here by night-long skirmish with 25 Union cavalrymen. See map on other side.

675 SAWYIER'S INSPIRATION
(Hall Rd. & US 27, S. of Camp Nelson Cem., Jessamine Co.)

Paul Sawyier, "The River Artist," painted scenes of Kentucky River gorge while living on houseboat near here, from 1908 to 1913. The noted artist created over 2,000 paintings, mostly landscapes of Central Kentucky–State Capitol, Kentucky River and Elkhorn Creek. Born in Ohio, 1865, he spent most of his life in Kentucky. Died in New York, 1917. Buried Frankfort.

676 CSA RETURNS TO TENN.
(Mt. Vernon, US 25, 150, Rockcastle Co.)

After Battle of Perryville, October 8, 1862, Confederate forces retired to Bryantsville. Union forces did not attack but destroyed sources of food. General Braxton Bragg began retreat, Oct. 13, in two columns under Generals Polk and Smith. Polk's moved thru here with USA pursuing. The CSA columns retired thru Cumberland Gap, October 19–24. See map on other side.

677 MORGAN'S FIRST RAID
(Somerset, Library lawn, Pulaski Co.)

CSA General John H. Morgan's first Kentucky raid covered 1,000 miles, July 4 to July 28, 1862–24 days. Left Tenn. with 900 men, returned with 1200, captured 17 towns, 300 horses, destroyed Union supplies. Here, July 21, Morgan took over telegraph line and countermanded USA orders to pursue. Destroyed commissary stores, wagons, arms. Moved on to Monticello. See map.

678 FOUNDER OF EDMONTON
(Edmonton, Courthouse lawn, US 68, Metcalfe Co.)

Edmund Rogers, 1762–1843. In the Virginia campaign of the war and the Revolution and at surrender of Cornwallis, 1781. As surveyor, joined General George Rogers Clark, his cousin, in 1783. A year later, came to area south of Green River. He made earliest surveys on Barren River and tributaries and settled here. Laid out Edmonton in 1800. Family burial ground to the south.

679 ROY STUART CLUKE
(6 mi. W. of Winchester on KY 1927, Clark Co.)

Site of home and farm from which Cluke enlisted in the Confederate army. Commissioned Colonel of 8th Regt. Ky. Cavalry CSA, Sept. 1862. Immediate action in Ky. won the confidence of Gen. John H. Morgan; was with Morgan in Dec. 1862 and July 1863 raids when captured in Ohio. He died December 31, 1863, in U.S. prison, age 39. Buried near Morgan in Lexington Cemetery.

680 ANGLES
(Blandville Rd., Paducah, McCracken Co.)

Home of Alben W. Barkley, 1937–56. A good example of Greek Revival architecture. Built in 1859 by Colonel Quintus Quincy Quigley. Location on sharp angles of three tracts of land source of its name. In early married life Barkley and his wife dreamed of owning it. Dream realized after 30 years. Beloved home for 19 years while Senator and Vice President. Over.
(Reverse)
"THE VEEP"
Alben W. Barkley, Vice President of United States, 1949–53. Member U.S. Senate, 1927–49 and 1955–56; Senate Democratic leader 13 years: House of Representatives 1913–27. Born in Lowes, Ky., 1877. Death came at Washington and Lee Univ., 1956. Last words of address to students, "I would rather be a servant in the house of the Lord than to sit in the seats of the mighty." Over.

681 ARTIST OF CONFEDERACY
(Louisville, Cave Hill Cem.—[Section 5], US 60, 460, Jefferson Co.)

Nicola Marschall designed the Stars and Bars, official flag of Confederacy, and gray uniform of the Southern army, March 1861. Born, 1829, St. Wendel, Germany, he came to U.S. (Alabama) in 1849 to continue professionally in art. Noted portraits: Jefferson Davis, other Confederates; Lincoln and other Presidents. In 1873 he came to Louisville where he died, 1917.

682 MURDOCH OF BUCKHORN
(Buckhorn, KY 28, Perry Co.)

Harvey Short Murdoch, 1871–1935, came from Brooklyn, N. Y. and as Field Secretary of E. O. Guerrant's Society of Soul Winners founded Witherspoon College in 1902. Became Presbyterian Child Welfare Agency. Log cathedral built 1907. Murdoch was pastor until his death. "To Buckhorn and Eastern Kentucky he brought a love for baseball, for education and for God."

683 INVASION AND RETREAT
(Pineville, US 25-E, Bell Co.)

On route of Gen. E. Kirby Smith's Confederate invasion of Kentucky, fall 1862, concurrent with that of Bragg to the west. At Richmond Kirby Smith defeated USA, then occupied Lexington, Sept. 2. The Battle of Perryville prevented CSA plan to take Central Kentucky. Kirby Smith's army joined Bragg's, moving through here, Oct. 19–24, on return to Tennessee. See map other side.

684 FIRST KENTUCKY CAVALRY
(Liberty, Courthouse lawn, Near US 127, Casey Co.)

Casey County, home of one-third of this Union regiment and of its commanders Col. Frank L. Wolford and Col. Silas Adams. Others came from eight nearby Ky. counties. Recruited July 1861, trained at Camp Dick Robinson. Saw active service from Wildcat Mt. battle, Oct. 19, 1861, until mustered out, Dec. 31, 1864. Became famous for skill and daring. See over.
(Reverse)
1ST KY. CAV.
Efficient in battle, infantry as well as cavalry.

Unsurpassed in fighting guerrillas and scouting. In Mill Springs, Perryville and Lebanon (Tenn.) battles and scores of other engagements. Led pursuit of CSA Bragg's retreat, Oct. 1862. First Kentucky was at surrender of John Hunt Morgan, Ohio, July 1863. Later that year in East Tenn. and Sherman's Atlanta campaign, 1864.

685 ON CONFEDERATE ROUTES
(Crab Orchard, US 150, Lincoln Co.)

CSA Gen. J. H. Morgan's cavalry on first Kentucky raid, returning from Cynthiana, burned Dix River bridge above here and camped on July 20, 1862. Burned 120 USA wagons here and at Somerset. (See map on other side.) After battle of Perryville Oct. 8, 1862, CSA retired to Bryantsville. Then retreated in two columns to Tenn. One of them moved thru here.

686 CSA AT FALMOUTH
(Falmouth, US 27, Pendleton Co.)

During Confederate invasion into Kentucky, CSA troops in area on threat to North. Sept. 18, 1862, 11 home guards met 28 CSA here. CSA casualties 6, home guard one. Col. Basil Duke's CSA cavalry camped here and on Sept. 27, 1862, attacked Augusta. CSA losses there forced return to Falmouth. Plan abandoned to cross Ohio River and threaten Cincinnati. See map.

687 SETTLES RIFLES
(SW of Glasgow, KY 252, Barren Co.)

Prized by frontiersmen, now rare collectors' items; they were made by three Settle generations in Barren County. Starting in 1800, William made flintlocks at Rocky Hill. A son, Felix, had shops in Glasgow, Roseville. Felix's sons, Simon and Willis, made rifles in Glasgow, Hiseville, and in Green and Logan counties. Name of maker and place made on all; some dated.

688 NEW MADRID EARTHQUAKE
(Near Miller, KY 94, Fulton Co.)

The greatest earthquake recorded in North America centered in this area Dec. 16, 1811 to Feb. 7, 1812. 1,874 quakes felt at Louisville, 250 miles away. Tremors also felt at Boston, Detroit, New Orleans. Reelfoot Lake, covering 25,000 acres, formed when some streams changed courses. New Madrid, Mo., destroyed; very few persons died, as population of area was sparse.

689 ON CIVIL WAR ROUTES
(Springfield, US 150, KY 55, Washington Co.)

CSA Gen. John H. Morgan's cavalry moved thru Springfield on raids, July 12 and December 30, 1862. On third raid, into Ohio, after battle of Lebanon, July 5, 1863, Union prisoners brought here but paroled to speed CSA movement. Confederate invasion force of 16,000 here before meeting Union Army in battle at Perryville, Oct. 8, 1862. See map other side.

690 STRATTON SETTLEMENT
(Jct. US 23 & Mare Creek Rd., Floyd Co.)

Founded, 1796, by Solomon Stratton, veteran of George Rogers Clark's expedition to Illinois, 1778. In Virginia militia, 1783. In 1788 he and son explored this region. Eight years later, he and kinsmen from Virginia settled here. In 1797, he, Matthias Harman, Andrew Hood, laid out Prestonsburg for Col. John Preston. Stratton died 1819; unmarked grave, 500 feet east.

691 MORGAN'S LAST RAID
(Mays Lick, US 68, Mason Co.)

On tragic last Kentucky raid, CSA Gen. John H. Morgan and Raiders entered state June 1, 1864, took Mt. Sterling June 8, lost it on 9th, took Lexington on 10th, and Cynthiana on 11th. USA under General S. G. Burbridge defeated CSA next day. Morgan retreated through here, reaching Virginia June 20. See map on other side. Raiders never recovered from this reverse.

692 MORGAN'S LAST RAID
(Claysville, US 62, Harrison Co.)

On tragic last Kentucky raid, CSA Gen. John H. Morgan and Raiders entered state June 1, 1864, took Mt. Sterling June 8, lost it on 9th, took Lexington on 10th, and Cynthiana on 11th. USA under General S. G. Burbridge defeated CSA next day. Morgan retreated through here, reaching Virginia June 20. See map on other side. Raiders never recovered from this reverse.

693 MORGAN'S LAST RAID
(Mt. Olivet, US 62, Robertson Co.)

On tragic last Kentucky raid, CSA Gen. John H. Morgan and Raiders entered state June 1, 1864, took Mt. Sterling June 8, lost it on 9th, took Lexington on 10th, and Cynthiana on 11th. USA under General S. G. Burbridge defeated CSA next day. Morgan retreated through here, reaching Virginia June 20. See map on other side. Raiders never recovered from this reverse.

694 MORGAN'S LAST RAID
(Wedonia, KY 11, 24, Mason Co.)

On tragic last Kentucky raid, CSA Gen. John H. Morgan and Raiders entered state June 1, 1864, took Mt. Sterling June 8, lost it on 9th, took Lexington on 10th, and Cynthiana on 11th. USA under General S. G. Burbridge defeated CSA next day. Morgan retreated through here, reaching Virginia June 20. See map on other side. Raiders never recovered from this reverse.

695 MORGAN'S LAST RAID
(Sardis, US 62, Mason Co.)

On tragic last Kentucky raid, CSA Gen. John H. Morgan and Raiders entered state June 1, 1864, took Mt. Sterling June 8, lost it on 9th, took Lexington on 10th, and Cynthiana on 11th. USA under General S. G. Burbridge defeated CSA next day. Morgan retreated through here, reaching Virginia June 20. See map on other side. Raiders never recovered from this reverse.

696 CSA AT PARIS, 1862
(Paris, Courthouse lawn, US 27, 68, Bourbon Co.)

Gen. John Hunt Morgan's cavalry on first Kentucky raid after its Cynthiana victory came to Paris, July 18, 1862. Citizens group had held out for days but surrendered. Warned of Union force nearby, CSA escaped pursuit, returned to Tenn. Paris occupied, Sept. 1862, during Confederate threat north. Capital at Frankfort, Georgetown, Lexington also held. See map over.

697 WARRIOR'S PATH
(Gray Hawk, US 421, Jackson Co.)

Along War Fork Creek, two miles east, coursed a primeval trail between the Shawnees of Ohio and Cherokees of east Tennessee. The Indians called it Athiamiowee, Path of the Armed Ones. On English map, 1755. Path was followed by Gabriel Arthur, when released by Indians, 1674; Thomas Walker, 1750; Christopher Gist, 1751; Daniel Boone and John Finley, 1769.

698 BEAR WALLOW
(At Hart Co. line, Bear Wallow, US 31-E, Barren Co.)

On CSA invasion of Kentucky, resulting in battle of Perryville, General Leonidas Polk's wing moved thru here, September 16, 1862, to attack USA troops at Munfordville. Two of Kentucky raids by CSA Gen. John Hunt Morgan's cavalry routed thru here, July 10 and December 25, 1862. On second raid, skirmish here failed to retard the CSA. See map other side.

699 HOME OF GOV. BRADLEY
(Lexington St., Lancaster, US 27, Garrard Co.)

Built about 1850, by A. A. Burton, Lincoln's Minister to Bogota; home of William O. Bradley, first Republican Governor of Kentucky, 1895–99. By special legislative action, 1865, permitted to take bar examination at 18 and passed. In 1904, seconded nomination of Theodore Roosevelt. 1908, elected U.S. Senator by Democratic legislature. Died 1914. Buried at Frankfort.

700 MORGAN'S LAST RAID
(Paintsville, South, US 23, 460, Johnson Co.)

On tragic last Kentucky raid, CSA Gen. John H. Morgan and Raiders entered state June 1, 1864, took Mt. Sterling June 8, lost it on 9th, took Lexington on 10th, and Cynthiana on 11th. USA under General S. G. Burbridge defeated CSA next day. Morgan retreated through here, reaching Virginia June 20. See map on other side. Raiders never recovered from this reverse.

701 GEORGETOWN RAIDED
(Georgetown, Courthouse lawn, KY 227, Scott Co.)

CSA Gen. John H. Morgan, on Kentucky raid here, July 15, 1862, camped two days. Destroyed rail bridges, USA stores, dispersed Home Guards. On 17th defeated USA at Cynthiana. Started back to Tenn. On last raid, Morgan was here, July 10, 1864, after taking Lexington. On 12th CSA met defeat at Cynthiana and retreated to Virginia. See map on other side.

702 FIRST KENTUCKY OIL WELL
(Whitley City, Courthouse lawn, US 27, McCreary Co.)

In 1818, Marcus Huling and Andrew Zimmerman were drilling salt wells along South Fork of Cumberland River. On land leased from Martin Beaty they struck oil. Attempts to market it downriver were not successful, so oil was barreled and carted away for medicinal use. This was the first commercial oil well; its production reached one hundred barrels daily. See over.
(Reverse)

MARTIN BEATY (BEATTY)

First came to this area in 1817 and bought land on the South Fork. Besides operating salt works, Beaty served as state senator, 1824–28, 1832; representative, 1848; and was elected to Congress in 1832. He was twice a Presidential elector; served locally on first Board of Common School Commissioners. Died in 1856. Beattyville, Lee County, was named for his family. Over.

703 MOUNTAIN MISSIONARY
(N. Main St., Hazard, KY 7, 15, Perry Co.)

The Rev. Asbel S. Petrey, born 1866, Whitley County, Ky. Ordained, 1891. Came here 1897, organized First Missionary Baptist Church of Hazard, 1898. Founder, 1902, and President of Hazard Baptist Institute, a public school since 1941. He organized 12 churches in area. Pastor of Petrey Memorial Baptist Church, 1922–40. Filled other pulpits until death, 1953.

704 CSA STARTS RETREAT
(Bryantsville, US 27, Garrard Co.)

In Sept. 1862, Confederates moved supply depot here from Lexington. After battle of Perryville, Oct. 8, CSA gathered here for council of war, Oct. 11. USA destroyed food sources. Oct. 13, under command of Gen. Braxton Bragg, retreat began in two columns under Generals Polk and Smith. With immaterial loss, they moved thru Cum-

berland Gap, Oct. 19–24. See map over.

705 MORGAN'S SECOND RAID
(Boston, US 62, Nelson Co.)

CSA Gen. John H. Morgan ordered Col. D. W. Chenault's regiment to burn the railroad trestle here, Dec. 29, 1862. This and destruction of two trestles at Muldraugh's Hill, the previous day, put L&N railroad, the main USA supply line, out of use for critical period. On 14-day Kentucky raid, Morgan destroyed $2,000,000 U.S. property, captured 1,877 USA troops. See map.

706 CONFEDERATE RAIDS
(Campbellsville, Courthouse lawn, US 68, Taylor Co.)

General John Hunt Morgan's cavalry, returning from second Kentucky raid, here, Dec. 31, 1862. Took supplies. Went on to Tenn. On raid Union's rail supply line wrecked and $2,000,000 property destroyed. Morgan thru here again after three-hour battle at Tebb's Bend, July 4, 1863. Continued raid into Indiana to NE Ohio, where captured, July 26th. See map other side.

707 CONFEDERATE RAIDS
(Columbia, Courthouse lawn, KY 61, 80, Adair Co.)

General John Hunt Morgan's cavalry, returning from second Kentucky raid, passed here on way back to Tennessee, Jan. 1, 1863. On raid, Union's rail supply line wrecked and $2,000,000 property destroyed. July 3, 1863, Morgan here again drove out small USA force. On July 8, at Brandenburg, crossed river into Indiana. Captured in NE Ohio, July 26. See map over.

708 COUNTY NAMESAKE
(Carlisle, Courthouse lawn, KY 32, 36, Nicholas Co.)

George Nicholas, 1743–99, born in Virginia. Colonel, Revolutionary War. Zealous advocate of Virginia adoption of Federal Constitution, 1788. He came to Kentucky, 1790. "Brightest luminary" in Kentucky's first constitutional convention. Became first Attorney General of State. First Transylvania law professor. Extensive landholder. Invested in cloth manufacture, iron furnace.

709 BENJ. LOGAN—PIONEER
(4 mi. W. of Shelbyville, US 60, 460, Shelby Co.)

In French and Indian, Dunmore's, Revolutionary Wars. In 1775 came to Kentucky with Boone, Henderson. Separated at Hazel Patch. Built Logan's Fort (St. Asaph's), 1776. In Virginia Assembly, 1781–87; Ky. conventions to separate from Va. and to draft Ky. state constitution. Defeated twice for Governor. Born Va., 1743; died 1802. Buried 2½ miles south. See other side. (Reverse)

JAMES KNOX—PIONEER

Led 40 "Long Hunters" to Kentucky in 1770. Knox, with nine, built camp in area now Green County. He returned to Virginia, 1771. Major in War of Revolution. Represented Kentucky in Virginia Assembly, 1788. State Senator from Lincoln County, 1795–1800. Born Ireland, came to Virginia at age 14 years. Died 1822. Buried in the Logan graveyard. See other side.

710 RARE 1860 TOMBSTONES
(3 mi. S. of Winchester, KY 15, Clark Co.)

In the burial ground, one-fourth mile east, are two rare Carrara marble tombstones carved in Italy by Joel Tanner Hart, the world renowned sculptor. He brought the stones to America, 1860, at time of unveiling of his great statue of Henry Clay in Richmond, Va. Visiting his birthplace near here, he placed stones in memory of his parents, Josiah and Judith Hart.

711 SKIRMISH HERE
(2 mi. S. of Sandy Hook, KY 7, Elliott Co.)

This burial ground is the final resting place of seven unnamed soldiers who were killed in a Civil War skirmish here in late Sept. 1862, between forces of USA Gen. George W. Morgan and CSA Gen. John Hunt Morgan. Union forces retreating from Cumberland Gap to Greenup were harassed by Confederates from West Liberty, thru here, to Grayson. See map.

712 DUTTON'S HILL BATTLE
(2 mi. N. of Somerset, KY 39, Pulaski Co.)

March 30, 1863, USA force of 1,250 under General Q. A. Gillmore overtook 1,550 Confederate cavalry under Gen. John Pegram, here. Five-hour battle resulted. CSA driven from one position to another, withdrew during night across Cumberland. Killed, wounded, missing, CSA 200 and USA 30. On nine-day expedition into Ky., CSA had captured 750 cattle and took 537 across river.

713 PLEASANT RETREAT
(S. of Lancaster, US 27, Garrard Co.)

Home of William Owsley and his son-in-law Simeon Anderson. Built about 1815. Owsley, 1782–1862, State House of Representatives and Senate; Court of Appeals; Kentucky Secretary of State and Governor of Kentucky 1844–48. Owsley County named for him. Anderson, born 1802; State House of Representatives; in 1839, U.S. Congress. Died 1840, in office.

714 HOME OF STATESMEN
(Paulding & Maple Sts., Lancaster, Garrard Co.)

Two hundred feet west John Boyle built log cabin, 1798, that is still part of home. He and three others, who later set up housekeeping in that cabin, were state legislators and represented the district in Congress 28 years. John Boyle, 1774–1834, also Chief Justice, Court of Appeals; U.S. District Judge. Boyle County named for him. See other side. (Reverse)

HOME OF STATESMEN
Continued from other side.

Samuel McKee, 1774–1826, also on Gen. Harrison's staff, War of 1812. George Robertson, 1790–1874, also Kentucky Secretary of State; Chief Justice Kentucky Court of Appeals. Robertson County named for him. Robert P. Letcher, 1788–1861, also Governor of Kentucky, 1840–44; Minister to Mexico, 1849–52. Letcher County named for him.

715 GREAT SALTPETER CAVE
(S. of Mt. Vernon, US 25, Rockcastle Co.)

"Big Cave," five miles SE, source of organic material for production of gun powder from 1797 through Civil War. Important supply during War of 1812. Great rooms with passageway through mountain and interior water stream permitted manufacture inside of the cave. Working by torchlight as many as 70 laborers were employed when production was at high point.

716 THE SHAKER TAVERN
(South Union, KY 73, Logan Co.)

Built 1869, nine years after the completion of the Louisville and Nashville railroad thru South Union land. Members approved tax to build line thru here, furnished material and constructed depot. Visitors increased and trustees built the hotel, replacing use of frame office building, center of village. One outside chimney for three fireplaces, unique feature.

717 GEN. SAMUEL HOPKINS
(Between Zion & Henderson, KY 351, Henderson Co.)

On Washington's staff and in many campaigns, War of the Revolution. Born in Va., 1753. Came to Ky., 1797, as Transylvania Company agent. With Col. T. Allen laid out town of Henderson. Chief Justice, First Court, 1799. Ky. House, 1800–06, Senate, 1809–13. Comm. in Chief, Western Frontier, 1812. Congress 1813–15. Hopkinsville and Hopkins County named for him. Died 1819.

718 CARDOME
(N. lawn of Cardome Center, US 25, Scott Co.)

Home of Gov. James F. Robinson, 1844 until death, at age 82, in 1882. He succeeded Beriah Magoffin who resigned as Governor, August 1862, after refusing Lincoln's call for troops. Robinson supported Union during year as Governor. Lawyer, jurist of distinction. Trustee, Georgetown College, 1831–81, and President of Board, 1864–81. House built, 1821: Cardome Academy, 1896.

719 LINCOLN'S MENTOR
(8 mi. N. of Greensburg, KY 61, Green Co.)

Three miles west, birthplace of Mentor Graham, 1800–86, "The Man Who Taught Lincoln." Sixty years a teacher. Green County 1818–26. After Illinois voted down slavery, moved to New Salem, 1826. There, from 1831–37, as tutor and friend, he had incalculable influence on Abraham Lincoln, his public life. Graham died at 86, South Dakota. Reburied at New Salem, Ill., 1933.

720 GREAT RIVER TRAGEDY
(Warsaw, 2nd & E. Main Sts., US 42, Gallatin Co.)

At midnight of Dec. 4, 1868 two cabined passenger steamers plying between Louisville and Cincinnati collided two miles above Warsaw. The *America* rammed deeply into the *United States*. Barrelled coal oil on deck of latter caught fire enveloping both boats in flames, spreading over surface of river. 162 lives, $350,000 property lost in terrible Ohio River holocaust.

721 OLD MULKEY CHURCH
(2 mi. S. of Tompkinsville, KY 1446, Monroe Co.)

First church in this area located 200 yards from here. Formed, 1773, by Philip Mulkey, other settlers from Carolinas. Church grew till this larger house built in 1804. Building in form of the Cross, 12 corners for Apostles, 3 doors for Trinity. Daniel Boone's sister, Hannah, and Revolutionary War soldiers buried in graveyard.

722 A CIVIL WAR REPRISAL
(Williamstown, Jct. of US 25, KY 36, Grant Co.)

Three Confederates were brought here from prison at Lexington and executed Aug. 15, 1864; reprisal for the guerrilla murder of Union sympathizers, Joel Skirvin and Anderson Simpson. Those executed were William P. and John L. Lingenfelter, brothers of Mrs. Simpson, and George Wainscott, lst Batt. Ky. Inf., CSA. Lingenfelter graves N.E. of Lusby's Mill, Owen County.

723 LOG CABIN PRE-1800
(Near Red Bird Hospital, KY 66, Clay Co.)

On these grounds of the Red Bird River Community Hospital of the Evangelical United Brethren Church Center is log cabin built before 1800. Erected by Dillion Asher. Born, 1774, died, 1844. Buried near log house. Asher was keeper of first tollgate in Kentucky, near Pineville. Established by legislature, 1795; fees paid for improvements on Wilderness Road.

Great river tragedy as two steamers collide, 1868. Kentucky Historical Society Collection.

724 JAMESTOWN SKIRMISHES
(Jamestown, US 127, Russell Co.)

Dec. 25, 1861, part of First Ky. Cav., USA, camped at Webb's Cross Roads to guard stored corn and forage and scout CSA operations. Detachment skirmished with enemy here resulting in one death, CSA. Both armies in area again, 1863. On June 2, 300 CSA attacked Union pickets, driving them into town. CSA retired when met by alert USA. One CSA man and weapons captured.

725 A CIVIL WAR REPRISAL
(2 mi. E of Lusby's Mill, Jct. KY 1330 & Keefer Rd., Owen Co.)

Three Confederates, imprisoned at Lexington, were executed at Williamstown, Aug. 15, 1864, in reprisal for guerrilla murder of Union sympathizers, Joel Skirvin and Anderson Simpson. Victims were from this area: William P. and John L. Lingenfelter, brothers of Mrs. Simpson, and George Wainscott. Lingenfelter graves are quarter mile north.

726 A WARFIELD SKIRMISH
(Warfield, KY 40, 971, Martin Co.)

A plundering, burning, Confederate detached force, under command of Col. V. A. Witcher, harassed east Kentucky and West Virginia during most of the Civil War. In fall, 1864, they took horses and cattle in this area from friend and foe. While Witcher's men made barbecue, Home Guards from Louisa attacked from hill to west. After exchange of fire, both withdrew. See over.
(Reverse)

WARFIELD
First Martin County seat, 1870. Established about 1850 as a coal, salt and lumber community by George Rogers Clark Floyd and John Warfield of Va. mountains. Products shipped by river boats to Catlettsburg. Floyd was son of one Governor of Virginia, brother of another. Coal mines used thru Civil War as hiding place against marauding by enemy. See over.

727 KNOWN BUT TO GOD
(Breaks Interstate Park, KY 80, Pike Co.)

Here rests the body of a soldier of the Confederacy, struck down by an unknown assassin in May of 1865–apparently on way to home in the South. He was buried in a coffin made of boards rived from a great oak by four men of this community. After the turn of the century, a rose bush marked this final resting place of a soldier who is "Known but to God."

728 KNOTT OF LEBANON
(Lebanon, Courthouse lawn, US 68, KY 49, Marion Co.)

J. Proctor Knott, 1830–1911. Born in this county. Missouri Legislature, 1851–59; Att. Gen., 1859–60. Came back here, 1863. U.S. Congress six terms, became famous as statesman, satirist, Governor of Kentucky, 1883–87. In 1891 Constitutional Convention, led keeping capital at Frankfort. First Dean Centre College Law School, 1894–1901. Knott County named for him.

729 PIONEER WARD
(Inez, Courthouse lawn, KY 3, 40, Martin Co.)

James Ward born in Virginia, 1758. He settled on Rockcastle Creek, three miles south of here, where he lived 50 years and died, 1848. Private, Virginia regiments, War of the Revolution, 1775–76, 1778. Came to Kentucky, 1779. With the Clark expedition against Indians, Chillicothe and Piqua, Ohio, 1780. In battles of Bryan Station, and Blue Licks, 1782. See other side.
(Reverse)

EDUCATOR WARD
William B. Ward, 1877–1952. Buried in Saltwell Cemetery. Known as educator, author and leader in the field of education, 50 years. Principal in schools of eastern and northern Kentucky; head of the Old Sandy Valley Seminary at Paintsville. Author *Outline of U.S. History*; publisher *The Mountain Journal* and *The New Day*. Descended from Pioneer Ward. See other side.

730 CIVIL WAR ACTION
(Scottsville, Courthouse lawn, US 31-E, 231, Allen Co.)

Confederate forces of 200 under Col. John M. Hughs attacked here, Dec. 8, 1863. Twelve days earlier he had attacked Monticello, Ky., captured then paroled garrison of 153 men; no supplies. Continuing to harass USA forces, seek stores, he came here, captured and paroled garrison of 86. Secured quantity of store, saddles, bridles, and 500 stand of small arms.

731 SCULPTOR'S BIRTHPLACE
(1 mi. E. of Winchester, US 60, Clark Co.)

Birthplace of Joel Tanner Hart, 1810, sculptor and poet. Began as stone-cutter, 1830. Went to Florence, Italy, 1840. Famed for busts: John Jordan Crittenden, Cassius M. Clay, Henry Clay, Andrew Jackson. Marble statues: Woman Triumphant, Il Penseroso, Henry Clay, Angelina and others. Died, Italy, 1871. By Legislative Act, reburied Frankfort, 1887.

732 SECESSION ABANDONED
(Mayfield, Courthouse lawn, US 45, KY 80, Graves Co.)

In May, 1861, delegates of seven Kentucky and twenty Tennessee westernmost counties, the Jackson Purchase, met in Mayfield. Belief in Southern cause, dissatisfaction with Kentucky adherence to Union, and Tennessee delay joining South, caused convention vote to secede and form a Confederate state. With Tennessee's vote to secede, June 8, 1861, proposal abandoned.

733 MORGAN'S FIRST RAID
(Versailles, US 60, 62, Woodford Co.)

On first Kentucky raid CSA Gen. John H. Morgan with 900 cavalry in Lawrenceburg July 14, 1862; came here that night. Sent out scouts in all directions and took 300 USA horses and mules. Next day moved to Georgetown, then to Cynthiana, after which returned to Tennessee. See map on other side. On raid Morgan covered 1,000 miles in 24 days, raiding 17 towns.

734 KENTUCKY DIAMOND
(6½ mi. W. of US 127 on KY 55, Russell Co.)

In the summer of 1888 on the farm of Henry Burris, two miles north, a brilliant stone was found. It was appraised gem quality diamond, octahedral in form, 0.776 carat by G. A. Schultz, a jeweler of Louisville, who bought it for $20. Diamond is now on display in the Smithsonian Institution. No other has been found in area although many have searched. See other side.
(Reverse)

OTHER U.S. DIAMONDS
Up to 1964, only Kentucky gem type diamond was found here: see over. Low grade ones in Elliott County, 130 miles northeast. In the Great Lakes Region, found at one

place each in Michigan, New York, Ohio; two places in Indiana, Tennessee; six in Wisconsin. Source of these probably glacial action, although Canadian origin not located. Also diamonds found in 10 other states.

735 JENNY (JENNIE) WILEY
(5 mi. S. of Paintsville, US 23, 460, Johnson Co.)

Captured by Indians in present Bland Co., Va., Oct. 1787 or '89. Four children and brother killed. A child born in captivity killed also. Harman party pursued, had to give up. Came here and joined by others built stockade. After nearly a year Mrs. Wiley escaped, followed "dream" to safety here. Reunited with husband in Va. They settled in this county in 1800.

736 HARMAN STATION
(5 mi. S. of Paintsville, US 23, 460, Johnson Co.)

The first settlement in Eastern Kentucky. Matthias Harman's party of hunters from Virginia built stockade near river bank, 1787. Indians forced evacuation in 1788, and burned blockhouse. Harman and others returned, 1789, and rebuilt an enduring fort. These men at Blockhouse Bottom broke Indian hold on Big Sandy Valley, opened Eastern Kentucky for settlement.

737 CSA RETURNS TO TENN.
(4-H Camp entrance, 4 mi. S. of London, KY 229, Laurel Co.)

After Battle of Perryville, Oct. 8, 1862, CSA gathered at Bryantsville on 11th. Pursuing Union force did not attack, but destroyed sources of food. CSA Gen. Bragg started moving forces south, Oct. 13. USA under Gen. Buell pursued to here, where he decided further pursuit was not expedient. CSA continued on, passing thru Cumberland Gap, Oct. 19-24. See map on other side.

738 KENTUCKY HISTORIAN
(Maysville, Courthouse lawn, US 62, 68, Mason Co.)

Lewis Collins, 1797-1870, born near Bryan's Station, author of Collins' *Historical Sketches of Kentucky*. He was presiding judge of Mason County, publisher-editor of the *Eagle*, lived here 52 years. His 1847 study of his own state—revised by Richard H. Collins,

Historian Lewis Collins. Kentucky Historical Society Collection.

his son, 1874 as Collins' *History of Kentucky*—is considered a basic source for the historian of today.

739 U.S. VICE PRESIDENT
(3 mi. W. of Georgetown, in Great Crossings Park, KY 227, Scott Co.)

Richard Mentor Johnson, 1780–1850, one of four Kentuckians—more than any state, except New York—who were U.S. Vice Presidents. Others were John C. Breckinridge, Adlai Ewing Stevenson and Alben W. Barkley. Johnson home 2 mi. north. Col., War of 1812. Congressman, 1807–19, 1829–37; Senate, 1819–29. Vice Pres. with President Van Buren, 1837–41. Ky. legislature, 1841–42.

740 U.S. VICE PRESIDENT
(S. Christian H. S., Herndon, KY 117, Christian Co.)

Adlai Ewing Stevenson, 1835–1914, one of four Kentuckians—more than any state, except New York—who were U.S. Vice Presidents. Others were Richard M. Johnson, John C. Breckinridge and Alben W. Barkley. Stevenson, born here, moved to Illinois, 1852. Member Congress two terms. Elected Vice President with Cleveland in 1892. Bryan's running mate in 1900.

741 U.S. VICE PRESIDENT
(Main St., Lexington, Courthouse lawn, Fayette Co.)

John Cabell Breckinridge, 1821–75, one of four Kentuckians—more than any other state, except New York—who were U.S. Vice Presidents. Others were Adlai E. Stevenson, Richard M. Johnson, and Alben W. Barkley. In U.S. Congress, 1851–55. Elected Vice-President in 1856. Candidate of Southern Democrats for President in 1860, carrying nine Southern States. See over.

(Reverse)

VICE PRESIDENT, CONT.

Breckinridge served as a major of Kentucky Volunteers, Mexican War. Elected to U.S. Senate in 1860. Became brig. general Confederate Army, 1861, and was expelled from the Senate. In battles of Shiloh, Chattanooga, Murfreesboro, and others. Confederate Secretary of War, Feb. 1865 until surrender of Lee at Appomattox, April 1865. He was born and died in Lexington.

742 OLD NEW LIBERTY
(New Liberty, KY 227, Owen Co.)

Settled before 1800, incorporated, 1827. Owen County formed, 1819. "Church on the Twins," organized 1801, first in the county. Now the New Liberty Baptist Church. One of earliest log cabins, built 1806 by John Gayle, stands as part of barn, two miles east. See other side.

(Reverse)

NEW LIBERTY—CONT.

Gayle House, built 1865. For 20 years famous retreat for Kentucky politicians. Torn down, 1920. Union Agricultural and Mechanical Fair, organized in 1859. Old Concord College, started 1867. Used until first high school, 1906. The *Owen News* started here, 1868.

743 FIRST COAL BY RAIL
(Owensboro, US 60 & Ewing Rd., Daviess Co.)

Robert Triplett built the first railway in Kentucky, 1826. Coal was moved from Bon Harbor hills to steamboats on the Ohio River. Triplett the first to get coal substituted for wood as fuel on river boats below Louisville. Coal was shipped south, sold by barrel. Built cotton, woolen mills and laid out town of Bon Harbor, 1842, 2½ mi. N., which failed.

744 BILL SMOTHERS PARK
(Park at 1st & St. Ann Sts., Owensboro, Daviess Co.)

Site of home of William Smeathers (Bill Smothers), who in 1797–98 made first permanent settlement at Yellow Banks, now Owensboro. Officer in Kentucky's "Corn Stalk" Militia in 1803 and on expedition up the Wabash River against the Indians in the War of 1812 under General Samuel Hopkins. He then went to Texas as an Indian hunter and guide. Died there, 1837.

745 PANTHER CREEK BATTLE
(7.5 mi. S. of Owensboro, US 431, Daviess Co.)

Sept. 19, 1862, Confederate force occupied Owensboro. USA troops at old Fairground refused demand for surrender. Skirmish followed. Union soldier swam Ohio River to summon help from Indiana Legion. CSA retired to here. Home Guards from Indiana crossed river and attacked next day. CSA retreated with 36 killed, 70 wounded. USA loss, 3 killed and 35 wounded.

746 GOVERNOR FROM WARSAW
(Warsaw, Courthouse lawn, US 42 & KY 35, Gallatin Co.)

Birthplace of Richard Yates, 1818. In Illinois legislature for three terms; U.S. Congress, 1851–55. As Governor of Illinois, 1861–65, he vigorously supported Lincoln and state exceeded the call for volunteers. Member of U.S. Senate, 1865–71. Delegate to conventions that nominated Lincoln and Grant for President. Yates died 1873. A son Illinois Governor, 1901–04.

747 COUNTY NAMED, 1798
(Warsaw, Courthouse lawn, US 42 & KY 35, Gallatin Co.)

For Albert Gallatin, 1761–1849, a Swiss, who came to U.S., 1780. Penn. Cons. Convention, 1789–90; Legislature, 3 yrs. Congress, 1795–1801. Leader in finance, constitutional and international law, Secretary of the Treasury, 1802–14; Comm., Treaty of Ghent, 1814; Minister to France, 1816–23, England, 1826–27. National (later Gallatin) Bank of New York, president, 1831–39.

748 CAPTURED AND BURNED
(9 mi. S. of Elizabethtown, US 31-W, Hardin Co.)

On second Kentucky raid CSA Gen. J. H. Morgan's cavalry came from Glasgow to Hammonville, Dec. 25, 1862. Next day sent some to Bacon Creek and others to Nolin to take stockades and burn trestles, both places. At Nolin, two miles west, 76 Union men taken prisoners and paroled. Stockades and trestles burned both places. Railroad out of use for critical time. See map.

749 CIVIL WAR 1862 INVASION
(N. of Phillips La., Hodgenville, KY 61, Larue Co.)

CSA under Gen. Braxton Bragg was through area late Sept. 1862, with plan to capture central Ky. Force under Gen. Joseph Wheeler here Sept. 23-27, scouting Union army along Louisville road to west. Ordered to Boston, many skirmishes with USA until Oct. 4. On Oct. 8, Confederate and Union forces met in battle at Perryville; then CSA retreated from state. See map.

750 A FOSTER INSPIRATION
(Frankfort & 5th Sts., Augusta, KY 8, Bracken Co.)

Stephen Collins Foster, as youth, visited here, May 1833. His uncle Dr. Joseph S. Tomlinson was then President of Augusta College. The musical, harmonious voices from the old Negro church on the hill floated softly over the town. "It can hardly be doubted" Foster was impressed by these since he "put into song at a later time the sorrow their voices reflected."

751 RANGER LEADER BLINDED
(6 mi. SE of Princeton, KY 91, Caldwell Co.)

Confederate Gen. Adam R. Johnson with 1700 Partisan Rangers were in area seeking recruits and supplies. Learning of Union troops under Gen. E. H. Hobson camped at Grubb's Cross Roads, Johnson attacked, Aug. 21, 1864. In the skirmish that followed, Johnson was wounded, losing sight of both eyes. CSA became demoralized and retreated to Paris, Tennessee.

752 A MASONIC LEADER
(La Grange, KY 53, 147, Oldham Co.)

Home of Dr. Rob Morris, 1818-88. In 1884 "crowned Poet Laureate of Freemasonry." Founded the Order of the Eastern Star. He was born near Boston, Mass., lived 28 years here. From 1861 to 1865 president of the Masonic College, located in La Grange, 1844-73. Author of many Masonic books and poems. Grand Master, 1858-59, the Grand Lodge of Kentucky. Died here in 1888.

753 SITE OF 1792 CHURCH
(3 mi. N. of Paris, US 68, Bourbon Co.)

Built of two-foot blue ash logs as home by Daniel Matheny, 1790. With Jacob Leer as class leader Mt. Gilead Methodist Society was organized here by Reverend Caleb Jarvis Taylor, author of revival hymns. Members were not allowed to buy slaves except to free them when their labor repaid the cost. Lot deeded for perpetual cemetery in 1878, after the church closed.

754 PRESBYTERIAN CHURCH
(500 W. Main St., Danville, US 127, 150, Boyle Co.)

One of three founded, 1784, by Reverend David Rice; earliest of this denomination west of Alleghenies. Here worshipped: James G. Birney, whose presidential candidacy in 1844 caused defeat of Henry Clay; John C. Breckinridge, whose 1860 candidacy resulted in election of Lincoln; Samuel D. Burchard, whose "Rum, Romanism and Rebellion" defeated James G. Blaine in 1884.

755 GRAYSON'S TAVERN
(lst & Walnut, Danville, US 127, 150, Boyle Co.)

Danville's first tavern, operated in this building before 1800 by Benjamin Grayson. Often within these walls the burning political issues of the day were discussed. The Danville Political Society, organized in 1786 and the first of its kind in the West, met and dined here at Grayson's Tavern to "plan the course of the empire" before blazing log fires.

756 COURTHOUSE A HOSPITAL
(Main St., Danville, Courthouse lawn, US 127, 150, Boyle Co.)

Boyle County's first courthouse erected here, 1842, destroyed by great fire of 1860. This building completed 1862. First occupied by Union forces as hospital after battle of Perryville, October 8, 1862. On 11th a Union force drove CSA from fairgrounds, thru town, skirmishing all way. CSA armies gathered at Bryantsville, started back to Tenn. on 13th. See over.

757 UNION SUPPLY BASE
(Fort Jefferson, US 51, Ballard Co.)

One of first Kentucky positions, Fort Jefferson, occupied by Union troops after Confederate seizure of Columbus, Sept. 1861. From this base, General Ulysses S. Grant directed demonstration against Columbus, Jan. 1862. Troops from here joined in capturing Ft. Henry, Feb. 1862. One of four river ports in area used as Union supply bases for operations in the western theater.

758 FOUNDER OF HAZARD
(Hazard, Courthouse lawn, KY 7, 15, Perry Co.)

Elijah Combs and seven brothers came with parents to Kentucky, 1790. He was first settler here; leader in forming county, named for Com. Oliver Hazard Perry, 1821. He deeded land on which Hazard stands to trustees, 1826. Member of Legislature, 1840.

759 UNCLE IRA
(Jeff, KY 7, 15, Perry Co.)

The Ira Combs Memorial Church–Little Zion Church, built in 1909 on land settled in 1790 by Mason Combs. Ira, a grandson, was Civil War veteran. Born 1844. In 1874 began preaching. For 60 years, without pay, he ministered to the Old Regular Baptists in Pine Mt. section. Died in 1934, buried on old homestead. Church dedicated in his honor on Easter Sunday, 1952.

760 COUNTY NAMED 1815
(Scottsville, Courthouse lawn, US 31-E, Allen Co.)

For Lieut. Col. John Allen, born in Va., 1771, came to Ky., 1779. Practiced law in Shelby County. State Representative, 1801–07, and State Senate, 1807–13. Killed in battle at River Raisin, Jan. 22, 1813, and one of nine officers at that battle for whom Kentucky counties named. Allen County formed by Act of Assembly, from Warren and Barren Counties.

761 MUHLENBERG HERO
(Greenville, US 62, Muhlenberg Co.)

Site of home of Ephraim M. Brank, 1791–1875. Born in North Carolina and came to Kentucky about 1808. Lieutenant, Kentucky militia, sent by Gov. Shelby in response to call of Gen. Andrew Jackson for troops to repel British at New Orleans. On January 8, 1815 Brank's daring coolness on breastworks at battle inspired Ky. and Tenn. riflemen to crucial defeat of the British.

762 COUNTY NAMED, 1829
(Hawesville, Courthouse lawn, US 60 & KY 69, Hancock Co.)

For John Hancock, 1737–93. Patriot, statesman and soldier. President of Continental Congress, 1775–77, and bold first signer of the Declaration of Independence. Mayor-general of Mass. militia in Revolutionary War, member of the Mass. Constitutional Convention, 1780, governor 1780–85, 1787–93. He presided over Mass. convention to ratify U.S. constitution, 1788.

763 COUNTY NAMED, 1886
(Bardwell, Courthouse lawn, US 51, 62, Carlisle Co.)

For John Griffin Carlisle. Born 1835, practiced law in Covington. Kentucky Legislator from 1859–71. Lt. Governor, 1871–75. U.S. Congress, 1877–91. House Speaker, 1883–89. U.S. Senate, 1890–93. Secretary of Treasury, 1893–97, under Pres. Grover Cleveland. Controversy over gold standard, 1896, caused him to move to New York. Died there, 1910. Buried Covington, Kentucky.

764 SITE OF BURNETT HOME
(W. of Cadiz, US 68, Trigg Co.)

Henry Cornelius Burnett, 1825–66, represented district, U.S. Congress, 1855–61. Presided at Russellville Convention in Nov., 1861, which formed Ky. provisional government. A member of Confederate Congress from Ky., 1861–65. After dispersal of CSA government from Richmond, sought pardon from President Andrew Johnson. When pardon was received, charges of treason were dropped.

765 COUNTY NAMED, 1836
(Bedford, Courthouse lawn, US 42, 421, Trimble Co.)

For Robert Trimble, U.S. Supreme Court Justice, 1826–28, appointed by Pres. John Quincy Adams. Born in Va., 1777, came to Ky., 1780. Capt., Bourbon Co. regiment, 1796. Practiced law in Paris, Ky., 1800. Member State Legislature, 1802–04. Ky. Court of Appeals, 1807–09. U.S. District Attorney, 1813–17. U.S. District Judge from 1817–26. Died in 1828, buried at Paris, Ky.

766 MORGAN'S RAIDERS CAMP
(KY 448, W. of Jct. KY 1638, Meade Co.)

Gen. John H. Morgan's CSA cavalry of 2,000 camped three miles east, July 7, 1863. Next day crossed river at Brandenburg on 2 captured steamers, repelling attacks by gunboat *Elk* and Indiana militia. Moved thru Indiana into NE Ohio where captured July 26. Escaped prison Nov. 24, returned south. Map other side. Raid sought to prevent USA move to Tenn. and Va.

767 JEFFERSON'S SISTER
(3 mi. N. of Smithland, US 60, KY 137, Livingston Co.)

Rocky Hill, one mile north, home of Lucy Jefferson Lewis, youngest sister, Thomas Jefferson, author of Declaration of Independence and third president of US. She was born in 1752, Albemarle Co., Va. Came to Ky., 1808, with her husband Dr. Charles L. Lewis, who served in Revolution, and their six children. Mrs. Lewis died in 1811, was buried near her home.

768 GRAYSON SPRINGS
(3 mi. E. of Leitchfield, KY 88, Grayson Co.)

Site of famous spa started in mid 1820's, owned by M. P. Clarkson, and known for healing powers of its mineral water springs. Resort reached its height in 1900 under ownership of Mercke brothers. Also home of St. Augustine's, first Roman Catholic Church in Grayson County, founded in 1815 by Father Charles Nerinckx, one of the great pioneer missionaries of Kentucky.

769 HOME OF THOMAS HINES
(US 31-W By-pass & 1210 Fairview Ave., at cemetery entrance, Warren Co.)

Capt. Thomas Henry Hines enlisted in the Confederate Army, 1861. With Brig. Gen John H. Morgan, 1862–63. Captured, July '63, in Ohio with Morgan. Led escape from Federal prison, Nov. '63. Leader of northwest conspiracy '64. Termed most dangerous man of Confederacy. Ky. Court of Appeals, 1878–98. Born Butler Co., 1838; lived here. Buried Fairview Cemetery, 1898.

770 BIRTHPLACE OF HINES
(Woodbury, KY 403, Butler Co.)

Capt. Thomas Henry Hines enlisted in the Confederate Army, 1861. With Brig. Gen. John H. Morgan, 1862–63. Captured, July 1863, in Ohio with Morgan. Led escape from Federal prison, Nov. 1863. Leader of northwest conspiracy 1864. Termed most dangerous man of Confederacy. Ky. Court of Appeals, 1878–98. Born, 1838; lived Bowling Green. Buried Fairview Cemetery, 1898.

771 HINDMAN SETTLEMENT SCHOOL
(Hindman, KY 160, E. of KY 80, Knott Co.)

Founded 1902 by May Stone and Katherine Pettit to provide an educational opportunity for the youth of the mountains and keep them mindful of their heritage.

772 COUNTY NAMED, 1860
(Catlettsburg, Courthouse lawn, US Business 23, 60, Boyd Co.)

For Linn Boyd. Born Tenn., 1800. Came to West Ky. in youth. Kentucky Legislature, 1827–1831. Congress, 1835–1837, 1839–55, and Speaker, 1851–55. Author of Resolution to annex Texas. The Kentucky delegation proposed Boyd for Vice President at Democratic Convention, 1856, but convention chose Breckinridge of Ky. Boyd elected Lt. Gov., 1859. He died before taking office.

773 FOR MOUNTAIN YOUTH
(College Campus, Berea, US 25, Madison Co.)

Berea College, founded 1855 by John G. Fee with the support of Cassius Marcellus Clay, in a one-room school built by the community. Its constitution, 1858, made it Christian, non-sectarian, anti-slavery. Compelled to close 1859 by pro-slavery factions, reopened 1865. Dedicated to the service of mountain areas, Berea is an historic monument to equality.

774 COUNTY NAMED, 1780
(Stanford, Courthouse lawn, Business US 150 & KY 1247, Lincoln Co.)

For Benjamin Lincoln, 1733–1810. Born Mass. In War of Revolution took Mass. Regts. to reinforce New York, 1776; at Saratoga, 1777, cut Burgoyne's communications with Canada; 1778, command of Southern Department. Commissioned by Washington to receive the sword of Cornwallis at British surrender, Yorktown, 1781. Secretary of War, 1781–84. Led forces that quelled Shays' Rebellion.

775 INSPIRATION MOUNTAIN
(N. of Harlan, US 119, 421, Harlan Co.)

Little Shepherd Trail, part of setting for: *Little Shepherd of Kingdom Come, Hell for Sartain, Trail of the Lonesome Pine,* by John Fox, Jr., famous for eleven novels of Ky. mountains and the Bluegrass, written 1893 to 1919. Born Paris, Ky., 1863. Harvard, 1883. Spanish-American War, 1898. Moved to Big Stone Gap, Va., 1886, had mining business. Died in 1919.

776 INSPIRATION MOUNTAIN
(N. of Cumberland, US 119, Harlan Co.)

Little Shepherd Trail, part of setting for: *Little Shepherd of Kingdom Come, Hell for Sartain, Trail of the Lonesome Pine,* by John Fox, Jr., famous for eleven novels of Ky. mountains and the Bluegrass, written 1893 to 1919. Born Paris, Ky., 1863. Harvard, 1883. Spanish-American War, 1898. Moved to Big Stone Gap, Va., 1886, had mining business. Died in 1919.

777 INSPIRATION MOUNTAIN
(S. of Whitesburg, US 119, Letcher Co.)

Little Shepherd Trail, part of setting for: *Little Shepherd of Kingdom Come, Hell for Sartain, Trail of the Lonesome Pine,* by John Fox, Jr., famous for eleven novels of Ky. mountains and the Bluegrass, written 1893 to 1919. Born Paris, Ky., 1863. Harvard, 1883. Spanish-American War, 1898. Moved to Big Stone Gap, Va., 1886, had mining business. Died in 1919.

778 ESCULAPIA SPRINGS
(Charters, KY 9, 989, Lewis Co.)

Site of one of the most popular health resorts along Ohio River, 1845–60, seven miles west. Mineral water from spring widely used for medicinal purposes. Resort was easy of access by boat and drew many out of state guests until destroyed by fire, 1860. Decline in use of spring water followed. Twenty other antebellum watering places flourished in Kentucky.

779 MINERAL MOUND
(2 mi. S. of Eddyville, KY 93, Lyon Co.)

Site of the home of Willis B. Machen, 1810–93, farmer, manufacturer, lawyer, legislator. A courageous leader of strong convictions and unimpeachable integrity. Member Ky. Constitution Convention 1849, State Senate 1853, House of Rep. 1856–60, Congress of Confederate States 1862–64, U.S. Senate 1872. A leader in Grange (Farmers') movement in Ky. for twenty years.

780 CIVIL WAR TERRORIST
(Albany, Courthouse lawn, US 127, Clinton Co.)

Champ Ferguson born here in 1821. Guerrilla leader with Confederate leaning, but attacked supporters of both sides thruout Civil War in southern Ky., Tenn. Over 100 murders ascribed to Ferguson alone. Hunted by both CSA and USA. Taken after end of war, convicted by US Army Court, Nashville, and hanged Oct. 20, 1865. Buried at home in White County, Tennessee.

781 COUNTY NAMED, 1806
(1 mi. N. of Liberty, Roadside Park, US 127, Casey Co.)

For Colonel William Casey, early Ky. pioneer and great-grandfather of Samuel L. Clemens, "Mark Twain." Casey born in Va. Came to Ky. in 1779. Built Casey's Station on the Dix River in 1791. Member of Convention, 1799, to frame second Ky. Constitution. Trustee, town of Columbia, 1802. 1813, Presidential elector. Lived Adair Co., died, 1816. County formed from Lincoln.

782 COUNTY NAMED, 1799
(Barbourville, US 25-E & KY 11, Knox Co.)

For Henry Knox, U.S. Sec. of War, 1785–96. Born Boston, 1750. Joined Continental

Army, 1775. Battles of Bunker Hill, Brandy-wine, Yorktown, and others. Command of artillery, 1775. Commissioned Major-General, 1781. Proposed a military academy in 1779, first commandant at West Point, 1782. Organized Society of Cincinnati, 1783. Sec. of War, 1785–96. Died in Maine, 1806.

783 COUNTY NAMED, 1860
(Dixon, Courthouse lawn, US Alt. 41 & KY 132, Webster Co.)

For Daniel Webster, 1782–1852, "Defender of the Constitution." Born in New Hampshire. Eight years United States House of Representatives, nineteen years U.S. Senate. A skilled legislator, persuasive debator, eloquent orator and constitutional lawyer. Five years Secretary of State, Presidents Harrison, Tyler and Fillmore. Buried at Marshfield, Mass.

784 COUNTY NAMED, 1803
(Greenup, Courthouse lawn, US 23, Greenup Co.)

For Christopher Greenup, governor of Ky., 1804–08. Born Va., 1750, officer in American Revolution. Began law practice in Ky., 1783. Clerk of Va. court for district of Ky., 1785–92. Member, conventions for Ky. statehood, 1784, '85, '88. Elected one of the first two Ky. members of U.S. Congress, 1793–97. Presidential elector, 1808. Died, 1818, buried in Frankfort Cemetery.

785 COUNTY NAMED, 1819
(Harlan, Courthouse lawn, US 119, 421, Harlan Co.)

For Major Silas Harlan, born Va., 1752, came to Ky. in 1774. Built Harlan's Station, 7 miles south of Harrodsburg on Salt River, 1778. Commanded spies, 1779, in Illinois campaign of Gen. George R. Clark, who said: "He was one of bravest soldiers that ever fought by my side." Killed, 1782, at the battle of Blue Licks while commanding his detachment. Buried at Blue Licks.

786 COUNTY NAMED, 1860
(Salyersville, Courthouse lawn, Jct. Church & Maple Sts., US 460, Magoffin Co.)

For Gov. Beriah Magoffin, born 1815, Harrodsburg. Centre College, 1835; Transylvania Law School in 1838. State Senate, 1850–52. Governor of Ky., 1859. Disagreement with the legislature over

enforcement of Ky. armed neutrality act caused resignation 1862, when agreement was reached on successor. In 1867–69, State Representative, Mercer Co. Died 1885, buried Harrodsburg, Ky.

787 MENIFEE COUNTY
(Frenchburg, Courthouse lawn, US 460, Menifee Co.)

Formed 1869 out of part of five joining counties; named for Richard H. Menefee, regarded as one of Kentucky's great orators. Born in Owingsville, 1808. Elected Commonwealth Attorney of 11th Judicial district, 1831; State Representative, 1836–37; U.S. Representative, 1837–39. Died at age of 32. Kentucky lost "one of her proudest and fondest hopes."

788 COUNTY NAMED, 1856
(Morehead, Courthouse lawn, US 60, Rowan Co.)

For Judge John Rowan, 1773–1843. Born Penn., came in 1783 to Ky. Admitted to bar, 1795. Member second Ky. Const. Convention in 1799. Secretary of State, 1804–1806. State Legislature, 10 years. Court of Appeals, 1819–1821. U.S. Senate from 1824 to 1830. First President of Ky. Historical Society, 1838–1843. Buried at his home, Federal Hill, "My Old Kentucky Home," Bardstown.

789 SITE OF FINLEY HOME
(Near Hill Top, KY 57, 170, Fleming Co.)

John Finley, 1748–1837, pioneer-surveyor who came to Ky. in 1773. Discovered Upper Blue (Salt) Licks, surveyed land to Ky. River near present Frankfort. Commissioned major, 1783, for notable service in Revolution. Judge Advocate of NW Terr., 1792. Came here with family, 1796, from Penn., farmed 1,000-acre land grant. Member Kentucky House of Representatives, 1800–04.

790 COUNTY NAMED, 1852
(Stanton, Courthouse lawn, KY 15, 213, Powell Co.)

For Governor Lazarus W. Powell, born Henderson Co., 1812. Graduated, 1833, from St. Joseph's College in Bardstown. Attended Transylvania law school. State legislature, 1836–38. Governor of Ky., 1851–55. U.S. Senate, 1859–65. Resolution for his expulsion for Southern sympathy, defeated 1862. Favored Kentucky neutrality. Died 1867, buried Fernwood Cemetery, Henderson, Ky.

791 COUNTY NAMED, 1884
(Hindman, Courthouse lawn, KY 80, Knott Co.)

For J. Proctor Knott during term as Governor of Kentucky, 1883–87. Knott was born Marion Co., Ky., 1830. Missouri Legislature, 1851–59. Atty. Gen., 1859–60. Returned Ky., 1863. U.S. Congress six terms. Famous as humorous and satirical orator. In the 1891 Const. Conv. took lead in keeping capital at Frankfort. First Law Dean, Centre College, 1891–1901. Died in 1911.

792 COUNTY NAMED, 1870
(Beattyville, Courthouse lawn, KY 11 & 52, Lee Co.)

For Gen. Robert E. Lee, 1807–70. "... he was fearless among men. As a soldier, he had no superior and few equal." West Point graduate, 1829. Declined command U.S. Army and resigned, 1861. Named military adviser to CSA Pres. Davis, 1861. Commander Army Northern Va., 1862. Highest ranking CSA officer, 1865. President, Washington College, now Washington and Lee Univ., 1865–70.

793 CHIEF PADUKE
(19th & Jefferson St., Paducah, McCracken Co.)

Chief of sub-tribe of Chickasaw Indians, who lived and hunted in this area until Jackson Purchase, 1818. Land here then owned by Gen. William Clark, who founded Paducah; named it in honor of the friendly chief. Statue sculptured by Lorado Taft, 1909, who combined features of various Indian tribes in its execution. *Marker sponsored by Junior Chamber of Commerce.*

794 IRON HORSE MEMORIAL
(Water St. & Kentucky Ave., Paducah, McCracken Co.)

This Mikado-type steam locomotive is dedicated to Illinois Central men and women, past and present, and to the importance of the railroad to Paducah's history and commerce. No. 1518 is the last "Iron Horse" owned by the ICRR. Engines built or rebuilt in the Paducah shops many years until 1960, played prominent role in

the age of steam. See other side.
(Reverse)
IRON HORSE MEMORIAL
Locomotive donated by Illinois Central Railroad. Maintenance funds provided under leadership of the Western Kentucky AFL-CIO Area Council. No. 1518 was moved from Barkley Park to its present site in 1985 when sponsored by city-county government and community action. The baggage car and caboose added at that time. *Marker presented by City of Paducah.*

795 "DUKE OF PADUCAH"
(6th & Broadway, Paducah, McCracken Co.)

Irvin Shrewsburg Cobb, 1876–1944. One of Paducah's famous sons. "A first-class humorist from a conversational gesture to a book wit who made all the world laugh with him." Author of more than sixty books, short story writer, recipient of O'Henry Award, movie actor, lecturer. Chevalier of the Legion of Honor, France, 1918. *Paducah Rotary Club, sponsor.*

796 COUNTY NAMED, 1869
(Sandy Hook, Courthouse lawn, KY 7, 32, Elliott Co.)

For John M. Elliott, born in Va., 1820. Came to this area, 1830. Admitted to bar, 1843. Kentucky Legis., 1847–53. U.S. Congress, 1853–59. Ky. Legis., 1861, but expelled for his southern sympathy. Congress of Confederate States, 1862–65. Circuit Judge, 1868, and Ky. Court of Appeals, 1876. Assassinated, 1879, by a disappointed litigant in a land case decided by court.

797 COUNTY NAMED, 1825
(Brownsville, KY 70, 101, Edmonson Co.)

For Captain John Edmonson, b. 1764, Va. In War of Revolution a private in company led by father. Battle of King's Mountain, 1782. Came to Ky., 1790. In War of 1812, raised rifle company in Fayette County. Killed at battle of River Raisin, Jan. 22, 1813. One of nine leaders killed then for whom Ky. counties are named. Edmonson formed from Grayson, Hart, Warren counties.

798 OLD POLLARD INN
(4 mi. N. of Pleasureville, US 421, Henry Co.)

Built c. 1790. Later a stage coach inn. James

G. Blaine when teacher at Western Military Institute, Drennon Springs, 1850–51, frequent guest. He was later Congressman, Senator, U.S. Secretary of State, candidate for President in 1884. Gen. John H. Morgan and Capt. T. H. Hines, Confederate Raiders, found shelter here, Dec. 1, 1863, after escape from prison in Ohio.

799 COUNTY NAMED, 1860
(Edmonton, Courthouse lawn, US 68, Metcalfe Co.)

For Thomas Metcalfe, 1780–1855. Born Va. Capt. Ky. Vol. War 1812; Congress 1819–28; Governor 1828–32; Ky. Senate 1834–38; U.S. Senate 1848–49, completing Crittenden's term. "Old Stone Hammer" laid the foundation, 1797, of Governor's Mansion, now home of Lieutenant Governors. Metcalfe County formed out of parts of Adair, Barren, Cumberland, Green & Monroe.

800 COUNTY NAMED, 1819
(Elkton, Courthouse lawn, Jct. US 68 & KY 181, Todd Co.)

For Col. John Todd. Born Pa., 1750. In battle of Point Pleasant, 1774. Came to Kentucky, 1775; in Va. legislature, 1776. On expedition led by Gen. George Rogers Clark that captured Illinois country from British, 1778. Named Civil Commandant of Illinois County. Va. legislature, 1780. Procured land-grants for public schools. Killed at Blue Licks, Aug. 1782.

801 COUNTY NAMED, 1798
(Smithland, Courthouse lawn, US 60, Livingston Co.)

For Robert R. Livingston, 1746–1813. N.Y. provincial convention, 1775; Continental Congress, 1775–77, 1779–81; one of committee to draft the Declaration of Independence. Sec. of Foreign Affairs, 1781–83. Administered oath to Washington, first president, 1789. Appointed minister to France by Jefferson, 1801–04. Partner of Robert Fulton in constructing first steamboat.

802 BROWNSVILLE
(Brownsville, KY 70, 101, Edmonson Co.)

Established 1828 and named for Jacob Brown, Commanding General of the United States army, 1821 until death, 1828, age 53 years. Defended New York state frontier against British in War of 1812, engaging them at Ogdensburg, Sackett's Harbor, Chippewa, Ft. Erie and Niagara. Gen. Brown was not a technical soldier; he was a natural leader of men.

803 COUNTY NAMED, 1806
(Vanceburg, Courthouse lawn, KY 59, 3037, Lewis Co.)

For Meriwether Lewis of Lewis and Clark expedition, sent out by President Jefferson to explore the northwest, 1804–05. Followed the Missouri River to source, crossed mountains, then Columbia River to Pacific. Lewis born Va., 1774. US army, 1795; captain, 1800. Private Secretary to Jefferson, 1801–03. Terr. Gov. of Louisiana, 1807–09. Died, 1809, buried in Tennessee.

804 COUNTY NAMED, 1800
(Monticello, Courthouse lawn, KY 90, 92, Wayne Co.)

For "Mad Anthony" Wayne, born in Penn., 1745. Officer in Revolution, given gold medal by Congress for capturing Stony Point, N.J., 1779. In command, U.S. forces at Fallen Timbers, 1794, and negotiated Treaty of Greenville, 1795, which ended Indian wars in Old Northwest and raids into Ky. Penn. Legis., 1784–1785. Moved to Georgia and elected Congressman, 1791–1792. Died, 1796.

805 COUNTY NAMED, 1798
(New Castle, Courthouse lawn, US 421, Henry Co.)

For Patrick Henry, 1736–99, patriot, orator. "Give me liberty or give me death." Va. House of Burgesses, 1765; the Continental Congress, 1774–76; Gov. of Va., 1776–79 and 1784–86. Opposed Va. ratification of U.S. Const., 1788, without Bill of Rights; later added. Declined appointments as U.S. Senator, Secretary of State, Chief Justice, Minister to France.

806 SITE OF CASEY HOME
(3 mi. SW of Columbia, KY 80, Adair Co.)

Home of Col. William Casey, early Ky. pioneer and great-grandfather of Samuel L. Clemens (Mark Twain). Born in Va., came to Ky. in 1779. Built Casey Station on Dix River. In 1791 moved to Russell Creek near here. Member second Kentucky Const. Conv., 1799. Trustee, town of Columbia,

1802. Presidential elector, 1813. Died here, 1816. Casey County named for him, 1806.

807 A FOUNDER OF D.A.R.
(Maxwell & Mill Sts., Lexington, Fayette Co.)

Mary Desha, one of four founders of the Daughters of the American Revolution in 1890, taught public school here, 1875–1885. Designer of society's seal. Taught in Alaska schools, returned to Washington, successfully advocated reforms. Granddaughter of Joseph Desha, Kentucky's tenth governor. Born, Lexington, 1850. Died, Washington, 1911. Buried, Lexington Cemetery.

808 COUNTY NAMED, 1821
(Pikeville, Courthouse lawn, Pike Co.)

For Zebulon M. Pike, 1779–1813. Born New Jersey. Entered army, 1794; served on frontier. Sent to trace Mississippi River source, 1805, and to explore headwaters of Arkansas and Red Rivers, 1806, when he discovered Pikes Peak. Brig. Gen. Pike killed in attack on York, Canada, April 27, 1813. Military burial, Sackett's Harbor on shore of Lake Ontario, N.Y.

809 COUNTY NAMED, 1842
(Near Whitesburg, US 119, Letcher Co.)

For Robert P. Letcher, during term as Governor of Kentucky, 1840–1844. Born Va., 1788; came Ky. in 1800. Ky. Mounted Militia, War of 1812. Legislature, 7 years, Speaker of House, two years. U.S. Congress, 1823–1835. Presidential elector in 1836. During term as governor he proclaimed first Thanksgiving. Minister to Mexico, 1849–1852. Died 1861; buried Frankfort Cemetery.

810 STATION CAMP
(West Irvine, KY 52, Estill Co.)

Indian Trading Post and camping ground. Called "Ah-wah-nee," a grassy place, by the Shawnees who hunted here and obtained their lead supply in this vicinity. In 1769, Daniel Boone, Squire Boone, and Joseph Proctor were first of many pioneers to use camp, which is located on an old buffalo trace known as War Road, then a direct route from Boonesborough to the East.

811 COUNTY NAMED, 1835
(Albany, Courthouse lawn, US 127, Clinton Co.)

For DeWitt Clinton, 1769–1828. In New York Senate, nine years; in U.S. Senate, 1802–03, where he introduced XII Amendment, present method of electing U.S. president, vice president. Mayor, New York, nine years; leader, tax supported school movement. Lieut. Gov., 1811–13; Gov., 1817-21, 25–28. Sponsor of Erie Canal, 1816–25. County from Cumberland and Wayne.

812 RENOWNED CONGRESSMAN
(Lawrenceburg, US 127 Business, Anderson Co.)

James Beauchamp (Champ) Clark born near here, 1850. Attended U. of K. Taught school in county, 1870–71. Pres. Marshall College, 1873–74. Congressman from Missouri 24 yrs. Led defeat of Cannonism, control of House by Speaker. Then Speaker, 1911–19. Candidate for nomination for president, 1912 Democratic Conv., through 46 ballots, but lost. Buried, 1921, Bowling Green, Mo.

813 COUNTY NAMED, 1843
(Booneville, Courthouse lawn, KY 11, 30, Owsley Co.)

For Judge William Owsley, who was prominent in the Old Court-New Court Controversy, 1823. Born in Virginia, 1782. Came with parents to Lincoln County, 1783. Studied law with Judge John Boyle. State Legislature, two terms. Appointed Court of Appeals; served 15 years. State Senate, 1832–34; Secretary of State, 1834–36; Governor of Kentucky, 1844–48. Died, 1862.

814 COUNTY NAMED, 1870
(Inez, Courthouse lawn, KY 3, 40, Martin Co.)

For Col. John P. Martin, born Va. 1811, came to Kentucky in 1828. State House of Representatives, 1841–43; U.S. Congress, 1845–47. State Senator, 1857–61. Delegate from State at large to Democratic National Convention, 1856. Delegate to futile Ky. Peace Convention in Sept., 1861. Floyd County citizen for seventeen years. Died there in 1862 at age 51.
(Reverse)
HENRY L. CLAY, D.D.
One of the distinguished natives of Martin

County. Teacher in the schools here and in Williamson, W. Va. Ordained into the Methodist Ministry, serving 33 yrs. in W. Va. Dist. Supt. in Ashland, Charleston and Huntington. On committee that formed The Methodist Church, 1939, uniting the Northern, Southern and Protestant Methodists. Rev. Clay born Inez 1875, died Florida 1964.

815 COUNTY NAMED, 1822
(West Liberty, Courthouse lawn, US 460, Morgan Co.)

For Daniel Morgan, 1736–1802. Born N.J. Moved to Va. Pontiac's War and Dunmore's expedition to Pa., 1774. Attack on Quebec, 1775. Colonel in command of Va. corps of 500 sharp shooters at Saratoga, Oct. 1777. A master of military art. As Brig. Gen. led victory at Cowpens, Jan. 1781. In command, suppression of Whiskey Rebellion, 1794. U.S. Congress, 1797–1799.

816 COUNTY NAMED, 1867
(Mt. Olivet, Courthouse lawn, US 62, Robertson Co.)

For George Robertson, 1790–1874. Born in Ky. In Congress, 1817–21, sponsored organization territory of Arkansas. Ky. Legislature eight years, six as Speaker; promoted the common-school system. Member Ky. Court of Appeals, 1829–34 and 1864–71. Professor of law in the Transylvania University, 1834–57. County was formed from parts of Bracken, Harrison, Mason, Nicholas.

817 COUNTY NAMED, 1799
(South Lake Dr., Prestonsburg, US 23, Floyd Co.)

For Col. John Floyd. Born Amherst County, Va., 1750. Led party to survey land now Kentucky, 1774. With George Rogers Clark's Indian expeditions. Back in Va., joined Colonial navy. Captured, taken to England. Escaped. Built Floyd's Station, 1779 or 1780, nearby what is now Louisville. Named Lieut. of Jefferson Co., part of Va., 1781. Killed in Indian ambush, 1783.

818 COACH AND FOUR
(Monticello, KY 90, 92, Wayne Co.)

Monticello-Burnside Stage, nine passenger stagecoach drawn by four horses. It was started in 1896 by Charles Burton, who had operated freight "jolt wagon." Route was 20 miles, uniting Monticello with railroad at Burnside. Mail also carried. Part of route followed was an old buffalo trace. This route, the last to operate in Kentucky, closed in 1915.

819 MOREHEAD HOUSE
(Main & Washington, Frankfort, Franklin Co.)

Built by Mark Hardin, Registrar, Ky. Land Office, in 1810. Before Civil War, home of six prominent Kentuckians; among whom were John Harvie, Pres., Bank of Ky., and, for 13 years, Charles S. Morehead, Governor (1855–59). Lawrence Tobin acquired it in 1874 and it was held by heirs to 1961. He built railroad, Lexington to Louisville, and was local merchant 48 years.

820 ROGERS STATION, 1780
(4 mi. W. of Bardstown, US 62, Nelson Co.)

Site of station located on 1,000-acre tract "marked and improved" in 1775 by Col. James Rogers. Born Va., 1742, died Ky., 1828. Fought in Dunmore's War, 1774, and Revolutionary War. Appointed Colonel, Nelson Co., Ky. Militia and the Justice of the Peace by Patrick Henry, Gov. of Va. Signer of "Petitions of Early Inhabitants of Ky." for separation from Va.

821 MUHLENBERG COUNTY
(Greenville, Courthouse lawn, US 62, Muhlenberg Co.)

Formed 1798 out of parts of Logan and Christian counties. Named for Gen. Peter Muhlenberg, 1746–1807, of Pa. Ordained minister, 1768. "A time to preach and a time to fight." Entered Revolutionary Army as Col., Eighth Va. (German) Regt. Active from 1776 to surrender of Yorktown. U.S. Congress, Senate. Collector of Customs, Phila. Many from his regiment pioneered here.

822 COUNTY NAMED, 1810
(Morgantown, US 231, Butler Co.)

For Gen. Richard Butler, b. 1743, Ireland. Came to America, 1760. Officer during Revolutionary War. Indian agent, 1784; Supt. Indian Affairs for Northern Dist., 1785. With George Rogers Clark negotiated Indian treaty, 1786. As Maj. Gen., second in

Stagecoach from Monticello to Burnside. Kentucky Historical Society Collection.

command, was killed on St. Clair's expedition against Indians into Ohio country, 1791. Butler out of Logan, Ohio counties.

823 BUTLER'S BIRTHPLACE
(S. of Camp Nelson Cem. entrance, US 27 & Jct. of Hall Rd., Jessamine Co.)

Gen. Wm. O. Butler, born here in 1791, died Carrollton, Ky. 1880. In War of 1812: the River Raisin, Pensacola, and New Orleans. Gen. Andrew Jackson's staff 1816–17. Cited for heroism in Mexican War 1846–48. U.S. Congressman 1839–43. Although defeated for Gov. 1844, Vice Pres. 1848, U.S. Senate 1851, he was one of the most prominent, best-liked Democrats in state.

824 HOME OF U.S. JURIST
(South Main St., Elkton, KY 181, Todd Co.)

Justice James Clark McReynolds, born here, 1862. His home through life. Law practice in Nashville and New York. Asst. U.S. Atty. General, 1903–07. Later, as U.S.

Attorney General, 1913–14, known for enforcement of Sherman Anti-Trust Law. For 27 years a distinguished Associate Justice of the U.S. Supreme Court, 1914–41; an opponent of New Deal measures. Died in Washington, D.C., 1946.

825 COUNTY NAMED, 1822
(Murray, Courthouse lawn, US 641, Calloway Co.)

For Col. Richard Calloway. Came to Ky. with Daniel Boone, 1776. One of founders of Boonesborough, he instilled confidence in success among other settlers. In one year, 1777, appointed Col. of Militia; Justice of the Peace; elected a representative of Ky. County in General Assembly of Va. Killed by Indians at Boonesborough 1780. County formed from Hickman.

826 COUNTY NAMED, 1842
(Wickliffe, Courthouse lawn, US 51, 60, Ballard Co.)

For Capt. Bland Ballard, 1759–1853. Born in Va. Came to Ky. in 1779. Devoted life to protecting frontier. Scout for George

Rogers Clark's Ohio expedition, 1780, '82; Wabash campaign, 1786. In the battles of Fallen Timbers, 1793; Tippecanoe, 1811; River Raisin, 1813. In Ky. Legis. for five terms. Legis. directed his burial in the Frankfort Cemetery. County from Mc-Cracken, Hickman.

827 LINCOLN'S PLAYMATE
(Pleasant Grove Baptist Church, E. of White City, KY 84, Larue Co.)

To the west, in Pleasant Grove Baptist Church Cemetery, is the grave of Austin Gollaher, 1806–98. Lincoln, while president, once said, "I would rather see (him) than any man living." They were schoolmates and playmates when the Lincoln family lived in this area, 1813 to 1816. Gollaher is credited with rescuing Lincoln from flooded waters of Knob Creek.

828 FORT ANDERSON
(Park, end of 4th St., Paducah, McCracken Co.)

Union fortification built, 1861, by Gen. Charles F. Smith. Manned by 5,000 troops. Jump-off for Grant's Miss. Valley Campaign. Fort was attacked March 25, 1864 by CSA Gen. Nathan B. Forrest's forces. Col. Albert P. Thompson, CSA, of Paducah killed. CSA burned riverfront warehouses. Next day USA troops under Col. S. G. Hicks burned homes in range of the fort. *Presented by Paducah Sun-Democrat.*

829 WELCOME TO PADUCAH, KY.
(Paducah Airport, McCracken Co.)

Founded by Gen. William Clark, 1827, at confluence of Tennessee, Ohio Rivers. Named for legendary Chickasaw Indian Chief Paduke. County seat McCracken County. Home Vice President Alben W. Barkley; this airport named in his honor. Nearby is Atomic Energy Plant. (See other side).
(Reverse)
BARKLEY FIELD, PADUCAH, KY.
Birthplace author Irvin S. Cobb; home Linn Boyd, member Congress, Speaker (1851–55), sponsor Texas Annexation Resolution. Town was first captured by Union Gen. Lew Wallace and Gen. Wm. T. Sherman. Railroad and river traffic cen-

ter. See other side. *Presented by Airport Board.*

830 UNION CAMP SITE
(KY 250, 2.2 mi. W. of US 431, McLean Co.)

In July 1864 Co. D, 35th Regt. Ky. Vol. Mtd. Inf. camped, north on Houston land. Muster, Owensboro Oct. 2, 1863. Guarded area between Cumberland and Green Rivers. Part of Union force that defeated CSA Gen. Adam R. Johnson's Partisan Rangers at Grubb's Cross Roads in Aug. 1864. Fought at Saltville, Va. Mustered out at Louisville, Dec. 29, 1864. Roster other side.
(Reverse)
McLEAN COUNTY RECRUITS, Co. D 35 REGT. KY. VOL. MOUNTED INF.
Chas. W. D. (Frank) Prange, Capt.
Geo. W. Mosley, Jas. T. Goode, Lieuts.
Wm. A. Short, John H. Taylor, Sgts.

James R. Baughn	Western Mitchell
Joseph F. Baughn	Thomas A. Nally
Allen H. Benton	James D. Nally
Granville Brown	Charles F. Prange
Michael Conley	Malvin Presley, Cpl.
Remos G. Cary	William L. Roads
Samuel A. Hudson	Mark L. T. Robertson
Hubbard V. Hicks	Lafayette Riley
George L. Jones	Alexander Stogner
John W. Little	James A. Taylor
Lucius L. Mitchell	William B. Taylor

831 COUNTY NAMED, 1819
(Owenton, Courthouse lawn, US 127 & KY 227, Owen Co.)

For Col. Abraham Owen. Born Va., 1769. Came to Ky., 1785. In Indian campaigns of 1790 and '91. Member of the Ky. Legislature, Senate and Constitutional Conv. of 1799. First Kentuckian to join command of Gen. Wm. Henry Harrison in Indian campaign, upper Wabash Valley. Nov. 7, 1811, Owen killed in the battle of Tippecanoe. Owen County out of Scott, Franklin, Gallatin.

832 MIDDLESBOROUGH
(Tourist Info. Center, North 20th St., Middlesboro, Bell Co.)

English colony founded in 1886 by Alexander Arthur. Project financed by English company, the American Association, because of timber and rich mineral deposits here. Almost 100,000 mountainous acres in Va., Tenn., and Ky. purchased for the settlement. Town was named for Middlesborough, England. Railroad to Knoxville and Cumberland Gap tunnel built by the company.

833 HELM CEMETERY
(Elizabethtown, Jct. US 31-W & KY 447, Hardin Co.)

This pioneer cemetery includes the graves of John LaRue Helm, who served two incomplete terms as Governor of Kentucky, and his son, Confederate Gen. Ben Hardin Helm, who fell at battle of Chickamauga, September 20, 1863. Gen. Helm and Abraham Lincoln married half-sisters, Emilie and Mary Todd, the daughters of Robert S. Todd of Lexington, Kentucky.

834 COUNTY NAMED, 1809
(Princeton, Courthouse lawn, US 62, Caldwell Co.)

For General John Caldwell. Born Va.; came Ky., 1781. Maj. Gen. in militia; Indian campaigns. With George Rogers Clark, 1786. Member Danville Conventions, 1787, 1788, which adopted petition "demanding admission into the Union." State Senator, 1792–96. Elected Lt. Gov. with Governor Greenup, 1804; served Sept. 4 to death, Nov. 19, 1804. Caldwell formed out of Livingston County.

835 LOCUST GROVE
1½ miles, Northwest
(US 42 & Blankenbaker Ln., Louisville, Jefferson Co.)

Home of Gen. George Rogers Clark from 1809 until his death, 1818. William and Lucy Clark Croghan built it about 1790. Visited by Presidents Monroe, Jackson, Taylor. Clark and his 175 frontiersmen defeated British-Indians during Revolution: won Northwest for U.S. He built first outpost at Falls of Ohio, 1778. Founder of Louisville.

836 COUNTY NAMED, 1806
(Manchester, Courthouse lawn, Court St., US 421, Clay Co.)

For Gen. Green Clay, 1757–1826. Born in Va. Came to Ky., 1777. In Va. Legislature, 1788–89, and Va. Convention that ratified Federal Constitution. From 1793 to 1808 in Ky. House, Senate, Const. Conv. In May, 1813, Gen. Clay with 3,000 Kentuckians,

at Ft. Meigs, held back British and Indians. Cousin of Henry Clay. County formed from parts of Madison, Floyd and Knox.

837 COUNTY NAMED, 1824
(Entrance to Taylorsville, KY 44, Spencer Co.)

For Capt. Spear Spencer, Kentucky "Corn Stalk" Militia, 1792–1801. With St. Clair and Wayne Indian campaigns. Captain of Militia of Harrison Co., Ind., 1809. Formed Spencer's "Yellow Jackets," joined Gen. Wm. Henry Harrison's command in Tippecanoe campaign in upper Wabash Valley. Spencer killed in battle, Nov. 7, 1811. County from parts of Nelson, Shelby, Bullitt.

838 EARLY PAPER MILL
(Roadside Park, 1½ mi. SW of Jamestown, US 127, Russell Co.)

Site of early Kentucky paper mill north on Greasy Creek. Erected by Joseph Crockett about 1800. Tax records indicate profitable operations. Large quantities of paper were shipped by river steamer in 1830's from Creelsboro to Nashville, Tenn. The mill operated for more than sixty years, apparently closed because of Civil War. See other side. (Reverse)

PIONEER BUSINESS
An early industrial area located along Greasy Creek. In addition to a paper mill, there were the Alex Dick and Geo. Lewis meat house, 1785; a grist mill, 1799; an iron furnace and forge, 1824; the Wooldridge's Roller Mill; a cotton and two woolen mills. The Farmers Woolen Mill, owned and operated by Esco Reese, was in operation until late 1940. See other side.

839 OLD JUDGE PRIEST
(Paducah, Courthouse lawn, McCracken Co.)

Here for six years presided William Sutton Bishop, the famed Judge Priest of Irvin S. Cobb's stories. Judge Bishop, 1839–1902, was First District Circuit Court Judge from 1891 to 1897. Served in 7th Ky. Conf. Inf. "This was a man," Paducah Bar Assn. *Presented by Southern Bell Telephone Company.*

840 PADUCAH, KENTUCKY
(Paducah Community College Campus, US 62-W, McCracken Co.)

McCracken county seat, founded by Gen.

William Clark, of Lewis and Clark Expedition, at confluence of Ohio and Tennessee rivers. Named for legendary Indian Chief Paduke. Home of Vice Pres. Alben Barkley and birthplace of Irvin S. Cobb. First occupied in Civil War by General U. S. Grant. Became supply base of his Miss. River campaign. Great Atomic Energy Plant nearby.
(Reverse)

McCracken County

Formed, 1824, from Hickman County. Named for Captain Virgil McCracken of Woodford County, Ky., who was killed in Battle of River Raisin near Detroit during War of 1812. Area 237 square miles. Ohio and Tennessee rivers brought industry dependent on river transportation. First county seat at Wilmington, 1825, and moved to Paducah, 1832. Government is County Commission. *Presented by Citizens Bank & Trust Company.*

841 Quicksand—1864
(Quicksand, Jct. KY 15 & 1111, Breathitt Co.)

Part of Co. I, 14th Ky. Inf., USA attacked Confederates camped here, night of April 5, 1864. CSA loss: eight killed or wounded, three prisoners and 24 horses taken. Gen. John Hunt Morgan's CSA men, on tragic last raid into Kentucky, moved by here. After two battles at Mt. Sterling, they met defeat in Cynthiana, June 12, 1864, and retreated to Va. Map other side.

842 Richards Home Site
(E. of Boxville, KY 56 & 983, Union Co.)

Lewis Richards, born Va., 1754. Sergeant with Gen. George Rogers Clark when he built first blockhouse at site of present Cincinnati. Went on, in attempt to save Kentuckians captured by English and Indians, 1779. Unable to overtake them, destroyed the Indian villages at Chillicothe and Piqua. Richards was a volunteer at battle of Blue Licks, 1782. Died here in 1846.

843 Swiss Colony Bernstadt
(Bernstadt, KY 1956 & Hawk Cr. Rd., Laurel Co.)

Founded 1881, this was Kentucky's largest foreign colony. Swiss farm crisis and high land prices caused mass emigration. Paul Schenk and Otto Bruner, agriculturalists, and Karl Imobersteg, owner of large passage office, promoted venture. These Swiss capitalists sold 4,000 acres to colonists, most from Bern. They improved farming; became known for wine and cheese production.

844 Home of Early Minister
(Greensburg, KY 61, near old courthouse, Green Co.)

Home of the Rev. David Rice, founder of first Presbyterian churches west of Alleghenies, 1784. Born in Va., 1733; moved to Danville, Ky. in 1788 after having founded "Rice's School," or Transylvania Seminary, near there, 1785. Member, State Constitutional Convention, 1792; urged gradual emancipation. Came here, 1798, forming in this area two churches. Died age 83.

845 County Named, 1823
(Brandenburg, KY 448, W. of KY 710, Meade Co.)

For Capt. James Meade, recognized for bravery and daring at Battle of Tippecanoe, 1811. Made captain in 17th US Infantry, March, 1812. Killed at River Raisin, Jan. 22, 1813, and one of nine officers at that battle for whom Kentucky counties named. Meade was formed out of parts of Breckinridge and Hardin counties, Dec. 17, 1823, by Act of Kentucky Assembly.

846 Lincoln's Law Partner
(Greensburg, old courthouse lawn, Green Co.)

Birthplace of William H. Herndon, 1818. Family moved to Illinois, 1820. An anti-slavery advocate and partner with Abraham Lincoln in practice of law, 1844–61. Herndon, Mayor of Springfield; State Bank examiner. After Lincoln's death, devoted life to biography of his friend. Wrote "Herndon's Lincoln: The True Story of a Great Life," 1889. Died 1891, Springfield, Illinois.

847 County Named, 1827
(North Main St., Lawrenceburg, US 62, Anderson Co.)

For Richard Clough Anderson, Jr., 1788–1826. Served in Ky. Legis. three terms. Elected Congress, 1817, for two terms. Returned Ky. Legis., 1822, chosen Speaker. Appointed Minister to Colombia by Pres. Monroe, 1823, where he negotiated first treaty with a South American nation, 1824. Interred, "Soldier's Retreat," family home, near Middletown, Ky.

848 PIONEER STATION
(2 mi. N. of Shelbyville, KY 55, Shelby Co.)

Squire Boone's Station or Painted Stone, half mile west on Clear Creek. Founded by Squire Boone and others, 1779. Born Penn., 1744, taken to N.C. as child. Came to Ky. with brother Daniel in 1769. In summer 1775 came here, returned spring 1776 painted name and date on creek stone which gave name of "Painted Stone." Aided in defense of Boonesborough in 1778. See over.
(Reverse)

SQUIRE BOONE
Captain, border militia stationed at Painted Stone Fort, 1780. Ky. delegate, Va. House of Burgesses, 1782. Member of Ky. Convention, 1785. Delegate, Va. ratification, United States Constitution, 1788. Given standing as Revolutionary soldier and officer by Congress in 1813. Moved to Indiana in 1806; built new settlement there, where he died, was buried, 1815. See over.

849 COUNTY NAMED, 1806
(Madisonville, Courthouse lawn, US 41-A, Hopkins Co.)

For Samuel Hopkins, 1753–1819. On Washington's staff and in many campaigns, War of the Revolution. Came to Ky., 1797, as Transylvania Company agent. In 1799, organized and named judge of first court held in original Henderson County, which included this area. In Ky. House, 1800–06; Senate, 1809–13. Commander in Chief, Western Frontier, 1812; U.S. Congress, 1813–1815.

850 EARLY SHIPPING POINT
(Cloverport, US 60, Breckinridge Co.)

Cloverport, an important shipping point beginning in 1798 when Joe Houston came from Va., built home and started trading and shipping business. Flatboats carried Ky. tobacco, other goods for sale in New Orleans. Boats sold as lumber. Men came back over Natchez Trace. Houston operated first ferry here in 1802. Shipping increased and steamboats came into use, 1820.

851 GENOA
(5 mi. S. of Hopkinsville, KY 107, Christian Co.)

Winston Jones Davie, 1824–87, home and burial site. Native of Christian County. He was Kentucky's first Commissioner of Agriculture, 1876–79. Appointed by Gov. James B. McCreary. Davie was an outstanding farmer, banker, legislator, and agricultural writer. Elected to Kentucky Legislature, 1850. Devoted life to improvement of agriculture and rural life.

852 DUTCH COLONY HERE
(1 m. S. of Pleasureville, US 421, Henry Co.)

In 1780 communal colonists came from Penn. to Mercer Co., Ky. In 1784 thirty of the families came here, purchased 10,000 acres from Squire Boone. Lived in log fort. Managed by Abraham Banta; George Bergen made trustee later. Shaker missionaries from New York tried to convert colonists, 1804. Their doctrine accepted by a few, who followed John Banta to Mercer Co.

853 WASHINGTON COUNTY
(Nelson County line, US 150, Washington Co.)

The first county formed by first Assembly of Kentucky, 1792. Named for Geo. Washington. Springfield, county seat, laid off, 1793, by Matthew Walton; veteran of War of Revolution, legislator. Courthouse built in 1816, oldest used as such in state (1965). First settlers in area, 1776. Pres. Lincoln's grandfather came this part Ky., 1782; parents married in county, 1806. Over.
(Reverse)

WASHINGTON CO. CONTD.
Col. John Hardin, Revolutionary soldier, laid claim in area, 1780. Settled, 1786. On peace mission in Ohio, 1792, murdered by Indians. First Dominican Priory in U.S., 1806, where Jefferson Davis went to school, 1815–16. John Pope, U.S. Senator, 1807–13, came to Springfield, 1820. Governor, Arkansas Terr., 1829–35; Congress, 1837–43. Home and grave in city. Over.

854 WASHINGTON COUNTY
(At Marion County line, KY 55, Washington Co.)

The first county formed by first Assembly of Kentucky, 1792. Named for Geo. Washington. Springfield, county seat, laid off,

1793, by Matthew Walton; veteran of War of Revolution, legislator. Courthouse built in 1816, oldest used as such in state (1965). First settlers in area, 1776. Pres. Lincoln's grandfather came this part Ky., 1782; parents married in county, 1806. Over. (Reverse)

WASHINGTON CO. CONTD.

Col. John Hardin, Revolutionary soldier, laid claim in area, 1780. Settled, 1786. On peace mission in Ohio, 1792, murdered by Indians. First Dominican Priory in U.S., 1806, where Jefferson Davis went to school, 1815–16. John Pope, U.S. Senator, 1807–13, came to Springfield, 1820. Governor, Arkansas Terr., 1829–35; Congress, 1837–43. Home and grave in city. Over.

855 IWO JIMA HERO
(Elizaville Cemetery, KY 170, Fleming Co.)

PFC Franklin Runyon Sousley USMCR. One of six of 28th Reg. 5th Marine Div. who raised flag on Suribachi 23 Feb. 1945. Immortalized in Joe Rosenthal's famed AP photograph. Sousley born Fleming County, 1925. Joined Marines, Jan. 1944. Landed on Iwo Jima 19 Feb. 1945, survived Suribachi, but killed month later. Reinterred, 1948, on hillside S.E. Purple Heart, 3 other medals. Over.
(Reverse)
Photograph of men raising flag on Suribachi. Caption under photograph reads: Uncommon valor was a common virtue.

856 UPPER BLUE LICKS
(Moorefield, Jct. KY 36 & 57, Nicholas Co.)

Aug. 12, 1782, Capt. John Holder and 17 militiamen overtook band of Wyandotte on Great Salt Creek (Licking River) six miles N.E. The Indians had captured two boys, Jones Hoy and Jack Calloway, near Boonesborough. In skirmish that took place Holder lost four men, and being outnumbered he withdrew without the boys. Hoy held captive seven years, Calloway not so long.

857 SAINT THOMAS FARM
(3 mi. S. of Bardstown, US 31-E, Nelson Co.)

The cradle of the Catholic Church in Ky., ½ mile east. In 1811, became residence of Bishop Flaget and Father David, when pioneering Saint Joseph's Cathedral, Saint Joseph's College and the old Bethlehem Academy in Bardstown. First home, 1812, of The Sisters of Charity of Nazareth. Founding site of Saint Thomas Seminary and Saint Thomas Orphanage, Louisville.

858 ROUTE OF LINCOLNS
(Vine Grove, KY 144, Hardin Co.)

In the autumn of 1816, Abraham Lincoln's family traveled this old pioneer trail through Vine Grove, established in 1802, when migrating from Knob Hill farm, Larue County, Ky., to Spencer County, Ind.

859 MARY INGLES
(Big Bone Lick State Park, KY 338, Boone Co.)

Reputed first white woman in Ky. Shawnees captured her and two sons in July 1755 at site Roanoke, Va. Led to village at mouth of Scioto, separated from sons, taken to Big Bone Lick. Compelled to make salt here; adopted by chief; given few liberties. Escaped late fall with another woman. After 40 days she reached home. Died 1813, age 83. A courageous, resourceful pioneer.

860 LINCOLN COUNTY
(Stanford, Courthouse lawn, Lincoln Co.)

Benjamin Logan built Logan's Fort at St. Asaphs, mile to west, 1776. Kentucky County, Virginia, formed 1776. First land court, St. Asaphs 1779. Kentucky was made into Lincoln, Jefferson, Fayette counties, 1780. In 1785 part of Lincoln taken for Madison and Mercer counties. Stanford named and made county seat, 1786. Records in courthouse from 1781, oldest in the state.

861 BRACKEN COUNTY, 1796
(Augusta, KY 8, Bracken Co.)

Formed from parts of Campbell and Mason. Named for William Bracken, hunter, fisherman, Indian fighter, came here 1773. Birthplace of John Gregg Fee, founder of Berea College, 1855. Birthplace and home of Dr. Joshua Taylor Bradford, 1819–71, world famous surgeon. Site Augusta College, first Methodist College in world, 1822. First White Burley tobacco, 1867, from Bracken seed.

862 GEN. HOOD BIRTHPLACE
(East Main St., Owingsville, US 60, Bath Co.)

John Bell Hood, 1831–79, graduate of West Point, 1853. Eight years Indian campaigns. Resigned, 1861, and joined CSA as colonel, heading Texas Brigade. He gained distinction at Sharpsburg, Fredericksburg, 1862, and at Gettysburg, Chickamauga, 1863. Appointed to command Army of Tenn. Met defeat: Atlanta in August, 1864; Franklin, Nashville in December. Lived in New Orleans after war.

863 CONFEDERATE DEFENSE LINE
(Nancy, W. of Somerset, KY 80, Pulaski Co.)

Late in 1861, Confederates sought to prevent Union forces from occupying strategic points in Kentucky and Tennessee, to maintain rail shipments of vital Confederate supplies from Virginia south and west, and to set up bases for future offensive thru Kentucky and Ohio to divide eastern and western Union states. With those aims the Confederate Defense Line was formed from the Big Sandy Valley in east Kentucky thru Cumberland Gap, Mill Springs on Cumberland River, Bowling Green on L & N Ry., to Columbus, Ky. on the Mississippi River.

THE FORCES MOVE IN

Brig. Gen. Felix K. Zollicoffer in Nov. 1861 built CSA bases at Mill Springs and across Cumberland at Beech Grove, as part of plan. Maj. Gen. George B. Crittenden took command, Dec. 13, 1861. On Jan. 11, 1862, Union forces under Brig. Gen. George H. Thomas started from Lebanon, Ky. to join the Federals under Brig. Gen. Albin Schoepf at Somerset and to attack the Confederate base at Mill Springs. On Jan. 19 Gen. Crittenden moved out with his CSA troops to prevent the Union forces under Gen. Thomas from joining US army at Somerset.
(Reverse)

BATTLE OF MILL SPRINGS

In first hour, Gen. Zollicoffer was killed, which threw his CSA regiments into confusion. Rallied by Gen. Crittenden, battle continued three hours. USA reinforcements arrived, CSA retreated, fighting all day to reach river. They evacuated camp during night and withdrew into Tennessee. Casualties: CSA 125 killed, 309 wounded and 99 missing; USA 39 killed and 207 wounded. Large quantity of supplies abandoned by CSA, as well as 150 wagons and more than 1,000 horses and mules. Battle also called Logan's Cross Roads or Fishing Creek.

AFTERMATH

The way was opened for the Union to advance into Eastern Tennessee. Lack of provisions, bad roads and difficulty of crossing river made such advance impractical. Gen. Thomas' command joined Gen. Buell's Union force in move on Nashville. This Mill Springs victory with defeat of Brig. Gen. Humphrey Marshall by USA Col. James A. Garfield in the Big Sandy Valley broke the right section of the Confederate Defense Line. Thus began a series of events bringing Union control of Kentucky and upper Miss. River in first year of war.

864 FAYETTE COUNTY FOUNTAINS
(Lexington, Courthouse lawn, Fayette Co.)

Dedicated to the men and women who developed Fayette County, these fountains were provided by:

Embry's	Standard Typewriter Co.
John G. King	Mrs. Morris Beebe, Sr.
Herndon J. Evans	Lexington Kiwanis Club
Edwin C. Gilson	The Lexington Herald
H. (Jack) Hagler	The Lexington Leader
Bank of Commerce	WLAP Radio Station

The Purcell Company, Inc.
Central Bank and Trust Company
New Union Building Association
Mr. and Mrs. Russell des Cognets, Jr.
Citizens Union Bank and Trust Company
Second National Bank and Trust Company
Ladies Auxiliary, Fraternal Order of Police
First Security National Bank and Trust Company
Presented by Fayette County Fiscal Court.

865 ORIGINAL BOUNDARY
(4th & Broadway, Paducah, McCracken Co.)

When Gen. William Clark platted town of Paducah in 1827, and when it was incorporated by Legislature, 1830, this was its west boundary. The 12 blocks in the plat were bordered by Oak St. (now Fourth), Clark St. on the south, Jefferson St. on the north and the river on the east. Original name of town, Pekin, changed by Clark to honor legendary Indian Chief Paduke. *Presented by Peoples First National Bank & Trust Co.*

866 GEN. LLOYD TILGHMAN
(Tilghman High School, Paducah, McCracken Co.)

Born Md., 1816. Graduated West Point, 1836. Built railways in South. In Mexican War, 1846–48. Resided Paducah, 1852–61. Built first R.R. here. Joined Confed. Army, July, 1861. Captured at Ft. Henry, Feb., 1862. Exchanged six months later. Formed new command at Jackson, Miss. Killed, May, 1863, Champion's Hill, near Vicksburg. *Communication Workers Local 3315, Sponsors.*

867 LEBANON
(Lebanon, Courthouse lawn, US 68, Marion Co.)

First settled and church built, 1789, by Va. Presbyterians led by Samuel and James McElroy. Town's main founder, 1815, and developer was Benedict Spalding, who gave the site of first Catholic Church organized 1815, church built 1825.
CENTER OF KENTUCKY
Three miles north-northwest, just east of Ky. 429. See over.
(Reverse)
COUNTY NAMED, 1834
For Gen. Francis Marion, 1732–95, "Swamp Fox" of the Am. Revolution. A South Carolina planter. In the Cherokee campaigns, 1759 and 1761. Member of South Carolina Prov. Cong., 1775. During Revolution, his men harassed and fought the British thruout South; became a symbol of resistance to tyranny. State Senate four terms. Commanded Ft. Johnson, 1784–90. South Carolina Const. Conv., 1790. See over.

868 FIRST BAPTIST CHURCH
(2980 Broadway, Paducah, McCracken Co.)

Organized as mission, New Bethel Church 1839; constituted as church Nov. 14, 1840. First met courthouse at 2nd and Kentucky;

lst building, 300 block Broadway; 2nd and 3rd buildings at 5th and Jefferson. Second building seized by Union army, 1861, for use as hospital during Civil War. Present, 4th, building dedicated May 9, 1965. *Presented by Church.*

869 COUNTY NAMED, 1823
(Mayfield, Courthouse lawn, US 45, KY 80, Graves Co.)

For Maj. Benjamin Franklin Graves. Born Va., 1771, came Ky., 1791. A farmer, settled in Fayette Co. Elected to the General Assembly, 1801, 1804. Enlisted at beginning War of 1812, commissioned Aug. 7. Presumed killed by Indians after being wounded and captured, battle of River Raisin, Mich., Jan. 22, 1813. County, part of Jackson Purchase, formed from Hickman.

870 HOME OF LUCY FURMAN
(Powell Street, Henderson, US 41, Henderson Co.)

Author, lecturer. Depicted life of Kentucky mountain people with dignity in books, serials. Born here, 1870, by age 23 she had been acclaimed for stories in literary magazines. First book in 1897. She worked and taught at Hindman Settlement School, Knott County, Ky., 1907–27. Continued writing. Death, 1958. Books include *The Quare Women* and *The Glass Window.*

871 JOHN LITTLEJOHN
(Russellville town square, US 68, 431, Logan Co.)

Born Eng., 1756, came America, 1767. Became Methodist preacher at age 20, riding the circuits in Md., Va., Ky. Came to Louisville from Leesburg, Va., 1818. Moved Warren Co., Ky., and then 7 miles south of Russellville in 1822. Died in 1836 after 60 years as minister. His priceless journals (1772–1832) are preserved by the Methodist Church. See over.
(Reverse)
JOHN LITTLEJOHN
Guardian of the Declaration of Independence, other state papers, which were entrusted to him by President James Madison in War of 1812. As the British advanced on Washington, Aug. 1814, the President ordered the national archives loaded onto a wagon and sent about 35 miles to Littlejohn, Methodist preacher, Leesburg,

and sheriff, Loudoun Co., Va. Over.

872 PRES. DAVIS' ESCORT
(Near Canton, KY 80, Trigg Co.)

CSA Pres. Jefferson Davis, when attempting to escape in closing days of Civil War, was captured with his family in south Georgia, May 10, 1865. Lt. Hazard Perry Baker, chief of escort, presented his sword to Union commander as symbol of surrender of President of the Confederacy. Baker, native of Trigg Co., enlisted at start of war. Grave, 4 mi. south, KY 1254.

873 COUNTY NAMED, 1810
(Leitchfield, Courthouse lawn, US 62, Grayson Co.)

For Col. William Grayson, 1740–90, aide-de-camp to Gen. Washington. Lawyer; in Revolutionary Army, 1776–79; Board of War, 1780–81; Virginia Assembly and Continental Congress, 1784–87; State Convention ratifying Federal Constitution, 1788; and first U.S. Senate, 1789–90. Washington once owned 5,000 acres in county, which was formed from Hardin and Ohio counties.

874 COUNTY NAMED, 1842
(Benton, Courthouse lawn, US 641, Marshall Co.)

For John Marshall, 1755–1835, Chief Justice of the United States, 1801–1835, "principal founder of judicial review and of American system of constitutional law." Area first settled about time of the Jackson Purchase in 1818. First church west of Tenn. River in Ky., started by Rev. H. Darnall, Baptist, in 1819 on Soldier Creek. Formed from Calloway County.

875 EARLY GUNPOWDER MILL
(New Linwood, US 31-E, Hart Co.)

Two miles east on Lynn Camp Creek John Courts built, 1811–12, first commercial gunpowder mill in the State of Kentucky. Located near two large springs that furnished power to grind the charcoal made on site. Mixed with saltpeter and sulphur, finer product made rifle powder and coarser for cannon and blasting powder. Used in War of 1812 through period of Civil War.

876 KARRICK-PARIS HOUSE
(Fourth and Buell, Perryville, US 68, Boyle Co.)

Bivouac for Confederate troops on Oct. 7, 1862, night before Battle of Perryville. Karricks ordered to vacate home the next day. Day after the battle they returned to survey damage, found little done. Officers, doctors lived in house for about 6 months. It was built early 1850s, bought in 1856 by James V. Karrick, who came from Shelby Co., Ky. See over.
(Reverse)

HARBERSON'S STATION

First settled, 1781 or 1782, by group from Pennsylvania led by James Harberson, who owned 1,400 acres. To protect against Indians they built fort to include spring and cave still found on this site. Plot for town laid out, 1815, by Edward Bullock and William Hall. Named Perryville for Commodore Oliver Hazard Perry. Established by legislature, 1817. See over.

877 ALEXANDER W. DONIPHAN
(Maysville, Clark's Run & US 68, Mason Co.)

Born, 1808, about five miles west. Moved to Mo., 1830. As Brig. Gen., Mo. Militia, quelled Mormon riots with no bloodshed, 1838; refused execute Prophet Smith and others court-martialed. In 1846, Mexican War, formed 1st Reg. Mo. Mounted Volunteers and led them through a brilliant 3,600-mile campaign, defeating larger Mexican armies with his poorly equipped force.

878 KIMMEL HOMESTEAD
(At Scott McGaw Motor Company, US 60, Henderson Co.)

Site of home of three generations of Kimmels. Indian fighter, Civil War Major (CSA) Manning M. bought it in 1872. His son, Husband E., born here, 1882. He graduated at Annapolis, 1904. Named Commander-in-Chief of US Fleet, February 1, 1941. Stationed at Pearl Harbor when infamous attack came Dec. 7, 1941. His three sons naval officers in WW II. Manning killed in action.

879 CHURCH-HOSPITAL
(Munfordville, US 31-W, Hart Co.)

Munfordville Presbyterian Church, founded, 1829. In Sept., 1862, during the siege of Munfordville, the Union Army commandeered this church for use as a hospital with nurses' quarters in house at left. Those who died in battle or of wounds removed to Nashville; 359 who died from other causes buried in scattered and unmarked graves. CSA casualties buried on field.

880 HDQRS. CSA COMMANDER
(Riverside Cem., Hopkinsville, US 41, Christian Co.)

Nathan Bedford Forrest, stationed in Hopkinsville during winter of 1861–62, resided, with wife and daughter, in log house, the third residence south. As colonel, in command 6 companies CSA Cavalry, reconnoitered Union forces between here and the Ohio River, defeated gunboat, CONESTOGA, at Canton, also US force at Sacramento. Withdrew when CSA left Bowling Green. Over.
(Reverse)

101 CSA UNKNOWN
Six companies CSA Cavalry under Col. Forrest were camped a mile to the north at the old fairgrounds, while reconnoitering this area in winter, 1861–62. A severe epidemic swept the camp and several hundred men died. When the city enlarged cemetery, 1887, John C. Latham, native of Hopkinsville, had bodies of 101 unknown reinterred and a large monument erected. Over.

881 CIVIL WAR SNIPER
(Jct. US 68 & KY 453, Trigg Co.)

In 1862 Jack Hinson swore revenge against Union Army when two sons were executed as bushwhackers. From ambush he picked off men in blue uniforms on gun boats and on land. With a price on his head, he continued his vendetta until his gun bore 36 notches at close of war. He guided General Nathan Bedford Forrest in his last campaign in area, Oct.–Nov., 1864.

882 UNION GENERAL'S GRAVE
(Riverside Cem., Hopkinsville, US 41, Christian Co.)

Brig. Gen. James S. Jackson, USA, killed in the battle of Perryville on Oct. 8, 1862, is buried in south end of cemetery. Born

Woodford Co., Ky., 1823. First Lt., Mexican War, then practiced law in Greenup. He came to Hopkinsville, 1855. Elected to Congress, 1861. Authorized by Lincoln, he recruited 3rd Ky. Cav. during fall 1861. In battles, Shiloh and others, before his untimely death.

883 CORNLAND
(Owensboro Belt Line & US 60, Daviess Co.)

Site of home, prior to 1809, of Colonel Joseph Hamilton Daveiss, killed at Tippecanoe, 1811. As US Dist. Atty. for Ky., he prosecuted Aaron Burr for treason in 1806. This county, others in Ind., Ill., Mo., named for this able, zealous patriot. George M. Bibb, twice US Senator, Sec., US Treas., 1884–85, and Philip Triplett, US Congressman, 1839–43, later owned Cornland.

884 PIKEVILLE COLLEGE
(Entrance to College, Hambley Blvd., Pikeville, Pike Co.)

Established by the Presbyterian Church in 1889 for the education of youth from the mountains of southern Appalachia. It now draws students from many states and foreign lands. The Celtic Cross, visible from many points of wide area, symbolizes its Christian aims and purposes.

885 LINCOLN'S FATHER HERE
(Burkesville, Courthouse lawn, KY 61, 90, Cumberland Co.)

Thomas Lincoln made claim for land in Cumberland County in May, 1801. In Jan., 1802 and again in 1804 he was appointed constable. On Sept. 5, 1802, he was commissioned ensign in Cornstalk Militia of Cumberland County. Returned to Washington County. Married Nancy Hanks 1806. To this union Pres. Lincoln was born. Thomas brought to Ky. from Va. as a child, 1782.

886 COUNTY NAMED, 1821
(Louisa, Courthouse lawn, US 23, Lawrence Co.)

For Capt. James Lawrence, whose charge, "Don't give up the ship," when mortally wounded in battle between USS CHESAPEAKE and HMS SHANNON off Boston, June 1, 1813, met highest traditions of US Navy and has inspired all Americans. Buried with honor by British in Halifax;

reinterred at Trinity Church, New York. Lawrence County was formed from Greenup and Floyd.

887 GIANT COOLING TOWER
(1 mi. N. of Louisa, US 23, Lawrence Co.)

Completion of this tower in 1962 was a historic event. First of its kind in Western Hemisphere and the largest capacity of any single tower in the world when it was built. The concrete, natural draft, hyperbolic structure cools 120,000 gallons water per minute for steam condensing. Its height is 320 feet and diameters 245 at base, 130 at neck and 139 at top.

888 COLONEL SILAS ADAMS
(Liberty, Courthouse lawn, US 127, Casey Co.)

A spirited USA Civil War leader. Enlisted July 11, 1861. Aided Col. Frank Wolford with recruiting of lst Ky. Cav. Distinctive service many campaigns. Succeeded Wolford in command, Mar., 1864. Mustered out, Dec. 31, 1864. Born, 1839, Pulaski Co. Elected Casey County Attorney two terms; Legislature, three terms; Congress, two terms. Buried, 1896, Brown Cem., Mt. Olive, Ky.

889 KENTUCKY'S NINETEENTH
(Alexandria, Courthouse lawn, US 27, Campbell Co.)

Campbell County formed, 1794, of parts of Mason, Scott, and Harrison counties, Ky., by legislative act. Named for Col. John Campbell, a Revolutionary War officer, and a Ky. pioneer and statesman. Boone, Kenton, parts of Pendleton and Bracken counties later taken from Campbell County. In 1796 county seat was established at Newport and in 1840 moved to Alexandria.

890 COUNTY NAMED, 1796
(Shepherdsville, Courthouse lawn, KY 44, 61, Bullitt Co.)

For Alexander Scott Bullitt, a leader in the political formation of Kentucky. Member conventions, 1788, seeking statehood and, 1792, drafting first Ky. Constitution. President Ky. Senate, 1792–99, and second constitutional convention, 1799. Elected first Lieut. Gov. of Ky., 1800–04, then re-elected to Senate, one term. Born in Va., 1762, came Ky., 1783, died, 1816.

891 MARVIN COLLEGE
(Clinton, US 51, Hickman Co.)

A Methodist school, built 1884–5, originally stood on this site. It operated until 1922 when it closed because of advance of free public schools. Alben W. Barkley, Congressman, Senator and United States Vice President, 1949–53, was graduated here in 1897. He worked his way through by doing janitorial work, giving rise to the phrase, "Barkley swept here."

892 LIVERMORE BRIDGE
(South end Livermore Bridge, US 431, McLean Co.)

When this structure was built, a unique contribution to history was made. It is claimed to be only river bridge in the world which begins and ends in the same county (McLean), spans two rivers (Green and Rough), and crosses another county (Ohio), a small point of which lies between the rivers. It is 1,350 feet long. Dedication of the bridge held Nov. 13, 1940.

893 BENJAMIN CRAIG
(Carrollton, Jct. KY 36 & US 42, Carroll Co.)

Grave of one of founders of Port William (now Carrollton). Craig laid off town on 613 acres which he and James Hawkins owned; the legislature incorporated it in 1794. He erected the first brick house in this county, 1792. Born in Va., 1751, Benjamin came to Ky. at age 30. He accompanied the Traveling Church, led by Lewis Craig, his brother. Died, 1822.

894 EBENEZER CHURCH
(Troy-Keene Rd., KY 1267, Jessamine Co.)

One-half mile west. Organized by Rev. Adam Rankin, 1793–95. Rev. Robert Bishop came 1803 when stone church replaced log house. From 1810–18, these two were opposing leaders in stormy controversy in early history of Presbyterianism in Ky. Ephraim January donated land. He, other Revolutionary War veterans buried there. Church abandoned 1875, restored 1953.

895 COUNTY NAMED, 1821
(Clinton, Courthouse lawn, US 51, Hickman Co.)

For Capt. Paschal Hickman who was massacred by Indians after River Raisin battle, Jan., 1813, one of nine Ky. officers killed in that action for whom counties named. Resided Franklin County, extensive landowner. Originally, Hickman comprised the Jackson Purchase in Ky. Later eight counties have been formed within initial area. First county seat was Columbus.

896 NAZARETH COLLEGE
(College entrance, N. of Bardstown, US 31-E, Nelson Co.)
Mother House of the Sisters of Charity of Nazareth since 1822. The first establishment was made in 1812 at St. Thomas Plantation five miles southwest of Bardstown. The site of Nazareth Academy, now Nazareth College of Kentucky, founded 1814, chartered 1829. Bishop John Baptist Mary David and Mother Catherine Spalding, co-founders, buried in cemetery.

897 PATRIOT—PIONEER
(Near Blue Licks Union Church, Old US 68, Nicholas Co.)
Site of home and grave of Major George M. Bedinger over on hilltop. Born Pennsylvania, 1756. Died 1843. Officer War of Revolution. In defense of Boonesborough, 1779, and at siege of Yorktown, 1781. In 1784 came back to Ky. First to survey this area. Indian campaign, 1791. Ky. legislator, 1792–94. US Congress, 1803–07. Opposed slavery. Freed his slaves at their age thirty.

898 FIRST WHITE MEN HERE
(1½ mi. N. of Williamsburg, KY 26, Whitley Co.)
Dr. Thomas Walker, employed by Loyal Land Co., in 1750 led five Virginians through Cumberland Gap. Built cabin at Barbourville site. Walker and two others went on to Rockcastle River, thence southwest to Young's Creek, up Cumberland River and Watt's Creek to Blake's Fork, Whitley County, and camped April 25. Joined party at cabin, returned to homes in Virginia.

899 FIRST CHRISTIAN CHURCH (DISCIPLES OF CHRIST)
(Blandville Rd., Paducah, US 62, McCracken Co.)
Organized, 1849, affiliated with Campbell-Stone Movement in plea for Christian Unity. Located at Seventh and Jefferson,

1895–1965. Tower Bell, cast in 1868, used on area river packets sixty years. Murrell Blvd. congregation merged following 1937 flood. A part of largest and oldest religious body indigenous to the United States. *Presented by Church.*

900 TIMBER TUNNEL
(4.8 mi. W. of Yamacrow, KY 92, McCreary Co.)
In 1899 Longsworth and Co. bought from Benj. F. Coffey the timber on 1,485 acres of Wolf Creek Valley. Built steam powered mill on creek and tramroad to Cumberland Fork, 10 miles. A 20-foot tunnel drilled thru rock 80 feet below here is still open. Mule drawn tramcars moved products to river, then by wagon to the railroad at Marshes Siding. Timber out in 15 years.

901 IVY POINT SKIRMISHES
(Near Salyersville city limits, KY 7 & US 460, Magoffin Co.)
During Civil War the Union Army's 14th Ky. Inf. operated in this area to scout and protect east Ky. On Oct. 30, 1863, 160 of these troops under Lieut. Col. Orlando Brown, Jr. repulsed Confederates here and captured 50 prisoners. Another skirmish occurred Nov. 30, 1863, when Capt. Peter Everett in command of 200 Confederates led surprise attack, captured 25 men.

902 REUBEN PATRICK GRAVE
(Bradley, 1½ mi. W. of Ivyton, KY 1888, Magoffin Co.)
Detachment leader 14th Vol. Inf. USA force engaged largely in this area. CSA camped near Ivyton in March, 1863. On night of 20th, as posted guard slept, Patrick boldly detached gun from carriage, hid it in woods. Their only artillery, a Williams Rapid Fire Gun. CSA moved on, left carriage. Gun has been displayed many years. Patrick a Ky. legislator, 1863–67.

903 THE WALKER EXPEDITION
(Paintsville, KY 40 at KY 581, Johnson Co.)
Doctor Thomas Walker led first expedition of record from Virginia into eastern Kentucky and camped at present site of Paintsville in 1750. Here, June 7, 1750, he discovered French cabins at mouth of Paint Creek and named river Louisa, honoring daughter of King George II and sister of

Duke of Cumberland for whom Walker named the Cumberland River and the Gap.

904 Breathitt Volunteers
(Jackson, Courthouse lawn, KY 15, 30, Breathitt Co.)

During World War I, this county attained national prominence by filling its quota of service men by volunteers. No men had to be drafted from Breathitt, the only county in U.S. with this record. During war 3,912 men registered, 405 volunteered; of 324 called, 281 were inducted and 43 rejected. Kentuckians ranked among highest in nation in physical fitness.

905 Little Floyd
(Jct. US 23 & Mare Creek Rd., Floyd Co.)

In 1845, Ky. Legislature put Mare Creek farm of Tandy R. Stratton in Floyd County. In Pike since it was formed from Floyd, 1821. Strip separates farm area from Floyd, forming "island" in Pike. Reported to be the only instance in U.S. His grandfather set up Stratton Settlement, 1796, at mouth of Mare Creek and with two others directed laying out of Prestonsburg, 1797.

906 Green Mill
(Falls of Rough, KY 79, 110, Grayson Co.)

Built in 1823, this mill operated continuously by the Green family for over 140 years. It was part of 6,000-acre farm-timber complex supporting several family-owned industries. Farmers from seven counties brought grain for milling into flour and cornmeal. Willis, first of family here, bought land, 1821. Member legislature, 1836–37, and of US Congress, 1839–45.

907 Mount Saint Joseph
(Saint Joseph, KY 56, Daviess Co.)

Mount Saint Joseph Motherhouse and Academy, the first motherhouse for Sisters in western Kentucky, the oldest operating girls' academy in Daviess County, founded August 14, 1874, by Rev. Paul Joseph Volk under auspices of Bishop George McCloskey of Louisville. Mother Aloysius Willett of Union County elected first Superior of the autonomous Ursuline house in 1912.

908 Chief Red Bird
(Big Creek Elem. School, KY 66, Clay Co.)

Was a legendary Cherokee Indian for whom this fork of the Kentucky River is named. He and another Indian, Jack, whose name was given creek to the south, were friendly with early settlers and permitted to hunt in area. Allegedly they were killed in battle protecting their furs and the bodies thrown into river here. The ledges bear markings attributed to Red Bird.

909 Westport
(Westport, KY 524, Oldham Co.)

First called Liberty, located on 1780 grant to Elijah Craig. Ferry operated here by Levi Boyer early as 1800 formed a link in route to Illinois country. Town became a port to the west–Westport. In the steamboat era, the town was a thriving port for shipping farm produce and receiving merchandise. The first county seat of Oldham, 1823–38, except nine months, 1827.

910 Marvel Mills Logan
(Near Fairview, KY 259, Edmonson Co.)

U.S. Senator from Kentucky, March 1931 until his death Oct. 1939. Born, 1875, on this farm, attended Brownsville schools. Admitted to Ky. bar, 1896, practiced here. State Attorney General, 1916–17. Judge on Ky. Court of Appeals, 1927–30. Grand Sire of the World, I.O.O.F. Pioneer promoter of Mammoth Cave as National Park, 1910. Taught Sunday School regularly 35 years.

911 Ghent
(Ghent, US 42, Carroll Co.)

Known as McCool's Creek Settlement, it was laid off in 1809 on land of Samuel Sanders, whose father was here early as 1795. Thirteen families came from Virginia, 1800. Traditionally, on visit here about 1816, Henry Clay, a member of the commission which negotiated the Treaty of Ghent ending the War of 1812, suggested the name Ghent in honor of historic Belgian town.

912 County Named, 1819
(Franklin, Courthouse lawn, W. Cedar St., Simpson Co.)

For Capt. John Simpson, one of the nine

officers killed at Battle of River Raisin, Jan. 22, 1813, for whom Ky. counties named. Fought under "Mad Anthony" Wayne, Battle of Fallen Timbers, 1794. Settled in Shelby Co., Ky. Speaker of Ky. House, 1811. U.S. Congressman. County formed from Allen, Logan, Warren. "Cut-Off" three-mile strip along Logan Co. added in 1869. Over.
(Reverse)
FRANKLIN

When Legislature formed county, it authorized commission to purchase site for county seat. Three owners of land sought to sell site. Water source essential. William Hudspeth dug well here, but it was dry. He hauled water secretly to fill well, sold 62 acres. Water primed well and it was used many years. Town surveyed, 1819, and made county seat by Legislature, Nov. 1820. Over.

913 CATHOLIC PIONEERS
(Holy Cross, KY 527, 457, Marion Co.)

Basil Hayden, Sr., led 25 Maryland Catholic families to settle near here, on Pottinger's Creek, 1785. Father Whelan said first Mass in Kentucky here in 1787. First Catholic church west of Alleghenies built here in 1792. First monks, 1805, Trappist Fathers (Cistercians). Present church erected in 1823, under direction of famous Belgian missionary, Charles Nerinckx.

914 MOUNT SAVAGE FURNACE
(E. of Grayson, Jct. US 60 & KY 1, Carter Co.)

Six miles south, site of famous iron furnace, erected, 1848, by R. M. Biggs and others. Operated 37 years, averaging 15 tons pig iron daily which was hauled by ox teams to Ohio River for shipment. Iron produced here was used for rails, plows, cannon, machines. Industry declined as limestone, charcoal, and ore supplies ran out. Last blast here occurred in 1885.

915 DAWSON SPRINGS
(Dawson Springs, US 62, Hopkins Co.)

In its heyday, from the start of the century until mid-1920's, this was one of best known spas, health resorts in the South. Thousands of the sick, the lame, the well

came for the curative waters and to enjoy the social activities. Six firms bottled and shipped the chalybeate water all over the U.S. W. I. Hamby, resident of Hopkins County, discovered springs, 1881.

916 PADUCAH, KENTUCKY
(North 8th & Julia Sts., Paducah, McCracken Co.)

McCracken county seat, founded by Gen. William Clark of Lewis and Clark Expedition at confluence of Ohio and Tennessee Rivers. Named for legendary Indian Chief Paduke. Home of Vice Pres. Alben W. Barkley and birthplace of Irvin S. Cobb. First occupied in Civil War by Gen. U. S. Grant. Became supply base of his Miss. River campaign. Great Atomic Energy plant nearby.
(Reverse)
McCRACKEN COUNTY

Formed, 1824, from Hickman County. Named for Capt. Virgil McCracken of Woodford County, Ky., who was killed in Battle of River Raisin near Detroit during War of 1812. Area 237 square miles. Ohio and Tennessee Rivers brought industry dependent on river transportation. First county seat at Wilmington, 1825, and moved to Paducah, 1832. Government is County Commission.

917 JOHN FRY
(N. of Liberty, US 127, Casey Co.)

Entered land on Carpenter's Creek 8 miles north, 1780, on a Treasury Warrant for service in Revolution. Land grant signed, 1783, by Gov. Benj. Harrison. Engaged in Battle of Point Pleasant, 1774. Served in Rockingham Militia, Va., during Revolution. With Kentuckians when killed at Blue Licks Battle, 1782, at age of 28. Four generations of family owned land over a century. *Presented by Mrs. Mary Frye Barley, Whittier, Calif.*

918 PADUCAH, KENTUCKY
(3100 South Beltline Highway, Paducah, McCracken Co.)

McCracken county seat, founded by Gen. William Clark of Lewis and Clark Expedition at confluence of Ohio and Tennessee Rivers. Named for legendary Indian Chief Paduke. Home of Vice Pres. Alben Barkley and birthplace of Irvin S. Cobb. First occupied in Civil War by Gen. U. S. Grant. Became supply base of his Miss. River campaign. Great Atomic Energy plant nearby. (Reverse)

McCracken County

Formed, 1824, from Hickman County. Named for Captain Virgil McCracken of Woodford County, Ky., who was killed in Battle of River Raisin near Detroit during War of 1812. Area 237 square miles. Ohio and Tennessee Rivers brought industry dependent on river transportation. First county seat at Wilmington, 1825, and moved to Paducah, 1832. Government is County Commission. *Anonymous sponsor.*

919 Pioneer Hero-Heroine

(11 mi. E. of Williamsburg, KY 92, Whitley Co.)

Graves of Capt. Chas. Gatliff and wife. During Revolution he fought against Indians on Va. frontier, came Ky., 1779. Wife, 4 children among 250 captives taken in 1780 at Martin's Station (Bourbon Co.) to Detroit by British and Indians. In 13 years wife made way back to Va. while Gatliff fought in many Indian campaigns. Reunited, they settled here on land grant, 1793.

920 Swango Springs Spa

(Hazel Green schoolyard, KY 191, Wolfe Co.)

Traditionally, healing properties of mineral water of a spring here discovered by owner when treating her pet dog for mange. Its use by humans spread and by 1895 three hotels and many boarding houses were hosts to people from all over America. Fire destroyed largest hotel, 1910. Visitors to resort dropped off. Mineral water bottled and widely shipped until 1943.

921 Indian Mounds

(13th & Galloway Sts., Ashland, US 23, 60, Boyd Co.)

One and one-half miles NE in Central Park is an irregular row of mounds, part of a chain built by prehistoric men who were the forerunners of American Indians. Many of remains of that ancient people which once dotted this area were leveled as the town expanded. Some of these were burial mounds; others contained artifacts such as arrowheads and stone utensils.

922 Moses Stepp

(10 mi. S. of Lovely, Pigeon Roost Valley Rd., Martin Co.)

Colorful frontiersman. An ancient headstone at grave shows he was born 1735, died 1855. Enlisted for three short periods in Revolution and fought Indians and Tories in west Carolinas and east Tennessee. Legend tells that he was captured by the Cherokees and tortured by nailing his ears to a tree. He tore loose and escaped. Came to this area, 1826, for rest of life.

923 Centre College

(Danville, Jct. US 127 & 150 at campus, Boyle Co.)

Founded on this campus in 1819 by pioneer Kentuckians who held that heart and mind must be trained together, and dedicated to the inculcation of ideals of culture and character in the hearts of American youth. Veritas Lux Mentis.

924 Grant's Proclamation

(Broadway at Riverfront, Paducah, McCracken Co.)

On this spot, September 6, 1861, Gen. Ulysses S. Grant read proclamation to citizens of Paducah announcing that the Union Army was taking possession of town "to defend you" against Confederate attack. The "enemy" had taken "possession of and planted his guns" at Columbus and Hickman on the Mississippi. Union troops moved in and the U.S. occupied city for duration of war.

925 Monterey

(Monterey, US 127, Owen Co.)

First named Williamsburg for James Williams, who came from Maryland, set up trading post about 1805. In 1847, legislature established town of Monterey, named for battle of Mexican War, on land owned by George C. Branham. Steamboats, in heyday on Ky. River, made regular stops at town wharf for passengers and cargo. Large tobacco market. Showboats visited town in summer.

926 Early Vital Junction

(Burgin school yard, KY 33, 152, Mercer Co.)

Crossroads for pioneer defense. Harrods-

burg, 1774, Harrod's Fort, 1775, and two miles east Bowman's Fort, 1777, earliest in area. In 1779–80 eight fortified stations built nearby–Crow's, Fisher's, Gordon's, Haggin's, McGary's, McMurtry's, Smith's, and Trigg's. Routes connecting them converged here in defense plan. All Indian attacks in area defeated. Over.
(Reverse)

COLONEL JOHN BOWMAN

Military Commander of Kentucky, appointed, 1776, by Gov. Patrick Henry of Va. and, 1778, by Gov. Thomas Jefferson. Built Bowman's Fort, 2 miles east of here, 1777. Brought 30 families, 1779, settling at fort. Leader of defense against Indians in period of hostilities. Directed attack into Ohio, 1779. On first court, Harrodsburg, 1777. A first Transylvania trustee. Over.

927 WILDERNESS ROAD INN
(½ mi. S. of Park entrance, KY 229, Laurel Co.)

Site of home-tavern built, 1804, by John Freeman on Revolutionary War land grant. The tavern stood beside historic Wilderness (wagon) Road built by Kentucky between Cumberland Gap and Crab Orchard in 1796. A principal highway, it promoted settlement of Ky. and the West. Operated as a toll road for about 80 years. Inn burned, 1962. Freeman (1761–1841) grave nearby.

928 McAFEE STATION
(McAfee, US 127, Mercer Co.)

Site of stockade built, 1779, by McAfee, McCoun, McGee, Curry and Adams families, 1½ miles west on Salt River on land owned by James McAfee. He and brothers, William, Robert, George, Samuel, in 1773–5, marked and improved land in area. 1785, New Providence Presbyterian Church formed. The third church erected by this continuous body stands one mile north. See over.
(Reverse)

PIONEER TEACHER, 1779

John May, first teacher in school at McAfee Station, 1779. One of four Ky. Dist. delegates, 1781, to Va. House of Burgesses. First clerk of Supreme Court, Ky. Dist., and one of original trustees of Transylvania Seminary, 1783. With Simon Kenton, famed frontiersman, he owned land where Maysville, Ky. was established by Va., 1787. It was named for May. See over.

929 McAFEE STATION
(McAfee, US 127, Mercer Co.)

Site of stockade built, 1779, by McAfee, McCoun, McGee, Curry and Adams families, 1½ miles west on Salt River on land owned by James McAfee. He and brothers, William, Robert, George, Samuel, in 1773–5, marked and improved land in area. 1785, New Providence Presbyterian Church formed. The third church erected by this continuous body stands one mile north. See over.
(Reverse)

PIONEER TEACHER, 1779

John May, first teacher in school at McAfee Station, 1779. One of four Ky. Dist. delegates, 1781, to Va. House of Burgesses. First clerk of Supreme Court, Ky. Dist., and one of original trustees of Transylvania Seminary, 1783. With Simon Kenton, famed frontiersman, he owned land where Maysville, Ky., was established by Va., 1787. It was named for May. See over.

930 JOHN POPE, 1770–1845
(S. of High St., Springfield, KY 53, Washington Co.)

Eminent Washington Co. citizen. Brilliant Kentucky lawyer, statesman. Born, Va. Represented Shelby Co., 1802, Fayette Co., 1806, in Leg.; U.S. Senate, 1807–13; Ky. Sec. of State, 1816–19; Ky. Sen., 1825–29; Gov. Arkansas Ter., 1829–35, named by Pres. Jackson; U.S. Congress, 1837–43. Federalist and Democrat. Built this home, 1839. Died here; buried in Springfield Cemetery.

931 JOHN HARDIN, 1753–92
(3 mi. E. of Springfield, US 150, Washington Co.)

Soldier, Indian fighter, surveyor. In Dunmore's War, 1774. Served under Gen. Daniel Morgan in the War of the Revolution. Cited for bravery, Saratoga. Explored this area, 1780; Q. M. for General Clark, Wabash expedition, 1787; Colonel, Nelson Co. Militia, 1789; Cmdr., Ky. troops, Maumee Campaign, 1790. In 1792, U.S.

peace envoy to Ohio Indians; foully murdered by them.

932 LINCOLN-HAYCRAFT MEMORIAL BRIDGE, 1936
(Elizabethtown at bridge, Hardin Co.)

Here along Severn's Valley Creek Samuel Haycraft, Sr., built mill raceway in 1796. Thomas Lincoln, father of Pres. Lincoln, employed in building it, received his first monetary wages when about 21 years of age. Abraham Lincoln, age 7, with his family on way to Indiana in 1816, crossed this creek about here and went thru Elizabethtown.

933 MATTHEW WALTON, 1759–1819
(2 mi. W. of Springfield, US 150, Washington Co.)

Home, office of political "father" of Washington Co. Born, Va. Came Ky., 1784. Danville Convs., 1785, 1787; Va. Fed. Const. Ratification Conv., 1788; Va. Assembly, 1790; Ky. Const. Conv., 1792; Legis., 1792, 1795, 1808; Ky. Sen., 1800–03; US Cong., 1803–07. Owned nearly 200,000 acres. This house erected about 1784. Manor house built here about 1791. It was razed in 1900.

934 TAR SPRINGS
(Cloverport, US 60, Breckinridge Co.)

Four miles south. A fashionable health resort of 1840s which had the unique attraction of a 100-foot cliff from which tar bubbled while from its base flowed eleven springs, each with different type of mineral water. Indians knew and used these curative waters. Wiley B. Rutledge, Justice of U.S. Supreme Court, 1943–49, was born, 1894, at Tar Springs resort.

935 OLD CONCORD CHURCH
(Near KY 36 & Dorsey St., Carlisle, Nicholas Co.)

Organized 1793, 2½ miles south. Site of Presbyterian Church and school made famous by its pioneer pastors: John Rankin, Barton W. Stone, Sam'l Shannon, John Rogers, John P. Campbell, Samuel Rannels, Robert Marshall, Robert Finley, James Welsh. In 1851 control of Old Concord was relinquished to Christian Church. Log structure replaced by present church, 1860.

936 AN INDIAN MASSACRE
(KY 491, west side of I-75, Crittenden, Grant Co.)

Three miles west. Reputedly scene of one of last massacres in Ky. McClures and Kennedys lived on hills above Bullock Pen Creek and the Bran family occupied cabin on creek at foot of hills. Around 1805, party of Indians burned the Bran home after scalping parents and children. All died except the mother, who crawled to the Kennedy house. She eventually recovered.

937 COUNTY NAMED, 1798
(Falmouth, Courthouse lawn, US 27, Pendleton Co.)

For Edmund Pendleton, 1721–1803. A patriot statesman. Virginian. Member House of Burgesses 1752–1774. In the First Continental Congress. Governor Colonial Virginia 1774–1776. President Virginia Constitutional Convention, 1776, and President of Virginia State Convention that ratified Federal Constitution, 1788. Chief, State Court of Appeals, 1779–1803. County from Bracken and Campbell.

938 GOWER HOUSE
(Smithland, US 60, Livingston Co.)

Erected about 1780: one of the luxury inns built to accommodate the travelers on the Ohio River. Host to many celebrities of that era including Presidents James K. Polk, Zachary Taylor; founder American Red Cross, Clara Barton; authors Charles Dickens and Lew Wallace; and Henry Clay. Lafayette was a guest here in May of 1825 while on his triumphal U.S. tour.
(Reverse)

NED BUNTLINE

Pen name of Edward Z. C. Judson, father of the dime novel, who came to Smithland to publish his works; lived here in 1845. He brought fame to "Buffalo Bill" (William Cody) thru stories and promotion of his renowned wild west show. He wrote of the marshals of the frontier west. In 1876, gave to Wyatt Earp, Bat Masterson, and others Colt "Buntline Special" revolvers.

939 TILGHMAN HOME
(7th & Ky. Sts., Paducah, McCracken Co.)

Gen. Lloyd Tilghman, soldier and rail builder, lived here, 1852–61. Born, Maryland, 1816. Graduated West Point, 1836. In the Mexican War (1846–48). Chief engineer, 1855–56, New Orleans and Jackson Railroad, first to enter Paducah. In Civil War joined Confed. Army, 1861. Killed, Battle of Champion's Hill near Vicksburg, May, 1863. *Sponsored by Tilghman High School Class of 1929.*

940 BATH COUNTY
(Owingsville, Courthouse lawn, US 60, Bath Co.)

Formed from Montgomery County, 1811. Named for its many mineral springs. The birthplace of CSA Gen. John B. Hood and US Senator Richard H. Menefee. Owingsville named for Col. Thomas D. Owings. Organizer US 28th Inf. Reg., 1812. Associate in ownership, operation of Bourbon Iron Works, 1795–1822. Host to Louis Philippe of France during part of his exile in U.S.

941 SAINT ROSE PRIORY
(3 mi. W. of Springfield, KY 152, Washington Co.)

Founded, 1806, by Fr. Fenwick from Maryland. First Dominican religious house and second oldest priory in the U.S. Site of first Catholic college west of Alleghenies, 1807. St. Thomas School here, 1809–28. Jefferson Davis, later President of Confederacy, student, 1815–16. In 1822 Fr. Wilson founded first community of Dominican Sisters in U.S. Present church built, 1852.

942 GRANT COUNTY
(Williamstown, Courthouse lawn, US 25, Grant Co.)

Formed from Pendleton County in 1820. Named for two brothers who came from N.C., 1779, established Grant's Station, Fayette County. John developed salt works on the Licking River. Samuel was killed by Indians in Indiana in 1794. William Arnold donated courthouse site. Williamstown named for him, a Capt. in Revolution and Lieut. in Maumee Indian Campaign of 1790.

943 A FRIEND TO MORGAN
(12 mi. N. of Monterey, KY 325 & 355, Owen Co.)

On his way south, escaping from a Union prison in Ohio, Confederate Gen. John Hunt Morgan stopped at home of J. J.

Alexander, mile east, for food and rest during daylight hours, Nov. 30, 1863. Morgan had been captured, July 26, in NE Ohio at end of his third and his farthest north raid. Morgan made way to Tenn., where he organized, led another raid into Ky., 1864.

944 STEAMBOAT INVENTOR
(Old Town Cem., Bardstown, US 31-E, Nelson Co.)

First burial place of John Fitch. Reinterred, 1927, in Court Square. Born Conn., 1743. Appointed Lt. of N.J. Co., 1st Reg. in Revolutionary War. Named Ky. deputy surveyor, 1780. Acquired 1,600 acres. Established home here in 1782. Conceived idea of steamboat 1785; built small one, 1786. Demonstrated larger one on Delaware River before framers of US Constitution, 1787. See over.

(Reverse)
STEAMBOAT INVENTOR

In Oct., 1788, he built boat which carried passengers on 20-mile trip from Philadelphia to Burlington. In 1790 constructed boat which ran regular schedule between those cities. On Aug. 26, 1791, patent granted to Fitch by US Congress. France also granted patent, 1791. Returned here, 1796, died in 1798. Robert Fulton developed his boat, *The Clermont,* in 1807. See over.

945 ARCHITECTS SHRYOCK
(Transylvania Univ. Campus, Broadway, Lexington, Fayette Co.)

"Best known surname in Kentucky architecture is Shryock." Family home, erected by Matthias Shryock (1774–1833), here. Designed first Episcopal church in city, 1814, and Mary Todd Lincoln home on W. Main. Son, Cincinnatus, born here, 1816. First Presbyterian Church, built 1872, considered his best. Also designed many homes. Died, 1888. Both buried in Lexington. Over.

(Reverse)
ANOTHER SHRYOCK

Gideon, "father of Greek revival movement in Ky. architecture," was also Matthias' son. Fine example of his classic style is Old State House, Frankfort, Ky., 1829. He also designed Morrison Hall on the Transylvania campus here, 1830,

Jefferson County Courthouse in Louisville, Arkansas State Capitol, Little Rock, 1830's. Born here, 1802; buried Louisville, 1880.

946 KELLY KETTLE
(Kuttawa, US 62, Lyon Co.)

One of many kettles made in this area by William Kelly, used for making sugar down South. In 1851, Kelly discovered process, known as Bessemer, for manufacture of steel. An Englishman, Bessemer, obtained patents on same process in England 1855 and in U.S. 1856. Kelly filed priority claim, 1857. U.S. awarded patent to Kelly and later refused renewal to Bessemer.

947 JESSAMINE COUNTY
(Nicholasville, Courthouse lawn, US 27, Jessamine Co.)

Formed from Fayette County, 1798. Named by Col. John Price, one of Representatives in Legislature, who stated he named it for flower which flourishes in region and for Jessamine Creek. A moving legend tells that the creek was named for Jessamine Douglass, daughter of an early settler, who was stealthily tomahawked by an Indian as she rested on the banks of the creek. (Reverse)

NICHOLASVILLE

County seat laid out in 1798 by Rev. John Metcalf, Methodist, who opened the first school in area, 1794. Chartered by legislature, 1812. Named for George Nicholas (1754–99); colonel in Revolution, "father of Kentucky constitution"; first Ky. Attorney General. John McLean, U.S. Supreme Court Justice, dissenter in Dred Scott case, 1857, spent part of boyhood years in vicinity.

948 SPRING HILL
(6½ mi. W. of Winchester on Colby Rd., Clark Co.)

Home of Hubbard Taylor, soldier, surveyor, politician. Born, Va., 1760; in Am. Revolution, 1776–78. Came to Ky. as surveyor, 1780. In 1790 brought family, built this home. In first Ky. Const. Conv., 1792; in Ky. Senate, 1796–1800 and 1815–19. Presidential elector six times. Died in 1840. His kinsman, Pres. James Madison, visited here; also Henry Clay, other statesmen.

949 SITE, AETNA FURNACE
(Jonesville, US 31-E, Hart Co.)

Built in 1816, first iron furnace in western half of Kentucky. Salt and iron sought by early settlers. Charles Wilkins, Ruggles Whiting, and Jacob Holderman were partners in this furnace until 1826, when Holderman became the sole owner. Property included 10,500 acres of land. Furnace operated until the 1850's. Holderman family cemetery located near site of furnace.

950 FLEMING COUNTY
(Flemingsburg, Courthouse lawn, KY 11, 32, Fleming Co.)

Kentucky's 26th, was taken out of Mason, 1798. Named for Col. John Fleming who came to area to mark, improve land, 1776. Officer in Rev. War. Built Fleming's Station, second in county, 1788. Closely associated with other pioneers, John Finley, Michael Cassidy, and George Stockton, his halfbrother, who owned the land and who laid out and named Flemingsburg, 1796.

951 HANSON HOME SITE
(Lexington Ave., Winchester, US 60, Clark Co.)

Here lived five Hanson brothers, Civil War soldiers, USA and CSA. For USA: Col. Charles S., hero of Battle of Lebanon, July, 1863; Pvt. Samuel K.–died in service. For CSA: Brig. Gen. Roger, mortally wounded in the Battle of Stone's River, Jan. 2, 1863; Pvt. Richard H. and Pvt. Isaac S. Sons of the Hon. Samuel and Matilda Hickman Hanson.

952 SAMUEL BOONE
(Gentry Rd., ¼ mi. NE of Athens, Fayette Co.)

Grave of Samuel Boone, the eldest brother of Daniel Boone, renowned Kentucky pioneer. Samuel was born in Penna., May 20, 1728. Came to Kentucky from South Carolina in 1779 with his family and settled Boone's Station. He joined in defense of Bryan's Station, 1782. His son, Thomas, was killed at Battle of Blue Licks, 1782. He died here, 1816, at the age of 88.

953 BRITISH, INDIAN RAID
(Falmouth, in front of Shell Refinery, US 27, Pendleton Co.)

In countermove, 1780, to control northwest, British Capt. Henry Bird with 150 troops and 1000 Indians came from Detroit, by river in June. From here, they marched to Ruddle's and Martin's Station, to the south, captured 470 settlers. Returned here, captives divided, families separated. The British took some to Detroit, remainder scattered among Indian villages.

954 RUSSELL COUNTY
(Jamestown, Courthouse lawn, US 127, Russell Co.)

Established, 1825, out of parts of Adair, Wayne, Cumberland. Named for Col. Wm. Russell (1758–1825). Lieut., Revolution; came Fayette Co., Ky. In Indian campaigns of 1791 and 1794. At Tippecanoe, 1811. Succeeded Gen. William H. Harrison in command Ind., Ill., Mo. frontier. Representative in Ky. Legislature for 13 sessions. Jamestown was established by Legislature, 1827.

955 OTTENHEIM
(Halls Gap, US 27 & KY 643, Lincoln Co.)

A German-Swiss settlement, 4 miles southeast, started by immigrants, early 1880s. Guided here by Joseph Ottenheimer "to this land of great opportunity" they found it to be a wilderness. Undaunted they built crude log cabins, then cleared the virgin land and developed it into a highly productive agricultural area. By 1886 a Lutheran and a Catholic Church had been built.

956 COUNTY NAMED, 1784
(Bardstown, Courthouse lawn, US 31-E, 62, Nelson Co.)

For Thomas Nelson, 1738–89. Member Va. House of Burgesses. In the first provincial convention, 1774; Continental Congress, 1775–77 and 1779. Signer of the Declaration of Independence. Commander of Va. Militia, 1777–81. Governor of Va., 1781. Commended for selfless patriotism in ordering guns to fire on his own home, the British headquarters, at Yorktown, 1781.

957 FUNK SEMINARY SITE
(LaGrange, KY 53, 146, Oldham Co.)

In 1841 William M. Funk bequeathed $10,000 to establish seminary. It was chartered by Legislature and erected here,

1842. In 1844 Grand Lodge of Ky. assumed control and changed it to Masonic College. In 1852 changed to Masonic Univ. of Ky. School reached its height in next decade. Civil War disrupted it. Reverted to high school in 1873. Building burned in 1911.

958 BOWIE, A KENTUCKIAN
(Russellville, Courthouse lawn, US 68, 79, Logan Co.)

James Bowie, Col. of Texas Rangers and co-commander at the Alamo, was native of Logan Co. With 187 others–P. J. Bailey, D. W. Cloud, W. Fountleroy of Logan Co. among them–he chose death rather than surrender. "Remember the Alamo" was battle cry of Texas victory and freedom from Mexico, 1836. The Bowie Knife, famed weapon of frontier days, designed by Bowie.

959 CUMBERLAND COUNTY
(Burkesville, Courthouse lawn, KY 61, 90, Cumberland Co.)

Established, 1798, taken out of Green County. Later, between 1800 and 1860, parts of Wayne, Monroe, Russell, Clinton, Metcalfe were taken from its original territory. First known white men here, 1769. Daniel Boone explored area, 1771. Burkesville, laid out in 1798 on land owned by Samuel Burks, was vital riverport for timber and farm produce during steamboat era.

960 HARDIN COUNTY
(Elizabethtown, Courthouse lawn, US 31-W, 62, Hardin Co.)

Formed from Nelson County by first Legislature, 1792. Named for Col. John Hardin, veteran of Dunmore's War, 1774, Am. Rev., Gen. Clark's Wabash Exped., 1787, and Maumee Indian campaign, 1790. Murdered by Ohio Indians while U.S. peace envoy to them in 1792. In 1780 Elizabethtown settled by Samuel Haycraft, Thomas Helm and Andrew Hynes, for whose wife town named.

961 BREATHITT COUNTY
(Jackson, Courthouse lawn, KY 15, 30, Breathitt Co.)

Formed from parts of Estill, Clay, Perry counties, 1839. Named for Gov. John Breathitt, who died in office, 1834. Breathitt born in Va., 1786. Family came to Logan

County, Ky., 1800. Representative in Ky. Legis. 3 terms, Lt. Gov. 1828, Gov. 1832–1834. County seat first named Breathitt; changed in 1845 to Jackson, honoring hero of New Orleans, the 7th U.S. President.

962 IRVIN S. COBB
(Oak Grove Cemetery, Paducah, McCracken Co.)

Native of Paducah, famed wit and humorist; newspaper reporter, war correspondent and feature writer; author of books, short stories, movie scripts and plays. Started career with local paper. Moved to New York, 1904; to Hollywood, 1934. Beloved, especially for his high tribute to Kentucky's proud folk in his writing and speeches. *Sponsored by Paducah Retail Merchants Association.*

963 A PADUCAH CSA HERO
(514 Park, Paducah, McCracken Co.)

Col. Albert P. Thompson fell here in Battle of Paducah, March 25, 1864, victim of Union cannonball. He commanded the 3rd Ky. Inf. CSA. The battle climaxed Gen. Nathan B. Forrest's memorable raid seeking medical supplies and munitions. Thompson, a respected lawyer here, joined Confederate cause in 1861. After war reinterred at Murray. *Sponsored by Paducah Lions Club.*

964 MEXICAN WAR, 1846–48
(Broadway at Riverfront, Paducah, McCracken Co.)

From this point a company of 90 Paducahans–3,500 population–formed by Lt. Harry Easton, left to take part in the Mexican War. The men lodged at old Fisher Hotel nearby during time of recruiting. Later they joined volunteers from other counties in the Jackson Purchase. Kentuckians led in turning tide, battle of Buena Vista. Over. *Sponsored by Paducah Colonial Baking Co.*
(Reverse)
LIBERTY OF TEXAS, 1836
From here 18 "Paducah Volunteers" led by Captain Amon B. King embarked for Texas in 1835 in response to Sam Houston's appeal for aid in fight for freedom from Mexico. Two weeks after the Alamo, in battle at Refugio, Urrea's Mexican troops captured and executed Capt. King and his

men. Many other Americans suffered same atrocities. See over. *Sponsored by Paducah Colonial Baking Co.*

965 CRAWFORD SPRINGS
(1 mi. E. of Perryville, US 68, Boyle Co.)

As Confederate and Union armies converged over to the west the day and night before great Battle of Perryville, Oct. 8, 1862, there was constant fighting for water. Almost unprecedented drought had made water so scarce that troops contended for pools in dry creeks. This spring provided continuous supply to CSA Gen. Bragg's hdqrs. and troops on this side of river.

966 COBB'S BIRTH SITE
(321 S. 3rd St., Paducah, McCracken Co.)

House in which Paducah's famed humorist, Irvin S. Cobb, was born in 1876 stood here until 1917. The home of Dr. Reuben Saunders, Cobb's maternal grandfather, a pioneer physician who practiced here 1847–1891. For discovery of a cure for cholera in epidemic of 1876, he was decorated by several foreign countries, cited by U.S. *Presented by Clyde Boyles.*

967 CHIEF PADUKE'S GRAVE
(1136 S. 3rd St., Paducah, McCracken Co.)

After Jackson Purchase in 1818 of land west of the Tenn. River, the Chickasaws moved to Mississippi. Traditionally, Chief Paduke, with 90 braves, returned in 1819 hoping to visit Gen. William Clark, founder of Paducah. Paduke died on way back. The braves returned his body and buried it where his wigwam had stood, 200 feet west of here. *Presented by Clyde Boyles.*

968 PADUCAH PICTORIAL
(Post Office grounds, 5th & Broadway, Paducah, McCracken Co.)

Paducah's colorful history from the time of the Chickasaw Indians through the age of steamboats and steam locomotives is depicted on a mural in Post Office building. History and legend of our city, painted by local artists, was presented to the United States by Paducah citizens group. Accepted officially on Oct. 14, 1961. *Marker presented by Paducah Moose Lodge No. 285.*

969 OLD BANK, ROBBED 1868
(South Main & 6th St., Russellville, Logan Co.)

Part of building erected about 1810 by Wm. Harrison, used as a residence by him and later by the Nortons. In 1857 front part built for Southern Bank of Ky. Building owned by Judge Hardy family sixty yrs. (1966). Mar. 20, 1868, it was scene of holdup by notorious Jesse James gang, who escaped with over $9,000 after they shot, slightly wounded bank president, N. Long.

970 WILMINGTON
(KY 358 between Paducah & Atomic Energy Plant, McCracken Co.)

Site of first McCracken County seat half mile south. Established in 1827, three years after county was formed. Town site covered 102 acres, on which there were only eight buildings. First court held home of Isaac Lovelace; courthouse completed, 1830. Floods caused the removal of county seat to Paducah in 1832. The county records had to be moved to Paducah in a skiff.

971 SCIENCE HILL SCHOOL
(Shelbyville, at school, US 60, Washington & 6th Sts., Shelby Co.)

For 114 continuous years, an outstanding school for girls. Directed by the founder 54 years then by one family 60 years, it ranked among nation's foremost college preparatory schools.

Principals

Mrs. Julia A. Tevis	1825–1879
W. T. Poynter, D.D.	1879–1896
Mrs. W. T. Poynter, A.B.	1896–1937
Juliet J. Poynter, A.B.	1937–1939

972 COURTHOUSE BURNED
(Morehead, Courthouse lawn, US 60, Rowan Co.)

Twenty-two Kentucky courthouses were burned during Civil War, nineteen in last fifteen months: twelve by Confederates, eight by guerrillas, two by Union accident. Courthouse at Morehead burned by guerrillas March 21, 1864, the easternmost damaged incident to war. Building was again burned in 1880. County records before 1880 all destroyed by fires.

973 ISHAM BROWDER'S GRAVE
(3 mi. W. of Fulton, near KY 116, Fulton Co.)

Enlisted, 1776, at age 14 in 2nd Virginia Reg., Cont. line. Wounded at Monmouth, discharged, 1779. Came to Ky., 1795. With family settled on Pond River grant, now Hopkins Co. When county formed, appointed on first County Court. Also sheriff. 1807 tax roll listed 2,100 acres. Leader in pioneer Methodist Church. Came here, home of two sons, 1828. Bought Fulton Co. land. Died 1830. *Presented by Mrs. Fred B. Cloys, Union City, Tenn.*

974 FORT WILLIAM
(St. Matthews, Jct. US 60, 460 & Whipps Mill Rd., Jefferson Co.)

Established in 1785 by William Christian and his wife, Anne, a sister of Patrick Henry. On this site one of earliest stone houses in Kentucky was a famous tavern, The Eight Mile House, on Harrods Trace to Falls of the Ohio. From here, Col. Christian directed the defense of Jefferson County. Killed by Indians, 1786. Buried on Middle Fork of Beargrass. Over.
(Reverse)

COL. WILLIAM CHRISTIAN

Pioneer leader, prominent in the development of Virginia, Kentucky. Born Virginia, 1743. Officer in French and Indian War, in Dunmore's War, the Revolution and defense of the frontier. He brought his family to Kentucky, 1785. Developed Bullitt Lick Saltworks, Kentucky's first industry. Trustee of Transylvania Seminary. County Lieut. Christian County named for him, 1796. Over.

975 ARGILLITE FURNACE
(Argillite, 7 mi. S. of Greenup, KY 1, Greenup Co.)

First of 97 iron furnaces in the Hanging Rock Iron Region of Ky. and Ohio, one of earliest in Ky. Built by John and David Trimble and Richard Deering in 1818. Stone stack was 25 feet high. Air blast machinery was water-driven. Charcoal fueled. Daily capacity two tons of iron, cast as utensils or shipped by river in pigs. Last blast in 1837. See other side.
(Reverse)

IRON MADE IN KENTUCKY

A major producer since 1791, Ky. ranked 3rd in US in 1830s, 11th in 1965. Charcoal timber, native ore, limestone supplied material for numerous furnaces making pig iron, utensils, munitions in the Hanging Rock, Red River, Between Rivers, Rolling Fork, Green River Regions. Old charcoal furnace era ended by depletion of ore and timber and the growth of railroads. See over.

976 BUFFALO FURNACE
(Entrance to Greenbo Lake Park, KY 1, Greenup Co.)

A major producer of iron in the Hanging Rock Region 1851–75, an important Union Army supplier in the Civil War. Built by H. Hollister and Ross. Stone stack originally was 36½ feet high, with a steam powered air blast. Employing about 150 men, it could produce 15 tons in 24 hours. Pig iron was shipped by steamboat on Ohio River. See the other side.
(Reverse)
IRON MADE IN KENTUCKY
A major producer since 1791, Ky. ranked 3rd in US in 1830s, 11th in 1965. Charcoal timber, native ore, limestone supplied material for numerous furnaces making pig iron, utensils, munitions in the Hanging Rock, Red River, Between Rivers, Rolling Fork, Green River Regions. Old charcoal furnace era ended by depletion of ore and timber and the growth of railroads. See over.

977 MARINE WAYS
(1st & Ky. Sts., Paducah, McCracken Co.)

400 feet south is Paducah's oldest continuous industry. Incorporated by act of the legislature Jan. 24, 1854. First ways, completed March that year in eight sections, were capable of holding boats 350 feet in length. During the more than century that the company has been operating, Paducah has been one of the important boat-and-barge building and repair centers. *Presented by Marine Ways.*

978 VIRGIL MUNDAY CHAPMAN
(Middleton, KY 100, Simpson Co.)

U.S. Congressman and Senator for a quarter century, born here, 1895. Acclaimed as champion of Kentucky farmers; promoter of legislation to aid tobacco growers. Sponsored revision of food, drug, cosmetic laws. Attended Franklin schools and

University of Kentucky. Practiced law, 1918–25; Congressman, 1925–29; 1931–49; Senator, 1949 until his death, 1951. Interred Paris, Ky.

979 BURNSIDE
(Burnside, US 27, Pulaski Co.)

First named Point Isabel. Settled about 1800 by pioneers from the Carolinas and Virginia. During the Civil War the Union army, in 1863, set up a troop rendezvous and supply base here as a prelude to East Tennessee campaign of Gen. Ambrose E. Burnside. The area became known as Camp Burnside in official dispatches and the name Burnside was retained after war.

980 BURNSIDE
(Burnside Island State Park, US 27, Pulaski Co.)

First named Point Isabel. Settled about 1800 by pioneers from the Carolinas and Virginia. During the Civil War the Union army, in 1863, set up a troop rendezvous and supply base here as a prelude to East Tennessee campaign of Gen. Ambrose E. Burnside. The area became known as Camp Burnside in official dispatches and the name Burnside retained after war.

981 McFADIN'S STATION
(Bowling Green, Cumberland Trace Elementary School, Warren Co.)

The first in this area, 1785. On north bank of Barren River, built by Andrew McFadin (McFadden), one of 8 brothers from N.C., all of whom fought in Revolutionary War. Five of them later came to Ky., settled along Barren River. Andrew made first surveys of much of the land in this region. McFadin's was stopover for Robert Moore, who founded Bowling Green about 1796.
(Reverse)
CUMBERLAND TRACE
McFadin's Station stood near the Cumberland Trace, an important artery in the development of this region, used by many who settled this area. The route branched off from the Wilderness Road near Harrodsburg, came past present sites of Greensburg and Glasgow, crossed the Barren River here and continued on to the Cumberland settlements, now Nashville, Tenn.

982 SPORTSMAN'S HILL
(At William Whitley House, US 150, Lincoln Co.)

Site of one of earliest circular racetracks. Crowd gathered within the half-mile track, able to see entire race. Built about 1780 by Col. Wm. Whitley, owner of estate. A fervent patriot, he built track to contrast with the British ones, using clay instead of turf and running races counter-clockwise instead of clockwise. Racing here ended with the Civil War. Over.
(Reverse)

WHITLEY HOUSE—1785

Located on the Wilderness Road, it was the first brick house in Ky. Situated so that racetrack was visible from it. Meetings held in fall, bringing elite of region here. After races, which started at dawn, lavish breakfast was served. Whitley, born Va., 1749. Famed Indian fighter; killed, Battle of the Thames, Canada, 1813. Whitley County, Ky., named for him. Over.

983 OXMOOR—1790 →
(St. Matthews, S. side US 60, 460, E. of Watterson Overpass, Jefferson Co.)

Built by Alexander Scott Bullitt and his wife, Priscilla, daughter of William Christian. Located on the 1000-acre Ware tract, surveyed by John Floyd in 1774. Bullitt born, Va., 1762; came Ky., 1783. With George Nicholas drafted first Ky. constitution, 1791. President 1799 Constitutional Convention. First Ky. Lieut. Gov. Died in 1816. Bullitt County named for him, 1796.

984 STURGUS STATION →
(St. Matthews, S. side US 60, 460, E. of Watterson Overpass, Jefferson Co.)

Named for Peter A'Sturgus, early Kentucky pioneer, who settled on 2,000-acre tract of land surveyed, 1774, and granted to Col. William Christian by patent dated June 2, 1780. One of the five important pioneer stations on Middle Fork of Beargrass Creek shown on John Filson's 1784 map. In 1780 it was a considerable fort and settlement of some twenty to forty families.

985 AMERICAN HISTORIAN
(Paintsville, US 23 Bypass, Johnson Co.)

William Elsey Connelley, born on Middle Fork, Jennie's Creek, 1855. Wrote: *The Founding of Harman's Station, The Wiley Captivity, History of Kansas* and 13 other major works; collaborated with Coulter on *History of Kentucky,* edited by Kerr. Contributed to journals on ethnology, folklore of Wyandots; prepared only written vocabulary of their language. Died, 1930.

986 FT. THOMAS ARMY POST
(Ft. Thomas Post, Ft. Thomas, Campbell Co.)

Established by Congress, 1887. Constructed at cost of $3,500,000 on about 111 acres, jurisdiction of which was ceded to U.S. by Kentucky Legislature, 1888. Post was designated Ft. Thomas, 1890. First commander was Col. Melville Cochran; first garrison two 6th infantry companies. Later parts of 2, 3, 4, 9, 10th Infantry Regiments were here. Now V.A. Hosp.
(Reverse)

ROCK OF CHICKAMAUGA

Gen. George Henry Thomas for whom post was named. Born Va., 1816; West Point graduate. In Indian campaigns and Mexican War. In the Civil War, from Mill Springs, Ky., Jan. 1862, to Nashville, Tenn., Dec. 1864, he successfully led Federal forces in many principal engagements. Rated one of four top Union generals. Pacific Div. Commander at death, 1870. Over.

987 WARREN COUNTY
(Bowling Green, Courthouse lawn, US 31-W, 68, Warren Co.)

Established by Legislature, 1796, as the 24th county of Kentucky. Formed from part of Logan County. Parts of Barren, Allen, Edmonson, and Simpson counties later taken from original Warren boundaries. Named for Maj. Gen. Joseph Warren who died at Bunker Hill in 1775. Two earlier courthouses, the first log and second brick, 1812, were built in present Fountain Square.
(Reverse)

PORTAGE RAILROAD

Built 1832, by company organized by J. Rumsey Skiles, early Bowling Green industrialist, was one of earliest railroads in Ky. It ran from this site to Barren River, over a mile. Its iron tramcars were pulled by mules. In 1836 a depot on this site and an elevator and warehouse on river bank were built. L & N bought Portage R. R., 1855. Part of it still used. Over.

988 PRICE'S MEADOW
(10 mi. N. of Monticello, KY 90, Wayne Co.)

This tract of land was once the home of Cherokee Chief Chuqualatague (Doublehead), the last chieftain along the Cumberland River. Camp site in 1770 of the Long Hunters; in 1774 of Daniel Boone and Michael Stoner; from 1775 until after 1800 site of Benj. Price's Station, one of the few in Ky. to withstand Indian attacks, 1777. In 1784 part of grant to George Rogers Clark.

989 MONTICELLO
(Monticello, KY 90, 92, Wayne Co.)

Established as county seat when Wayne County formed, 1800. Named for home of Thomas Jefferson, who became third President of U.S. that year. Name was suggested by Col. Micah Taul, the first county clerk, later Congressman and Col. of Wayne County volunteers, War of 1812. Town laid off by surveyor Joshua Jones, Revolutionary War veteran. Land owned by Wm. Beard.

990 SAMUEL WOODFILL
(Samuel Woodfill School, Ft. Thomas, US 27, Campbell Co.)

"Outstanding soldier of the AEF," Gen. Pershing. "The first soldier of America," Marshall Foch. Given Congressional Medal of Honor, the French Croix de Guerre and Legion of Honor. Alone he destroyed three machine gun nests, killing 19 foe at Cunel, France, on Oct. 12, 1918. Born, Ind., 1883. Campbell County, Ky., farmer. Major, World War II. Interred Arlington Cemetery, 1951.

991 LONG RUN MASSACRE
(Eastwood, US 60, Jefferson Co.)

One mile south. Scene of massacre, undoubtedly the bloodiest in early Kentucky, which took place, 1781. A Miami Indian party killed over 60 pioneers en route from Squire Boone's Painted Stone Station to safety of forts at Falls of Ohio. Next day, reinforced by British Capt. McKee's Hurons, they killed 16 of 25 militia led by Col. John Floyd to bury massacre victims.

992 CHENOWETH MASSACRE
(Jct. US 60 & English Station Rd., Jefferson Co.)

One mile north. Scene of one of many Indian raids which plagued this area from time of earliest settlements to 1795. On July 17, 1789 Shawnees attacked the fort-springhouse built (1785) by one of Louisville's founders, Richard Chenoweth. Five were massacred—one, Bayless, burned at stake and Chenoweth's wife scalped; however, she survived and lived to age 80.

993 BOURBON IRON WORKS
(3 mi. S. of Owingsville, KY 36, 965, Bath Co.)

Jacob Myers from Richmond, Va. took up land grants here on Slate Creek, 1782. He built the first iron blast furnace in Ky., 1791. John Cockey Owings and Co. formed to operate furnace. Utensils and tools supplied settlers. Began to make cannon balls, grape shot for US Navy 1810. Furnished munitions for US victory, New Orleans 1815. First blast 1791, last 1838. Over.
(Reverse)
IRON MADE IN KENTUCKY
A major producer since 1791, Ky. ranked 3rd in US in 1830s, 11th in 1965. Charcoal timber, native ore, limestone supplied material for numerous furnaces making pig iron, utensils, munitions in the Hanging Rock, Red River, Between Rivers, Rolling Fork, Green River Regions. Old charcoal furnace era ended by depletion of ore and timber and the growth of railroads. See over.

994 DRUMMER BOY AT 7
(6 mi. S. of Golden Pond, off US 68, Trigg Co.)

Nathan Futrell, reputed to be the youngest drummer boy in War of the Revolution, was born, N.C., 1773. Joined N.C. Continental Militia. Married, 1798, came to Ky., 1799. Settled here on Ford's Creek, 1820, where he farmed, set out the first apple orchard, built one of area's first grist mills, was official surveyor. Died, 1829. He and his wife, Charity, buried on adjacent hill.

995 CAMPBELLSVILLE
(Campbellsville, Courthouse lawn, US 68, Taylor Co.)

First settled about 1800. Town, established by Legislature, 1817, was made seat of gov-

ernment when county was formed. It was named for Adam and Andrew Campbell who with three brothers came from Va., settling on father's land grants. Adam and Andrew among founders of town. Andrew died, 1819; Adam was prominent farmer and leader in Taylor County affairs. See over.
(Reverse)

TAYLOR COUNTY

Kentucky's 100th. Established by Legislature, 1848, formed from a part of Green County. Named for Gen. Zachary Taylor, famed Kentucky soldier. Noted as Indian fighter: Ft. Harrison, War of 1812; Black Hawk War, 1832; Florida Seminoles, 1837. Defeat of superior Mexican forces at Battle of Buena Vista, 1847, made him a national hero. Elected US President, 1848. Over.

996 CASTO-METCALFE DUEL
(Bracken Co. on Mason Co. line, KY 8, Bracken Co.)

On the Ohio River shore near here one of the last duels fought in Kentucky under the "code duello" took place on May 8, 1862, between William T. Casto, former Maysville mayor, and Col. Leonidas Metcalfe, U.S. Army, son of former Gov. Thomas Metcalfe. Colts rifles were used at 60 yards. On the first fire Casto was mortally wounded. Metcalfe was not hit. See over.
(Reverse)

CAUSE OF THE DUEL

The duel (see other side) climaxed a bitter Civil War episode. In Oct., 1861, Metcalfe was ordered to arrest 7 men, including Casto, for aiding the Confederates. They were sent north to Union prisons; all were later released, Casto in Feb., 1862. His belief that Col. Metcalfe was responsible for his arrest led Casto to challenge him to duel which ended his own life.

997 BOWLING GREEN
(Chestnut St. & Spring Alley, Main Place, US 31-W, 68, Warren Co.)

Founded in 1796 by Robert Moore who built cabin at the Big Spring located here. This spring water was nucleus around which the town grew. Moore, his brother, George, and James Stewart posted bond of 1,000 English pounds to establish town

in 1797. First courts met in Moore's home. Named "Bolin Green," 1798, traditionally because of bowling grounds located on site.

998 LAURA FURNACE
(6 mi. S. of Golden Pond, US 68, Trigg Co.)

Site of one of several furnaces operated in this region between the rivers, now lakes. This one, Laura, built 1855 by Tennesseans at cost of $40,000. Produced iron successfully, employing as many as 130, until Civil War forced it to close down. After the war it was in blast intermittently, but it could not be made profitable; was closed in 1872. See over.
(Reverse)

IRON MADE IN KENTUCKY

A major producer since 1791, Ky. ranked 3rd in US in 1830s, 11th in 1965. Charcoal timber, native ore, limestone supplied material for numerous furnaces making pig iron, utensils, munitions in the Hanging Rock, Red River, Between Rivers, Rolling Fork, Green River Regions. Old charcoal furnace era ended by depletion of ore and timber and the growth of railroads. See over.

999 TANNER'S STATION 1789
(Petersburg, Elem. Schoolyard, KY 20, Boone Co.)

First settlement in Boone County. The Rev. John Tanner built blockhouse, and town began on 2,000 acres he and John Taylor owned. Shawnees captured Tanner's 9-year-old son here, held him until grown. An ardent Baptist, Tanner preached in Carolinas, Virginia; came to Kentucky in 1781; moved to Missouri, 1798; died there, 1812, age about 80. Town was named Petersburg, 1818.

1000 SAVOYARD
(Savoyard, KY 314, Metcalfe Co.)

Birthplace of Eugene W. Newman, whose pen name was given to the town, formerly Chicken Bristle. A noted Washington columnist for several metropolitan newspapers and author of sketches about the Pennyrile of Kentucky. Known as great political writer, praised by contemporaries for understanding of people and versatility. Newman lived 1845–1923; buried Edmonton.

1001 ELLERSLIE
(Lexington, 2440 Richmond Rd., US 25, Fayette Co.)

The home which stood on this site from 1787 to 1947 was built by Levi Todd (1756–1807), who named it for his ancestral village in Scotland. He was one of a party of hunters who named Lexington in 1775; first Fayette County clerk; aide to George Rogers Clark, 1779, Kaskaskia Expedition; Maj., Battle Blue Licks; trustee, Transylvania; grandfather of Mary Todd Lincoln.

1002 JOSEPH A. ALTSHELER
(KY 218, Three Springs, Hart Co.)

Author, newspaperman. Wrote more than 40 books based on American history and designed especially for young people. A native of Three Springs, educated at Glasgow, Ky., and Vanderbilt Univ. On staff of the Louisville *Courier-Journal*, 1885–92; joined New York *World*, 1892, as editor of its tri-weekly edition. His books reached peak of popularity about 1918. Died, 1919.

1003 SHELTER FOR LINCOLNS
(S. of city limits of Hardinsburg, KY 261, Breckinridge Co.)

In the autumn of 1816 the family of Abraham Lincoln, then 7 years old, migrating to Indiana, rested and recuperated for about three weeks in a cabin that stood here. Local residents gave them food. Lincoln route in Kentucky started near Hodgenville and went through Elizabethtown, Vine Grove, Harned, here to Cloverport, river ferry. Lincolns traveled by ox-cart.

1004 FRONTIER JUSTICE
(N. of Dixon, US 41, Webster Co.)

Big Harp's head displayed here as warning to outlaws, about 1800. Mother and child murdered in cabin west of Dixon by Big (Micajah) and Little (Wiley) Harp, who were then pursued to Muhlenberg County where Big Harp was shot. His head was brought here, at that time a crossroad. Harps and wives roamed Kentucky in 1798–99 on crime spree. Little Harp was executed in Miss. later.

1005 SITE OF ROSE HILL ACADEMY, 1901–1918
(Rose Hill St., Versailles, US 62 West, Woodford Co.)

Whose headmaster was Professor Matt Gay Jesse, a superb educator and builder of character of his students. *Presented by his grateful alumni–1967.*

1006 JACKSON PURCHASE
(300 yds. S. of Irvin Cobb Bridge, Paducah, US 45, McCracken Co.)

8,500 square mile area, former tribal lands of Chickasaw Indians. United States paid $300,000 for tract in 1818 after negotiations by General Andrew Jackson and Governor Isaac Shelby. Bordered by Tennessee, Ohio and Mississippi Rivers, now comprises Kentucky's eight and Tennessee's twenty westernmost counties.

1007 FIRST BOY SCOUT TROOP
(Burnside, US 27, Pulaski Co.)

Before Boy Scouts of America was organized, 1910, a troop of 15 had been formed here, spring of 1908, by Mrs. Myra Greeno Bass. Using the official handbook of English scouting, she guided them hiking and camping, like scouting today. Known as Eagle Troop, Horace Smith was troop leader. Insignia was a red bandanna around neck. Reputed the first American Boy Scout Troop.

1008 STEAM FURNACE
(Wurtland, US 23 at KY 503, Greenup Co.)

Built by Shreve Brothers in 1824, stood 3¼ mi. south. First blast furnace in the Hanging Rock Iron Region to operate blowing engines by steam power rather than water. Charcoal-fueled, 28 ft. high, 8½ ft. across, produced 3 tons of iron in 24 hours, mostly cast at furnace into utensils. Abandoned after 1860. See other side. *Marker presented by Armco Steel Corp.*
(Reverse)

IRON MADE IN KENTUCKY

A major producer since 1791, Ky. ranked 3rd in US in 1830s, 11th in 1965. Charcoal timber, native ore, limestone supplied material for numerous furnaces making pig iron, utensils, munitions in the Hanging Rock, Red River, Between Rivers, Rolling Fork, Green River Regions. Old charcoal furnace era ended by depletion of ore and timber and the growth of railroads. See over.

1009 RACCOON FURNACE
(Greenup, US 23 at KY 2, Greenup Co.)

Built in 1833 by D. Trimble and J. T. Withrow, six miles south. Originally 35 ft. high with a maximum inner diameter of 10.5 ft. In 1873, this furnace produced 1467 tons of iron. It owned about 10,000 acres of land, mining its own ore and limestone, and making its own charcoal. Not operated after 1884. See other side. *Marker presented by Armco Steel Corp.*
(Reverse)
IRON MADE IN KENTUCKY

A major producer since 1791, Ky. ranked 3rd in US in 1830s, 11th in 1965. Charcoal timber, native ore, limestone supplied material for numerous furnaces making pig iron, utensils, munitions in the Hanging Rock, Red River, Between Rivers, Rolling Fork, Green River Regions. Old charcoal furnace era ended by depletion of ore and timber and the growth of railroads. See over.

1010 BUENA VISTA FURNACE
(KY 5 at KY 784, Boyd Co.)

Built by William Foster and Co. in 1847, 2¼ miles west, named for Mexican War battle that year. It was an important factor in the Hanging Rock iron industry until dismantled in 1876. Its 1874 iron production was 4113 tons. Stone stack was 40 feet high with a maximum inner diameter of 10 ft., and burned charcoal. See over. *Marker presented by Armco Steel Corp.*
(Reverse)
IRON MADE IN KENTUCKY

A major producer since 1791, Ky. ranked 3rd in US in 1830s, 11th in 1965. Charcoal timber, native ore, limestone supplied material for numerous furnaces making pig iron, utensils, munitions in the Hanging Rock, Red River, Between Rivers, Rolling Fork, Green River Regions. Old charcoal furnace era ended by depletion of ore and timber and the growth of railroads. See over.

1011 PINE GROVE FURNACE
(Near South Shore, Jct. KY 7 & 784, Greenup Co.)

Smallest blast furnace in Hanging Rock Iron Region, 17 feet high with a maximum inner diameter of six feet. Built 1881, six miles west, by Joseph Spriggs, who owned the land, and a sawmill operator named Sanders, whose steam engine drove the air blast. Produced only 26 tons of iron altogether. See other side. *Marker presented by Armco Steel Corp.*
(Reverse)
IRON MADE IN KENTUCKY

A major producer since 1791, Ky. ranked 3rd in US in 1830s, 11th in 1965. Charcoal timber, native ore, limestone supplied material for numerous furnaces making pig iron, utensils, munitions in the Hanging Rock, Red River, Between Rivers, Rolling Fork, Green River Regions. Old charcoal furnace era ended by depletion of ore and timber and the growth of railroads. See over.

1012 ASHLAND FURNACE
(Winchester Ave. at 6th St., Ashland, Boyd Co.)

When dismantled in 1962, world's oldest known operating blast furnace. Built in 1869 by Ashland Coal and Iron Railway Co., then 60 ft. high, 15 ft. diameter inside. Daily capacity 40 tons of iron, increased by rebuilding to 550 tons. Operated after 1921 by Armco Steel Corp. as Sixth Street Furnace. See other side. *Marker presented by Armco Steel Corp.*
(Reverse)
IRON MADE IN KENTUCKY

A major producer since 1791, Ky. ranked 3rd in US in 1830s, 11th in 1965. Charcoal timber, native ore, limestone supplied material for numerous furnaces making pig iron, utensils, munitions in the Hanging Rock, Red River, Between Rivers, Rolling Fork, Green River Regions. Old charcoal furnace era ended by depletion of ore and timber and the growth of railroads. See over.

1013 BOONE FURNACE
(KY 2 at KY 1773, Carter Co.)

A stone blast furnace 3.5 miles west, built by Sebastian Eifort and others in 1856. Its

last blast was in 1871. It produced 1400 tons of iron that year. It was originally 44 feet, 7 inches high, with a maximum diameter inside of 10.5 feet and a single tuyere, or pipe, for the steam-powered air blast. See over. *Marker presented by Armco Steel Corp.*
(Reverse)

IRON MADE IN KENTUCKY

A major producer since 1791, Ky. ranked 3rd in US in 1830s, 11th in 1965. Charcoal timber, native ore, limestone supplied material for numerous furnaces making pig iron, utensils, munitions in the Hanging Rock, Red River, Between Rivers, Rolling Fork, Green River Regions. Old charcoal furnace era ended by depletion of ore and timber and the growth of railroads. See over.

1014 IRON HILL FURNACE
(Iron Hill, KY 7, Carter Co.)

Later Charlotte, built in 1873 by Iron Hills Furnace and Mining Co. It has an iron shell stack 49 ft. high, with a maximum diameter inside of 12½ ft. Largest blast furnace intended to use charcoal fuel in the Hanging Rock Iron Region, it produced only 962 tons of iron for first owners. Ceased operating before 1884. See over. *Marker presented by Armco Steel Corp.*
(Reverse)

IRON MADE IN KENTUCKY

A major producer since 1791, Ky. ranked 3rd in US in 1830s, 11th in 1965. Charcoal timber, native ore, limestone supplied material for numerous furnaces making pig iron, utensils, munitions in the Hanging Rock, Red River, Between Rivers, Rolling Fork, Green River Regions. Old charcoal furnace era ended by depletion of ore and timber and the growth of railroads. See over.

1015 KENTON FURNACE
(Load, KY 7, Greenup Co.)

Built, 1856, by John Waring six miles west, and named for Simon Kenton, Ky. pioneer and Indian fighter. Originally 37 feet high and 10½ feet in maximum inside diameter, burning locally-made charcoal fuel. In 1874 it produced 3525 tons of iron. Operated until 1882. See other side. *Marker presented*

by Armco Steel Corp.
(Reverse)

IRON MADE IN KENTUCKY

A major producer since 1791, Ky. ranked 3rd in US in 1830s, 11th in 1965. Charcoal timber, native ore, limestone supplied material for numerous furnaces making pig iron, utensils, munitions in the Hanging Rock, Red River, Between Rivers, Rolling Fork, Green River Regions. Old charcoal furnace era ended by depletion of ore and timber and the growth of railroads. See over.

1016 PENNSYLVANIA FURNACE
(Argillite, KY 1 at Culp Creek Rd., Greenup Co.)

Stood 3¼ miles west. Built 1845 by George and Samuel Wurts, later owned by Eastern Kentucky R. R. which shipped its production to Ohio River. Operated until 1881, producing 2213 tons of iron in 1873. Its stone stack was 38 ft. high with a maximum diameter inside of 10¼ ft., using charcoal for fuel. See other side. *Marker presented by Armco Steel Corp.*
(Reverse)

IRON MADE IN KENTUCKY

A major producer since 1791, Ky. ranked 3rd in US in 1830s, 11th in 1965. Charcoal timber, native ore, limestone supplied material for numerous furnaces making pig iron, utensils, munitions in the Hanging Rock, Red River, Between Rivers, Rolling Fork, Green River Regions. Old charcoal furnace era ended by depletion of ore and timber and the growth of railroads. See over.

1017 HUNNEWELL FURNACE
(US 60 at KY 207, Carter Co.)

Originally Greenup Furnace five miles north. Built 1845 by John Campbell, John Peters and John Culbertson. As rebuilt in 1870, it was 47 ft. high, 12 ft. across inside. Its yearly capacity 6000 tons of iron, mainly carried to Ohio River in ox carts, later by E. K. Railroad, which bought furnace. Last blast 1885. See other side. *Marker presented by Armco Steel Corp.*
(Reverse)

IRON MADE IN KENTUCKY

A major producer since 1791, Ky. ranked

3rd in US in 1830s, 11th in 1965. Charcoal timber, native ore, limestone supplied material for numerous furnaces making pig iron, utensils, munitions in the Hanging Rock, Red River, Between Rivers, Rolling Fork, Green River Regions. Old charcoal furnace era ended by depletion of ore and timber and the growth of railroads. See over.

1018 STAR FURNACE
(2 mi. W. of Boyd Co. line, US 60, Carter Co.)

Built in 1848 by A. McCullough and Lampton Brothers. Its stone stack was 36 feet high, 11½ feet across inside at widest point, and burned "stone coal" rather than charcoal. It was served by its own railroad spur. In 1866 it produced 2600 tons of iron, 1958 tons in 1871. The last blast was in 1874. See other side. *Marker presented by Armco Steel Corp.*
(Reverse)
IRON MADE IN KENTUCKY
A major producer since 1791, Ky. ranked 3rd in US in 1830s, 11th in 1965. Charcoal timber, native ore, limestone supplied material for numerous furnaces making pig iron, utensils, munitions in the Hanging Rock, Red River, Between Rivers, Rolling Fork, Green River Regions. Old charcoal furnace era ended by depletion of ore and timber and the growth of railroads. See over.

1019 LAUREL FURNACE
(Oldtown, KY 1 & Laurel Creek Rd., Greenup Co.)

Built 4 miles west by George and Samuel Wurts in 1849. The bottom half of the stack, originally 39 feet high, is carved from one block of stone cliff. The maximum inner diameter is 10½ feet. It made 2150 tons of iron in 31 weeks of 1855, consuming 376,250 bushels of charcoal fuel. The last blast was in 1874. See other side. *Marker presented by Armco Steel Corp.*
(Reverse)
IRON MADE IN KENTUCKY
A major producer since 1791, Ky. ranked 3rd in US in 1830s, 11th in 1965. Charcoal timber, native ore, limestone supplied material for numerous furnaces making pig iron, utensils, munitions in the Hanging

Rock, Red River, Between Rivers, Rolling Fork, Green River Regions. Old charcoal furnace era ended by depletion of ore and timber and the growth of railroads. See over.

1020 BELLEFONTE FURNACE
(Greenup-Boyd Co. line, KY 5, Greenup Co.)

The most successful of pioneer Kentucky charcoal furnaces in the Hanging Rock Iron Region. Built by Archibald Paull, George Poague and others in 1826. Its stone stack was 34 feet high with a maximum inner diameter of 10½ ft. In 1874, a typical year, produced 3600 tons of iron. Operated until 1893, leaving an accumulated slag heap of 300,000 tons. See over.
(Reverse)
IRON MADE IN KENTUCKY
A major producer since 1791, Ky. ranked 3rd in US in 1830s, 11th in 1965. Charcoal timber, native ore, limestone supplied material for numerous furnaces making pig iron, utensils, munitions in the Hanging Rock, Red River, Between Rivers, Rolling Fork, Green River Regions. Old charcoal furnace era ended by depletion of ore and timber and the growth of railroads. See over.

1021 MILE STONE, CA. 1835
(Cox's Creek, US 31-E, 150, Nelson Co.)

Along the early turnpikes the law required mile posts. Some were cut from stone and some cast in iron. They showed the distance to each end of the turnpike. Typical of the stone markers are 14 along the east side of the present highway, at their approximate initial locations beside the old Bardstown-Louisville Turnpike. See over.
(Reverse)
AN EARLY TURNPIKE
The Bardstown-Louisville Turnpike Company, chartered by the Kentucky Legislature in 1831, was capitalized at $130,000, increased to $200,000. Shares owned half by individuals, half by state. Turnpike completed July 1, 1838, at cost of $203,598. Length of road 29 miles, width 60 feet cleared with 40 graded. Tolls collected during the year ended Oct. 1841: $9,755. See over.

1022 MILE STONES, CA. 1835
(Near Mt. Washington Baptist Church, US 31-E & 150, Bullitt Co.)

Along the early turnpikes the law required mile posts. Some were cut from stone and some cast in iron. They showed the distance to each end of the turnpike. Typical of the stone markers are 14 along the east side of the present highway, at their approximate initial locations beside the old Bardstown-Louisville Turnpike. See over.
(Reverse)

AN EARLY TURNPIKE
The Bardstown-Louisville Turnpike Company, chartered by the Kentucky Legislature in 1831, was capitalized at $130,000, increased to $200,000. Shares owned half by individuals, half by state. Turnpike completed July 1, 1838, at cost of $203,598. Length of road 29 miles, width 60 feet cleared with 40 graded. Tolls collected during the year ended Oct. 1841: $9,755. See over.

1023 NORTON FURNACE
(Winchester Ave. at 23rd St., Ashland, US 23, 60, Boyd Co.)

In 1967, the world's oldest known operating blast furnace. Built by Norton Iron Works Co. in 1873, an iron shell stack 67 ft. high with maximum inner diameter of 18 ft., burning "stone coal." It produced 10,502 tons of iron in 1874. Its 1884 capacity was 20,000 tons yearly. Operated after 1928 by Armco Steel Corp. See other side. *Marker presented by Armco Steel Corp.*
(Reverse)

IRON MADE IN KENTUCKY
A major producer since 1791, Ky. ranked 3rd in US in 1830s, 11th in 1965. Charcoal timber, native ore, limestone supplied material for numerous furnaces making pig iron, utensils, munitions in the Hanging Rock, Red River, Between Rivers, Rolling Fork, Green River Regions. Old charcoal furnace era ended by depletion of ore and timber and the growth of railroads. See over.

1024 CIVIL WAR OCCUPATIONS
(Fountain Square, Bowling Green, Warren Co.)

Threatened by Union forces to the west, CSA, who had occupied city five months and fortified hills, planned to evacuate Feb. 14, 1862. Other Federals came from north and bombarded from across the river. CSA set fire to depot and warehouses, as planned, night of 13th. Federals resumed bombardment next day, but ceased and entered city when informed CSA had gone.

1025 IRVIN S. COBB SAID:
(3rd & Broadway, Paducah, McCracken Co.)

"Here in Paducah one encounters, I claim, an agreeable blend of Western kindliness, and Northern enterprises, superimposed upon a Southern background. Here, I claim, more chickens are fried, more hot biscuits are eaten, more corn pone is consumed, and more genuine hospitality is offered than in any town of like size in the commonwealth."
(Reverse)

ALBEN W. BARKLEY SAID:
"Paducah is a town with a distinct flavor. It was—and is—a good place, an interesting place, in which to live. A great part of its personality is derived from such colorful citizens as Judge Bishop (the living prototype of Cobb's fictional Judge Priest), Irvin Cobb and others." *Marker presented by Shiva Artist Colors.*

1026 SAINT MARY'S COLLEGE
(Marion Adjustment Center, KY 84, Marion Co.)

Oldest extant Catholic College for men west of the Alleghenies and third oldest in the nation. Founded in 1821 by the Reverend William Byrene. Conducted by the Jesuit Fathers, 1833–1846, by the Holy Cross Fathers, 1846–1848, by the Diocesan Fathers, 1848–1869. Closed 1869–1871. Directed by the Resurrection Fathers since 1871.

1027 SECOND COURTHOUSE
(2nd & Ky., Paducah, McCracken Co.)

First courthouse at Wilmington, 1824–32. Second courthouse, a two-story brick structure, 36 feet square, built near here at a cost of $3,049, on land given by Gen. William Clark, founder of Paducah. Courthouse also provided meeting place for various early churches. Replaced after 25 years by third courthouse at 6th and Washington. *Marker presented by Harry Harris.*

1028 RESTORATION PROJECT
(Downtown Jeffersontown, KY 155, Jefferson Co.)

Cemetery of the German Reformed Presbyterian Church 1799–1909. A Community Service Project of the Rotary Club of Jeffersontown. Commenced 1964. Completed 1967. *Marker presented by Rotary Club of Jeffersontown.*

1029 BROADWAY METHODIST
(Broadway at 7th, Paducah, McCracken Co.)

Paducah's oldest institution. Founded 1832. First edifice erected 1842 on northwest corner Broadway at 4th. Relocated 1875 on southeast corner Broadway at 7th. Moved to present site 1896. Destroyed by fire 1929; rebuilt 1930. Judge Wm. Sutton Bishop, the "Old Judge Priest" of Irvin Cobb's stories, and Vice-Pres. Alben W. Barkley held membership here. *Presented by Louis Igert.*

1030 BARKLEY'S LAW OFFICE
(510 Broadway, Paducah, McCracken Co.)

Alben W. Barkley, Congressman, U.S. Senator, and Vice President, began practice of law here, 1901. He had read law for two years in offices of Rep. Charles K. Wheeler and Judge William Sutton Bishop, the "Old Judge Priest" of Irvin Cobb's stories. Barkley supplemented his income by acting as court reporter. *Presented by BPO Elks No. 217 Paducah, of which Mr. Barkley was a member.*

1031 COL. HICKS' HDQRS.
(Broadway, between 2nd & 3rd Sts., Paducah, McCracken Co.)

Here stood the headquarters of Colonel Stephen G. Hicks, commander of the USA occupation forces here during Battle of Paducah March 25, 1864. Next day Col. Hicks ordered sixty private homes that had been used by CSA forces as cover near the fort burned to the ground. Most owners filed suits but were never repaid for their homes. *Marker presented by William Clark Market House Museum.*

1032 CLARA BARTON'S VISIT
(2nd & Broadway, Paducah, McCracken Co.)

The organizer of the American Red Cross in 1881, Clara Barton, came to Paducah March 13, 1884, on the steamboat "Josh V. Throop" to help direct relief work during the Ohio River flood. Relief boats traveled from Pittsburgh to Cairo in first flood relief operation of the American Red Cross. *In memory of Charles and Anna Sullivan.*

1033 EASTERN STATE HOSPITAL
(Newtown Pike, Lexington, KY 922, Fayette Co.)

The second State Mental Hospital built in the U.S. Established by legislative act of Dec. 4, 1822, which named commissioners to buy and operate it in Fayette County. They acquired The Fayette Hospital organized in 1816. "The Lunatic Asylum" opened May 1, 1824. It has been continuously operated by the Commonwealth since. By 1913, it was named Eastern State Hospital.

1034 MOONLIGHT SCHOOLS
(Morehead, Wilkinson Blvd., US 60, Rowan Co.)

Established in Rowan County, Ky., in 1911, by Mrs. Cora W. Stewart, "to emancipate from illiteracy those enslaved in its bondage." Because the people had to labor by day it was decided to have the schools on moonlight nights so the moon could light the way. The schools were taught by volunteer teachers. Movement soon spread nationally and internationally.

1035 CHURCH OF CHRIST
(2855 Broadway, Paducah, McCracken Co.)

Organized in Paducah in 1906 from a six-week tent meeting. Oldest of Churches of Christ in area. Until one-room structure on Goebel Ave. was built in Aug., 1906, meetings held under tree. Second location, 19th and Broadway, dedicated 1924 and present building Aug., 1959. "Serving God and man in restoring New Testament Christianity." *Presented by Church.*

1036 $5 BOUGHT PADUCAH
(2nd & Broadway, Paducah, McCracken Co.)

In 1827, Gen. Wm. Clark purchased 37,000 acres of land, including the site on which Paducah now stands, for $5. This land, part of a Revolutionary War grant to his brother, George Rogers Clark, was secured from

Cora Wilson Stewart's "moonlight schools" inspired literacy programs throughout the nation. Kentucky Historical Society Collection.

George Woolfolk, of Louisville, who had been named administrator of George Rogers Clark's estate when he died. *Marker presented by Hart's Bread, 1967.*

1037 COL. ED MURRAY'S HOME
(6th & Ohio Sts., Paducah, McCracken Co.)

Site of home of Col. Ed Murray who built the *USS Merrimac*, 1855. Ship was taken by Confederates at Norfolk, April 20, 1861. Rebuilt as "ironclad," the CSS *Virginia.* On March 8, 1862, it sank two US ships off Hampton Roads, Va. Next day engaged in famous five-hour battle with USS *Monitor. Virginia* was burned May 10, 1862, to prevent capture by Union forces.

1038 JESSE HEAD HOMESITE
(Lincoln Park Road, Springfield, KY 528, Washington Co.)

On June 12, 1806 he performed the marriage of Thomas Lincoln and Nancy Hanks, who, in 1809, became the parents of Abraham Lincoln, 16th President of the U.S. Head, born in Maryland in 1768, "came-a-preaching" to Kentucky in 1798. Cabinet maker, justice of peace, on Sundays he preached fearlessly. Moved shop to Harrodsburg, 1810, kept on preaching, began newspaper.

1039 BELL'S TAVERN
(Park City, 2 blocks off US 31-W, Barren Co.)

Erected by Wm. Bell, 1830. Stage stop for his lines that brought visitors to Mammoth Cave when first promoted. Famed in U.S. and Europe for elite patrons, cuisine and magic peach and honey brandy for "Joy before the journey's end," until it burned 1860. Civil War doomed completion of new tavern begun by grandson, Wm. F. Bell, and his stepfather, George M. Proctor.

1040 ELMWOOD
(3 blocks S. of Courthouse, Lebanon Hill, Springfield, Washington Co.)

Built in 1851, by Wm. S. Davison, son of the town's first merchant. Typical Italianate style employed by Blue Grass architect Lewinski. Purchased by Hugh McElroy, 1858. In early Oct., 1862, Union forces moved through Springfield before Battle of Perryville. Gen. Buell made hdqrs. here. Forced owner's son to map water sources in area because of bad drought condition.

1041 PEACE PARK
(Hopkinsville, at park site, US 68 & 41, Christian Co.)

Bequest to city of Hopkinsville with funds for beautification and maintenance by John C. Latham of New York, a native of

Hopkinsville. A generous and forgiving gift. Mr. Latham was owner of a large tobacco warehouse on this site that was destroyed, when burned by Night Riders, disgruntled tobacco growers, Dec. 8, 1907. The next year death came to Mr. Latham.

1042 THE TRAIL OF TEARS
(E. 9th St. at Little River, Hopkinsville, US 41, Christian Co.)

A camping ground, Oct. 1838, for a part of the Cherokee Indians who were forcibly moved from their homes in the Smoky Mountain region of N. Car. and Tenn. to Indian Terr., now Okla. Badly clothed and fed, hundreds became ill and many died, among them the aged and highly respected chiefs, Fly Smith and Whitepath. Their graves on bank of Little River.

1043 GEN. LLOYD TILGHMAN
(Lang Park, Fountain Ave., Paducah, McCracken Co.)

Heroic statue of this Confederate erected in 1909 by his sons and United Daughters of Confederacy. Born in Maryland. Chief engineer, 1855–56, New Orleans and Jackson Railroad, first to enter Paducah. Joined Confederates July 5, 1861. Killed in battle near Vicksburg, Miss., on May 16, 1863. Sculptor was Henry H. Kitson of Boston, Mass. *Marker presented by Tilghman Class of 1929.*

1044 IMMANUEL BAPTIST
(3465 Buckner Lane, Paducah, McCracken Co.)

Organized in 1887, as mission of First Baptist Church. Constituted as the Second Baptist Church in January 1894, with twenty-two members. First building located 9th and Ohio. Moved to Murrell Boulevard in February 1922, and changed to present name. Building program started October 1958, on this location. Church dedicated November 6, 1966. *Presented by Church.*

1045 FIRST PRESBYTERIAN
(9th & Liberty Sts., Hopkinsville, US 41, 68, Christian Co.)

Organized in 1813, traditionally by the Reverend Gideon Blackburn, a pioneer minister and missionary to the Cherokee Indians. Present church building, not including later additions, was built during the period 1848–1852. Used as a hospital during severe epidemic that swept the camp of Confederates under Colonel Nathan Bedford Forrest through the winter of 1861–62.

1046 ELENORES
(510 North Walnut, Springfield, KY 53, Washington Co.)

Home of Elizabeth Madox Roberts, novelist, poet. Best known works, *Time of Man*, 1926, *Great Meadow*, 1930, both written here. The latter also published in England, Germany, Spain; made into successful movie. She wrote all of her novels, short stories and most poems, 1922–37. Born, Perryville, 1881. Family home here, 1904, Elenores added, 1928. Buried in Springfield Cemetery, 1941.

1047 CAPT. JOHN STRODE
(1 mi. W. of Winchester, US 60, Clark Co.)

Came from Va. to Boonesborough, 1776. Builder of Strode's Station, 1779, the largest and most important fortified area in Clark County during the early settlements and bloody Indian wars. Indians attacked station 1781, and later. Two men killed first attack, none in later ones. Old burial ground unearthed, 1965, and the remains reinterred in Winchester Cemetery.

1048 CAPTAIN JOHN HOLDER
(Athens-Boonesboro Rd., Howard's Creek, Clark Co.)

An outstanding pioneer at Fort Boonesborough, 1776–81. Among the rescuers of Callaway and Boone girls captured by Indians. Named colonel of militia, 1779. Engaged in expeditions against Indians. In 1781 built Holder's Station and operated boatyard at the mouth of Howard's Creek. Led in the Battle of Upper Blue Licks, 1782. Trustee of Winchester, justice Co. Court.

1049 BAKER HILL
(N. of Bowling Green, Old Louisville Rd., Warren Co.)

One of nine hills fortified by CSA making Bowling Green a strong Confederate defense center, 1861. Feb. 14, 1862, day after CSA left the area, USA forces in command of Gen. Ormsby Mitchell bombarded the town from here. It continued until a civilian bearing flag of truce advised Federals CSA had gone. Residence on hilltop used as hospital by USA to end of war.

1050 CLEAR CREEK FURNACE
(Salt Lick, US 60 at KY 211, Bath Co.)

Built in 1839, 5 miles south, by W. A. Lane and W. S. Allen. Stone stack originally 40 ft. high and 10½ ft. across inside, burning charcoal. Air blast powered by steam. Its iron was used mainly for railway car wheels. Operated until about 1857, then idle until rebuilt and renamed Bath Furnace 1872–73. In 1874 produced 1339 tons. Last blast 1875. See over.

(Reverse)

IRON MADE IN KENTUCKY

A major producer since 1791, Ky. ranked 3rd in US in 1830s, 11th in 1965. Charcoal timber, native ore, limestone supplied material for numerous furnaces making pig iron, utensils, munitions in the Hanging Rock, Red River, Between Rivers, Rolling Fork, Green River Regions. Old charcoal furnace era ended by depletion of ore and timber and the growth of railroads. See over.

1051 COLLEGE HILL
(Main & Park Sts., entrance to Reservoir Park, Warren Co.)

Now known as Reservoir Hill, one of nine key fortifications of CSA defense during 1861 Civil War occupation of Bowling Green. Felled trees with sharpened ends were placed as cavalry barriers. Stones from a college building under construction went into the fortifications. The Bowling Green system was manned by approximately 4,000 Confederates.

1052 FIRST LOG CABIN
(lst & Broadway, East side of flood wall, Paducah, McCracken Co.)

Here in April 1821, three years after the Jackson Purchase, the first home, a round-log cabin, was built by James and William Pore. Only a few Indians remained. James Davis, his wife, and three sons built a shelter soon after. In next five years a score or more settled along the Tennessee River. Town was first named Pekin. See over. *Marker by Greater Paducah Chamber of Commerce.*

(Reverse)

FIRST FRAME HOUSE

Was built by Albert Hayes in 1826 a few feet south of here. It had three rooms, was "quite attractive in those days" and bore the name "Fox House." Tradition is that Gen. William Clark stayed here when he platted town, May 26, 1827, and changed its name, Pekin, to Paducah, in honor of Chief Paduke. Over. *Marker by Greater Paducah Chamber of Commerce.*

1053 THE 1937 FLOOD
(29th & Jefferson, Paducah, McCracken Co.)

The Ohio Valley Flood of 1937 was the greatest natural disaster in the history of the U.S. and drove over one million citizens from their homes. This location marks the water's western edge in Paducah at the height of the flood, February 2, 1937. Over 90% of the city was inundated, 27,000 people were evacuated and damage exceeded $22,000,000. Over.

(Reverse)

THE 1937 FLOOD

The 1937 Flood could not happen again in Paducah because of the flood wall, the chain of TVA Dams, and other upstream reservoirs. In all, flood control has cost TVA almost $200,000,000. Paducah's $8,000,000 flood wall was built by the U.S. Corps of Engineers, is twelve miles long and protects the city to a height of three feet above the 1937 flood level. Over. *Presented by Gresham Hougland.*

1054 RED RIVER IRON WORKS
(8 mi. NE of Ravenna, KY 52, Estill Co.)

Blackstone and Chandler Furnaces, a single stone structure 60 ft. high, 40 x 60 ft. Twin stacks 50 ft. high, 12½ ft. across inside. Three miles north. Built in 1869 by Sam Worthley, designed by Fred Fitch, with steam-powered air blast, burning charcoal. Operated until 1874, producing 16,072 tons of iron. Fitchburg, chartered in 1871, no longer exists. See over.

(Reverse)

IRON MADE IN KENTUCKY

A major producer since 1791, Ky. ranked 3rd in US in 1830s, 11th in 1965. Charcoal timber, native ore, limestone supplied material for numerous furnaces making pig iron, utensils, munitions in the Hanging

Rock, Red River, Between Rivers, Rolling Fork, Green River Regions. Old charcoal furnace era ended by depletion of ore and timber and the growth of railroads. See over.

1055 ESTILL STEAM FURNACE
(5 mi. NE of Ravenna, Jct. KY 52 & 213, Estill Co.)

Six miles north. A stone stack, built, 1830, by Thomas Deye Owings, a leader in the once thriving Red River iron industry. Originally 34 ft. high, 10 ft. across inside with a steam-powered air blast, burning charcoal. Produced 1967 tons of iron in 1872. Last blast in 1874. Pig iron was made into finished products at Clay City forge and rolling mill. See over.
(Reverse)
IRON MADE IN KENTUCKY
A major producer since 1791, Ky. ranked 3rd in US in 1830s, 11th in 1965. Charcoal timber, native ore, limestone supplied material for numerous furnaces making pig iron, utensils, munitions in the Hanging Rock, Red River, Between Rivers, Rolling Fork, Green River Regions. Old charcoal furnace era ended by depletion of ore and timber and the growth of railroads. See over.

1056 COTTAGE FURNACE
(5 mi. NE of Ravenna, Jct. KY 52 & 213, Estill Co.)

Built, 1856, operated until 1873, when 1950 tons of iron were made. Six miles north. A stone stack, originally 38 ft. high, maximum inner diameter 10½ ft. Fuel was charcoal. Steam-driven air blast. Iron was made into bars, nails and other products at Clay City forge and rolling mill, or cast into utensils at furnace for sale here and in Bluegrass. See over.
(Reverse)
IRON MADE IN KENTUCKY
A major producer since 1791, Ky. ranked 3rd in US in 1830s, 11th in 1965. Charcoal timber, native ore, limestone supplied material for numerous furnaces making pig iron, utensils, munitions in the Hanging Rock, Red River, Between Rivers, Rolling Fork, Green River Regions. Old charcoal furnace era ended by depletion of ore and timber and the growth of railroads. See over.

1057 DR. REUBEN SAUNDERS
(Broadway near 3rd, Paducah, McCracken Co.)

On this site stood the office of Reuben Saunders, M.D., credited with discovering that hypodermic use of morphine-atropine halted cholera during epidemic here in 1873. Telegraphed prescription to other plague-stricken areas. Accepted by Materia Medica, world over. Honored by American Medical Association and in Europe. See other side. *Marker presented by the McCracken County Medical Society.*
(Reverse)
DR. REUBEN SAUNDERS
Born in Frankfort, Kentucky, September 6, 1808. Outstanding pioneer physician in Western Kentucky for fifty years. Discovered treatment for cholera. First to advocate fresh air for pneumonia and tuberculosis. First President, West Ky. Medical Association. Grandfather of Irvin S. Cobb. Died in Paducah, Dec. 13, 1891. See other side. *Marker presented by McCracken County Medical Society.*

1058 TEMPLE ISRAEL
(28th & Monroe, Paducah, McCracken Co.)

An organized Jewish community has existed in Paducah since 1864, when Paducah Chevra Yeshurun Burial Society was chartered. The first Jewish house of worship in Paducah was established in 1871, located on the east side of South Fifth between Clark and Adams. In 1873, the Paducah Jewish congregation became charter member, Union of American Hebrew Congregations. See over.
(Reverse)
TEMPLE ISRAEL
In 1893 a new structure was built on the southeast corner of Seventh and Broadway and incorporated as Temple Israel. That temple served as home for the congregation until May, 1963 when Temple Israel on southeast corner of Madison and Joe Clifton Drive was dedicated. Temple Israel Cem. is located on Lone Oak Highway. See over. *Presented by Temple.*

1059 HON. HENRY STANBERY
(2126 N. Ft. Thomas Ave., Ft. Thomas, US 27, Campbell Co.)

Site of his home, 1857 to 1881. Attorney-

General of U.S., 1866–68. Resigned to become one of counsel for President Andrew Johnson in impeachment trial by U.S. Senate, 1868. Johnson reappointed him, but Senate refused to confirm. Resumed practice of law, Cincinnati, 1868. First Att. Gen. of Ohio, 1846–51. Member Ohio Const. Conv. of 1850. b. N.Y., 1803. Buried Cin., 1881.

1060 FLOYD'S STATION
(Breckinridge Ln. at Hillsboro Ave., Louisville, Jefferson Co.)

This pioneer fort, begun in 1779, one of five on Beargrass Creek, was situated 500 ft. west. Three were owned by Col. John Floyd who made his headquarters here. He served as first County Lieut. of Jefferson County, 1780 until killed by Indians, 1783. From these forts, of defense and refuge, war was carried on against the British and the Indians in Ohio.

1061 FIRST PRESBYTERIAN CHURCH
(7th & Jefferson, Paducah, McCracken Co.)

Organized October 29, 1842, at home of Judge James Campbell on Broadway, with eight charter members. Reverend A. W. Campbell served as first pastor. Met in homes and courthouse until 1848, when church was built near corner of Third and Kentucky. Moved to this location, 1888. Dedication of present building, Dec. 3, 1933. *Presented by James Rhodes.*

1062 GUNSMITH FERD HUMMEL
(4th St. near Broadway, Paducah, McCracken Co.)

Site of a one-story frame store, Hummel's Gunshop. He came here in 1861. Federal soldiers occupying Paducah in Civil War brought their firearms to him for repair. When the Confederates raided the city, March, 1864, they looted his shop, but he had secreted best arms in his home. Hummel, continuing as a gunsmith, was granted a patent on a breech-loading firearm in 1881.

1063 OLD UNION CHURCH
(7 mi. E. of Woodburn, US 31-W, KY 240, Warren Co.)

Legislative Act of 1795 gave right to 200 acres for each settler in Green River country. This brought many from Carolinas.

Among them were Baptists, two preachers, who constituted Union Church in 1795. John Hightower, first pastor, served until 1813. Meeting house shared with other denominations. Services through Civil War while most did not. The present building erected in 1866.

1065 HISTORIC RIVERFRONT
(Riverfront near Broadway, Paducah, McCracken Co.)

Here the Tenn. River flows into the Ohio. Owen's Island opposite Kentucky Ave. There in 1779 George Rogers Clark's small army landed to prepare for its defeat of the British in the Illinois country. In 1780 Col. John Donelson landed 30 boats with 30 families that had floated down river from east Tenn. After stopover went up Ohio and Cumberland, founded Nashville. Over. (Reverse)

HISTORIC RIVERFRONT

Here Captain Nicholas Roosevelt's *New Orleans* made port, 1811. First steamer to ply the rivers from Pittsburgh to New Orleans. In 1861 Union troops under Gen. U. S. Grant landed here to occupy Paducah for duration of the war. Clara Barton arrived, 1884, on the *Josh V. Throop* during American Red Cross' first major flood relief operation. See over. *Marker presented by Downtown Paducah Kiwanis Club.*

1067 COUNTY NAMED, 1818
(Williamsburg, Courthouse lawn, US 25-W, Whitley Co.)

For Colonel William Whitley, famous leader in over 17 Indian battles. By 1794 had driven Indians from S.E. Ky. Joined Ky. militia in War of 1812. Killed at Battle of the Thames, 1813. Whitley County formed from Knox. Williamsburg, seat of government, also named for Col. Whitley. First court held, 1818, in home of Samuel Cox, first citizen of Williamsburg.

1068 OLD PROVIDENCE CHURCH
(5 mi. S. Winchester-Richmond Rd., at Old Stone Rd., Clark Co.)

Daniel Boone attended; Squire, Jr., Samuel and Mary Boone baptized here. Church name changed, 1790, from Howard's Creek to Providence. William Bush, a member of Boone's second Kentucky expedition, built the present stone structure of native limestone. United Baptists formed here in 1801. Building was passed to Negro Baptists, 1870. Restored after slight fire damage, 1949.

1069 DEATH VALLEY SCOTTY
(S. of Cynthiana, US 27, Harrison Co.)

Native of Cynthiana. Walter E. Scott (Death Valley Scotty), gold prospector, whose fabulous tales of Death Valley, Calif., lost gold mines fooled investors. Stories supported by $3,000,000 castle in desert provided by millionaire of Chicago, who "got it all back in laughs." Old miner was found out in 1941 but had become a legend. Died in 1954, at age 81.

1070 UNCLE TOM'S CABIN
(4 mi. W. of Paint Lick, KY 52, Garrard Co.)

Harriet Beecher Stowe, author of *Uncle Tom's Cabin*, visited the Kennedy home–see other side–while gathering some of the material for her book. Legendary cabin of Uncle Tom was behind the mansion, which was torn down about 1926. The book inflamed anti-slavery sentiment throughout the North and deep resentment in the South, with its publication in 1851.
(Reverse)
GEN. THOMAS KENNEDY

One mile south to home site of No. Car. Rev. War veteran who came to Ky., 1780. Member first Ky. Const. Conv.; first Senate; Comm. which named Frankfort as capital. Appointed Brig. Gen. of Militia. Leader in forming Garrard County and its Representative for eight terms. At the time of his death, 1836, he owned a plantation of 7,000 acres and 200 slaves. Over.

1071 CEDAR HOUSE
(Bowling Green Rd., Russellville, US 68, 431, Logan Co.)

Site of the seat of justice for all Western Ky., 1793-1798. Logan Co. citizens erected two story, four room house of cedar logs, 1792, for first Logan Co. sheriff, Wesley Maulding. First court was held here, 1793. Also used as inn and tavern where members of court and visitors lodged. Then it was considered to be the most elegant house in the Green River country.

1072 ST. PAUL LUTHERAN CHURCH (MISSOURI SYNOD)
(2100 Kentucky Ave., Paducah, McCracken Co.)

Organized on Pentecost Sunday, May 24, 1868, by the Rev. B. Sickel. The Congregation was incorporated January 26, 1869. First church building on South Fourth Street dedicated Jan. 7, 1872. Present early English Gothic building was dedicated November 26, 1939. Over.
(Reverse)
ST. PAUL LUTHERAN CHURCH

First church building 416 South Fourth St. abandoned because of 1937 flood damage. Bricks and some lumber of old structure used in erecting present building. The 1500-pound bell, almost 6 ft. in diameter, was removed and placed in the tower of the new church where it continues to ring out its call for all to worship. Over. *Presented by Church.*

1073 JEFFERSON DAVIS' SALUTE TO KENTUCKY
(Fairview, on monument grounds, US 68, Todd Co.)

"Kentucky, my own, my native land. God grant that peace and plenty may ever run throughout your borders. God grant that your sons and daughters may ever rise to illustrate the fame of their dead fathers and that wherever the name of Kentucky is mentioned, every hand shall be lifted and every head bowed for all that is grand, all that is glorious, all that is virtuous, all that is honorable and manly." From address made here on his last visit to his birthplace in Nov. 1886. At that time he presented the site of the cabin in which he was born to the Bethel Baptist Church. He also presented a communion service, which is still kept in church. Marker erected in the 175th anniversary of the Commonwealth of Kentucky.

1074 ROBBERS' ROOST CAVE
(2½ mi. W. of Strunk, Jct. new US 27 & KY 1470, McCreary Co.)

Hideout of bandits, 1819-22, two miles west. They preyed on salt dealers returning to Beatty's salt mine along nearby trails. Legend is that Beatty, trying to outwit bandits, sent a young Harmon girl to the salt market, but she was kidnaped. Friendly Cherokee Chief Little Jake, son of Big Jake and Princess Cornblossom, rescued her and drove the outlaws out of area.

1075 PRINCESS CORNBLOSSOM
(Near Stearns, US 27, McCreary Co.)

Burial site of daughter of Chief Double-head. Legend is that as a young girl she accompanied her father at signing of Treaty of Sycamore Shoals, 1775, transferring Cherokees' land between Ohio and Cumberland rivers to Transylvania Society. As'Quaw tribe settled in region south of river. Protecting tribe's secret mine, she killed a renegade. Married Big Jake, trader.

1076 BENNETT'S MILL BRIDGE
(8 mi. S. of South Shore, KY 7, Greenup Co.)

One of Kentucky's longest wooden, one-span, covered bridges, length 195 feet. B. F. Bennett and his brother Pramley built the bridge in 1855 or 1856 to accommodate customers at their mill. It has withstood severe floods through the years. Original footings and frame are intact. The bridge was never painted and has weathered to its present rustic appearance.

1077 ROMANTIC 1825 TRAGEDY
(Bloomfield, at Cemetery, US 62, KY 44, Nelson Co.)

Jereboam Beauchamp and wife Anna buried here in same coffin at own request. To avenge her alleged seduction by Col. Solomon Sharp, Beauchamp murdered him at Sharp's Frankfort home, 1825. Beauchamp and Anna were held in Frankfort jail. She was released but joined her husband in his cell, refusing to be separated even by force. He was sentenced to hang. See over.
(Reverse)
ROMANTIC 1825 TRAGEDY
On execution day, they attempted suicide by stabbing themselves. Her wound was fatal, but he lived to be hanged that day, the first legal hanging in Ky., 1826. Col. Sharp's political prominence caused case to have widespread newspaper publicity. Edgar Allan Poe and many other authors wrote of the tragedy, inspired by Beauchamps' deep devotion and love. See over.

1078 CEDAR CREEK BAPTIST
(4 mi. W. of Bardstown, US 62, Nelson Co.)

One mile south, site of The First Cedar Creek Baptist Church, second Baptist church constituted in Ky., July 4, 1781, fifth anniversary of Declaration of Independence. Pioneer settlers of nearby Rogers Station, 1780, Col. James Rogers, first judge, Nelson Co., Atkinson Hill, Judge James Slaughter, and Mathew, William, Jonathan Rogers among founders of the church. Over.
(Reverse)
CEDAR CREEK BAPTIST
First pastor, 1781, was Reverend Joseph Barnett, assisted by John Garrard. They were followed in about 1785 by Joshua Morris, who served the church many years. First structure was a log cabin replaced by brick when Peter Able and Saml. Ross, trustees, secured two and one-half acres from John Troutman in 1856. Additions to brick building, 1949, 1962. Over.

1079 HOME OF THOMAS CLAY
(2 mi. from Jct. US 60 on KY 405, Daviess Co.)

Revolutionary War Captain. Member, from Madison Co., 1792 and 1799, Ky. Constitutional Conventions; Ky. House of Rep., 1792–93, and 1796–98; Ky. Senate, 1793–95. Came here in 1812. Cousin of John Clay, father of renowned Ky. statesman Henry Clay, and uncle of Cassius Marcellus Clay, famed Kentuckian of Civil War period. Grandfather of U.S. Senator T. C. McCreery.

1080 IRON IN GREEN COUNTY
(N. of Brush Creek, KY 61, Green Co.)

Three iron furnaces built along Brush Creek after iron ore was found in 1815. Jacob Holderman and Charles Wilkins built furnace and forge in 1816, 10 miles downstream. Joseph Harrison erected furnace, 1819, downstream 7 miles. Forge produced household wares, tools. 2 miles from here, Green Springs Furnace built, 1832. All operated until late 1830s. See other side.
(Reverse)
IRON MADE IN KENTUCKY
A major producer since 1791, Ky. ranked 3rd in US in 1830s, 11th in 1965. Charcoal

timber, native ore, limestone supplied material for numerous furnaces making pig iron, utensils, munitions in the Hanging Rock, Red River, Between Rivers, Rolling Fork, Green River Regions. Old charcoal furnace era ended by depletion of ore and timber and the growth of railroads. See over.

1081 GEORGE MASON
(E. of Owensboro at Green River Steel Mill, US 60, Daviess Co.)

About 60,000 acres along Panther Creek and Green River owned by George Mason, author of Virginia Bill of Rights and Constitution, 1776. Designed Virginia State Seal. Member Continental Congress, 1777, and United States Constitutional Convention. A Virginian, friend and neighbor of George Washington. Died, 1792, without visiting Kentucky. Grandson George W. Mason lived near here.

1082 UNIQUE FATHER AND SON
(Greensburg, US 68 opposite "Old Courthouse," Green Co.)

Reuben Creel, Greensburg native, appointed by Lincoln as consul from U.S. to Chihuahua, Mexico, 1863. Served until 1866. His son Enrique C., in turn, served as ambassador from Mexico to U.S., 1907–09. Reuben went to Mexico with Gen. Ward, Greensburg native, serving as his interpreter during Mexican War. Remained after the war. Early home stands here. See over.
(Reverse)
UNIQUE FATHER AND SON
Enrique Creel born in Mexico, 1854. Wealthy banker. Member Mexican National Congress, 1898–1904. Was ambassador to U.S., 1907–09. Governor of Chihuahua. Served as official interpreter at meeting of Pres. Taft and Mexican Pres. Diaz in 1912. Minister of Foreign Affairs until Revolution of 1913, when his property was confiscated. Fled to United States. Died in Mexico, 1931. Over.

1083 MERCER COUNTY BEFORE KENTUCKY BECAME A STATE
(Harrodsburg, Courthouse lawn, Chiles St., Mercer Co.)
(Left panel of marker)
HARRODSBURG

1774–Laid off as Harrodstown by James Harrod and companions. First permanent English settlement west of the Allegheny Mountains.

1776–Virginia Legislature formed Kentucky County, the area now Commonwealth of Kentucky; named Harrodsburg seat of government.

1777–First Court held in the area.

1780–Virginia Legislature divided Kentucky County into Lincoln, Fayette and Jefferson Counties with Harrodsburg seat of Lincoln County government.

1785–Virginia Legislature formed Mercer County out of Lincoln, the area shown on map, which was the same when Kentucky became a state in 1792. Harrodsburg was continued as the county seat.

(Center panel—Map)

(Right panel of marker)
Here was the center of organization that held the Northwest against outside attack. George Rogers Clark planned campaign of 1778. Hdqrs. of Col. John Bowman, military commander of Kentucky County, 1775 to 1780. Stations shown on map were defense against Indians.

Mercer County FIRSTS in Kentucky
1774 Kentucky's first settlement. James Harmon's corn crop.
1775 Rev. John Lythe's services. Dr. George Hart, physician.
1776 Mrs. Jane Coomes' school. William Poage's plow and loom. Ann McGinty's linsey-woolsey. Wheat sown, reaped
1777 John Cowan's census.
1782 Capt. McMurtry's grist mill.
1783 Horse racing. Humble's "Race Paths"; Jail; Road to Squire Boone's Station "viewed" and opened.

1084 STONY CASTLE
(Near Berry, KY 1054, Harrison Co.)

Here was first post office between Lexington and Covington. Built by Postmaster John Smith in 1807 on land granted by Patrick Henry, Governor of Commonwealth of Virginia. Home withstood Civil War and was commandeered by CSA raider John Hunt Morgan for his wounded and weary troops. Postal room located in large closet in front parlor, right of main entranceway.

1085 A KENTUCKY GOVERNOR
(5 mi. E. of Albany, KY 90, Clinton Co.)

Birthsite of Preston H. Leslie. Lived here, 1819–1835. Admitted to bar, 1840. Moved to Monroe Co., 1841. Kentucky Representative, 1844–1851. State Senator, 1851–1855, 1867–1871. Chosen Speaker, 1869. Succeeded Governor Stevenson, Feb., 1871. Elected governor, August, 1871. Montana Territorial Governor, 1887–1889. Died, 1907, and buried in Montana. Leslie Co., Ky., was named for him.

1086 AIRDRIE FURNACE SITE
(Drakesboro, US 431, Muhlenberg Co.)

East five miles. Furnace, 55 ft. high, and stone machinery house built by Robert Alexander, 1855. Brought in Scottish workers, unfamiliar with American ores. Never produced any salable iron. Alexander named town of Airdrie for his Scottish home. Incorporated, 1858. Union General Don Carlos Buell lived there, 1866–98. His plan for industrial city at Airdrie never materialized. Over.
(Reverse)
IRON MADE IN KENTUCKY
A major producer since 1791, Ky. ranked 3rd in US in 1830s, 11th in 1965. Charcoal timber, native ore, limestone supplied material for numerous furnaces making pig iron, utensils, munitions in the Hanging Rock, Red River, Between Rivers, Rolling Fork, Green River Regions. Old charcoal furnace era ended by depletion of ore and timber and the growth of railroads. See over.

1087 MIDWAY JUNIOR COLLEGE—PINKERTON HIGH SCHOOL
(Midway, entrance to college, US 62, Woodford Co.)

Operated by Kentucky Female Orphan School since 1944. Orphan school was founded by James Parrish and Dr. Lewis L. Pinkerton. It was the first female orphan school in the United States. Chartered by 1846 Kentucky Legislature. Opened in 1849 with 14 students present, and for over a century has provided for deserving young women.

1088 MAJ. BLAND W. BALLARD
(US 60 at Cross Keys Rd., Shelby Co.)

Hunter, Indian fighter and scout for George Rogers Clark in Wabash expeditions. Born in Va., 1761. With Wayne at Fallen Timbers. Wounded at River Raisin. Survived Long Run, Tick Creek Massacres, Floyd's Fork Ambush. State Legislator. Died in 1853 in Shelby County, buried in the State Cemetery at Frankfort.
(Reverse)
TICK CREEK MASSACRE
Near Tyler Station, three miles north, Bland Ballard, his wife, and three children were massacred at Ballard's cabin on Tick Creek in October 1788. His son, Major Bland W. Ballard, killed six Indians, and survived attack. Two other children survived. Tyler Station was established in 1781 by Ballard and Robert Tyler. It was abandoned shortly after the massacre.

1089 THE BLOCKHOUSE
(5th and Main Sts., Shelbyville, US 60, Shelby Co.)

Built in 1858 by townspeople for civil defense against guerrillas. Located in middle of intersection. Measured 12 by 18 feet with loopholes on all sides. Manned by townsmen when alarm sounded. Several encounters with gangs attempting to raid town. Torn down in 1870 when civil law and order were assured, and marauders had been dispersed.
(Reverse)
MARTIN'S RAID
In August 1864 Captain David (Black Dave) Martin and gang attempted raid on courthouse to secure guns stored there. Thomas C. McGrath, merchant, J. H. Masonheimer, tailor, and others defended town against raiders. Three guerrillas were killed, and McGrath wounded. Mission failed. Martin died in 1896 and was buried in Grove Hill Cemetery.

1090 GRACE EPISCOPAL
(820 Broadway, Paducah, McCracken Co.)

Grace Church was organized in 1848 in

the home of Adam Rankin, led by the Rev. N. N. Cowgill of Hickman. The first structure, built of lumber cut in Louisville and floated downstream, was located on riverfront near Market Street. Consecrated on April 21, 1851. During Civil War property was confiscated by U.S. government and church was used as hospital.
(Reverse)

GRACE EPISCOPAL

Cornerstone for present Gothic edifice, one of Paducah's oldest landmarks, was laid on April 26, 1873 under rectorship of the Rev. W. M. Pettis who envisioned a building large enough to serve a growing city. Dedication and first service held June 21, 1874. Restoration of property after ravages of 1937 flood was led by the Rev. Custis Fletcher, rector. *Presented by Church.*

1091 "UNCLE" CHARLIE MORAN

(Centre College Campus, Danville, US 127, 150, Boyle Co.)

Colorful college football coach and National Baseball League umpire. Coached Praying Colonels of Centre College into national football spotlight, 1916–23. See other side. First coached, 1898–99, at Bethel College, Russellville, Ky. Then held four other coaching positions before going to Texas A. and M., where he coached, 1908–13, and at Carlisle Indian School, 1914–15. After seven years at Centre, then went to Bucknell Univ., 1923–25; Catawba College, 1929–39. National League umpire, 1917–39. Officiated at four baseball World Series–1927, 29, 33, 38. Born in Nashville, Tennessee, 1879. University of Tenn., 1897. Resident of Horse Cave. Died, 1949. Interred Horse Cave Cemetery.
(Reverse)

COACH MORAN'S BANNER FOOTBALL RECORD AT CENTRE

Centre	Opponent	Centre	Opponent
1919		1920	
95 Hanover	0	66 Morris Harvey	0

Centre	Opponent	Centre	Opponent
1919		1920	
12 Indiana	3	120 Howard	0
57 St. Xavier	0	55 Transylvania	0
69 Transylvania	0	14 Harvard	31
46 Virginia	7	0 Georgia Tech	24

14 W. Virginia	6	34 DePauw	0
56 Kentucky	0	49 Kentucky	0
56 DePauw	0	28 VPI	0
77 Georgetown	7	103 Georgetown	0
		77 Tex. Christian	7

1921 National Champions

14	Clemson	0
14	VPI	0
28	St. Xavier	6
98	Transylvania	0
6	Harvard	0
55	Kentucky	0
21	Auburn	0
25	Wash. and Lee	0
21	Tulane	0
38	Arizona	0
	Post season	
14	Texas A and M	22

1922			1923		
72	Carson-Newman	0	14	Carson-Newman	0
21	Clemson	0	28	Clemson	7
55	Mississippi	0	29	Oglethorpe	0
10	VPI	6	0	Pennsylvania	24
10	Harvard	24	10	Kentucky	0
32	Louisville	7	20	Sewanee	6
27	Kentucky	3	17	Auburn	0
27	Wash. and Lee	6	19	Wash. and Lee	0
0	Auburn	6	3	Georgia	3
42	S. Carolina	0			

1092 THE ROBERT E. LEE WON WITH STURGIS COAL

(Sturgis, US 60, Union Co.)

Nearby coal fields supplied fuel to power steamboat *Robert E. Lee* in race against the *Natchez*, 1870. Greatest race in river history began in New Orleans and ended at St. Louis. *Robert E. Lee* won the championship of Mississippi River by 6 hours and 15 minutes. Both steamboat captains were natives of Kentucky.

1093 MONROE COUNTY—TOMPKINSVILLE

(Tompkinsville, Courthouse lawn, KY 63, 100, Monroe Co.)

The only county of the 2,957 in the United States named for a President where the county seat is named for the contemporary Vice-President. County formed in 1820; named for James Monroe the fifth President, author of the Monroe Doctrine. The county seat named for Daniel Tompkins.

The steamboat Robert E. Lee *won the "greatest race in river history," 1870. Kentucky Historical Society Collection.*

Two terms for each covered 1817–25.

1094 SCOTT'S BLOCKHOUSE
(Carrollton, Point Park, US 42, Carroll Co.)

Blockhouse built here, 1789, by General Charles Scott for protection of settlers against Indians who had massacred and driven off earlier families. Scott came from Virginia, 1785. He was in the French and Indian Wars. Organized first company south of James River in the Revolution. Indian fighter, in Battle of Fallen Timbers, 1794. Gov. of Kentucky, 1808–12.

1095 SAINT CATHARINE
(3 mi. W. of Springfield, US 150, Washington Co.)

Cradle and Mother House of the Dominican Sisters in U.S. First settlement at St. Rose Farm, 1822. Known as St. Magdalen Academy from 1823 to 1851. Renamed, 1851, St. Catharine of Sienna. Mother Angela Sansburgy, O.P., and Reverend S. T. Wilson, O.P., co-founders. Former buried in Columbus, Ohio. Latter in St. Rose. The Academy was chartered, 1839. College in 1931.

1096 HODGENVILLE
(Hodgenville, KY 61, Larue Co.)

Established in Feb., 1818, by order of Hardin County Court on 27 acres and owned by Robt. Hodgen, tavern keeper and native of Pa. He erected a gristmill on Nolin River, 1789, within protection of Phillips Fort. Hodgenville had its first Post Office in 1826. It was incorporated in 1839 and in 1843, when Larue County was formed, became the seat of government.

1097 CENTERVILLE
(US 641 at Caldwell County line, Crittenden Co.)

County seat, 1804, of the original Livingston County. A Presbyterian Church was started, 1797, by the Rev. Terah Templin. County seat moved to Salem, 1809. U.S. Army used earlier buildings as supply depot on the "Trail of Tears," Cherokee relocation, 1834 to '38. By Civil War days little remained of the town. Landmarks today are only the foundations and earth depressions.

1098 PHILLIPS FORT
(Hodgenville, Jct. KY 210 and Phillips Ln., Larue Co.)

A half mile east on North Fork of Nolin

River is site of this fort, first settlement in Larue County, built in 1780 by Philip Phillips, surveyor, and company of settlers from Pennsylvania. Used as place of refuge from Indians, it was abandoned and removed about 1786, when it became safe for settlers to build homes. Nearby lie many pioneers in unmarked graves.

1099 PETTICOAT ABOLITIONIST
(Jct. US 421 & KY 1255, Trimble Co.)

"Underground railroad" station, a mile west, run by Delia Webster on land bought with funds provided by Northern abolitionists, 1854. Slaveholders filed charges against her. After refusing to leave Ky., she was imprisoned. Following her release she was indicted again but escaped into Indiana. For similar activities in Lexington she had served term in penitentiary, 1844.

1100 ST. JOSEPH'S PARISH
(Triangle at Golden Pond, US 68, Trigg Co.)

Settlement of German immigrants founded the first Catholic Church in the county, 1882, a mission of the Louisville diocese. Prussian agriculture, architecture, and traditions flourished under their influence. Due to migration the parish declined about 1900, and the church was razed in 1925. Now the parish cemetery is all that remains of the European colony.

1101 EDGEWOOD
(5th St. at site of home, Bardstown, US 31-E, 150, Nelson Co.)

Right wing built, 1815, main part, 1819, by Ben Hardin, noted lawyer, statesman, member Kentucky Legislature and U.S. Congress. Hardin born in Penn., 1784; his daughter married John L. Helm, twice Ky. Governor and President L&N R.R. Their son Ben Hardin Helm, CSA Gen., born here, 1831, married Emilie Todd, sister of Mary Todd Lincoln, wife of 16th U.S. President. See over.
(Reverse)

EDGEWOOD

General Leonidas Polk used this as headquarters during Confederate occupation of Bardstown. Barbecues here in the 1840's brought Henry Clay, Judge John Rowan and John J. Crittenden as speakers. Other notable visitors included Cassius M. Clay, Gen. William Preston, Felix Grundy, Jesse Bledsoe. In rear of place is site of famous Rowan-Chambers 1801 duel. See over.

1102 FEDERAL HILL—MY OLD KENTUCKY HOME
(Entrance to Park, Bardstown, US 150, Nelson Co.)

Inspiration for the state song of Kentucky by Stephen Collins Foster in 1853. Judge John Rowan, cousin, owned and had built back wing in 1795 and the front in 1818. Federal Hill became renowned as a center of legal, political and social activity. In Senate Rowan led amending US judicial system and ending imprisonment for debt.

1103 ARMY OF SIX
(Arch & Spring Sts., Madisonville, Hopkins Co.)

Union troops, 300, ordered to burn the CSA Madisonville sympathizers' homes, 1862; withdrew, bluffed by CSA Gen. Adam Johnson and six men. CSA went on to Henderson, crossed river to Newburg, taking medical supplies, arms and rations for the Confederates. Johnson and his Breckinridge Guards became famous for daring raids until he was blinded in battle, 1864.

1104 MADISONVILLE
(Madisonville, Jct. KY 70 & US 41, Hopkins Co.)

Named for former President James Madison. One year after Hopkins County established, Madisonville made county seat, 1807, on 40 acres given by Daniel McGary and Solomon Silkwood. Incorporated in 1810. Home of Maurice K. Gordon, who gave The American Legion its name when founded at Paris, France, in March, 1919, and later led in its organization in Kentucky.

1105 LINN BOYD HOME—1853
(1726 Broadway, Paducah, McCracken Co.)

Home of Linn Boyd, 1800–59, stood 500 ft. south. Served in Kentucky Legislature, U.S. Congress, wrote resolution to annex Texas. House Speaker, 1851–55. Proposed for Vice President by Kentucky delegates at Democratic Convention, 1856, which chose Breckinridge of Ky. Elected Lt. Governor, 1859, but died before taking office. Boyd County, Kentucky, is named for him.

1106 St. Francis de Sales
(530 Broadway, Paducah, McCracken Co.)

St. Francis de Sales Catholic Church is the oldest church in Paducah located on original site. Property purchased May 8, 1848, for $225 by Father Elisha Durbin. First church built 1849 and was enclosed with a fence as livestock roamed at large at the time. First pastor was Rev. William Oberhulsman, 1850–54. Second church built in 1870 by Rev. Ivo Schacht, 1869–71.
(Reverse)

St. Francis de Sales

Rev. Herman W. Jansen, pastor from 1882–1909, built present church at cost of $30,000. Cornerstone laid June 5, 1899. Rev. Henry Connolly was pastor 1909–1927. Reverend John D. Fallon served 1927–38. Reverend Albert J. Thompson 1938–57. Rev. Charles DeNardi 1957–63. Rev. Robert T. Wilson named pastor 1963. Members of six generations under eighteen pastors have worshiped here. *Presented by Henry Puryear.*

1107 American Red Cross
(300 Broadway, Paducah, McCracken Co.)

McCracken County Chapter chartered May 14, 1917. Organized by Mrs. A. R. Meyers, with W. F. Paxton as first chairman. Initial WWI fund drive raised $42,000. During great Ohio Valley Flood of 1937 carried on an amazing evacuation and relief program. World War II fund campaigns raised $164,530. Serving McCracken County for over fifty years. *Marker in memory of Mr. and Mrs. D. E. Wilson, Sr.*
(Reverse)

Red Cross Serves McCracken County

Flood	1929	$	3,021
Drought	1929–31	$	12,851
Flood	1936	$	812
Flood	1937	$	1,189,141
Tornado	1938	$	2,061
Flood	1939	$	751
Fire	1939	$	979
Flood	1945	$	865
Flood	1950	$	7,281
Flood	1963	$	4,590

Presented by Tom Wilson

1108 The Flood Wall
(1st & Broadway next to Flood Wall, Paducah, McCracken Co.)

Paducah's $8,000,000 flood wall was built by the U.S. Corps of Engineers, is twelve miles long and protects the city to a height three feet above the 1937 flood level. The Flood of 1937 could not recur again in Paducah because of the flood wall, TVA's dams, and other upstream reservoirs. In all, flood control has cost TVA almost $200,000,000. Over.
(Reverse)

The 1937 Flood

The Ohio Valley Flood of 1937 was the greatest natural disaster in the history of the U.S. and drove over one million citizens from their homes. When the Ohio River reached its crest in Paducah on Feb. 2, 1937, the water stood at 60.8 feet. Over 90 per cent of the city was inundated, 27,000 people were evacuated, and damage exceeded $22,000,000. Over.

1109 Creelsboro
(Creelsboro, KY 1313, Russell Co.)

Laid out, 1809, named for Elijah and Elza Creel, pioneers whose son, Reuben, served US in Mexico; his son Enrique served Mexico in US. An interpreter for General W. T. Ward during Mexican War, Reuben stayed on there, was appointed US Consul, 1863, by Pres. Lincoln. Enrique was Governor of Chihuahua State, 1903 to 1906, and Mexican Ambassador to US, 1906 to 1909.

1110 U.S. President, A Day
(Lansdowne Shopping Center, Tates Creek Rd., Lexington, Fayette Co.)

David R. Atchison born, 1807, in Frogtown, 2¼ miles S.W. Graduated, Transylvania Univ., 1825. Admitted to Ky. bar, 1829. Moved to Mo., 1830. U.S. Senator, 1843–55. As Pres. pro tem he became President of U.S., noon Sun., Mar. 4, 1849, end of Polk's term, until Taylor's inauguration, Mon., Mar. 5. He was an organizer of the Atchison, Topeka and Santa Fe Railroad. Died, 1886.

1111 Paducah's Indian Name
(415 Broadway, Paducah, McCracken Co.)

Paducah, only major Kentucky city with an Indian name, was named in honor of legendary Indian Chief Paduke by Gen. William Clark when he platted town in 1827. Village was first named Pekin. The Paducahs, Chief Paduke's sub-tribe of Chickasaw Indians, had lived and hunted in this area until land was taken by Jackson Purchase in 1818. Presented in Memory of Lee Anna Rhodes. *Presented by James Rhodes.*

1112 BARKLEY'S GRAVE
(Entrance to Mt. Kenton Cem., Paducah, McCracken Co.)

Alben W. Barkley, "The Veep," was Senate majority leader under President Franklin D. Roosevelt, and Vice-President under President Harry S. Truman. He died on April 30, 1956, while addressing a mock Democratic Convention at Washington and Lee Univ. His last words were: "I would rather be a servant in the house of the Lord than sit in the seats of the mighty."
(Reverse)

ALBEN W. BARKLEY

Alben W. Barkley, Vice President of United States, 1949–53. Member U.S. Senate, 1927–49 and 1955–56; Senate Democratic leader 13 years; House of Representatives 1913–27. Born in Lowes, Ky., 1877. Came to Paducah 1898. Elected to first public office as McCracken County Attorney, 1905. County Judge, 1909. Buried in Mt. Kenton Cemetery, in 1956. Loved and honored by nation. *Presented by McCracken County Fiscal Court.*

1113 NELSON FURNACE
(E. of Nelsonville, KY 52, Nelson Co.)

Organized by William and Mordecai Miller and John Irwin in 1836. The blast furnace had two forty-foot pyramidal stone stacks with six-foot hearths. Output of iron in 1857 was 12 tons daily. The Civil War boom in iron brought the merger with Belmont Furnace, Bullitt County, in 1865. After nine years, Nelson and Belmont furnace closed down, 1874. Over.
(Reverse)

IRON MADE IN KENTUCKY

A major producer since 1791, Ky. ranked 3rd in US in 1830s, 11th in 1965. Charcoal timber, native ore, limestone supplied material for numerous furnaces making pig iron, utensils, munitions in the Hanging Rock, Red River, Between Rivers, Rolling Fork, Green River Regions. Old charcoal furnace era ended by depletion of ore and timber and the growth of railroads. See over.

1114 FIRST BAPTISM IN KY.
(S. of South Fork Baptist Church, Hodgenville, US 31-E, Larue Co.)

Seven persons baptized in Nolin Creek, 1782, first in Ky., by Rev. Benjamin Lynn who founded South Fork Church, the second church in Ky. Originally at Phillips Fort, 13 members. Moved to South Fork of Nolin, where church was constituted and cemetery located. Church has assumed style of United, Separate, Regular and Missionary Baptists. Later split by slavery.
(Reverse)

INDIAN FIGHTER GRAVE

John Walters came to Phillips Fort in 1780–81. Commissioned Lt., 2nd Regiment of Ky. Militia by Governor Isaac Shelby in 1792. In local skirmishes, 1794 Battle of Brown's Run under Col. Patrick Brown, War of 1812. Was born April 4, 1770, Beacon Town, Pa., in valley of Monongahela. Died April 17, 1852, at home 2½ miles south. Buried South Fork Cemetery, ½ mi. west.

1115 LARUE COUNTY
(Hodgenville, US 31-E, KY 61, Larue Co.)

Was established March 1, 1843 from part of Hardin County after debate over selection of name. An act to create Helm County honoring John LaRue Helm, then Speaker of the House, was amended by Senate to give the honor instead to Gabriel Slaughter. Compromise resulted in naming it Larue for those of that family who were among the early explorers and settlers of area.
(Reverse)

COUNTY OFFICIALS—1843

Joseph Abell, Abraham Miller, Thomas Brown, Lewis Reed, Squire LaRue, John McDougal, Marshall Scott and Jesse Rodman, Justices; Stephen Stone, Clerk; Jonathan F. Cessna, Sheriff; Wm. Elliott,

Isham R. Twyman, Jediah Ashcraft, John C. Nevitt and William B. Read, Constables; James Redman, Jailer; William Cessna, Representative. Court first met on March 25, 1843.

1116 ELIZABETHTOWN BATTLE
(Elizabethtown, at Cemetery, US 31-W, 62, Hardin Co.)

Confederate Gen. John Hunt Morgan on his second raid into Kentucky, with 3,900 men, was met by 652 Union troops under Lt. Col. H. S. Smith, Dec. 27, 1862. Object of raid was destruction of L&N R.R., main artery for USA troop movement south. Morgan surrounded town and placed artillery on the cemetery hill. Elizabethtown garrison was destroyed. Federals surrendered.

1117 MT. UNION CHURCH
(1 mi. N. of Jct. US 231 & KY 1332, Allen Co.)

Organized in 1864 under the name of Mulberry Hill General Baptist Church. In 1869 the original log building burned. The congregation rebuilt on present site, changed the name to Mt. Union. Thirteen churches were invited from Mt. Union to form Portland Association in 1921, making Mt. Union the mother church of two associations. *Marker presented by Bonner Memorial Fund.*
(Reverse)
M.J. BONNER
Burial site about 65 feet east of here; born on Dec. 17, 1825 and died Nov. 21, 1907. Rev. Bonner organized the Mt. Union General Baptist Church which stands on these grounds. He is known as the founder of 3 associations: the Mt. Union, Green River Union, New Harmony Assoc. of Gen. Baptists. *Marker presented by Bonner Memorial Fund.*

1118 DRIPPING SPRINGS
(6 mi. W. of Edmonton, US 68, KY 80, Metcalfe Co.)

Organized as Baptist "Sinks of Beaver Creek," 1789, at William Blakely home. Services continuous since first building about 1799, log cabin. In 1874, hand dressed yellow poplar structure replaced original. Present building erected in 1961. Name changed, but same organization continued. Over the years members have withdrawn to form other churches in the area.

1119 PIONEER EDUCATOR
(Hindman, KY 80, Knott Co.)

In 1889, George Clarke came to Hindman, licensed to practice law. Seeing the need of education, Clarke established a subscription school with the help of the students and citizens. Educator, State School Inspector, member State Board of Examiners. Died, 1940. His epitaph reads: "Let God be praised and let Eastern Kentucky rejoice that so great a man once graced its soil."

1120 BEAVER DAM FURNACE
(Scranton, KY 1274, Menifee Co.)

Erected in 1819 by J. T. Mason. It began operations under Robert Crockett, ironmaster. The furnace was a big truncated pyramid of sandstone blocks, 35 feet high with a 28 foot square base. Some products were nails, "plough plates," kettles, skillets, flat irons. The goods were "flat-boated" down river to the markets. The furnace went out of business, 1870–73.
(Reverse)
IRON MADE IN KENTUCKY
A major producer since 1791, Ky. ranked 3rd in US in 1830s, 11th in 1965. Charcoal timber, native ore, limestone supplied material for numerous furnaces making pig iron, utensils, munitions in the Hanging Rock, Red River, Between Rivers, Rolling Fork, Green River Regions. Old charcoal furnace era ended by depletion of ore and timber and the growth of railroads. See over.

1121 McCALL'S SPRING
Formerly Cove or Lillard Spring. (½ mi. S. of Bluegrass Pky., US 127, Anderson Co.)

The McAfee brothers, James McCoun, Jr., and Samuel Adams, first white men to explore this area, 1773. Cove Spring and Cove Spring Branch in Franklin County boundary line, 1794. Maj. Gen. E. Kirby Smith, CSA, and troops camped here on their way to join General Bragg Oct. 9, 1862. Only known time Spring's supply was exhausted.

1122 HEBRON CHURCH
(½ mi. S. of Bluegrass Pky., US 127, Anderson Co.)

A Cumberland Presbyterian Church organized by Rev. Laban Jones in 1827 in log cabin on Thomas McCall farm, overlooking McCall Spring. The itinerant pastor traveled his circuit on horseback visiting his "preaching places twice a year." This church was built in 1844 on the old family burying ground. Interments prior to 1816. *Presented by Emery Frazier and Frank Routt.*

1123 COUNTY NAMED
(Calhoun, Courthouse lawn, KY 81, McLean Co.)

For Judge Alney McLean, lawyer and politician. Established in 1854, from parts of Daviess, Ohio, and Muhlenberg counties. Solomon Rhoads and James Inman settled in 1788. First county officers were: Sanders Eaves, judge; Alfred Tanner, clerk; Henry Griffith, sheriff; Frank McLean, county attorney; Jacob Davis, surveyor; James Hinton, jailer. See over.
(Reverse)

CALHOUN
Named for John Calhoun, circuit judge, Congressman, 1835 to 1839. Formed in 1784 as Rhoadsville, it became known as Fort Vienna, 1785, when Solomon Rhoads built a fort here. Boyhood home of the builder and master of "My Old Kentucky Home," Senator John Rowan, Esq. Calhoun incorporated, 1852. Made county seat, 1854. Called "Capital of Green River Country." See over.

1124 BIG HILL SKIRMISH
(N. of US 421, near Jct. of Madison, Jackson & Rockcastle Counties, Madison Co.)

Aug. 23, 1862, 650 cavalry of Gen. E. Kirby Smith's invading CSA army routed small Federal force under Col. Leonidas Metcalfe here on way to seize Ky., cooperating with CSA army under Gen. Braxton Bragg. Central Ky. captured, but plans to take Cincinnati and Louisville failed. CSA retired from Kentucky after Battle of Perryville, October 8, 1862.

1125 COUNTY NAMED, 1843
(½ mi. N. of Paintsville, near high school, US 23, Johnson Co.)

For Richard M. Johnson, native of Kentucky, US Vice-President, 1837 to 1841, US Rep. 1807–19, 1829–37, US Senator 1819–29, intimate of President Jackson. His tactics as Colonel of Ky. Mounted Riflemen, War of 1812, won Battle of the Thames and earned him title: "Father of American Cavalry." Johnson was formed from parts of Lawrence, Floyd and Morgan counties.

1126 PAINTSVILLE
(Paintsville bypass, Jct. Jefferson Ave. & US 23, Johnson Co.)

The second oldest settlement in Eastern Kentucky, at first named Paint Lick Station. Established in 1790 by Col. John Preston. Dr. Thomas Walker probably camped at mouth of Paint Creek, near some abandoned log cabins, in 1750. Rev. Henry Dixon laid out town and built first house in 1826. Paintsville incorporated in 1872, but city government much older.

1127 HOBSON HOUSE
(1100 West Main St., Bowling Green, US 31-W, 68, Warren Co.)

Located at the west end of Main St. Home of Col. Atwood G. Hobson, lawyer, banker and Union officer, begun 1860. During the Confederate occupation of Bowling Green, 1862, CSA Gen. Simon B. Buckner saved house at request of his friend, USA General W. E. Hobson, son of owner. Used as munitions depot. After the war, Col. Hobson made that his home until death, 1898.

1128 CAPT. JOHN SIMPSON
(Simpsonville, US 60, Shelby Co.)

Simpsonville and Simpson County, Kentucky, were named for the Captain who fought with Wayne at Fallen Timbers, practiced law in Shelbyville, and was elected to the State Legislature four times. Elected to Congress in 1812. He and another Shelby Countian, Colonel John Allen, raised a company of riflemen in the War of 1812. Both killed at Battle of River Raisin.

1129 THE ARMSTRONG HOTEL
(6th & Main Sts., Shelbyville, US 60, Shelby Co.)

Established in 1859 by George A. Armstrong and was known for its good food and lodgings. Guerrilla leader Ed Terrell stopped here briefly, May 26, 1866.

Attempting to escape, he was mortally wounded nearby. Brig. Gen. Henry H. Denhardt was slain here, Sept. 20, 1937. When the hotel was destroyed by fire on February 7, 1944, the owners decided not to rebuild.

1130 NEW HAMPSHIRE FURNACE
(N. of Lynn, KY 7 at Brushy Creek Rd., Greenup Co.)

Built 6 mi. west in 1846 on a tract of 30,000 acres by Samuel Seaton and others. Stone stack is 35 ft. high, 10 ft. across inside. Charcoal-fueled, steam-powered air blast. In 22 weeks of 1854, produced 970 tons of iron, hauled in pigs by oxcarts to the Ohio River. It was probably not operated after 1854. See over. *Marker presented by Armco Steel Corp.*
(Reverse)

IRON MADE IN KENTUCKY

A major producer since 1791, Ky. ranked 3rd in US in 1830s, 11th in 1965. Charcoal timber, native ore, limestone supplied material for numerous furnaces making pig iron, utensils, munitions in the Hanging Rock, Red River, Between Rivers, Rolling Fork, Green River Regions. Old charcoal furnace era ended by depletion of ore and timber and the growth of railroads. See over.

1131 SANDY FURNACE
(KY 3 at KY 773, Boyd Co.)

Built 1853 by Young, Foster & Co. (Dan and John Young, Wm. Foster, Irwin Gilruth), 4 mi. west on a 19,000 acre tract. Stone stack originally 32 ft. high, 10½ ft. across inside. In 1854, its last year of operation, made 1000 tons of iron, which had to be hauled by oxcart across country to Big Sandy River. See other side. *Marker presented by Armco Steel Corp.*
(Reverse)

IRON MADE IN KENTUCKY

A major producer since 1791, Ky. ranked 3rd in US in 1830s, 11th in 1965. Charcoal

Barker's 1795 map of Kentucky showing the area around Paint Lick. Kentucky Historical Society Collection.

timber, native ore, limestone supplied material for numerous furnaces making pig iron, utensils, munitions in the Hanging Rock, Red River, Between Rivers, Rolling Fork, Green River Regions. Old charcoal furnace era ended by depletion of ore and timber and the growth of railroads. See over.

1132 CAROLINE FURNACE
(4 mi. W. of Raceland city limits, US 23 at Caroline Furnace Rd., Greenup Co.)

Stood 1½ mi. south. Built 1833 by Henry Blake & Co. Stone stack was 35 ft. high, with a maximum inner diameter of 10 ft.; burned charcoal. Air blast powered by steam. In 1838, produced 750 tons of iron, consuming 2062 tons of ore, 225,000 bushels of charcoal. Made 1200 tons of iron,

1857. Furnace operated until 1890. See over. *Marker presented by Armco Steel Corp.* (Reverse)
IRON MADE IN KENTUCKY
A major producer since 1791, Ky. ranked 3rd in US in 1830s, 11th in 1965. Charcoal timber, native ore, limestone supplied material for numerous furnaces making pig iron, utensils, munitions in the Hanging Rock, Red River, Between Rivers, Rolling Fork, Green River Regions. Old charcoal furnace era ended by depletion of ore and timber and the growth of railroads. See over.

1133 CONFEDERATE CONGRESSIONAL MEDAL OF HONOUR
(Glasgow, Courthouse lawn, US 31-E, 68, Barren Co.)

The President (CSA), in 1862, was authorized to confer a Medal of Honour upon one enlisted man of each company for "every signal victory." At first dress-parade, thereafter, the men engaged in the battle chose, by vote, the soldier most worthy to receive this honour. More Confederates from Barren than any other Kentucky county received this medal. See over. (Reverse)
BARREN COUNTY CSA MEDALISTS
STONE'S RIVER
Dec. 31, 1862–Jan. 2, 1863
Enoch S. Jones
Corp., Co. D, 6th Ky. Inf.
James Beverly Lewis
1st Sgt., Co. C, 6th Ky. Inf.
Thomas W. Payne
Pvt., Co. E, 6th Ky. Inf.
George Walter Rogers
Corp., Co. A, 4th Ky. Inf.
CHICKAMAUGA
Sept. 19–20, 1863
Marcellus Smith Mathews
Pvt., Co. D, 6th Ky. Inf.
Bayard Taylor Smith
2nd Lt., Co. A, 4th Ky. Inf.
Ephraim R. Smith
Corp., Co. A, 4th Ky. Inf.

1134 HISTORIC RAILROAD
(1500 Ky. Ave., Paducah, McCracken Co.)

The Illinois Central is successor to Paducah's original railroad, the New Or-

leans and Ohio, which on July 4, 1854, ran its first train. The most prominent railroad landmark in Paducah is company's large shops, on a 110-acre site, begun in 1925, finished two years later. Since then Paducah Shop has been principal Illinois Central locomotive facility. See over. (Reverse)
ILLINOIS CENTRAL
Charles H. Markham was president of the railroad when he dedicated the new shop in 1927. His bust is on the shop grounds. The Illinois Central serves Paducah from all points of compass, including the great coal fields to the east. Its main north-south freight line, the Edgewood Cutoff, crosses the Ohio River over Metropolis Bridge a few miles downstream. See over. *Presented by Illinois Central R.R.*

1135 PRINCESS FURNACE
(Princess, KY 5, Boyd Co.)

Built here in 1876–77, by Thomas W. Means (1803–90), for 50 years the leading figure in the iron industry of this area, owner of furnaces in Ky., Ohio, Va., Ala. This iron-jacketed stack burned "stone coal" because Buena Vista Furnace nearby had used all the charcoal timber on 6000 acres. Last blast, 1878. See the other side. *Marker presented by Armco Steel Corp.* (Reverse)
IRON MADE IN KENTUCKY
A major producer since 1791, Ky. ranked 3rd in US in 1830s, 11th in 1965. Charcoal timber, native ore, limestone supplied material for numerous furnaces making pig iron, utensils, munitions in the Hanging Rock, Red River, Between Rivers, Rolling Fork, Green River Regions. Old charcoal furnace era ended by depletion of ore and timber and the growth of railroads. See over.

1136 BELMONT FURNACE
(Across from Belmont, KY 61, Bullitt Co.)

Stone stack 500 yds. east, 33 ft. high originally, 10 ft. across inside. Built in 1844, perhaps by John H. Baker, rebuilt in 1853, it burned charcoal fuel, smelted iron ore from Cane Run. The air blast machinery was powered by steam. In six months dur-

ing 1857, it produced 1140 tons of pig iron, shipped to Louisville, mainly for making nails. See other side.
(Reverse)

IRON MADE IN KENTUCKY

A major producer since 1791, Ky. ranked 3rd in US in 1830s, 11th in 1965. Charcoal timber, native ore, limestone supplied material for numerous furnaces making pig iron, utensils, munitions in the Hanging Rock, Red River, Between Rivers, Rolling Fork, Green River Regions. Old charcoal furnace era ended by depletion of ore and timber and the growth of railroads. See over.

1137 MAULDING'S FORT
(10 mi. S. of Russellville, KY 663, Logan Co.)

Site of stockade, built in 1780 on the Red River as protection against Indians. Named for the James Maulding family, immigrants from Virginia and leaders in Russellville's early development. Morton Maulding was the first representative of Logan County to Kentucky legislature, 1794. In 1782, Indians compelled a temporary abandonment of fort.

1138 COUNTY NAMED, 1792
(Russellville, Courthouse lawn, US 68, 431, Logan Co.)

For Gen. Benjamin Logan (1743–1802), pioneer and Indian fighter who called the Danville Assembly, 1784, leading to ten conventions preceding Kentucky's separation from Virginia, 1792. Logan served as a delegate in all ten, later in the legislature. Logan County was formed from part of Lincoln County, and organized immediately after Ky. admitted to the Union.

1139 COUNTY NAMED, 1801
(Columbia, Courthouse lawn, KY 61, 80, Adair Co.)

For Gen. John Adair, Governor of Kentucky 1820–24. Born, 1757, in South Carolina, came to Ky., 1788. Member of Kentucky Constitutional Convention, 1792. Served in Ky. House of Representatives, 1793–95, 1798, 1800–03, 1817. US Senator, 1805–06, Congressman, 1831–33. At Battle of Thames, 1813. Commanded Kentucky troops in Battle of New Orleans, 1815. Died, 1840.

1140 CLARK'S STATION
(SE of Danville, US 150 & KY 52, Boyle Co.)

Early pioneer settlement erected before 1779. Developed by George Clark, brother-in-law of William Whitley, whose party came to Ky. about 1775. Located on Clark's Run Creek, named for George Clark, it was one of the first stations built in the vicinity of the forts at Harrodsburg and Stanford. Clark raised a crop here as early as 1775, improved the site in 1776.

1141 KENTUCKY NOVELIST
(6.7 mi. E. of Paris, KY 627, Bourbon Co.)

Site of birthplace and early home of John Fox, Jr., famous Kentucky author, born 1862, graduated from Harvard in 1883. Died, 1919. His understanding of mountain life in Ky. and Va. revealed in 12 novels and 45 short stories, including *The Little Shepherd Of Kingdom Come*, among first books published in US to sell one million copies, and *Trail Of The Lonesome Pine*.

1142 AMANDA FURNACE
(Approx. 1 mi. W. of Boyd Co. line, US 23, Greenup Co.)

A stone stack 35 ft. high, 10 ft. across inside, built in 1829 by James E. McDowell, John Culver, John H., Edwin P., Robert C. and Wm. L. Poage; later owned by the Paull family, buried on hillside above. In 196 days of 1838 made 100 tons of iron. Produced 200 tons in 1854, its last year of operation. See other side. *Marker presented by Armco Steel Corp.*
(Reverse)

IRON MADE IN KENTUCKY

A major producer since 1791, Ky. ranked 3rd in US in 1830s, 11th in 1965. Charcoal timber, native ore, limestone supplied material for numerous furnaces making pig iron, utensils, munitions in the Hanging Rock, Red River, Between Rivers, Rolling Fork, Green River Regions. Old charcoal furnace era ended by depletion of ore and timber and the growth of railroads. See over.

1143 HOPEWELL FURNACE
(Hopewell, KY 1, Greenup Co.)

In 1824, William Ward built here a bloomery forge, converting it, 1832–33, to a blast

furnace, also known as Camp Branch Furnace. Air blast was waterpowered. In 1838, this stone stack made 600 tons of iron, consuming 1500 tons of ore, and burning 165,000 bushels of charcoal fuel. Operations ceased in 1844. See other side. *Marker presented by Armco Steel Corp.*
(Reverse)

IRON MADE IN KENTUCKY

A major producer since 1791, Ky. ranked 3rd in US in 1830s, 11th in 1965. Charcoal timber, native ore, limestone supplied material for numerous furnaces making pig iron, utensils, munitions in the Hanging Rock, Red River, Between Rivers, Rolling Fork, Green River Regions. Old charcoal furnace era ended by depletion of ore and timber and the growth of railroads. See over.

1144 COUNTY NAMED, 1798
(Hartford, Courthouse lawn, US 231, Ohio Co.)

For the Ohio River, originally its northern boundary. From this territory has been formed Butler, Grayson, Daviess, Hancock, McLean counties. Two settlements were Hartford Station, about 1785, and Barnett's Station, founded by Col. Joseph Barnett in 1790. The first Ohio County Court was organized, 1799. Christopher Greenup was its Circuit Judge, 1803. Elected Gov., 1804.

1145 COUNTY NAMED, 1858
(McKee, Courthouse lawn, US 421, Jackson Co.)

For Andrew Jackson, the 7th US President, 1829–37, first to be elected from west of Appalachians. First Representative in Congress from Tenn., 1796–97. In US Senate twice, 1797 and 1823. Victorious commander at New Orleans, 1815. County formed from small parts of Madison, Estill, Owsley, Clay, Laurel and Rockcastle, every adjoining county, except Lee.

1146 UNITY CHURCH—THE UNITED CHURCH OF CHRIST
(4600 Buckner Ln., Paducah, McCracken Co.)

Organized August, 1874 as "German Evangelical Unity Church" with the Rev. Daniel Eschenbrenner, first pastor. German services held in "Old School House Church"

on So. 3rd St. New church at 423 So. 5th St. dedicated August, 1894 and renamed Unity Evangelical Church. Services in English begun in 1905. Located here in June, 1961. Over.
(Reverse)

UNITY CHURCH—THE UNITED CHURCH OF CHRIST

Evangelical and Reformed Churches of German origin united in 1934. Both have heritage dating to the Reformation in 1517. Merger with Congregational-Christian, English origin, 1957. This merger first in our nation of denominations of different governing styles and of national backgrounds. See over. *Presented by Church.*

1147 ENTERPRISE FURNACE
(US 23 at KY 1215, Greenup Co.)

Stood 5 miles south. Built, 1826, by Richard Deering, James McCoy and Jacob Clingman, on the site of a bloomery forge erected in 1824. Its air blast was operated by water power, and it burned charcoal fuel, producing as much as 3 tons of iron daily, mostly cast into utensils. Not in blast after 1833. See other side. *Marker presented by Armco Steel Corp.*
(Reverse)

IRON MADE IN KENTUCKY

A major producer since 1791, Ky. ranked 3rd in US in 1830s, 11th in 1965. Charcoal timber, native ore, limestone supplied material for numerous furnaces making pig iron, utensils, munitions in the Hanging Rock, Red River, Between Rivers, Rolling Fork, Green River Regions. Old charcoal furnace era ended by depletion of ore and timber and the growth of railroads. See over.

1148 PACTOLUS FURNACE
(Pactolus, KY 1, Carter Co.)

Built in 1824 by Joseph McMurtry and David L. Ward, on the site of an earlier bloomery forge. Its stone stack used charcoal fuel, and its air blast machinery was powered from a dam, 5½ ft. high, in Little Sandy River. Capacity was about three tons of iron daily, mainly shipped via Ohio River. Last blast before 1835. See over. *Marker presented by Armco Steel Corp.*

(Reverse)
IRON MADE IN KENTUCKY
A major producer since 1791, Ky. ranked 3rd in US in 1830s, 11th in 1965. Charcoal timber, native ore, limestone supplied material for numerous furnaces making pig iron, utensils, munitions in the Hanging Rock, Red River, Between Rivers, Rolling Fork, Green River Regions. Old charcoal furnace era ended by depletion of ore and timber and the growth of railroads. See over.

1149 BELLEFONTE FURNACE
(US 23, just W. Boyd Co. line, Greenup Co.)
The 96th blast furnace built in Hanging Rock Region since 1818. Considered most highly perfected in existence when erected, 1942, by Armco Steel Corp., with hearth 25 ft. across, producing 1000 tons of iron daily, later increased to 2600 tons, with 28¾ ft. hearth. Named for pioneer charcoal-fueled furnace a mile south. See over. *Marker presented by Armco Steel Corp.*
(Reverse)
IRON MADE IN KENTUCKY
A major producer since 1791, Ky. ranked 3rd in US in 1830s, 11th in 1965. Charcoal timber, native ore, limestone supplied material for numerous furnaces making pig iron, utensils, munitions in the Hanging Rock, Red River, Between Rivers, Rolling Fork, Green River Regions. Old charcoal furnace era ended by depletion of ore and timber and the growth of railroads. See over.

1150 AMANDA FURNACE
(E. of Greenup Co. line, US 23, Boyd Co.)
When built, 1963, by Armco Steel Corp., rated as the ideal blast furnace, with a hearth diameter of 30½ ft., daily capacity of 3340 tons of iron. Set American record of 110,515 tons in March, 1966. Rebuilt, in 1968, to produce 4020 tons daily with 33½ ft. hearth. Named for pioneer furnace a mile west. See other side. *Marker presented by Armco Steel Corp.*
(Reverse)
IRON MADE IN KENTUCKY
A major producer since 1791, Ky. ranked 3rd in US in 1830s, 11th in 1965. Charcoal

timber, native ore, limestone supplied material for numerous furnaces making pig iron, utensils, munitions in the Hanging Rock, Red River, Between Rivers, Rolling Fork, Green River Regions. Old charcoal furnace era ended by depletion of ore and timber and the growth of railroads. See over.

1151 ST. PAUL'S CHURCH
(Newport, across from Courthouse, US 27 South, Campbell Co.)
For a century and a quarter, a St. Paul's Episcopal Church has stood on this corner. Since 1871, the bell in the towering spire atop this native stone church has rung for services. Here worshipped Gen. James Taylor, War of 1812; Henry Stanbery, who defended President Andrew Johnson at his impeachment trial, 1868; Brent Spence, 37 yrs. in Congress, a lifetime member.

1152 CARR CREEK CENTER
(9 mi. S. of Hindman, KY 160, Knott Co.)
Olive V. Marsh and Ruth E. Watson, from Mass., aided by the Daughters of the American Revolution, carved this center of learning out of a wooded hillside overlooking rustic "Singing Carr." When organized, September 1, 1920, it was dedicated to the education of mountain youth and is maintained by the contributions of many friends and the Knott Co. Board of Education.

1153 JOSHUA JONES
(Wayne Co. Public Library, S. Main St., Monticello, Wayne Co.)
Native of Pennsylvania. Appointed surveyor of public lands by Gov. Isaac Shelby. Came to Kentucky in 1794. Surveyed Monticello site in 1801. Owner of iron works in Virginia. Built bloomery on Elk and Beaver Creeks in 1800. He was granted 1,000 acres in 1801 by the Legislature to aid his iron works in Kentucky in manufacture of pig iron. Died here in 1816.

1154 AN EMINENT STATESMAN
(Main & Washington Sts., Frankfort, Franklin Co.)
John Jordan Crittenden, 1787–1863, lived here, 1819–1863. Legislator, 15th Kentucky Governor. Attorney General under three Presidents. Five times a U.S. Senator. Noted

for Crittenden Compromise, 1860, futile effort to avert Civil War and preserve the Union. His last words: "Let all the ends thou aimest at be thy country's, thy God's and truth's." See over.
(Reverse)
CRITTENDEN HOUSE
This building, before west portion was added, was the home of John J. Crittenden, 1819 until death, 1863. Built in 1800 by Dr. Joseph Scott on land once owned by Aaron Burr. In May, 1837, Daniel Webster and family visited here. In Feb. 1849, President-elect Zachary Taylor was guest here on way to inauguration. Carriage step is from the first Kentucky state capitol. Over.

1155 CLINTON FURNACE
(US 60 at KY 538, Boyd Co.)

Stood one mile east. Its stone stack was 10 ft. across inside, about 35 ft. high, built in 1832 by George, William, Thomas H., and Hugh A. Poage. In 270 days of 1838, it used 2992 tons of ore, 247,000 bushels of charcoal to make 950 tons of iron. In 1857, produced 1500 tons. Operations ceased before 1867. See over. *Marker presented by Armco Steel Corp.*
(Reverse)
IRON MADE IN KENTUCKY
A major producer since 1791, Ky. ranked 3rd in US in 1830s, 11th in 1965. Charcoal timber, native ore, limestone supplied material for numerous furnaces making pig iron, utensils, munitions in the Hanging Rock, Red River, Between Rivers, Rolling Fork, Green River Regions. Old charcoal furnace era ended by depletion of ore and timber and the growth of railroads. See over.

1156 GLOBE FURNACE
(At Bennett's Mill Bridge, KY 7 at KY 1215, Greenup Co.)

Stood just across this stream, which provided power for its air blast machinery. It was built by George W. Darlington and others in 1830. In 1838 it produced 600 tons of iron from 1800 tons of ore, burning 165,000 bushels of charcoal. Ceased operating before 1855; its stones used in bridge abutments here. See the other side. *Marker presented by Armco Steel Corp.*

(Reverse)
IRON MADE IN KENTUCKY
A major producer since 1791, Ky. ranked 3rd in US in 1830s, 11th in 1965. Charcoal timber, native ore, limestone supplied material for numerous furnaces making pig iron, utensils, munitions in the Hanging Rock, Red River, Between Rivers, Rolling Fork, Green River Regions. Old charcoal furnace era ended by depletion of ore and timber and the growth of railroads. See over.

1157 OAKLAND FURNACE
(US 23 at KY 538, Boyd Co.)

Stood 2 miles west. Built in 1834 by John C. and Jacob Kouns, it was a stone stack with air blast machinery powered by steam. It made 600 tons of iron in 1838, consuming 2100 tons of ore and 180,000 bushels of charcoal fuel. The iron was shipped in pigs by river boat. Furnace not operated after 1849. See other side. *Marker presented by Armco Steel Corp.*
(Reverse)
IRON MADE IN KENTUCKY
A major producer since 1791, Ky. ranked 3rd in US in 1830s, 11th in 1965. Charcoal timber, native ore, limestone supplied material for numerous furnaces making pig iron, utensils, munitions in the Hanging Rock, Red River, Between Rivers, Rolling Fork, Green River Regions. Old charcoal furnace era ended by depletion of ore and timber and the growth of railroads. See over.

1158 DAVIESS COUNTY
(N. of entrance to Daviess Co. H. S., US 231, Daviess Co.)

Formed in 1815 out of Ohio County. Named for Col. Joseph Hamilton Daveiss. As US attorney for Ky., he prosecuted Aaron Burr in 1806 for treason, in plotting to seize Spanish territory, a friendly nation; but he did not obtain a conviction. Joined army of Gen. William Henry Harrison. Killed at Battle of Tippecanoe, 1811, in a charge made at his own urging.

1159 COUNTY NAMED, 1820
(Cadiz, Courthouse lawn, US 68, Trigg Co.)

For Col. Stephen Trigg, Virginian. Came

to Ky. as member of Court of Land Commissioners, 1779. Settled Trigg's Station near Harrodsburg, 1780. In Va. Legislature was active in establishing town of Louisville, 1780. Justice of Peace, on first Lincoln Co. court, 1781. Trigg killed at Battle of Blue Licks, Aug. 19, 1782. Trigg County formed from Caldwell and Christian.

1160 COUNTY NAMED, 1842
(Marion, Courthouse lawn, US 60, 641, Crittenden Co.)

For John Jordan Crittenden, 1787–1863, one of Kentucky's great statesmen. 15th Governor of state. Attorney General under three Presidents. United States Senator five times. Noted for Crittenden Compromise, 1860, futile effort to avert Civil War and preserve the Union. Crittenden, the 91st county established in state, was formed out of eastern part of Livingston.

1161 RIDE ROUND THE RIVERS
(Riverfront near Flood Wall & Ky. Ave., Paducah, McCracken Co.)

This unique pleasure-boat tour is an eighty-mile loop from Paducah up the Tennessee, through Kentucky Lock, up Kentucky Lake, through the Land-Between-The-Lakes Canal, down Barkley Lake, through Barkley Lock, down the Cumberland to Smithland, and down the Ohio back to Paducah. West Kentucky has greatest concentration of major navigable rivers in world. Over.
(Reverse)

PADUCAH HARBOR
The deep protected water between Owens Island opposite and the Kentucky shore has been a major base for commercial navigation throughout Paducah's history. Every type of barge and boat used in the Mississippi Valley has been built, repaired, manned, and supplied here. It was a famous ice-free winter harbor for steamboats from the northern rivers. *Presented by Crounse Corp.*

1162 SALT RIVER FURNACE
(Beech Grove Rd. & KY 61, Bardstown Junction, Bullitt Co.)

Stood one mile west. It was a stone stack 33 ft. high with a maximum inner diameter of 10 ft. Its fuel was charcoal, and its air blast machinery was driven by a steam engine, blowing preheated air through the stack. Built in 1832, perhaps by John H. Baker, it produced 700 to 800 tons of iron and castings annually until operations ended, 1853. See over.
(Reverse)

IRON MADE IN KENTUCKY
A major producer since 1791, Ky. ranked 3rd in US in 1830s, 11th in 1965. Charcoal timber, native ore, limestone supplied material for numerous furnaces making pig iron, utensils, munitions in the Hanging Rock, Red River, Between Rivers, Rolling Fork, Green River Regions. Old charcoal furnace era ended by depletion of ore and timber and the growth of railroads. See over.

1163 FAYETTE COUNTY HEMP
(Newtown Pk. near Jct. of Iron Works Rd., Fayette Co.)

Consistently the leader in hemp production and cordage making in Kentucky. In 1803, Hunt and Brand Co. produced first hemp bagging made in U.S. In the early 1840s the county had 63 ropewalks; they were long, narrow sheds for the spiral winding of hemp fibers. In 1871, 2,000 tons of fiber were harvested, $1/3$ of yield for entire state in that year. See over.
(Reverse)

HEMP IN KENTUCKY
First crop grown, 1775. From 1840 to 1860, Ky.'s production largest in U.S. Peak in 1850 was 40,000 tons, with value of $5,000,000. Scores of factories made twine, rope, gunny sacks, bags for cotton picking and marketing. State's largest cash crop until 1915. Market lost to imported jute, freed of tariff. As war measure, hemp grown again during World War II. See over.

1164 FRANKLIN COUNTY HEMP
(Wilkinson Blvd., Frankfort, US 421 Bypass, Franklin Co.)

Kentucky River Mills began making hemp yarns for backs of Brussels carpets in 1878, and started producing binder twine in 1879. Finest quality imported machinery used. Employed 125 persons year round. In 1941, received contract from Navy for $148,500 worth of marine oakum. This was the last hemp factory to operate in Ky., closing down in 1952. See over.

(Reverse)
HEMP IN KENTUCKY

First crop grown, 1775. From 1840 to 1860, Ky.'s production largest in U.S. Peak in 1850 was 40,000 tons, with value of $5,000,000. Scores of factories made twine, rope, gunny sacks, bags for cotton picking and marketing. State's largest cash crop until 1915. Market lost to imported jute, freed of tariff. As war measure, hemp grown again during World War II. See over.

1165 HEMP IN MASON COUNTY
(Near entrance to Maysville Community College, US 68, Mason Co.)

The only major hemp-producing Ky. county outside the Blue Grass area. The 1810 crop income was $70,000. Maysville second to Louisville in finished hemp products, 1830s. Nicholas Arthur's factory, using horsepower, was one of several ropewalks, long buildings for spiral winding of hemp fibers. It processed yearly 600,000 lbs. of rope worth $41,000. See over.
(Reverse)
HEMP IN KENTUCKY

First crop grown, 1775. From 1840 to 1860, Ky.'s production largest in U.S. Peak in 1850 was 40,000 tons, with value of $5,000,000. Scores of factories made twine, rope, gunny sacks, bags for cotton picking and marketing. State's largest cash crop until 1915. Market lost to imported jute, freed of tariff. As war measure, hemp grown again during World War II. See over.

1166 HEMP IN SCOTT COUNTY
(N. lawn of Cardome Centre, US 25, Georgetown, Scott Co.)

Rev. Elijah Craig established at Georgetown, in 1789, one of the earliest ropewalks, which were long sheds for spiral winding of hemp fibers. Also started fulling mill in 1793. Both factories made cordage and rigging for vessels built on the Ohio and Kentucky Rivers. Peak production in 1839; over 1,000 tons processed yearly with value of $120,000. See over.
(Reverse)
HEMP IN KENTCKY

First crop grown, 1775. From 1840 to 1860, Ky.'s production largest in U.S. Peak in 1850 was 40,000 tons, with value of $5,000,000. Scores of factories made twine,

rope, gunny sacks, bags for cotton picking and marketing. State's largest cash crop until 1915. Market lost to imported jute, freed of tariff. As war measure, hemp grown again during World War II. See over.

1167 WOODFORD COUNTY HEMP
(1 mi. E. of Versailles, US 60, Woodford Co.)

One of chief producing counties, crop income reached a yearly high of $125,000 in the 1840s. During these peak years, there were 19 ropewalks, long sheds for spiral winding of hemp fibers. In 1941, Kentucky-Illinois Hemp Co. built a breaking plant at Versailles, with 2,000 acres of hemp under contract, using 4 binders and 16 reapers to harvest crop. See over.
(Reverse)
HEMP IN KENTUCKY

First crop grown, 1775. From 1840 to 1860, Ky.'s production largest in U.S. Peak in 1850 was 40,000 tons, with value of $5,000,000. Scores of factories made twine, rope, gunny sacks, bags for cotton picking and marketing. State's largest cash crop until 1915. Market lost to imported jute, freed of tariff. As war measure, hemp grown again during World War II. See over.

1168 COUNTY NAMED, 1840
(Independence, Courthouse lawn, KY 17, Kenton Co.)

For General Simon Kenton, 1755–1836. Pioneer of area. Born in Virginia. At 16, thinking he had killed a man, fled beyond Alleghenies, becoming companion of Daniel Boone and other early pioneers of Ky. Scout for Governor Dunmore of Va. Returned to Kentucky, 1782. Frequently engaged in Indian warfare. Fought with Kentucky troops at Battle of Thames. Kenton Co. formed out of Campbell.

1169 FULTON COUNTY
(Fulton, Courthouse lawn, US 45, 51, Fulton Co.)

Formed, 1845, out of Hickman Co. Part of Jackson Purchase from the Chickasaw Indians in 1818. Named for Robert Fulton, whose CLERMONT, best known of early steamboats, went up the Hudson River in 1807. Far western part of the county, known as Madrid Bend, separated from rest by bend of Mississippi River. Hickman, county seat, was founded as Mills' Point in 1834.

1170 COUNTY NAMED, 1799
(Hardinsburg, Courthouse lawn, US 60, Breckinridge Co.)

For John Breckinridge, 1760–1806. Attorney General of Ky., 1793–97. Representative in Kentucky Legislature, 1797–1801. Coauthor with Jefferson of 1798 Kentucky Resolutions, opposing U.S. Alien and Sedition Acts. Appointed Attorney General of the U.S. in 1805. He was a key figure in the writing of the Kentucky Constitution, 1799. He served in the U.S. Senate, 1801–05.

1171 COUNTY NAMED, 1793
(Cynthiana, Courthouse lawn, US 27, 62, Harrison Co.)

For Colonel Benjamin Harrison, who came to area, 1776. Served as Col. in Revolution from Penn. He was a member, 1787 and 1788 Kentucky Conventions, 1792 Constitutional Convention at Danville. Elected to Kentucky Legislature in 1793. County formed from Bourbon and Scott. Portions of Campbell, Boone, Pendleton, Owen, Grant, Kenton, Robertson taken from Harrison.

1172 GRANVILLE ALLEN
(Logansport Rd., Morgantown, KY 403, Butler Co.)

First Union soldier killed in west Kentucky, while skirmishing on the Big Hill with CSA scouting party Oct. 29, 1861. A stone monument erected, 1894, by Granville Allen, Post 98, G.A.R., marks the place. Member of Co. D, 17th Kentucky Inf., enrolled by Col. John H. McHenry, Calhoun, Oct. 3, 1861. Union army volunteers south of Green River risked danger for home and family.

1173 BEAUMONT COLLEGE 1895–1915
(Beaumont Inn, Harrodsburg, US 68, 127, Mercer Co.)

Col. and Mrs. Thomas Smith owned and ran this famous girls' school, which offered "art, eloqution, a conservatory of music and the strongest of literary courses in preparation for the best American and European schools." Beaumont motto: "Exalted character graced by elegant culture and refined manners." *This marker erected by Beaumont College Alumnae–1968.*

(Reverse)
HISTORIC SITE, 1806 TO 1916

1806–27	Greenville Springs Spa
1806–28	Christian Baptist School
1830–33	Christian Baptist School
1834–41	Boyhood home, Supreme Court Justice John Harlan
1841–56	Greenville Institute
1856–93	Daughters' College
1893–94	Young Ladies College
1895–1915	Beaumont College
1916	Daughters' College
from 1917	Beaumont Inn. See over.

1174 FIRST PUBLIC WELL
(119 Broadway, Paducah, McCracken Co.)

July 22, 1833, the City Council authorized John Hynes and David Smith "to let a contract for a public well." In 1835 the old well was ordered cleaned and a new one built with "windlass, chain, and hook for the bucket." The well required constant care, and misuse of the bucket led to adoption of an ordinance July 11, 1834. Over. *Marker presented by Paducah Tourist Commission.*
(Reverse)
PUBLIC WELL ORDINANCE

"Persons drawing water are in the habit of starting the windlass and letting the bucket run down with great speed by which the bucket is frequently broken. Resolved that if this occurs hereafter, he or she...shall pay 4 dollars fine...[or]...shall receive on the lower back ten stripes well laid." Over. *Marker presented by Paducah Tourist Commission.*

1175 CONFEDERATE FLAG OF WELCOME
(310 Broadway, Paducah, McCracken Co.)

With the Confederate occupation of Hickman and Columbus in the late summer of 1861, Paducahans were thrilled and flew a large Confederate flag to welcome Southern Army thought on way. As General Grant's Union forces, backed by gunboats, moved to occupy Paducah on Sept. 6, it was feared flag would be seized. See over.
(Reverse)
RESCUE OF FLAG

Mrs. Emily Jarrett, whose husband and sons were fighting for the CSA, rushed to save the banner. Under Union gunboat fire, she had a small slave boy climb the pole, retrieve the flag, and drop it to her. Union troops searched her home but failed to find flag's hiding place. Some thirty years later, the faded cloth was laid to rest with its loyal rescuer. Over.

1176 LAUREL COUNTY
(Levi Jackson State Park, at Mt. Life Mus., US 25, Laurel Co.)

Formed in 1825 out of portions of Clay, Rockcastle, Whitley, and Knox counties. The abundance and beauty of laurel shrub impressed the early pioneers so much that they named the county for it. Dr. Thomas Walker's party, exploring for the Loyal Land Company of England, first came to the area in 1750, naming the streams after different members of his party.

1177 BECKHAM COUNTY
(Olive Hill, US 60, Carter Co.)

Created from parts of Carter, Lewis and Elliott counties with county seat here by legislative act signed February 9, 1904, by Governor J. C. W. Beckham, for whom it was named. C. C. Brooks appointed County Judge. On April 29, 1904, the Court of Appeals ruled that it failed to meet constitutional standards of size and population and ordered it dissolved.

1178 E.K. RAILWAY
(Jct. US 23 & KY 1, Greenup Co.)

A major factor in development of this area, the Eastern Ky. Railway opened from the Ohio River here to Argillite in 1867; finally reached Webbville, Lawrence Co., 1889. It hauled local timber, iron ore, and coal, but never fulfilled its owners' plans to connect southern coal fields with Great Lakes. Total trackage: 36 mi. Abandoned by 1933. *Presented by Eastern Ky. Railway Historical Society and Greenup County Fiscal Court.*

1179 CHURCH HILL GRANGE HOUSE
(Church Hill, 5 mi. S. of Hopkinsville, Christian Co.)

Built 1878 by the Grange. Used ever since for public meetings. Kentucky's first farm cooperative, the Church Hill Grange operated a livestock market here. Leading this pioneer cooperative were two Christian County farmers, Winston J. Davie, first Ky.

Commissioner of Agriculture, 1876–79, and his brother Montgomery Davie, Master of the Kentucky Grange.

1180 PADUCAH GASEOUS DIFFUSION PLANT
(Main entrance to Noble Park, Paducah, US 60, McCracken Co.)

A key facility in producing the Uranium 235 needed for fuel in nuclear electrical generating stations and other peaceful uses. The $785,000,000 plant was built in 1951–4 and is operated by the Union Carbide Corp. Nuclear Div. for the Atomic Energy Commission 17 miles west of Paducah off US 60. Can be seen from the access road. *Presented by Union Carbide Corp.*

1181 PATRIOT—PIONEER
(Jct. KY 227 & KY 325, Owen Co.)

Colonel Joshua Baker, b. 1762, d. 1816. Home site and graves 2 miles south. His wife, Mary Callaway, cousin of Boonesborough girls, kidnapped by Indians, 1776. Scouted across the Ohio with Simon Kenton in 1787. They led attempt to capture Chief Tecumseh in 1792. He was officer in Cornstalk Militia, 1792–1811. A delegate to convention framing second Kentucky Constitution, 1799.

1182 SITE OF LOVE HOUSE
(Wapping & Wilkinson Sts., Frankfort, Franklin Co.)

First meeting of the Legislature, after Frankfort made capital, held here, 1793, when owned by Andrew Holmes. Built about 1786 by Gen. James Wilkinson. Purchased in 1797 by Maj. Thomas Love and wife. It was for years an inn and center of political and social life for the capital. The exiled French Prince Louis Philippe and Aaron Burr were among guests. In use until 1870.

1183 CONFEDERATE CONGRESSIONAL MEDAL OF HONOUR
(3rd & Frederica Sts., Owensboro, Courthouse lawn, Daviess Co.)

The President, CSA, in 1862, was authorized to confer a Medal of Honour upon one enlisted man of each company for "every signal victory." At first dress-parade, thereafter, the men engaged in the battle chose, by vote, the soldier most worthy to receive this honour. 72 Kentuckians com-

ing from 34 counties were so honoured. Three were from Daviess County. Over.
(Reverse)

DAVIESS COUNTY CSA MEDALISTS

STONE'S RIVER
Dec. 31, 1862–Jan. 2, 1863
Albert M. Hathaway
2nd Lt., Co. K, 4th Ky. Inf.

CHICKAMAUGA
Sept. 19–20, 1863
John L. Bell
2nd Lt., Co. K, 4th Ky. Inf.
Killed in action
Mathias Garrett
Corp., Co. K, 4th Ky. Inf.

1184 GRASS HILLS →
(Ghent-Eagle Station Rd., Sanders, just off I-71, Carroll Co.)

Home and family cemetery of Lewis Sanders, 1781–1861. House built 1819, on land wife inherited from Col. George Nicholas, key drafter of Ky. Constitution and the first state Attorney General. Sanders organized first Ky. fair on his farm in Fayette Co., 1816. With Henry Clay, 1817, made the first importation of shorthorn cattle from England, west of Alleghenies.

1185 A PIONEER ROUTE
(Mattoon, 4½ mi. NE of Marion, US 60, 641, Crittenden Co.)

The "Chickasaw Road," part of the old Saline Trace, used by Indians in pursuit of the vast herds of bison, deer, elk which came this way to the salt licks in Illinois. Flynn's Ferry began operating at the Ohio crossing of this trail in 1803, making it an important route of migration and commerce. Movement of Civil War troops was the last major use of this road.

1186 PIONEER METHODIST
(KY 210 at 462, Larue Co.)

John Baird (Beard) was born 1768. In 1791, became a Methodist circuit rider in Maryland. Immigrated to Kentucky in 1795. Preached first sermon in this area at house of Phillip Reed, Aug., 1796, that led to organization of the Level Woods Methodist Church. He died in 1846. Buried in the family cemetery near Level Woods Church. "An able expounder of the Word of God."

1187 LONG HUNTERS
(Bowling Green, Courthouse lawn, US 68, 231, Warren Co.)

An exploring party of 13 "Long Hunters," so named because of the long periods of time spent away from home, camped along Barren River in 1775. Their names were carved on a beech tree, a silent record of the first white men in this area. Henry Skaggs and Joseph Drake of this group had been among first Long Hunters, 1769–71, whose exploring helped open mid-Kentucky.

1188 SCUTTLE HOLE GAP ROAD
(Near Whitesburg, 7 mi. S. of Jct. KY 15 on KY 931, Letcher Co.)

Indians or buffalo probably were the first to follow this gap and make a trail across Pine Mountain. First white settlers, about 1800, made trail into treacherous wagon road, their only route to Virginia for supplies of flour, salt, and sugar. Called Scuttle Hole Gap, meaning deep gorge through cliffs. Trail goes 7 miles from here into the Cumberland River Valley.

1190 ON WASHINGTON'S GUARD
(At Three Forks Baptist Church, Hammonsville, KY 357, Hart Co.)

Sergeant Joseph Timberlake, born in Va., 1752; buried here, 1841. Revolutionary soldier. One of the members of General Washington's bodyguard. All were chosen as being "sober, young, active and well built, men of good character that possess pride of appearing soldier like, those having family connection in this country, and men of some property."

1191 PIONEER SURVEYOR
(Covington Woods Park, Bowling Green, US 31-W, 68, Warren Co.)

General Elijah M. Covington of the Kentucky Militia came here from North Carolina in 1795 to farm and survey. Acquired 23,000 acres in Warren, Logan, Edmonson counties. He became Warren County's first sheriff and surveyor. Helped to select the early site of Bowling Green and made the first survey of Mammoth Cave. This park named for him, purchased by city, 1933.

1192 SASSAFRAS TREE
(2100 Frederica St., Owensboro, Daviess Co.)

This giant tree, first mentioned for its size in 1883, has been an historic landmark in Daviess County for several centuries. Believed to be 250 or 300 years old, it measures over 100 feet tall, with a circumference of 16 feet. It is probably the largest of its kind in the world, and is registered with American Forestry Association as largest in U.S.

1193 OWINGS HOUSE
(Owingsville, US 60, Bath Co.)

Built 1811–14 for Colonel Thomas Deye Owings by Benjamin Latrobe, who redesigned the interior of the US Capitol after the British burned it, War of 1812. This house was a center of social life during early 1800's. Henry Clay, while US Sec. of State, attended a grand ball here. Reputedly, in 1814, someone posing as Prince Louis Philippe was a guest here. See over.
(Reverse)

THOMAS DEYE OWINGS

Came to Bath County in 1800 from Maryland. An early ironmaster, he operated the Bourbon Iron Works, Slate and Maria forges. Iron Works Pike, Owingsville to Lexington, built to haul iron from this area to the Bluegrass, there being no nearby river route. Owings was four times a state representative and a state senator, 1823–27. Town named for him, 1811. See over.

1194 MAJOR JOHN P. GAINES
(KY 338, 2½ mi. W. of I-75, Boone Co.)

Home site of John Pollard Gaines, 1795–1857. Fought in War of 1812. In state legislature, 1825–36. Major in the 1st Ky. Cavalry and an aide-de-camp to Gen. Winfield Scott in Mexican War. Elected to Congress, 1847–49, while prisoner of war. Governor of the Territory of Oregon, 1850–53, appointed by President Zachary Taylor, who was a comrade in arms in Mexico.

1195 SITE OF FORT HARTFORD
(N. of Hartford at Rough River Bridge, US 231, Ohio Co.)

Settled before 1790, this area was often scene of bloody strife with Indians. There is evidence that a settlement was made at present site of Hartford in 1782, first fortified place in the lower Green River Valley. Land was donated by Gabriel Madison, part of 4,000-acre Virginia grant in 1782. Name Hartford derived from the river ford where animals crossed.

1196 FIRST PUBLIC BUILDING
(Hartford, Courthouse lawn, US 231, Ohio Co.)

Ohio County's first jail and courthouse, a combined two-story, log structure, built 1799–1800. The second-story courtroom was of "well-hewed logs, with a raised bench for the court, a bar for the attorneys, with bannisters and rails." This building collapsed in 1813. The material salvaged was burned to celebrate the victory of Commodore Perry on Lake Erie.

1197 PIONEER ANCESTOR
(Near Isom, 4 mi. S. of Jct. KY 15 on KY 7, Letcher Co.)

James Caudill, born in Virginia in 1753, first came to Big Cowan Creek in 1787. Because of Indians, he took his family back to North Carolina. Returning here in 1792 with his family, he built a cabin, stayed several years, went back to North Carolina. They settled here permanently in 1811. He was progenitor of a large, widespread mountain family. He died in 1840.

1199 CORP. JAMES BETHEL GRESHAM MEMORIAL BRIDGE
(Rumsey, S. end of Green River Memorial Bridge, KY 81, McLean Co.)

Erected, 1928, honoring the first American killed in action in World War I on Nov. 3, 1917, at Battle of Sommerviller. Enlisted in 1914 in Indiana. With Pershing in Mexico, 1916. Sent overseas, June 14, 1917, with first American soldiers of AEF. Born McLean Co., Aug. 23, 1893. Buried in France; reinterred, Evansville, Ind., 1921.

1200 ED PORTER THOMPSON
(Center, Masonic Lodge, KY 314, Metcalfe Co.)

Born near Center, Metcalfe Co., in 1834. Elected Kentucky Superintendent of Public Instruction, 1891 to 1895. Noted educator, mathematician, and linguist, the author of 6 books, including 2 state adopted texts: *Academic Arithmetic* and *Young People's History of Kentucky*. His *History of the Orphan Brigade* is a most complete and valuable

Civil War record. He died in 1903.

1201 WARREN COUNTY'S CHIEF USA CIVIL WAR OFFICERS
(Bowling Green, Courthouse lawn, US 31-W, 68, Warren Co.)

Brig. Gen. William E. Hobson
    1st Brig., 2nd Div., 23rd Corps
Col. Benj. C. Grider, 9th Ky. Inf.
Col. J. H. Grider, 52nd Ky. Inf.
Col. P. B. Hawkins, 11th Ky. Inf.
Col. Atwood G. Hobson, 13th Ky. Inf.
Col. E. L. Mottley, 11th Ky. Inf.
(Reverse)

WARREN COUNTY'S AWARDS—CONFEDERATE MEDALS OF HONOUR
Conferred by President Davis on enlisted man selected by company at the first dress parade after "every signal victory."
Sgt. Wm. E. Kinman
Co. H, 9th Ky. Inf.
    at Stone's River, 1863.
Pvt. Benjamin F. Parker
Co. A, 2nd Ky. Inf.
    at Chickamauga, 1863.   Over.

1202 JONATHAN E. SPILMAN
(Greenville, near Jct. US 62 & KY 601, Muhlenberg Co.)

Birthplace of Kentucky lawyer, minister, and composer. While at Transylvania Law School, 1837, he wrote the music for Robert Burns' "Flow Gently, Sweet Afton," best remembered of his seven melodies. An adaptation of this music used in one of the tunes to "Away in a Manger," words by Martin Luther. Lawyer 18 years. Became minister when 46. Born 1812. Died 1896.

1203 CARPENTER'S STATION
(2 mi. W. of Hustonville, KY 78, Lincoln Co.)

Established near this site, 1780, by the brothers Adam, Conrad and John Carpenter. All were American Revolutionary soldiers, sons of George Carpenter, Sr., who died while serving with the First Virginia Regiment. One of early stations through which the settlement of Kentucky was achieved. Carpenters once owned 3,000 acres in vicinity of this station.

1204 SALEM
(US 60, KY 133, Livingston Co.)

County seat, 1809–42, of Livingston, which

included present Crittenden. First courthouse, of hewn logs, was built by William Rodgers on land donated by him. On August 8, 1864, 35 Federal troops under Captain Hugh M. Hiett repelled a Confederate force of 300 commanded by Major John T. Chenoweth in a six-hour skirmish here. See the other side.
(Reverse)

LIFE OF A COUNTY
This area was part of different counties as they were developed.

1780 Lincoln, county seat at Harrodsburg. One of three original Ky. counties.
1792 Logan, county seat at Logan Court House, now Russellville.
1797 Christian, county seat at Hopkinsville.
1799 Livingston, county seats at: 1800 Eddyville–1804 Centerville–1809 Salem–1842 Smithland.

1205 BIBB-BURNLEY HOUSE
(Wapping St., Frankfort, Franklin Co.)

Site of first house lived in on street, 1786, by John Instone, who came here from England to build boats for Gen. Wilkinson. Wapping Street named by Instone for one of that name in London. John B. Bibb, Lt., War of 1812, represented Logan Co. in Ky. House, 1827–28, Senate, 1830–34. Bought property and built present house, 1845. He developed Bibb variety of lettuce here.

1206 COUNTY FORMED, NAMED
(Transylvania Park, Henderson, US 41, 60, Henderson Co.)

By Kentucky Statute, Dec. 1798, effective, May 1799, the county of Henderson was formed out of part of Christian. Named to honor Colonel Richard Henderson, founder of the Transylvania Land Company, which was granted land on Green and Ohio Rivers by Va. Gen. Assembly, 1778, to compensate for voiding purchase of land from Cherokees in Eastern Kentucky. Park named for Company.

1207 LT. CHARLES MORAN—USAF
(Horse Cave, Jct. US 31-W & KY 218, Hart Co.)

Shot down a lead plane of first invading flight of the Korean War, June 27, 1950. Four of enemy's nine fighter planes destroyed. Lt. Moran was killed in action 40 days later, Aug. 7, 1950. Member of 68th Fighter (AW) Squadron. Born in Horse Cave in 1924. Grandson of "Uncle Charlie" Moran, Centre's famous football coach. Lt. Moran buried in Horse Cave Cemetery.

1208 THE OLD MANSION
(High & Clinton Sts., Frankfort, US 127, Franklin Co.)

Home of thirty-three Governors during their terms of office and scene of elaborate political and social functions, 1797 to 1914. Thomas Metcalfe, who laid the stone foundation in 1797, later occupied the mansion as the tenth Kentucky Governor, 1828–32. Not used from 1914 to 1956. Then it was renovated and made residence for the Lieutenant Governors.

1209 PIONEER SPIRIT
(State Line Rd., Fulton-Graves Co. Line, Fulton Co.)

Nearby gravesite of Lucy Flournoy Roberts, believed to be the first woman of French Huguenot lineage to come to this area. Her husband and 25 dependents are also buried here. She was a descendant of one of the founders of Manakintown, Va., a Huguenot settlement. One of many brave women who left family ties to go with their husbands to a new life in the wilderness. *Presented by descendants.*

1210 CRITTENDEN FURNACE
(2½ mi. N. of Dycusburg, Crittenden Co.)

Built a mile west by Gideon D. Cobb in 1847, 9 feet across inside, 30 feet high, charcoal-fueled, with steam-powered machinery. In 1855 made 1300 tons of iron. Named for newly formed county, it was last of several ironworks operated by the Cobb and Lyon families, who came to area about 1800, when Andrew Jackson told them of iron ore deposits here. See over.
(Reverse)
IRON MADE IN KENTUCKY
A major producer since 1791, Ky. ranked 3rd in US in 1830s, 11th in 1965. Charcoal timber, native ore, limestone supplied material for numerous furnaces making pig iron, utensils, munitions in the Hanging Rock, Red River, Between Rivers, Rolling Fork, Green River Regions. Old charcoal furnace era ended by depletion of ore and timber and the growth of railroads. See over.

1211 ASHLAND
(Greenup Ave. at 17th St., Ashland, US 23, 60, Boyd Co.)

Settled by 1799 by members of the Poage family of Virginia. Known as Poage's Landing until named in 1854 for Henry Clay's Lexington estate, by the owners, Ky. Iron, Coal and Manufacturing Company. It engaged M. T. Hilton to lay out a town, then auctioned lots. City incorporated by act of Ky. Legislature, Feb. 13, 1856. *Presented by the City of Ashland.*

1212 PULASKI COUNTY, 1799
(Somerset Community College, US 27, Pulaski Co.)

Kentucky's 27th formed, its territory taken from Lincoln and Green Counties, was named for Count Casimir Pulaski, Polish patriot and soldier of liberty. He came to US when he learned of the Colonies' fight for freedom. A brigadier general in Revolution, he gave his life to the cause of America, Oct. 11, 1779. Counties in 7 states named for him. Over.
(Reverse)
SOMERSET
Established as county seat, 1801, on 40 acres given by William Dodson. This site picked because of nearby spring; the path to it became the town's most traveled street. The first courthouse built of logs in 1801. Three have since been built, present one in 1871. Kentucky's first raw silk produced here, 1842, by Cyrenius Wait. City incorporated in 1888. See over.

1213 BRACKEN COUNTY WINE
(Augusta, KY 8, 19, Bracken Co.)

During the 1870s, leading wine-producing county of US, furnishing over 30,000 gallons annually, half the entire national production. Germans, finding soil here similar to that in France and Spain, brought grape cultivation and wine production to this area. This last remaining wine cellar has 3-foot-thick walls of native limestone and a vaulted ceiling.

1214 PADUCAH, KENTUCKY
(City Hall grounds, Paducah, McCracken Co.)

Located at the confluence of Ohio and Tennessee Rivers. Named for legendary Indian Chief Paduke. Settled in 1821, it was platted in 1827 by General William Clark, incorporated in 1830, and made McCracken county seat in 1832. During Civil War, Confederates seized Hickman and Columbus. Gen. U. S. Grant occupied Paducah, 1861, keeping Kentucky in the Union. Nathan Bedford Forrest raided here, March 25, 1864, in action called Battle of Paducah. Home of Alben Barkley, Vice President, 1949–53, and birthplace of Irvin S. Cobb, world-famous author. From village to town in 1856, to second-class city by 1902, Paducah grew as market, steamboat port, and railroad hub. In the early 1950s Paducah entered the atomic age when the $785,000,000 gaseous diffusion plant was built. Over. *Presented by Tilghman Class of 1928.*
(Reverse)

PADUCAH'S CITY HALL

One of the nation's most attractive, a gleaming symbol of pride and progress, designed by world-famous Edward Durell Stone and Associates of New York City; associate architect Lee Potter Smith. The building, two-story and basement, rises from a 216-foot-square podium encircled by a moat, has over 60,000 square feet of floor space, and cost over $1,500,000. Highlight of the interior is the pyramidal lantern enclosing a two-story-high, 60-foot-square atrium, rising above the centrally located fountain. Ground was broken on June 20, 1963, while Robert Cherry was Mayor. Dedication ceremonies were held on February 28, 1965, during Mayor Tom Wilson's administration, marking the beginning of a renaissance for downtown Paducah. See over. *Presented by Tilghman Class of 1928.*

1215 MAN O' WAR
(Near Man o' War statue at Ky. Horse Park, Fayette Co.)
Fair Play—Mahubah by Rock Sand

Greatest race horse and leading money winner of his day. Winner of twenty of twenty-one starts with lifetime earnings of $249,465. Foaled March 29, 1917, at August Belmont's Nursery Stud a few miles away. Sold at auction as yearling for $5,000 to Samuel D. Riddle, his owner throughout his racing career and later retirement. "Big Red" sired 62 stakes winners, his get earning over $3.5 million. War Admiral, Triple Crown winner, was most famous of his offspring. Man o' War died November 1, 1947; lies buried beneath this statue by noted sculptor Herbert Haseltine. *Plaque presented by The Thoroughbred Club of America.*
(Reverse)

RACES WON BY MAN O' WAR
2 year old, 1919

Futurity	Tremont
Grand Union Hotel	U.S. Hotel
Hopeful	Youthful
Hudson	Purse Race, at Belmont
Keene Memorial	

Won all entered as a 2 year old, except second in Sanford Memorial.

3 year old, 1920

Belmont	Potomac
Dwyer	Preakness
Jockey Club	Stuyvesant
Kenilworth Gold Cup	Travers
Lawrence Realization	Withers
Miller	

Won all entered as a 3 year old, eight in record time. *Plaque presented by The Thoroughbred Club of America.*

1216 MONTGOMERY COUNTY, 1797
(Mt. Sterling, Courthouse lawn, US 60, Montgomery Co.)

Named for General Richard Montgomery, Revolutionary War officer. Born in Ireland, 1738. An advocate of colonial freedom, he commanded continental forces in the north, capturing first British colors in war, Fort St. Johns, 1775. Killed in Quebec attack, December 31, 1775. Original county taken from Clark; included area of 2 present counties and parts of 8 others.

1217 COUNTY NAMED, 1793
(Winchester, Courthouse lawn, US 60, Clark Co.)

For General George Rogers Clark, who came to Kentucky territory from Virginia, 1775. He commanded expedition into Illinois territory in 1778–79, taking the British forts which held the northwest for future

US settlement, and capturing commander of area. Originally taken from Bourbon and Fayette; covered area of 5 present counties and parts of 8 others.

1218 COUNTY NAMED, 1842
(Main St., Danville, Courthouse lawn, US 127, 150, Boyle Co.)

For Judge John Boyle, 1774–1834. State representative, 1800; U.S. Congress, 1803–9; Kentucky Court of Appeals, Chief Justice, 1810–26; U.S. District Judge for Kentucky, 1826–34. The Judge "lived for his country," setting many important legal precedents for the new state. The 94th county, formed from parts of Mercer and Lincoln, with Danville named the county seat.

1219 COUNTY NAMED, 1808
(Irvine, Courthouse lawn, KY 52, 89, Estill Co.)

For Captain James Estill, gallant soldier and frontiersman. Fought one of bloodiest Indian battles, Estill's Defeat, on March 22, 1782, in what is now Montgomery County. He and 7 of his 25 pioneers were killed in violent combat with a band of marauding Wyandots. The 50th county, formed out of parts of Clark and Madison. Parts of 5 counties were taken from Estill.

1220 LINDSEY CEMETERY
(1½ mi. N. of KY 36 on KY 1743, Harrison Co.)

Located one-half mile east, this pioneer cemetery is the burial place of settlers, among them four Revolutionary War veterans, Rangers of the Frontiers, 1778–83: Capt. Thomas Moore, Capt. William Moore, Lt. David Lindsey, John Makemson. This plot set aside about 1800 by David Lindsey, who brought his family here about 1780. See over. *Marker presented by descendants, 1968.*
(Reverse)
MAKEMSON MILL AND DISTILLERY
Operated in the early 1800s and located on adjacent Mill Creek, on land purchased in 1795 by the Makemson (McKemson) family, who intermarried with the Lindseys. David Lindsey appointed Harrison County's first coroner, 1794. John and Andrew Makemson appointed surveyors in 1807. See over. *Marker presented by descendants, 1968.*

1221 WOODFORD COUNTY, 1789
(Versailles, US 60, Woodford Co.)

Last of nine formed by Virginia before Kentucky became a state in 1792. Original county taken from Fayette and extended as far north as the Ohio River; included the area of 7 present counties and parts of 4 others. Versailles was established as county seat by the first Kentucky legislature, 1792, and was named for Versailles, France. See over.
(Reverse)
COUNTY NAMED
For General William Woodford, a Virginian, commander of the First Brigade of the Continental army. Active in campaign to drive out Lord Dunmore, the colonial governor of Virginia, who later left the colonies and returned to England. Woodford was taken prisoner at fall of Charleston, later died in captivity under the British at New York, 1780. Over.

1222 AVIATION PIONEER
(US 60 & KY 182, Carter Co.)

Matthew Sellers, among first to experiment with gliding and power flight. Did this research at his home and laboratory, 6 mi. south, 1897–1911. Built most advanced wind tunnel of his day, 1903, to study lift and drag of various wing designs; and developed first use of retracting wheels, 1908, on powered plane said to be lightest ever flown. See over.
(Reverse)
MATTHEW B. SELLERS
Born in Baltimore, 1869, of parents who were Kentuckians. He was educated in Germany and France, receiving law degree at Harvard, 1892. Died in 1932. Among patents he received: 1908, airplane-type kite, prototype for later models; 1909, four-wing glider, basis for powered plane; 1911, power plane with retractable wheels; 1914, steering and wheel retraction improvements. See over. *Presented by sons of Matthew Sellers.*

1223 COUNTY NAMED, 1786
(Richmond, Courthouse lawn, US 25, 421, Madison Co.)

For James Madison, Virginia patriot whose political foresight led to the formation of

many of our basic democratic principles. He was a member of Virginia's Constitutional Convention and her First Assembly, 1776. He was also influential in framing the Constitution of the United States and was 1 of 39 to sign it. He became the fourth US President, 1809–17. See over.
(Reverse)

COUNTY FORMED

One of nine created by Virginia before Kentucky became a state. Taken from Lincoln, it covered the area of 5 present counties and parts of 9 others to southeast. Richmond, made county seat in 1798, is 4½ miles from original one at Milford, established in 1789. Richmond was settled by John Miller in 1785; first court was held in his barn. See over.

1224 COUNTY NAMED, 1797
(Hopkinsville, Courthouse lawn, US 41, 68, Christian Co.)

For Col. William Christian, native Virginian, soldier, politician, and pioneer. Served as Colonel in Revolution, member Va. Legislature. Moved family to Jefferson County in 1785, where his Virginia land grants totaled 9,000 acres. Killed 1786, defending frontier against Indians. Original county, taken from Logan, included area of 16 present-day counties and parts of 4 others.

1225 HURRICANE FURNACE
(2 mi. E. of Tolu, KY 135, Crittenden Co.)

Built ¼ mile southeast in 1850 by Andrew Jackson, Jr. Also known as Jackson Furnace. As rebuilt in 1856, it was 34 ft. high, with a maximum inner diameter of 10 ft. In 6 months of 1857, made 1200 tons of iron from ores of the Jackson Bank, two mi. south. Its soft iron was prized by rolling mills. Operations ceased in the early 1860s. See other side.
(Reverse)

IRON MADE IN KENTUCKY

A major producer since 1791, Ky. ranked 3rd in US in 1830s, 11th in 1965. Charcoal timber, native ore, limestone supplied material for numerous furnaces making pig iron, utensils, munitions in the Hanging Rock, Red River, Between Rivers, Rolling Fork, Green River Regions. Old charcoal

furnace era ended by depletion of ore and timber and the growth of railroads. See over.

1226 CANEY FURNACE
(Midland, Old River Rd., US 60, Bath Co.)

Stood five miles south. This stone stack, built 1837–38 by Harrison Connor and Joshua Ewing, Sr., was among first iron furnaces west of the Alleghenies to be equipped with a hot-blast oven, a device to preheat the air blown through the stack. Charcoal-fueled and steam-powered, it operated until 1849, and made iron again briefly in 1857–58. See the other side.
(Reverse)

IRON MADE IN KENTUCKY

A major producer since 1791, Ky. ranked 3rd in US in 1830s, 11th in 1965. Charcoal timber, native ore, limestone supplied material for numerous furnaces making pig iron, utensils, munitions in the Hanging Rock, Red River, Between Rivers, Rolling Fork, Green River Regions. Old charcoal furnace era ended by depletion of ore and timber and the growth of railroads. See over.

1227 MOUNTAIN VISION
(W. Cumberland Ave., Middlesboro, US 25, Bell Co.)

Alexander Arthur, 1846–1912, an outstanding figure in history of Middlesboro. He came here in 1885 to prospect, discovering coal and iron ore deposits. President of American Association, formed to carry out his plans for a mining and manufacturing city. Watts Steel and Iron Company was one of the largest concerns, having blast furnaces, brick works, steel mills. *Presented by American Assoc. Limited.*

1228 OLDEST HOUSE
(N. of 19th St., Middlesboro, US 25, Bell Co.)

Built about 1800 in Yellow Creek Valley, the second brick house in the county, and the oldest one still standing. The bricks were made from clay by slave labor. Home of Rev. John Calvin Colson, "Patriarch of Yellow Creek Valley," preacher, teacher, lawyer, doctor, farmer, miller, merchant, "being gifted along these lines but not educated for such pursuits." *Presented by Chamber of Commerce.*

1229 HOME OF FOUNDER
(202 E. Chestnut at Brook St., Louisville, Jefferson Co.)

Home of Col. Reuben T. Durrett, 1876–1913. Founder of The Filson Club and author of its first publication, in 1884, *John Filson, the First Historian of Kentucky,* and the *Centenary of Kentucky,* 1892. Designed by Henry Whitestone, noted Kentucky architect. Built by Dr. Thomas Edward Wilson and his wife, Caroline Bullitt, after 1856. Later, The Home of the Innocents.
(Reverse)

THE FILSON CLUB
Named for John Filson, author of first history of Kentucky, *The Discovery, Settlement and Present State of Kentucke,* 1784. Founded by Col. Reuben T. Durrett. Formed in his home here May 15, 1884 by: Reuben T. Durrett, George M. Davie, John Mason Brown, Basil W. Duke, Thomas W. Bullitt, Alex P. Humphrey, Wm. Chenault, James S. Pirtle, Richard H. Collins, Thomas Speed.

1230 COL. DANIEL BOONE, 1734–1820
(5½ mi. N. of Carlisle, US 68, Nicholas Co.)

Daniel Boone's last home in Ky. In spring of 1795, Daniel Boone and his wife returned from Va. and built log cabin. Restored cabin →. Boone and family lived here until they moved to Louisiana Territory (Missouri), 1799. Boone fought in last battle of Am. Revolution in the West, August 19, 1782, at Lower Blue Licks, 7 miles north.

1231 LAST SKIRMISH IN KY.
(State Penitentiary overlook, Eddyville, KY 730, Lyon Co.)

Overlooking site, now underwater, where last significant Civil War skirmish east of the Miss. River occurred, Apr. 29, 1865. US force under Captain S. M. Overby driven back after attacking about 140 Confederates from Army of Northern Virginia, under Colonel L. A. Sypert. Casualties on both sides; supplies captured. By May 6, most of the Confederates killed or captured.

1232 GOV. RUBY LAFFOON
(Madisonville, Courthouse lawn, US Alt. 41, KY 70, Hopkins Co.)

Born January 15, 1869, Madisonville. Began law practice, 1892. Served as chairman of the first Insurance Rating Board, 1912. Circuit Court Judge, 1921–31. While Governor, 1931–35, he reorganized charitable and penal boards; recodified the educational laws; was responsible for building of more highways and bridges than in the previous 15 years. He died March 1, 1941.

1233 CHALYBEATE SPRINGS
(Russell Springs, Corner Jamestown & Main Sts., Russell Co.)

A health resort long known as Big Boiling Springs, operated before 1850 by family of Sam Patterson, among the earliest settlers. Log cabins (12) called Long Row were built for guests who came here for amusement, pleasure, and the medicinal iron and sulphur water. In 1898, large hotel built which burned in 1942. The spring has been capped for use as a well.

1234 EARLIEST CHURCH
(Main St. at Harvey Helm Lib., Stanford, US 27, 150, Lincoln Co.)

The Stanford Presbyterian Church, founded 1788 on this site, on Old Wilderness Trail. Land given by Mary Briggs, sister of Gen. Benjamin Logan. Church moved to its present site, 1838; land given by Logan, one of founders. In 1797, David Rice, father of Presbyterianism in Kentucky, preached here. The original log church now part of this library building.

1235 MORGAN INDUCTED—CSA
(US 31-W & KY 88, Hart Co.)

On site, 1200 feet west, stood the church, his headquarters, where Gen. John Hunt Morgan and 84 of his men were formally sworn in, October 27, 1861, as the Second Cavalry Regiment, Kentucky Volunteers, CSA. Formerly part of the Lexington Rifles, they joined Confederates at Green River, and their daring exploits earned them the sobriquet "Morgan's Raiders."

1236 HART COUNTY, 1819
(Munfordville, Courthouse lawn, US 31-W, Hart Co.)

The 61st formed in Kentucky, from parts of Hardin, Barren counties. Home of the Buckners. Simon Bolivar Buckner, graduate of West Point, captain in Mexican War, CSA general in the Civil War, governor of

Kentucky, 1887–91, candidate for US Vice-President, 1896. His son S. B. Buckner, Jr., commanding general 10th US Army, killed Okinawa, 1945. Both buried Frankfort, Ky., Cemetery.

1237 OLD AMERICAN OIL WELL
(3 mi. N. of Burkesville, KY 61, Cumberland Co.)

Site of early American gusher that covered Cumberland River with oil and created spectacular "river of fire," March, 1829. Oil bottled from this well was widely sold for medicinal use in United States and Europe under trade name, "American Oil." The claims of the superior qualities of this oil merited it the name of Old American Oil Well. Original boring was for salt well.

1238 SHELBY COUNTY, 1792
(Shelbyville, Courthouse lawn, 5th & Main Sts., US 60, 460, Shelby Co.)

Formed from a part of Jefferson County, it was the third created after Kentucky became a state. Named in honor of Isaac Shelby, 1750–1826, first Kentucky governor, 1792–96; elected again 1812–16. In the Revolutionary War, Indian campaigns, and War of 1812. He came to Kentucky in 1783. Member of the Kentucky Constitutional Conventions at Danville, 1784–92.

1239 GREEN COUNTY, 1792
(Greensburg, Courthouse lawn, KY 61, Green Co.)

Formed from parts of Lincoln and Nelson counties. The last of seven formed during first legislature. Named for General Nathanael Greene, who, in the Revolutionary War, commanded a unit at Boston, 1776; helped plan defense of New York; fought at Trenton, Brandywine and Monmouth. Sent south by Washington. Greene's Carolina campaign forced British to leave Charleston, 1782.

1240 GARRARD COUNTY, 1797
(Lancaster, Courthouse lawn, US 27, KY 52, Garrard Co.)

Taken from parts of Lincoln, Madison, and Mercer, it was the 25th county formed. Lancaster, county seat, established in 1798. Named for James Garrard, then governor of Kentucky, 1796–1804. A native of Virginia, served as militia officer in Revolu-

tion. He came to Kentucky in 1783. Member statehood and Constitution conventions at Danville, 1784–92.

1241 UNCLE TOM LIVED HERE
(2.5 mi. E of KY 405 on US 60, Daviess Co.)

Site of Riley family homeplace, owners of Josiah Henson, one of the characters on which Harriet Beecher Stowe based her 1852 novel *Uncle Tom's Cabin*. Henson served as overseer of Amos Riley's farms, 1825–29. On learning owner planned to sell him "down the river," he escaped to Canada, living there rest of life. Invited to visit Mrs. Stowe in Andover, Mass., 1849.

1242 MADISON'S LAND
(2 mi. E. of Sorgho, KY 54, Daviess Co.)

James Madison, 4th U.S. president, and wife, Dolly, owned 2,000 acres along Panther Creek, now Daviess County. Land held by them until sold in smaller acreages, 1832–34. Madison was member of Continental Congress, 1780–83, 86–88, and of Federal Constitutional Convention, 1787. Member of first Congresses, 1789–97. Sec. of State, 1801–09. President of United States, 1809–17.

1243 McCREARY COUNTY, 1912
(Whitley City, Courthouse lawn, US 27, McCreary Co.)

Taken from parts of Pulaski, Wayne, and Whitley counties, it was the last formed of Kentucky's 120 counties. Named for James B. McCreary, 1838–1918. Lawyer, Col., 11th Ky. Cavalry, CSA. State legislature, 1869–75. Twice governor of Kentucky, 1875–79 and 1911–15. Delegate to International Monetary Convention, Brussels, 1892. US Congressman, 1885–97, 1903–09.

1244 MASON COUNTY, 1788
(S. end of Simon Kenton Bridge, Maysville, US 62, 68, Mason Co.)

Established by the Va. Legislature, original county taken from Bourbon; included area of 16 present-day counties and parts of 3 others. Named for George Mason, Virginian, author of the Va. Declaration of Rights, 1776, foundation for the US Bill of Rights. He also drafted the Va. Constitution. Delegate to Continental Congress, 1777, US Constitutional Convention, 1787.

1245 LYON COUNTY, 1854
(Eddyville, Courthouse lawn, US 62, 641, Lyon Co.)

The 102nd Kentucky county. Formed from a part of Caldwell, it was named for Col. Chittenden Lyon. Born in Vermont, 1787. Came here with father, Col. Matthew Lyon, in 1801. Had large mercantile and farming interests. Member state legislature, 1813–14, 1822–25; US Congress, 1827–35. Eddyville first settled, 1799, and became county seat in 1854.

1246 BOURBON COUNTY, 1786
(Paris, Courthouse lawn, US 27, 460, Bourbon Co.)

Named for the royal French family who aided the colonies in the War of Independence. Bourbon was one of nine Virginia counties formed before Kentucky became a state in 1792. From its original area all of twenty-four counties and parts of ten other new ones were made. At this site the first courthouse in 1787 marked the county seat. Known as Hopewell, renamed Paris.

1247 COUNTY NAMED, 1838
(Grayson, Courthouse lawn, US 60, Carter Co.)

For Col. William Grayson Carter, state senator, 1834–1838. The 88th Ky. county formed, 32nd in area, Carter was created from Greenup and Lawrence. Noted in early years for 5 iron furnaces, its clay products industry developed in late 1800's. Carter Caves, a major source of saltpeter during War of 1812, has been important tourist attraction since 1924.

1248 SCOTT COUNTY, 1792
(Georgetown, Courthouse lawn, US 25, 460, Scott Co.)

Formed out of a part of Woodford County, it was the second created after Kentucky became a state. Named for Gen. Charles Scott, 1739–1813, a Va. native. Officer in Revolution, saw service at Trenton, 1776, Germantown and Monmouth, 1777, Stony Point, 1779. Came to Kentucky in 1785. Represented Woodford Co. in the Va. Assembly, 1789–90. Fourth governor of Ky., 1808–12.

1249 PERRY COUNTY, 1821
(Hazard, Courthouse lawn, KY 15, 80, Perry Co.)

Formed from parts of Clay and Floyd counties. Both Hazard, the county seat, and the county named for Commodore Oliver Hazard Perry, 1785–1819, the commander and hero in battle of Lake Erie, 1813, which he reported in famous message: "We have met the enemy and they are ours." Victory gave United States control of the Lake and advanced its claims to the great Northwest.

1250 UNION COUNTY, 1811
(Morganfield, Courthouse lawn, US 60, 641, Union Co.)

The 55th Kentucky county created, it was formed entirely out of Henderson County. "It was possibly so named because of the unanimity of its citizens for division of the old county." Morganfield made county seat. Named for Gen. Daniel Morgan, who owned the land. Officer throughout the Revolutionary War, from 1775 at Quebec to 1781 at Cowpens, S.C.

1251 OLDHAM COUNTY, 1824
(La Grange, Courthouse lawn, KY 53, 146, Oldham Co.)

Taken from parts of Jefferson, Shelby, and Henry counties, it was the 74th formed. Named for Col. William Oldham, native Virginian, officer in War of Revolution. Commanded regiment of Kentucky militia in ill-fated Indian campaign on Wabash River in 1791, led by General St. Clair. Oldham was one of over 800 killed in battle, half of troops engaged.

1252 DROMGOOLE'S STATION
(lst St., Adairville, US 431, Logan Co.)

Site of station, built 1788, one of several erected in this area. James Dromgoole came from Tenn. with Philip Alston, whose daughter he had married, and settled at Alston's Station, on the Red River, about 1785. After three years he established his own station here on the Nashville to Russellville route. Dromgoole Station's name changed to Adairville, Nov. 1818.

1253 BOONE COUNTY, 1798
(Southbound rest stop, I-75, Boone Co.)

Formed by legislative act from a part of Campbell County. Named for Daniel Boone, renowned Kentucky pioneer-explorer. Big Bone Lick, graveyard of the mammoth, was discovered in 1729 by Captain M. de Longueuil. In 1756, Mary Inglis was brought here by Shawnees, the first white woman in Kentucky. In 1765–66, extensive bone collection sent to England.

1254 ROCKCASTLE COUNTY, 1810
(Mt. Vernon, Courthouse lawn, US 25, 150, Rockcastle Co.)

The 52nd Kentucky county created, out of Knox, Lincoln, Madison, Pulaski counties. Isaac Lindsey, who came here with a hunting party in 1767, observed a lone rock which resembled an ancient castle. From this the river was named, later the county. Dr. Thomas Walker and party, first white men to visit the interior of Kentucky, were at this rock as early as 1750.

1255 BARREN COUNTY, 1798
(Glasgow, Courthouse lawn, US 31-E, 68, Barren Co.)

Taken from parts of Green and Warren counties. Glasgow, county seat, was founded in 1799. County received name from the "barrens" or prairies of this region. Early explorers and settlers came through this area. In Civil War, first two of Morgan's Raids moved through here, 1862. The CSA invasion of Kentucky under Gen. Braxton Bragg entered here, 1862.

1256 WOLFE COUNTY, 1860
(Campton, Courthouse lawn, KY 15, Wolfe Co.)

Formed from parts of Breathitt, Morgan, Owsley, and Powell counties, it was the 110th created. Named for Nathaniel Wolfe, 1810–65, a native of Virginia, reported to be first graduate of University of Virginia. In Kentucky, he was Commonwealth's Attorney for Jefferson County, for 13 years, 1839–52. Member of State Legislature, 1853–55, 1859–63.

1257 WILLIAM HENRY NEWMAN
(Edmonton Public Square, US 68, Metcalfe Co.)

"One of the foremost railroad managers in the country." He was an associate of the great railroad builders. President of New York Central R.R., 1901–09, successor to Cornelius Vanderbilt. He merged 14 lines into New York Central System; planned Twentieth Century Lmtd. and Grand Central Terminal. Born in Metcalfe County,

1848. Died in New York City, 1918.

1258 MERCER COUNTY
(Harrodsburg, Courthouse lawn, Main St., US 68, 127, Mercer Co.)

Formed by Virginia Act in 1785, before Kentucky became a state. Included most of present Anderson and Boyle, part of Franklin, Casey, Garrard counties. First permanent English settlement west of the Alleghenies, founded as Harrodstown by James Harrod, 1774. Harrodsburg seat of government of Kentucky County, 1776; Lincoln County, 1780; Mercer County, 1785. Over.
(Reverse)
COUNTY NAMED
For Gen. Hugh Mercer, ca. 1725–77. A native of Scotland, he came to America about 1746. Officer in French and Indian War, 1755–59. Served with Washington. Was the commandant at Fort Pitt. Hero in Revolution. Instrumental in success at Trenton, 1776, and Princeton, 1777, where he was bayonetted to death by Hessians. He owned 13,000 acres in Ky. District. Over.

1259 FIRST BRIDGE
(Just outside Hartford city limits, N. side of Rough River, US 231, Ohio Co.)

Site of the first covered bridge here, built in 1823, thought to be the first across the Rough River. This was later replaced by another similar one after the decay of the first. Earlier crossings were by ford or ferry. An iron bridge was constructed here, 1875; removed 23 years later to Barnett's Creek. The present bridge was opened to traffic in 1934.

1260 GOVERNORS FROM LOGAN
(Russellville, Courthouse lawn, US 68, 79, Logan Co.)

Seven residents of Logan County became governors in four states:

KY.	John Breathitt	1832–34
	James T. Morehead	1834–36
	John J. Crittenden	1848–50
	Charles S. Morehead	1855–59
FLA.	Richard Call	1836–39, 41–44
ILL.	Ninian Edwards	1826–30
TEX.	Fletcher Stockdale	1865

1261 O'BANNON HOUSE
(Russellville, S. Main St., site of house, US 68, 79, Logan Co.)

Lt. Presley N. O'Bannon, USMC, the first American to raise our flag on foreign soil, April 17, 1805. Barbary coast pirates who were holding 180 American seamen for ransom were overcome in an attack led by O'Bannon. He came to Logan County in 1807. Served in state legislature 1812, 17, 20–21, and Senate 1824–26. Died in 1850. His remains moved to Frankfort, 1920.

1262 MIDDLESBORO GOLF CLUB
(Middlesboro, at Golf Club, US 25, Bell Co.)

One of the oldest in US, founded 1889. The present nine-hole course located on site where original was laid out by the English developers who came 1886 and brought the golf game to this mountain region. In 1899, a financial crash in England took most of the immigrants home, leaving the club with only sporadic golf until 1916, when it was reorganized by local citizens. *Presented by Kiwanis, Lions & Rotary Clubs.*

1263 FIRST COURTHOUSE
(Murray State Univ. Campus, Chestnut St., Murray, KY 121, Calloway Co.)

First public building in Jackson Purchase area. Built in 1823 for $100, it was originally erected at Wadesboro, Calloway county seat, 1822–42, where its first session of court was held, Feb. 13, 1823. Remained in use till new one built in 1831. Murray became county seat in 1843 and the log building was moved here then. It has been used as a residence for over a century.

1264 RUMSEY
(Jct. KY 81 & 138, McLean Co.)

Founded in 1834. Named for James Rumsey, steam navigation pioneer, at request of his nephew Edward Rumsey, US Congressman from this area, 1837–39. James Rumsey had first boat successfully operated by steam to carry both freight and passengers, Potomac River, 1786. The first steamboat on Green River, LUCY WING, was built here in 1846 by the Jones Brothers.

1265 GUNSHOP SITE
(Reedville, KY 185, Butler Co.)

William Stephens, Sr., gunsmith by trade, came to America from England with his two sons, 1832. They traveled overland, then down the Ohio to the Green River, where they bought 150 acres in 1854. The gunshop operated from 1855–61, when Stephens' two sons joined CSA as gunsmiths and ordnance workers. Shop reopened after the Civil War. Operations discontinued in 1868.

1266 THE OHIO COUNTY NEWS
(Center St., at newspaper office, Hartford, US 231, Ohio Co.)

Formed by merger, 1926, of *Hartford Herald,* founded by John Barrett in 1875, and *Hartford Republican,* established in 1888 by Col. Cicero Barnett. For 50 years "The Herald of a Noisy World" was masthead of the *Hartford Herald.* McDowell Fogle and Wilburn Tinsley were the first co-editors of *The News.*

1267 EARLY SURGERY
(Hartford, Ohio Co. Museum, 415 Mulberry St., Ohio Co.)

The first known successful removal of an entire collarbone, performed in 1813, by Dr. Charles McCreery. The patient, a 14-year-old boy, "made a complete recovery with perfect use of his arm, living past middle age." Dr. McCreery was born, 1785, trained under Dr. John Goodlett of Bardstown, settled in Hartford about 1807, the area's first real doctor. He died in 1826.

1268 PIONEER GRAVEYARD 1812–1858
(301 W. 13th Street, Hopkinsville, US 41, 68, Christian Co.)

Within this enclosure are buried 185 named persons, and many more unknown, all early settlers of Christian County. The land for this cemetery was donated in 1812 by Bartholomew Wood, the first settler in Hopkinsville. He also donated land and timber for the first public buildings, 1797. He died in 1827 and was buried here.

1269 BETHEL COLLEGE
(Site of college, 15th Street, Hopkinsville, US 41, 68, Christian Co.)

Organized by the Bethel Baptist Association and opened in 1854 as Bethel Female High School. Used by CSA as hospital during Black Measles epidemic, 1861–1862. Bethel Women's Jr. College, 1917. Closed 1942–1945; rooms rented to Camp Campbell Army officers. Became co-educational in 1951; name changed to Bethel College. Closed, 1964. Buildings razed, 1966.

1271 BEVERLY L. CLARKE
(Main St., Franklin, Courthouse lawn, US 31-W, Simpson Co.)

Born in Va., 1809. Came to Simpson County in 1827. Studied law under the noted Kentucky lawyer George Robertson. Served in the Kentucky Legislature, 1841–42; US Congress, 1847–49. Delegate to Kentucky Constitutional Convention, 1849. US Minister to Guatemala, 1857 until his death, 1860. State legislature authorized reinterment in the Frankfort Cemetery in 1868.

1272 WALLSEND MINE
(Pineville, US 25-E, Bell Co.)

The first to begin operations in Bell County, starting in 1889, with 1500 acres of coal land. Extension of the Louisville and Nashville Railroad to this area in 1888 marked the beginning of a new industrial era. This mine was not a financial success until it was purchased by Wallsend Coal and Coke Co., 1904, a Ky. corporation, but stock held mostly in England. *Presented by Pineville Chamber of Commerce*

1273 KAVANAUGH SCHOOL
(Woodford St., Lawrenceburg, US 62, Anderson Co.)

"The Sun Never Sets on Kavanaugh"

Kavanaugh Academy	1904–09
Anderson Co. High School	1909–20
Kavanaugh High School	1920–49

Rhoda C. Kavanaugh, A.B., founder and principal 41 years. Under her direction it ranked among the nation's foremost preparatory schools for Annapolis and West Point. Over.
(Reverse)
MRS. "K"
Rhoda C. Kavanaugh dedicated her life to teaching boys and girls, and built the school into an institution recognized nationwide for the quality of its instruction. This plaque is erected in memory of her power to instill in the minds of her students a hunger

for and a pride in achievement. *Presented by The Kavanaugh Association.*

1274 INDIAN OLD FIELDS
(11 mi. SE of Winchester, KY 15, Clark Co.)

Site of Eskippakithiki, sometimes called "Kentake," located on the Warrior's Path. This meeting place for traders and Indian hunters was the last of the Kentucky Indian towns. Occupied by the Shawnees, ca. 1715–1754. John Finley had a store here and traded with the Indians, 1752. Daniel Boone viewed "the beautiful level of Kentucky" from this point on June 7, 1769.

1275 WEST-METCALFE HOUSE
(Mill Springs Roadside Park, KY 1275, Wayne Co.)

One mile south. First brick house in area. Built by Capt. Isaac West, Revolutionary soldier, who came here about 1798, received land grant in 1799, and built this house, in 1800, of bricks he made himself. Gen. Felix Zollicoffer, CSA, had headquarters here, 1861. Used as hospital after Battle of Mill Springs, 1862. Confederates buried then in family cemetery.

1276 WASHINGTON STREET MISSIONARY BAPTIST CHURCH
(721 Washington St., Paducah, McCracken Co.)

Organized 1855 in log cabin near this site, led by George Brent, member Paducah First Baptist Church. Second was frame building, built by slaves, under leadership of Rev. George W. ("Pappy") Dupee, the first pastor constituted on Feb. 4, 1855. See over. *Marker donated by the Brotherhood of 1969.*
(Reverse)
WASHINGTON STREET MISSIONARY BAPTIST CHURCH
Colonial brick structure built in 1893 under Rev. Dupee, rebuilt in 1942 after fire, when Rev. D. E. King pastor. Cornerstone this edifice laid June 18, 1967 under pastorate of Rev. H. Joseph Franklin, who envisioned building adequate for worship, Christian education. Dedicated August 1969.

1277 FORREST'S BIVOUAC
(6 mi. S. of Paducah, KY 310 at Jct. of Bogard Rd., McCracken Co.)

Gen. Nathan B. Forrest and his CSA troops bivouacked one mile southwest of this spot after Battle of Paducah, March 25, 1864. Forrest moved to Mayfield next day where he paroled his men in order that they could visit their homes in western Kentucky and Tennessee. After three-day furlough troops joined Forrest at Trenton, Tennessee, without loss of a man.

1278 PREACHER TO PIONEERS
(Princeton, KY 293 at Dogwood La., Caldwell Co.)

Bishop Asbury named two itinerant Methodist preachers to Kentucky in 1786. One, Rev. Benjamin Ogden, had dedicated himself to religion after the Revolution. He preached in what is now Kentucky and Tennessee area. While inspiring countless pioneers, he endured a lifetime of sacrifice and suffering. Born in New Jersey in 1764, he died here in 1834. Monument, gravesite .3 mile east.

1279 FIRST CROP
(Danville, Courthouse lawn, US 127, Boyle Co.)

Kentucky's first recorded hemp crop, 1775, was on Clark's Run Creek, near Danville. Grown by Archibald McNeill, who brought the first seed with him when he located here. Hemp production spread slowly throughout the area, but Boyle County later became one of ten Bluegrass counties which together produced over 90 percent of entire US yield in 1889. Over.
(Reverse)
HEMP IN KENTUCKY
First crop grown, 1775. From 1840 to 1860, Ky. production largest in U.S. Peak in 1850 was 40,000 tons, value of $5,000,000. Scores of factories made twine, rope, gunny sacks, bags for cotton picking and marketing. State's largest cash crop until 1915. Market lost to imported jute, freed of tariff. As war measure, hemp grown again during World War II. See over.

1280 DANIEL BOONE BRYAN, 1758–1845
(Higbee Mill Pk. at Waveland Mus., .5 mi. W. of US 27, Fayette Co.)

Kentucky pioneer, Revolutionary War soldier, a founder and defender of Bryan Station; developed Waveland estate and community; agricultural leader; operated

gunshop, made gunpowder; established paper mill; promoted education; church and civic leader, pioneer historian. Son of William Bryan; nephew of Daniel Boone. Son Joseph built Waveland mansion, once home of Ky. Life Museum.

1281 ROWAN-CHAMBERS DUEL
(S. of Bardstown, US 31-E, Nelson Co.)

Site in valley to east, one of most famous duels in Kentucky because of prominent men involved. John Rowan, later jurist, and US Senator. His second, George M. Bibb, Kentucky Chief Justice, US Senator, Secretary of Treasury. Dr. James Chambers was popular physician. An argument on Jan. 29, 1801, climaxed in duel on Feb. 3. Dr. Chambers was killed in the second round of firing.

1282 SUCCESSFUL SURGERY
(Bardstown, Courthouse lawn, US 31-E, 62, Nelson Co.)

The first successful amputation of a leg at the hip joint in US. Done here by Dr. Walter Brashear in 1806 without any precedent to guide him. The patient was a seventeen-year-old boy whose leg had been badly mangled. Dr. Brashear was born in 1776, came to Kentucky, 1784, and studied medicine under Dr. Frederick Ridgely of Lexington. He died in 1860.

1283 JOHNSTON'S INN
(5 mi. W. of Paris, KY 627, Bourbon Co.)

Robert Johnston, a Revolutionary War captain, was born in Virginia in 1749. He and his wife operated a tavern in their house here from 1796–1812. Located on what was the main road between Maysville and Lexington, this inn served stage and horseback passengers in its 30-foot tavern room with sleeping accommodations overhead. This house appears on first Ky. map of 1784.

1284 PERRYVILLE
(Perryville at Chaplin River Bridge, US 150, Boyle Co.)

Established as Harberson's Fort before 1783 by James Harberson, Thomas Walker, Daniel Ewing and others at the crossroads of Danville-Louisville and Harrodsburg-Nashville routes. Town laid out by Edward Bullock and William Hall, 1815, named for

Commodore Oliver Hazard Perry, victorious at Battle of Lake Erie in 1813. Incorporated by act of Ky. Legislature, January 17, 1817.

1285 SALEM ACADEMY
(517 N. 3rd St., Bardstown, US 31-E, Nelson Co.)

Bardstown's first school, 1788, formed by Va. act. James Priestley, the noted educator, in charge. One class of Kentuckians later noted in life consisted of John Rowan, Judge and US Senator; Joe Daveiss, lawyer and hero in Battle of Tippecanoe; John Pope, US Senator; Felix Grundy, Appeals Court Chief Justice; Rev. Archibald Cameron, noted preacher.

1286 HENDERSON SETTLEMENT
(S. of Pineville at Bert Combs Forestry Bldg., KY 190, Bell Co.)

Rev. Hiram M. Frakes founded this Methodist Settlement in 1925. Begun in a cabin with 13 students, it became an institution for spiritual and educational development of mountain youth. Frakes guided and influenced the entire Middle Laurel Fork Valley. Their simply expressed gratitude for his work was, "Parson, we're glad you came." Settlement is 17 miles west on KY 190.

1287 FORREST'S HEADQUARTERS
(1501 Broadway, Paducah, McCracken Co.)

In a grove of trees at this site, CSA Gen. Nathan B. Forrest had headquarters, Battle of Paducah, on March 25, 1864. USA Fort Anderson attacked, warehouses burned, about 60 homes destroyed by USA after battle. CSA lost 300 men, withdrew that night. This battle climaxed Forrest's memorable raid seeking horses, ammunition, and medicines. *Presented by Western Kentucky Gas Company.*

1288 WOOLDRIDGE MONUMENTS
(Maplewood Cem., US 45 North, Mayfield, Graves Co.)

Those enshrined here are Keziah Nichols, mother of Col. Henry Wooldridge; his brothers, W.F., Alfred, Josiah and John; his sisters, Narcissa, Minerva and Susan; small statues of great nieces, Maud and Minnie. His favorite hunting dogs, Tow-Head and Bob, a deer and fox along with Henry, himself, astride his favorite horse, Fop. See over.

(Reverse)
WOOLDRIDGE MONUMENTS

This rare statuary, a memorial to loved ones, was conceived by Colonel Henry Wooldridge, whose central marble image was carved in Italy. Devoted to the memory of his family and his life. Animal lover, famous fox hunter and member of the Masonic order, only he is entombed here. Details at Chamber of Commerce.

1289 SAM AND NOLA OF MORRIS FORK
(At Morris Fork Presby. Church, Morris Fork, KY 28, Breathitt Co.)

Samuel VanderMeer came here from New Jersey in 1923. "Uncle Sam" to generations of Ky. youngsters, he became pastor of the Morris Fork Presbyterian Church in 1927, the year he married nurse Nola Pease. Missionaries, community builders. They gave a total of 98 years of service and love to this area, until retirement in 1969. Church and Community Center, 1 mile → .

1290 FORT WILLIAMS
(W. of Glasgow Municipal Cem., between Cem. & US 31-E bypass, Barren Co.)

Site of Civil War fort built in spring of 1863. Attacked Oct. 6 by Confederate Col. John M. Hughs and his 25th Tenn. Infantry. US troops under Maj. Samuel Martin surprised. Over 200 horses captured, part of fort burned, and 142 men taken prisoner, later paroled. In nearby cemetery is buried Gen. Joseph H. Lewis, Commander of lst Kentucky (Orphan) Brigade, CSA.

1291 JAMES TANDY ELLIS
(Main St., Ghent, US 42, Carroll Co.)

Birthplace of poet, humorist, columnist, raconteur, soldier. He brought pleasure to thousands with his dialectal stories and banjo songs of the Blue Grass, and his unique fictional character of "Uncle Rambo." For 20 years did daily column, "Tang of the South," for 3 papers. The Adjutant-General of Ky., 1914–1919, World War I. Born in 1869. He died here, 1942.

1292 CAMP BINGHAM 1969
(Near Jabez, KY 196, Wayne Co.)

Kentucky's first state 4-H Camp was established at Tatham Springs, Washington County, in 1940, by Barry Bingham as a memorial to his father, Robert Worth Bingham. This camp is dedicated to the training of 4-H youth in leadership, citizenship, and as a continuing memorial to Robert Worth Bingham. Over.

(Reverse)

ROBERT WORTH BINGHAM, 1871–1937

Born near Hillsboro, N.C. Resident of Louisville, Ky. A lawyer, civic and political leader, diplomat and philanthropist. President and publisher, the *Courier-Journal and Times*. Ambassador to the Court of Saint James (Great Britain), 1933–7. Organized Burley Tobacco Growers Assn. Secured passage of Bingham Cooperative Marketing Act. Over.

1293 OLD THRESHING ROCK

(9 mi. S. of Manchester at Lee Hacker Memorial Park, Clay Co.)

This large rock was used by the settlers of this area for threshing of grain as early as 1800. There were indications that Indians from a nearby settlement used the rock. For many years it was used for flailing grain by farmers of the area. It was often necessary to stand guard protecting the grain from both birds and animals.

1294 KINGDOM COME

(KY 931, near Kingdom Come Rd. Jct., Letcher Co.)

Early settlers, ca. 1816, were deeply religious and God-fearing. They chose a name for this beautiful and fertile valley from the words in "The Lord's Prayer." History of this area is typical of that of many communities along the creeks and hollows where descendants of the first settlers still live. It was immortalized by John Fox, Jr., in *Little Shepherd of Kingdom Come.*

1295 AN EARLY DERBY WINNER

(Young's Park on Linden Ave., Harrodsburg, Mercer Co.)

Leonatus, the 1883 Kentucky Derby winner, owned by Col. Jack Chinn and George Morgan, at old Leonatus Farm, 7 mi. east, in Mercer Co. By Longfellow, out of Semper Felix, by *Phaeton, as a three-year-old, within a period of 49 days, won ten stakes races. All these races were in Kentucky and Illinois. He was retired to Runnymede Stud, Paris, Kentucky. See over.

(Reverse)

ANOTHER DERBY WINNER

George Smith, 1916 Kentucky Derby winner, was bred by Christopher "Kit" Chinn and Fred Forsythe. Foaled at Fountainblue Stud, 5 mi. north, in Mercer Co. This colt, by *Out of Reach, out of *Consuelo II, won considerable money for that time, $42,884 in 31 starts. Besides the Derby, won 10 other stakes between 1915–1918, most in Maryland and Canada. See over.

1296 L & N BRIDGE IN CIVIL WAR

(Near Shepherdsville, KY 61 at crossing of Salt River, Bullitt Co.)

Destroyed three times by CSA. Partially razed on Sept. 7, 1862, by troops under Col. John Hutcheson. During the occupation of Shepherdsville, Sept. 28, Braxton Bragg's troops again destroyed it, but new bridge was up by Oct. 11. After Battle of Elizabethtown, Dec. 27, John Hunt Morgan's men moved along tracks, destroying everything on way to trestle works at Muldraugh's Hill.

1297 GRAHAM SPRINGS

(Young's Park on Linden Ave., Harrodsburg, Mercer Co.)

As early as 1807, springs in this area were used as a spa. In 1827, Dr. Christopher C. Graham purchased the springs. This "Saratoga of the West" flourished until 1853, when sold to US Gov't. as a military asylum. Fire later destroyed main buildings and the place fell into disuse. Judge Ben C. Allin opened a resort called "Graham Springs" on these grounds, beginning 1912.

1298 WESTON

(Mattoon, US 60, Crittenden Co.)

West-town, as early name implies, was most important river port for western Kentucky pioneers before Jackson Purchase opened in 1820s. Incorporated as a town in 1854. It developed around Flynn's Ferry at Ohio River crossing of the old Saline Trace. With the passing of the golden age of river trade, the town's prosperity faded. Site of Weston, 10 mi. north. Over.

(Reverse)
VITAL JUNCTION

George Flynn improved the north-south trace, previously used by animals on way to salt licks, into a wagon road. This intersection of the two main roads of that day, Weston to Princeton and Caseyville to Marion, was vital to the free movement of troops during Civil War. Hotly contested by Confederate raiding parties and US occupation forces until war's end. See over.

1299 AN INDIAN AMBUSH
(Bonnieville, Jct. US 31-W & KY 728, Hart Co.)

In 1788, William Smuthers, Gilbert LeClerc and his wife, pioneers, were on their way to settle the land they had bought, which later became the site of Munfordville. The men were killed by Indians, about 4 miles SE of here. The deed taken as part of the booty. Land resold before title was found not to be clear. Original deed found and building in town was resumed.

1300 RICHMOND PRELUDE
(US 421, 1.2 mi. S. of Jct. US 25 at Terrill, Madison Co.)

Confederates in Tennessee under Gen. E. Kirby Smith planned an invasion of the Blue Grass area. Finding Cumberland Gap protected, they entered through Rogers' Gap, heading for Lexington. US Gen. William Nelson sent Gens. M. D. Manson and Charles Cruft to oppose the invasion. The 2 armies, US 7,000, CSA 5,000, confronted each other 6 mi. below Richmond. See over.
(Reverse)
RICHMOND-BATTLE

On Aug. 30, 1862, CSA forces repulsed the enemy in three separate engagements. Confederate Generals T. Churchill and P. Cleburne and Colonels P. Smith and John Scott led in battles at Mt. Zion Church, White's Farm, and at Richmond. The total dead, wounded, missing of both sides was 5,804. Federals retreated and scattered. The CSA moved on to Lexington. See over.

1301 CIVIL WAR ACTIONS
(Freedom, Jct. KY 55 & US 127, Russell Co.)

On April 19, 1863, US Lt. Col. William

Riley ordered to Creelsboro, 5 mi. west, to scout enemy strength. Surprised CSA, took 12 prisoners. On December 31, 1863, USA troops under Lt. Col. A. J. Cropsey arrived at Creelsboro with two gunboats, forty sharpshooters. They came on scouting expedition from Nashville, turned back because of rapidly falling waters. See over.
(Reverse)
ZOLLICOFFER HERE

On November 22, 1861, CSA Gen. Felix Zollicoffer reached Jamestown, 4 mi. north, anxious to secure strong defensive position on Cumberland River to protect approaches to SE Ky. His plan to seize 9 ferryboats along river was defeated. Federal troops under Colonel Thomas Bramlette, Kentucky governor, 1863–1867, had destroyed them earlier in their effort to confine the CSA. Over.

1302 MARTIN JOHN SPALDING
(Calvary, KY 208, Marion Co.)

Born May 23, 1810, near Calvary on the banks of the Rolling Fork. Graduated St. Mary's College, 1826. Ordained in 1834 at Urban College, Rome. Christian education and charity were his main interests. Established St. Vincent de Paul Society in 1854, for Christian charity. Appointed by the Pope as Archbishop of Baltimore in 1864. He died at Baltimore, Feb. 7, 1872.

1303 EMINENT THEOLOGIAN
(Spalding Ave., Lebanon, KY 55, Marion Co.)

Bishop John Lancaster Spalding, also sociologist and writer, born here on June 2, 1840. Graduated St. Mary's College, 1856, at age 16. He was ordained at American College, Louvain, Belgium, in 1863. Organized first Louisville Negro parish, St. Augustine's, in 1866. Consecrated first Bishop of Peoria, Ill., in 1877. "A great influence on US Catholic education." Died 1916 at Peoria.

1304 SENATOR MCCREERY HOME
(Griffith Ave., Owensboro Public Lib., Daviess Co.)

Homesite of Thomas Clay McCreery. Born in 1816. He died in 1890. He was one of Daviess County's most distinguished natives, an accomplished lawyer, orator, and farmer. A presidential elector 1852, 1856, 1860. United States senator from 1868–71, elected to fill an unexpired term, and from 1873–1879. Grandson of Thomas Clay, a Revolutionary War officer, legislator.

1305 SILAS WESLEY, 1852–1931
(Bethelridge, KY 70, Casey Co.)

A community and church leader, businessman and farmer, he opened first general store in 1876. Gave Bethelridge its name, 1890, and was the first postmaster. Sponsored first telephone. Helped establish banks at nearby Middleburg and Eubank. His ancestors were among the first settlers in this area. *Presented by a committee of his descendants.*

1306 GOVERNOR'S BIRTHPLACE
(4 mi. S. of Albany, US 127, Clinton Co.)

Thomas E. Bramlette born near here on Jan. 3, 1817. State legislature in 1841. Appointed by Gov. John Crittenden as the commonwealth's attorney, 1848. Circuit judge, 1856–1860. Accepted Federal Army commission in 1861. Raised and commanded 3rd Ky. Inf. Resigned in 1862. Appointed by Pres. Lincoln as US district attorney. Elected governor in 1863. He died, 1875.

1307 BUFFALO ROAD
(1st & Frederica Sts., Owensboro, Daviess Co.)

Buffalo herds opened first road in wilderness to present site of Owensboro. Bill Smothers, the pioneer settler of Yellow Banks, followed trail from Rough Creek, near present day Hartford, to Ohio River. Built his cabin at end of road, near here, 1797–98. An old court record says the buffalo road was a "place of great resort for that kind of game."

1308 GOLDEN POND
(Golden Pond, at park in town, US 68, KY 80, Trigg Co.)

A town from 1882–1969. Named for nearby pond which gives a golden reflection from the sunrays. It was originally two settlements, Fungo and Golden Pond, later becoming one. Twice destroyed by fire and rebuilt, 1898 and 1936. The town prospered from abundant natural resources in

Thomas Clay McCreery, U.S. senator from Daviess County. Kentucky Historical Society Collection.

the area, the rich valley soils, the timbered hills, cool springs, iron ore, wildlife.

1309 FORT JEFFERSON SITE
(1 mi. S. of Wickliffe, US 51, Ballard Co.)

Built in 1780 by George Rogers Clark as part of impressive plan of settlement, conceived by Governor Patrick Henry of Virginia, later pursued by and named for Gov. Thomas Jefferson. The fort was to protect US claim to its western border and to be a key trading post. It was abandoned, 1781. Resettled after Jackson Purchase. Important Union post in Civil War. Over. (Reverse)

INDIAN MASSACRE

In 1781, the Chickasaws, led by a Scotchman, Colbert, aroused by use of their land without consent, besieged the fort for five days. Many settlers killed. Those left became desperate for provisions, already low because of the difficulty in reaching the fort. Gen. Clark arrived with reinforcements and supplies. The Indians withdrew. Fort was abandoned thereafter. Over.

1310 SEN. ED P. WARINNER
(Seventy-Six Falls Rd., at roadside park, N. of KY 90 near Lake Cumberland, Clinton Co.)

Born near here in August, 1909. Served 16th district in state senate, 1952–1959. In 1954 sponsored both Minimum Foundation Act (school support) and lowering of the voting age to 18. In 1958 he promoted the veterans bonus legislation and public assistance program. He also advocated Bookmobile system. He died in 1959 and is buried in Albany. See over.
(Reverse)

SEVENTY-SIX FALLS
Birthplace of the late Senator Ed P. Warinner (see over), whose ancestors settled here over 100 years ago. This area named for the height of the falls, at that time 76 feet, now 38 feet because of backwater of the lake. Settled in 1800, the community was laid out in 1817. The senator led in development of this roadside park as attraction for Clinton County. See over.

1311 CUMBERLAND TRACE
(1 mi. N. of Greensburg, KY 61 at Trace Creek, Green Co.)

The road over which most pioneers traveled westward across Kentucky. After Declaration of Independence, pioneers moved westward at an ever-increasing rate to claim frontier. This offshoot of the Wilderness Road turned west at Logan's Fort, Lincoln Co., passing through here. Glover's Station, now Greensburg, and Pittman's Station were settled along this trail in 1779 and 1780.

1312 OUR LADY CHURCH
(Rudd Ave. at Cedar Grove Terrace, Louisville, Jefferson Co.)

Congregation organized in 1837–38 by Father Stephen Badin, the first priest ordained in US. He saw to Portland's spiritual welfare when it was first a community of French immigrants. Also helpful in forming church were Bishop Flaget, first bishop west of Alleghenies, and Bishop Chabrat, first to be ordained in Ky. Bricks in original church, 1841, used for this one. Over.
(Reverse)

PORTLAND
French immigrants established a community here in 1806. In 1814 it was surveyed and platted. By 1837 it was incorporated as a suburb of Louisville. It was an early river port and boatbuilding center—41 steamers had been built by 1855. Portland was site of first tramway in US, connecting it with Louisville, and once famous hostelry of South, St. Charles Hotel. Over.

1313 FAMOUS PROPHET
(Entrance to Riverside Cem., Hopkinsville, US 41, Christian Co.)

Edgar Cayce—a psychic counselor and healer. Accepted nationally, he was one of the best known in this field. A humble and religious man, Cayce never profited from his predictions. Used reputed gift of extrasensory perception, including medical diagnosis, to better man's understanding of God's purpose for him here on earth. Born near here, 1877. Died, Va., 1945. Buried here.

1314 REVOLUTIONARY WAR WIDOW
(2 mi. SE of Russellville, KY 100, Logan Co.)

Abigail, wife of General Daniel Morgan, died in 1816 and was buried in family cemetery ½ mi. south. Her husband, one of Washington's chief strategists during the Amer. Revolution, campaigned from Boston and Quebec, 1775, to the Carolinas, 1781. After Morgan's death and burial in Va., 1802, Mrs. Morgan came here and lived in this area about 10 years.

1315 JESSAMINE COUNTY HEMP
(Nicholasville, Courthouse lawn, US 27, Jessamine Co.)

One of chief producing counties, it was third in value of product and also in the number of cordage factories, with 14 in 1840. Peak production reached in late 1800s, yielding over 1,000 tons per year, with a value of about $125,000. In 1899, it was one of the three Bluegrass counties which together produced more than one-half of hemp grown in the entire country.
(Reverse)

HEMP IN KENTUCKY
First crop grown, 1775. From 1840 to 1860, Ky.'s production largest in U.S. Peak in 1850 was 40,000 tons, with value of $5,000,000. Scores of factories made twine, rope, oakum to caulk sailing ships and cotton bagging. State's largest cash crop until 1915. Market lost to imported jute, freed

of tariff. As war measure, hemp grown again during World War II. See over.

1316 WILLIAM McCOY, SR.
(Inez, Courthouse lawn, KY 3, 40, Martin Co.)

Noted local attorney. Born at Pleasant, 1873. Read law, was admitted to bar in 1896. Martin County attorney, 1906–1914. Considered an expert on old land patents and deeds of eastern Ky. Interest in education led to appointment by Gov. Flem Sampson as a commissioner on first State Textbook Commission, 1928. Promoted education as great hope for county. Died, 1950. See over.
(Reverse)
LEWIS DEMPSEY
Financier and developer of this region. He was born in 1852, near Warfield. Founded Inez Deposit Bank and served as its president for 33 years. Owned vast coal and timber lands which he kept for the county's future development. Often loaned money to promising young people for education and helped start many in business. He died here in 1937. See over.

1317 GEN. JOSEPH H. LEWIS, 1824–1904
(Cave City, US 31-W, Barren Co.)

Confederate Brigadier General, commanded famous "Orphan Brigade" in Civil War. In 1861 he conducted recruiting and training camp here. State legislature, 1850–54, 69–70. US Congress, 1870–73. Member of Kentucky Court of Appeals for 24 years, 1874–98. Its chief justice six years. Born in Barren County, he is buried in Glasgow Cemetery.

1318 CAVELAND
(Jones Nursery Rd., 7 mi. N. of Hootentown-Fayette Co. Line Rd., Clark Co.)

Home of Richard Hickman. Born in Va., 1757. Built house in 1797. Clark County's first legislative representative, 1793–98. Member 1799 Ky. Constitutional Convention. General in the Kentucky Militia. State senator, 1800–8, 1811–12, 1819–22. Lt. Gov., 1812–16, serving briefly as Governor in 1813 while Gov. Shelby led Ky. troops in War of 1812. Died in 1832. Buried here.

1319 CLARK COUNTY HEMP
(5 mi. W. of Winchester, US 60, Clark Co.)

One of the ten Bluegrass counties which produced over 90 percent of the entire country's yield in late 1800s. Production increased from 155 tons in 1869 to over 1,000 tons in 1889, valued at about $125 per ton. In 1942, Winchester selected as site of one of 42 cordage plants built throughout country to offset fiber shortage during war. See over.
(Reverse)
HEMP IN KENTUCKY
First crop grown, 1775. From 1840 to 1860, Ky.'s production largest in U.S. Peak in 1850 was 40,000 tons, with value of $5,000,000. Scores of factories made twine, rope, oakum to caulk sailing ships and cotton bagging. State's largest cash crop until 1915. Market lost to imported jute, freed of tariff. As war measure, hemp grown again during World War II. See over.

1320 SHELBY COUNTY HEMP
(3½ mi. E. of Shelbyville, Jct. US 60 & KY 714, Shelby Co.)

One of chief producing counties. Crop income reached a yearly high of $150,000 in 1860. Nine hundred tons of hemp were consumed to produce 2,000 bales of twine and 5,000 coils of rope this same year. One of the ten Bluegrass counties which accounted for more than 90 percent of the yield of the whole country in the late 1800s.
(Reverse)
HEMP IN KENTUCKY
First crop grown, 1775. From 1840 to 1860, Ky.'s production largest in U.S. Peak in 1850 was 40,000 tons, with value of $5,000,000. Scores of factories made twine, rope, oakum to caulk sailing ships and cotton bagging. State's largest cash crop until 1915. Market lost to imported jute, freed of tariff. As war measure, hemp grown again during World War II. See over.

1321 AUDUBON HERE
(Road through Otter Creek Park, 1 mi. off KY 1638, Meade Co.)

Artist, naturalist, ornithologist. John James Audubon often came through this county on sketching trips in 1820. His frequent and wide excursions took him into all parts of the neighboring territory where he combined a love of art and science to produce his now-famous prints. Many done in this area were in *Birds of America*, to which he owes his fame.

1322 LT. GEN. FIELD HARRIS, USMC, 1895–1967
(Pisgah-Mt. Vernon Rd., 1 mi. N. of US 60, Woodford Co.)

Commanding general of US Marine Air Wing at invasion of Guadalcanal, 1942, WW II; and Korea, 1950. US Naval Academy, 1917; WW I. A courageous and inspiring leader. Harris' 21 combat decorations included army and navy Distinguished Service Medals, Legion of Merit with 3 Gold Stars, Order of British Empire. Buried in Pisgah Cemetery.
(Reverse)
MILITARY FOREBEARS
Lt. Gen. Field Harris, USMC, ancestors included:
William Field, came to Ky. with Harrod, then fought in Dunmore's War, 1774.
Col. John Field, killed at Point Pleasant, Dunmore's War, 1774.
Capt. Benjamin Field, Revolution, 1780–81.
Col. Ezekiel Field, Revolutionary War, died at Battle of Blue Licks, 1782.
Gen. E. H. Field, a parade marshal at ceremonies of Boone reinterment, 1845. Fought in Mexican War, 1847.
Gen. Charles Field, CSA, great Civil War leader who commanded half Lee's army, the only effective fighting force left to surrender at Appomattox.

1323 JUSTICE TODD HOUSE
(Wapping and Washington Sts., Frankfort, Franklin Co.)

Home of Thomas Todd, built 1812. Clerk, the 10 Danville conventions leading to Kentucky statehood. Court of Appeals, 1801–1806. Its chief justice, 1806–1807. Justice on the US Supreme Court, 1807–1826. Born in Virginia, 1765. Died in 1826. His second marriage was to Lucy Payne Washington, sister of Dolley Madison, in the first recorded White House wedding, 1812.

1324 SHERMAN HERE
(Lebanon Junction, KY 434 at railroad crossing, Bullitt Co.)

USA General William T. Sherman with 4,000 troops made headquarters here, late September, 1861. Object to secure Muldraugh's Hill against anticipated onrush of Confederates toward Louisville and to rally Kentuckians to Union cause. CSA Gen. Simon B. Buckner took Bowling Green, establishing Confederate line across Ky., but failed to push north. No major action occurred.

1325 NEIGHBORS—GOVERNORS
(5 mi. NE of Harrodsburg, US 68, Mercer Co.)

← Former home, grave, of Gabriel Slaughter, governor 1816–20. Born in Virginia, 1767. Died here, 1830. While in office, advocated state support for the public schools.
→ Former home of John Adair, governor 1820–24. Born in S.C., 1757. Died here, 1840. As governor, he promoted expansion of higher education, prison reform, abolition of imprisonment for debt. Over.
(Reverse)
MERCER GOVERNORS
Three other governors have been residents of Mercer County:
Christopher Greenup, 1804–8, with prestige of governor's office backed establishment of Bank of Kentucky.
Robert Letcher, 1840–44. In 1844, proclaimed first state Thanksgiving.
Beriah Magoffin, 1859–62, refused Lincoln's call for troops, 1861, in effort to keep Ky. neutral. See over.

1326 EDDYVILLE FURNACE
(1 mi. E. of Kuttawa, KY 295, Lyon Co.)

Also called Jim and I. A brick blast furnace for smelting iron, burning charcoal fuel, built 1832 by John and Samuel Stacker and Thomas Tennessee Watson. Later owned by members of Cobb family, then by William Kelly, inventor of the so-called Bessemer process for making steel. Much of its iron was forged at Kuttawa. Last blast about 1850. See other side.
(Reverse)
IRON MADE IN KENTUCKY
A major producer since 1791, Ky. ranked 3rd in US in 1830s, 11th in 1965. Charcoal timber, native ore, limestone supplied material for numerous furnaces making pig iron, utensils, munitions in the Hanging Rock, Red

River, Between Rivers, Rolling Fork, Green River Regions. Old charcoal furnace era ended by depletion of ore and timber and by the growth of railroads. See over.

1327 SUWANEE FURNACE
(1½ mi. W. of Kuttawa, US 62, 641, at Jct. with Suwanee Road, Lyon Co.)

Was built by 1851, 200 yds. NW, by William Kelly, whose experiments there perfected his invention of the so-called Bessemer method of making steel, for which Kelly was granted the patent. The blast furnace was a brick stack 35 ft. high, 10 ft. maximum inner width, steam-powered, charcoal fueled. Made 1700 tons of iron in 1857, its last year. See other side.
(Reverse)

IRON MADE IN KENTUCKY
A major producer since 1791, Ky. ranked 3rd in US in 1830s, 11th in 1965. Charcoal timber, native ore, limestone supplied material for numerous furnaces making pig iron, utensils, munitions in the Hanging Rock, Red River, Between Rivers, Rolling Fork, Green River Regions. Old charcoal furnace era ended by depletion of ore and timber and the growth of railroads. See over.

1328 CAPT. GEORGE GIVENS
(Jct. KY 1273 & US 150, Lincoln Co.)

Homesite and grave 1 mile west. B., Orange Co., Va., 1740. D., 1825. 40 years service to his country. Lt. at Fort Pitt, Dunmore's War, 1774. Captain, Botetourt County militia, 1776. Northwest Campaign of George Rogers Clark, 1778. Came to Ky., 1781. He received military land grant, 1781. In War of 1812. *Presented by Jane Craig Reichlein and Mrs. Birdie Givens Pickle.*

1329 LINCOLN SPOKE HERE
(Morganfield, Courthouse lawn, KY 56, Union Co.)

Abraham Lincoln's only political speech in his native state, here, 1840, at age 31. An elector from Illinois, he campaigned for Whig presidential candidate William Henry Harrison. From Shawneetown, across river, Lincoln led parade. Young ladies rode on floats drawn by white horses. Cannon for salute burst upon firing. Its

breech is at Kentucky Historical Society.

1330 BEAVER DAM
(Beaver Dam, US 231, Ohio Co.)

Named for an unusually large dam made by beavers across a nearby stream. First settlers came in 1798 and founded the first Baptist Church here, in year Ohio County formed. Town incorporated, 1873. In early times, area was covered by canebrakes and inhabited by bear, deer and buffalo. Pioneers enroute to Ohio River followed buffalo trace from area as early as 1797.

1331 CIVIL WAR ROBBERY
(Main & Bank Sts., Mt. Sterling, Montgomery Co.)

In this building is the Farmers Bank vault, which was robbed of $60,000 as "Morgan's Raiders" were on their last raid through Kentucky. Later the night of June 8, 1864, several of Morgan's men went to the house of J. O. Miller, cashier, and took the vault key from him. The money was never recovered. It was believed it went to Confederate cause. See over.
(Reverse)

BANK SUES
In 1866, a civil suit was filed in Anderson Co. by Farmers Bank against Lt. J. F. Witherspoon. The bank was awarded a judgment of $59,057.33 for damages. On appeal, Witherspoon found not liable. Court of Appeals said that under laws of war robbery was not unlawful. Furthermore, there was no proof Witherspoon more guilty than any other in Morgan's command. Over.

1332 NEW UNION FORGE
(Kuttawa, KY 295, Lyon Co.)

Stood ¼ mile SE. Built 1846–47 on site of older facilities by Wm. Kelly to process pig iron from nearby blast furnaces. Kettles to refine sugar, boiler-plate iron among products. Here Kelly began to develop the so-called Bessemer steel-making process, for which he received the patent. Closed in 1857. Chas. Anderson laid out the town of Kuttawa here in 1870.
(Reverse)

IRON MADE IN KENTUCKY
A major producer since 1791, Ky. ranked

3rd in US in 1830s, 11th in 1965. Charcoal timber, native ore, limestone supplied material for numerous furnaces making pig iron, utensils, munitions in the Hanging Rock, Red River, Between Rivers, Rolling Fork, Green River Regions. Old charcoal furnace era ended by depletion of ore and timber and the growth of railroads. See over.

1333 A GOVERNOR FOR TENNESSEE
(Owensboro-Daviess Co. Airport, Daviess Co.)

Albert Smith Marks birthplace site, October 16, 1836. Moved to Tennessee at age 19. Served as the 24th governor of that state, 1879–81, following distinguished service in Civil War. Enlisted early in the Confederacy, rising to rank of colonel. Battle of Perryville, 1862. Severely wounded Battle of Murfreesborough, December 31, 1862. "One of best officers in division."

1334 BOYHOOD HOME, 1793–1802
(Adairville, KY 591, Logan Co.)

The Rev. Peter Cartwright, 1785–1872. A dedicated itinerant Methodist preacher in Kentucky for 22 years. Saved from "sins of his youth" and "licensed to exhort" during the Great Revival of 1800. Ordained 1808. He was Presiding Elder for 50 years and delegate to 13 General Conferences. Moved to Illinois in 1824. Defeated by Abraham Lincoln in race for Congress, 1847.

1335 EARLY GUN SHOP SITE
(Moreland Ave., Harrodsburg, Mercer Co.)

Here Benjamin Mills made some of finest rifles in US, ca. 1830–50. His muzzle loaders famous for dual trigger system. Used by Kit Carson and Dr. Christopher Graham, conceded to be best rifle shot in world at that time. Used at The Alamo and on Fremont expeditions. The Boone Shooting Club, of which Graham and Gov. Beriah Magoffin were members, held matches behind this shop. Over.
(Reverse)

CIVIL WAR ARMORER

At raid of Harpers Ferry arsenal by John Brown, 1859, Mills, as armorer, was captured. Rescued next day by Marines under Col. Robert E. Lee, US offered position as chief armorer at Springfield, Mass., if he would stay with the Union. Declined offer, casting his lot with the South. During the war, he worked at Palmetto, South Carolina, arsenal. Over.

1336 SINCE 1842
(Frankfort Ave., Louisville, Jefferson Co.)

The Kentucky School for the Blind, third such state-supported school in U.S. Dr. Samuel G. Howe, of Boston, a pioneer educator of blind, was invited to Kentucky to give public demonstration with his own pupils. Displayed before Kentucky Legislature and in Louisville demonstrating they could be trained for useful life, "free from crushing weight of dependence, ever their lot." Over.
(Reverse)

SINCE 1858

American Printing House for the Blind, the oldest non-profit agency for blind in US and largest publishing house for blind in world. Since 1879, the official school-book printery for all such students in US. The only institution devoted solely to publishing literature and developing and manufacturing manual aids for them. See over.

1337 PATRIOT'S STAGE STOP
(White Sulphur, Jct. of Ironworks Pk. & KY 227, 460, Scott Co.)

This house, 1800–32, a stagecoach stop owned by Julius Gibbs. On the Iron Works Pike, route for hauling iron products from furnaces in Bath County to Kentucky River. Gibbs enlisted 1775, in first Va. Regiment under Col. Patrick Henry. Served until 1781. Pioneer settler of Great Crossings, 1782. Charter member of its Baptist church, 1785. *Presented by Mrs. Lena Gibbs Ransdell and Gibbs' Descendants.*

1338 CENTURY OF COAL MINING
(Earlington, US 41-A & KY 112, Hopkins Co.)

Earlington founded in 1870 by St. Bernard Coal Co. Named for John Baylis Earle, who discovered No. 11 coal vein not far from this site, in 1869. John Bond Atkinson, the president of St. Bernard Coal, planned free public schools, free public library, Loch Mary Reservoir, an arboretum, home and church sites. In 1870, L & N Railroad be-

Kentucky School for the Blind, the third such state-supported school in the U.S. Kentucky Historical Society Collection.

gan coal shipments from this area.

1339 CARTWRIGHT'S STATION
(3 mi. N. of Lebanon, KY 55, Marion Co.)

Here, in 1779, Samuel Cartwright located his station on the trail from Wilderness Road to Falls of the Ohio. Earlier, in 1774, he and Simon Kenton explored Big Sandy-Ohio River region. Stopped for a while at Harrodsburg, then settled here. Kenton came here in 1782 to get Col. Philemon Waters as a scout for Gen. George Rogers Clark's attack on the Indians.

1340 FULTON FURNACE
(Jct. KY 453 & Lookout Tower Rd., 1.2 mi. N. of Conservation Center Sta. Rd., Lyon Co.)

Built 2 miles east in 1845 by Thomas Tennessee Watson, Daniel Hillman. A brick stack 33 ft. high, 11 ft. across at the widest point, it produced 1044 tons of iron in 22 weeks of 1857. After 1856, it had ovens to heat the air for its blast, which was powered by steam. Charcoal fuel made and ore mined locally. Last blast 1860. See other side.
(Reverse)

IRON MADE IN KENTUCKY

A major producer since 1791, Ky. ranked 3rd in US in 1830s, 11th in 1965. Charcoal timber, native ore, limestone supplied material for numerous furnaces making pig iron, utensils, munitions in the Hanging Rock, Red River, Between Rivers, Rolling Fork, Green River Regions. Old charcoal furnace era ended by depletion of ore and timber and the growth of railroads. See over.

1341 GOVERNOR'S HOME SITE
(1 mi. S. of Lebanon, KY 49, Marion Co.)

J. Proctor Knott, Governor of Kentucky, 1883–1887, lived at this site until 1902, when house burned. He then gave this land to be used for chautauquas. These gatherings combined entertainment, education, and religion. For 27 years, 1906 to 1932, they flourished here. Central Kentucky Chautauqua Association formed, 1906. Renamed Proctor Knott Chautauqua Association in 1908.

1342 OLYMPIAN SPRINGS
(Olympian Springs, KY 36, Bath Co.)

This famous resort, known by 1791 as Mud Lick Springs, was favored for a century by such prominent visitors as Henry Clay. First stagecoach route in Kentucky began in 1803 between here and Lexington. Many Lexingtonians fled here from cholera epidemic of 1833. 28th US Infantry camped here during War of 1812. Civil War cavalry battle was fought here, Oct. 19, 1864.

1343 BOONE'S CAVE
(3 mi. E. of Harrodsburg, Jct. of Handy Pike & US 68, Mercer Co.) Not open to public

Only cave in Kentucky historically verified as used by Daniel Boone. He spent rest of winter in cave alone after companion, John Stuart, was killed in January, 1770, the first recorded white man killed by Indians in Ky. Boone joined in summer by brother Squire. Together they continued to explore and hunt before returning to North Carolina.

1344 LOCAL AUTHORESS
(School grounds on Lexington St., Lancaster, US 27, Garrard Co.)

Eugenia Dunlap Potts, daughter of George Dunlap, US Congressman and lawyer, was born in Garrard County in 1840 and pursued her literary career here, where she died, 1912. The first of her nine works was "Song of Lancaster," a metrical history in style of Longfellow's "Hiawatha." In 1892, she became editor of "Illustrated Kentuckian."

1345 YOUNG MEMORIAL PARK
(7 mi. S. of Russellville, US 79, Logan Co.)

Honoring Paul Everett Young, Sr., in recognition of his dedication to roadside beauty and conservation. Directed his interest, energy, and influence toward development of these parks. Logan County native, 1904–1966. Served this 20th District in Kentucky House of Representatives 12 years, 1954–1966. Lawmaker, county official, banker, farmer. *Presented by Judge Robert Brown and Fiscal Court members.*

1346 SALT WORKS
(17 mi. S. of Hazard, KY 7, Perry Co.)

Here in 1835, the Brashears' well produced salt from a fine brine. For half century it supplied area with that commodity so nec-

essary to their livelihood. These wells were drilled by hand. Salt was sold both here and in Virginia, transported for $1.00 a bushel over treacherous mountain trails by mule and oxen. The wells were destroyed by flood in 1892.

1347 FREE-TOWN CHURCH
(2 mi. W. of Gamaliel, KY 100, Monroe Co.)

Built in 1846 by freed slaves of William Howard, who gave them 400 acres on which to build homes, known since then as Free-Town. Albert Martin gave them the land for the church. No replacements of the original building material of this church, except for metal roof in place of old wooden one. The logs are held together by wooden pegs and chinked with clay.

1348 UNDERWOOD FURNACE
(8 mi. E. of Smithland at Mint Springs Church, KY 70, Livingston Co.)

Built ¾ mile north in 1846–47 by James C. Sloo and Leonard White. It was a brick structure with a steam-powered air blast, using locally made charcoal fuel to produce pig iron from ore mined nearby. Iron was shipped by steamboat to fabricators. After 1848, operations were transferred to the neighboring Hopewell Furnace. See the other side.

(Reverse)
IRON MADE IN KENTUCKY
A major producer since 1791, Ky. ranked 3rd in US in 1830s, 11th in 1965. Charcoal timber, native ore, limestone supplied material for numerous furnaces making pig iron, utensils, munitions in the Hanging Rock, Red River, Between Rivers, Rolling Fork, Green River Regions. Charcoal-furnace era ended in 1880s with depletion of ore and timber and use of modern methods. Over.

1349 HOPEWELL FURNACE
(8 mi. E. of Smithland at Mint Springs Church, KY 70, Livingston Co.)

Also called Ozeoro, built ½ mile north in 1848 by Wm. L. Hiter, Wm. Lewis and Henry F. Given. A brick stack 30 ft. high, 9 ft. in maximum inner diameter, it was charcoal-fueled with air blast powered by steam. In 33 weeks of 1856 it produced 1096 tons of pig iron from locally mined

ore. It was rebuilt in 1857, and ceased operating in 1859. See other side.
(Reverse)
IRON MADE IN KENTUCKY
A major producer since 1791, Ky. ranked 3rd in US in 1830s, 11th in 1965. Charcoal timber, native ore, limestone supplied material for numerous furnaces making pig iron, utensils, munitions in the Hanging Rock, Red River, Between Rivers, Rolling Fork, Green River Regions. Charcoal-furnace era ended in 1880s with depletion of ore and timber and use of modern methods. Over.

1350 LOUISVILLE AND NASHVILLE RAILROAD
(10th and Broadway, Louisville, Jefferson Co.)

Chartered by the Kentucky General Assembly, March 5, 1850. First track was laid near here in July, 1855. First train ran in August, 1855. First passenger station dedicated at 9th and Broadway in 1858. From it in 1859 ran first through train from Louisville to Nashville. During Civil War L & N was Western sector's only North-South rail link, a vital part of Union supply route. Used by Generals Grant and Sherman to move men and supplies as Union rolled deeper into South. It was prime target for marauding Confederate units. Gen. John Hunt Morgan raided extensively along its tracks and bridges. But despite difficulties the railroad continued to operate.
(Reverse)
L & N EXPANSION
First Train:
1859 Louisville to Nashville (Map showing 1867 Memphis expansion)
1872 Birmingham, Montgomery
1880 New Orleans, St. Louis, Pensacola, Mobile
1881 Cincinnati
1902 Knoxville
1905 Atlanta
1957 Paducah, Chattanooga
1969 Chicago

1351 BELLEVUE, KENTUCKY
(24 Fairfield Ave., Bellevue, KY 8, Campbell Co.)

Incorporated March 15, 1870, on part of original land grant to Gen. James Taylor, pioneer, for whose farm this city was

named. A general in War of 1812, banker, and statesman, whose farm was an underground railroad station. President of the first town trustees was George D. Allen. Hometown of Anna E. Wolfram, one of Kentucky's first women doctors.

1352 CLARK'S LAND
(Entrance to roadside park, adjacent to Jct. of US 60 & 68, McCracken Co.)

George Rogers Clark was original patentee of land on which Paducah is now located. Two grants totaling 73,962 acres were conveyed to Clark by Virginia, a portion of this representing money owed him for services rendered. Land deeded to brother William (of Lewis and Clark fame) in 1803, "in consideration of $2,100 for sundry services." Clark later developed Paducah. See over.
(Reverse)
CLARK'S ARMY CAMPED
On June 27, 1778, George Rogers Clark's army of about 200 faithful followers landed on nearby Owen's Island, just 4 days after starting from Corn Island at Falls of Ohio. A small hunting party appeared soon afterwards, giving valuable information about Kaskaskia. Clark recruited them and proceeded under severe hardship to defeat British and save Illinois country for US. Over.

1353 TOLLGATE HOUSE
(6 mi. W. of Carlisle at Bourbon Co. line, Nicholas Co.)

One of last to operate in Kentucky. There were 13 of these, spaced 5 miles apart and at edge of each town, along Maysville to Lexington Road. The Maysville, Washington, Paris and Lexington Turnpike Co. built road, 1829–1835, owned toll houses. In late 1890s, "tollgate war" raged against system until the counties bought turnpikes. Most gates had been abolished by 1900.

1354 PIONEER FURNACE
(US 23, S. of Louisa at Jct. of KY 644, Lawrence Co.)

The southernmost blast furnace in the Hanging Rock Iron Region. Built in 1881, 4½ miles south, by Jay H. Northup, George C. Peck and Thomas Cummings. A stone stack 18 ft. high with a maximum inner diameter of 4½ ft., it began operations in

1882, using locally mined ore and charcoal fuel made nearby. Production had ceased by 1884. See the other side.

(Reverse)

IRON MADE IN KENTUCKY

A major producer since 1791, Ky. ranked 3rd in US in 1830s, 11th in 1965. Charcoal timber, native ore, limestone supplied material for numerous furnaces making pig iron, utensils, munitions in the Hanging Rock, Red River, Between Rivers, Rolling Fork, Green River Regions. Charcoal-furnace era ended in 1880s with depletion of ore and timber and use of modern methods. Over.

1355 BRISTOW, THE SOLDIER-BIRTHPLACE

(South Main St., Elkton, KY 181, Todd Co.)

Benjamin Helm Bristow, 1832–1896, Federal officer and staunch Unionist during secession. Active recruiter of 25th Volunteer Militia, of which he was Lt. Col., and 8th Ky. Cavalry, which he served as Col. At Fort Donelson and Shiloh battles, 1862. A leader in capture of Morgan and raiders, 1863. Elected state senate while still in field, 1863. Over.

(Reverse)

BRISTOW, THE LAWYER

Practiced law here until 1858. (See over for military career.) From 1866–70, US attorney for district of Kentucky. First US Solicitor General, 1870–72. As Secretary of Treasury, 1874–76, exposed frauds in "Whiskey Ring" operating in mid-west. In 1876, lost Republican presidential nomination to Rutherford B. Hayes. Leading member Ky. Bar Assn. until 1878, when he moved to New York.

1356 STEPHEN'S OLD MILL

(4 mi. E. of Pine Knott, KY 92, McCreary Co.)

Standing for over a century, this mill was used on occasion until recently. Original poplar rafters and millstones are still intact. In 1952, new metal 16-foot overshot wheel replaced old wooden one. During the Civil War, Confederates took mill in hopes of finding grain. Similar mills were in most early communities. "Toll" for grinding usually an eighth of the grain.

1357 EMPIRE FURNACE

(7½ mi. NW of Cadiz, KY 274, Trigg Co.)

Stood 1 mile west. Built 1843 by Thomas Tennessee Watson, it was a brick stack with a maximum inner diameter of 9½ ft., 35 ft. high. It burned charcoal fuel, and its air blast was powered by steam. In 45 weeks of 1856, made 1836 tons of pig iron. Operations transferred to Center Furnace in 1861 because of floods, Civil War military actions. See other side.

(Reverse)

IRON MADE IN KENTUCKY

A major producer since 1791, Ky. ranked 3rd in US in 1830s, 11th in 1965. Charcoal timber, native ore, limestone supplied material for numerous furnaces making pig iron, utensils, munitions in the Hanging Rock, Red River, Between Rivers, Rolling Fork, Green River Regions. Charcoal-furnace era ended in 1880s with depletion of ore and timber and use of modern methods. Over.

1358 COLBYVILLE TAVERN

(5 mi. W. of Winchester, Colby Rd., KY 927, at Jct. of Becknerville Rd., Clark Co.)

Built in 1820s by Colby Taylor as a place of rest and entertainment on stage road from Winchester to Lexington. In 1832, President Andrew Jackson visited here on his trip to Winchester. During antebellum heyday in late 1840s, popular stop for those on way to Olympian Springs in Bath Co. These grounds were used as muster-and-drill area for the Winchester Light Infantry.

1359 FRANKLIN COUNTY, 1795

(Frankfort Overlook, US 60, Franklin Co.)

Taken from portions of Woodford, Mercer and Shelby counties. Ky. had become a state 3 years earlier, with Frankfort as capital, 1792. First meeting of the legislature's second session met here, 1793. Frankfort made county seat, 1795. Named for Benjamin Franklin, one of the leaders for independence and creation of United States.

1360 OGDEN COLLEGE

(State St. at 15th St., Ogden Campus, Western Ky. Univ., Warren Co.)

Founded here, 1877, with funds left by Robert Ogden, local businessman. Filled educational gap, as there were no public schools here until 1882. Prep school accredited in 1919. Ogden's criteria: regular attendance, gentlemanly deportment, diligent study. Consolidated with Western Ky. Univ., 1927. Its name is retained in the Ogden College of Science and Technology.

1361 SANDERS
(Railroad St., Sanders, Jct. KY 36 & 47, Carroll Co.)

Gen. George Rogers Clark used route through here, ca. 1780s, called Clark's War Road, from Drennon's Lick to Ohio River. First called Rislerville, then Liberty Station. In 1874, renamed Sanders, for "Wash" Sanders, local citizen active in state politics. In the early 1900s, it became a noted resort. Guests came to enjoy healing waters of nearby wells.

1362 MADISON HEMP AND FLAX CO.
(5.4 mi. W. of Eastern By-pass in Richmond, KY 52 at Silver Creek Bridge, Madison Co.)

Began operations here on Silver Creek in 1806. The machinery for spinning hemp and flax was run by water power. In 1808, received permission from the legislature to incorporate and sell stock. Factory produced thread which was sold or used here for weaving. One hundred and six spindles were in operation, each capable of spinning daily ½ lb. thread suitable for linen. Over.
(Reverse)
HEMP IN KENTUCKY
First crop grown, 1775. From 1840 to 1860, Ky.'s production largest in U.S. Peak in 1850 was 40,000 tons, with value of $5,000,000. Scores of factories made twine, rope, oakum to caulk sailing ships and cotton bagging. State's largest cash crop until 1915. Market lost to imported jute, freed of tariff. As war measure, hemp grown again during World War II. See over.

1363 BEN HARDIN, 1784–1852.
GRAVE →
(3 mi. S. of Springfield, KY 55, Washington Co.)

One of the ablest orators, lawyers, lawmakers in early Ky. Moved to Nelson, now Washington Co., with parents. In 1808, he settled at Bardstown where his career

earned him the title "last of race of giants." Member state legislature 9 yrs.; U.S. congressman, 10 yrs.; Ky. Constitutional Convention, 1849. Requested his children to bury him beside his parents.

1364 MAMMOTH FURNACE
(Land Between The Lakes, Bethlehem Church Rd., KY 58, Lyon Co.)

Built 3 1/4 miles west in 1845 by Charles and John Stacker, a stone stack 31 1/2 ft. high, 9 ft. across inside at widest. Steam-powered, charcoal-fueled, it made white unusually hard pig iron from ore deposits near furnace, producing 1514 tons in 48 weeks, 1857. CSA Army obstructed Tenn. River at Fort Henry with iron spikes made here. Last blast 1874. See over.
(Reverse)
IRON MADE IN KENTUCKY
A major producer since 1791, Ky. ranked 3rd in US in 1830s, 11th in 1965. Charcoal timber, native ore, limestone supplied material for numerous furnaces making pig iron, utensils, munitions in the Hanging Rock, Red River, Between Rivers, Rolling Fork, Green River Regions. Charcoal-furnace era ended in 1880s with depletion of ore and timber and use of modern methods. Over.

1365 PARTISAN PROTECTED
(Park, Jct. KY 571 & 740, Barren Co.)

Civil War's first Kentucky Federal death, Oct. 10, 1861, 4 miles east. A Union company slipped through graveyard at night to arrest C. B. Hutcherson, a local Southern sympathizer. Ten poorly equipped recruits from CSA camp of Gen. Joseph Lewis, sent to guard him, were attacked, but defeated enemy. Federals fled with one dead, seven wounded. There was no CSA loss.

1366 CENTER FURNACE
(7½ mi. NW of Cadiz, KY 274, Trigg Co.)

Sometimes called Hematite, furnace was built by 1852 by Daniel Hillman 2 1/2 mi. west; 35 ft. high, 10 ft. across inside at widest point. Operated, although not continuously, until 1912, burning charcoal fuel. Its air blast was powered by steam. In 46 weeks of 1856, it produced 2,139 1/2 tons of pig iron, mostly shipped by steamboat to fabricators. See other side.

(Reverse)

IRON MADE IN KENTUCKY

A major producer since 1791, Ky. ranked 3rd in US in 1830s, 11th in 1965. Charcoal timber, native ore, limestone supplied material for numerous furnaces making pig iron, utensils, munitions in the Hanging Rock, Red River, Between Rivers, Rolling Fork, Green River Regions. Charcoal-furnace era ended in 1880s with depletion of ore and timber and use of modern methods. Over.

1367 STACKER FURNACE

(Linton, KY 164, Trigg Co.)

Also called Olive Landing and Line Island, was built here by William Ewing and French Rayburn in 1845-46, and it afterward owned by Samuel Stacker. It had a steam-powered air blast. Using ore from deposits nearby and locally made charcoal fuel, it produced pig iron at intervals until 1856, when it was finally abandoned. See the other side.

(Reverse)

IRON MADE IN KENTUCKY

A major producer since 1791, Ky. ranked 3rd in US in 1830s, 11th in 1965. Charcoal timber, native ore, limestone supplied material for numerous furnaces making pig iron, utensils, munitions in the Hanging Rock, Red River, Between Rivers, Rolling Fork, Green River Regions. Charcoal-furnace era ended in 1880s with depletion of ore and timber and use of modern methods. Over.

1368 GRAND RIVERS FURNACE

(Grand Rivers, KY 453 at Commerce Ave., Livingston Co.)

Built ½ mile west, 1890–91, by the Grand Rivers Coal, Iron and Railroad Co. Two stacks, each one 60 ft. high with a maximum inner diameter of 13½ ft., together could produce 45,000 tons of iron yearly, using coal for fuel until 1901, and coke thereafter. These blast furnaces operated intermittently until dismantled in 1921. See the other side.

(Reverse)

IRON MADE IN KENTUCKY

A major producer since 1791, Ky. ranked 3rd in US in 1830s, 11th in 1965. Charcoal timber, native ore, limestone supplied material for numerous furnaces making pig iron, utensils, munitions in the Hanging Rock, Red River, Between Rivers, Rolling Fork, Green River Regions. Charcoal-furnace era ended in 1880s with depletion of ore and timber and use of modern methods. Over.

1369 GOODNIGHT MEMORIAL LIBRARY

(Franklin, South Main St., US 31-W, Simpson Co.)

Mrs. Goodnight (1858–1935), wife of I.H. Goodnight, in her will made possible the erection of this municipal building containing library, auditorium, assembly room, museum, kitchen. With aid of federal funds, WPA did the work. Assembly room used by Ella Hoy Goodnight Music Club. Sen. Alben W. Barkley, later Vice President, dedicated building in 1937. Over.

(Reverse)

ISAAC HERSHEL GOODNIGHT

State representative, congressman, circuit judge. Born Allen County 1849, he came here in 1870 and began practice, 1873. Served as state representative, 1877–1878, U.S. Congressman from 1889–95. Chairman of the Democratic State Convention of 1891. Elected judge of Kentucky's seventh circuit in 1897, serving till his death here in 1901. See over.

1370 CERALVO

Three miles South

(Centertown, Jct. KY 85 and old Ceralvo Road, Ohio Co.)

Name derived from Spanish word meaning deer. Traditionally deer watered and crossed the river there. Town was laid out by H. D. Taylor, in March 1851. Ceralvo took its place as thriving river town. Became an important shipping point for both passengers and freight serving many communities in this area. Incorporated February 1870 by an act of the Kentucky Legislature.

1371 JAMES THOMPSON, 1750–1825

(Dick's River Baptist Church, N. of Lancaster, US 27, Garrard Co.)

Burial site of first Lincoln Co. surveyor,

commissioned Jan., 1781. Surveyed this area, then part of Lincoln Co. Daniel Boone was made Deputy Surveyor under him, 1783. Thompson, nephew of Isaac Shelby, was State Rep., Garrard Co., 1803; State Senator, 1804–06. First Lt. with 12th Va. Militia in Rev. War. Trustee of Kentucky Academy, 1794, and the Lancaster Academy, 1798.

1372 VETERANS OF AMERICAN REVOLUTION ELECTED GOVERNOR OF KENTUCKY
(Old State Capitol, Frankfort, Franklin Co.)

Isaac Shelby, 1792–96, 1812–16; Col., Va. Militia

James Garrard, 1796–1800, 1800–4; Col., Va. Militia

Christopher Greenup, 1804–8; Col., Va. Militia

Charles Scott, 1808–12; Brevet Maj. Gen., Cont. Army

George Madison, 1816–died same year; Capt., Caroline Militia, Va.

John Adair, 1820–24; Brig. Gen., S.C. Line

Presented by Ky. Soc. Sons of the Revolution.
(Reverse)

VETERANS OF AMERICAN REVOLUTION ELECTED U.S. SENATOR FROM KY.

John Brown, 1792–1805; Private, Va. Militia

John Edwards, 1792–95; Drummer, Pa. Line

Humphrey Marshall, 1795–1804; Capt., Va. Militia

John Breckinridge, 1801–5; Subaltern, Va. Militia

George Walker, 1814; Pvt., Morgan's Rifle Corps

John Adair, 1805–6; Brig. Gen., S.C. Line

Presented by Ky. Soc. Sons of the Revolution.

1373 GERARD FURNACE
(Mt. Carmel Church, KY 121, Calloway Co.)

Built 2¼ miles east in 1854 by Browder, Kennedy and Co. Inside it was 24 ft. high and 10½ ft. across at widest point, burning locally made charcoal fuel. Its air blast machinery was powered by steam. In 34 weeks of 1857, it produced 1,595 tons of pig iron, mostly shipped by steamboats on Tennessee River. Did not operate after 1858. See the other side.

(Reverse)
IRON MADE IN KENTUCKY

A major producer since 1791, Ky. ranked 3rd in US in 1830s, 11th in 1965. Charcoal timber, native ore, limestone supplied material for numerous furnaces making pig iron, utensils, munitions in the Hanging Rock, Red River, Between Rivers, Rolling Fork, Green River Regions. Charcoal-furnace era ended in 1880s with depletion of ore and timber and use of modern methods. Over.

1374 BLANDVILLE COURTHOUSE
(Blandville, Courthouse sq., KY 1837, Ballard Co.)

Site of the first courthouse in Ballard Co., Kentucky, which, until 1886, was comprised of present Ballard and Carlisle Counties. Blandville, like Ballard Co., was named for Captain Bland Ballard. Established as the county seat by Kentucky Legislature in 1842, and continued as such for 40 years until 1882, when courthouse burned. Wickliffe then became county seat.

1375 JAMES THOMAS, SR.
(3.5 mi. W. of Jct. KY 139 & 807, Trigg Co.)

Served in Revolutionary War, 10th Regiment, Donoho's Company under General Nathanael Greene. Born in Bertie County, N.C. in 1760. Married Mary Standley in 1790. He migrated to Donaldson Creek, 1806, and settled on 200-acre Kentucky land grant. Built cabin 50 yards south of here. Died 1832; buried with wife in family graveyard ½ mile south. See over.
(Reverse)
JAMES THOMAS, SR.

First Thomas to settle permanently in area. Active in county affairs and served as justice of the peace. Seven children were: Cullen, Temperance, Starkie, Mary, Perry, and James, Jr., all born in N.C.; and Stanley, born in Kentucky. His descendants, who present this marker in his honor, have migrated to a number of states, although many still live in Trigg Co. Over.

1376 OLD CROW INN
(Danville city limits, US 150, Boyle Co.)

The oldest existing stone house in Kentucky, built 1784, is part of this building.

The house has been enlarged and Doric pillars added. Land purchased from John Crow by James Wright, 1781. Next owner, Colonel Joshua Barbee, who built original house. In 180 years only three families have been owners. Adams family since 1899. *Presented by Joshua B. Adams.*
(Reverse)
JOHN CROW
Came to Harrodsburg in 1774 with James Harrod and his group of 32. Settled near here in 1776. Founded Crow's Station, 1782, which became the political and cultural capital for District of Kentucky when Supreme Court met there, 1783–85. John Crow sold to Walker Daniel, 1784, land on which he established Danville in 1788. Over. *Presented by Joshua B. Adams.*

1377 MCCRACKEN COUNTY COURTHOUSE
(Paducah, 6th St., McCracken Co.)

First courthouse on this site finished 1861 and occupied almost immediately by Union Army. Used as a Civil War hospital. Present building erected 1940–43 with help of Works Progress Administration. Total cost of courthouse $344,919. *Marker presented by McCracken County Civic Beautification Board.* Over.
(Reverse)
MCCRACKEN COUNTY COURTHOUSE
1825– First courthouse built of logs at Wilmington.
1832– County seat moved to Paducah. Courthouse at Second and Ky.
1861– First courthouse at this site, then at edge of town.
1943– Present building occupied.
Marker presented by McCracken County Civic Beautification Board. Over.

1378 VALLEY VIEW FERRY
(12 mi. N. of Richmond at Ky. River, KY 169, Madison Co.)

The oldest continuous business of record in Ky. On land acquired by John Craig in 1780 through a military warrant, the Virginia Assembly granted a perpetual and irrevocable franchise to establish ferry in 1785. Ferry is presently named for the location in picturesque Valley View community. *Presented by Claude C. Howard and Family. Owners since 1950.*

1379 SHELBYVILLE FOUNTAIN
(Shelbyville public sq., 5th & Main Sts., US 60, Shelby Co.)

This fountain was purchased jointly in 1895 by city and county from J. L. Mott Iron Works, New York. It was erected at intersection of Fifth and Main Sts. upon the completion of Shelbyville's first public water works. Moved in 1914 to public square to clear the street after construction of new courthouse. Figure chosen for top of fountain is "Atlantis" pattern.

1380 TRIGG FURNACE
(2.4 mi. E. of Rockcastle, KY 274, Trigg Co.)

Built here in 1871 by the Daniel Hillman Iron Co. was a brick-and-stone blast furnace producing pig iron from locally mined ore. It burned charcoal fuel, and used steam power to blow preheated air through the stack. Most iron made here was processed at the works of the Tennessee Rolling Mills, 3 miles NW. Operations ceased by 1878. See the other side.
(Reverse)
IRON MADE IN KENTUCKY
A major producer since 1791, Ky. ranked 3rd in US in 1830s, 11th in 1965. Charcoal timber, native ore, limestone supplied material for numerous furnaces making pig iron, utensils, munitions in the Hanging Rock, Red River, Between Rivers, Rolling Fork, Green River Regions. Charcoal-furnace era ended in 1880s with depletion of ore and timber and use of modern methods. Over.

1381 HIGH BRIDGE
(4 mi. SW of Wilmore, KY 29, Jessamine Co.)

Highest railroad bridge in US over a navigable stream (308 feet). Planned as suspension bridge for Lexington and Danville R.R. by John Roebling, designer of famous Brooklyn Bridge (N.Y. City). Huge stone towers to hold cables built in 1851. Work on bridge abandoned during Civil War. Towers removed in 1929 by Southern Railroad to permit double tracks. Over.
(Reverse)
HIGH BRIDGE
First cantilever bridge built on the American continent. Most remarkable bridge in US when constructed in 1876. Marked the

beginning of modern scientific bridge building. It was designed by Charles Shaler Smith and built for the Cincinnati Southern Railroad. Bridge was replaced in 1911, using same foundations without stopping rail service. See over. *Presented by Southern Railway System.*

1382 OLD JOE CLARK BALLAD
(Jct. KY 577 & 1350, Clay Co.)

Mountain ballad, about 90 stanzas, sung during World War I, and later wars by soldiers from eastern Kentucky. Early version, as sung in Virginia, printed in 1918. Joe Clark, born 1839, lived here; shiftless and rough mountaineer of that day. His enemies were legion; he was murdered in 1885. In the moonshining days of 1870s, he ran government-supervised still.

1383 CUMBERLAND TRACE
(Campbellsville, Courthouse lawn, US 68, KY 55, Taylor Co.)

As early as 1779 and 1780, many settlers traveled over the trace, passing through what is now Taylor County. The Cumberland Trace branched off from the Wilderness Road near Logan's Station in Lincoln County (40 mi. east). It was the trail traveled by the pioneers who came through the Cumberland Gap to settle the then new lands of Ky. and Tenn. Over.
(Reverse)
CUMBERLAND TRACE
Turning west from Logan's Station, the trace crossed the Rolling Fork River; went down to Robinson Creek in what is now Taylor County; then near Buckhorn Creek, and down the south side of the Trace Fork of Sinking Creek (Pittman Creek). It crossed the Green River at Pittman's Station and went south across the Cumberland River to the site that is now Nashville. Over.

1384 FIRST RFD IN KENTUCKY
(Post Office, Allensville, KY 102, Todd Co.)

First rural free delivery of mail in Kentucky was established at Allensville Post Office on Jan. 11, 1897. Three carriers, with horse and buggy, over dirt roads, traveled 15 miles per day; covered an area of 24 square miles with population of 220, at $300 an-

nually. RFD enabled farmers to receive daily mail and avoid a drive to the post office.

1385 SAND CAVE
(Old entrance road to Cave area, KY 255, Edmonson Co.)

Floyd Collins was first to explore Sand Cave. Fallen rock trapped him in narrow passage 150 ft. from entrance, Jan. 30, 1925. Rescuers reached him with food and heat for short time. Aid cut off by shifting earth closing passage. Engineers sank 55-foot shaft but were unable to reach Collins' body until February 16. Rescue attempt publicized worldwide. Aroused sympathy of nation.

1386 DR. THOMAS HINDE
(Court & York Sts., Newport, Campbell Co.)

Northern Kentucky's first doctor. Born in Oxfordshire, England, on July 10, 1737. Graduate of Royal College of Physicians. Served at Quebec with Gen. James Wolfe. In 1765 settled in Virginia; the personal physician to Patrick Henry. Chief Surgeon, in 1775, for the "Gun Powder Expedition." Practiced medicine in Newport from the early 1800s until his death Sept. 28, 1828. *Presented by Campbell-Kenton County Medical Society.*

1387 RICHWOOD PRESBYTERIAN CHURCH
(KY 338, 2 mi. W. of I-75, Boone Co.)

Services have been held by this old church continuously since it was founded in 1834 by Joseph Cabell Harrison, first pastor. He and cousin John Breckinridge in 1824 founded early religious paper in Ky. Cousin of Pres. William Henry Harrison. Pastor's wife, Sophia Rice Harrison, granddaughter of David Rice, father of Presbyterian Church in Ky. Harrisons buried here.

1388 MICHAEL CASSIDY (1755–1829)
(2 mi. W. of Flemingsburg, Jct. KY 32 & Cassidy Rd., Fleming Co.)

A fearless Indian fighter in over 30 battles, Michael Cassidy built Cassidy Station (site—one mile south) in later 1780s. A native of Ireland, he came to Va. as cabin boy at age 12. Enlisted early in Revolution and was with Washington at British surrender at Yorktown, 1781. Settled in Fleming Co., Ky.; served 1800–06 as first senator and several terms as representative.

1389 BUCKNER-CHURCHILL FURNACE
(Approx. 5½ mi. S. of Greenville, KY 181, Muhlenberg Co.)

A round stone blast furnace built a mile northwest in 1837 by Aylette Hartswell Buckner and Cadwallader Churchill. Using local ore and charcoal fuel, it produced pig iron, which was hauled eighteen miles to South Carrollton for shipment on Green River, and kettles, shovels, tongs and andirons for sale in this vicinity. Last blast was in 1842. See the other side.
(Reverse)

IRON MADE IN KENTUCKY
A major producer since 1791, Ky. ranked 3rd in US in 1830s, 11th in 1965. Charcoal timber, native ore, limestone supplied material for numerous furnaces making pig iron, utensils, munitions in the Hanging Rock, Red River, Between Rivers, Rolling Fork, Green River Regions. Charcoal-furnace era ended in 1880s with depletion of ore and timber and use of modern methods. Over.

1390 HENRY CLAY FURNACE
(Adjacent to Courthouse, Munfordville, US 31-W, Hart Co.)

Furnace built 7¼ miles east in 1832 by Aylette Hartswell Buckner, S. V. Leedom, Cadwallader Churchill. A stone stack about 35 ft. high, 9 ft. across at widest inside, it burned charcoal fuel to produce pig iron and utensils from local ore. Its air-blast machinery was powered by a water wheel. Its operations were discontinued in 1837. See the other side.
(Reverse)

IRON MADE IN KENTUCKY
A major producer since 1791, Ky. ranked 3rd in US in 1830s, 11th in 1965. Charcoal timber, native ore, limestone supplied material for numerous furnaces making pig iron, utensils, munitions in the Hanging Rock, Red River, Between Rivers, Rolling Fork, Green River Regions. Charcoal-furnace era ended in 1880s with depletion of ore and timber and use of modern methods. Over.

1391 CAMP ANDERSON
(2 mi. S. of Flippin, KY 1366, Monroe Co.)

Camp established by Union Army to train and drill troops and as a place of rendezvous. In October 1861, Col. S. S. Stanton, 25th Tenn. Infantry, Confederate Army, was ordered to capture the encampment. He marched his regiment into the county and burned Camp Anderson, which had already been abandoned by the Federal troops.

1392 FIRST KENTUCKY CONSUMER RURAL COOPERATIVE ELECTRICITY
(6 mi. S. of Henderson, US 41 Alt., Henderson Co.)

Here in October 1937 Frank T. Street became first member-consumer to receive rural electric cooperative power in Ky. Energy was provided by Henderson RECC, first rural electric system in state to be energized. Cooperative electricity has provided a more stable and diversified economy and a higher standard of living in rural areas.

1393 MAGNIFICENT PIN OAK
(1 mi. E. of Charters, N. of KY 10, Lewis Co.)

One of the largest and oldest pin- or swamp-oak trees in the world. In 1970, when the highway was relocated, it was about one hundred and fifty years old; its trunk circumference was 16.2 feet; the diameter at breast height was five feet, and the total height was 58 feet. This historic oak is preserved as one of nature's beautiful achievements.

1394 FAMOUS TREE
(Indian Creek Church, Flippin, KY 249, Monroe Co.)

In 1894, a huge Tulip Poplar tree was felled about 1½ miles south of this site. It measured 11 ft. in diameter, 35 ft. in circumference. Two six-foot saws were welded together to cut it. A four-foot log from the tree was transported to Chicago for exhibition at the 1893–94 Columbian World's Fair and Exposition, where it won a first prize. Over.
(Reverse)

INDIAN CREEK CHURCH
The main log from this tree supplied lumber to build the second Baptist Church house of Indian Creek, and a part of the

Methodist Church. The first Baptist Church housed on this site was destroyed by fire in 1893. The second church house burned in 1921, and a third building was erected here. Over.

1395 LICKING FURNACE
(4th St., in front of Newport Mall, KY 8, Campbell Co.)

Built three blocks east in 1859 by Swift's Iron and Steel Works. As rebuilt in 1869, it was 65 feet high, with a maximum diameter inside of 16 feet. Its annual capacity was 17,000 tons of iron, using Connellsville coke as fuel. Iron mostly converted to steel at same works. Furnace ceased operating by 1888. See over. *Presented by Newport Works Interlake, Inc.*
(Reverse)

IRON MADE IN KENTUCKY

A major producer since 1791, Ky. ranked 3rd in US in 1830s, 11th in 1965. Charcoal timber, native ore, limestone supplied material for numerous furnaces making pig iron, utensils, and munitions throughout the northern and western portions of the Commonwealth of Kentucky. Old charcoal-furnace era ended by depletion of ore and timber and the growth of railroads. See over.

1396 NOLIN FURNACE
(Information Center at Moutadier Camp Ground, KY 2067, Edmonson Co.)

Also called Baker Furnace after its ironmaster, John H. Baker; was built in 1848, a mile north, by Craddock & Co. The top of the stone stack, about 40 ft. high originally, is still visible when water in Nolin Reservoir is low. Using steam power, charcoal fuel, it produced pig iron, kettles, andirons and other articles from local ore. Last blast in 1850.
(Reverse)

IRON MADE IN KENTUCKY

A major producer since 1791, Ky. ranked 3rd in US in 1830s, 11th in 1965. Charcoal timber, native ore, limestone supplied material for numerous furnaces making pig iron, utensils, munitions in the Hanging Rock, Red River, Between Rivers, Rolling Fork, Green River Regions. Charcoal-furnace era ended in 1880s with depletion of ore and timber and use of modern methods. Over.

1397 CEDAR CRAG
(Manchester Memorial Hospital, Marie Langdon & Memorial Dr., off KY 421, Clay Co.)

Site of home of David Yancey Lyttle, 1822–1904. Attorney who practiced in First Ky. Judicial District. As state senator from 1867–1871, he was an active member of Standing Committee on Education. In 1871 named a member of special committee to study and revise common school laws. Leader in passage of legislation for the improvement of the school system.

1398 COLUMBUS
(Columbus, KY 58, Hickman Co.)

First entire town in Kentucky to be moved from one site to another. In 1927, after the most severe flood in its history, Columbus was moved from the banks of the river to this bluff, 200 feet above, by the American Red Cross at a cost of $100,000. The relocation was under the supervision of Marion Rust, national Red Cross representative.

1399 EAST BROADWAY CEMETERY
(E. Broadway & Park Ave., Winchester, Clark Co.)

In 1833 town trustees bought about an acre for $45 for public burial ground. First cholera epidemic in U.S. reached here. Seventy-five victims were buried here in 1833. John Ward, town trustee and a leader in forming cemetery, and his wife were both plague victims. The cemetery used until 1854. Maintained as a memorial of that terrible tragedy.

1400 GUERRILLA RAIDS ON CLINTON
(Clinton, US 51, Hickman Co.)

Federal troops garrisoned in area between 1862 and 1865 were often harassed by enemy guerrillas. March 10, 1864, Clinton was first raided by about forty who took supplies and horses that had been purchased for Union army. On July 10, 1864, guerrillas nearing Clinton on another raid lost 3 men killed and 5 wounded in a skirmish with USA infantry.

1401 WILLIAM TAYLOR RUNNER ROADSIDE PARK
(3 mi. S. of Bowling Green, US 31-W, Warren Co.)

Runner (1890–1969) planned this, first roadside park in area, 1948. Officer U.S. Army, Mexican Campaign and World War I. Employed by Highway Department in 1930; Superintendent of Roadside Improvement for this District (1947–1960). Dedicated worker in the cause of highway beautification.

1402 WATTS FURNACES
(Middlesboro, US 25-E at KY 441, Bell Co.)

Stood ½ mi. SW. A pair of blast furnaces built by the Watts Steel and Iron Syndicate, Ltd., 1890–93, and operated until 1898. Each iron shell stack was 75 ft. high with a maximum inner diameter of 17 ft. Using coke fuel and local ore, they had a planned capacity together of 400 tons of iron daily, converted to steel at the same site. See the other side.
(Reverse)

IRON MADE IN KENTUCKY
A major producer since 1791, Ky. ranked 3rd in US in 1830s, 11th in 1965. Charcoal timber, native ore, limestone supplied material for numerous furnaces making pig iron, utensils, munitions in the Hanging Rock, Red River, Between Rivers, Rolling Fork, Green River Regions. Charcoal-furnace era ended in 1880s with depletion of ore and timber and use of modern methods. Over.

1403 MELMONT
(2 mi. N. of Burkesville, KY 704, Cumberland Co.)

The home of Brig. Gen. John Edwards King (1757–1828). Revolutionary War land grant for service through war attaining rank of Capt., 1780. Born in Va. Settled here 1799. Outstanding military tactician in War of 1812. Commended by Shelby for leadership in Battle of the Thames, 1813. Served as clerk of both county and circuit courts, 1803–24. His gravestone here.

1404 CAVE SPRING
(8 mi. SE of Lexington, Walnut Hill Rd. near Jct. with US 25, 421, Fayette Co.)

Home of Capt. Robert Boggs, born 1746, Mill Creek Hundred, Del. Moved to Va. Soldier in Revolution. Came to Ky., 1774, as chainman on Col. John Floyd's survey party. One of founders of Boonesborough. Officer, Cherokee Expedition, 1776. Under Washington, 1777–81. Took up Ky. land totaling 2,276 acres. Cave Spring was begun 1784, completed 1792. Quaint, substantial Georgian stone house.

1405 "OAK HILL"
(26 Aspen St., Calvert City, Marshall Co.)

Calvert City was named for Potilla Calvert, who built "Oak Hill" in 1860. He gave the land to railroad company so that the railroad might run by his home. He also saw to it that provisions were made for food and shelter for those who chose this site for settlement. Calvert was one of the founders of Calvert City's First Baptist Church. *Presented by citizens of Kentucky.*

1406 OLD MORRISON
(Transylvania University campus, 3rd St., Lexington, Fayette Co.)

An early Greek Revival design by Kentucky architect Gideon Shryock. Trustee and teacher Henry Clay guided construction supported by bequest of Col. James Morrison. Work on building slowed by cholera epidemic of 1833. Dedication was Nov. 4, 1833. Damaged by fire 1969. Morrison was rededicated May 9, 1971. See over.
(Reverse)

TRANSYLVANIA ALUMNI
Jefferson Davis, John Hunt Morgan, Stephen F. Austin, Cassius M. Clay, Albert Sidney Johnston, James Lane Allen and John Fox, Jr., all were students here. Among past Transylvanians are two U.S. Vice-Presidents—Richard M. Johnson and John C. Breckinridge—50 U.S. Senators, 101 Representatives, three House Speakers, 36 Governors, and 34 Ambassadors. See over.

1408 CIVIL WAR RAID
(SE of Hickman at State Line, Jct. KY 116 & 125, Fulton Co.)

On March 24, 1864, forces under Gen. Nathan B. Forrest captured the Federal garrison at Union City, eight miles southeast. On the same day a detachment of Forrest's cavalry crossed the state line here. This band of about 1,200 men proceeded seven miles northwest to Hickman which they raided, taking large quantities of supplies.

1409 GEN. JOSEPH WINLOCK (1758–1831)
(KY 55, approx. 2½ mi. S. of I-64, Shelby Co.)

Soldier and statesman. Served entire Revolutionary War, rising from private to captain. Came to Ky., 1787. Delegate to first Ky. Constitutional Convention, 1792. State senator from 1800 to 1810. Commissioned a Brig. Gen. in State Militia, 1812. Commanded regiments to aid Gen. William Henry Harrison in Northwest Territory. Buried in family cemetery. See other side.
(Reverse)

DR. JOHN KNIGHT (1748–1838)
Skilled surgeon and physician. First to practice in Shelby Co. Born in Scotland. Came to America, 1773. Served in Revolution under Col. William Crawford; with him when captured by Indians in Ohio, 1782. Crawford burned at stake. Knight escaped. Settled in Kentucky, 1789. Member of state legislature, 1796. Buried in Winlock family cemetery. See other side.

1410 CONFEDERATE BIVOUAC
(Cayce, KY 94, near Jct. with KY 239, Fulton Co.)

In the winter of 1861–62, the Sixth Battalion of Tennessee Cavalry commanded by Lieutenant Colonel T. H. Logwood constructed and occupied a camp of wooden huts near here. The winter was spent in scouting and patrolling in this area. In March 1862, a surprise attack by a Federal force from Hickman was repulsed after a vigorous skirmish.

1412 ZACHARY TAYLOR NATIONAL CEMETERY
(Entrance to cem. on Brownsboro Rd., Louisville, US 42, Jefferson Co.)

Gen. Zachary Taylor (1784–1850), distinguished lifetime soldier and twelfth President of United States, buried here in family cemetery. Commissioned Lt. 1808. Served in War of 1812; Black Hawk War, 1832; Seminole War, 1836–43. Major Gen., 1846. Active leader in Mexican War, 1846–47. Western Army Command, 1847. Elected President, 1848. Died in office.

1413 MORGAN—ON TO OHIO
(Near bridge crossing Salt River, KY 61, Bullitt Co.)

July 2, 1863, CSA Gen. J. H. Morgan began raid to prevent USA move to Tenn. and Va. Repulsed at Green River, July 4. Defeated a USA force at Lebanon, July 5. Moved through Bardstown, July 6. After night march, crossed here July 7. Rested troops few hours and proceeded to Brandenburg. Crossed to Indiana, July 8. He continued raid until captured in northeast Ohio, July 26.

1414 LAST RECORDED INDIAN RAID
(½ mi. NE of Legrande, KY 436, Hart Co.)

In Oct. 1792, ten Indians attacked party of travelers at Oven Spring. Two men and one woman were killed, a girl and woman captured, five pack horses taken. Settlers under leadership of Capt. William Edgar pursued raiding party four days, overtook them at Roberts Spring, killed all the Indians and rescued the woman and girl. Records show no later raid in area.

1415 MYSTERY CEMETERY
(KY 245 near Jct. with KY 1604, Bullitt Co.)

Decades-old graveyard discovered near here. Graves, with unmarked headstones, believed to be those of itinerant railroad workers struck down by cholera epidemic during the construction of the Bardstown-Springfield-Louisville Railroad around 1854, or burial ground for Civil War soldiers killed during one of the many skirmishes occurring in this area.

1416 PRESBYTERIAN CHURCH
(Winchester Ave. at 16th St., Ashland, Boyd Co.)

Organized June 11, 1819, at home of Maj. Jas. Poage, north of this spot, as Bethesda Presbyterian Church by Rev. Robert Wilson with 20 members. First a mile SW on Pollard Rd.; moved 1828 to Beech Grove, ½ mile W, and in 1858 to this corner as First Presbyterian Church, oldest Boyd County church building and congregation, 1971. *Marker presented by Church members.*

1417 POTTER COLLEGE
(Western Ky. Univ., entrance to grounds of Potter College of Arts and Humanities, Bowling Green, Warren Co.)

School for girls founded 1877 as Cedar Bluff Female College near Woodburn. Part of the staff moved to Bowling Green in 1899 and began Potter College. Located on Vinegar Hill, now part of the campus of Western Kentucky University. School closed in 1909. Name perpetuated in Potter College of Arts and Humanities of Western Kentucky University.

1418 BOWLING GREEN COLLEGE OF COMMERCE
(Western Ky. Univ., entrance to grounds of Bowling Green College of Commerce, Warren Co.)

Became a college of Western Kentucky University in 1963. Founded as part of Glasgow Normal Institute in 1875. School moved to Bowling Green in 1884. Was named Southern Normal School and Business College. In 1907 the schools separated. The Business University moved downtown, then to College Street. Flourished as a private school for over 50 years.

1419 WHITNEY M. YOUNG, JR. (1921–1971)
(Residential Manpower Center, Simpsonville, US 60 West, Shelby Co.)

Civil rights leader born here. Son of distinguished educator, Dr. Whitney M. Young, Sr. Served in US Army, World War II. Graduated Ky. State College, 1941; Univ. of Minn., 1947. Director of Urban Leagues in Minn. and Neb., 1947–53. Dean of School of Social Work, Atlanta Univ., 1954–60. Director National Urban League, 1961 until death. Originally buried Lexington, Ky.
(Reverse)
WHITNEY M. YOUNG, JR. (1921–1971)
Devoted his life to overcoming injustice to and furthering economic progress for blacks. As Director of National Urban League, helped thousands find employment. Declined cabinet post in 1968 to remain with League where he believed could accomplish more. Gravesite eulogy delivered by President Nixon; first civil rights leader so honored. Over.

1420 "FATHER OF KENTUCKY HISTORICAL SOCIETY HIGHWAY MARKER PROGRAM"
(Old State Capitol, Broadway, Frankfort, Franklin Co.)

Still dynamic after a full career of diversified public service, W. A. Wentworth directed rapid expansion of Kentucky Historical Highway Marker Program as Chairman, 1962 until his death, 1971. Born New Hampshire, 1888. Public Relations executive with Borden Co., N.Y., for 27 years. President General, Natl. Society Sons of the American Revolution.
(Reverse)
"FATHER OF KENTUCKY HISTORICAL SOCIETY HIGHWAY MARKER PROGRAM"
In 1962, eighty percent of the few markers in Kentucky were located in the Bluegrass area. Under W. A. Wentworth's leadership, markers were erected in every county with more than 1100 in the state. Affection for his "adopted state" was displayed by dedication to this program. These historical markers will remain a monument to his scholarship and integrity.

1421 PADUCAH FURNACE
(3rd & Norton, Paducah, McCracken Co.)

Built here 1889 by Paducah Iron Co., 70 ft. high with a maximum inner diameter of 14 ft. Rated annual capacity 30,000 tons of iron, using coke fuel. Operations began in 1900, smelting ore from Lyon, Trigg, Livingston counties in Ky., and from Missouri. It was in blast intermittently until 1903, when the furnace ruptured. Razed 1907. See the other side.
(Reverse)
IRON MADE IN KENTUCKY
A major producer since 1791, Ky. ranked 3rd in US in 1830s, 11th in 1965. Charcoal timber, native ore, limestone supplied material for numerous furnaces making pig iron, utensils, munitions in the Hanging Rock, Red River, Between Rivers, Rolling Fork, Green River Regions. Charcoal-furnace era ended in 1880s with depletion of ore and timber and use of modern methods. Over.

1422 GOVERNOR OWSLEY HOME
(1½ mi. N. of Danville, US 127, Boyle Co.)

Mansion built by William Owsley at close of term as Governor of Kentucky, 1844–48. Tract on which house stands part of land claimed by James Harrod prior to 1785. Owsley (1782–1862) served as Judge on the Court of Appeals, State Senator, and Secretary of State before elected Governor. Owsley County named for him. *Marker presented by Charles E. Beck.*

1423 TENN. ROLLING MILLS
(Near Confederate, KY 274, Lyon Co.)

Moved from Nashville to a site one mile west, 1845–46, by Thomas Tennessee Watson and Daniel Hillman. Pig iron from charcoal-fueled blast furnaces in this vicinity was processed into boiler plate, sheets, beams and other articles here for shipment all over the Mississippi Valley. Operations transferred to Louisville in 1884 by the L. P. Ewald Iron Co.

1424 CAMP BRECKINRIDGE
(Main entrance to Camp Breckinridge, US 60, Union Co.)

Army post built in 1942, on 36,000 acres, at a cost of $39,000,000. Named for John C. Breckinridge, US Vice President, 1856–60; Confederate Secretary of War, 1865. Created as infantry training center for up to 40,000 men. Used during WW II, 1943–46, as prisoner of war camp for as many as 3,000 enlisted men of German Army. Camp deactivated in 1949. Over.
(Reverse)

CAMP BRECKINRIDGE
During Korean War, 1950–54, camp reopened for training of infantry. From 1954 to 1963 used for summer training of 4,500 National Guard troops. Disposal of camp by Army began in 1963. Dept. of Labor obtained 853 acres for Job Corps Training Center opened in 1965. Remaining acreage acquired by individuals, city of Morganfield and state of Kentucky. Over.

1425 THE HOCKERSMITH HOUSE
(218 South Scott, Madisonville, Hopkins Co.)

The home of L. D. Hockersmith, Captain, 10th Ky., General John Hunt Morgan's Cavalry, CSA. Hockersmith captured by Federal troops during Morgan's Ohio raid, July 20, 1863. Held with Morgan in Ohio State Prison at Columbus. Helped dig tunnel by which he and five other officers escaped with Morgan on Nov. 27, 1863. This

escape was one of most daring of all time.

1426 CUMBERLAND FORD
(KY 66 & Pine St., Pineville, Bell Co.)

One of the most important points on the Wilderness Road marked by Daniel Boone in 1775. Ford first used by Indians, then by early explorers and the Long Hunters. After Boone opened the way west, more than 100,000 settlers used the crossing as a gateway to Ky. During Civil War ford occupied by both Union and CSA troops because of its strategic location.

1427 MURRAY STATE UNIVERSITY
(West side of Murray campus, KY 121 Alt., Calloway Co.)

Established 1922. Founder, Rainey T. Wells (1875–1958). His home, where the idea of the University was born, 350 feet SE of here. Dr. Wells second president of Murray State. Gov. Morrow signed bill authorizing two "normal schools"—one in east Ky., other in west Ky., on March 8, 1922. Murray chosen as site in west Ky., Sept. 17, 1922. Doors opened Sept. 24, 1923. Dr. John W. Carr (1859–1960) was first president. His home 285 feet SW. To locate school at Murray, citizens of Calloway Co. gave to Ky. $17,000 to acquire land for campus and $100,000 to construct Administration Building 150 feet NE of here.

1428 THE OLD CEMETERY
(At cem., adjacent to Main St., US 27, Harrison Co.)

Only burial ground in Cynthiana from 1793 to 1868. Located on four acres deeded to the city by Robert Harrison, owner of land on which Cynthiana founded. Samuel January, first Mayor, and other prominent early citizens buried here. First school in city, Harrison Academy, situated on corner of this plot. Cynthiana named for Harrison's daughters Cynthia and Anna.

1429 CARNEAL HOUSE, CA. 1815
(406 E. Second St., Covington, Kenton Co.)

Built by Thomas Carneal, a founder of Covington, on land purchased in 1814 from Thomas Kennedy. First brick house in the city. Georgian in concept, style reveals the influence of the great Italian architect Andrea Palladio. In 1825 Lafayette visited as a guest of owner William W. Southgate. Other famous visitors were Henry Clay, Daniel Webster and Andrew Jackson.

1430 SALT RIVER CHURCH, ½ MILE →
(2 mi. S. of Lawrenceburg, Old US 127, Anderson Co.)

Mother church of Baptist witness in area. Constituted Feb. 3, 1798, by William Taylor and John Penney with seven charter members. John Penney, first pastor, served until his death, 1833. Great-grandfather of J. C. Penney, founder of Penney Stores. In 1842, log meetinghouse was replaced by present building. Last church member died in 1965.

1431 WESTMINSTER UNITED PRESBYTERIAN CHURCH
(28th and Broadway, Paducah, McCracken Co.)

Incorporated March 3, 1851, by an act of Kentucky General Assembly as Cumberland Presbyterian Church. Merged with Presbyterian Church USA, 1906, and became Kentucky Avenue Presbyterian Church. In 1951 the congregation moved to the modified Gothic structure here and changed name to Westminster Presbyterian Church.

1432 FELICIANA
(KY 94, 1½ mi. from US 45 at Water Valley, Graves Co.)

Site of a settlement established in 1830s. By 1838 it was most important trading point in the county. After a state road was built through Feliciana in 1845, it became one of the greatest commercial centers in western Ky. This community remained prominent until bypassed by the railroad in 1858. Abandoned when business interests moved to other towns.

1433 POTTINGER'S STATION
(Near Gethsemani, KY 52, 1 mi. E. of Jct. KY 247 & 52, Nelson Co.)

Site of one of the forts which protected the early settlement of Bardstown. Built by Samuel Pottinger, soldier in Revolution, who first saw the land in 1778 when he came from Maryland with troops of Capt. James Harrod. In 1781 Pottinger returned with his family and built station. It was often used as a refuge for other settlers migrating to Kentucky.

1434 KENTON FURNACE
(4th & Park Ave., Newport, Campbell Co.)

Built at foot of Park Avenue in 1869 by the Kenton Iron Co., to supply iron to a foundry making pipe and structural materials. It was 58 ft. high and 15 ft. across at widest point inside, burning coke fuel and powered by steam. In 1877, the machinery was taken down, and assembled again at Greendale, Ohio, beginning to operate in 1879. See other side.
(Reverse)

IRON MADE IN KENTUCKY

A major producer since 1791, Ky. ranked 3rd in US in 1830s, 11th in 1965. Charcoal timber, native ore, limestone supplied material for numerous furnaces making pig iron, utensils, and munitions throughout the northern and western portions of the Commonwealth of Kentucky. Old charcoal-furnace era ended by depletion of ore and timber and the growth of railroads. See over.

1435 ISAAC HITE'S HOME
(12215 Lucas Ln., Anchorage, Jefferson Co.)

This log house, which appears as Hite's house on John Filson's map printed in 1784, was on the plantation, Cave Spring, owned by Isaac Hite, an early surveyor. Hite (1753–1794) was born in Virginia. He came to Kentucky in 1773 in Capt. Thomas Bullitt's party which was the first to survey Jefferson Co. and the land on which Louisville now stands.
(Reverse)

ISAAC HITE

In 1775 Isaac Hite represented the Boiling Spring Settlement at Transylvania Convention that met at Boonesborough in first attempt to form government in Ky. He fought beside Boone, Todd and Stoner defending Boonesborough, being wounded on April 24, 1777. He served with Gen. George Rogers Clark in the Indian Campaigns of 1780 and 1782. Hite died in 1794.

1436 GEORGE GRAHAM VEST
(Owensboro, Courthouse lawn, US 60, Daviess Co.)

Established Owensboro's second newspaper, *The Gazette*, near here in 1852, with Robert S. Triplett, an Owensboro businessman. Vest was U.S. Senator from Missouri, 1879–1903. Author of world famous "Tribute To A Dog." This spontaneous oration in court in defense of a backwoodsman's dog, "Old Drum," won case for the client and gained George G. Vest world fame. (Reverse)

"TRIBUTE TO A DOG"

"The one absolutely unselfish friend that man can have . . . the one that never deserts him and the one that never proves ungrateful or treacherous is his dog. . . . He guards the sleep of his pauper master as if he were a prince. When all other friends desert he remains."–From a pleading before a jury by George Graham Vest.

1437 OLDEST HOUSE IN LEXINGTON
(317 S. Mill St., Lexington, Fayette Co.)

Built in 1784 for Adam Rankin, minister of Lexington's pioneer Presbyterian Church. Samuel D. McCullough, born here in 1803, was a teacher, astronomer, antiquarian and maker of world-famous Burrowes mustard. In 1971, the Blue Grass Trust for Historic Preservation moved this house from its original location, at 215 West High Street, to prevent its destruction.

1438 SHERBURNE BRIDGE
(KY 11 at bridge, Fleming-Bath Co. line, Fleming Co.)

The most unusual of Kentucky's covered bridges is the Sherburne "suspension" bridge, built 1867–68 at a cost of $3,500. In the early days a stagecoach route from Mt. Sterling to Maysville crossed the bridge, then privately owned. This bridge is 266 ft. long and has a single roadway 14 ft. wide. The heavy steel suspension cables and reinforcing timbers added in 1951.

1439 DOVER COVERED BRIDGE
500 ft. south (Tuckahoe Rd. near Jct. with KY 8 at Dover, Mason Co.)

One of the oldest covered bridges in Kentucky still in use. Erected in 1835, it was originally a toll bridge. The 62-foot span was built in an unusual Queenpost truss design similar to early barn construction. Major repairs were made by Bower Bridge Co. in 1928. Restoration of bridge completed by

the Kentucky Highway Dept., 1966.

1440 FAYETTE COUNTY
(Main St., Lexington, Courthouse lawn, Fayette Co.)

One of three original counties formed when Kentucky Co., Va., was divided by Va. act in 1780. Included area north and east of Ky. River, 37 present-day counties and parts of 7 others. Reduced to its present boundaries 1799. Named for Marquis de Lafayette, French champion of liberty, who came to America in 1777 to assist with our war for independence.

1441 JEFFERSON COUNTY
(Louisville, Courthouse lawn, Jefferson Co.)

One of three original counties formed when Kentucky Co., Virginia, was divided by Va. act in 1780. Other 2 counties were Lincoln and Fayette. Jefferson included 19 present-day counties; parts of 11 others. By 1811 reduced to present boundaries. Named for Thomas Jefferson, then governor of Va.; author of Declaration of Independence; and third U. S. President, 1801–1809.

1442 TRINITY EPISCOPAL CHURCH
(Main St., Danville, US 127, 150, Boyle Co.)

One of the oldest church buildings in Danville. Erected in 1830 after Trinity parish founded in 1829. Rebuilt on the original walls following fire which swept central part of town, 1860. James Birney and Ephraim McDowell members of first vestry. In churchyard is tombstone of first rector, Rev. Gideon McMillan, a victim of the cholera epidemic of 1833.

1443 DANIEL BOONE'S TRACE
(Northbound rest area on I-75, Madison Co.)

Two miles east is location of the trail blazed in 1775 by Daniel Boone, who was then an agent for the Transylvania Co. This famous road was used by thousands of settlers traveling to Kentucky. Boone's Trace entered Ky. at Cumberland Gap, crossed the Cumberland River at Pineville, ran northwest past London, and ended at the fort at Boonesborough on the Ky. River.

1444 "GLEN WILLIS"
(Wilkinson Blvd., Frankfort, US 421 Bypass, Franklin Co.)

Willis A. Lee, Jr., built a double two-story log house here in 1793. Tract of land on which the house stood was given to Lee by his uncle, Hancock Lee, founder of Leestown, the first settlement in Franklin County. In 1815 Lee erected a story and a half brick house, "Glen Willis," on same site and resided there until his death in 1824. See over.
(Reverse)
"GLEN WILLIS"
In 1832 the Lee family sold "Glen Willis" to Humphrey Marshall, officer in Revolution, lawyer, extensive landowner, legislator, Federalist leader. In 1809 he fought a duel with Henry Clay over political differences. Marshall wrote one of the earliest histories of Kentucky. Died in 1841. House then bought and enlarged by Henry H. Murray. See over.

1445 SCHOOL OF MEDICINE
(2nd & Broadway, Lexington, Fayette Co.)
Site of the world-renowned Medical Hall of Transylvania University. Erected 1839 and dedicated November 2, 1840. Massive building of Grecian architecture with facilities not surpassed at that time by any school in America or Europe. Constructed on a lot purchased for $5,000, of which citizens of Lexington contributed $3,000. *Marker presented by George G. Greene, M.D.*
(Reverse)
SCHOOL OF MEDICINE
The magnificent structure built here was used by Transylvania University until Medical College disbanded in 1857. Building was destroyed by fire in 1863 while being used as military hospital by the Union Army. Over 6,400 of America's early physicians received training at Transylvania during its illustrious existence. *Marker presented by George G. Greene, M.D.*

1446 HOUSE OF HISTORY
(301 Walnut St., Springfield, KY 555, Washington Co.)
Built on part of Matthew Walton's land used to establish Springfield. Deeded, 1817, to John Thompson by the town trustees. Bought same year by John Bainbridge, who operated a tavern there. Sold in 1830 to D. H. Spears, noted silversmith. Later owned by James Calhoun, who boasted he cast only vote for Lincoln tallied in county, 1860. Named Ky. Landmark House in 1969.

1447 FAIRLAWN, CA. 1845
(904 Broadway, Lexington, Fayette Co.)
Home of Dr. Benjamin W. Dudley from 1846 until 1870. Small white cottage to south purchased by Dr. Dudley, 1839, used for instruction in anatomy and surgery while on faculty of Transylvania Medical School. William T. Withers, a CSA Colonel, purchased Fairlawn, 1874. General U. S. Grant and King Kalakaua of Hawaii were entertained here. *Presented by Lexington Surgical Society.*
(Reverse)
DR. BENJAMIN DUDLEY
Eminent Kentucky surgeon and outstanding lithotomist of 19th century. Born Spotsylvania Co., Virginia, April 12, 1785. Died in Lexington, Ky., January 20, 1870. Dr. Dudley served as professor of anatomy and surgery at Transylvania Medical School, 1817–50. After retirement, practiced occasionally at Fairlawn. *Presented by Lexington Surgical Society.*

1448 SANDERS TAVERN
(6 mi. E. of Campbellsville, US 68, Taylor Co.)
Site of tavern owned by Henry Sanders, Jr., and operated by him as early as 1814. The 30-room inn was a famous stop for the six-horse stage coaches traveling the old Lexington and Nashville Road. Many notable persons were guests at the tavern, the most prominent of whom was Pres. Andrew Jackson on his way to Washington, September 27, 1832. See over.
(Reverse)
SANDERS TAVERN
Henry Sanders, Jr., 1776–1844, settled in this county in 1795. Besides building Sanders Tavern, parts of which stood until about 1947, he also built "Clay Hill," the home of his son James Sanders. He assisted in the survey of the road built through Muldraugh's Hill, and in 1837 gave the land for Pleasant Hill Baptist Church, located nearby. See over.

1449 THE BIG SPRING
(Back of Harrodsburg High School, US 68 & 127 Bypass, Mercer Co.)

This spring, with its abundant, never-failing flow of water, was reason for the location of Harrodsburg. Capt. James Harrod with his party, on June 16, 1774, began building first settlement in Kentucky along this "town branch." Harrod in the previous year had visited the area and after choosing this site returned to build town bearing his name.

1450 DEER CREEK FURNACE
(Approx. 4 mi. SE of Tolu at Jct. KY 135 & 1668, Crittenden Co.)

Stood one mile south. It was a brick blast furnace, smelting iron ore from the numerous small pits still visible nearby, using locally made charcoal fuel, and having a steam-powered air blast. Built in 1850 by Alleniah Cole and Carey Allen Darlington, but operated only briefly. Land owned later by Hurricane Furnace, one mile west. See over.
(Reverse)
IRON MADE IN KENTUCKY
A major producer since 1791, Ky. ranked 3rd in US in 1830s, 11th in 1965. Charcoal timber, native ore, limestone supplied material for numerous furnaces making pig iron, utensils, munitions in the Hanging Rock, Red River, Between Rivers, Rolling Fork, Green River Regions. Old charcoal-furnace era ended by depletion of ore and timber and the growth of railroads. Over.

1451 LEWIS & CLARK EXPEDITION
(At the Wharf, 4th St., Louisville, Jefferson Co.)

Exploration of the Northwest Territory was the first expedition undertaken by U.S. Government. Planned by President Thomas Jefferson. Led by Army Captains Meriwether Lewis and William Clark. Lewis began voyage at Pittsburgh; descended River to falls of the Ohio, Louisville, where he met Clark. On Oct. 26, 1803, they set out on historic journey westward. Over.
(Reverse)
WILLIAM CLARK (1770–1838)
Brother of George Rogers Clark. Born in

Va. Came to Louisville in 1785. He was commissioned Lt. in Army in 1792 and served four years, two years in same division with Meriwether Lewis. After leaving Army, he returned to Louisville. From 1803 to 1806 was with Lewis on expedition. In 1807, he moved to St. Louis. Named Gov. of Missouri Territory, 1813. Over.

1452 DR. REUBEN SAUNDERS (1808–1891)
(Entrance to Oak Grove Cem., Paducah, McCracken Co.)

Physician credited with discovery that hypodermic use of morphine-atropine halted cholera during epidemic here, 1873. Telegraphed prescription to other plague-stricken areas. Honored by Medical Association in U.S. and Europe. First to advocate fresh air for pneumonia and tuberculosis. Grandfather of Irvin S. Cobb. *Presented by John Pearce Campbell IV.*
(Reverse)
DR. REUBEN SAUNDERS (1808–1891)
Outstanding pioneer physician in Western Kentucky for 50 years. Born in Frankfort; died in Paducah. Buried in this cemetery beside his son, Dr. John Bartlett Saunders (1840–1873), also a physician of eminence. John migrated to Honolulu, where he did research on leprosy. He was personal physician to King of Hawaii at the time of his death. *Presented by John Pearce Campbell IV.*

1453 CUMBERLAND PRESBYTERIAN COLLEGE
(Near Jct. US 62 & KY 91, Princeton, Caldwell Co.)

Site of college founded March, 1826, by the Cumberland Presbyterian Church. First president was Rev. F. R. Cossitt. School opened with six students on some 500 acres of land bought for $6,000. A manual-labor school, students required to work 2 hours a day on farm. Classes in theology aided those interested in ministry. College merged 1858 with Cumberland Univ., Lebanon, Tenn.

1454 SCOTT COUNTY COURTHOUSE
(Georgetown, Courthouse lawn, US 25, 460, Scott Co.)

Present structure, 4th courthouse of Scott County, erected in 1877 at a cost of $34,600. It is an outstanding example of the French "Second Empire Style," known

in U.S. as "Gen. Grant Style." Built of materials obtainable in this area. Distance from ground to top of steeple is 185 ft. Designed by Thomas Boyd of Pittsburgh, who served as supervising architect.
(Reverse)

GOEBEL TRIAL HERE

Scott County courthouse chosen by Judge J. E. Cantrill for trials of the 20 persons accused of being involved in the assassination of Governor William Goebel. Although the murder was in Frankfort, the hearings were held in Georgetown to insure fair trials to the indicted. Three of the principal suspects were found guilty and sentenced to life imprisonment.

1455 SHAKER COLONY
(South Union, near Jct. US 68 & KY 73, Logan Co.)

Organized 1807, as Gasper Society of United Believers in Christ's Second Appearing. Building program started and trade established in textiles, seeds, mill products, and purebred cattle. Peak membership 350; acreage 6,000. Most prosperous period 1840–60. Last western colony to disband, 1922. Museum moved here, in 1972, with handicrafts and furniture of the Shakers.

1456 DAVIESS COUNTIANS WHO SERVED
(Owensboro, Courthouse lawn, US 60, Daviess Co.)

During World War I approximately 80,000 men enlisted from Kentucky. Of this number 1,747 that answered the call to serve, between April 1917 and November 1918, were from Daviess County. Seventy-one were killed in action and seventy-six others wounded. This marker erected to honor these soldiers for all time to come. *Sponsored by 82 buddies of Yellow Banks Barracks 2429.*

1457 INDIAN CREEK BAPTIST CHURCH
(In front of church, KY 32 & 36, Harrison Co.)

This is original building erected on this site by pioneer families of Indian Creek Settlement. Church constituted in 1790; in continuous use until 1965. Buried in church cemetery are Rev. Charles Webb, an early minister; Revolutionary soldiers, Moses Endicott, Edward McShane, Henry Talbert, and Hugh Wilson; and many of first settlers.

1458 FORT WEBB
(Beech Bend Rd. & Country Club Dr., Warren Co.)

Constructed by CSA during early days of Civil War. One of numerous fortifications in Bowling Green area used by CSA and Union forces. Located at head of navigation on Barren and Green River systems, Bowling Green became an important stronghold with two railroads to Memphis and Nashville. Threats from Union forces caused CSA to abandon town on February 14, 1862. Over.
(Reverse)

CIVIL WAR FORTIFICATIONS OF BOWLING GREEN
(A map showing fortifications)

1459 CLAY VILLA, CA. 1845
(221 Forest Avenue, Lexington, Fayette Co.)

Home of James B. Clay, son of Henry Clay. Designed by Major Thomas Lewinski, as an Italianate villa. Floor plan consisted of central hall with 4 rooms on each floor. Thomas Clay's home, Mansfield, on Richmond Rd. designed at same time. James Clay (1817–64) practiced law with his father; charge d'affaires in Portugal, Congressman and member of Peace Commission, 1861.

1460 MOTHER OF GOD CHURCH
(119 W. 6th St., Covington, Kenton Co.)

Full title: The Annunciation of the Ever Virgin Mary, Mother of God. Organized 1841 by the Rev. Dr. Ferdinand Kuhr. Mother Church of German parishes and second parish in Covington. First church built 1842. One-story brick school erected 1843. Present Renaissance church built 1871. The towers rise 200 ft.; the cupola, 150 ft. *Presented by members of Parish.*
(Reverse)

"CRADLE OF THE ARTS"

Five murals by Johann Schmitt. Wall frescoes painted in 1890 by Wenceslaus Thien. Stained-glass windows imported from Munich. The 38-rank Koehnken and Grimm organ was built in 1876. English mosaic sanctuary floor installed, 1903, and the German Mettlach tile floor in 1921. The famed artist Frank Duveneck baptized here, 1848. *Presented by members of the Parish.*

1461 HOWELL LAND
(5 mi. W. of Centertown, KY 85, Ohio Co.)

Adjacent area, so-called Howell Land, was 7,472-acre plantation of Capt. John Howell, one of county's earliest settlers. The old blazed road from Hartford to Vienna and old buffalo road passed through here. Howell, 1756–1830, fought in the Revolutionary War battles of Brandywine, Germantown, Yorktown, and Monmouth. Buried across road. Remains moved to Frankfort, 1874.

1462 RUDDELL'S MILLS
(Ruddell's Mills, KY 1940, Bourbon Co.)

Near his home Isaac Ruddell built a gristmill in 1788 on the north side of Hinkson bridge, and a sawmill in 1795 to be operated by his son, Abram. A 720-spindle cotton mill erected 500 feet west by Thomas and Hugh Brent in 1828, burned 1836. Soon rebuilt by Abram Spears, it also spun wool until about 1855. Ruddell gave land for Stoner Mouth Church and cemetery.

1463 BARNETT'S STATION
(2 mi. E. of Hartford on Barnett's Station Rd., just off KY 69, Ohio Co.)

Site of one of the earliest forts erected in this area. Established by brothers Joseph and Alexander Barnett who came from Virginia to Kentucky in early 1780s. Settlement was frequently raided by Indians. During an attack in April 1790, two children were killed and Hannah Barnett, the ten-year-old daughter of Joseph, carried off and held captive for six months.

1464 FIRST BAPTIST CHURCH
(100 West Clinton St., Frankfort, Franklin Co.)

Organized in 1833, issuing from an integrated worship, this church was established by John Ward and Ziah Black. Ward donated first lot. Members worshipped in private homes before occupying the first structure. Construction for present church began, 1904. Distinguished religious, educational, and civic leaders have held membership here.

1465 LT. PRESLEY N. O'BANNON, USMC
(Frankfort Cemetery, E. Main St., US 60, Frankfort, Franklin Co.)

First American to raise U.S. flag on foreign soil at Battle of Derne on shores of Tripoli, April 27, 1805. Led attack that overcame Barbary Coast pirates who were holding 180 American seamen for ransom. O'Bannon came to Logan County in 1807. Served in State Legislature 1812, 17, 20–21, and Senate 1824–26. Died in 1850. Remains moved to Frankfort, 1919.
(Reverse)
MARINE CORPS EMBLEM
(Image)

1466 DR. LUKE P. BLACKBURN CORRECTIONAL COMPLEX
(At Complex, 1 mi. W. of US 25 on Spurr Road, Fayette Co.)

Originally Kentucky Village, this complex renamed in honor of Dr. Luke P. Blackburn, 26th Governor of Ky., in recognition of his pioneer efforts in prison reform. Elected Governor in 1879, after campaigning to relieve conditions at Frankfort Penitentiary, he asked for drastic changes in penal system in first message to legislature.
(Reverse)
BLACKBURN CORRECTIONAL COMPLEX
In 1880 prison reform finally began. Abolition of the lessee system soon followed. Governor Luke P. Blackburn's efforts resulted in creation of the Kentucky State Penitentiary at Eddyville. Dr. Blackburn also noted for treating epidemics in parts of U.S. and other countries. Native of Woodford County, born 1816, he singlehandedly fought great epidemic of cholera there, 1835.

1467 JAMES FORGY—PIONEER
(Near Quality Church of Christ, KY 106, Butler Co.)

Born in Ireland, 1752; fought in the Revolutionary War under General Francis Marion. One of first settlers in N. Logan County, Ky., 1794. Charter member Caney Fork and Concord churches. Died 1828. Grandson, James N. Forgy, 1826–1923, built early grist mill on Muddy River. Established Forgytown (Quality); built the Quality Church of Christ. Buried there. *Presented by William H. Forgy Wood.*

1468 LINCOLN HERITAGE HOUSE

(Elizabethtown, ¼ mi. E. of US 31-W, Hardin Co.)

Pioneer homes of the Hardin Thomas family. One-room log cabin built circa 1789. Thomas Lincoln, the father of 16th President, did the carpentry and cabinet work on the four-room log structure built ca. 1805. For several years Thomas Lincoln was a resident of Hardin County, which then included other present-day counties. Restoration was made possible by Hardin County Historical Society.

1469 WEST KENTUCKY INDUSTRIAL COLLEGE

(1400 Thompson Ave., Paducah, McCracken Co.)

Ground broken for this college on December 9, 1909, by Dr. Dennis H. Anderson, who had a determination to improve education for Negroes in Kentucky. The cornerstone for first building laid, 1911. Dr. Anderson failed to get bill passed in 1912 legislature to make the school a state institution. It did become state-supported in 1918 and by 1938 had grown to be the third largest Negro junior college in the United States. *Presented by the National Alumni Association: Lorenzo Goatley, President, J. D. Marks, Jr., Secy.*
(Reverse)

WEST KENTUCKY INDUSTRIAL COLLEGE

Before it merged with Ky. State, 1938, this college was served by Presidents D. H. Anderson, 1909–37, and H. C. Russell, 1937–38. A vocational school established in 1938. The following have served as its president: M. H. Griffin, 1938–43; H. C. Russell, 1943–47; M. J. Sleet (Acting Pres.), 1947–48; C. L. Timberlake, 1948–57; and H. C. Mathis since 1957. School has continued to meet the vocational needs of Kentuckians. *Presented by the National Alumni Association.*

1470 WING COMMANDER

(Iron Works Pike, Jct. KY 1973 & Mt. Horeb Pike, Lexington, Fayette Co.)

Famous five-gaited saddle horse. Won first championship as 3-year-old in Chicago International Show. Undefeated for 7 yrs., 1948–54. Won over 200 championships at state fairs in 9 years of competition. De-

feated only twice in lifetime. After retiring from show ring, he sired many world champions. Foaled at Dodge Stables, 1943. Trained and shown by Earl Teater.
(Reverse)

FAMOUS SADDLE HORSE

(Photograph of Wing Commander)

1471 GOODWIN (GOODIN) FORT

(Near Boston, KY 52, north of Jct. with Stillwell-Patton Rd., Nelson Co.)

Established by Samuel Goodwin in 1780 at the site of Old Boston. Important link with other stations encircling future Bardstown, and became refuge for pioneers in area. Fort raided by Indians, July 1781. Peter Kennedy led the reprisal against Indians, but captured. He escaped after two years. Though pursued by Indians, he warned settlers, who repelled the attack.

1472 THE POINT

(George Rogers Clark Park, Riverside Dr., Covington, Kenton Co.)

Confluence of Ohio and Licking Rivers. Christopher Gist, Agent of the Ohio Company, was first white man known to have set foot on Point, 1751. The Lieutenant of Kentucky Co., Va., Col. John Bowman, led expedition from here against Shawnee Indians in Ohio, 1777. Governor Isaac Shelby rendezvoused 4,000 Ky. troops here before his victory at the Thames, 1813. Over.
(Reverse)

PIONEER LEADERS HERE

Many other pioneer leaders made the Point a base for military operations, among them Benjamin Logan, Daniel Boone, Simon Kenton and George Rogers Clark. In 1780 and 1782 Clark and his 2 regiments met here before crossing the Ohio to attack the Shawnees. Second expedition was to avenge the Battle of Blue Licks; 5 Indian towns were destroyed. See over.

1473 DR. PHILLIP'S BIRTHPLACE

(303 S. Main St., Nicholasville, Jessamine Co.)

Dr. Lena Madesin Phillips, founder of National Federation of Business and Professional Women's Clubs, 1919, born here, September 15, 1881. Her work with the YWCA, 1917, led to interest in organization of business women. Instrumental in organizing and first President of the International Federation of B. and P. W., 1930. Died 1955; buried Maple Grove Cem., Nicholasville.

1474 LYNDON
(Lyndon, KY 146, Jefferson Co.)

An early settler, Alvin Wood, named this community in 1871. One of America's oldest military schools, Ky. Military Institute, founded, 1845; moved here, 1896. Points of interest in area: Central State Hospital, founded on site of Isaac Hite's home, and Oxmoor, home of Alexander Scott Bullitt, who helped draft first Ky. State Constitution. *Presented by Lyndon Homemakers Club.*

1475 TRAINER AND JOCKEY
(Town Square at Jeffersontown, Jefferson Co.)

Roscoe Goose, 1891–1971, rode the 1913 Derby Winner Donerail, which paid biggest odds in Derby history. Born near here, Goose became a trainer and aided many jockeys. Active in all aspects of racing. One of first 10 men named to Ky. Athletic Hall of Fame, March 14, 1957. Pres., Kentucky Thoroughbred Breeders Assn., 3 yrs. Buried Cave Hill Cemetery, Louisville, Ky.

1476 FIRST METHODIST CHURCH
(211 Washington St., Frankfort, Franklin Co.)

Organized by Rev. William Holman in 1821. First Methodist Conference in Kentucky, 1790, made Frankfort, then a frontier station, part of the Lexington Circuit. The first small church built on Ann Steet. Present site of church purchased, 1856; building completed, 1858. Bishops H. H. Kavanaugh and E. L. Tullis served as pastors of church. *Presented by John B. Browning Memorial Class.*

1477 HORSE HOLLOW CABIN
(Michigan Ave., at First Christian Church, Monticello, KY 92, Wayne Co.)

Built before 1814 by Elder "Raccoon" John Smith, 1784–1868. Associate of Alexander Campbell and Barton W. Stone in the establishment of the Christian Church in this area.

1478 STIRMAN'S FOLLY
(519 Locust St., Owensboro, Daviess Co.)

This imposing Victorian structure built circa 1860 by Dr. William Doswell Stirman, who was a successful physician. Received its name because he spent a fortune building it. In 1915, Samuel R. Ewing, civic leader and tobacco farmer, purchased and remodeled the house. He entertained Clara Barton, founder of the American Red Cross, and other notables here.

1479 DISTINGUISHED NAVAL OFFICERS— ALUMNI OF KAVANAUGH
GRADUATES OF U.S. NAVAL ACADEMY, ANNAPOLIS
(Woodford St., Lawrenceburg, US 62, Anderson Co.)

	Class of
ADMIRAL Edmund Tyler Wooldridge	1920
VICE ADM Charles K. Duncan	1933
REAR ADM (Ret) John Huston Brady	1923
REAR ADM (Ret) Rhodam Yarrott McElroy	1935
REAR ADM (Ret) Andrew Irwin McKee	1917
REAR ADM (Ret) Logan McKee	1921
REAR ADM (Ret) Elliott West Shanklin	1924
CAPT J. Wade Adams, Jr.	1924
CAPT (Ret) Warfield Clay Bennett, Jr.	1936
CAPT Fred "Buzz" Borries, Jr.	1935
CAPT (Ret) James Beattie Denny	1933
CAPT (Ret) Hugh Murrey Durham	1942
CAPT (Ret) James Gilbert Franklin	1933
CAPT (Ret) Joseph Howard Gibbons, Jr.	1924
CAPT (Ret) George Russell Lee	1935
CAPT (Ret) Percy Anthony Lilly, Jr.	1941
CAPT (Ret) Malcolm Wood Pemberton	1922
CAPT (Ret) Hugh Trent MacKay	1930
CAPT (Ret) William S. Manning	1939
CAPT (Ret) Frank Smith	1935
CAPT (Ret) Ronald Francis Stultz	1939

(Reverse)

DISTINGUISHED ARMY OFFICERS—ALUMNI OF KAVANAUGH
GRADUATES OF U.S. MILITARY ACADEMY, WEST POINT

	Class of
MAJ GEN William Mattingly Breckinridge	1928
BRIG GEN William Robards Buster	1939
COL (Ret) Robert Pepper Clay	1925
COL John Hiley Cobb, Jr.	1943
COL (Ret) John Richard Knight	1940
COL (Ret) Thomas Washington Woodyard	1935

(Graduates of Kavanaugh often remarked

Rhoda C. Kavanaugh's school in Lawrenceburg was dubbed "Little Annapolis." Kentucky Historical Society Collection, photo by Cusick.

that the academic courses and the physical discipline at this school were more strenuous than at the service academies.)

KAVANAUGH SCHOOL

Rhoda C. Kavanaugh founded school on Woodford Street which became known as "Little Annapolis." First boarding student came to prepare for Naval Academy in 1914. From then until 1945, Mrs. Kavanaugh launched 150 future Navy officers from her "dry-land harbor." She also instructed students for West Point. Fifteen later became Army officers. Success of the school was due to her superior teaching methods. Students also received rigorous physical training coupled with stern but impartial discipline. Kavanaugh School merged with city schools in 1949.

1480 DR. ROBERT PETER

(Newtown Pike, approx. 1 mi. N. of KY 1273, Lexington, Fayette Co.)

Pharmacist, physician, chemist, teacher

and author. Born in England, 1805, he came to Lexington in 1832. Dr. Peter was associated with Transylvania Univ. more than 50 yrs.; elected to chair of chemistry and pharmacy and Dean of Medical School. Also Professor of chemistry at Kentucky University. He lectured daily in both schools. *Presented by the Lexington Surgical Society.*
(Reverse)

DR. ROBERT PETER

Chemist for Kentucky Geological Survey, 1854–93, when survey was suspended. Among Dr. Peter's many writings were: *History of Fayette County*, articles in *Transylvania Journal of Medicine*. In Civil War he was surgeon in charge of U.S. military hospitals at Lexington. Married Frances Dallam; later moved to "Winton," where he died, 1894. *Presented by the Lexington Surgical Society.*

1481 SHAKERTOWN AT PLEASANT HILL
(Shakertown at Pleasant Hill, US 68, Mercer Co.)

Mother Ann Lee and small band of converts came from England to New York, 1774. She was founder of Shakerism in America. Shakerism introduced in Mercer County by Elisha Thomas, Samuel and Henry Banta. After attending a Revival at Concord, Bourbon Co., Ky., Aug. 15, 1805, they were converted by missionaries to acceptance of the doctrine of United Society of Believers in Christ's Second Appearance.

1806—Believers located at Shawnee Run on Thomas' farm near each other for religious worship and protection. Dec. 3, first family covenant signed by 44 converts, agreeing to mutual support and common property ownership.

1808—First meeting house built. Name "Shaker" came from vigorous worship practice. The Shakers were devout, orderly and followed celibacy; excelled in architecture, farming and inventions. At its height there were 500 members, 5,000 acres of land with 25 miles of rock fence.

1910—Last 12 members deeded land to private citizen; he to care for them during life.

1923—Sister Mary Settle, last Shaker in Mercer County, died.

1961—Present restoration was begun.

1482 ABRAHAM LINCOLN'S FIRST SCHOOL
(Athertonville, US 31-E, Larue Co.)

Lincoln's formal education began in a primitive log cabin near this site. While the Lincoln family was living on Knob Creek, he and his sister Sarah attended ABC schools for a short period of time. First school taught by Zachariah Riney; the second by Caleb Hazel. The Lincolns' home stood 2 miles south on the old Cumberland Road.

1483 PIONEER LEADERS FOUNDED CHURCH
(Walnut Hill Rd., W. of US 25, Lexington, Fayette Co.)

General Levi Todd and the Reverend James Crawford were instrumental in the founding of Walnut Hill Presbyterian Church. Crawford organized church in 1785 on land given by Todd, one of founders of Lexington. First place of worship was a log cabin near the church cemetery, where Crawford is buried. Present church was built in 1801.

1484 SANDFORD HOUSE
(1026 Russell Street, Covington, Kenton Co.)

Built in early 1800s by Major Alfred Sandford. Land originally owned by his father, Gen. Thomas Sandford, who was first member of Congress from Northern Ky. In 1835 house purchased by the Western Baptist Theological Institute for home of President. The building housed Miss Bristow's Boarding and Day School in the 1890s. *Presented by the Sanders and Eilerman Families.*

(Reverse)

WESTERN BAPTIST THEOLOGICAL INSTITUTE

Incorporated by a Special Act of the General Assembly in 1840. Opened, 1845. Conflict between Northern and Southern trustees over slavery issue forced its closing in 1853. Arbitration by Supreme Court Justice John McLean led to equal division of property between the parties. *Presented by the Sanders and Eilerman Families.*

1485 FAMOUS KENTUCKY ARTIST
(Hartford, Ohio Co. Mus., 415 Mulberry St., Ohio Co.)

Charles Courtney Curran, a Hartford native, became well known as an artist. Born in 1861; at age 27 received the 3rd Hallgarten prize for his painting "A Breezy Day." In 1890 his "Lotus Lilies of Lake Erie" won honorable mention in Paris salon. One painting hangs in White Hall Shrine, near Richmond. Elected full member of National Academy of Design, 1904. Died 1942.

1486 FORAGE DEPOT—CIVIL WAR
(Poplar Grove Church, US 127, Russell Co.)

In Dec. 1861, Col. Frank Wolford, USA, with Companies A, B, C and H left Camp Billy Williams enroute to Webbs Cross Roads. Here they guarded forage collected and stored by Lieutenant Silas Adams, Regimental Quartermaster of First Ky. Cavalry. July 4, 1862, the First Ky. Cavalry bivouacked here one night; next day Col. Wolford marched with them on to Lebanon.

1487 GEORGETOWN COLLEGE
(Entrance to College, East Main St., Georgetown, US 62, 460, Scott Co.)

First Baptist College west of the Alleghenies. Chartered in January, 1829, by "The Trustees of the Kentucky Baptist Education Society." Later named Georgetown. The site of Rittenhouse Academy, Georgetown, chosen for the College, July, 1829. Giddings Hall was first building erected. Under leadership of Pres. Howard Malcom, in 1840s, a permanent program was formed.

1488 NOTED HISTORIAN
(502 Scott St., Covington, Kenton Co.)

Richard Collins became famous for his authoritative *History of Kentucky*. Continued the work of his father, Lewis Collins, who in 1847 published a history of the state. Born in Maysville in 1824, Richard became a newspaper editor and lawyer. Founded *Danville Review*, 1861. Practiced law in Cincinnati and lived in Covington, 1862–71, '74. Died Missouri, 1888.

1489 CAVE CITY RAID
(Cave City at Public Park, KY 70, Barren Co.)

CSA General John Hunt Morgan and a company of troops arrived here, May 11, 1862. They seized a train reported to be carrying some of Morgan's men captured at Lebanon, Tenn. Instead, it carried railroad employees whom he released. Morgan burned the train; later detained a second one carrying passengers. Among them were two officers of the command of Col. Frank Wolford, USA.

1490 STATE ARSENAL
(At Arsenal, East Main St., Frankfort, US 60, Franklin Co.)

Erected 1850 to replace Arsenal, on Old State House grounds, that burned in 1836. It was seized by Confederates in Sept., 1862, but recaptured by Union in Oct. Scene of a second skirmish, 1864. Fire destroyed building, 1933, but outer walls remained intact. Rebuilt and used by the Department of Military Affairs until conversion to Military History Museum, 1973.

1491 LT. GOV. JAMES G. HARDY
(Near Barren County line, US 31-E, Hart Co.)

Politician and outstanding orator who came to Barren Co. at an early age. He was born in Virginia in 1795, and is buried near here. A surveyor and teacher who for many years represented Barren Co. in the Kentucky Legislature. Town of Hardyville in Hart County named for him. Hardy was elected Lieutenant Governor in August, 1855. Served one year until his death, 1856.

1492 NOTED HISTORIAN
(McDonald Parkway, Maysville, Mason Co.)

Richard Collins, born in Maysville in 1824, became famous for his authoritative *History of Kentucky*, published in 1874. Continued the work of his father, Lewis Collins, who in 1847 published a history of the state. Richard was editor of *Maysville Eagle* and founded *Danville Review*. Practiced law in Maysville and Cincinnati. Died in 1888; buried in Maysville.

1493 FAMOUS INVENTOR, 1877–1963
(Tenth & Vine Sts., Paris, KY 627, Bourbon Co.)

Sites of birthplace of Garrett A. Morgan, and Branch School, which he attended, are ¼ mile south. He invented the tri-color traffic signal, forerunner of the present type, and a gas mask worn in rescue work at Cleveland, Ohio, 1916. His mask was the basis for one used in World War I. In his honor the Claysville area is renamed "Garrett Morgan Place."

1494 VAN METER FORT
(½ mi. W. of Elizabethtown, US 62, Hardin Co.)

Site of fort, erected 1780, by Jacob Van Meter, Sr., who led a party of 100 settlers from Va. to "the Falls of the Ohio." They made their journey on 27 flatboats and suffered many hardships during their trip. One member of group, John Swan, was killed by Indians. Van Meter built his fort by the spring which supplied water for Elizabethtown for many years. Over.
(Reverse)
VAN METER FORT
Van Meter brought seed wheat from Virginia; built a grist mill. The fort, October, 1790, was scene of an Indian skirmish. Van

Meter was a founder of Elizabethtown and Hardin County. Helped organize Severn's Valley Baptist Church, 1781; served in Revolutionary War as Captain in Clark's Northwest expedition. Buried at fort; remains later moved to Elizabethtown Cemetery.

1495 EARLY CONGREGATION
(210 W. Clinton St., Frankfort, Franklin Co.)

The A.M.E. Church was established in Frankfort, 1839, by Negroes before days of emancipation. First structure built on Lewis Street. Building and ground given by Mrs. Triplett, a white lady, to her servants, Benjamin Dunmore and Benjamin Hunley. In 1881, Rev. D. S. Bentley gave the name "St. John" to the A.M.E. Church. Present church built in 1893.

1496 REV. ROBERT STOCKTON
(2 mi. W. of Edmonton, US 68, KY 80, Metcalfe Co.)

Site of the home and grave of this Revolutionary War chaplain and pioneer Baptist preacher. Born in Va., 1743. "Submitted to believer's baptism" in 1771. Captured by the British at Brandywine, 1777, and held prisoner two years. Came to this area, 1799. Stockton helped form Strawberry and Green River Baptist Associations of which he was moderator. He died here, 1824.

1497 CLINTON SEMINARY
(Clinton, Courthouse lawn, US 51, Hickman Co.)

First high school in Ky. west of Tenn. River established at Clinton, 1846. Frame structure erected; burned 1854. In 1850, Clinton Female Seminary was incorporated. Organized as Clinton Academy as charter made no mention of only women students. Professor G. W. Ray was early educational leader in Hickman County. Clinton was known as "Athens" of West Kentucky.

1498 NEW PROVIDENCE
(7 mi. N. of Harrodsburg at Church, US 127, Mercer Co.)

The McAfee Company first visited Salt River in 1773 to choose a location for settlement. While returning to Virginia, they were near starvation until Robert McAfee killed a deer which provided food for them. Later when they built their church on Salt River, it was named New Providence to

commemorate this act of divine providence in their behalf. See over.
(Reverse)
HOUSE OF WORSHIP
The McAfee Company returned to Salt River, 1779, to establish their permanent settlement. In 1785 the first building to serve as meeting place and school house was erected ¾ mi. east. Present church building was started in 1861; Civil War delayed completion until 1864. Continuous worship services have been held since church's founding. See over.

1499 SENATOR W. J. DEBOE
(South Main St., Marion, US 60 & KY 91, Crittenden Co.)

Born 1849, eight mi. SE of here. Deboe was elected County School Superintendent and opened law office, 1889. State Senator, 1893–97. Elected by Legislature to U.S. Senate, 1897. He sponsored the 17th Amendment to the U.S. Constitution which provided for the popular election of U.S. Senators. Marion Postmaster three years. Died, 1927. Over.
(Reverse)
SENATORS FROM MARION
Marion's two U.S. Senators lived one block east at College and Depot Streets. The home of W. J. Deboe, first Kentucky Republican Senator, was on the northwest corner. Senator Ollie M. James, a Democrat, resided on southwest corner. Both were prominent political leaders. Their graves are in cornering lots in Mapleview Cemetery, ½ mile west. Over.

1500 OLD TRINITY CENTRE
(403 W. Fifth St., Owensboro, US 231 Daviess Co.)

Erected in 1875, this building is the oldest example of Gothic architecture in Western Kentucky. Served as Trinity Episcopal Church, oldest brick church building in Owensboro, until 1964, when it was occupied by The Cliff Hagan Boys' Club. The property was acquired by the city of Owensboro, and, in 1973, the building was dedicated to be used as a community center.

1501 HOTEL LATHAM
(7th & Virginia Sts., Hopkinsville, US 41, Christian Co.)

Erected on this site, 1894, and named for Hopkinsville native and philanthropist, John C. Latham, Jr. Structure was Italian Renaissance style. It became a well-known tourist stop, social and civic center. Among its famous guests: Vice President Charles Curtis, William J. Bryan, John Philip Sousa, Ethel Barrymore, and Capt. Eddie Rickenbacker. Hotel burned, 1940.

1502 FOUNDER OF AUGUSTA
(Powersville, KY 10 & 19, Bracken Co.)

Captain Philip Buckner, Revolutionary War soldier, gave 600 acres of land to establish Augusta in 1797. He received many land grants, one in present Bracken County, for service as Commissary Officer in Va. Capt. Buckner was member of 2nd Ky. Constitutional Convention, 1799; represented Bracken Co. in Legislature. Lived at "Woodlawn" many years; died here in 1830.

1503 LOCAL HUMANITARIAN
(Summer Shade, Jct. Nobob-Summer Shade Rd. & KY 90, Metcalfe Co.)

Dr. C. C. Howard, an outstanding physician and citizen of Barren County, was born in Summer Shade, Kentucky, 1888. Began his medical career in Glasgow. He opened a private hospital there, 1914, and later helped build Glasgow's first community hospital. Dr. Howard encouraged passage of an act which created 6 regional tuberculosis hospitals in Kentucky. See over.
(Reverse)

LOCAL HUMANITARIAN

Dr. Howard was instrumental in the establishment of Rural Kentucky Medical Scholarship Fund. Among the numerous awards he received were the Governor's Medallion for outstanding leadership in the field of rural medicine and the Kentucky Medical Association's first Distinguished Service Award. In 1947, he opened the Howard Clinic. Died, 1971. Over.

1504 BATTLE OF ROWLETTS STATION
(2 mi. S. of Munfordville, US 31-W, Hart Co.)

Four hundred yards west of this site, December 17, 1861, Colonel B. F. Terry, 8th Texas Cavalry, CSA, was killed. He was leading his Rangers in a charge against troops, formed in a hollow square, of the 32d Indiana Volunteers under the command of Colonel August Willich. *Presented by Texas Division, Sons of Confederate Veterans.*

1505 BROWN-PUSEY HOUSE
(128 N. Main St., Elizabethtown, KY 61, Hardin Co.)

This Georgian mansion was built in 1825 by John Y. Hill. It is known as "Hill House" and as "Aunt Beck Hill's Boarding House." Jenny Lind sang here in 1851 and General George Armstrong Custer and wife boarded here, 1871–73. Doctors William Allen and Robert Brown Pusey gave the house to Elizabethtown in 1923 for a Community House and library.

1506 BELLEVUE LANDMARK
(Taylor Ave. & Division St., Bellevue, Campbell Co.)

For many years the tower and nave of this edifice have served as an historic feature of Bellevue. The Sacred Heart Church, built 1874, was first house of worship in this city. Present building, erected 1892–93, was originally called Herz Jesu Kirche. At that time the parish ministered chiefly to the German-speaking population.
(Reverse)

BELLEVUE LANDMARK

This structure, which resembles the provincial Bavarian churches, was designed by Cincinnati architect Louis Picket. Altars with ogee arches, elaborate niches, finials, architraves, and bar tracery were hand-carved in Germany. The triple clerestory windows have stained glass of European narrative type. Murals created by local artists Leon Lippert and Theodore Brasch.

1507 BATTLE OF IRVINE
(Irvine, Courthouse lawn, KY 52 & 89, Estill Co.)

Only Civil War battle in this area. Col. John S. Scott, CSA, and troops arrived here July 30, 1863, with plan to capture 14th Ky. Cavalry. Held Irvine only a few hours. Col. W. P. Sanders, USA, and his force pursued Scott, capturing some of rear guard. Col. Scott's troops crossed river at Irvine but fought with Col. Sanders' men from other side. Scott soon departed.

1508 KENTUCKY AUTHORS
(303 S. Main St., Dixon, US 41-A, Webster Co.)

Birthplace of Rice brothers, Cale Young, 1872–1943, noted poet and author; Laban Lacy, 1870–1973, well-known educator and author. Lacy published *The Best Poetic Works of Cale Young Rice* after Cale's death. Included in famous collection is poem, "The Mystic." Cale married Alice Hegan, also a distinguished Kentucky writer. Home overlooks Memorial Garden.

1509 OLD GRIST MILL—DISTILLERY
(At Distillery, approx. 10 mi. NW of Lebanon, KY 52, Marion Co.)

Formerly known as Burks' Mill and distillery. At the site of the present still house, Charles Burks erected, Sept. 1805, a water-powered grist mill. The limestone walls of that early structure still stand, providing foundation support for the present stillhouse. Except during time of prohibition, milling of grain has been continuous since 1805. Over.
(Reverse)

OLD GRIST MILL—DISTILLERY

Charles Burks began a distillery operation, circa 1805–1815, in connection with the family grist mill. It was located near the present stillhouse. Burks died in 1831, and the distillery was in operation until then. In 1889, distilling was begun again by George R. Burks, a great-grandson. He erected present plant now known as Maker's Mark Distillery. Over.

1510 ROSINE
(Rosine, US 62, Ohio Co.)

Post office here was established as Pigeon Roost, January 16, 1872. The name was changed to Rosine, June 10, 1873, in honor of Jennie Taylor McHenry, 1832–1914, a poet who wrote under the pen name of "Rosine." A collection of her poems was published. She was the wife of Henry D. McHenry, prominent lawyer and banker. The town was incorporated September 15, 1873.

1511 BIG SPRING CHURCH
(121 Rose Hill, Versailles, US 62, Woodford Co.)

Organized as Baptist congregation in 1813.

Present building erected, 1819. Their first preacher, Jacob Creath, Sr., was called greatest orator in the West by Henry Clay. With his able guidance the church grew and prospered. Under Creath's leadership the members became followers of Alexander Campbell's doctrines and changed to Christian Church. Restoration began in 1970.

1512 FOLK MUSIC SCHOLAR
(East Main St., Hindman, KY 550, Knott Co.)

Dr. Josiah H. Combs, born in Hazard, 1886, lived here from 1893–1920s. He distinguished himself as an educator and collector of American folk music. Began his study of folklore at Hindman Settlement School; one of two students in first graduating class, 1904. Combs collected mountain ballads and gave recitals from New York to Texas with his three-string dulcimer.
(Reverse)

DR. JOSIAH H. COMBS, 1886–1960

Dr. Combs received Ph.D. degree from the Sorbonne in Paris in 1925. Married Charlotte Benard of France. He was a professor of foreign languages in many universities and a pioneer in research and the preservation of folklore, folk songs, and U.S. dialects. Combs had great affection for his fellow mountaineers. His father, John W. Combs, was state senator, 1904–06.

1513 CAMP NELSON COVERED BRIDGE
(In park at Camp Nelson, US 27, Jessamine Co.)

Site of first bridge across the Kentucky River. Designed in 1838 by famous bridge builder, Lewis V. Wernwag. With two lanes, each 12 feet wide, it was a single span structure; 240 feet between the abutments which still stand. A main artery between the North and South during Civil War. Condemned, 1926. Longest wooden cantilever bridge in America when razed, 1933.

1514 TOWN HOUSE OF MAJ. RICHARD BIBB
(Eighth & Winter Sts., Russellville, US 431, Logan Co.)

Bibb, a Revolutionary War soldier, was born in Va. in 1752. He came to Lexington, Kentucky, in 1798; moved to Logan Co. the next year where he built Bibb's Chapel. Later, erected this house for his wife. Maj. Bibb freed 29 of his slaves in 1829 and sent them to Liberia. He died in 1839, and his will provided for the release of his other slaves and gave them land.

1515 CAMP NELSON
(In park at Camp Nelson, US 27, Jessamine Co.)

Named for Major General William Nelson, who established first Union recruiting center south of Ohio River, 1861. Original camp, Garrard Co., called Camp Dick Robinson. For better protection from invading CSA armies of Tenn., camp moved to Jessamine side of Ky. River. Major General George H. Thomas renamed it Camp Nelson. Occupied until end of war; now U.S. military cem. Over.
(Reverse)

MAJ. GEN. WILLIAM NELSON

A navy lieutenant when he founded Camp Dick Robinson, Gen. Nelson was the only naval officer, CSA or USA, to become full-rank Civil War major general. He persuaded Lincoln to abandon "hands off" policy in Ky. and to supply 5,000 guns to Union supporters. Killed by fellow Union officer, Jeff C. Davis, in personal dispute at Galt House in Louisville, September 29, 1862.

1516 PIONEER SETTLER
(Albany, Courthouse lawn, US 127, Clinton Co.)

William Wood (1773–1851), native of Virginia, was a founder of Cumberland and a leader in Clinton Co. He represented Cumberland Co. (when Clinton was part of it) in the General Assembly for 23 years. One of the founders of Clear Fork Baptist Church, first in Clinton County. Wood served with distinction in the War of 1812; commissioned brevet major.

1517 KIWANIS TRAIL
(Entrance to DuPont Lodge in Cumberland Falls State Park, KY 90, Whitley Co.)

Corbin-Cumberland Falls Road built by the Kiwanis Club of Corbin. July 10, 1927, first round trip by auto through wilderness from Corbin to Falls stimulated idea for trail. Members of Kiwanis Road Committee were Tom Gallagher, I. O. Chitwood, Robert A. Blair and Wade Candler. Trail completed Sept. 22, 1927. The highway was dedicated in 1931, opening Cumberland Falls to public.

1518 BURKS CHAPEL A.M.E. CHURCH
(635 Ohio St., Paducah, McCracken Co.)

Organized ca. 1871 at home of Dinah Jarrett with 12 members. Named for its founder, Moses Burks. On this site was first structure, a frame church. Brick church built, 1874. In 1911, under the Rev. P. A. Nichols, the present edifice was constructed. Rev. G. H. Matthews became pastor in 1960 and made many worthwhile improvements. *Presented by The Gleaners Club, Catherine Means, Pres.*

1519 EARLY STAGE—MAIL ROUTE
(Washington, US 68, Mason Co.)

This route follows the Buffalo Trace from the Ohio to Licking rivers and was first known as "Smith's Wagon Road." In 1829, President Andrew Jackson's Postmaster General, Wm. T. Barry, planned mail stage route, extension of branch of "National Pike," from Zanesville through Lexington to New Orleans. Maysville to Washington was the first macadamized road west of the Alleghenies.

1520 FORT BOONESBOROUGH
(At Fort, Boonesborough, KY 388, Madison Co.)

Boonesborough, "Capital of the Colony of Transylvania," was setted April, 1775, by Daniel Boone as the first fortified settlement in Kentucky. Near the fort under the "Divine Elm Tree" in May, 1775, Colonel Richard Henderson held the first legislative assembly of frontier settlers of Harrodsburg, St. Asaph, Boonesborough and Boiling Springs settlements.
(Reverse)

FORT BOONESBOROUGH

In 1778, the Kentucky frontier was saved by two major military victories: The settlers withstood the Great Siege of Boonesborough and George Rogers Clark defeated British and Indians at Kaskaskia and Vincennes. This fort became the first town chartered in Kentucky, October, 1779, by the Virginia Assembly. See other side. *Presented by Ky. Soc. Sons of the Revolution.*

1521 Hunt Settlement
(At New Hebron Church Rd., near Penrod, KY 949, Muhlenberg Co.)

John Hunt, a Revolutionary War soldier, came here with his family in the early 1800s. Area became known as Hunt Settlement. He acquired large land acreage for his service in the Revolutionary War. His son, Daniel, gave land for the cemetery and Old Hebron Church, first log chapel in Hunt settlement. John and his wife Charity are buried in this cemetery.

1522 Family of Judges
(225 W. Bellville St., Marion, KY 91, Crittenden Co.)

T. J. Nunn, 1846–1917, represented Crittenden and Livingston counties in 1890 Convention which framed present constitution of Kentucky. He was Judge of Kentucky's Court of Appeals, 1903–1914; resigned because of ill health. His son, C. S. Nunn, appointed to complete his father's term. C. S. was State Senator, 1920–24. T. J. lived in this house many years; C.S. born here.

1523 Artist-Naturalist
(John James Audubon State Park, 2 mi. N. of Henderson, US 41, Henderson Co.)

John James Audubon, 1785–1851, was one of America's most famous ornithologists. From 1810–1819 he lived in Henderson roaming the woods in this area, finding and painting birds in their natural habitat. While here two of his children, John Woodhouse and Lucy, were born. Lucy is buried in Samuel Hopkins cemetery. Audubon State Park named in his honor.

1524 Old State House
(Old State Capitol grounds, Broadway, Frankfort, Franklin Co.)

Kentucky's third capitol on this site was built in 1827–1829 of Kentucky River marble. The two previous capitols were destroyed by fire. Gideon Shryock of Lexington, one of the state's most distinguished architects, designed the building which introduced Greek Revival style to Kentucky. Its most outstanding feature is the self-supporting, stone circular stairway. Joel Scott, keeper of penitentiary, invented a wire saw to cut the rough stone to expedite construction. This building, Shryock's masterpiece, served as seat of government for eighty

years until completion of New Capitol in 1909. Daniel Boone and wife Rebecca lay in state here in 1845 before their reinterment in Frankfort. Only state capitol in U.S. captured by Confederate forces, September 1862. Gov. William Goebel assassinated here, January 30, 1900. Home of the Kentucky Historical Society since 1920; restored, 1973–75. Extensive museum—open to public.

1525 Fort Paint Lick
(Paint Lick, KY 52, Garrard Co.)

500 ft. north is site of log fort and stockade built by Lt. Col. Wm. Miller. Born in Virginia, he came to Kentucky with Daniel Boone's party and helped mark a trace to Boonesboro; served with Capt. James Estill in Battle of Little Mountain. Miller surveyed land for the fort in 1776. Other early settlers were George Adams, Wm. Champ, and Alexander Denny. Over.
(Reverse)

Fort Paint Lick

First settlers found Indian signs painted on trees along creek banks and around the nearby salt lick. They gave settlement the name of Paint Lick. The fort was built over a spring that was entered by steps leading down to it. Jinney Adams was killed by Indian Chief Thunder in 1791. She is buried in the first marked grave in fort cemetery. See over.

1526 Chapel Hill Presbyterian Church
(W. of Crayne, KY 688, Crittenden Co.)

Organized in 1883 at the home of John A. Hill. Services were held in an old school house until this building was constructed on T. M. Hill's land in 1884. Rev. A. J. Thomson was first pastor. Provision for the perpetual upkeep of the nearby cemetery was made in the will of N. T. Bigham. *Presented by relatives of Chapel Hill members.*
(Reverse)

Pioneer Church

The frontier religious revival of the early 1800s led to Bethany USA Presbyterian church in 1803. This church moved to Marion in 1846; remained there until 1882 when a majority of its members seceded to the US church. The USA Presbyterian church was reorganized at Chapel Hill, 1883. *Presented by relatives of Chapel Hill members.*

1527 TRINITY EPISCOPAL CHURCH
(Madison Ave., Covington, Kenton Co.)

Parish organized, Nov. 24, 1842. Cornerstone of first church laid, June 24, 1843. Gothic window of the church sanctuary dedicated to vestryman John W. Stevenson, governor and U.S. senator. Bishop Benjamin B. Smith consecrated the building in 1860. Bell tower erected in 1888. First Covington School of Industrial Arts was taught here in 1903.

1528 CAPT. JOHN "JACK" JOUETT, JR.
(Owingsville, Courthouse lawn, US 60 & KY 36, Bath Co.)

This famous Revolutionary War hero, who rode 40 miles to warn Jefferson, Patrick Henry and other legislators of British approach, June 3, 1781, is buried in Bath Co. Jack Jouett of Va. galloped all night from Cuckoo Tavern to Monticello to Charlottesville. Moved to Kentucky, 1782. Represented Mercer County in Va. Assembly, and Mercer and Woodford counties in Ky. Assembly.

1529 GREENUP "TOWN FATHERS"
(Greenup, Courthouse lawn, US 23 & KY 2, Greenup Co.)

Vital leaders of Greenup County and town were Thomas Waring, Seriah Stratton, Jesse Boone (Daniel's son), Andrew and Thomas Hood. In Andrew Hood's home they organized court of quarter sessions (1804) and circuit court (1806). Waring and Boone were justices on both; Stratton, on sessions court. Andrew Hood and Boone were active in the planning of early roads.

1530 WILDERNESS REVIVAL
(East Lexington St., Harrodsburg, US 68, Mercer Co.)

Scene of the first of a series of religious revivals conducted in Kentucky during April and May of 1776. The Rev. Thomas Tinsley, a Baptist minister, was assisted by William Hickman in meetings held here under a spreading elm tree. The tree was only a short distance from "Big Spring," where Capt. James Harrod and men started Kentucky's first settlement.

1531 GRACE UNITED CHURCH OF CHRIST
(819 Willard St., Covington, Kenton Co.)

Organized as a Reformed Church and German-language day school. Cornerstone laid July 13, 1862. Victorian Gothic church second oldest in Covington still used by founding congregation. Dedicated Palm Sunday, 1863. Construction interrupted when this area was threatened by Morgan's Raiders. Name of Grace Reformed Church adopted during war in 1918.

1532 FOUNDER'S SHACK—1917
(Pippa Passes, KY 899, Knott Co.)

Built for Alice Geddes Lloyd by Caney Creek residents to educate their children. Mrs. Lloyd worked to educate leaders for service to the people of this area. Friends helped, and through Mrs. Lloyd's leadership, the Caney Creek Community Center, Alice Lloyd College and over 100 schools in Eastern Kentucky were formed. *Presented by East Kentucky Health Services Center.*

1533 PIKEVILLE COLLEGIATE INSTITUTE
(College St. at Kilgore Lane, Pikeville, US 119 & KY 80, Pike Co.)

Established by the Presbyterian Church. Building erected, 1889. The brick was fired on the site, using clay from nearby riverbank. Structure served as school, chapel, and community center for many years. Designated on National Register, 1974; used since then as the Center for Local Arts and History. Oldest surviving school building in Pike County, 1975.

1534 COMMODORE JOSHUA BARNEY
(201 N. Main St., Elizabethtown, KY 61, Hardin Co.)

Famous American privateer and naval hero in War of 1812. Barney owned many acres of land in Hardin Co. A friend of George Washington, John Paul Jones and Napoleon Bonaparte. His greatest desire was to bring his family to Elizabethtown but he died en route, December 1, 1818. Buried, Pittsburgh. His wife came on to Elizabethtown and lived in this house a few years.
(Reverse)

FIRST BRICK HOUSE

Site of Elizabethtown's first brick house,

built 1801–1803 for Major Benjamin Helm. He was a prominent court clerk and town's first bank president. Helm rode horseback to Lexington, 90 miles, for nails. Sold the house and two acres of land to Joshua Barney, who wanted to end his days here. Later, home of Elizabethtown's historian, Samuel Haycraft.

1535 FIRST BAPTIST CHURCH
(201 St. Clair St., Frankfort, Franklin Co.)

Second church in city; organized, February 25, 1816, with 13 members. Met in homes, then in House of Public Worship on southwest corner of Old Capitol square. An early pastor, Silas M. Noel, helped to establish Georgetown College. He was followed by the Rev. Porter Clay, brother of Henry Clay. First church was built on Lewis Street, 1827. It burned in 1867. Present site chosen, 1868.

1536 BRIG. GEN. ELIAS BARBEE
(Broadway, Campbellsville, Courthouse lawn, US 68, Taylor Co.)

Born 1763. Died 1843. Served in Rev. War from Culpeper Co., Va. His five brothers, Daniel, John, Joshua, Thomas and William, also served in Revolution. Elias Barbee came early to what is now Taylor County. Lived eight miles N.W. of Campbellsville. He was appointed Major in 1792, Colonel in 1797, and Brig. General, in 1799, in Ky. Militia, 16th Regt., Green Co., Ky.
(Reverse)
BRIG. GEN. ELIAS BARBEE
Represented Green Co. in Kentucky Senate. In 1822, Senator Barbee introduced a bill in the Senate calling for establishment of the present Kentucky School for the Deaf at Danville, Ky. Bill drawn up by Judge John Rowan, passed by Legislature and signed by Gov. Adair, establishing on April 10, 1823, first state-supported school for the deaf in the United States.

1537 THE CHURCH OF THE ASCENSION
(311 Washington St., Frankfort, Franklin Co.)

In January 1836 the first Bishop of Kentucky, the Rt. Rev. Benjamin Bosworth Smith, received from the Church of the Ascension on Canal Street in New York City a "gift or loan" to found an Episcopal Church in Frankfort. The present church building was erected in 1850 with funds donated by Judge John Harris Hanna, first president of the Farmers Bank. Over.
(Reverse)
THE CHURCH OF THE ASCENSION
First full-time rector was the Reverend John N. Norton. Throughout the Civil War, the parish remained united. The parish founded first free school for the poor in Frankfort and furnished a home for orphans from 1859 to 1939 on this site. It sponsored the first library in Frankfort. Many of Kentucky's Governors have worshipped here. See over.

1538 KENTUCKY WRITER
(Main St. on court square, Benton, US 641 & KY 58, Marshall Co.)

Born in Benton, 1918, Joe Creason often spoke of his birthplace as "the only town in Kentucky where I was born." He became an outstanding journalist. His daily column, "Joe Creason's Kentucky," in Louisville *Courier-Journal* won him wide recognition and acclaim. Creason, a "goodwill ambassador," wrote fondly of his native state. Died, 1974; buried at Bethel, Ky.

1539 OLD LOG COURT HOUSE
(10 Court St., Cynthiana, Harrison Co.)

Oldest house in Cynthiana, built 1790. Young Henry Clay practiced law here, 1806. In 1817, city's first newspaper, the *Guardian of Liberty*, was printed by Adam Keenan, assisted by H. H. Kavanaugh, later a noted Bishop, and Dudley Mann, who became a diplomat to France. *Guthrie's Arithmetic*, first to be published west of Alleghenies, was also printed here.

1540 FIRST PRESBYTERIAN CHURCH
(416 West Main, Frankfort, Franklin Co.)

Organized, 1815, Presbyterians built first denominational church in city, 1824, on north side of Wapping, near St. Clair. This was outgrowth of Sunday School, begun in 1810 by Margaretta Brown. In 1849, the present modified Gothic church was built under guidance of the Rev. Stuart Robinson. During Civil War church remained united because of strong Union sympathies.

1541 CAPT. JOHN (JACK) JOUETT HOUSE
(4 mi. SW of Versailles, Craigs Creek Pike, Woodford Co.)

Erected circa 1797. Jack Jouett (1754–1822), hero of the Revolution. Famed for tortuous all-night ride to save Va. legislators, including Gov. Thomas Jefferson, Patrick Henry and 3 signers of the Declaration from capture. Member of Kentucky Separation Convention, of Va. and Ky. Gen. Assemblies; distinguished early leader; father of Matthew Jouett, famous portrait painter.

1542 JOE CREASON
(Longview Cem., Bethel, KY 11, Bath Co.)

Longview Cemetery, Bethel, is grave site of one of the most noted and best-loved Kentucky journalists. Born 1918 in Benton, he gained renown from his column, "Joe Creason's Kentucky," in the Louisville *Courier-Journal.* His popular book by same name contained stories from column. With friends in all 120 counties, he was known as state's "goodwill ambassador."

1543 CORDIA SCHOOL
(Cordia, KY 1088, Knott Co.)

Lotts Creek Community School was founded by Alice Slone from Caney Creek, 1933. Sent to Cleveland, Ohio, by Alice Lloyd for education; returned home to teach. A year later she started the Cordia High School, uniting the people for a common goal—education. Includes all 12 grades; average 200 pupils. Supported by gifts and volunteers as well as by Knott County.

1544 BEARGRASS BAPTIST CHURCH
(US 60 at Shelbyville Road Plaza, Jefferson Co.)

Site of first known church in greater Louisville area; formed Jan. 1784, by John Whitaker, aided by James Smith. It served until 1842, when members dispersed among Beargrass Christian Church and others. Whitaker helped found most early churches near city. In 1780, he and son, Aquilla, were in George Rogers Clark's campaign against Indians. *Presented by Kentucky Baptist Historical Society.*

Joe Creason, popular journalist from Benton. Courtesy Bill Creason.

1545 LOUISVILLE WESTERN BRANCH LIBRARY
(604 South Tenth St., Louisville, Jefferson Co.)

This Carnegie-endowed library was one of the first in the nation to extend privileges to the black community. The library was first in William M. Andrews' residence at 1125 West Chestnut, now gone. The present library was designed by the architectural firm of McDonald and Dodd and was opened in October of 1908.
(Reverse)

LOUISVILLE WESTERN BRANCH LIBRARY
Thomas F. Blue (1866–1935), a theologian by training, joined the branch in 1908 as librarian. He designed a training program for blacks in library science which was instituted on a national scale. The library has served also as a community and cultural center for many years.

1546 ST. JOHN'S EVANGELICAL CHURCH
(637 East Market St., Louisville, Jefferson Co.)

German congregation founded, 1843. The first local church to join Evangelical Church Society of the West, 1856, pioneer of Evangelical Synod of North America. Hosted first general conference of Society, 1859, at church on Hancock Street, built, 1848. Maintained school, 1849–1882; from 1869,

in schoolhouse on site of present Parish Hall. Over. *Dedicated to memory of Rev. Theodore S. Schlundt, D.D.*
(Reverse)

ST. JOHN'S EVANGELICAL CHURCH

Cornerstone laying for present Gothic structure, June 24, 1866. Completion and dedication were in October, 1867. English services begun, 1893. Longest of the 14 pastorates was held 1936–67 by the Reverend Theodore S. Schlundt, D.D. Denominational mergers in 1934 and 1957 brought present membership in The United Church of Christ. See over. *Dedicated to memory of Rev. Theodore S. Schlundt, D.D.*

1547 MORGAN SPRINGS
(Main St. in front of City Hall, Morganfield, KY 56, Union Co.)

Under the municipal building lies the old Morgan Springs, named for General Daniel Morgan of Revolutionary War fame. Water from spring furnishes a portion of the supply used by fountain in front of building. The city of Morganfield was established in 1811 on part of a military grant that was given to Daniel Morgan; Morganfield named for him.

1548 MAN OF COURAGE
(415 Mulberry St., Hartford, Ohio Co.)

William Smeathers took part in American Revolution and War of 1812; helped erect fort here and at Vienna (later Calhoun) in early 1780s. He was the subject of a sketch by Washington Irving, 1797. Smeathers served on first grand jury of Court of Quarter Sessions at Hartford, 1803. Joined Stephen F. Austin in Texas, 1821, as one of "Old Three Hundred."

1549 TRANSYLVANIA PAVILION
(Gratz Park, 253 Market St., Lexington, Fayette Co.)

This building was one of two dependencies for Transylvania University's elaborate, three-storied 1816 structure designed by Lexington architect Matthew Kennedy. Main building burned in 1829. Nine-bayed, it had center pavilion of 5 bays surmounted by a broad pediment. The hip roof had octagonal, baroque-manner cupola. *Presented by Lexington-Fayette Co. Historic Commission.*

1550 LEXINGTON CEMETERY
(West Main St., Lexington, US 421, Fayette Co.)

Incorporated in 1849, Lexington Cemetery was laid out as a natural landscape park. Both Confederate and Union soldiers are buried in this cemetery. Towering over Henry Clay's grave is a 120-foot monument surmounted by his statue. Other noted men, including James Lane Allen, John C. Breckinridge, and John Hunt Morgan, interred here. *Presented by Lexington-Fayette Co. Historic Commission.*

1551 FIRST INAUGURATION
(Main St. between Mill and Broadway, Lexington, US 25, 421, Fayette Co.)

Isaac Shelby was inaugurated as 1st governor of Kentucky, June 4, 1792, at building on West Main Street; built as a market house, 1791–92. After Kentucky's admission to Union, the structure was also used as a State House during the legislative sessions of 1792. The Lexington Library was organized in same building in January, 1795. *Presented by Lexington-Fayette Co. Historic Commission.*

1552 PIONEER BURYING GROUND
(W. Main & Felix, Lexington, US 25, 421, Fayette Co.)

Lexington's first burial ground was on this site, part of "first hill" on route from fort toward Georgetown. In 1781, this square was set aside by town trustees for house of worship and graveyard. The cemetery was used until end of cholera epidemic in 1833. Since 1788, there have been four Baptist churches here. *Presented by Lexington-Fayette Co. Historic Commission.*

1553 CHEAPSIDE
(Main at Cheapside, Lexington, US 25, 421, Fayette Co.)

A log schoolhouse on east side of public square was one of first buildings outside fort walls, 1782. Here, the first teacher, John McKinney, was attacked by a wildcat. A stone market house was built in 1795, and the surrounding square became a popular trading center. Court day was held each month until 1921. See over. *Presented by Lexington-Fayette Co. Historic Commission.*
(Reverse)

LEXINGTON COURTHOUSES

East of Cheapside is the public square, where courthouses of Lexington have stood since 1788. The present edifice is fifth courthouse, the fourth on this site. It was built during 1898–1900, after fire destroyed fourth courthouse and the famous statue "Woman Triumphant" by Kentucky sculptor Joel Tanner Hart. Over. *Presented by Lexington-Fayette Co. Historic Commission.*

1554 BLOCKHOUSE AND FORT
(Main & Mill Sts., Lexington, US 25, 421, Fayette Co.)

First Lexington blockhouse and stockade built, April 1779, near SW corner of Main and Mill streets, close to "the public spring." After many Indian uprisings in Kentucky, Colonel John Todd in 1781 led in building new artillery-proof fort: 94 ft. sq., walls of rammed earth seven ft. thick, enclosed in timber and surrounded by a wide ditch. *Presented by Lexington-Fayette Co. Historic Commission.*

1555 KENTON'S BLUE HOLE
(Parkers Mill Rd., Lexington, KY 1968, Fayette Co.)

In this valley is a deep spring known as the Blue Hole. It was discovered in 1775 by William McConnell who built a cabin and later traded the 400-acre claim to Simon Kenton, who was known as Simon Butler at that time. Joseph Frazer then bought it; his son George built the house, "Rose Hill," southwest of the spring. *Presented by Lexington-Fayette Co. Historic Commission.*

1556 TOWN BRANCH
(Vine St., Lexington, US 25, 421, Fayette Co.)

Under Vine Street flows the Town Branch of Elkhorn, the stream upon whose banks Lexington was established in 1779. Used in the early days to bring merchandise to Lexington from Ohio River. On Town Branch was launched Edward West's steamboat in 1793. Heavy floods troubled Lexington until a large underground channel was built in 1930s. *Presented by Lexington-Fayette Co. Historic Commission.*

1557 PRESTON'S CAVE SPRING
(Dunkirk Dr., Lexington, Fayette Co.)

The stream in this valley emerges from a cave. It was part of 1,000-acre Cave Spring Tract, on waters of South Elkhorn Creek, owned by Col. William Preston. The water is connected underground with sinking spring of William McConnell. Colonel Preston was official surveyor for Fincastle Co. who directed military surveys in Kentucky for colony of Virginia. *Presented by Lexington-Fayette Co. Historic Commission.*

1558 EARLY LAND GRANT
(Viley Rd. between Leestown & Old Frankfort Pk., Lexington, Fayette Co.)

This spring 900 feet to the west was discovered in 1775 by Joseph Lindsay, who was killed at the Battle of Blue Licks. Spring and surrounding 2,000 acres were later surveyed for Evan Shelby, father of the first governor of Kentucky. The house on this site, "Lewis Manor," was built by Thomas Lewis, circa 1800. *Presented by Lexington-Fayette County Historic Commission.*

1559 GODDARD "WHITE" BRIDGE
(Maddox Rd., just off KY 32 at Goddard, Fleming Co.)

This covered bridge is the only surviving example of Ithiel Town Lattice design in Ky. The timbers are joined with wooden pegs (tree-nails); its date of construction and original builder are unknown. The 63-foot span was restored in 1968 under the supervision of L. S. Bower of Flemingsburg. Goddard Bridge was listed on the National Register of Historic Places, 1975.
(Reverse)
COVERED BRIDGES
Covered bridges were first built in the 1790s but did not become widely popular until after 1814. They were covered to protect them from the weather. At one time there were more than 400 covered bridges in Ky. The timbered spans have played a romantic role in our history. Some were destroyed during the Civil War. The remaining ones are a nostalgic link with the past.

1560 THE OLD CHURCH ON THE DRY RIDGE
(Warsaw Ave., Dry Ridge, Grant Co.)

Organized 1791 as Baptist Church by Elders Lewis Corban and John Conner. Indians threatened early services. Squire Boone preached here, in 1798. Reorganized in 1826 as Williamstown Particular Baptist Church by William Conrad, imprisoned as Confederate sympathizer, 1864; pastor 54 yrs. Present building erected, 1892. Affiliated with Presbyterian Church in 1975.

1561 HOME OF JOHN LOGAN
(1 mi. E. of Stanford, Jct. US 150 and Goshen Rd., Lincoln Co.)

Pioneer, soldier, statesman, John Logan established land claim for 1400 acres in Lincoln County and built stone house here. He was in Lincoln County Militia; member of first Kentucky Court, 1781; Lincoln Co. delegate to Virginia Assembly and to 1787 Danville Convention. Logan was state senator and elected first state treasurer in 1792. Served until his death in 1807.

1562 PAINT LICK PRESBYTERIAN CHURCH
(3 mi. W. of Paint Lick, KY 52, Garrard Co.)

Founded 1784 by Rev. David Rice. Early elders of the church: Thomas Maxwell, Alexander Henderson, James Woods, Samuel Woods, Robert Brank, George Denny, Robert Henry. First located in Paint Lick Cemetery. Second building erected circa 1830 on present site. During Civil War several skirmishes here; membership split. Present building was erected, 1875; church reunited.
(Reverse)
PAINT LICK CEMETERY
In this cemetery are soldiers from Revolutionary and Civil wars. There are eight Revolutionary soldiers, including Thos. Kennedy, John Slavin, John Courtney, Robert Brank, Walter Burnside, William Miller, Humphrey Bates, and John Provine. The last was a charter member of Paint Lick Presbyterian Church, and his is oldest marked grave in cemetery, 1792.

1563 ROB MORRIS, 1818–1888
(5 mi. W. of Fulton, KY 94, Fulton Co.)

A Mason and Poet Laureate of Freemasonry, Rob Morris lived here in 1854 when he wrote "The Level and the Square," the best-loved of over 400 poems which earned him the laureateship. He was also the Master Builder of the Order of the Eastern Star, an international fraternal order.

1564 BIRTHPLACE OF NAVAL AVIATION PIONEER
(1 mi. N. of Stanford, US 150, Lincoln Co.)

Lt. Richard Caswell Saufley's Naval flights were the first official demonstrations in U.S. using aeroplanes for scouting purposes. This innovation revolutionized warfare. Born in Stanford, 1885, he attended school there and at Centre College. Graduated from U.S. Naval Academy, 1908. Killed while making endurance flight in Florida, 1916.
(Reverse)
LT. RICHARD CASWELL SAUFLEY
This aviation pioneer was awarded two Aviation Medals of Merit by the Aero Club of America: one for efficient air service in an expedition, 1914, and another for breaking the world's altitude record twice in succession, 1915. U.S. Navy Saufley Field in Pensacola, Florida, and World War II destroyer named for him.

1565 WALCOTT COVERED BRIDGE
(5 mi. N. of Brooksville, KY 1159, Bracken Co.)

This scenic bridge, also known as The White Bridge, is a 75-foot span over Locust Creek and has served Walcott community from 1824–1954. It is of King and Queen type, timber truss construction with hand-hewn joints and beams. First restored by A. L. Murray. Bridge was listed on the National Register of Historic Places, 1975.
(Reverse)
COVERED BRIDGES
Covered bridges were first built in the 1790s but did not become widely popular until after 1814. They were covered to protect them from the weather. At one time there were more than 400 covered bridges in Ky. The timbered spans have played a romantic role in our history. Some were destroyed during the Civil War. The remaining ones are a nostalgic link with the past.

1566 COLVILLE COVERED BRIDGE
(4 mi. NW of Millersburg, US 68, Bourbon Co.)

Built in 1877, this bridge spans Hinkston Creek. It is of Burr truss construction, which is the multiple king post type. The single span is 124 feet long and 18 feet wide. It was restored by Louis Bower in 1913 and

by his son "Stock," 1937. In 1976, Colville is the last surviving bridge in Bourbon Co. Listed on the National Register of Historic Places, 1974.
(Reverse)

COVERED BRIDGES

Covered bridges were first built in the 1790s but did not become widely popular until after 1814. They were covered to protect them from the weather. At one time there were more than 400 covered bridges in Ky. The timbered spans have played a romantic role in our history. Some were destroyed during the Civil War. The remaining ones are a nostalgic link with the past.

1567 JOHNSON CREEK BRIDGE

(Alhambra, KY 1029, 1¾ mi. NE of KY 165, Robertson Co.)

This covered bridge was erected, 1874, by the noted bridge builder Jacob N. Bower. It is 114 ft. long, 16 ft. wide and has a Smith-type truss reinforced with arches. With 2 spans, it crosses Johnson Creek over an old Buffalo Trace, near Blue Licks Battlefield. Partially destroyed by fire; rebuilt, 1910. Bridge was listed on the National Register of Historic Places, 1976.
(Reverse)

COVERED BRIDGES

Covered bridges were first built in the 1790s but did not become widely popular until after 1814. They were covered to protect them from the weather. At one time there were more than 400 covered bridges in Ky. The timbered spans have played a romantic role in our history. Some were destroyed during the Civil War. The remaining ones are a nostalgic link with the past.

1568 RINGOS MILL COVERED BRIDGE

(KY 158, 3.2 mi. SE of Jct. with KY 111, Fleming Co.)

This bridge and the surrounding community developed because of a grist mill operating on Fox Creek in the mid-1800s. The single span structure is 86 ft. long and built, 1867, on popular Burr truss design. The original yellow pine trusses remain. Abutments are of "red stone" covered with a concrete facing. Listed on the National Register of Historic Places, 1976.
(Reverse)

COVERED BRIDGES

Covered bridges were first built in the 1790s but did not become widely popular until after 1814. They were covered to protect them from the weather. At one time there were more than 400 covered bridges in Ky. The timbered spans have played a romantic role in our history. Some were destroyed during the Civil War. The remaining ones are a nostalgic link with the past.

1569 HILLSBORO COVERED BRIDGE

(Fox Creek, KY 111, Fleming Co.)

Built circa 1865–70, this bridge is a single 86 ft. span and a good example of Theodore Burr's truss employing multiple king posts. The yellow pine timbers have double-shouldered braces. Abutments are of "red stone"; corrugated sheet metal covers roof and sides. It was originally double-sided with yellow poplar. Listed on National Register of Historic Places, 1976.
(Reverse)

COVERED BRIDGES

Covered bridges were first built in the 1790s but did not become widely popular until after 1814. They were covered to protect them from the weather. At one time there were more than 400 covered bridges in Ky. The timbered spans have played a romantic role in our history. Some were destroyed during the Civil War. The remaining ones are a nostalgic link with the past.

1571 SWITZER COVERED BRIDGE

(Switzer, KY 1262, Franklin Co.)

Franklin County's only covered bridge spans North Elkhorn Creek and is 120 ft. long and 11 ft. wide. It was built by George Hockensmith circa 1855. Each entrance has a sawtooth edge; the lattice is pinned with trunnels (treenails). Restored in 1906 by Louis Bower. Closed to traffic in 1954. This bridge was listed on the National Register of Historic Places, 1974.
(Reverse)

COVERED BRIDGES

Covered bridges were first built in the 1790s but did not become widely popular until after 1814. They were covered to protect them from the weather. At one time there were more than 400 covered bridges in Ky. The timbered spans have played a romantic role in our history. Some were destroyed during the Civil War. The remaining ones are a nostalgic link with the past.

1572 CABIN CREEK BRIDGE
(4.5 mi. NW of Tollesboro, KY 984, Lewis Co.)

Built ca. 1870, this 114 ft. covered bridge spans Cabin Creek. The name of the builder is unknown. It was constructed on Burr truss design, with laminated arches and truss rods added later. Louis Bower employed arches in early 1900s. Lack of siding creates a window effect along entire length. Bridge was listed on the National Register of Historic Places, 1976.
(Reverse)

COVERED BRIDGES
Covered bridges were first built in the 1790s but did not become widely popular until after 1814. They were covered to protect them from the weather. At one time there were more than 400 covered bridges in Ky. The timbered spans have played a romantic role in our history. Some were destroyed during the Civil War. The remaining ones are a nostalgic link with the past.

1573 OLD STAGECOACH STOP
(8 mi. NE of Bowling Green, US 31-W, Warren Co.)

Built in 1841 by Samuel Murrell, this house was a well-known inn and stagecoach stop on Louisville-Nashville road until the L&N Railroad was completed in 1859. This property previously belonged to Susannah Henry Madison, wife of General Thomas Madison and sister of Patrick Henry. She was buried here and was later moved to a cemetery in Smiths Grove.

1574 CAMP GROUND METHODIST CHURCH
(Approx. 7 mi. S. of London, KY 229, Laurel Co.)

Known as camping ground as early as 1811, this was a favorite spot for both Indians and whites. Bishop Francis Asbury, en route to first Methodist conference in Kentucky, 1790, held worship near here. First church was of logs, erected by a generous gift from Amos Shinkle, who was president of The Covington-Cincinnati Bridge Company. Present building was constructed in 1876.

1575 JOHN HAMMON
(Near Mussel Shoals Baptist Church, 8 mi. E. of Owenton, KY 330, Owen Co.)

Born in Virginia, 1760, John Hammon was a Revolutionary War soldier. He served in the battle of King's Mountain, and was also a defender of Bryan's Station in Kentucky, 1782. Shortly afterwards, Hammon joined Colonel Benjamin Logan's expedition against Indian towns in Ohio. Helped establish Mussel Shoals Baptist Church in 1817; buried in churchyard, 1868.

1576 CASSIUS MARCELLUS CLAY, U.S. MINISTER TO RUSSIA (1861–62; 1863–69)
(Entrance to Richmond Cemetery, US 25 & KY 52, Madison Co.)

Buried in this cemetery is Cassius Marcellus Clay. As a result of his diplomacy in Russia, friendship between the two powers reached its highest peak. This helped prevent intervention of England and France during Civil War and provided an atmosphere which made possible purchase of Alaska, 1867.

1577 HOME OF CAPT. NATHANIEL HART
(Approx. 1 mi. S. of Main Entrance to Ft. Boonesborough State Park, KY 388, Madison Co.)

This old log house was built by Captain Nathaniel Hart, one of the proprietors of Transylvania Company. Hart settled near this spot in 1779 and named his settlement "White Oak Springs." He was joined here by some Dutch families from Pennsylvania. This structure is the oldest house still standing in Madison County. *Presented by Society of Boonesborough.*
(Reverse)

NATHANIEL HART
Nathaniel Hart was born in Hanover County, Virginia, in 1734. A key figure in the purchase of land in Kentucky from Cherokee Indians, he came to Boonesborough in 1775. Killed in 1782 by Indians near this old house, and buried across the road. His daughter, Susannah, became wife of Isaac Shelby, first and fifth Governor of Kentucky. *Presented by Society of Boonesborough.*

1578 FIRST FERRY IN KENTUCKY

(Approx. 500 ft. N. of Main Entrance to Ft. Boonesborough State Park, KY 388, Madison Co.)

License for first ferry established in state, Oct. 1779, was granted to Col. Richard Callaway by the Virginia legislature. The fare for a man or a horse was three shillings (50 cents). Ferry operated until 1931, when the present bridge was constructed. Its last owner was Colonel David J. Williams. Ferry road remains nearby. *Presented by Society of Boonesborough.*
(Reverse)

COL. RICHARD CALLAWAY

Born in Caroline County, Virginia, in June, 1722, Richard Callaway served in French and Indian wars and as a colonel in Revolutionary War. He was a member of Virginia House of Burgesses and one of the first settlers of Boonesborough. In process of building this ferry, Callaway was killed by Indians, Mar. 8, 1780, and buried near here. *Presented by Society of Boonesborough.*

1579 "SYCAMORE HOLLOW"

(Ft. Boonesborough State Park near picnic shelter, off KY 388, Madison Co.)

The area surrounding this marker was known as "Sycamore Hollow." Daniel Boone and his small group came here ca. April 1, 1775, and began construction of rough log huts. When Col. Richard Henderson arrived on April 20, 1775, fear of flooding caused him to have the location of the fort moved 300 yards to higher ground. *Presented by Society of Boonesborough.*
(Reverse)

"SYCAMORE HOLLOW"

This hollow became the center of activity for Boonesborough. Located here were several sulphur and fresh water springs. Area around stream was known as the Salt Lick, where animals came for water and salt. This marks site of last giant sycamore tree, removed in 1932. Four or five men could stand in its shell. *Presented by Society of Boonesborough.*

1580 MIDWAY

(Railroad St., Midway, US 62, Woodford Co.)

First Kentucky town established by a railroad. In 1831, Lexington and Ohio Railroad Co. began railroad between Lexington and Frankfort and first train reached midway point, 1833. John Francisco farm bought by L&O in 1835; town of Midway laid out by R. C. Hewitt, civil engineer for railroad. Many streets named for L&O officials. Midway incorporated, 1846, by Ky. legislature.

1581 MT. ZION COVERED BRIDGE

(KY 458, 2.2 mi. N. of Jct. with KY 55, Washington Co.)

The covered bridge over Little Beech Fork is 211 feet long and 16 feet wide. It utilizes the Burr truss design and is one of the longest multi-spans in Ky. The contractors were H. I. and William F. Barnes of Mount Washington. Original cost of structure was $5,000; completed on November 6, 1871. Listed on the National Register of Historic Places, 1976.
(Reverse)

COVERED BRIDGES

Covered bridges were first built in the 1790s but did not become widely popular until after 1814. They were covered to protect them from the weather. At one time there were more than 400 covered bridges in Ky. The timbered spans have played a romantic role in our history. Some were destroyed during the Civil War. The remaining ones are a nostalgic link with the past.

1582 "DIVINE ELM"

(Ft. Boonesborough State Park near camping area, off KY 388, Madison Co.)

Near this site, close to the walls of the fort, stood the "Divine Elm," a majestic tree, under whose boughs 100 persons could be seated. The old tree served as both council chamber and church in the development of this state. On May 23, 1775, it was site of the first legislative session held in Kentucky, presided over by Colonel Richard Henderson.
(Reverse)

"DIVINE ELM"

Here, May 28, 1775, the first official Christian worship service in Kentucky was conducted by the Reverend John Lyth, representing the Church of England. To replace the original which fell in 1828, this elm tree was planted by the Boone Family Assn. on

Sept. 2, 1927, near site of the "Divine Elm." At its roots was placed earth from thirty-seven historic American shrines.

1583 YATESVILLE COVERED BRIDGE,
½ MILE →
(N. of Louisa at Yatesville, KY 3, Lawrence Co.)

Built ca. 1900 of William Howe's truss design, the single-span wooden structure is 130 feet long and crosses Blaine Creek. The board-and-batten siding is open at the top under the eaves in a window effect, and corrugated tin provides roofing. Bridge was in general use until 1965. Listed on the National Register of Historic Places, 1976.
(Reverse)
COVERED BRIDGES
Covered bridges were first built in the 1790s but did not become widely popular until after 1814. They were covered to protect them from the weather. At one time there were more than 400 covered bridges in Ky. The timbered spans have played a romantic role in our history. Some were destroyed during the Civil War. The remaining ones are a nostalgic link with the past.

1584 EAST FORK COVERED BRIDGE
½ MILE →
(Near Fallsburg, KY 3, Lawrence Co.)

Built in 1924 by John and George Riffe, this covered bridge is 42 feet long and has modified king posts. The single-span, wooden structure crosses the East Fork of Little Sandy River near Fallsburg. The bridge has concrete abutments and a corrugated tin roof. It was listed on the National Register of Historic Places in 1976.
(Reverse)
COVERED BRIDGES
Covered bridges were first built in the 1790s but did not become widely popular until after 1814. They were covered to protect them from the weather. At one time there were more than 400 covered bridges in Ky. The timbered spans have played a romantic role in our history. Some were destroyed during the Civil War. The remaining ones are a nostalgic link with the past.

1585 OLDTOWN COVERED BRIDGE
(Approx. 9 mi. S. of Greenbo Lake State Park, KY 1 near Frazer Branch Rd., Greenup Co.)

Crossing Little Sandy River near here is the 194-foot Oldtown Covered Bridge. Built on Burr's patented design, it was completed in 1880 at cost of $4,000. Commissioners in charge of project were J. C. Irvin, John Conley and W. A. Womack. It has withstood floods of 1913 and 1937. Restored in 1972–73 by Green Thumb Program. Listed on National Register of Historic Places, 1976.
(Reverse)
COVERED BRIDGES
Covered bridges were first built in the 1790s but did not become widely popular until after 1814. They were covered to protect them from the weather. At one time there were more than 400 covered bridges in Ky. The timbered spans have played a romantic role in our history. Some were destroyed during the Civil War. The remaining ones are a nostalgic link with the past.

1586 KINCHELOE'S STATION
(7 mi. E. of Bardstown, US 62, Nelson Co.)

Near here is site of Kincheloe's Station. Named for Capt. William Kincheloe, one of the leaders who established station in early 1780s. Later called Polke's Station for Chas. Polke, who claimed the land. Indians made a surprise attack in Sept., 1782, and massacred many men, women and children. Known as "Burnt Station" after Indians captured and burned it.

1587 FOUNDING FATHER
(Carr St., Fulton, US 45-E, Fulton Co.)

Nearby is grave of Benj. Franklin Carr, one of first settlers of Fulton, Kentucky. He bought first land grant here, 1828; accumulated over 1100 acres in Fulton, West Fulton and Riceville. The Carr home is one block west. His family gave land for the first railroad in area, First Baptist and First Christian churches. *Presented by William Skeen Carr and Mary N. Carr Weaks.*

1588 NALLY SPA
(Jct. KY 56 & 758, Union Co.)

Four miles south of here stood the old Chalybeate Springs Resort Hotel featuring Sulphur Water Springs and a fresh water spring on its grounds from 1850 to 1890. The fresh water spring was renamed "Nally Spa" in 1975 to honor Union Countian James P. (Jimmy) Nally.

1589 LOUISVILLE LEGION
(Near Gen. John B. Castleman monument, Cherokee Rd., Louisville, Jefferson Co.)

The founding of this Legion dates to 1837, when a company was formed as the "Louisville Guards." The next year three more companies were organized. They were the "Washington Grays." These military organizations were combined into the Louisville Legion by a charter enacted by the Kentucky Legislature in 1839.
(Reverse)

LOUISVILLE LEGION
This organization served the nation under various designations. They participated in many conflicts, among which were: the Mexican War, 1846–47; the Civil War, 1861–64; Spanish-American War, 1898–99; Mexican Border, 1916; World War I, 1917–19; World War II, 1942–45; and Vietnam War, 1968–69. Legion is now represented by Hqs. XXIII Corps Arty. and 138th Arty. Group.

1590 MCCORMACK CHRISTIAN CHURCH
(6 mi. W. of Stanford, KY 1194, Lincoln Co.)

Daniel McCormack donated land for church, graveyard and school, 1819, to replace log church built by Baptists, circa 1785. Structure was used by several denominations. In 1830 most of original members became affiliated with the Disciples of Christ, founded by Alexander Campbell. Has served continuously as Christian Church since then. *Presented by Friends of McCormack Christian Church.*
(Reverse)

MCCORMACK CHRISTIAN CHURCH
Bricks laid in Flemish bond on stone foundation reflect Campbell's belief in simplicity of design and worship. Galleries for slaves were at each end. Stipulation by McCormack was that church was to be open to all denominations and people. It was listed on National Register of Historic Places, 1976. *Presented by Friends of McCormack Christian Church.*

1591 THOMAS LINCOLN'S FLATBOAT TRIP
(Elm St., West Point, Hardin Co.)

In early spring of 1806, Thomas Lincoln, who was to become the father of Abraham Lincoln, took a flatboat loaded with produce from the West Point boat landing to New Orleans. The trip, requiring about sixty days, was a profitable one and enabled Thomas to make final plans for his marriage to Nancy Hanks, June 12 of that year.

1592 REVOLUTIONARY WAR SOLDIER
(S. of main entrance to Rough River Dam State Park, KY 79, Grayson Co.)

George Eskridge, born in Virginia in 1763, served in Revolutionary War, having enlisted in the Virginia Continental line at an early age. Eskridge came to Kentucky and settled in Grayson County, circa 1811. Built a log house at Falls of Rough River and established a ferry which connected a road known as Eskridge Ferry Road. He died in 1827.

1593 ST. FRANCIS CHURCH
(At church, White Sulphur, US 460, Scott Co.)

The oldest parish in Covington Diocese, this was a pioneer mission center for East Kentucky. Parish, second oldest in the state, was formed by Maryland settlers who arrived in 1786. First church built circa 1794; resident pastor was Reverend Stephen Theodore Badin, first priest ordained in U.S. Present church constructed in 1820 at a cost of $3,600.
(Reverse)

ST. FRANCIS CHURCH
Dedicated to Francis de Sales. Four priests who served here became bishops: Edward Fenwick (1822), Guy Chatbrat (1834), F. P. Kenrick (Phila., 1830, and Balt., 1851) and F. Brossart (1915). Bishop G. A. Carrell, also pastor here, established first seminary of Diocese, 1856. Visitation nuns located school and convent here, 1875; moved to Cardome, 1896.

1594 GRANT HOUSE
(520 Greenup St., Covington, Kenton Co.)

From 1859 to 1873 this was the home of Jesse Root and Hannah (Simpson) Grant,

parents of General Ulysses S. Grant, 18th President of the United States. Jesse served as the Postmaster of Covington from 1866 to 1872. Gen. Grant's sister, Mary, lived here with her husband, Rev. Michael Cramer, who served as United States Minister to Denmark. *Presented by family of A. L. Eilerman.*
(Reverse)

GRANT HOUSE

President Grant visited this house on several occasions. In January 1862, he sent his wife and children here to live. The children attended local schools. Among the famous persons to visit here were Generals William T. Sherman, A.H. Terry, George Stoneman and John Rawlins, who was later Secretary of War. *Presented by the family of A. L. Eilerman.*

1595 SAMUEL BROWN, M.D. (1769–1830)
(190 Market St. at Ridgely Bldg., Lexington, Fayette Co.)

This building was office of Dr. Samuel Brown, first professor of chemistry, anatomy and surgery at Transylvania Medical School. He was a pioneer in cowpox vaccination against smallpox and introduced it in Lexington, 1801. His scientific knowledge led him to apply steam distillation to the manufacture of whiskey. *Presented by Samuel Brown Journal Club.*
(Reverse)

DR. SAMUEL BROWN

Dr. Brown's analyses led to the use of Kentucky cave nitre in manufacture of gunpowder. This added to Kentucky's role in winning War of 1812. Jefferson appointed him to advise Lewis and Clark Expedition on Indian lore. He was first man in the United States to envision a national medical organization. *Presented by Samuel Brown Journal Club.*

1596 SILAS BAPTIST CHURCH
1 mile west
(Russell Cave Road, KY 353, Bourbon Co.)

Organized by 20 members of the Cooper's Run Church in 1800, with the help of Ambrose Dudley, George Eve and Augustine Eastin. They built at this site on land given, 1798, by Charles Smith, Sr. The log

structure was replaced by a brick house of worship in 1850 and redecorated in 1902. It is the oldest church in the county continuing without interruption.

1597 BAYOU DE CHINE CHURCH
(2 ½ mi. E. of Water Valley, KY 2422, Graves Co.)

Named after a stream which flows nearby, this church congregation is the oldest of Mayfield Presbytery. It was organized circa 1826; original log church used until 1866. During Civil War part of CSA Army located near here at Camp Beauregard. When a measles epidemic swept camp, Bayou de Chine was used as hospital. Many soldiers are buried in community graveyard at site of the camp.

1598 DR. GEORGE M. HUGGANS
(Water St., Eddyville, KY 730, Lyon Co.)

Home of G. M. Huggans (1815–1866), an early doctor of Eddyville. He was asked to judge sanity of William Kelly. Kelly's dream of a material more malleable and stronger than iron and experiments using cold air led to charges of insanity. Huggans, familiar with iron ore, found Kelly sane and judged his idea practical. Kelly won patent to manufacture steel in U.S. in 1857.

1599 ADAIR COUNTY COURTHOUSE
(Columbia, Courthouse lawn, KY 55 & 80, Adair Co.)

On June 28, 1802, court ordered permanent seat of justice on the public square. First courthouse built in 1806. Present structure was designed by McDonald Bros., Louisville, and built by William H. Hudson and Columbus Stone in 1887. A unique architectural feature is the carving of faces on the south columns. Listed on National Register of Historic Places, 1974.

1600 FLAT LICK, KENTUCKY
(8 mi. S. of Barbourville at Flat Lick, US 25-E, Knox Co.)

This area was first used as an Indian camp and later as a Long Hunters' camp. Daniel Boone was here by 1769. At this point three historic roads—Boone's Trace (to Boonesborough), Wilderness Road (to Crab Orchard) and the Warrior's Path (to mouth of Scioto River)—converge and become one road to Cumberland Gap.

(Reverse)
FLAT LICK, KENTUCKY

On path of Gen. Felix Zollicoffer when he took Barbourville, Sept. 19, 1861; one of first Civil War skirmishes in Kentucky. Union Gen. G. W. Morgan had sick camp here, 1862. In Aug., Gen. Kirby Smith captured Pineville, Barbourville and Flat Lick, cutting off Morgan's forces at Cumberland Gap. In Sept., Morgan escaped along Warrior's Path to here, Manchester and on to Ohio.

1601 ROEBLING SUSPENSION BRIDGE
(Riverside Dr. & Riverside Place, Covington, KY 17, Kenton Co.)

First bridge to span Ohio River, connecting Kentucky and Ohio. John Augustus Roebling, engineer; Amos Shinkle, president of Covington-Cincinnati Bridge Co. The formal opening of this bridge was celebrated, January 1, 1867. A prototype for famed Brooklyn Bridge, the Suspension Bridge remained open during tragic flood of 1937. Listed on National Register of Historic Places, 1975.

1602 "THE CEDARS"
(2 mi. E. of Leitchfield at Rogers Springs, KY 1214, Grayson Co.)

Built in 1847 by Benjamin Lone Rogers, around a log cabin that dates back to 1789. Mansion took its name from a cluster of trees that originally grew in front of the house. This transitional Greek Revival structure is one of the oldest brick houses in Grayson County. It was center of Rogers Springs community, named for its mineral and fresh-water springs.

1603 REVOLUTIONARY WAR SOLDIERS BURIED IN NEW PROVIDENCE PRESBYTERIAN CHURCH CEMETERY

1 mile →
(McAfee, at New Providence Presbyterian Church, US 127, Mercer Co.)

James Cardwell	George McAfee
Robert Coleman	Samuel McAfee
Isaac Coovert	John McGee
Richard Holman	Thomas Smithey

1604 WICKLAND
(Near city limits of Bardstown, US 62, Nelson Co.)

This Georgian mansion, built ca. 1815 by Charles A. Wickliffe, is known as the home of 3 governors: the builder, gov. of Ky., 1839–40; his son, Robert C. Wickliffe, gov. of Louisiana, 1856–60; and his grandson, J. C. W. Beckham, gov. of Ky., 1900–07. Based on designs of John Rogers and John M. Brown, it has hand-carved woodwork and stairway with no visible support.

1605 RENFRO VALLEY, KENTUCKY
(E. side of entrance to Renfro Valley Barn, Renfro Valley, US 25, Rockcastle Co.)

From Renfro Valley in November of 1939 originated the first series of radio broadcasts aimed at preserving the customs, culture and music of pioneer America. The Renfro Valley Barn Dance and Sunday Morning Gatherin', carried by network radio, consisted of local people and unknowns who later became nationally prominent in country music. Over.
(Reverse)
RENFRO VALLEY, KENTUCKY

Among those who started their careers here are Red Foley, Homer and Jethro, Lily May and The Coon Creek Girls, Old Joe Clark, Merle Travis and numerous others. John Lair, producer of Renfro Valley broadcasts, took group representing American country music to a White House party Mrs. F. D. Roosevelt gave in honor of the King and Queen of England when they visited U.S.

1606 JOHN MARSHALL HARLAN (1833–1911)
(Weisiger Park, Main St., Danville, Boyle Co.)

Born in Boyle Co. and a graduate of Centre College, 1850, Harlan practiced law in central Ky. after 1853. Although against Lincoln and abolition in 1860, he was a strong Unionist during Civil War; recruited 10th Ky. Infantry. Elected Attorney General of Kentucky in 1863. Supported rebuilding Union and amendments 13–15. Named to Supreme Court by Pres. Hayes; served nearly 34 yrs.
(Reverse)
KENTUCKY'S "GREAT DISSENTER"

During John Marshall Harlan's Supreme Court tenure, he authored 1161 opinions, spoke for the Court 745 times and wrote

The Coon Creek Girls appeared regularly at the Renfro Valley Barn Dance. Special Collections, Berea College.

316 dissents. Harlan was a highly respected jurist because of his individualism, dedication, and courage. He dissented with vigor, often alone, on issues of civil rights, interstate commerce, and income tax. Many of his dissents became the law of the land.

1607 TOWN SPRING
(South Vine St., Somerset, Pulaski Co.)

Near the site of this spring Somerset was established as the county seat in 1801 on forty acres given by William Dodson. The path to it became the town's most traveled street in order to drink from the Old Town Spring. Thus a saying became popular, "Whoever drinks from the Old Town Spring will have wisdom and will always return to Somerset." Over.
(Reverse)

PULASKI COUNTY, 1799

As Kentucky's 27th county, its territory was taken from Lincoln and Green counties and named for Count Casimir Pulaski, a Polish patriot and soldier, who came to America when he learned of the Colonies'

fight for freedom. A brigadier general in Revolution, he gave his life to the cause of America, Oct. 11, 1779. Counties in seven states are named for him.

1608 GEN. WASHINGTON'S GUARD
(Monterey, US 127, Owen Co.)

3rd Corp. Henry Sparks (1753–1836) was Revolutionary War soldier from Virginia; served with Commander-in-Chief's Guard, "the flower and pick of American army." While with this bodyguard Sparks fought at the battles of Brandywine and Germantown. Discharged at Valley Forge in 1778. Came to Kentucky, 1795; settled in present Owen Co., 1800. Buried at Sparks Bottom.

1609 OLD GREENVILLE CEMETERY
(Entrance to cem. on Court Row, Greenville, Muhlenberg Co.)

Land for this cemetery given to Presbyterian Church by Charles and Nancy Wing in two deeds, 1825 and 1826. One plot deeded by Jas. Weir, 1827. Trustees of the Church—Ephraim M. Brank, M. C. Hay and Alney Dennis—deeded cemetery to city of Greenville, 1874. Ephraim M. Brank, distinguished war hero of 1812, and other pioneer citizens of Greenville are buried here.

1610 CAMP NELSON NATIONAL CEMETERY
(Camp Nelson, US 27, Jessamine Co.)

One of 40 burial grounds listed by Congress in 1866 to become National Cemetery sites. Although no battles were fought in immediate area, a large camp hospital was located here. There were 1,183 men buried in this cemetery between July 28, 1863, and February 4, 1866. This included disinterments from several battlefields. The stone wall was built in 1867–68.
(Reverse)
CAMP NELSON NATIONAL CEMETERY
In June and July of 1868, after the Civil War, over 2,000 dead were removed from five areas of Kentucky and reburied here. This included 975 bodies from the battle of Perryville. Also buried here are soldiers from the Spanish-American War, World Wars I and II, Korea, and Vietnam. Expansion of the cemetery was made possible by a ten-acre donation in May of 1975.

1611 CLINTON COLLEGE
(Clinton, Hickman Co. Elem. School, E. Clay St., KY 123, Hickman Co.)

Established in 1873 under auspices of West Union Baptist Assoc. First building was erected on this site, 1874. Rev. Willis White pioneered educational work in Hickman County and led movement to secure college charter. Under leadership of Prof. T. N. Wells and Miss Amanda Hicks, college contributed much to the Purchase area. Closed, 1913; used for Clinton High School, 1918–35.

1612 CMDR. D. W. "MUSH" MORTON, USN
(In front of Nortonville City Building, US 62, Hopkins Co.)

This World War II hero spent his early youth and attended elementary school in Nortonville; high school at Madisonville. Graduated from U.S. Naval Academy, Annapolis, Md., 1930. Became Commanding Officer of the submarine, *Wahoo*. Morton received his first award of the Navy Cross for extraordinary heroism during action against enemy forces in the Pacific area. See over.
(Reverse)
WAHOO
The *Wahoo*, with "Mush" Morton as its Commanding Officer, sank 31,890 tons of Japanese shipping. *Wahoo* left Pearl Harbor Sept. 9, 1943, headed for Sea of Japan but was lost through enemy action. Morton was awarded 4 Navy Crosses and the Army Distinguished Service Cross; his submarine won the Presidential Unit Citation for outstanding performance in combat.

1613 PATTERSON CABIN
(Near corner of 3rd & Broadway, Transylvania Univ. campus, Lexington, Fayette Co.)

Built by Robert Patterson prior to his marriage in April 1780 to Elizabeth Lindsay, this small cabin has been a home, servant's quarters and tool shed. It has had many sites, including original on Cane Run; farm of Patterson's grandson, Dayton, Ohio, 1901–1939; and several on Transylvania campus. Returned to Lexington by request of Kentucky, this city and D.A.R.
(Reverse)
COL. ROBERT PATTERSON (1753–1827)
A large landholder, Patterson took part in founding Lexington, Cincinnati and Dayton. Chose site of Lexington, helped erect fort, April 1779, and laid off town; on Board of Trustees for many years. He helped charter Transylvania Univ. Urged separation from Va., 1784; elected representative from Fayette County, 1792, and served eight years. Moved to Dayton, 1803.

1614 KENTON AMBUSHES INDIANS
(Foster, KY 8, Bracken Co.)

In summer of 1793 Indians crossed Ohio River, hid canoes at mouth of Holt's Creek, site of Foster, and proceeded to Bourbon Co. to steal horses. Simon Kenton secured a small group to ambush them on their return. After lying concealed for four days, Kenton's men were successful; they killed six of the enemy, scattered the others, and retrieved the horses.

1615 ELLIS' OLD STONE TAVERN
(2 mi. S. of Blue Licks, US 68, Nicholas Co.)

Near here, Ellis Station, Boone stopped enroute to Battle of Blue Licks. House built ca. 1807 by James Ellis, Revolutionary War soldier; it was well-known point on "Smith's Wagon Road" and Ohio-to-Alabama mail stagecoach line. Ellisville named county seat of Nicholas Co., 1805. Across road stood county's first courthouse, 1806–1816. Seat moved to Carlisle.

1616 MAYSVILLE ACADEMY
(West Fourth St., Maysville, Old US 68, Mason Co.)

Ulysses S. Grant entered this academy in fall of 1836, at the age of 14. Grant's home was in Georgetown, Ohio; he stayed with his uncle nearby while attending school. One of the most famous institutions in Ohio Valley, it was taught by two eminent scholars, Jacob W. Rand and W. W. Richeson. This building erected circa 1829 by Thomas G. Richardson, contractor.

1617 FORKS OF DIX RIVER BAPTIST CHURCH
(6 mi. N. of Lancaster, US 27, Garrard Co.)

Constituted at Forks of Dix River, 1782, by Lewis Craig of "Traveling Church." Log church built here on Sugar Creek. John Routt gave one-acre tract for church and stone edifice erected, 1823. It was later torn down and used for foundation of present brick church, dedicated 1850. Randolph Hall, the first pastor, served in Rev. War.

1618 FELIX GRUNDY (1777–1840)
(Springfield, Courthouse lawn, US 150, Washington Co.)

Grundy gained prominence in Ky. as a celebrated criminal lawyer and political leader. He practiced law on Main St., Springfield, took part in 2nd Constitutional Conv., served Washington County in legislature (1800–02); Nelson Co. (1804–1806). Became judge to Court of Appeals, then Chief Justice of Ky., in 1807. In U.S. Senate, from Tenn. 1829–38; 1839–40; was U.S. Attorney General, 1838–39.

1619 CLEAR FORK BAPTIST CHURCH
(At Church, KY 738, 1 mi. S. of courthouse in Albany, Clinton Co.)

Isaac Denton, Sr., first preacher in region,

1798. He founded the Stockton Valley Church, 1801, and constituted Clear Fork Baptist Church, April 1, 1802; founded Stockton Valley Assn., 1805. Organized first school in area, 1806. Oldest church in Clinton Co., and fountainhead for many churches in Kentucky and Tenn. *Presented by Friends of Clear Fork Baptist Church.*
(Reverse)

SOME MINISTERS OF CLEAR FORK

Isaac Denton, Sr.	W. R. Bradshaw
Joseph C. Denton	T. L. Cummins
Alvin Bertram	Ora C. Jones
O. G. Lawless	Arnold Cool
Isaac Hucaby	Morris M. Gaskins

William Cross, ordained by Clear Fork, founded Bethlehem Assn., was captain in War of 1812 and the first judge of Clinton County. *Presented by Friends of Clear Fork Baptist Church.*

1620 CARLOW'S STONE WALL
(304 Union St., Madisonville, Hopkins Co.)

This wall was originally located at Carlow, on the main Madisonville-Henderson route. It was built by Thomas J. Jackson in 1857 to enclose his stage coach inn, a general store, Masonic Lodge No. 314 and post office. This work of art, reconstructed here in 1975, is hand quarried, hand cut and hand carved with all joints friction fitted.

1621 SEVERNS VALLEY BAPTIST CHURCH
(112 West Poplar St., Elizabethtown, Hardin Co.)

The oldest continuing Baptist congregation west of Allegheny Mts., organized June 17, 1781, near Hynes Station. Preceded by log structures, this edifice completed, 1834, by John Y. Hill. Sold to First Baptist Church, 1897, and services held until 1974, except when USA soldiers used building as hospital, 1865. Listed on National Register of Historic Places, 1974.

1622 SKAGGS TRACE
(At Ft. Sequoyah Indian Village, near Rockcastle River bridge, US 25, Rockcastle Co.)

This trail, from the Hazel Patch to Crab Orchard, crosses Rockcastle County. It was a widely used land route through Kentucky for several years and became part of the

Wilderness Road. Daniel Boone crossed the Rockcastle River near here in 1775 in blazing Boone's Trace from Cumberland Gap to Boonesborough. See over.
(Reverse)

SKAGGS TRACE

This trace was named for Henry Skaggs, a Long Hunter. Many famous pioneers, including John Floyd, Benjamin Logan and William Whitley, traveled over it. On Oct. 21, 1861, the first Kentucky Civil War battle occurred near here at Camp Wildcat. This first Union victory took place in the Rockcastle Hills. Over.

1623 "ELMWOOD"
(Near Dennis, KY 80, Logan Co.)

This was last home of Capt. John Lewis, born 1747 in Va., son of Col. Fielding Lewis and Catherine Washington, first cousin of George Washington. Col. Lewis and John supplied Va. troops with gunpowder during Rev. War. In 1811, John and daughter Mary Ann moved to Warren Co. Losing his land to squatters, he came to his sons' home, died in 1825, and was buried here.

1624 CAPT. JOHN CRAIG'S FORT
(At church, near Jct. KY 33 & 169, Woodford Co.)

John Craig, who was Commander during siege at Bryan's Station in August, 1782, and one of the first trustees of Transylvania Seminary, built a fort and settled near here on Clear Creek in early 1783. He gave land inducements in exchange for assistance in building the fort and blockhouse. Many descendants of these settlers still live in the area. Over.
(Reverse)

CLEAR CREEK BAPTIST CHURCH

Land for this church was deeded to the trustees of Clear Creek by John Craig, whose fort was nearby. Church was established in April, 1785; John Taylor was the first pastor. During Great Revival its membership grew to about 500. Outgrowths of this congregation have been Hillsborough, Griers Creek and Versailles Baptist churches. See over.

1625 UNIVERSALIST CHURCH
(14 mi. NW of Hopkinsville, KY 109, Christian Co.)

Near this site, the Consolation Universalist Church was organized by a traveling preacher, William Lowe, in the home of James E. Clark in May 1819. It was the first Universalist Church organized west of Allegheny Mountains. Early ministers were L.T. Brasher, J.E. McCord, D.M. Wooldridge, W.E. McCord, Joab Clark, and L.M. Pope. *Presented by the Kentucky Universalists.*

1626 TIMBERLAKE
(108 Stevenson, Erlanger, KY 236, Kenton Co.)

In 1826 this two-story brick home was built beside an Indian trail. Its builder, Maj. William Thornton Timberlake, in War of 1812, helped to develop toll road which became Dixie Highway. Home of son-in-law, Dr. John H. Stevenson, first to practice medicine in Boone and Kenton counties. Five generations of Timberlakes, Stevensons and Taylors have lived in this house.

1627 BIRTHPLACE OF EARLE B. COMBS
(Pebworth, KY 11, Owsley Co.)

Centerfielder for Yankees, 1924–35, and coach, 1936–43, Combs helped New York win 11 pennants and 9 World Series. Lifetime batting average .325. This Pebworth native (1899–1976) elected to the Ky. Athletic Hall of Fame in 1963 and to the Baseball Hall of Fame, 1970. With Louisville Colonels, 1922–23. On Board of Regents at Eastern Kentucky University, 1956–75.

1628 CHILDHOOD HOME OF DR. DRAKE
(Main St., May's Lick, Old US 68, Mason Co.)

Dr. Daniel Drake (1785–1852) came to May's Lick with his parents at the age of two. He described this area in *Pioneer Life in Kentucky*. After studying medicine with Dr. Wm. Goforth (Cincinnati), he was first resident doctor of May's Lick. Drake was a professor at Jefferson Medical College, Philadelphia; Louisville Medical Inst.; and Transylvania Univ. Medical Dept.
(Reverse)

PIONEER DOCTOR AND EDUCATOR

Known as "Father of Medicine" in Cincinnati, Drake founded Medical College of Ohio, Medical Dept. of Cincinnati College and Cincinnati Eye Infirmary. Author of more than seven hundred articles and books of which his *Principal Diseases of the Interior Valley of North America* is a medical classic. This 40-year collection of data was monumental contribution to medical knowledge.

1629 JOHN B. CASTLEMAN—SOLDIER
(Near Gen. John B. Castleman monument, Cherokee Rd., Louisville, Jefferson Co.)

Castleman, one of Morgan's men, led attempt in 1864 to free CSA prisoners at Camp Morton. He was imprisoned until end of the war, exiled, then pardoned by President Johnson. A native of Fayette Co., he came here in 1867. Colonel, Louisville Legion, 1st Regt., Ky. State Guard, reorganized in 1878. Served with 1st Regt. as Brigadier General in Puerto Rico, 1898–99.
(Reverse)

JOHN B. CASTLEMAN—CITIZEN
After the Civil War, Castleman studied law and graduated from University of Louisville in 1868. Known as Father of Louisville Park System, he was responsible for Cherokee, Shawnee, Iroquois and Central parks. Castleman also organized and was president of American Saddle Horse Assn., 1892. Appointed Adjutant General by both governors Knott and Beckham.

1630 SKIRMISH AT GRUBB'S CROSSROADS
(6½ mi. S. of Princeton, KY 91, Caldwell Co.)

Most Caldwell County Confederates enlisted in Gen. Adam Johnson's Co. K, 10th Ky. Partisan Rangers. His purpose was to gather recruits and supplies, to secure state for CSA. In August, 1864, he attacked a Union regiment here, was blinded permanently. Rangers then retreated over Cumberland and Tennessee rivers to Paris, Tenn., where they reorganized for another Ky. raid.

1631 CIVIL WAR DRILLING CAMP
(3 mi. S. of White City, KY 470, Larue Co.)

Site of Camp Wickliffe, named for Gov. Charles A. Wickliffe. Brigadier General William Nelson, U.S.A., chose location, near supply depot at New Haven, for observation purposes. His division (4th) made winter camp here (Dec. 14, 1861–Feb. 14,

1862), drilling daily. His strict efficiency led to wholesome food, warm clothing, and improved hospital facilities.

1632 JOHN C.C. MAYO—"DREAMER"
(3rd & Court Sts., Paintsville, Johnson Co.)

Mayo (1864–1914) migrated to this county with his family at an early age. He foresaw the wealth in coal and with meager savings from teaching, he and two others bought mineral rights in Johnson Co. Soon his holdings extended throughout the valley. By early 1900s he had interested Eastern capitalists in Big Sandy coal fields; served as primary link in their development.
(Reverse)

JOHN C.C. MAYO—"DOER"
Mayo promoted railroads and helped organize banks to assist rail and coal companies. Having gained extensive wealth, he established many religious, educational and financial institutions to help the mountain people. He built his home on this corner, 1904–11, and Mayo Memorial Methodist Church. Mayo State Vocational School had its beginning with the Mayo College.

1633 SANDHILL 4-H CONSERVATION CAMP
(7 mi. from Cumberland Falls State Park, KY 700, 4½ mi. off US 27, McCreary Co.)

Established in 1959, this was first county 4-H conservation camp in Ky. Its purpose, teaching youth the appreciation and care of natural resources, is a cooperative program of the U.S. Forest Service, County Board of Education, and U.K. Extension Service. The camp, in the heart of Daniel Boone National Forest, is used during all seasons.

1634 JACK THOMAS HOUSE
(East Main St., Leitchfield, Grayson Co.)

First story, east wing of house, was the earliest brick residence in Grayson County. It was built ca. 1810 by Jack Thomas, first county and circuit court clerk. He added two-story brick wing on north, Federal style. Despite alterations of the 1870s–80s, original walls remain. A striking feature of construction is uniform log joists supporting first floor.

1635 MAN O' WAR
CHESTNUT, 16.2 HANDS TALL, FOALED 1917
BY FAIR PLAY—MAHUBAH, BY ROCK SAND
(4 mi. N. of Lexington, US 25, adjacent to old August Belmont Farm, Fayette Co.)

Of all the great horses which have thundered over the American Turf, Man o' War remains the standard by which thoroughbreds are judged. Foaled east of this marker, on the farm then known as August Belmont's Nursery Stud, Man o' War was purchased as a yearling at Saratoga by S. D. Riddle and was trained by Louis Feustel. A 2-year-old champion, he won 9 of 10 races, finishing second once to Upset, a horse he defeated soundly in their 6 other meetings. As a 3-year-old in 1920, he was unbeatable in 11 races; he did not run in the Kentucky Derby but won the Preakness and Belmont Stakes. He set or equaled 8 track records, establishing American records for 1, $1^1/8$, $1^3/8$, $1^1/2$ and $1^5/8$ miles, winning the latter by 100 lengths. In his last race, he defeated older champion Sir Barton, first Triple Crown winner, by 7 lengths, and was retired as a 3-year-old with then-record earnings of $249,465 from his 20 victories in 21 races. He then became one of America's greatest sires. See other side.
(Reverse)

MAN O' WAR (1917–1947)
CHAMPION AND SIRE OF CHAMPIONS

Standing at S. D. Riddle's Faraway Farm about 10 miles east of this marker, Man o' War, "as close to a living flame as a horse can be," passed on his great racing ability to his progeny. Man o' War topped the sire list in 1926 when his offspring earned a then-record $408,137 in purses. In his 22 years at stud, Man o' War sired 379 foals, of which 220 were winners, and an extraordinary number, 64, were stakes winners, including War Admiral, 1937 Triple Crown winner and leading sire of 1945; Battleship, winner of the 1934 Grand National in America and of the 1937 Grand National Steeplechase in England; American Flag, Crusader, Bateau, Scapa Flow, Edith Cavell, Maid at Arms, and Florence Nightingale. Man o' War also sired Blockade, three-time Maryland Hunt Cup winner;

and Holystone, a race winner later developed into a champion show jumper. Although limited by the quantity and quality of mares bred to him, Man o' War still proved to be an exceptional sire.

1636 SOUTH ELKHORN CHRISTIAN CHURCH
(5 mi. south of Lexington, US 68, Fayette Co.)

An outgrowth of Lewis Craig's "Traveling Church," this is oldest continuous congregation north of Ky. River. It arrived here from Gilbert's Creek in 1783. Originally Baptist, became Christian Church, ca. 1830, influenced by B. W. Stone and Alex. Campbell. Prominent pastors include Jacob Creath, Sr., Jacob Creath, Jr., and Elder John Smith. Present sanctuary rebuilt, 1870.

1637 ORIGINAL FORT HARROD SITE
(Across from Ft. Harrod State Park, Lexington & Fort Sts., Harrodsburg, Mercer Co.)

A crude fortification was located at "The Big Spring," 1774. Warned of impending Indian war, Harrod and his men were ordered east to participate in Dunmore's War. They returned in 1775 and chose this site on high ground; it was more defensible and did not flood. The fort was later used as school and jail; finally deteriorated. Replica constructed on present site, 1927.
(Reverse)

ORIGINAL FORT HARROD SITE

(Metal photograph of original fort with description of items in and around it.) © 1977 by *Reader's Digest* Staff Artist, Nick Calabrese.

1638 CONFEDERATE FINANCIER
(Dixie Highway at Beechwood Rd., Ft. Mitchell, US 25 & 42, Kenton Co.)

Eli Metcalfe Bruce, a vital link to equipment and food for Southern cause, is buried nearby in Highland Cemetery. He amassed a fortune in meatpacking before War, then moved plants south. He acquired blockade runners to export cotton and bring supplies. Twice elected to CSA Congress; on staff of Gen. John C. Breckinridge as noncombatant. *Presented by the Bruce Family.*
(Reverse)

CONFEDERATE BENEFACTOR

Eli M. Bruce (1828–1866) used his wealth to assist destitute Confederate soldiers and their families after the War. He helped many stranded Kentuckians home and provided funds for education of disabled CSA Ky. soldiers. Pardoned by President Andrew Johnson, Bruce then bought and renamed Southern Hotel in N.Y.C. for penniless ex-Confederates. *Presented by the Bruce Family.*

1639 CATHEDRAL OF THE ASSUMPTION

(443 S. Fifth St., Louisville, Jefferson Co.)

Parish first gathered in 1805; founded by Father Stephen Badin, the first Roman Catholic priest ordained in U.S. Congregation moved to this site, 1830. In mid-1830s Catherine Spalding founded orphanage and academy here. In 1841, center of America's oldest inland diocese transferred from Bardstown to Louisville.
(Reverse)

CATHEDRAL OF THE ASSUMPTION

Benedict Flaget, "First Bishop of the West," moved here and is buried in crypt. Present church was begun in 1849 under leadership of Bishop Martin John Spalding and dedicated, October 3, 1852. Building was planned by architect William Keely. Cathedral witnessed 1855 Bloody Monday riot and Civil War funeral services. On the National Register of Historic Places, 1977.

1640 CENTER OF POPULATION OF U.S. IN 1880

(Exit 184 off of I-75, then .2 mi. W. on KY 236 [Donaldson Highway], Boone Co.)

The exact center of the population of the United States in 1880 was located within a few hundred yards of this plaque.
North latitude   39°   4'   8"
West longitude   84° 39' 40"
Population base in 1880 was 49,371,340.

1641 CRITTENDEN CABIN

(2 mi. E. of Versailles, US 60, Woodford Co.)

This cabin moved from its original site approximately ¼ mi. north and restored in 1978. Built by Maj. John Crittenden ca. 1783. It was birthplace of his son, John Jordan Crittenden, who became one of Kentucky's ablest statesmen: in 1809, ap-

pointed Atty. Gen. for Illinois Territory; 1811, elected to state legislature, reelected 6 times, became Speaker. See over.
(Reverse)

JOHN J. CRITTENDEN (1787–1863)

Crittenden was on Gov. Shelby's staff at Battle of the Thames; a U.S. Senator five times; Sec. of State under Gov. James Morehead; Atty. Gen. under two Presidents; 1848, Gov. of Kentucky; 1860, introduced Crittenden Compromise, designed to save Union. One son, Thomas Leonidas, Maj. Gen., USA; another, George Bibb, Maj. Gen., CSA. Over.

1642 GRANT'S LICK

(Grant's Lick, at Grant's Lick Funeral Home, Old US 27, Campbell Co.)

Ca. 1793, salt water found here by Samuel Bryan, a nephew of Daniel Boone. John Grant, another Boone nephew, and Charles Morgan helped him drill well, which supplied salt to interior of Ky. This territory was owned by John Grant and named for him. John Breckinridge, who also claimed land in area, formed partnership with him. In 1804, James Taylor became third partner.
(Reverse)

GRANT'S LICK

First Court of Quarter Sessions met in John Grant's home, in nearby Wilmington, June 1795. James Taylor was appointed first clerk of Campbell County; Samuel Bryan was among those appointed Justices of the Peace. Grant was authorized to keep a ferry and to build a mill. All three men took part in marking out and planning local roads. Over.

1643 PFC DAVID M. SMITH

(At Livingston Pentecostal Church, Livingston, US 25, Rockcastle Co.)

Homesite of this Congressional Medal of Honor winner, born in Livingston, Ky., November 10, 1926. Church built here, 1974. Smith served with U.S. Army, Co. E, 9th Inf. Regt., 2d Inf. Div., during Korean Conflict. The honor was awarded Private Smith posthumously for his gallantry and outstanding courage in saving five men's lives near Yongsan, Korea. See over.

(Reverse)
MEDAL OF HONOR WINNER

During the Korean War, Pvt. Smith was a gunner in mortar section of Co. E and under attack in rugged mountainous terrain. Encircled by enemy, mortar section was unable to withdraw. Observing a grenade thrown near him, he threw himself on it to smother the explosion and saved the lives of five men. This display of valor cost him the supreme sacrifice, Sept. 1, 1950.

1644 BOONE WAY
(Mt. Vernon, Courthouse lawn, US 25, Rockcastle Co.)

The 96-mile stretch of road from Crab Orchard to Cumberland Gap was known as the Boone Way. Colonel James Maret, an early advocate of road improvement, was responsible for cutting of roadbed and its first paving. As L & N railroad agent and telegraph operator in Mt. Vernon, Maret developed a concern for road conditions. Highway was in use by 1918; the Boone Way became US 25.
(Reverse)
COL. JAMES MARET (1855–1936)

Born in Garrard Co., Maret came here in 1877. He established this county's first telephone exchange and newspaper; was town clerk for 25 years. Maret served as executive secretary of Kentucky's Good Roads Association, and in 1929 published a routing guide, listing over 1200 points in U.S. and Canada. He died in Old Masonic Home, Shelbyville; buried Elmwood Cem., Mt. Vernon.

1645 AUDUBON SAW AND GRIST MILL
(Second & Water Sts., Henderson, Henderson Co.)

In 1816 John James Audubon and his wife's brother, Thomas Bakewell, built a steam mill here. The 45' x 65' structure cost $15,000; Audubon supplied over half the money. In operation 1817–19, it failed due to defective machinery and scanty wheat crops. Audubon then devoted himself to painting and found success. Mill was used later as tobacco warehouse; burned in 1913.

1646 PIATT'S LANDING
(East Bend Bapt. Church, .3 mi. off KY 338 on Lower River Rd., Boone Co.)

Near here on the north bank of the Ohio River at mile 510.5 was a riverboat landing, ferry and road to the courthouse at Burlington. The landing and large brick home that once stood near, later called Winnfield Cottage, were built ca. 1814 by Robert Piatt. He was the grandfather of Brevet Major General Edward R. S. Canby, who was born nearby. See over.
(Reverse)
GENERAL E.R.S. CANBY

In a cabin at East Bend, Brevet Maj. Gen. Edward Richard Sprigg Canby was born, November 9, 1817. A West Point graduate, in 1839, he accepted the final surrender of the Confederacy from Generals Richard Taylor and Kirby Smith in Alabama and Louisiana in May 1865. He was killed in California at a peace conference with Modoc Indians, April 11, 1873. Over.

1647 SITE OF OLD GILBERTSVILLE
(Roadside park area at Ky. Dam State Park, Gilbertsville, KY 641, Marshall Co.)

Gilbertsville was settled in 1870 and named for lawyer Jesse Gilbert, who encouraged its incorporation. Its post office known as Clear Pond until 1874. The old town was demolished when TVA built Kentucky Dam, 1938–44; relocated west of original site. Illinois Central Railroad bridge rebuilt over the dam. This TVA project acquired 35,133 acres in Marshall Co.

1648 INUNDATED SITE
(At Fairdealing Church of Christ, Fairdealing, Jct. US 68 & KY 962, Marshall Co.)

Birmingham, six miles north, was one of the oldest settlements in Marshall County and a major early boat landing. Settled 1849; named by British settlers for Birmingham, England. Town covered as Kentucky Lake formed; Kentucky Dam built, 1938–1944. The Birmingham Cemetery was relocated at Briensburg. This TVA project acquired 35,133 acres in Marshall County.

1649 OFFUTT-COLE TAVERN
(Nugent's Cross Roads, Old Frankfort Pike & US 62, Woodford Co.)

Site first owned by Hancock Taylor, early surveyor. Features of log section date it to 1780s–1790s. Major John Lee lived here, then leased to Horatio Offutt, who built brick section, 1802, for use as tavern. He rented building to John Kennedy and William Dailey, who opened famous stagecoach inn, 1804. Tavern operated by Richard Cole, Jr., 1812–1839. See over. (Reverse)

OFFUTT-COLE TAVERN

Richard Cole, Jr.'s son, James, was father of Zerelda (Cole) James, mother of notorious Jesse and Frank James. Tavern later known as "Black Horse Tavern." It was operated as a tollgate house, 1848–80. Owned by Lexington, Versailles and Midway Road Co.; acquired by McCabe family in 1916 which deeded property to Woodford Co. Historical Society, 1979, for restoration. Over.

1650 JOHN YOUNG BROWN (1835–1904)
(E. side of US 31-W, just S. of KY 1357, Hardin Co.)

Born at Elizabethtown (Claysville section), this Ky. statesman and orator was admitted to bar, 1857, and began law practice here. Brown was a state elector on Douglas ticket, 1860. He was elected to Congress four times and governor, 1891–95; helped state comply with Constitution of 1890. He ran for governor in 1899, unsuccessfully, against Goebel and Taylor.

1651 THREE FORTS
(Adjacent to Elizabethtown City Cem., Elizabethtown, US 31-W, Hardin Co.)

Elizabethtown began in 1780 when three forts were built by Samuel Haycraft, Sr., Col. Andrew Hynes and Capt. Thomas Helm for common defense against Indians. The forts were one mile apart, the only settlements between falls of Ohio and Green River. Hynes laid out 30 acres for public buildings, 1793. In 1797 County Court established the town named for Hynes' wife.

1652 EARLY MEADE COUNTY LEADER
(Main St., Old Courthouse lawn, Brandenburg, Meade Co.)

Most of the original plot of this town owned by Solomon Brandenburg, an early settler who served in War of 1812. He built the Old Walnut Log Tavern, a double log house which served as courthouse, hotel, schoolhouse and home. Among the earliest

steamboats built were three at his landing and ferry. A leading promoter, he helped town become a major river port. Over. (Reverse)

MEADE COUNTY COURTHOUSE

When Brandenburg became county seat in 1825, the Old Walnut Log Tavern was used as a courthouse. Among visitors to the tavern were James Wilkinson, Aaron Burr and John James Audubon. The brick courthouse built on this site, 1872–73, was destroyed by tornado on April 3, 1974. A new courthouse was built on Fairway Drive and dedicated on April 3, 1976. Over.

1653 LIBERTY HALL
A NATIONAL HISTORIC LANDMARK
(218 Wilkinson, Frankfort, Franklin Co.)

This Georgian mansion was begun 1796, by John Brown and named for Lexington, Va., academy he attended. His wife Margaretta and Elizabeth Love began first Sunday School west of Alleghenies in garden. Guests have included James Monroe, Zachary Taylor, Andrew Jackson and Gen. Lafayette. In 1937 property deeded to Liberty Hall, Inc. Over. (Reverse)

JOHN BROWN (1757–1837)

A member of the Continental Congress and one of Kentucky's first two U.S. senators, 1792–1805, John Brown was in the Revolutionary War under Washington and served as aide to Lafayette. After reading law with Thomas Jefferson, he came to Kentucky and purchased this square from Andrew Holmes. In 1799 John married Margaretta Mason of New York; brought her here, 1801.

1654 LOUISVILLE FREE PUBLIC LIBRARY
(Fourth & York Sts., Louisville, Jefferson Co.)

Louisville Library Company founded in 1816 by Mann Butler and 4 others but failed, 1822. Later library attempts: Franklin Lyceum, 1840; Public Library of Ky., 1871, and the Polytechnic Society, 1876. Louisville Free Public Library was founded, 1903. Building on York St. given by Andrew Carnegie opened, 1908. North Building opened, 1969. *Presented by Friends of the Library.*

(Reverse)
REPRESENTATIVE LOUISVILLE AUTHORS FROM KY. COLLECTION

John Mason Brown, Madison Cawein, Joseph Seaman Cotter, Mrs. George Madden Martin, Clark McMeekin, Alice Hegan Rice, Cale Young Rice, Henry Watterson, Annie Fellows Johnston, Robert Emmett McDowell, Gwen Davenport, John Jacob Niles, Eleanor Mercein Kelly, Abraham Flexner and Amelia B. Welby. *Presented by Friends of the Library.*

1655 THE GAITSKILL MOUND
(Northern Bypass, KY 686, Montgomery Co.)

Indian Mound attributed to Adena people, who inhabited Ohio Valley ca. 800 B.C. to A.D. 700. They began cultivating simple crops, bringing about a mixed hunting and farming economy. Central to Adena life were rituals involving cremation and mound building. Engraved stone tablets found here indicate mound to be Adena. Listed on the National Register of Historic Places, 1975.

1656 THREE TANYARDS
(Kinniconick, KY 344, Lewis Co.)

Lewis Co., rich in tanbark, has had several tanneries. The father of Ulysses S. Grant was a manufacturer of leather associated with three tanyards in this area. Jesse Grant in 1846 bought a tanyard near the celebrated Esculapia Springs. He later operated a large tannery with Grimes family, relatives in Concord. Third tanyard he owned was at mouth of Grassy at Kinniconick.

1657 ZION BAPTIST CHURCH
(22nd & Walnut Sts., Louisville, Jefferson Co.)

Congregation was organized by 18 blacks in Aug., 1878. First church on Center Street, 1882; present church bought in 1927. Notable pastors have been W. H. Craighead, D. E. King, A. D. Wms. King (brother of Dr. Martin Luther King, Jr.) and H. D. Cockerham. Zion was base for local and state civil rights activities; Ky. Christian Leadership Conference office was in adjoining building.

1658 FIRST COUNTY SEAT
(Hesler, KY 227, Owen Co.)

Owen County was organized and Heslerville, now Hesler, chosen as its county seat in 1819. Jacob Hesler owned land where town was established. County court met in Hesler's home. An early justice of peace, Hesler later served as sheriff. In 1821, Ky. Legislature changed boundaries; a year later the county seat was moved to a new location, where Owenton developed.

1659 FIRST UNITED METHODIST CHURCH
(5th & Greenup Sts., Covington, Kenton Co.)

Congregation first used public school house, ca. 1805. The first building was erected, 1832, on Garrard St., then replaced by one on Scott St., 1843. Church split over slavery, 1846. M. E. Church South remained on Scott St.; Union M. E. group located at Fifth and Greenup. Two churches reunited, 1939. Jesse Grant, father of U. S. Grant, had a pew here. Over.
(Reverse)
FIRST UNITED METHODIST CHURCH

This Gothic structure erected, 1867, with Amos Shinkle as liberal donor. Burned; rebuilt, 1947. Pastors elected bishops: H. H. Kavanaugh, D. W. Clark, and U. V. W. Darlington. Pastors 1939–1979: J. L. Murrell, W. A. E. Johnson, J. W. Worthington, W. P. Davis, C. A. Nunnery, A. J. Roberts, C. S. Perry, W. R. Yates, A. W. Gwinn. *Presented by a Friend.*

1660 WM. "UNCLE BILLIE" ADAMS
(Salyersville, Courthouse lawn, Old US 460, KY 40, Magoffin Co.)

Town founder "Uncle Billie" Adams owned extensive farm land, a hotel, gristmill, tannery and blacksmith shop. The village which grew up around his home and businesses was called Adamsville until 1860. It was then renamed Salyersville for legislator who sponsored creation of Magoffin Co. In 1871 Adams and his wife gave land for courthouse and other public buildings.

1661 SIMMONS UNIVERSITY
(1811 Dumesnil, Louisville, US 60, Jefferson Co.)

School proposed by Gen. Assoc. of Colored Baptists in Kentucky and chartered

through legislature in 1873 as Ky. Normal and Theological Institute. Frankfort was the first site suggested but Assoc. selected Louisville. Charter amended in 1882, changing name to State Univ. Became Simmons Univ. in 1919 in honor of Wm. J. Simmons, eminent president from 1880 to 1890. Over.
(Reverse)
SIMMONS UNIVERSITY
By 1919 Simmons had grown from 3 to 10 departments, including Music, Theology, Law, Insurance, Social Service and Industrial Education. Medical School founded, 1888. First site at 7th and Kentucky sold to University of Louisville for Municipal College in 1930. Simmons moved to Dixie Highway, 1935, and to 1811 Dumesnil, 1949. Name changed to Simmons Univ. Bible College, 1967.

1662 KNIGHTS OF PYTHIAS TEMPLE
(930 W. Chestnut St., Louisville, Jefferson Co.)
The Knights of Pythias Lodge was organized in 1893 and the state headquarters built, 1915, at a cost of $130,000. The same prominent leaders organized the Lodge and Chestnut Street YMCA. Among those founding fathers were Albert Mack, W. H. Wright, and Albert Meyzeek. Known for their social and civic activities, the Pythians served as role models for black youths. Over.
(Reverse)
HUB OF CULTURE AND HISTORY
The Pythias Temple housed many professional offices and facilities for serving the community. It included USO for blacks and office of James Bond, civil rights leader. Some 25,000 blacks attended the National Pythian Convention in this city, 1925. Lodge declined after Depression; Temple sold to Chestnut St. YMCA, 1953. Listed on National Register of Historic Places, 1978.

1663 DR. JAMES BOND (1863–1929)
(930 W. Chestnut St., Louisville, Jefferson Co.)
Born in Woodford County during slavery, James Bond was raised in Knox Co. He led a young steer to Berea College for his tuition. In 1896, became a trustee of Berea.

After Day Law passed, he joined college's staff as fund raiser for Lincoln Institute. Served as Dir. of State YMCA for blacks and the first Dir. of Kentucky Commission on Interracial Cooperation. Over.
(Reverse)
EARLY LEADER AND EDUCATOR
James Bond, a student of theology, obtained his B.D. from Oberlin in 1895 and D.D. from Berea in 1901. He was YMCA Service Director at Camp Taylor during World War I, traveled state in civil rights endeavors and facilitated compromise which established Chickasaw Park. Bond was the Kentucky delegate to YMCA Convention in Finland, 1926. Over.

1664 BIRTH OF TRUTH IN ADVERTISING
(First & Main Sts., Louisville, Jefferson Co.)
The Associated Advertising Clubs of America met at Galt House, on this site, for their fifth annual convention, 1909. Led by Samuel C. Dobbs, the convention took united action to challenge false advertising. This stand began concept of the Better Business Bureau. By 1918, the Louisville Better Business Bureau, third in the nation, received its charter.

1665 McFADIN'S STATION
(KY 1402, Porter Pike, Warren Co.)
First settlement in Warren County, ¼ mi. east, was on north side of Barren River near mouth of Drake's Creek. Andrew McFadin, Rev. War soldier from N.C., surveyed area and established station, 1785. It was a popular stopover on Cumberland Trace. Emmett Logan, a *Louisville Times* editor, once owned land where station stood. Henry Watterson was frequent visitor to his home.

1666 JOHN W.I. GODMAN
(Near entrance to Cem., South Carrollton, US 431-North, Muhlenberg Co.)
As an infant Godman was brought from Va. to this county by his cousin, Col. Moses Wickliffe, ca. 1800, after his parents died. A protege of Wickliffe and friend of Henry Clay, he was first judge of Muhlenberg County to be elected. Versatile and largely self-educated, he read and practiced both

law and medicine. His farm was in north-east part of county, near Green River.

1667 OLD CALVARY CEMETERY—¼ MILE →
(Calvary, KY 208 at the road leading to cem., Marion Co.)

Early Catholic settlers came to Rolling Fork area after 1790 and established Calvary Settlement. Among those buried in the Catholic cemetery, later renamed Holy Mary, are Revolutionary War soldiers, originally from Maryland: John Barton Abell, Henry Hudson Wathen, and Bene-dict Spalding. Another soldier-settler, Samuel Abell IV, died 1795, before cem-etery created.

1668 BARDSTOWN
(Bardstown, Courthouse square, US 62, 150, Nelson Co.)

Bardstown area was explored in mid-1770s. William Bard came here in 1780 as agent for his brother David and John C. Owings, and laid off the town. Settlement was first called Salem. A land grant of 1000 acres was issued by the Virginia General Assem-bly in 1785. Of this land 100 acres, includ-ing Salem, were set aside for county seat. Over.

(Reverse)

BARDSTOWN

William Bard laid off the town and granted two acres for erection of courthouse and other public buildings in the name of his brother David, who remained in Pennsyl-vania. The first courthouse, of hewn logs, was built 1785; by then the town was called Baird's Town, a variation of family name. It was designated Bardstown when incor-porated in 1788. Over.

1669 MILL HOLE FARM—PREHISTORIC SITE
(4 mi. S. of Park City, US 31-W, Edmonson Co.)

One mile west is an archaeological site lo-cated about 200 yards southeast of Federal style house built in early 1800s. Variety of stone implements found on this five-acre site indicates long span of occupation. There is evidence of hunting, stone tool manufacturing and domestic activities; ear-liest non-cave site in region. Listed on the National Register of Historic Places, 1978.

1670 SCOTTSVILLE PUBLIC SPRING
(South First St. at Locust St., Scottsville, Allen Co.)

Allen County was formed in April 1815. Scottsville was named for Gen. Charles Scott, 4th governor of Ky. In 1816, loca-tion was chosen for county seat because of abundant water supply from this spring. County bought 100 acres, which were laid off in lots and sold to build a courthouse. Renovation of springhouse and premises sponsored by local Garden Club, 1973–1979.

1671 KEENE SPRINGS HOTEL
(Keene, Jct. KY 169 & 1267, Jessamine Co.)

This two-story frame building was erected by Mason Singleton. White sulphur water was discovered circa 1848; its medicinal qualities made hotel and adjoining tavern popular summer resort of 1840s and 1850s. Captain G. L. Postlethwait was its most noted host. This was place of safety during cholera panic in Lexington. Site sold to A. McTyre in 1857; to F. S. Wilson in 1868.

1672 PFC WESLEY PHELPS
(Rosine, US 62 near KY 1544, Ohio Co.)

This Congressional Medal of Honor win-ner, born in Grayson County, June 12, 1923, is buried in Rosine Cemetery. Phelps served with Third Battalion, Seventh Ma-rines, FIRST Marine Divison, during World War II. The honor was awarded Phelps posthumously for gallantry at the risk of his life that another might be spared serious injury on Paleliu Island, Japan. See over.

(Reverse)

MEDAL OF HONOR WINNER

Pvt. Phelps was in WW II action against enemy Japanese forces during a savage counterattack. He and another Marine were in an advanced position when a hand grenade landed in his foxhole. Phelps shouted a warning to his comrade and rolled over on deadly bomb, absorbing impact of explosion with his body. He cou-rageously gave his life, Oct. 4, 1944. Over.

1673 RAYWICK
(Between school & church, Raywick, KY 84, Marion Co.)

Settlers here, 1778, included Henry Prather

and James and John Ray. After marriage of Lloyd Ray and Nancy Wickliffe in 1811, town known as Raywick. Gov. J. Proctor Knott was born nearby. His grandfather, Thos. P. Knott, came in 1796 and taught first school in area. His father, Joseph P., was surveyor of Marion County. State legislature established Raywick in 1838.

1674 McHenry
(McHenry, US 62 near the post office, Ohio Co.)

The town was named for Henry D. McHenry, lawyer, banker, state representative and senator. His influence brought railroad—and coal-burning locomotives—to Ohio Co. Member of Convention, 1890–91, which framed Kentucky's present (4th) Constitution. McHenry was incorporated Feb. 26, 1880. First trustees: W. G. Duncan, G. Render, J. Kelly, S. Williams, and O. Roll.

1675 Mantle Rock—½ mile →
(3 mi. W. of Joy, KY 133, Livingston Co.)

During winter of 1838–1839, the Cherokees were forced to leave their Smoky Mountain homes for Oklahoma territory. Mantle Rock, a 40-foot sandstone arch, was used for shelter on their "Trail of Tears." Since the icy Ohio River had no ferry traffic, the Indians sought cover beneath the arch. Many died there. Mantle Rock was also campsite for ancient Indians.

1676 Bowman Field
(Bowman Field, Taylorsville Rd., KY 155, Jefferson Co.)

Kentucky's oldest civil airport was first used in 1919. Army Air Corps Reserve unit established three years later. Double hangars (west) housed 325th Observation Squadron. Terminal building, erected in 1929, was used by airlines through 1947. Concrete runways were installed in 1938. Operated by Louisville and Jefferson County Air Board since 1928. *Presented by Ky. Aviation Association, Inc.*
(Reverse)
Bowman Field
Land first owned by pioneer Col. John Floyd, later by German Baron von Zedwitz. Confiscated as alien property during World War I. Local businessman and aviation enthusiast Abram H. Bowman found-

ed flying service with Robt. H. Gast on this site in 1920. Property purchased by City of Louisville in 1928 for development as municipal airport. *Presented by Ky. Aviation Association, Inc.*

1677 Center Street C.M.E. Church (Chestnut St. C.M.E. Church)
(At Church, 809 W. Chestnut St., Louisville, Jefferson Co.)

Center Street C.M.E. was outgrowth of M.E. Church South. Became first of denomination in Louisville during early 1870s and hosted 3rd General C.M.E. Conference in 1874. Under leadership of Dr. L. H. Brown, church moved to present site in 1907 and became Chestnut St. C.M.E. Last known work of Gideon Shryock. *Presented by the Trustee Board.*
(Reverse)
Brown Memorial C.M.E. Church
In May 1954, congregation renamed church Brown Memorial C.M.E. as a tribute to Dr. Brown, minister. Two pastors became bishops: C. H. Phillips and C. L. Russell. Edifice built for Chestnut Street M.E. South, 1863–64. Architecture blends Romanesque and Greek Revival styles. Listed on the National Register of Historic Places, 1979. *Presented by the Trustee Board.*

1678 First Court Proceedings
(4½ mi. SW of Hawesville, KY 1389, Hancock Co.)

Site of Hancock's first county court, 300 yds. south, held in home of James Dupey, Mar. 1829. The two-story log structure also scene of first circuit court, in April. Samuel C. Jennings appointed clerk; John Sterett, sheriff. County seat was to be on Richard Hawes' land and named Hawesville. The surveyor of Breckinridge Co. was designated to lay out Hancock's county lines.

1679 Burgin Christian Church
(2nd & Main Sts., Burgin, Mercer Co.)

This congregation was constituted in 1830 by dissenters from Baptist faith who chose to follow teachings of Alexander Campbell. They met at Shawnee Run Baptist and Cane Run school house on alternate Sundays until 1847, when they built Cane Run Christian Church. By 1895, when Cane Run needed costly repairs, members built present church. Dedication was in November. Over.

(Reverse)

BURGIN CHRISTIAN CHURCH

Site of Cane Run Church, forerunner of Burgin Christian, is .8 mile east of here. The village was incorporated in 1878 and named for church member Temple Burgin, whose gift of land in 1874 to Cincinnati Southern Railway helped to bring about its establishment. This church occupies a portion of Temple Burgin's original land. The name Burgin Christian Church first used, 1896.

1680 PRESTON PARK SEMINARY

(At Bellarmine College, Newburg Rd., Louisville, Jefferson Co.)

This land was part of a grant for French-Indian War service. Surveyed in 1774 by Wm. Preston, it was granted to James McCorkle by Gov. Thomas Jefferson in 1779. Bought by Bishop Wm. McCloskey, 1869, as site of diocesan seminary, which functioned until 1910. Orphanages of St. Vincent (1892–1901) and St. Thomas (1910–1938) were also here. *Presented by Bellarmine College Alumni Association.*

(Reverse)

BELLARMINE COLLEGE

Founded by Archbishop John A. Floersh, Bellarmine opened as a Catholic men's college in 1950. Merged with Ursuline College in 1968 and became coeducational. The international Thomas Merton Studies Center housed on campus. College visitors have included John F. Kennedy, Thomas Merton, Karl Rahner and Henry Cabot Lodge. *Presented by Bellarmine College Alumni Association.*

1681 LOUISVILLE'S STEAMBOAT ERA

(At the Wharf, 4th St., Louisville, Jefferson Co.)

River navigation in 18th century was by flatboat and keelboat. First steamboat, NEW ORLEANS, arrived in Louisville in autumn of 1811. City soon became steamboat center with six lines operating here. Hundreds of these boats were built in area. Wharf teemed with traffic through Civil War. Eight U.S. presidents arrived on this wharf or "levee." *Presented by The Louisville Historical League.*

(Reverse)

VISITORS AT LOUISVILLE WHARF

James Monroe	June 1819
Andrew Jackson	June 1819
Alexis de Tocqueville	Dec. 1831
Washington Irving	Sept. 1832
Abraham Lincoln	Sept. 1841
Charles Dickens	Apr. 1842
Walt Whitman	Feb. 1848
Ralph Waldo Emerson	June 1850
Oliver W. Holmes	Sept. 1855
Herman Melville	Jan.1858

Presented by Bellarmine College Alumni Association.

1682 FANCY FARM

(Fancy Farm, KY 80, Graves Co.)

The town which grew up around St. Jerome's Church was named ca. 1845 for farm of John Peebles. Samuel Willett and Elizabeth Hobbs, from St. Rose's, Washington Co., were first permanent Catholic settlers in 1829. First church was built 1835–1836 by Rev. Elisha Durbin. The present church blessed by Bishop Wm. McCloskey in November 1893. Annual picnic is fundraiser for parish. Over.

(Reverse)

CENTENNIAL PICNIC, AUG. 2, 1980

This blend of politics, community spirit and home cooking puts Fancy Farm in Kentucky headlines. First picnic in 1881; Reverend R. Feehan, pastor. Centennial picnic hosted by Reverend W. Hancock. First resident pastor was Reverend A. Hagan. Reverend C. Haeseley built present church, brick school and rectory. Other noted pastors include Msgr. A. Thompson, Msgr. E. Russell and Reverend C. Denardi.

1683 WARREN CASH (1760–1850)

(SE corner of Jct. of KY 1136 & 1868, near Gilead Baptist Church, Hardin Co.)

With Va. Militia from 1776–1780, Cash took part in the battles of Brandywine and Monmouth, several skirmishes, and was with Washington at Valley Forge. Married Susannah Baskett, who taught him to read. They came to Ky., joined Baptist Church, and Cash became a minister. Moved to Hardin Co. in 1806. Among churches he organized was Gilead, 1824. Both he and wife buried here.

1684 HOME OF GOVERNOR MORROW
(208 East Oak St., Somerset, Pulaski Co.)

Edwin P. Morrow (1877–1935), a native of Somerset, built this house soon after marrying in 1903; he began his Somerset law practice same year. Morrow served in Spanish-American War; appointed U.S. District Attorney for eastern Kentucky by Pres. Taft and elected governor in 1919. A popular orator, he was nephew of Governor Wm. O. Bradley. Buried in Frankfort Cem.

1685 GRAVE OF HANCOCK TAYLOR
(Approx. 1 mi. W. of Richmond, KY 52, Madison Co.)

On Taylor's fork of Silver Creek, .7 mi. east, is burial place of Hancock Taylor. This pioneer was at Falls of Ohio in 1769 enroute to New Orleans and surveying in Ky. by 1773. A deputy surveyor under Wm. Preston, he was near mouth of Ky. River when shot by Indians in July 1774. Taylor rejoined party, and these companions brought him just south of Richmond, where he died.

1686 BEN JOHNSON HOUSE
(1003 North Third St., US 31-E, Bardstown, Nelson Co.)

Well-known representative and state senator Ben Johnson (1858–1950) was born and lived most of his life here. This native son was a member of Congress for 20 consecutive years and served on Ky. Highway Commission under 4 administrations. The house was built in 1856 for Ben's father, William Johnson, who was state senator and lieutenant governor of Kentucky. Over.
(Reverse)
CONFEDERATE FLAG RAISING
Nancy Johnson, mother of Ben Johnson, was a member of the committee to select flag of the Confederacy. The one chosen, designed by Nicola Marschall, was unfurled here in 1861 before some 5,000 people. Gen. John Hunt Morgan, escaping from northern prison, stayed here overnight. The house listed on National Register of Historic Places, 1979. Over.

1687 MT. HOREB PRESBYTERIAN CHURCH
(At Church, Iron Works Pike at Mt. Horeb Pike, Lexington,

Fayette Co.)

This church was organized April 21, 1827, at nearby "Cabell's Dale," home of Mary Cabell Breckinridge, widow of John Breckinridge, U.S. Senator and Attorney General in Thomas Jefferson's cabinet. The original brick church, constructed in 1828 on this site, burned in 1925. Present building of similar design was dedicated in 1926. *Presented by Kentucky Breckinridge Committee.*

1688 JOHN HAMPTON HOUSE
(101 West Main St., Frankfort, Franklin Co.)

Earliest surviving stone house in city. Built before 1840, it is constructed of patterned river limestone with jack arches over windows and doors. The builder, John Hampton, was a tavern owner and operator in the county by 1818. His licenses extended into the 1820s. Several members of his family owned and operated taverns. *Presented by Mrs. Fred W. Burch.*
(Reverse)
EARLY STONE HOUSE
This house, built by John Hampton, was later the home of Col. Mason H. P. Williams, Franklin County sheriff. He entertained Judge John M. Elliott of Ky. Court of Appeals in this house the night before the judge's assassination across street at the Capital Hotel, March 26, 1879. Listed on National Register of Historic Places. *Presented by Mrs. Fred W. Burch.*

1689 WATER WORKS PUMPING STATION
(Near entrance to water tower, off River Rd. & Zorn Ave., Louisville, Jefferson Co.)

Louisville Water Co. incorporated in 1854. Its first pumping station, in Classical Revival style, blends beauty and utility. The classic structures were designed and built by Theodore R. Scowden and his assistant, Charles Hermany. Built 1857–60, it could pump 12 million gallons in 24 hours. Site was away from industry, well elevated, with good landing for coal boats. Over.
(Reverse)
WATER TOWER
The 169-foot tower encloses a water standpipe. It represents a Roman column in the Doric order. The base is surrounded by Corinthian columns, nine topped by

Greek classical figures and one by an American Indian. Tower damaged by a tornado in 1890. The station and its water tower were named National Landmarks in Nov. 1971. *Presented by Friends of the Water Tower.*

1690 GRACE EPISCOPAL CHURCH
(Liberty St., US 41 southbound, at Sixth St., Hopkinsville, Christian Co.)

Organized in 1831 by local laymen with aid of George P. Giddinge, Md. missionary, who became first rector, and Benjamin B. Smith, later first Bishop of Ky. and Presiding Bishop of the Episcopal Church. First church was built ca. 1850 on Virginia St. On Oct. 10, 1875, Jefferson Davis, an Episcopalian and native of Christian Co., worshiped there. Over.
(Reverse)

GRACE EPISCOPAL CHURCH
Present church built 1883–84. Liberal contributor was John C. Latham, Jr. Under rectors John W. Venable, 1883–94, and George C. Abbitt, 1902–29, church became center for social and cultural community activities. Parish house, a memorial to Emma Glass Gaither, built 1906. Tower destroyed in 1978 by tornado, restored in 1979. *Presented by Grace Episcopal Church.*

1691 HOLMES HIGH SCHOOL
(25th St. & Madison Ave., Covington, Kenton Co.)

Holmes is one of Kentucky's earliest tax-supported, coeducational, public high schools. It was founded as Covington High School in 1853, at Scott and 11th Sts. Present name adopted when moved to this site. Campus is former estate of New Orleans merchant, Daniel Henry Holmes, and site of Union Army activity during Civil War. Over. *Presented by Holmes High School PTA.*
(Reverse)

HOLMES DALE ESTATE
Holmes Castle, home of Daniel Henry Holmes, erected here in 1866. His son, Daniel Henry, Jr., was noted 19th century poet. The 32-room, English-Gothic manor was acquired by Covington Board of Education; from 1919–36 the mansion was part of Holmes High School. In 1936, it was razed and replaced by a new administration building. Over. *Presented by Holmes High School PTA.*

1692 MEMORIAL AUDITORIUM
(Fourth & Kentucky Sts., Louisville, Jefferson Co.)

Construction began in 1927 as a tribute to Louisvillians who died in First World War. Architect of the Greek Revival building was Thomas Hastings, assisted by E. T. Hutchings. On Decoration Day, May 30, 1929, the War Memorial Auditorium was dedicated. Within its walls Louisville's cultural life flourished, despite the dismal years of the Great Depression.
(Reverse)

PERFORMERS AT MEMORIAL

Sergei Rachmaninoff	Nov. 1931
Ignace Paderewski	Mar. 1933
George Gershwin	Feb. 1934
George M. Cohan	Feb. 1935
Helen Hayes	Mar. 1935
Ethel Barrymore	Oct. 1935
Marian Anderson	Dec. 1939
Artur Rubinstein	Feb. 1948
Mikhail Baryshnikov	Nov. 1978
The Peking Opera	Oct. 1980

Presented by Bellarmine College Students.

1693 GREEN STREET BAPTIST CHURCH
(519 East Gray St., Louisville, Jefferson Co.)

This church was constituted on Green Street, Sept. 29, 1844, with Brother George Wells as pastor. A noted trustee and treasurer was Ben Duke, who lived to age 110. Present church built 1930 by Samuel Plato under pastorate of H. W. Jones. Scene of August 1967 rally led by Dr. Martin Luther King, Jr., to promote voter registration. *Presented by Mr. Till Lecian.*

1694 LOUISVILLE CONVENTION, 1845
(Fourth St., between Market & Jefferson, Louisville, Jefferson Co.)

The Methodist Episcopal Church was first church to divide over issues which led to Civil War. Fourth St. Church, formerly at this site, hosted Lousville Convention in May 1845. Delegates of southern and southwestern conferences formed the M.E. Church, South, following separation plan adopted by General Conference, 1844. *Pre-*

sented by Southeastern Jurisdiction Historical Society.
(Reverse)

UNITED METHODIST CHURCH

National leaders Henry Clay, Daniel Webster, and John C. Calhoun saw M.E. separation as significant rift in American society. This was largest religious denomination in USA. Efforts to reconcile began in Louisville in 1874 at another site. Division healed, 1939. These branches of Methodism became parts of United Methodist Church in 1968. *Presented by S.E. Jurisdiction Historical Society.*

1695 CALVARY EPISCOPAL CHURCH
(821 S. Fourth St., Louisville, Jefferson Co.)

Calvary's congregation was derived from Sehon Methodist Chapel; it was admitted as an Episcopal parish at Diocesan Convention of 1861. The church was incorporated by Ky. General Assembly in 1869. Outstanding rectors have included W. H. Platt, James G. Minnegerode, and F. Elliott-Baker. Over. *Presented by Calvary Episcopal Church.*
(Reverse)

CALVARY EPISCOPAL CHURCH

This building was erected in two stages (1872–76, 1886–88) and is the product of two architects, W. H. Redin and Henry P. McDonald. One of only two cut stone spires in the United States caps the south tower. Calvary Episcopal Church was listed on the National Register of Historic Places, 1978. *Presented by Calvary Episcopal Church.*

1696 WASHINGTON BAPTIST CHURCH CEMETERY
(Washington, US 68, Mason Co.)

Site of Limestone Baptist Church (renamed Washington), organized in 1785 by Wm. Wood, first pastor. He and Arthur Fox, Sr., bought land from Simon Kenton and laid out Washington that year. Wood gave land for the church and cemetery. Church burned twice; not rebuilt after 1889. Part of Washington Historic District. See over.
(Reverse)

WASHINGTON BAPTIST CEMETERY

Buried here are pioneers, Indians, Revolutionary War soldiers and—in a common grave—some 40 early Presbyterians of Washington and Murphysville. The first two Presbyterian pastors, Robert Wilson and Paradise Lost McAboy, are here; also Arthur Fox, Sr., Indian fighters Charles and James Ward, and Abigail H. Johnston, mother of Albert Sidney Johnston.

1697 JEFFERSON COUNTY COURTHOUSE
(Sixth & Jefferson Sts., Louisville, Jefferson Co.)

Designed by Gideon Shryock in the Greek Revival style. Construction began ca. 1837, and building first used by city and county, 1842. Completed in 1860 by Albert Fink and Charles Stancliff, it housed legislature briefly during Civil War. Structure renovated by Brinton Davis after 1905 fire. Seven U.S. Presidents have spoken here. On National Register of Historic Places, 1972.
(Reverse)

CITY AND COUNTY NAMED

Louisville, at the Falls of the Ohio, was founded in 1778 by George Rogers Clark. Site first served as a military outpost; the city which developed was named for Louis XVI. Kentucky Co., Virginia, was divided in 1780 into Jefferson, Fayette, and Lincoln counties. Jefferson County was named for Governor Thomas Jefferson, who signed the first town charter of Louisville. Over.

1698 GRAVE OF JOHN T. SCOPES
(In front of Oak Grove Cem., Park Ave., Paducah, McCracken Co.)

Here is buried the man who, at age 24, taught Darwin's theory of evolution to a Dayton, Tennessee, biology class. The Paducah native and University of Kentucky graduate violated a Tennessee law forbidding the teaching of evolution. This test case, tried in Dayton, gained international attention. Popular play, *Inherit the Wind*, is based on the famous Scopes trial. Over.
(Reverse)

SCOPES "MONKEY TRIAL"

The July 1925 trial of John T. Scopes had at issue academic freedom, separation of church and state, and reconciling of science and religion. Scopes' defender was Clarence Darrow; his prosecutor, William Jennings Bryan. Scopes was convicted and fined $100. Later worked as geologist in S.

America and La. Law he violated was repealed in 1967. Scopes died, 1970. Over.

1699 "VAUCLUSE"
(Jct. KY 155 & Yoder Station Rd., Spencer Co.)

House built by Jacob Yoder circa 1806 and known as "Beechland" until his death. This Rev. War soldier and Indian fighter left Fort Redstone (Pa.), 1782, on first flatboat to descend Mississippi River. Yoder arrived in New Orleans with cargo of produce. He bought hides and furs to sell in Baltimore. Buried on farm, 1832. Listed on National Register of Historic Places, 1976.

1700 EARLY SETTLER
(2 mi. E. of Whitesburg at Ermine, Jct. KY 119 & 2034, Letcher Co.)

Archelous Craft of Wilkes Co., N.C., was with small band of pioneers who immigrated to Upper Ky. River Valley in 1804. Born December 25, 1749, in Roanoke River area, Craft was a veteran of Revolutionary War; he fought in battles of Hanging Rock and Eutaw Springs. He died November 8, 1853. His unmarked grave is three miles north of Crafts Colly. *Presented by Craft Family Reunion Assoc.*

1701 OXFORD CHRISTIAN CHURCH
(5 mi. from Georgetown on Oxford Rd., US 62, Scott Co.)

Organized at the Old Sugar Ridge Schoolhouse in July 1831. In 1847 new, frame church was built under supervision of Elders John A. Gano, Sr., and "Raccoon" John Smith. The original membership was about 100. Church was repaired in 1881 under the pastorate of Elder C. F. Forscutt. Present brick church built 1900–01 by E. C. Muddiman. *Presented by Oxford Christian Church.*
(Reverse)

OXFORD HISTORIC DISTRICT
Oxford was laid out and settled by landowner named Patterson. The village was a busy settlement by 1847. Hart Boswell tavern typifies rural commercial buildings of period. Historic District includes nineteenth as well as early twentieth century architecture. Leading influence in Victorian style was stonemason and bricklayer E. C. Muddiman. *Presented by Oxford Christian Church.*

1702 PRESENTATION ACADEMY
(861 S. Fourth St., Louisville, Jefferson Co.)

The city's first Catholic school and Louisville's oldest existing school, founded 1831, by Mother Catherine Spalding. Recognized as co-founder of Sisters of Charity of Nazareth with Bishop J. B. David, she began a hospital and city's first orphan asylum at school's original site on Fifth St. during the 1830s cholera epidemic. *In Memory of Joe Valla by Marlene Valla Bohn.*
(Reverse)

PRESENTATION ACADEMY
The actress Mary Anderson attended classes at Presentation Academy in the 1870s. In 1892, the Sisters bought Thomas Jacobs house on this site. The new Presentation, erected in 1893 and designed by D.X. Murphy in Richardsonian Romanesque style, is listed on the National Register of Historic Places. It observed school's sesquicentennial in 1981. *In Memory of Joe Valla by Marlene Valla Bohn.*

1703 ST. PAUL'S EPISCOPAL CHURCH
(At Church, Green & Center Sts., Henderson, Henderson Co.)

The design of this English Gothic church was supervised by Bishop Benjamin Bosworth Smith; church consecrated by him in May 1869. Stained glass memorial windows from Munich, Germany, donated. Congregation organized in 1831; first church, erected in 1838, at Third and Main. Listed on National Register of Historic Places, 1978. *Presented by St. Paul's Church.*

1704 LOUISVILLE CITY HALL
(Sixth & Jefferson, Louisville, Jefferson Co.)

This building, a merger of the French Second Empire and Italianate style, was erected, 1871–73, from plans of John Andrewartha. Mansard clock tower designed by Henry Whitestone to replace one that burned in 1875. The Annex was added in 1909; its architect was Cornelius Curtin. Louisville City Hall Complex was listed on the National Register of Historic Places, 1976. Over.
(Reverse)

SIXTH AND JEFFERSON
This area has been Louisville's civic cen-

ter since 1784, when log courthouse was begun on south side of Jefferson near Sixth. In 1788 it was replaced by a stone structure. Brick courthouse stood here, 1811–1837. Across Sixth Street was "gaol," whipping post and pillory. Abraham Lincoln visited Pirtle and Speed law offices nearby in summer of 1841.

1705 LOTTIE MOON (1840–1912)
(At First Baptist Church, 317 W. Broadway, Danville, Boyle Co.)

This dynamic Southern Baptist missionary spent almost forty years (1873–1912) teaching and ministering in China. She was a member of First Baptist Church, Danville, 1868–71, and taught at Caldwell Female Institute, later a part of Centre College. Lottie Moon's life inspired Christmas offering for Baptist foreign missions; fund named for her, 1918.

1706 "TOMMYGUN INVENTOR"
(3rd St. between Monmouth & York, Newport, US 127, Campbell Co.)

Brig. Gen. John T. Thompson, USA, inventor of Thompson submachine gun, was born here in 1860. A West Point graduate of 1882, he was early advocate of automatic weapons and improved many small arms. Awarded Distinguished Service Medal as Director of Arsenals in World War I. General Thompson died in 1940, lamenting the notoriety of the Tommygun as a gangster weapon.

1707 EARLY SOUTH FRANKFORT
(507 W. Second St., Frankfort, Franklin Co.)

This site is part of 500-acre land grant (1782) to Rev. War soldier Geo. Campbell, who served with Geo. Rogers Clark. Property has been owned by noted persons including early legislators Otho Beatty, Wm. Murray and Baker Ewing; State Auditor Thomas Page; and lawyer philanthropist John Hanna. South Frankfort, a separate town 1810–50, included most of Campbell survey.
(Reverse)

EARLY FAMILIES HERE
Owners whose families lived in the original house here – J. W. Denny, State Attorney General; Thomas Loughborough and son Judge Preston Loughborough, Chief

U. S. Postal Inspector; Sally S. Jouett, widow of Col. William R. Jouett; and Thomasine Jouett, granddaughter of Rev. war hero Jack Jouett. This Queen Anne house was built by John Meagher, 1889–90. Over.

1708 CALEB WALLACE'S LAW OFFICE
(Lansing Lane, Midway, Woodford Co.)

Woodford's first county court met here, May 16, 1789. Caleb Wallace (1742–1814), Presbyterian minister from Va., was in Kentucky by 1783. He served on Supreme Court of District of Ky. and on Ky. Court of Appeals for 30 years. A founder of several colleges and a trustee of Transylvania University, Wallace was called the "Father of the Academy System of Kentucky."

1709 WILLIAM GOEBEL—LAWYER
(Goebel Park, 6th & Philadelphia Sts., Covington, Kenton Co.)

Goebel began his legal career in this building and advanced through ties to notable leaders. Born in Pa. in 1856, Goebel rose from poverty. Elected to state senate in 1887, he served as president pro tem of that body, 1894–1900. In the 1890–91 constitutional convention, and later, Goebel was active in his support of railroad regulation and other reforms. Over.
(Reverse)

WILLIAM GOEBEL—GOVERNOR
Nominated for governor in 1899, Democrat Goebel lost close race to Republican William Taylor. The election was contested and, during that debate, Goebel was shot on January 30, 1900, near the Old Capitol. Before his death four days later, he was declared gov. by legislature. Three convicted in the murder were later pardoned and killer's identity uncertain. Over.

1710 FIRST CHRISTIAN CHURCH
(316 Ann St., Frankfort, Franklin Co.)

Organized December 2, 1832, by noted minister and educator Philip S. Fall, aided by John T. Johnson. Services held at various locations until 1842 when church erected on this site. Alexander Campbell preached here. Church burned, 1870; Emily T. Tubman gave money to erect second building. Part of it utilized in present edifice, completed, 1924. *Presented by First Christian Church.*

1711 RINEYVILLE NAMED
(Rineyville, KY 220, just west of KY 1600, Hardin Co.)

Sylvester Riney gave land for Illinois Central R.R., 1874, and town named for family. Zachariah, his father, was Abraham Lincoln's first teacher while living on Rolling Fork. Zachariah moved to Rineyville site, 1830; built this double log house, later enlarged and clapboarded. Lived here nearly 25 years with his son, Sylvester. His grandson, Mancil G., was first postmaster.

1712 ALVAN DREW SCHOOL
(Pine Ridge, KY 15, Wolfe Co.)

The Methodist-sponsored Alvan Drew school was here, 1913–1947. Started by missionary Mrs. M. O. Everett, and named for supporter of rural education, it began as a one-room school and later added a student-operated farm, blacksmith and print shops, grist and planing mills. Closed after 1947 fire. Dessie Scott Children's Home, formerly in Breathitt Co., moved here, 1950.

1713 THOMAS EDISON BUTCHERTOWN HOUSE
(729 E. Washington St., Louisville, Jefferson Co.)

Designated the official Edison Museum in the Commonwealth of Ky. by an Act of the General Assembly, 1982. Thomas A. Edison lived in Louisville, 1866–67. Moved to N. J. where he perfected the incandescent light. Edison returned to Louisville in 1883 for opening of Southern Exposition, where 4600 of his lights were on display. See over.
(Reverse)

THOMAS EDISON BUTCHERTOWN HOUSE
Edison (1847–1931) rented a room in this house. As a young man he conducted experiments, often all night, then walked to his job as a telegraph operator at 58 West Main Street. Experimenting at work, he spilled acid and was fired. He left Louisville and later developed over 1000 patents for such devices as phonograph and microphone. Over.

1714 THOMAS HUNT MORGAN
(210 N. Broadway, Lexington, Fayette Co.)

Winner of 1933 Nobel Prize was born in Hunt-Morgan house, 1866; grew up here. A nephew of John Hunt Morgan, he attended State College of Ky. (Univ. of Ky.). Taught at Columbia Univ. and there, influenced by Mendel's work, left embryology, his main field, for genetics. Headed up research team studying inbreeding of fruit flies. Observing offspring led to discovery of genes. Over.
(Reverse)

GENETIC RESEARCH
Morgan's research team confirmed Mendel's laws, proved reality of gene as part of chromosome, showed sex determined by chromosomes, demonstrated dominant and recessive traits. At 62, Morgan went to Cal. Institute of Technology, Pasadena, as biology dept. head to research cell differentiation. Died there, 1945. University of Kentucky named new school of biological sciences for him.

1715 ALICE VIRGINIA COFFIN (1848–88)
(Jefferson St., between Preston & Floyd Sts., Louisville, Jefferson Co.)

Born on this street, Alice Virginia was one of seven founders of P.E.O., an international philanthropic and educational organization for women. It began as a sorority at the Iowa Wesleyan College, 1869; owns Cottey College in Missouri, and provides monetary assistance for education of women. Miss Coffin designed P.E.O. seal. *Presented by Ky. P.E.O. Chapters.*

1716 FIRST BAPTIST CHURCH
(209 W. Jefferson St., Georgetown, Scott Co.)

Organized 1811, its first meeting house erected here, 1815. Howard Malcom, pastor and president of Georgetown College, urged relocation of church near college and lease of original site to black congregation, 1842. G. W. Dupee, a slave, was first official pastor; 19 have served church. Reuben Lee was pastor when present edifice built, 1870. *Presented by First Baptist Church.*

1717 ST. VINCENT'S ACADEMY
(Between Waverly and Morganfield, near Jct. US 60 & KY 141,

Union Co.)

Sisters of Charity from Nazareth–Angela Spink, Frances Gardner, and Cecily O'Brien–arrived here, 1820. They began a girls boarding school on this site on land of Alvey family. With aid of Father Elisha Durbin, school gained renown. It operated until 1967. First Catholic cemetery in county joins the school site. Buried here are several Revolutionary War soldiers.

1718 HOME OF ARTHUR KROCK
(East Main St., KY 90, at May St., Glasgow, Barren Co.)

Called dean of Washington newsmen, Glasgow's native son (1886–1974) grew up here with his grandparents, Emmanuel and Henrietta Morris. He began his career in journalism with the Louisville *Herald*, then went to Washington, D.C., as a correspondent for the *Times* and *Courier-Journal*. Krock won French citation after his coverage of the Versailles peace conference. Over.
(Reverse)
HISTORIC HOME
In 1927, Krock joined the New York *Times*; soon became its Washington correspondent and bureau chief. His column, "In the Nation," was noted for its opinions on public policy. Over his 60-year career, Arthur Krock knew 11 presidents and won four Pulitzer Prizes. Joel Cheek, who also lived here, was one of two founders of the Maxwell House Coffee Company. Over.

1719 HENRY WATTERSON (1840–1921)
(525 W. Broadway, Louisville, Jefferson Co.)

Born in Washington, D.C., son of a Congressman and editor, Watterson gained wide newspaper experience. He succeeded Prentice as the editor of Louisville *Journal*, which merged with W. N. Haldeman's *Courier* and the recently acquired *Democrat*, 1868. For most of "Marse Henry's" 51-year tenure, the *Courier-Journal* was at Fourth and Liberty. It attained prominence under Watterson. Over.
(Reverse)
JOURNALIST-POLITICIAN
Watterson was a major force in Democratic Party. He enlisted in the Confederate Army, but believed in Union; was foe of sectionalism and often blasted it in writings. He opposed prohibition and League of Nations. His style influenced three generations; editorials hailing U.S. declaration of war earned him a Pulitzer Prize, 1917. He retired to "Mansfield" in Jeffersontown, 1919.

1720 KENTUCKY RAILWAY MUSEUM
(Ormsby Station, on Dorsey Lane at LaGrange Rd., Louisville, Jefferson Co.)

Officially designated Kentucky Railway Museum by Act of General Assembly. Began, 1954, on River Rd. Search for new location started after 1964 flood; moved here, 1977. Exhibits of rail relics given by many regional railroads and industries. One engine, L & N No. 152, pulled Theodore Roosevelt's campaign train; listed on National Register of Historic Places.

1721 PADUCAH COMMUNITY COLLEGE
(In front of College, Paducah, US 62, McCracken Co.)

Founded at 707 Broadway in 1932, this is oldest nondenominational two-year college in Ky. Originally private, Paducah Jr. College was a municipal institution, 1936–1968. In 1949–1953 college became focal point of NAACP'S successful efforts to integrate higher education. Since 1968, school has been part of Community College System of the University of Kentucky.

1722 JOHN EDWARDS, 1748–1837
(Paris, Courthouse lawn, US 27 & 68, Bourbon Co.)

As early legislator, Edwards was member of the Virginia House of Delegates in 1781–83, 1785, 1786. He was a delegate to the convention to ratify Federal Constitution, June 1788, and to conventions that separated Kentucky from Virginia. Edwards served as a representative to the 1792 convention which framed the first constitution of Ky. Over.
(Reverse)
WESTWOOD
Six miles west on Brentsville Road on Cooper's Run is the site of the home of John Edwards, one of Kentucky's first two United States senators, 1792–1795. In Virginia he married Susannah Wroe and came to Ky. in 1780. He served in militia and became

first clerk of Bourbon County. Elected to Ky. House of Representatives, 1795; then to Ky. Senate, 1796–1800. See over.

1723 EARLY FOURTH STREET
(Near south entry to the Galleria, Louisville, Jefferson Co.)

Louisville's earliest map (1779) included Fourth Street. At first a street of residences and churches, it had become by the early 1900s the dominant commercial and social avenue of the city. Here arose prominent landmarks: Kaufman's (1903) and Stewart's (1907); the Seelbach (1905) and the Brown (1923) hotels; Starks Building (1912). *Presented by the City of Louisville.*
(Reverse)
LATER FOURTH STREET
On Fourth Street in 1870s stood a Polytechnic Library and in 1880s a Renaissance Customs House. In 1920s, "Movie Row" grew here with such "palaces" as Mary Anderson, Rialto, and Loew's theaters. Many U.S. presidents have paraded here, including Theodore and Franklin Delano Roosevelt. Down Fourth "Avenue" Louisvillians marched to war and celebrated peace. See over.

1724 FOURTH STREET
(Near north entry to the Galleria, Louisville, Jefferson Co.)

During Civil War, "Newspaper Row" stood in this area along Green (Liberty) St. On north side was pro-Union *Journal*; on south side, pro-southern *Courier*. Union Army Hq. was on west side of Fourth near Walnut. Macauley Theater opened in 1873 near Fourth and Walnut. It hosted Sarah Bernhardt in 1880. Mark Twain spoke in the area, 1885. *Presented by the City of Louisville.*
(Reverse)
A CIVIL WAR COMPASS
From Galleria, all compass points have Civil War personality ties. One block *west,* Abe Lincoln visited James Speed's law office (1841). One block *east* is Christ Church, whose rector, Rev. Ashe, married Jeff Davis and Sarah Knox Taylor (1835). One block *south,* U. S. Grant visited Henry Watterson (1879). One block *north,* John Wilkes Booth performed on stage (1864). Over.

1725 THE MASTERSON HOUSE
(Highland Ave., 2 mi. E. of downtown Carrollton, US 42, Carroll Co.)

Oldest brick house still standing in county, this was home of Richard and Sarah Masterson. Bricks laid in Flemish bond. House was center of town's activities. Mastersons, leading Methodists, opened their home for services before church erected in 1810. Masterson was among early trustees of Port William, now Carrollton, which was incorporated in 1794. See over.
(Reverse)
THE MASTERSON HOUSE
First court of Gallatin County held here May 14, 1799. Bishop Francis Asbury visited "Widow Masterson" in 1808. Sarah and Richard Masterson are buried in the family cemetery nearby. The house was listed on the National Register of Historic Places, 1975. It was restored by the Port William Historical Society, 1979–1980. Over.

1726 REV. JESSE R. ZEIGLER HOUSE
(FRANK LLOYD WRIGHT HOUSE)
(509 Shelby St., Frankfort, Franklin Co.)

The design for this house came from a chance shipboard meeting in 1910 of Rev. Zeigler of this city with Frank Lloyd Wright, the internationally known architect. The Presbyterian minister had local contractor Scott begin construction that year. This is an example of Wright's "prairie house," utilizing open floor plans. See over.
(Reverse)
FRANK LLOYD WRIGHT, (1869–1959)
Famous primarily as a residence architect, Wright also planned many impressive public structures, including the Imperial Hotel in Tokyo and Guggenheim Museum in New York City. This is the only building of his design erected in Ky. during his lifetime. House was listed on National Register of Historic Places in 1976. Over.

1727 GALLANTRY IN ACTION
(Elizabethtown, Courthouse lawn, US 31-W & 62, Hardin Co.)

Sergeant George E. Larkin, Jr., a native of Colesburg, Hardin Co., took part in Doolittle's raid on Japanese mainland, April 18, 1942. He was awarded the Distinguished Flying Cross and decorated by the Chinese government; won award for being first Kentuckian to bomb enemy capital. Famous raid boosted American morale. Six months later, the 23-year-old was killed in Asia.

1728 McCoy Graves Here
(Dils Cem., Pikeville Bypass, Pikeville, US 23 & 119, Pike Co.)

Among some 500 graves in Dils Cemetery are the resting places of Randolph McCoy, clan leader in the Hatfield-McCoy feud; his wife, Sarah; their daughter and son, Roseanna and Sam; and Sam's wife, Martha. This Appalachian vendetta, from Civil War to 1890s, became well known. Dils Cemetery is part of the Hatfield-McCoy Feud Historic District. See over.
(Reverse)

Hatfield-McCoy Feud

The feud resulted, in part, from Civil War conflicts, romantic entanglements, family-oriented discord, property and election disputes, mixed with mountain pride. Violence surrounding clan leaders Anderson Hatfield and Randolph McCoy eventually involved governors of Kentucky and West Virginia. Deaths and time brought an end to the feud. See over.

1729 Campbellsville Baptist Church
(420 N. Central Ave., Campbellsville, KY 527, Taylor Co.)

Taylor County's oldest congregation began with Pitman Creek, organized 1791, and Robinson Creek, founded by 1793. They combined to form the "Church Pitman," which became Campbellsville Baptist Church, 1852, located on No. Columbia Ave. Frame building there was used by court during the Civil War after Confederates burned the courthouse. *Presented by Campbellsville Baptist Church.*
(Reverse)

Campbellsville Baptist Church

In 1889, Shuttleworth Memorial Baptist Church, now the Library, replaced 1852 building. In 1915–1916, a church with domed ceiling and four walls of stained glass windows was erected; destroyed by fire, 1962. The present Greek Revival edifice was erected in 1963. Of group's origin, only Pitman and Robinson church

cemeteries still remain. *Presented by Campbellsville Baptist Church.*

1730 Early Schoolhouse
(Northern Kentucky University, Highland Heights, Campbell Co.)

A part of cabin, moved here from Grants Lick area, stood adjacent to Gosney School, and typifies first schoolhouses of Campbell County. Forty-two were erected. Two of them—John's Hill (ca. 1880–1906) and St. John's (ca. 1847–1857)—were within three miles of here. This site is part of land patent of David Leitch, early settler. *Presented by Northern Kentucky University.*
(Reverse)

Northern Kentucky University

Northern Ky. University began as an extension center of University of Ky., 1948. It became community college, 1962, and by 1976 was a state university. It moved here from Covington in 1972. The 300-acre NKU campus is part of land first surveyed in April and June 1785, and issued as land patents by Isaac Shelby in 1792. See over. *Presented by Northern Kentucky University.*

1731 Godman Field
(Park Rd. and Pilot St., Ft. Knox, Hardin Co.)

First airfield in Kentucky, used since October 1918 when built for 29th Aero Sqdn. Operated by 31st Balloon Co. 1920–21. Largely inactive until 1937, when 12th Observation Sqdn. assigned here through early 1942. World War II units included the 73rd Reconnaissance Group and the 387th, 391st, 477th Bombardment Groups with Martin B-26 aircraft. See other side. *Presented by Kentucky Aviation Assn. and Kentucky Historical Society.*
(Reverse)

Godman Field

Named for Lt. Louis K. Godman who was killed in airplane crash at Columbia, S.C., 28 September 1918. Original 4 hangars were located ½ mile N.E. of this site. Two moved ca. 1922 to Louisville's Bowman Field; one is now Bldg. 1338 on Angel Alley, and one is Bldg. 1328 on Briggs St. Present main hangar and runways constructed in 1941. *Presented by Kentucky Aviation Assn. and Ky. Historical Society.*

1732 PILOT—SPY—HERO
(Whitesburg, Courthouse lawn, Letcher Co.)

Francis Gary Powers and the "U-2 Incident" catapulted activities of the United States into world view. This Burdine native, with other pilots directed by CIA, flew U-2's (high altitude jet gliders) over Russia, photographing missile and industrial sites and nuclear tests. On May 1, 1960, when his plane was diasabled 1300 miles over Russia, Powers parachuted to safety. Over.

(Reverse)
FRANCIS GARY POWERS, 1929–1977

Taken prisoner, Powers stated his compass had malfunctioned on a weather flight. Finding film intact in plane's wreckage, the Russians told him he would stand trial for espionage. Sentenced to ten years imprisonment, Powers was released in 1962 in exchange for a Soviet spy. Later decorated by CIA. Died in civilian helicopter crash.

1733 BIRTHPLACE OF CARRY A. NATION
(KY 34 at its Jct. with Fisher Ford Rd., Lancaster, Garrard Co.)

With hatchet in hand, this famous Kentuckian harassed saloon owners across U.S. Four miles from here on Carry Nation Rd. is house where she was born, 1846; lived there five years and in other Ky. towns before moving west. After Kansas banned liquor, Carry began crusade there in 1899, smashing furniture, mirrors, bottles. Home on National Register of Historic Places. Over.

(Reverse)
LADY WITH THE HATCHET

Carry Nation gave direction to the antiliquor movement, which led to Prohibition, 1920–33. Driven by bitterness from first marriage to an alcoholic, she had "visions" which commanded militant pursuit of temperance. Carry's methods put her in jail some 30 times. She died in 1911 and was buried in Belton, Mo. The words, "She hath done what she could," engraved on her monument.

1734 WARD HALL
(1 mi. W. of Georgetown, US 460, Scott Co.)

Junius R. Ward had this mansion (75 ft. by 75 ft.) built circa 1855. Striking features are its coquina (coral and fossils) foundation, 40 ft. columns, and stone window and door frames. A frequent guest was his niece—noted southern belle Sallie Ward. After the Civil War devastated his fortune, Ward sold estate in 1867. Listed on National Register of Historic Places. Over.

(Reverse)
WARD HALL

Built as summer home, Greek Revival house in Corinthian motif has two roofs. Bottom is slate; top, once copper, had a huge copper tank for water. Deep rubbed walnut woodwork, variety of Greek trim on cornices, and an elliptical staircase are part of mansion's lavish detail. Among past owners was Col. Milton Hamilton, who offered house to legislature for state capitol. Over.

1735 REVOLUTIONARY WAR SOLDIERS
(Greenville, Courthouse lawn, Muhlenberg Co.)

Those who settled in Muhlenberg County:

Josiah Arnold	Andrew Glenn
Elisha Atkinson	Isaiah Hancock
John Bone	John Harper
James Craig	Nathan Harper
Albritain Drake	Michael Hill
David Edward	Richard Hill
Joshua Elkin	Hardy Hines
David Engler	William Hopkins
Mathew Ganey	John Hunt
Sikes Garris	Edward Jarvis

(Reverse)
REVOLUTIONARY WAR SOLDIERS

Peter Kincheloe	Michael Roll
John Littlepage	Thomas Tetterton
Ephraim McLean	Abraham Unsell, Jr.
John McMahon	Frederick Unsell
Hugh Martin	Henry Unsell
Benjamin Neal	Lewis Webb
Abraham Newton	Arrington Wickliffe
Jesse Oates	Britton Willis
Joseph Pitt	William Worthington
William B. Rice	William Young
Richard D. Reynolds	Matthew Zimmerman
Henry Rhoads	

1736 JOHN F. DAY (1913–1982)
(Flemingsburg, Courthouse lawn, Fleming Co.)

A native of Fleming County, this prize-winning journalist began his career with the Lexington *Leader*, later worked with Washington Bureau of Louisville *Courier-Journal*. Director and Vice President of CBS News, 1955–61, where he won two Emmy awards. Wrote *Bloody Ground*, 1941, on Eastern Kentucky. John Day spent his last years in England publishing a weekly newspaper.

1737 LOUISVILLE MEDICAL COLLEGE
(Louisville, 101 West Chestnut St., Jefferson Co.)

Founded in 1869, the college was one of four medical institutions in city which merged with Medical Dept. of University of Louisville, 1908. College built this limestone Richardsonian Romanesque structure 1891–1893. Building was designed by firm of Clarke and Loomis. It housed U of L School of Medicine, 1909–1970. Listed on National Register of Historic Places, 1975.

1738 HAWESVILLE
(Hawesville, Main St., KY 3101, Hancock Co.)

Hancock County and Hawesville were created by Ky. law January 3, 1829. County seat was named for Richard Hawes, who donated land for town. His son, Richard, Jr., became Confederate governor of Kentucky, 1862. Hancock's first cannel coal produced commercially, 1832; mine operated by Charles Landers. Venture drew workers and investors from as far away as England and Ireland.

1739 SCOTTISH RITE TEMPLE
(Louisville, 200 East Gray St., Jefferson Co.)

Home of Grand Consistory of Ky., a branch of Freemasonry. Chartered 1852 in Louisville by Supreme Council of Ancient and Accepted Scottish Rite of Freemasonry, Southern Jurisdiction of U.S. of America. Oldest Body under Supreme Council in continued existence. John C. Breckinridge was the first Ky. Sovereign Grand Inspector Gen. *Presented by The Louisville, Ky., Scottish Rite.*
(Reverse)

GRAND CONSISTORY OF KENTUCKY

Albert G. Mackey, Sec.-Gen. of Supreme Council, issued warrant "To open and hold Consistory of Sublime Princes of the Royal Secret" for Ky. in Louisville, Aug. 21, 1852.

A dispensation was given to H. Gray, Grand Cmdr.; H. Hudson, 1st Lt. Cmdr.; J. H. Howe, 2nd Lt. Cmdr.; J. Cromie, Grand Treas.; and F. Webber, Grand Sec., to serve as Charter Officers of the Grand Consistory.

1740 BETHLEHEM ACADEMY
(In front of Bethlehem Academy, KY 1357, Hardin Co.)

Sisters of Loretto began girls' school here in 1830; the official contract made, 1831. John L. Helm, twice gov. of Ky., sold 580 acres for $2,240 to Rev. Chas. J. Cecil. Sisters used Helm mansion as main building; wings added ca. 1848. With facilities for 75 boarding and 25 day students, Academy had grade through high school levels. Closed 1959; mansion restored in 1981.

1741 LEITCHFIELD LANDMARKS
(Leitchfield, Clinton & Market Sts., Grayson Co.)

Leitchfield was laid off 1810, and named for David Leitch, prominent landowner and founder of Leitch's Station. His estate gave land for Grayson's county seat. Site chosen because of fresh water springs, particularly "Big Spring" nearby. Grayson's first circuit court met under large oak tree on this hill; Judge Henry P. Broadenax presided. Town was incorporated in 1866.

1742 BRECKINRIDGE'S LAST HOME
(Lexington, 429 W. Second St., Fayette Co.)

Built circa 1866, this house was occupied by John C. Breckinridge in 1874–1875. The former U.S. senator and youngest U.S. vice-president was also a Confederate general and secretary of war. After exile, he returned to Lexington in 1869 and resumed the practice of law. He rented this house the last year of his life and died here May 17, 1875.

1743 VEST-LINDSEY HOUSE
(Frankfort, Wapping & Washington Sts., Franklin Co.)

Erected before 1820, this house is linked to several prominent men. It was childhood home of George Graham Vest, a famous orator, debater and three-term senator from Missouri; member CSA Congress 3 years. Also home of Daniel W. Lindsey, who, during the Civil War, was Union regimental and brigade commander, and later Inspector General and Adjutant General of Kentucky.

1744 BEECHLAND
(Louisville, #2 Rebel Rd., just off Brownsboro Rd., Jefferson Co.)

On June 17, 1835, the daughter of Zachary Taylor, Sarah Knox, married Jefferson Davis in the house that originally stood on this site. The home was owned by Zachary Taylor's sister. Soon after their marriage, while visiting Davis' relatives in Louisiana, the couple contracted malaria. In September of that year, the young bride died. The present house built ca. 1870.

1745 CHARLES WALLACE HOME →
(2 mi. E. of Hartford, adjacent to KY 69, Ohio Co.)

Builder and owner Charles Wallace erected first two courthouses in Ohio Co. The carpenter-contractor and his brother operated county's first water mill. Wallace came to area in 1798 and built his home ca. 1820, ½ mi. north. House had movable wall, which the Wallaces often raised for early Methodist meetings. Home listed on National Register of Historic Places.

1746 UNION STATION
(Owensboro, 1035 Frederica, US 431, Daviess Co.)

Built 1905–6, on site of the Louisville, Henderson and St. Louis depot. It represents an agreement between the Louisville, Henderson and St. Louis; the Louisville and Nashville; and the Illinois Central railroads to provide Union Station for Owensboro. The plans were drawn by John B. Hutchings and Henry F. Hawes; contractor, Walter Brashear.

1747 HAZEN A. DEAN (1899–1984)
(Owensboro, at Settle Memorial Methodist Church, Daviess Co.)

First Kentuckian to receive "70 Continuous Years of Service Award" from Boy Scouts of America, 1983. Scoutmaster for over 50 years; with Owensboro's oldest troop, 24, from 1949 till death. Among many honors, he received Scoutmaster's Key and Silver Beaver awards. Recognized for having 86 Eagle Scouts, most in nation; received Lt. Governor's Outstanding Kentuckian Award, 1982.

1748 TAYLORSVILLE
(Taylorsville, KY 55, Spencer Co.)

Named in honor of Virginia native Richard Taylor, who donated sixty acres of land in 1799 for a town at forks of Brashear's Creek and Salt River. Taylor operated a grist mill nearby. Town became county seat of Spencer in December 1824. Four of earliest trustees of Taylorsville were Robert Jeffries, George Cravinston, Philip W. Taylor, and Benjamin Bourne.

1749 JAMES R. LEMON (1848–1919)
(Benton, 1309 Main St., Marshall Co.)

Owner and editor of Benton *Tribune* and Mayfield *Messenger* and author of a Marshall County history lived here. Lemon, in 1884, also founded Big Singing Day. This evolved from Southern Harmony, a hymn-singing custom popular in early 1800s, continuing today. Using only four "shaped notes," it simplifies music reading and has no accompaniment. House listed on National Register.

1750 CAMP DICK ROBINSON
(US 27, just SE of Jct. with KY 34, Garrard Co.)

Major General William Nelson was authorized by President Lincoln to establish, Aug. 1861, first camp south of Ohio River for recruitment of federal troops in Civil War. Named for Richard M. Robinson, a Union supporter, who offered house and farm as campsite. Noted stagecoach stop, the house was also Nelson's headquarters. Camp later moved to Camp Nelson in Jessamine County.

1751 WARWICK
(Approx. ½ mi. S. of Salvisa, US 127, Mercer Co.)

On Kentucky River, 2½ miles from here, James Harrod and party landed in 1774, before founding Harrodsburg. Called "Harrod's Landing," this location was major rendezvous for militia, 1780. It became site of Warwick, founded 1787. Trustees included early surveyor Samuel McAfee, future governor Christopher Greenup, and the noted Indian fighter Hugh McGary. Over.
(Reverse)
WARWICK/OREGON

Warwick flourished for some 50 years and was succeeded by Oregon. Both were early shipping ports. Flatboats, during Warwick era, and later steamboats, at Oregon, ran regularly between here and New Orleans. This point was at head of slackwater navigation on Kentucky River. The creek is still called Landing Run because of significance to James Harrod.

1752 KENTUCKY STATE UNIVERSITY

(Frankfort, Maryland Ave. entrance to Kentucky State University, Franklin Co.)

John H. Jackson, before becoming first president of college, headed black teachers' assoc. in Kentucky and promoted establishment of schools for instruction of black teachers. His efforts led to legislation founding college which became Ky. State. He served 1887–1898 and 1907–1910. First permanent building, Jackson Hall, was named for him. Hall listed on the National Register.
(Reverse)

KENTUCKY STATE UNIVERSITY

School was chartered 1886; opened 1887 with three teachers and 55 students. The first state-supported institution of higher education for blacks, school gained funds from legislature for building and teachers, and from Frankfort city council for site and clearing of grounds. Ky. State accredited as four year college in 1931; achieved university status 1972. Over.

1753 GEORGE ROGERS CLARK

(Louisville, Cave Hill Cem.—Section P, Jefferson Co.)

In 1776, Clark, delegate to Va. Gen. Assembly, prompted recognition of Ky. as county of Va. By 1778, he set up outpost on Corn Island, at Falls of Ohio, from which he launched invasion of Northwest. He captured three British forts, reduced Indian power, and crippled English strategy, thus helping secure territory for U.S. Over. *Presented by Louisville-Thruston Chap., Ky. Soc. S.A.R.*
(Reverse)

GEORGE ROGERS CLARK

After fall of Ruddle's and Martin's stations, Clark led expeditions against Indians in 1780 and 1782. In later years Clark was plagued by poor health and war debts incurred for his country. He died at Locust Grove, his sister's home. Buried there and afterwards reinterred in Cave Hill Cem., 1869. Outpost he founded grew into Louisville.

1754 WHITEHAVEN

(Paducah, Whitehaven Tourist Welcome Center, US 45 & I-24, McCracken Co.)

Main part of house, two-story brick structure, built in 1860s by Edward Anderson. Edward Atkins bought it in 1903 and had noted Paducah architect A. L. Lassiter transform Victorian farmhouse into Classical Revival mansion. He added the Corinthian-columned front portico, and named the house Whitehaven. See over. *Presented by McCracken County Civic Beautification Board.*
(Reverse)

WHITEHAVEN

In 1908, Paducah Mayor James P. Smith bought and renamed home "Bide-A-Wee," Scottish adage for "Come Rest A While." Smith family members lived here until 1968. After mansion restored, it opened on June 23, 1983, as Whitehaven Tourist Welcome Center. Listed on the National Register of Historic Places in 1984. See over. *Presented by McCracken County Civic Beautification Board.*

1755 DOE RUN CREEK HISTORIC DISTRICT

(S. of Brandenburg, at Doe Run Inn, KY 448, Meade Co.)

Listed on the National Register of Historic Places. Creek discovered by Squire Boone and John McKinney, 1778. District includes one of oldest mills in Ky., built before 1792 by Jonathan Essery. Mill operated until 1900 when converted to resort; became Doe Run Inn, 1927. Another mill, three houses (one log) and county's first hydroelectric plant also in district.

1756 CAPTAIN JOHN W. CANNON

(Hawesville, 2nd scenic overlook on US 60, 1½ mi. E. of KY 69, Hancock Co.)

Below is view of river bottom land where John Cannon, riverboat pilot and builder of fine steamboats for lower Mississippi trade, was born in 1820. By 1840 this skilled pilot began his career as steamboat entrepreneur. His most famous achievement was the ROBERT E. LEE, which won over the NATCHEZ in celebrated steamboat race from New Orleans to St. Louis in 1870.

1757 PITTSBURG AND WILDERNESS ROAD
(Pittsburg, Old Richmond Rd. & Crab Orchard, just off US 25, Laurel Co.)

The "Madison Branch" of Wilderness Road was last 18th-century link from Cumberland Gap to central Kentucky. By legislative act of March 1, 1797, Joseph Crockett built new road from Milford, then seat of Madison Co., to intersect with improved Wilderness Road at present-day Pittsburg. This point became new "forks of the road" and replaced Old Hazel Patch crossing.

1758 GEN. ORMSBY MACKNIGHT MITCHEL
(Ft. Mitchell, Grandview Dr., Kenton Co.)

This park named for General Mitchel (1809–62), who assisted in Union defense of Cincinnati during Civil War. Fort Mitchell, one of 7 forts erected around city, named for him. Born in Ky.; graduate of West Point and served in Mexican War. A noted astronomer, he founded Cincinnati Observatory; later director of the Dudley Observatory, N.Y. Died of yellow fever while in the service.

1759 NO-TILLAGE FARMING
(Approx. 2 mi. S. of Herndon, KY 107, Christian Co.)

First practice of no-tillage crop production in Ky. occurred on this farm in 1962. Harry and Laurence Young, of Christian Co., were among first in nation to experiment with no-tillage techniques, which use herbicides in providing seed bed in residue stubble. Conserves soil and water; saves time, labor, fuel, and often produces higher crop yields. *Presented by the Du Pont Agricultural Chemicals Dept.*

1760 JACKSONIAN HOTEL
(Scottsville, Public Sq. at Library, Allen Co.)

Built in 1919 during an oil boom, Jacksonian gained wide prominence. It was third hotel on site and stood here for 54 years. Closed in 1973. Hotel received name because of its location on Jackson Highway, now 31-E, one of oldest roads in Kentucky. This was route Andrew Jackson sometimes traveled between Nashville and Washington, D.C. *Presented by the Scottsville Woman's Club.*

1761 REV. VALENTINE COOK (1763–1822)
(4 mi. NE of Russellville, Jct. KY 1588 & John Rob Williams Rd., Logan Co.)

Pioneer Methodist preacher who settled on Muddy River in 1806 where Camp Meeting was held, 1800. A teacher, orator and organizer of churches, he attended Cokesbury College in Md. and began ministry, 1788. Presiding Elder of Cumberland Dist., 1798. Married Tabitha, niece of Gov. Slaughter, same year. Buried near Camp Meeting site. *Presented by Rena Milliken.*

1762 BASEBALL GREAT
(2¼ mi. from Morganfield at entrance to Earle C. Clements Job Corps Center, US 60, Union Co.)

Jackie Robinson (1919–1972) began his professional baseball career while a lieutenant at Camp Breckinridge, 1944. The next year Branch Rickey, Brooklyn Dodgers general manager, signed the four-sport letterman from UCLA for Montreal Royals, top Dodger farm club. In 1947, Robinson promoted to Dodgers team, breaking major league color barrier. Elected to Baseball Hall of Fame in 1962.

1763 YOUNG'S INN
(West Point, Second & Elm Sts., Hardin Co.)

This famous stagecoach stop on the old Louisville & Nashville Turnpike was built ca. 1797 by James Young, founder of West Point, Ky. At this inn John James Audubon wrote about seeing large flocks of passenger pigeons. Jenny Lind stopped here briefly in 1851 and sang from inn steps. Other guests have been Henry Clay, Andrew Jackson, James Buchanan, and Wendell Willkie.

1764 CARLISLE PASSENGER DEPOT
(Carlisle, 101 Market St., Nicholas Co.)

Built in 1912 by L & N soon after original frame depot burned. The Lexington and Maysville Railroad was completed to

Carlisle by 1871; railroad joined L & N system, 1891. Land donated for depot by thirteen citizens and businesses in 1882. Depot purchased in 1978 by Nicholas Co. Historical Society and listed on National Register of Historic Places in 1979. Renovated 1981.

1765 ABNER GAINES HOUSE →
(Walton, US 25, Boone Co.)

In 1790s Abner Gaines built this Federal style mansion and became owner of first stage line between Lexington and Cincinnati, 1818. House used as inn and stagecoach stop. It has 3 stairways and 10 carved mantels. Abner's son, John P. Gaines, was appointed governor of Oregon Territory in 1850. House listed on National Register of Historic Places, 1980.

1766 EARLY BLACKSMITH SHOP
(Louisville, 3612 Brownsboro Rd., Jefferson Co.)

This historic property has served as a blacksmith shop, wagon making shop and general store. Begun by John and Barbara Bauer in 1870, their businesses flourished here, on a main turnpike to Louisville, and finally in 1918 evolved into the Bauer family restaurant. This building was erected 1868–1869. Renovated in 1984.

1767 CHURCH OF CHRIST, UNION
(In front of the Church, across from Boone Tavern Hotel, Berea, KY 21, Madison Co.)

Founded 1853 by the Rev. John G. Fee of Bracken County on the invitation of local citizens and Cassius M. Clay, who projected an antislavery community here. Open in full equality to all races and nonsectarian, the church had a leading part in establishment of Berea College, 1855, and in cause of racial equality in this area. *Presented by Congregation.*

1768 GOV. KEEN JOHNSON, 1896–1970
(KY 453 & Brandon Chapel Road, Lyon Co.)

Born at Methodist parsonage at Brandon Chapel, he was son of the Rev. Robert and Mattie H. Johnson. Entered politics from Madison Co., where he was editor-publisher. Elected lt. gov., 1935; gov., 1939–1943. A frugal administrator, Johnson supported legislation which brought cheap TVA electric power to state. He was appointed first Under Secretary of Labor by President Truman.

1769 ADMIRAL CLAUDE C. BLOCH
(Woodbury, KY 403, Butler Co.)

The career of this naval officer spanned Spanish-American War and World Wars I and II. A native of Butler County, he attended public schools and Ogden College in Bowling Green; graduated from Annapolis, 1899. Assumed command of USS *Plattsburg* in 1918; received the Navy Cross for hazardous transporting of troops and supplies to Europe. Over.
(Reverse)
ADMIRAL CLAUDE C. BLOCH
Bloch's duties included Commander, Mine Force, Pacific Fleet; Chief of Staff to Commander, Battleship Divisions; Chief of Bureau of Ordnance—all in 1920s; Commander in Chief, U.S. Fleet, 1938–40; Commandant of 14th Naval Dist. at Pearl Harbor, 1940–42. As chairman of Navy Board for industrial production awards, he was given Legion of Merit. Retired, 1945.

1770 THE COOPERATIVE PROGRAM
(Murray, 203 S. Fourth St., Calloway Co.)

Under leadership of H. Boyce Taylor, First Baptist Church, Murray, began in 1900 a new approach to church finance. Taylor, pastor 1897–1931, avidly promoted this unified budget plan; appointed chairman of a State Baptist Committee, 1913, "to consider . . . unifying our work" under one budget. During 1914–1915 Taylor and layman F. D. Perkins toured the state promoting unified plan. Over.
(Reverse)
THE COOPERATIVE PROGRAM
The Gen. Assoc. of Baptists in Ky. (now Ky. Bapt. Conv.) adopted first "budget plan for the collection of funds" in 1915. Taylor served as chairman of first budget committee. This was Kentucky's part in the development of world mission budget plan adopted by Southern Baptist Convention in Memphis, 1925, known as the Cooperative Program. See over. *Presented by Kentucky Baptist Convention.*

1771 ALEXANDER WALTERS (1858–1917)
(Bardstown, at the A.M.E. Zion Church, 219 East Brashear Ave., Nelson Co.)

This 24th bishop of A.M.E. Zion Church was born in Bardstown and educated under church auspices. Local A.M.E. Zion Church sponsored him for ministry. Licensed to preach, 1877; elected bishop, 1892. Served as president of National Afro-American Council and Pan African Conference. He was a leader of National Negro Committee, which later became NAACP.

1772 PIONEER METHODIST PREACHER
(W. of Danville, US 150, Boyle Co.)

Reverend Francis Clark organized first Methodist Society in Ky., 1783; such groups formed Methodist Episcopal Church, established 1784. Clark, from Virginia, settled near here. A local preacher, he was assisted by John Durham, lay leader. Society, led by Clark and Durham, began westward movement of Methodism. Grave is north on Quirk's Run Road. *Presented by United Methodists-Ky. Conference.*

1773 BOONE'S CREEK BAPTIST CHURCH
(Athens, KY 1973 [Cleveland Rd.], Fayette Co.)

Organized November 1785, by Elders John Taylor and John Tanner with 18 original members. Church part of Elkhorn Assn.; in 1823 joined Boone's Creek Assn. Sunday School organized ca. 1866. Present church is on same land as the first log church of 1785. Prominent among the founders were Daniel Boone's brother Samuel with wife Sarah. *Presented by Boone's Creek Baptist Church.*

1774 FRANKFORT CHOSEN AS CAPITAL
(Near New Capitol, Capitol Ave., just south of Todd St., Franklin Co.)

After Kentucky became a state, five commissioners were appointed on June 20, 1792, to choose a location for the state capital. They were John Allen and John Edwards (both from Bourbon Co.), Henry Lee (Mason Co.), Thomas Kennedy (Madison Co.), and Robert Todd (Fayette Co.). A number of communities competed for this honor, but Frankfort won by perseverance and, according to early histories, the

offer of Andrew Holmes' log house as capitol for seven years, a number of town lots, £50 worth of locks and hinges, 10 boxes of glass, 1500 pounds of nails, and $3000 in gold.
(Reverse)

FRANKFORT CHOSEN AS CAPITAL

Other contenders for the honor of being selected as the permanent seat of Kentucky state government had offered, as was customary, lists of contributions. These hopeful towns were Legerwood's Bend (Mercer County), Delany's Ferry and Petersburg (Woodford County), Louisville, Lexington, Leestown, and Frankfort. After thorough examination of all sites, the commissioners, following a majority vote, met with the legislature in Lexington on December 5, 1792, and gave their recommendation–that Frankfort was the most suitable site for the state capital. See over.

1775 MARION RUST (1879–1958)
(Columbus-Belmont State Park, Columbus, Hickman Co.)

Red Cross agent Marion Rust came to Columbus after its destruction in 1927 by Mississippi floods. Noting river bank cave-ins, Rust directed relocation of town. Exploring area, he found remains of Confederate garrison and envisioned Civil War memorial park. With CCC camp labor, he partially restored fort area, 1934–37, providing major step in development of present state park.

1776 BRENT SPENCE (1874–1967)
(Newport, Carothers Rd. & Monmouth St, US 27, Campbell Co.)

As chairman of U.S. House Banking and Currency Committee, Spence was a delegate to 44-nation Bretton Woods (N.H.) Conference, 1944, to promote fair commerce. This led to creating the International Monetary Fund and Bank, and Spence's sponsoring legislation in Congress. A Newport native and University of Cincinnati law graduate, he served in Ky. Senate, 1904–08; and U.S. House, 1931–63.

1777 AUGUSTUS OWSLEY STANLEY
(Henderson, Main St., Henderson Co.)

A dynamic orator, Stanley became nationally known for investigation of U.S. Steel

Corp., while serving six terms in U.S. House, 1903–15. Born in Shelbyville, 1867, he moved to Henderson in 1898, and entered politics. Gov. of Ky., 1915–19; U.S. Senator, 1919–25. Chaired International Joint Commission to mediate disputes arising along U.S.-Canadian border. Died 1958.

1778 GRAVE OF STEAMBOAT CAPTAIN
(Bank St., W. of 34th St. at entrance to Portland Cem., Jefferson Co.)

Mary M. Miller of Louisville, a pioneer among women, was issued license as master of a steamboat on inland waters, Feb. 16, 1884, in New Orleans. License authorized her to navigate waters of Quachita, Mississippi, Red, and other western rivers. She and her husband George, a pilot and master, owned steamboat SALINE, built nearby. Died 1894; buried in Portland Cem.

1779 NEW CAPITOL
(Frankfort, Capitol Ave., just south of Todd St., Franklin Co.)

Gov. J. C. W. Beckham promoted construction of New Capitol due to overcrowding and disrepair in Old Capitol. Federal funds for Civil and Spanish-American War claims paid half of $1,820,000 cost. In 1904, Frank M. Andrews selected as architect. Cornerstone laid 1906. Capitol completed during Gov. A. E. Willson's term. Legislature met January; building dedicated June 1910.
(Reverse)
NEW CAPITOL
Building's style is neo-classic, with seventy Ionic monolithic columns. North pediment shows a heroine–Kentucky–with Progress, History, Law, Art, and Labor as attendants. French influence portrayed by dome and rotunda, designed like tomb of Napoleon, and white marble stairs with banisters, copies of those in Paris Opera House. Murals in east and west wings by Gilbert White.

1780 THOMAS SATTERWHITE NOBLE
(539 W. Third St., Lexington, Fayette Co.)

Boyhood home of prominent American historical painter and portraitist. Noble (1835–1907) was first Director of the Art Academy of Cincinnati. He studied in Louisville under Samuel W. Price, in France

under Thomas Couture, and at the Munich Academy. His pupils include Paul Sawyier, Kentucky watercolorist, and Gutzon Borglum, sculptor of Mt. Rushmore. *Presented by John Bradford Society.*

1781 WILLIAM S. TAYLOR (1853–1928)
(Morgantown, Courthouse lawn, Logan St., Butler Co.)

This Republican governor from Butler Co. was declared winner over William Goebel and inaugurated Dec. 12, 1899. When Democrats contested the election, controversy and extreme bitterness led to Sen. Goebel's being shot in front of Old Capitol, Jan. 30, 1900. In a disputed move, Goebel was then declared governor. His February 3 death brought J. C. W. Beckham as successor. See over.
(Reverse)
WILLIAM S. TAYLOR
For some 160 days Taylor served as governor, two-thirds of that time unofficially, with Kentucky torn between two functioning state governments. When courts decided for Beckham in May, Taylor left the state and went to Indianapolis. There the former teacher and attorney general of Kentucky practiced law and became vice-president of an insurance company.

1782 DANIEL TRABUE (1760–1840)
(299 Jamestown St., Columbia, Adair Co.)

A founder of Columbia, Trabue built original house (SW corner of this structure) ca. 1823. He served as trustee, sheriff, and justice of peace; operated grist mill, inn and retail store. Here Trabue wrote memoirs, 1827, of pioneer era, which included events at Logan's Station, Boonesborough, and service under Anthony Wayne. These accounts part of famous Draper Manuscripts.

1783 CEDAR HALL-HELM PLACE
(2575 Bowman's Mill Rd., Lexington, Fayette Co.)

This antebellum Greek Revival home was part of Bowman estate. Col. Abraham Bowman commanded 8th Va. Regt. in Revolution. Behind house was Todd's Station, built 1779 by Levi Todd, grandfather of Mary Todd Lincoln and Emilie Todd Helm. Mrs. Helm, wife of CSA Gen. Ben H. Helm, bought house, 1912. Later owned

by William H. Townsend, Lincoln authority. Listed on National Register, 1978.

1784 SILVERSMITH SHOP
(Corner Mill & Short Sts., Lexington, Fayette Co.)

On this site, 1810–1838, was shop of Asa
Blanchard, the most noted of Kentucky's
silversmiths. Blanchard silver was as prized
in Kentucky as that of Paul Revere in New
England. Among his customers were the
most prominent families in the Bluegrass.
A master craftsman who trained many
apprentices, Blanchard was a goldsmith as
well as a watch and clockmaker. He died
in 1838.

1785 ST. JEROME SESQUICENTENNIAL
(Fancy Farm, Jct. KY 80 & 339, Graves Co.)

Site of first St. Jerome, completed 1836 by
the Rev. Elisha Durbin; first Catholic
Church in the Jackson Purchase. Second
church dedicated, 1858; present church in
1893. St. Jerome settlers were mainly de-
scendants of Maryland Catholics from
Washington Co., Ky. Missions: St. Charles
in Carlisle Co., 1891; St. Denis in Hickman
Co., 1913. *Presented by St. Jerome Parish.*
(Reverse)
ELISHA JOHN DURBIN, 1800–1887
A missionary for over 50 years, Father
Durbin aided in building ten Catholic
churches, including St. Jerome. Born 1800,
Madison Co.; ordained 1822; given pasto-
ral care of Catholic population of western
and southwestern Ky. (now Owensboro
Diocese) in 1824. Headquarters at Sacred
Heart in Union County. Buried in St. Louis
Cem., Louisville, Ky. *Presented by St. Jerome
Parish.*

1786 AUGUSTUS E. WILLSON (1846–1931)
(Louisville, Cave Hill Cem.—Section L, Jefferson Co.)

As governor, 1907–1911, Willson acted to
quell civil unrest caused by Night Riders
in tobacco growing areas of western Ky. A
native of Maysville, Willson began career
in Louisville. He became the protege and
law partner of U. S. Supreme Court Justice John Marshall Harlan. Active in civic
affairs until death, Willson was buried in
Cave Hill Cemetery, Louisville.

1787 GEORGE HUSTON
(205 N. Brady St., Morganfield, Union Co.)

A Harvard graduate and lawyer who spe-
cialized in land litigations, George Huston
helped found city's first bank in 1869. He
owned and enlarged this antebellum house
from the early brick section where Dr.
Brady, Huston's father-in-law, lived. At
Civil War's end, Union soldiers camped
here. In 1846 ex-President Tyler stayed
here while Huston checked his land boundary.

1788 DRURY BRIDGES (BRIDGERS, BRIDGER) 1765–1840
(Maple Grove, 8 mi. S. of Cadiz, KY 1062, Trigg Co.)

This Trigg County pioneer came to Ky.
from N.C. in 1804 and built a cabin here,
near Beechy Fork Creek, on 85½-acre land
grant. Born 1765; son of Wm. Bridgers,
patriot who helped N.C. troops during Rev.
War. Direct descendant of Joseph Bridger
(1628–1686), influential Royalist and member of Virginia House of Burgesses. See
over.
(Reverse)
DRURY BRIDGES (BRIDGERS, BRIDGER)
1765–1840
Bridges married Charity Calhoun in 1790;
they had seven children. Active in the community, the couple became charter members of Donaldson Creek Baptist Church,
1814. Their home was later site of Maple
Grove post office. Drury Bridges died in
1840; his wife in 1852. Both are buried in
family cemetery nearby. *Presented by The
Thomas-Bridges Assn.*

1789 FOUNDING OF LEWISPORT
(Lewisport, Jct. KY 334 & 657, Hancock Co.)

Formerly called Little Yellow Banks, town
was renamed Lewisport in 1839 in honor
of John Lewis, one of the first permanent
settlers in area. He was an early surveyor
of land between Salt and Green rivers.
Original town plat drafted by James and
John Prentis, 1837; town was incorporated
in 1844. Logging and building of flatboats
were first chief industries here.

1790 JACOB HUNTER
(Owenton Cem., US 127, Owen Co.)

This Rev. War soldier entered U.S. service from Boone's Station, 1780. Served as garrison guard there and as Indian spy; under Geo. Rogers Clark on raids at Old Chillicothe and Piqua. Marched with Benj. Logan to reinforce troops at Blue Licks; joined survivors of battle to bury the dead. Moved to Owen County ca. 1817. Hunter lived on Big Twin Creek; died and buried there, 1856.

1791 LOGAN COUNTY JAIL, 1874–1977
(W. Fourth St., Russellville, Logan Co.)

This building replaced an old jail three blocks east which burned. To finance construction of new jail, a property tax was passed, 1869. By December 1874, jail operated on this site. Jail restored, 1979–1980. County records stored here by order of Fiscal Court. Logan County Genealogical Society designated to clean and file the records. *Presented by Rena Milliken.*

1792 JACOB SKILES AND THREE SPRINGS
(At Warren Co. Parks & Recreation Office, 2055 Three Springs Rd., Warren Co.)

Pioneer merchant Skiles started to Ky. in 1790 by Ohio River flatboat, surviving Indian capture en route. He settled in Bowling Green, 1803, and later moved to Three Springs on the Cumberland Trace. Here he established a thriving mercantile business. Skiles died, 1816. Three Springs declined as an area trade center in 1820s when travel was diverted through Bowling Green.

1793 OLD CATHOLIC HIGH SCHOOL
(428 S. 8th St., Louisville, Jefferson Co.)

Site of Kentucky's only Catholic high school for blacks. It existed at this location from 1928–1958, operated by the Archdiocese of Louisville. Founded in 1921, the school was administered by pastors of St. Augustine and St. Peter Claver churches, with Sisters of Charity of Nazareth and lay staff as teachers. Desegregation led to the school's closing in 1958.

1794 WALKER FOXHOUNDS
(Site of Walker homeplace, KY 1647, approx. 6 mi. E. of Lancaster, Garrard Co.)

Site of John W. Walker's home where he and George Washington Maupin, avid hunters, bred and developed famous Walker foxhounds. With red fox migration into central Ky., ca. 1852, Virginia hounds were crossed with "Tennessee Lead," a dog noted for speed and stamina needed to hunt red fox. English hounds "Rifler" and "Marth" brought color and conformation to breed.

1795 JOHN CURD
(3 mi. from Wilmore on High Bridge Pike, KY 29, Jessamine Co.)

A Rev. War soldier, John Curd lived here. The Va. Gen. Assembly established tobacco inspection warehouse on Curd's land, 1786, at mouth of Dix River, as well as a public ferry across Ky. River. Curd's 1½-story Federal house, with Flemish bond brickwork and original interior woodwork, is on National Reg. of Historic Places. *Presented by Descendants of John Curd, 1986.*

1796 GARRARD/CRITTENDEN HOUSE
(300–302 Wilkinson Blvd., Frankfort, Franklin Co.)

This early 19th century house is architecturally notable because of brick and log construction. It has series of timbers filled in with brick and mortar and covered with clapboard, a technique uncommon to central Kentucky. Owned by several prominent Kentuckians, including Thomas L. Crittenden and James Garrard families. Later acquired by the Commonwealth in 1973.

1797 JACKSON STAGE STOP
(4 mi. NW of Hanson, KY 1069, Hopkins Co.)

Original two-room brick building, unusual in design, was constructed in 1830 of handmade brick from clay on farm. It served as a stagecoach stop between Hopkinsville and Henderson before completion of the Evansville, Henderson, and Nashville Railroad, 1871. Beckley Jackson, who came from Va. by 1815, provided extra horses and mail distribution point for stage line.

1798 WATKINS TAVERN
(Main St., Versailles, Woodford Co.)

Site of stone tavern/inn built by stonemason Thomas Metcalfe, later governor of Ky.

Formation of the Kentucky River at confluence with the South Fork. Kentucky Historical Society Collection.

Owned by Henry Watkins and wife Elizabeth, widow of Rev. John Clay and mother of Henry Clay. Lafayette, traveling from Frankfort to Lexington, was entertained here on May 15, 1825; greeted friends and veterans and had to address crowd from upper balcony. Tavern burned in 1886.

1799 AMOS KENDALL (1789–1869)
(413 West Broadway, Frankfort, Franklin Co.)

This noted journalist-politician lived here. A Massachusetts native, he migrated to Kentucky in 1814 and spent one year with the family of Henry Clay as tutor. From 1816–28, Kendall resided in Frankfort as editor of the *Argus of Western America.* First a supporter of Henry Clay, he later promoted Andrew Jackson and helped carry Kentucky for him in 1828. See over.
(Reverse)

AMOS KENDALL

Amos Kendall moved to Washington with Jackson administration, 1829. Joined group of close presidential advisors known as "Kitchen Cabinet" and served five years as postmaster general. He gained wealth as business agent for Samuel F. B. Morse, 1845–1869; his generous donations helped to found school for deaf and mute, later Gallaudet College in Washington, D. C. Over.

1800 LAURA CLAY (1849–1941)
(9 mi. N. of Richmond at White Hall, off US 25, Madison Co.)

Woman's rights leader, born here, was pres. of Ky. Equal Rights Assn. 1888–1912. Daughter of Cassius M. Clay, Laura won coeducational, property, and joint guardianship rights for Ky. women and held key positions in National American Woman Suffrage Assn. Her associates included Susan B. Anthony. Woman suffrage gained by 19th Amendment, 1920. Laura Clay buried Lexington.

1801 CUMBERLAND FALLS MOONBOW
(Cumberland Falls State Resort Park, KY 90, Whitley Co.)

The Moonbow that appears here is the only one in the Western Hemisphere. It may be observed under a full moon and a clear sky. An arch of white light is usually produced at base of Falls and continues downstream. Generations of people have visited here to see this natural phenomenon. Last hotel on this site, Moonbow Inn, was named for the moonbow.

1802 PHELPS ACRES FARM
(At farm, N. of Jamestown, KY 92, Russell Co.)

John Phelps served in the Revolutionary War as defender of Boonesborough. He and son Shadrach were still at fort with Daniel Boone in 1795. Shadrach and Celia (Stapp) Phelps settled here circa 1798. This farm continuously owned and operated by their descendants. Original log house was home for 3 generations. Two-story structure built by grandson John Quincy Phelps, 1875.

1803 LYNCH
(Lynch, KY 160, Harlan Co.)

Built by U.S. Steel Corp., 1917–25, this was largest company-owned town in Kentucky through World War II. Crucial need for steel during WW I led to founding of town, site of millions of tons of high-quality coal. With largest coal tipple then in existence, Lynch had first fully electrified coal mine in U.S. Much of the self-contained, model city dismantled in 1960s by U.S. Steel.

1804 JENKINS
(Jenkins, at city limits, US 23, Letcher Co.)

Land bought by John C. C. Mayo and sold to Consolidation Coal Co. to develop town and coal mines. Coal company laid out streets and built houses, stores, hospital, churches, and schools. Town named for George C. Jenkins, a promoter and Baltimore banker. The railroad reached Jenkins ca. 1912. With Consolidation's 14 tipples, Letcher Co. was largest coal producer in Kentucky in 1916.

1805 KENTUCKY RIVER FORMS HERE
(Beattyville Bypass, Lee Co.)

North and Middle Forks unite below St. Helens, then join South Fork at Beattyville to form Kentucky River, which flows 255 miles to the Ohio. Kentucky River played primary role in early commerce of Lee Co. Steamboats came to Beattyville, near head of navigation, and river traffic increased with building of locks and dams. Coal and timber were shipped to various ports.

1806 HISTORIC LAND
(540 West Maxwell St., Lexington, Fayette Co.)

The land upon which Pleasant Green Baptist Church stands was conveyed in 1822 by Dr. Frederick Ridgely, a white surgeon in Lexington, to trustees Harry Quills, Benjamin Admon, and Solomon Walker, all slaves, for purpose of erecting an African church. From date of deed, black congregation has continued to worship at this site.

1807 HARRIETTE SIMPSON ARNOW (1908–1986)
(Burnside, US 27, Pulaski Co.)

The author of such celebrated Appalachian novels as *The Dollmaker* and *Hunter's Horn*; social histories include *Seedtime on the Cumberland* and *Flowering of the Cumberland*. Born in Wayne County, Arnow spent most of her childhood in Burnside. Moved to Michigan during World War II, but continued to chronicle Appalachian life and people.

1808 JESSE STUART (1906–1984)
(Jct. W-Hollow Rd. & KY 1, Greenup Co.)

This Kentucky Poet Laureate was born and lived most of his life in W-Hollow, near Greenup. An educator and prolific writer, Stuart authored books, short stories, and poems which portray Appalachian Ky. He received Guggenheim fellowship, 1937; nominated for Pulitzer Prize in Poetry, 1977. Works include *The Thread That Runs So True* and *Man with a Bull-Tongue Plow*.

1809 JOHN HUNT MORGAN (1825–1864)
(Fayette Co. Courthouse, Lexington, Fayette Co.)

Known as the "Thunderbolt of the Confederacy," Morgan was born in Huntsville, Alabama; in 1831 moved to Lexington. After attending Transylvania, he fought in the Mexican War. In Lexington, he prospered as owner of hemp factory and woolen mill. Morgan organized Lexington Rifles Infantry, 1857; later led them to aid Confederacy. See over.

(Reverse)

JOHN HUNT MORGAN (1825–1864)

Leading cavalry raids behind the enemy lines, General J. H. Morgan disrupted Union supplies and communications. For southerners, he was the ideal romantic hero. Captured in Indiana-Ohio raid, he escaped and was killed in Greeneville, Tennessee, September 4, 1864. Buried in Lexington Cemetery. Morgan became a courageous symbol of the Lost Cause.

1810 FORT SOUTHWORTH
(Louisville, 4522 Algonquin Parkway, Jefferson Co.)

Here was westernmost fort of 11-fort system designed to protect Louisville from the Confederates during Civil War. Construction began August 1, 1864; almost complete at war's end. Funded by the city and the federal government, Fort Southworth, 19,000 sq. ft., was composed of earth and designed by John R. Gillis. *Presented by Louisville-Jefferson Co. Metropolitan Sewer District.*

1811 JAMES D. BLACK (1849–1938)
(North Main St. at Union National Bank, Barbourville, Knox Co.)

Kentucky's 39th governor, native of Knox Co., served for seven months in 1919. As lieutenant governor, he succeeded A. O. Stanley when that official became U.S. senator. Black, a teacher and lawyer, was representative in Ky. House and superintendent of Knox Co. schools. A co-founder of Union College (1879), he named the institution Union to show community support.

1812 WILLIAM WORTHINGTON (1761–1848)
(Jct. US 431 & KY 85 at Baptist Church, Island, McLean Co.)

This early settler owned large tract of "Island" territory, cut off during times of high water. He served in Revolutionary War under George Rogers Clark, 1781. Became circuit court judge, 1803, then postmaster of Worthington (now Island) in 1829. Judge Worthington was a member of Ky. Senate, 1812–25. Buried north of town. Chapel bears family name.

1813 JANICE HOLT GILES (1905–1979)
(Near Janice H. Giles home, KY 76 and Spout Springs Rd., Adair Co.)

Historical novels by this talented author have sold more than three million copies. Most settings of her some twenty books reflect her adopted home, the Green River area where she lived with her husband Henry, and the Indian territory of Okla. and Ark. where Giles spent early years. Her

works, noted for action and imagery, include *The Enduring Hills* and *The Believers.*

1814 JESSE STUART (1906–1984)
(Roadside park near Jesse Stuart Mem. Bridge, US 23, north of Greenup, Greenup Co.)

This Kentucky Poet Laureate was born and lived most of his life in W-Hollow, near Greenup. An educator and prolific writer, Stuart authored books, short stories, and poems which portray Appalachian Ky. He received Guggenheim fellowship, 1937; nominated for Pulitzer Prize in Poetry, 1977. Works include *The Thread That Runs So True* and *Man with a Bull-Tongue Plow.* (*Presented by Transportation Cabinet*).

1815 GOV. SIMEON WILLIS (1879–1965)
(Between 1608 and 1612 Bath Ave., Ashland, Boyd Co.)

Judge on Kentucky's highest court 1927–1933; Governor 1943–1947. His administration extended State Park System, increased funding for education, expanded TB hospitals, ended most toll bridge charges, founded Postwar Planning Comm. and Comm. on Negro Affairs. Born in Ohio, he moved to Ky. as a child and later practiced law in Ashland, living at 1608 and 1612 Bath Ave.

1816 OLD MAIL STAGE ROUTE
(Shakertown at Pleasant Hill, US 68, Mercer Co.)

Completed by 1839, Lexington-Harrodsburg-Perryville Turnpike (KY 68) ran through center of Pleasant Hill. Road became part of interstate Zanesville (Ohio)-Florence (Ala.) mail stage route. Stages discontinued here by 1877. Turnpike brought the reclusive Shakers communication and trade, as well as Confederate and Federal invaders during the Civil War.

1817 SHAKER FERRY ROAD
(Shakertown at Pleasant Hill, Jct. US 68 and Shaker Ferry Rd., Mercer Co.)

Begun 1826, this two-mile section of road was Shaker lifeline to trade on Kentucky River. Although improved by Shakers in 1840s, the present road, cut from stone cliff by star drills and sledgehammers, was not completed until 1861. Evidence of drill holes is still visible. Frequent use by heavy

Jesse Stuart at his home in W-Hollow, with wife Naomi Dean and daughter Jane. Courtesy Jesse Stuart Foundation.

Civil War equipment caused severe damage, but Shakers made repairs.
(Reverse)

SHAKER LANDING

At foot of this road is landing purchased by Shakers, 1830. Site made Pleasant Hill busy river port and ferry crossing. Quality Shaker products left here for downriver markets as far away as New Orleans. During Civil War, ferry confiscated by Federal forces; it was soon retrieved and back in use. By 1873, ferry could transport two wagons and horse teams at each crossing.

1818 HAYFIELD
(3000 Bunker Hill Dr., Louisville, Jefferson Co.)

This Greek Revival mansion was the home of world-renowned botanist Dr. Charles Wilkins Short from 1847 to 1863. Front section of Hayfield built by Col. George Hancock ca. 1834. Rear L-shaped part of house dated by some as late 1700s. Among the first property owners were Col. John Thruston, a trustee of Louisville, and

David L. Ward, a prominent landowner.

1819 FIRST RURAL ELECTRIC IN COUNTY
(6 mi. N. of Owenton, Jct. US 127, 227 & KY 36, Owen Co.)

Gov. A. B. Chandler threw switch at New Liberty Substation, Jan. 29, 1938, to energize some 130 mi. and brought electricity to 370 homes and businesses by Dec. Owen Co. R.E.C.C. now includes 9 counties. Charter members, 1937, were: J. H. Satterwhite, Lister Ransdell, J. W. McElroy, J. L. Tackett, Ira Kemper; manager, Chester Clayton Roland. *Presented by Owen County R.E.C.C.*

1820 WOODLAWN RACE COURSE
(Perryman & Westport Roads, Louisville, Jefferson Co.)

Opened in 1859 and drew national attention. Closed after Civil War. R. A. Alexander, noted breeder, was major figure in buying estate for National Racing Association. He contracted with Tiffany's to design Woodlawn Vase; used in 1861 and 1862. It was buried for safety during war.

Vase is now winner's trophy at the Preakness Stakes, where a replica is given each year.

1821 JACOB PRICE
(Jacob Price Homes, Greenup St., Covington, Kenton Co.)

This prominent black businessman owned and operated a lumberyard at 426–428 Madison Avenue. As a Baptist minister, Price was major figure in development of city's black churches. He was also a leader in obtaining free public education for blacks in northern Kentucky. Died in 1923. Jacob Price housing project named to honor his accomplishments.

1822 TRIMBLE COUNTY JAIL
(Bedford, Courthouse Square, US 42, Trimble Co.)

Old stone jail erected ca. 1850 on site of original jail; second story added in 1899. For some 133 years, until 1983, this building was a physical symbol of law and order in Trimble County. Its most noted prisoner, ardent abolitionist Delia Webster, was incarcerated here briefly during 1854. The jail is listed on the National Register of Historic Places.

1823 BEDFORD SPRINGS AND HOTEL
(Near Nursing Home, Bedford, US 42, Trimble Co.)

Mineral springs discovered ca. 1840 by Mr. and Mrs. Noah Parker, who found water unusual in taste and of medicinal value. The Parkers soon erected hotel and, with son Nathan, owned and managed noted antebellum health resort, which fostered Bedford's growth. After the 1851 cholera epidemic, resort declined. The former hotel burned in 1967.

1824 EADES TAVERN
(421 High St., Paris, Bourbon Co.)

This log building lined with adz-hewn cherry was built as a tavern. In 1795 it became first post office in Paris. Thomas Eades then served as tavern owner and postmaster. Robert Trimble had home and law office here before becoming U.S. Supreme Court justice, 1826. It became site of Lizzie Walker's private school. Listed on National Register of Historic Places, 1973.

1825 CIVIL WAR FIELD HOSPITAL
(Approx. 4 mi. S. of Richmond, US 421, Madison Co.)

Built in 1852, this building was adjacent to location of the Battle of Richmond, August 29–30, 1862, and became field hospital for Gen. Wm. Nelson's 1st and 2nd brigades, USA. Mortality was high, and about forty Union soldiers were buried in mass grave near church. Reinterred in Camp Nelson National Cem., 1868. After war, building again served as Mt. Zion Christian Church. Over.
(Reverse)

CIVIL WAR FIELD HOSPITAL

On August 30, 1862, this building was struck by fire from Captain John T. Humphrey's Arkansas Artillery Battery, with Churchill's (3rd) Division of E. Kirby Smith's Provisional Army of Ky., CSA. Scar is still visible on south wall. Battle of Richmond brought a Confederate victory. After Battle of Perryville in October, Confederates retired from state.

1826 ADOLPH F. RUPP (1901-77)
(Memorial Coliseum, Lexington, Fayette Co.)

"Winningest" coach in history of college basketball. Native Kansan who played under famed coach "Phog" Allen. Head coach at UK, 1930–72. Won 4 NCAA titles, won or tied SEC crown 27 times; coach of 1948 US Olympic team that won gold medal. Natl. coach of yr. 4 times. Never a losing season; 879 wins-190 losses. Nicknames include "Man in Brown Suit" and "Baron of the Bluegrass."

1827 BENEDICT JOSEPH FLAGET (1763-1850)
(Bardstown, Courthouse lawn, Nelson Co.)

A priest for 62 years, the "First Bishop of the West" became Bishop of Bardstown, 1810; of Louisville, 1841. Jurisdiction embraced area of Ky., Tenn., and old Northwest Territory. Flaget directed founding of colleges, congregations, and St. Joseph's Cathedral; witnessed ten dioceses formed from region. Bishop buried in Louisville.

1828 PIONEER FAMILY
(KY 224, E. of KY 479, Millerstown, Grayson Co.)

Millerstown, settled before 1800, founded

by Jacob Miller, Jr. He owned 500 acres along Nolin River and built grist mill. Christopher, a brother, was prisoner of Indians for 11 years; rescued by spies of Anthony Wayne, he then helped Wayne secure peace, 1794. Christopher and brother Nicholas both served in Ky. House of Rep. Town was at peak ca. 1900, with population of 150.

1829 JOHN C. THOMAS HOUSE
(Hartford, 415 Mulberry St., Ohio Co.)

This house erected in 1880 on land originally donated to the town by pioneer Gabriel Madison in 1799. Now owned by Ohio County Historical Society, the home is its museum. It was the former home of John C. Thomas, early Hartford merchant. With two brothers, he operated Thos. Bros. Hardware & Saddlery on Main and Union Streets. That structure is also still standing.

1830 BETHEL ACADEMY
(Entrance to Asbury College, Wilmore, KY 29, Jessamine Co.)

This was second Methodist school in United States. In 1790 Bishop Francis Asbury laid plans for Bethel Academy, four miles southeast of Wilmore on cliffs above Kentucky River. It was operating by 1794; closed ca. 1804, due to lack of funds and Indian hostilities. Second site was in Nicholasville, 1820–93.
(Reverse)

ASBURY COLLEGE

Established in 1890, this school was named for Francis Asbury, first Methodist bishop and circuit rider in United States. Asbury Theological Seminary was established at Asbury College, 1923. Original Bethel Academy site and Asbury College Administration Building are listed on National Register of Historic Places.

1831 HOME/OFFICE OF DUNCAN HINES 1941-1959
(3098 Louisville Rd., Bowling Green, Warren Co.)

Authority on restaurants and lodgings in U.S. Born in Bowling Green, 1880. From places visited on business trips, he noted good eating places and inns. That led to annual editions of *Adventures in Good Eating* and *Lodging for a Night*. Also authored *Vacation Guide* and *Adventures in Good Cooking*. Died in 1959; buried Fairview Cem.

1832 UPPER DONALDSON SCHOOL
(KY 1175 [Old Dover Road] & Donaldson Creek Rd., 9 mi. S. of Cadiz, Trigg Co.)

Organized 1813, this grade school operated for 135 years. First teacher was Ephriam Cowand, whose salary was 4 barrels of corn and $2.00 per pupil. School met first at Donaldson Creek Church 1½ mi. west; later used nearby log cabin, 1815–1910. One-room concrete block structure built 1911; used until 1948, when school consolidated. *Presented by former students, teachers, and friends.*

1833 SPENCER HOUSE
(Taylorsville, Main St., Spencer Co.)

This popular rest stop on the Louisville-Taylorsville stage route was famous hotel and tavern for many years. Built ca. 1838 by Frederick B. Mathis, this 20-room brick structure was later owned by Isaiah Yocum, Confederate veteran, who settled here after Civil War. For 58 years he and his wife Kate served guests, calling them to meals by bell atop the hotel.

1834 REV. WILLIAM DOWNS
(415 Mulberry St., Hartford, Ohio Co.)

This orator, debater, and minister was also a teacher, Bible scholar, and hymn composer. He preached near the Lincoln home on Knob Creek and baptized Abraham's father, Thomas Lincoln. William Downs was born 1782 in old fort at site of Hartford. Father killed by Indians. William's brother Thomas also became pioneer Baptist preacher. William died 1860, near Hartford.

1835 CASEY COUNTY COURTHOUSE
(Courthouse lawn, Liberty, Casey Co.)

Present seat of justice, built 1888, was preceded by log building, 1809, and brick structure, 1837. Architects for current courthouse were the noted McDonald Bros. of Louisville. Its asymmetrical design and lavish use of stone trim (by T. D. Dunhauser of Germany) are unusual features among courthouses of McDonald firm. Listed on

Nat'l Register of Historic Places, 1977.

1836 HAVEN GILLESPIE (1888-1975)
(Goebel Park, 5th & Philadelphia Sts., Covington, Kenton Co.)

The composer of "Santa Claus Is Comin' To Town" was a native of Covington. He attended local school, became a printer, and later employed by Cincinnati *Times-Star* and N.Y. *Times*. Gillespie's songs carried Americans through Great Depression and World War II; they include "Breezin' Along With The Breeze," "You Go To My Head," "Honey," and "That Lucky Old Sun."

1837 CUMBERLAND COLLEGE
(At College, Main St., Williamsburg, Whitley Co.)

Founded as Williamsburg Institute in 1889 under the leadership of General Green Clay Smith and R. C. Medaris to provide affordable Christian education for mountain people. Early supporters were James P. and Thomas B. Mahan, Ancil Gatliff, Edwin S. Moss, John W. Siler, and John D. Rockefeller. Name changed to Cumberland College, 1913. Over. *Presented by Centennial Com. of Cumberland College.*
(Reverse)

CUMBERLAND COLLEGE

Alumni include U.S. congressman, Kentucky governors, military officers, medical doctors, missionaries, and university presidents. Among them: Cong. Eugene Siler, Governors Bert Combs and Edwin Morrow, Vice Adm. Charles Blakely, Maj. Generals Ben Baker, Charles Calloway, and Floyd Parks, Brig. Gen. Roy Easley, folk artist Jean Ritchie, and educators William McCall and Cratis Williams.

1838 FIRST COURT OF TRIGG COUNTY
(4 mi. W. of Cadiz, US 68/80, Trigg Co.)

On May 15, 1820, justices of the peace, commissioned for the newly formed Trigg County, met at the log home of Samuel Orr, in the vicinity of this well, in town of Warrington. Composing the court were: Samuel Orr, Abraham Boyd, Ferdinand Wadlington, John Goode, William Scott, Presley Slaughter, James Daniel, Beman Fowler and Richard Dawson.

1839 STANLEY F. REED (1884-1980)
(At Stanley Reed's summer home, US 68 Extension, Maysville, Mason Co.)

This Mason Co. native was Associate Justice of U.S. Supreme Court from 1938 to 1957. Served in Ky. General Assembly, 1912-16. Under Hoover and Roosevelt, Reed helped rescue nation from the Depression, as General Counsel of Federal Farm Board and as Solicitor Gen. for New Deal programs. Appointed to Supreme Ct. by Roosevelt. Retired, 1957. Died, New York; buried in Maysville.

1840 MAPLE GROVE SCHOOL
(7 mi. S.W. of Cadiz, Maple Grove Rd., ¼ mi. off KY 1062, Trigg Co.)

An early log schoolhouse first was opened by teacher William Bridges (1800–1844), son of settlers Drury and Charity Bridges. Education continued in new concrete block school, erected in 1913. After serving the Trigg County community for many years, the school closed, 1949. Maple Grove Baptist Church was organized at school site, 1943. *Presented by The Thomas-Bridges Association.*

1841 EARLY EDUCATION IN GEORGETOWN
(Broadway & College, Georgetown, Scott Co.)

The roots of Georgetown College go back to 1788, when Baptist minister Elijah Craig began an academy which offered classical education—Latin, Greek, and sciences. This early school was in large log house near corner of South Broadway and West College Streets. Ten years later, Craig's school was absorbed by Rittenhouse Academy. Its assets taken over by Georgetown College.

1842 PHILIP BUCKNER (1747-1820)
(Augusta Public Square, Bracken Co.)

Captain Philip Buckner, an Englishman, was a Revolutionary War veteran. He came to Va., served adopted colony as issuing commissary, received extensive land grants, then settled here. In 1797, he donated this lot for Augusta Public Square as part of land for town. It became the site of the courthouse until it burned, 1848; pioneer jail still standing.

1843 COL. ALGERNON S. THRUSTON
(Thruston Elem. School, 4 mi. E. of Owensboro, KY 144, Daviess Co.)

Lawyer, soldier and farmer. Born in Louisville 1801, died 1864 at Thruston. Went to Texas with company of volunteers in 1836. Commissary General of Purchases (1837) and Quartermaster General (1838) for the Republic of Texas. Political ally of President Sam Houston. Practiced law in Houston. Returned to Daviess County in 1854. *Presented by Nettie Sweeney Rhodes.*
(Reverse)

ALGERNON SIDNEY THRUSTON
This community became known as Thruston. Algernon's father, Col. John Thruston, at age 16, served at Kaskaskia and Vincennes with General Clark in Revolutionary War. Algernon's grandfather, Rev. and Col. Charles Mynn Thruston of Va., was "a fighting parson" of the Revolution. Charles received 15,000 acres in Daviess and Ohio counties for military services.

1844 EARLE C. CLEMENTS (1896–1985)
(Morganfield City Park, KY 56 East, Union Co.)

This Union Countian became governor following service in World War I, then as sheriff, county clerk and judge, state senator. As governor, 1947–1950, Clements spurred massive industrialization effort as well as road and state parks development. Resigned to serve a term in U.S. Senate; ally of Lyndon Johnson. Later Ky. highway commissioner.

1845 CALVARY BAPTIST
(28th & Woodland Ave., Louisville, Jefferson Co.)

Black members of Walnut Street Baptist Church formed own congregation by 1829, and began worshipping on Market St. They acquired lot on Fifth & York, 1833; held services there until 1957. The church played an especially prominent role under the ministry of educational and civil rights leader C. H. Parrish, 1885–1931. Present site purchased, 1958. *Presented by The Versatilia Club of Calvary.*

1846 GOV. JAMES B. MCCREARY
(527 W. Main St., Richmond, Madison Co.)

This was home of James McCreary, twice gov. of Ky., 1875–79 and 1911–15. He was only governor to serve at both capitols and live as chief executive in both governor's mansions. McCreary served with South in Civil War, then in the state legislature, 1869–75. Later, as member of U.S. House and Senate, he aided in obtaining the Federal Building, now Richmond City Hall.

1847 WOODFORD COUNTY COURTHOUSES
(Main & Court Sts., Versailles, Woodford Co.)

On this courthouse square in 1790 Jesse Graddy built, of logs, first of county's four courthouses. Total cost was $22.50. James and Henry Thompkins completed second one, of stone, 1794. Third hall of justice, built of brick in 1812–13, cupola with clock added by 1846; other additions later. Structure burned in 1965. Present courthouse completed 1970 by Gault Bros. of Lexington.

1848 LOW DUTCH STATION
(At Jct. of Brown's Ln., Bowling Pkwy., & Kresge's Way, St. Matthews, Jefferson Co.)

In 1780 Hendrick Banta led large group of Dutch pioneers from Pa. They rented land from John Floyd and built Low Dutch (New Holland) Station here, one of six pioneer forts on Beargrass Creek. Fleeing from Indians, group later bought land from Squire Boone in Henry and Shelby counties. This property was acquired in 1810 by James Brown of Md., a leading agriculturalist.

1849 ZACHARY TAYLOR HOME
(5608 Apache Rd., off Blankenbaker Ln., Louisville, Jefferson Co.)

Col. Richard Taylor of Va., veteran of French and Indian War and the Revolution, built original part of "Springfield" ca. 1790. Boyhood home of son "Old Rough and Ready" Zachary Taylor (1784–1850), veteran of 1812 and Black Hawk wars. Mex. War hero and 12th U.S. pres. (1849–50). Zachary's daughter Sarah Knox married Jefferson Davis, future CSA president. Son Richard was Confed. Gen.

1850 TRIANGULAR JOG
(Ky.-Tenn. State Line, US 31-W South, Simpson Co.)

The Simpson County jog in Kentucky-Tennessee boundary was error of Dr. Thomas Walker's 1780 survey party. Luke Munsell and James Bright resurveyed region fifty years later, but the controversy continued until survey by Austin P. Cox and Benjamin Peebles in 1858–1859. This stone-marked line set official boundary between the two states and ended an 80-yr. dispute.

1851 LOUISVILLE GIRLS HIGH SCHOOL
(Second & Lee Sts., Louisville, Jefferson Co.)

Serving girls' education for almost 100 years, school was originally known as Female High School and provided women of Louisville with a strong educational base. Opened on April 7, 1856 at Center and Walnut, school functioned on 1st Street and at 5th and Hill before moving to this site in 1934. Architect was J. M. Colley. It consolidated with DuPont Manual Boys School in 1950.

1852 JOHN W. STEVENSON HOME
(314 Greenup St., Covington, Kenton Co.)

Scene of early political career, 1847–65. From this home and office base, Stevenson represented Kenton County in legislature and 1849 Constitutional Convention and served in U.S. House. He became lt. governor, 1867, and governor upon Helm's death. Left office 1871, after election to U.S. Senate. Pres. of American Bar Association, 1884. Died 1886; buried in Cincinnati.

1853 LATONIA RACE TRACK
(Winston Ave., Covington, Kenton Co.)

This track, 1883–1939, known as one of world's foremost race tracks; two yearly meets, spring-summer and late fall. Leonatus won Hindoo Stakes, 1883. Greatest attraction was Latonia Derby, 1½ mile event. Winners included Broadway Jones, Gallant Knight, and Upset. Here, Handy Mandy in 1927 beat record of Man o' War for 1½ mile distance. *Presented by City of Covington.*
(Reverse)
LATONIA RACE TRACK
Extended west from Winston Ave. with main entrance at head of Latonia Ave. Generous purses attracted such equine greats as Epinard, Clyde Van Dusen, Zev,

Black Gold, and Equipoise. After amassing substantial debts in the 1930s, Latonia Race Track closed after its last race on July 29, 1939. See over. *Presented by City of Covington.*

1854 FRANK DUVENECK (1848–1919)
(Goebel Park, Covington, Kenton Co.)

City was home to internationally known artist. Early artistic work was painting and carving altars for Catholic churches. At age 21, he went to Munich to study; in 1878, founded art school there. Married Elizabeth Boott, also an artist, who died two years later. Sculpted an outstanding bronze memorial for her grave in Florence, Italy. Over. *Presented by City of Covington.*
(Reverse)
EMINENT ARTIST
Frank Duveneck, major American portrait, genre, and landscape painter, returned home to teach after wife's death. Joined faculty of Cincinnati Art Academy and remained active in international exhibitions. Received special gold medal at Panama-Pacific Exposition, San Francisco, 1915. Buried Mother of God Cem., south of Covington. *Presented by City of Covington.*

1855 HOPEWELL
(At church, 102 Hutchison Station Rd., Paris, US 27 & 68, Bourbon Co.)

Hopewell, one of the oldest Presbyterian churches in Bourbon County, has held worship services since 1785. The first congregation included Dutch settlers. It was recognized by the Transylvania Presbytery in 1787. Original church was located near Grant's Fort, one mile from this site. After fort and church burned, the church was rebuilt here in 1823 and in 1904.

1856 HAWESVILLE RAILROAD STATION
(Hancock Co. Mus., Water St., Hawesville, Hancock Co.)

Rails of Louisville, St. Louis, and Texas Railroad laid here June 9, 1888. First passenger train ran between Owensboro and Stephensport Oct. 7, 1888. Service between Evansville and Louisville began in April 1889. Rail line later became Louisville, Henderson, St. Louis R.R. and then part of L&N system in 1929. See over. *Presented*

by National-Southwire Aluminum Co.
(Reverse)
HAWESVILLE RAILROAD STATION
Present station constructed 1902; additions made ca. 1919. During heyday, six L&N trains stopped here daily. Embarkation point for Army troops during World War I. Pres. Harry S. Truman spoke here during an election campaign whistlestop, Sept. 30, 1948. Local passenger service ended in the late 1950s. See over. *Presented by National-Southwire Aluminum Co.*

1857 U.S BULLION DEPOSITORY
(3 mi. N. of Radcliff at Gold Vault entrance, Bullion Blvd., Hardin Co.)

In 1935, portions of property in Fort Knox military reservation were set aside for use as U.S. Bullion Depository. Constructed in 1936, it was placed under supervision of Dir. of the Mint, a U.S. Treasury official. First gold brought here by railroad in 1937, and depository continues to be storage site for most of the nation's gold. By law, not open to public visits or tours.

1858 RICHARD PARKS BLAND
(Ohio Co. Mus., 415 Mulberry St., Hartford, Ohio Co.)

This fiery native son of Hartford, later a Missouri congressman for 24 years, embraced bimetallism, or "Free Silver," as solution to widespread indebtedness. "Silver Dick" (1835–99), a noted orator, also denounced monopolies, high protective tariff, and imperialism. Richard Parks Bland was forerunner of another famous champion of "Free Silver," William Jennings Bryan.

1859 MADRID BEND
(Near head of Madrid Bend, Jct. KY 313 & Hart's Service Rd., Fulton Co.)

Kentucky claimed land to the westernmost middle of Mississippi River—to this bend. Kentucky and Tennessee disagreed over boundary line until the Cox-Peebles survey, 1858–59, brought compromise. Nearby village of Compromise prospered during steamboat era but was eroded by the river ca. 1880. Neck joining bend to Tenn., once three miles wide, is now less than one mile across.

1860 COMPROMISE
(Kentucky-Tennessee line, KY 313, Fulton Co.)

To end Kentucky-Tennessee boundary dispute, Cox-Peebles survey began at Compromise, Ky., west of this point. Surveyors marked boundary eastward every 5 miles to Cumberland mountains. The 1858–59 line, for the first time, verified border to inhabitants, as well as to county and state officials. In 1860, Ky. and Tenn. recognized it as official boundary between the two states.

1861 GEN. BASIL W. DUKE, C.S.A.
(Georgetown courthouse square, Main St., Scott Co.)

A close associate of brother-in-law John Hunt Morgan, Duke provided tactics, discipline, and spirit, major elements of success of famous 2nd Ky. Cavalry. Wounded in battle twice, 1862; captured July 1863 in Ind.-Ohio raid; exchanged August 1864. After Morgan's death, Basil Duke appointed to command brigade. Later led part of the escort for Jefferson Davis in April–May 1865.
(Reverse)
BASIL W. DUKE (1838–1916)
Scott County native Basil Duke–attorney, politician, and author–is most noted for Civil War service to Confederacy. Admitted to bar in 1858, he began law practice in St. Louis. After Civil War he settled in Louisville. Elected to Ky. House of Rep. Duke led powerful railroad lobby and was bitter enemy of Wm. Goebel. Writings include *History of Morgan's Cavalry*. Buried Lexington.

1862 FIRST CITY HALL
(Covington, 3rd St., Kenton Co.)

Covington's first permanent city hall erected on this site in 1843; one of first in entire Ohio Valley. During Republican State Convention in 1860, fiery emancipationist Cassius M. Clay spoke here. Almost eighty years later, on June 3, 1938 (in the courtyard of later city hall), Kentucky's last execution by hanging took place. *Presented by City of Covington.*
(Reverse)
FIRST CITY HALL
City Hall doubled as a hospital in 1848 for returning Mexican War veterans. It was site

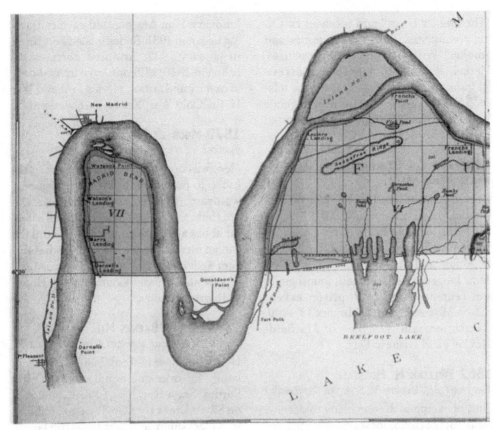

Madrid Bend from Kentucky Geological Survey's Map of the Jackson Purchase, 1885. *Kentucky Historical Society Collection.*

of many antislavery meetings. This prominent nineteenth-century social and political center also served as the location for pro-Union military and political activities during the Civil War. *Presented by City of Covington.*

1863 SLAVE ESCAPE
(Covington, 6th & Main Sts., Kenton Co.)

On a snowy night in January 1856, seventeen slaves fled, at foot of Main Street, across frozen Ohio River. Margaret Garner was in this group. When arrested in Ohio, she killed little daughter rather than see her returned to slavery. This much publicized slave capture became focus of national attention because it involved the issues of federal and state authority.
(Reverse)

CONTROVERSIAL JUDGMENT

Decision regarding Margaret Garner fueled fires of abolition. Fugitive Slave Law supporters wanted her returned to master.

Garner wished to remain in Ohio, even at risk of death for her crime. She was returned to Ky., with master's agreement to extradite her to Ohio. But soon afterward Garner was sent south and never heard from again. *Presented by City of Covington.*

1864 JOHN BRADFORD
(1916 Iron Works Pike, Lexington, Fayette Co.)

Built on this property Flemish bond brick home, "Fairfield," ca. 1785–1800. Earlier a surveyor, Bradford became publisher and editor of *Kentucky Gazette*, state's first newspaper, printed Aug. 11, 1787. Active in public life, he served as trustee of city and Transylvania Univ., in Ky. legislature, and as Fayette Co. sheriff. His early Ky. "Notes" are a valued source on era.

1865 UNA MERKEL—FILM STAR
(Goebel Park, 5th & Philadelphia Sts., Covington, Kenton Co.)

This Covington native won a Tony Award in 1956 for performance in Broadway's

"The Ponder Heart" and received an Oscar nomination, 1962, for "Summer and Smoke." With her 66 motion pictures, Merkel (1903–1986) represented successful transition from silent films to "the talkies." She played opposite film legends W. C. Fields and Marlene Dietrich. Buried Highland Cem., Kenton Co.

1866 PIKE CO. COURTHOUSE AND JAIL
(Main St., Pikeville, Pike Co.)

Courthouse erected 1888–89 by McDonald Bros.; later renovated 1932–33. Here was scene of Hatfield clan trials for murders of Tolbert, Randolph, Jr., Pharmer, Alifair, and Calvin McCoy. The defendants lodged in adjacent jail; found guilty and sentenced to life in prison except Ellison Mounts, hanged February 18, 1890. Courthouse and jail part of Hatfield-McCoy Feud Historic Dist.

1867 WILLIAM H. HORSFALL
(Evergreen Cem., Alexandria Pk., Southgate, Campbell Co.)

One of youngest Kentuckians to receive the Medal of Honor for service during Civil War is buried in Evergreen Cem. Horsfall, born in Newport, 1847, was a drummer in Co. G, First Ky. Infantry (USA). Medal was awarded for saving the life of a wounded officer lying between the lines during combat at Corinth, Mississippi, May 21, 1862. This war hero died in 1922.

1868 KENTUCKY-TENNESSEE BOUNDARY
(At Kentucky-Tennessee Boundary, Bell Co.)

The easternmost boundary between Ky. and Tenn. began at seven pines and two black oaks, surveyor's point of reference, about 1½ mi. south of Cumberland Gap. Surveys by Steele and Looney (1821) and Matthews (1826) were among those run before controversy settled by Cox and Peebles, 1858–59. Stone-marked line became official boundary between the two states.

1869 CAMP KNOX
(Chaffee Ave., near Main Gate, Fort Knox, Hardin Co.)

Established in 1918 as artillery range and named for Major General Henry Knox, who organized artillery during the Revo-

lutionary War. Mechanized cavalry training began in 1931. Redesignated Fort Knox in January 1932. Armored Force established in 1940. Millions have trained here in cavalry and armor, serving in World War II, the Cold War, Korea, and Vietnam.

1870 MODREL'S STATION
(Near crossing of Laurel River, KY 229, Laurel Co.)

Here was one of four defense posts established to protect emigrant parties moving westward. Approximately five miles south of London, Modrel's Station offered safety for about a year, during 1793–94, until the Indian menace ended. Robert Modrel was later active in settlement of Somerset and represented Pulaski County in Ky. House of Representatives.

1871 SITE OF BARNES MILL
(Barnes Mill Rd., approx. 8 mi. from Richmond, Madison Co.)

Here a mill operated continuously by same family for over one hundred years. Elias Barnes, Sr., a Rev. War soldier, built mill on Silver Creek by 1796. It passed to Elias, Jr., a blacksmith, and then to his son James, a captain in the Mexican War. Other family members operated Barnes Mill until ca. 1913. Barnes Mill Pike is all that remains. *Presented by Mrs. Jamie Bronston Long.*

1872 FRANCES E. BEAUCHAMP (1857–1923)
(Presbyterian Church, Main St., Richmond, Madison Co.)

This Madison Co. native spearheaded the antiliquor crusade in Ky. and was a leading figure in temperance movement nationwide. A protegee of famed Frances E. Willard, Beauchamp lectured on dry cause throughout the country. Among other causes she championed were prison reform and woman suffrage. See over.
(Reverse)

PROHIBITION ADVOCATE

Frances Beauchamp was preeminent leader of dry cause in Kentucky. Pres. of Ky. Women's Christian Temperance Union from 1895 until her death in 1923. She served ten years as chairman of state Prohibition party at a time when women were denied the vote. Largely through Beauchamp's efforts, a prohibition amendment to Kentucky constitution was adopted in 1919.

1873 BETHABARA BAPTIST CHURCH
(7 mi. SE of Owensboro at Habit, Jct. KY 142 & 762, Daviess Co.)

This congregation was organized on Oct. 5, 1825, in log house. New meeting house, on the site of present cemetery, built 1832. Current brick church erected in 1854, with clay from the original site. Six churches have grown from Bethabara: Macedonia, Sugar Grove, Hopewell, Karn's Grove, Friendship, and Dawson. *Presented by Bethabara Baptist Church.*

1874 GABRIEL SLAUGHTER, 1767–1830
(US 68 & Curry Pk., Harrodsburg, Mercer Co.)

Called "lieutenant governor and acting governor," Gabriel Slaughter directed the Commonwealth, 1816–20, after death of Gov. Madison. In spite of succession controversy, the Mercer Co. farmer-soldier, Ky. congressman, and twice lt. gov. earned esteem, if not support. His advanced ideas regarding education, roads, and the state penitentiary met strong resistance.

1875 JAMES LANE ALLEN
(Gratz Park, Lexington, Fayette Co.)

This Transylvania honor graduate, who later taught there, won an international audience with his nostalgic stories and novels of Bluegrass region. Allen was born near Lexington. By 1893, after his work became popular, he moved to New York City. He died there, and was buried in Lexington Cem. His will provided funds for fountain nearby, for children of the city.

1876 MADELINE M. BRECKINRIDGE
("Ashland," the estate of Henry Clay, Lexington, Fayette Co.)

This descendant of Henry Clay and Ephraim McDowell was born 1872 in Franklin Co.; grew up at "Ashland," Clay's home; and married Desha Breckinridge, editor of Lexington *Herald.* Ill with tuberculosis, she promoted its treatment and cure; advanced educational opportunities for poor children in Lexington and entire state; and helped gain voting rights for women. Over.

(Reverse)
KENTUCKY SUFFRAGE LEADER
Madeline McDowell Breckinridge saw woman suffrage as a way to advance social reform. Served as pres. of Ky. Equal Rights Assoc. 1912–15 and 1919–20; vice pres. of National American Woman Suffrage Assoc., 1913–15. Ratification of 19th amendment by Ky. legislature, 1920, largely credited to her efforts. She died same year, after amendment passed. Buried in Lexington Cem.

1877 JAMES HARROD
(Across street from present Ft. Harrod, Harrodsburg, Mercer Co.)

Born in Pa., this explorer and military leader came here in 1774. Chose Big Spring as site of Ky.'s first settlement. When that area flooded, he and his men built Fort Harrod on higher ground. James Harrod led in protecting area and promoting statehood. Served in Va. legis., 1784 Danville Conv., and as Harrodsburg trustee. Never returned from a hunting trip ca. 1792.

1878 JOSEPH DESHA (1768–1842)
(Near Washington, US 68, Mason Co.)

As governor, Desha became major proponent of debtor relief. The Pa. native, under Wayne and Harrison, fought Indians and led troops at Battle of Thames, 1813. Elected from Mason Co. to Ky. legislature and Congress. During his 1824–28 term as governor, he favored the controversial reorganization of Ky. Court of Appeals. Desha was buried in Georgetown, Ky. Over.

(Reverse)
OLD COURT-NEW COURT ISSUE
After Panic of 1819 and depression, the Ky. Court of Appeals struck down numerous relief measures as unconstitutional. Prorelief Desha forces in state legislature abolished Old Court and created a New Court. Angered, Old Court refused to vacate. Both courts sat simultaneously. By 1826, New Court canceled and court reorganization repealed. Issue gradually faded.

1879 ROBERT PENN WARREN, 1905–1989
(Third & Cherry Sts., Guthrie, Todd Co.)

A native of Guthrie, Warren was one of nation's most prolific writers, a world-renowned man of letters. Graduate of Vanderbilt Univ., summa cum laude, 1925; member of the Fugitives (writers group). Rhodes scholar at Oxford, 1928–1930; and twice a Guggenheim Fellow. He was professor of English at La. State, Minnesota, and Yale universities.
(Reverse)

ROBERT PENN WARREN, 1905–1989

Designated "First Poet Laureate of the United States" by Congress on February 26, 1986. To date only person to receive a Pulitzer Prize in both fiction and poetry. Warren was a three-time winner of the Pulitzer Prize: 1947 in fiction for *All the King's Men;* 1958 in poetry for *Promises;* 1979 in poetry for *Now and Then: Poems 1976–1978.*

1880 LOUIS DEMBITZ BRANDEIS, 1856–1941

(Entrance to Univ. of Louisville Law School, Louisville, Jefferson Co.)

U.S. Supreme Court Justice, 1916–1939, born on Center Street (now Armory). Brandeis attended public school in Louisville and later Harvard Law School. Pres. Woodrow Wilson nominated him for Supreme Court, 1916. He actively supported rights of speech and assembly, consumer protection, and women's rights. See over.
(Reverse)

U.S. SUPREME COURT JUSTICE

Brandeis was first Jew named to high court. Oliver Wendell Holmes, Jr. was often his ally there. Brandeis championed such causes as low-cost life insurance through savings banks; opposed trusts, monopolies, and "the curse of bigness" in government and business. Brandeis Univ. in Mass. named for him. His ashes interred at Univ. of Louisville Law School.

1881 ROBERT L. SURTEES, 1906–1985

(Goebel Park, 5th & Philadelphia Sts., Covington, Kenton Co.)

This famous cinematographer won three Academy Awards during a 54-year career in the motion picture business. Surtees, a Covington native, distinguished himself as a specialist in color photography. He won Academy Awards for "King Solomon's Mines" (1950), "The Bad and the Beautiful" (1952), and "Ben-Hur" (1959). See over.
(Reverse)

ACADEMY AWARD WINNER

Surtees spent early years, 1928–30, in Germany perfecting his craft, then returned to the United States. This Director of Photography received sixteen Academy Award nominations. Among his film credits are "Oklahoma," "Doctor Dolittle," "The Graduate," "Summer of '42," "The Last Picture Show," and "The Sting." Died in Monterey, California, 1985. Over.

1882 JAMES T. MOREHEAD, 1797–1854

(Courthouse, Bowling Green, Warren Co.)

Ky.'s first native son to become governor was born in Bullitt Co. but reared in Logan Co. He read law under John J. Crittenden; began practice in Bowling Green. Served in Ky. House of Rep., and elected lt. gov. At Gov. Breathitt's death, Morehead became chief executive, 1834–1836. A close Whig ally of Henry Clay, he was in U.S. Senate, 1841–1847. Buried in Frankfort.

1883 JAMES GUTHRIE (1792–1869)

(City Hall, Railroad St., Bloomfield, Nelson Co.)

Guthrie—lawyer, statesman, and financier—became a noted leader interested in both the development of resources and politics. In Gen. Assembly he promoted legislation for Bank of Kentucky and framed its charter. Guthrie strongly advocated railroad construction. During Civil War, he was conservative Unionist. As L&N pres., he placed railroad in service of U.S. government. Over.
(Reverse)

JAMES GUTHRIE (1792–1869)

This railroad promoter and U.S. Secretary of Treasury was born near Bloomfield. Appointed, at age 28, Commonwealth's Attorney by Governor Adair. He represented Jefferson Co. and Louisville in General Assembly, 1827–40. Guthrie served as president of Kentucky Constitutional Conv., 1849; as U.S. Treasurer, 1853–57, under Pierce; and in U.S. Senate, 1865–68. Over.

Churchill Downs on Derby Day, 1927. Kentucky Historical Society Collection.

1884 FLEM D. SAMPSON (1875–1967)
(Barbourville, Courthouse lawn, Knox Co.)

This Ky. Governor, born in Laurel County, attended Union College. Began law practice here; among partners was Caleb Powers, accused assassin of Wm. Goebel. Sampson served as co. and dist. judge, on Ky. Court of Appeals, and as its chief justice. As gov. (1927–1931) Sampson had to face the problems of Great Depression. Later practiced law here. Buried Barbourville Cem.

1885 CHURCHILL DOWNS
(Ky. Derby Museum, 704 Central Ave., Louisville, Jefferson Co.)

Organized in 1874 as Louisville Jockey Club by sportsman Col. M. Louis Clark. Track built on land leased from Clark's uncles, John and Henry Churchill. Twin-spired grandstand, a National Historic Landmark, first used in 1895. Col. Matt Winn (1861–1949) assumed management in 1902, saving track from bankruptcy. Under his leadership, Churchill Downs

known worldwide as Ky. Derby site.
(Reverse)

KENTUCKY DERBY

Referred to as the "Run for the Roses," the first Kentucky Derby was run on this track, May 17, 1875. Black jockey Oliver Lewis rode H. P. McGrath's Aristides to victory. The 1¼ mile race for three-year-old Thoroughbreds is the oldest continuously run stakes race in America, "greatest two minutes in sports," and the first jewel in racing's Triple Crown.

1886 GARRETT DAVIS (1801–1872)
(Link Ave., Winchester Rd., KY 627, Paris, Bourbon Co.)

This lawyer, state legislator, and congressman, who played leading role in preventing 1861 secession of Kentucky, lived 1 block north. Davis represented Bourbon Co. in legislature. In Congress, 1839–47, 1861–72; Ky. Const. Conv., 1849. A Whig ally of Henry Clay, he joined the American (Know-Nothing) party but refused their nomination for pres., 1856; later a Democrat.

1887 HOLY CROSS PARISH
(3600 Block of Church St., Covington, Kenton Co.)

This parish, established in 1890, spurred the growth of Latonia community. Benedictine Sisters came here to teach in 1891. Original two-story church and school on west side of Longworth, now Church St. Present church was completed, 1908, under Fr. John B. Reiter. Dominated by bronze-domed twin towers, church is of German Romanesque influence.
(Reverse)

HOLY CROSS CHURCH

Church's vast interior features handsome detailing and vaulted ceiling unobstructed by columns. Marble imported from Africa and Italy. Main altar inlaid with gold; stained glass from Germany, France, Belgium, and England. Transcept windows depict lives of St. Helen and St. Paul. Restored, 1990. On Natl. Register of Historic Places. *Presented by The Holy Name Society and City of Covington.*

1888 MATTHEW H. JOUETT (1788–1827)
(Georgetown Rd. [US 25] & Nandino Blvd., Lexington, Fayette Co.)

Master portrait painter Matthew Harris Jouett was born in Mercer Co., a son of Capt. Jack Jouett. He graduated from Transylvania and studied law under Judge George M. Bibb. Served in War of 1812 as paymaster of infantry regiment. Vouchers were lost during battle, and Jouett was thrown into debt. After leaving army he abandoned law and devoted himself to art. Over.
(Reverse)

MATTHEW H. JOUETT (1788–1827)

Jouett was noted for his ability to paint men, women, and children equally well. His portraits reflect unusual ability to memorize faces. Depicted eminent people of era, including Lafayette. Jouett studied briefly with Gilbert Stuart in Boston. Struggled to support large family; paid war debt before he died at farm near Lexington. Judged one of Kentucky's greatest artists.

1889 OLD STONE INN
(Simpsonville, US 60 W, Shelby Co.)

This structure on Midland Trail has been a tavern, stagecoach inn, and home since built in early 1800s. Erected from stone quarried nearby. Oldest stone residence in Shelby County still standing and occupied. Operated as early tavern; among its owners was Fleming P. Rogers, 1817–27. After serving as private home for many years, Old Stone Inn opened as a restaurant in 1922.

1890 LOWER DONALDSON SCHOOL
(Approx. 10 mi. S. of Cadiz, near shore of Lake Barkley, Trigg Co.)

One-room structure known as Dixon School, built 350 yds. S.W. in 1881. After building burned, new school was constructed in 1913; approximately 50 students attended each year. Pupils often competed with other schools in athletic and scholastic matches. Second building withstood 1937 Ohio Valley flood despite water that reached eaves. *Presented by Former Students and Teachers.*
(Reverse)

LOWER DONALDSON SCHOOL

School operated during seven-month school terms that began in July. Lower Donaldson also served as community center, with pie suppers and political meetings. School closed in 1958 and building razed in 1962, after U.S. Army Corps of Engineers bought property for Barkley Dam and Lake project. *Partially funded by Ky. Bicentennial Commission.*

1891 CEDAR CREEK BAPTIST CHURCH
(7709 Bardstown Rd., Fern Creek, Jefferson Co.)

First named Chenoweth Run, church formally organized June 16, 1792, about 12 mi. S.E. of Louisville. Log church built in 1798 on land given by William Fleming to Moses Tyler, trustee. Moved to this community after changing name to Cedar Creek, 1846. Present church completed in 1962. Congregation continuously active since 1792 organization. *Presented by Cedar Creek Baptist Church.*

1892 DONALDSON
(8 mi. S. of Cadiz, Jct. KY 807 & 1062, Trigg Co.)

This community was first settled ca. 1798. Among the prominent Revolutionary War veterans who settled here were John Cohoon, James Thomas, Sr., and Nathan

Futrell. These early pioneers cleared forests, planted crops and orchards, set up lumber and grist mills and distilleries. Donaldson post office, established 1855, was on this site 1894–1913. See over.
(Reverse)

DONALDSON

This seven-mile-long valley has numerous fresh-water springs that feed Donaldson Creek. It was once a hunting ground for the Chickasaw Indian tribe. Area was part of Christian County until Trigg was created in 1820. Donaldson precinct formed in 1917; citizens voted here for more than forty years. Over.

1893 WILLIAM G. KENTON (1941–1981)
(Maysville High School, 2nd & Limestone, Maysville, Mason Co.)

This Maysville native was elected to Kentucky House in 1969. Became Speaker in 1976 at age 34 and served until death. Achievements include leading legislative independence movement and increasing public participation in government. William Kenton's legislative service continued tradition of grandfather W.T. and great-grandfather Eldrige Kenton.

1894 EAST KY. POWER COOPERATIVE
(4758 Lexington Rd., Winchester, Clark Co.)

On July 7, 1941, thirteen of Kentucky's rural electric co-ops formed East Kentucky Power Cooperative to relieve the electric power shortage common in rural areas. In 1951, Hugh L. Spurlock became EKPC's first general manager. Construction began soon after on its first power plant, William C. Dale Station.
(Reverse)

EAST KY. POWER COOPERATIVE

Before 1937, only 3% of rural homes in Ky. had electricity. Today, electricity is available to all. EKPC supplies wholesale power to 18 electric co-ops that serve electricity needs of farms, homes, and businesses in eastern 2/3 of state. With headquarters here, EKPC operates three coal-fired generating plants in Somerset, Ford, and Maysville.

1895 DISCOVERY OF SULPHUR WELL
(Roadside park, KY 70, Sulphur Well, Metcalfe Co.)

This artesian well was discovered in 1845 by Ezekiel Neal, who was drilling for salt water. When he reached 180 ft. depth, pressure shot water, auger, and shafting over top of large sycamore tree. Besides salt, water contained sulphur, magnesium, and iron; used by many for its medicinal value. Constant water supply not affected by cold, heat, rain, or draught.
(Reverse)

BEULA VILLA HOTEL

Built in 1903 by Catlett W. Thompson, across from sulphur well. Two main buildings with guest rooms were noted for spacious, wide verandas. A swinging bridge was erected from the main veranda to the well. Next owner was King C. Crenshaw. Business thrived until 1960, when Crenshaw's health failed. After 65 years of serving the community, this popular hotel closed in 1968.

1896 GOV. GEORGE MADISON (1763–1816)
(330 W. Broadway, Frankfort, Franklin Co.)

A youthful Rev. War. soldier from Va., Madison was appointed auditor of Ky. public accounts by Governor Shelby; served some 20 years. His heroic service in the War of 1812 helped propel him to governorship, 1816; died shortly after taking office. Lt. Gov. Slaughter finished term of first Ky. gov. to die in office. Madison is buried in the state section of the Frankfort Cem.

1897 SPALDING HALL
(114 N. Fifth, Bardstown, Nelson Co.)

Erected in 1826 and later named for Bishop M. J. Spalding. Until 1889, it was part of St. Joseph College, founded by Bishop B. J. Flaget. Jesuits took charge of celebrated college, 1848–1868. During Civil War, St. Joseph was a military hospital. Spalding Hall has served as college and seminary, as orphanage, and as St. Joseph Prep School directed by Xaverian Brothers from 1911–68.

1898 NOTED SCHOOL SITE
(550 W. Kentucky St., Louisville, Jefferson Co.)

Designed in 1873 by B.J. McElfatrick, architect, as first black public school in Ky. Central Colored School served as cultural and educational center for city's black community until 1894. Then, because of over-crowding, Central relocated. Education continued here for eight more decades. From 1916 to 1970, this was the Mary D. Hill School, named for kindergarten pioneer.

1899 IRENE DUNNE (1898–1990)
(Ky. Center for the Arts, Louisville, Jefferson Co.)

Born in Louisville, this actress appeared on Broadway in 1920s and then starred in forty-one comedy, dramatic, and musical films of the 1930s and 40s. Nominated five times for an Academy Award. Her noted films included "Show Boat" (1936), "Anna and the King of Siam" (1946), and "I Remember Mama" (1948). Irene Dunne received Kennedy Center Honors in 1985.

1900 GOV. ALBERT B. CHANDLER (1898–1991)
(Jct. Pisgah Pike & US 60, Woodford Co.)

Known as "Happy," this Henderson Co. native was state senator and lt. gov. before becoming governor in 1935 and 1955. U.S. senator, 1939–45. As baseball commissioner, he approved Jackie Robinson's contract, making Robinson the first black player in major league baseball, 1947. Chandler elected to Baseball Hall of Fame, 1982. Over.
(Reverse)
ALBERT BENJAMIN CHANDLER
This colorful orator and two-term governor began his law practice in Versailles. As governor, he was the driving force behind the establishment of the University of Kentucky Medical Center, later named in his honor. "Happy" Chandler lived in Versailles and is buried in the Pisgah Cemetery in this county. →

1901 BOWMAN FIELD—EAST
(Sidney Park St. near corner of Cannon Lane, Louisville, Jefferson Co.)

The east side of Bowman Field airport was expanded in 1940 to become the Bowman Field Air Base. It was a training facility with 124 buildings used by the U.S. Army Air Force throughout World War II. One hangar survives. Bowman Field was first used to train bomber crews and later was assigned to the first troop carrier command.

Presented by WW II Flight Nurses Assoc., Inc.
(Reverse)
BOWMAN FIELD—EAST
Troop carrier units were organized and combat glider pilots trained at Bowman Field. Only school of Air Evacuation in Air Force here, 1942–44. It taught surgeons, flight nurses, and medical technicians the procedures for the care of patients in the air. Some gave their lives caring for sick and wounded soldiers worldwide. *Presented by WW II Flight Nurses Assoc., Inc.*

1902 SHANDY HALL (PRINCETON)
(Big Spring Park, E. Washington St., Princeton, Caldwell Co.)

Shandy Hall, two-story frame home built on bluff above Big Spring, built by William Prince on his 200-acre survey made in 1798. Prince, a Rev. War veteran from S.C., began town on waters of Eddy Creek. In 1817, Princetown became county seat of Caldwell Co. Changed to Princeton the next year, it was situated on 50-acre donation of Prince heirs. *Presented by Caldwell Co. Bicentennial Committee and The Ky. Bicentennial Commission.*

1903 HISTORIC EDUCATIONAL SITE
(US 60 & KY 91 [W. Main St.], Princeton, Caldwell Co.)

Six educational institutions have flourished here since 1860. Local citizens gave $20,000 and Dr. T.L. McNary six acres to establish Princeton College, 1860–80. Youth also served by Princeton Collegiate Inst., 1880–1911; Princeton High, 1911–23; Butler High 1924–54; Caldwell Co. H.S. until 1972; then Caldwell Middle School, 1972–92. *Presented by Caldwell Co. Bicentennial Committee and The Ky. Bicentennial Commission.*

1904 THE HAYCRAFT INN
(2315 S. Wilson Ave., Radcliff, Hardin Co.)

Oldest portion of inn constructed ca. 1814. Building enlarged to its present size when purchased by Daniel Haycraft, ca. 1820. On the Louisville-Nashville Turnpike, the inn was popular stopping place for stagecoaches. In spite of railroads and resulting declines in stagecoach travel, inn was still operating in 1884. Private home by 1917. On Natl. Register of Historic Places.

1905 MERRITT JONES/WAYSIDE TAVERN

(16 mi. S. of Richmond; 6½ mi. SE of Berea, US 421, Madison Co.)

Down this lane was a log tavern and overnight stop on the Old State Road from Cumberland Gap to Lexington by 1830s. The older half of building dates back to ca. 1800. During Civil War, Jones Tavern was held alternately by Confederate and Union forces. In Jan. 1864, Gen. U.S. Grant and staff stayed overnight on their way from east Tennessee to Lexington. Over.

(Reverse)

JONES TAVERN/CSA CEMETERY

During the Battle of Richmond, Aug. 29–30, 1862, this building was a Confederate field hospital for men wounded while fighting farther north near Mt. Zion Church. Thirteen who died here, including a boy soldier only fifteen years old, are buried in a small cemetery in the woods above the house. See over.

1906 LT. DARWIN K. KYLE

(Near Jenkins, US 23 & 119, Letcher Co.)

This Congressional Medal of Honor winner fought in Korean War. Born in Jenkins, June 1918, Second Lt. Kyle in U.S. Army with Co. K, 7th Inf. Regt., 3d Inf. Div. Lt. Kyle rallied his men amid intensive fighting to renew attacks on enemy machine-gun positions. He killed 7 men in 2 assaults, then was slain by enemy fire, February 16, 1951. *Presented by Letcher County Historical and Genealogical Society.*

1907 TYLER SETTLEMENT

(Sweeney Ln. & Taylorsville Rd., Jeffersontown, Jefferson Co.)

By 1785, Edward Tyler patented some 1,000 acres on Chenoweth Run. Sons Moses, William, Edward III, and nephew Robert Tyler established farms on this land, each productive and self sufficient by the 1790s, forming a rural community. The three surviving homesteads retain many original structures, including log and stone houses, springhouses, barns, and a family cemetery. Over.

(Reverse)

TYLER SETTLEMENT

In 1986, a 600-acre area was designated the Tyler Settlement Rural Historic District, including portions of Moses, Edward III,

and Robert Tyler's farms. Moses ran one of the state's earliest licensed distilleries. A portion of his land (170 acres) is now Blackacre State Natural Preserve, one of the oldest working farms in Jefferson Co. and an environmental education center.

1908 FREDONIA

(Fredonia, US 641, Caldwell Co.)

Town founded 1835 as a voting precinct. Established between Princeton and Salem stage stops, it was first called Midway; name changed to Fredonia two years later. In 1887, the Ohio Valley Railroad ran one-half mile west of town. Kelsey was established there; the two post offices combined in 1906, and retained Fredonia name.

1909 FISHER'S GARRISON

(Near 391 McDowell Dr., Lexington Rd., Danville, Boyle Co.)

Stephen Albert Fisher, Rev. War soldier from Va., assigned in 1775 to active duty and wounded while serving with Colonel John Bowman's militia. Returned to Ky. in 1779 with wife Mary Magdalene Garr. He established garrison of military significance in vicinity of 400-acre settlement tract. Bros. Adam (in Rev.) & Barnett followed to Ky. *Presented by Col. Richard Hampton Fisher, S.A.R.*

1910 CHARLES S. MOREHEAD, 1802–1868

(Pioneer Cem., W. 13th St., Hopkinsville, Christian Co.)

This Ky. governor and congressman was born near Bardstown. A graduate of Transylvania, he began law practice in Hopkinsville. Morehead served in state legislature, as attorney general, in U.S. House of Rep., and as governor of Ky., 1855–59. During his administration, geological survey completed, state prison enlarged, and funds allotted for annual state fair. See over.

(Reverse)

CHARLES SLAUGHTER MOREHEAD

Hoping to avert civil war, Morehead attended Washington Peace Conf., 1861. Although neutral, he sympathized with Confederacy and criticized Lincoln's policies. Arrested by federal leaders and imprisoned for several months. Warned of another arrest, he fled to Canada, Europe, and

Mexico. Died at his Mississippi plantation, 1868. Buried in Frankfort Cem.

1911 JOHN WALLER (1758–1823)
(3 mi. S. of Falmouth, US 27, Pendleton Co.)

This Rev. War soldier helped build Kenton's Station near Maysville, 1784. Commissioned capt. of militia for Bourbon Co.; later trustee and tavern owner at Millersburg. Served in Va. and Ky. legislatures. A founder of Falmouth, 1793, he owned gristmill and sawmill on south fork of Licking. Buried family cem.; Waller monument nearby. *Presented by Capt. John Waller Chapter, Daughters of American Revolution.*

1912 JOHN LARUE HELM, 1802–1867
(Elizabethtown, Jct. US 31-W & KY 447, Hardin Co.)

This Hardin Co. native was one of Kentucky's most celebrated lawyers. In legislature 17 yrs.; rose to House Speaker. Elected lt. gov., he became gov. when John J. Crittenden resigned, 1850. Pres. of L&N R.R., 1854–60, when railroad completed. A harsh critic of Pres. Lincoln, Helm favored neutrality for Ky. in the Civil War. Elected gov., 1867. Died after five days in office.

1913 FEUDISTS ON TRIAL
(Kentucky Ave., Pikeville College campus, Pikeville, Pike Co.)

Hanging site of Ellison Mounts, Feb. 18, 1890. Seven other Hatfield supporters indicted for murder of Alifair McCoy were sentenced to life in prison. By the time of his trial, Mounts had confessed. He was also found guilty, but the jury recommended the death penalty. Pike County sheriff carried out sentence. This was one of the last episodes in Hatfield-McCoy feud.

1914 THOMPSON FERRY
(Jct. KY 334 & Emmick Rd., Lewisport, Hancock Co.)

Thompson Ferry is the site where many biographers of Abraham Lincoln say Thomas Lincoln family crossed the river to Indiana in 1816. A river ferry in area established Feb. 1804, by Daniel Lewis; later operated by Hugh Thompson. Ferry run by John and Lin Dill in 1827, when they charged Abe Lincoln with illegally ferrying passengers on river. Lincoln later acquitted.
(Reverse)

THOMPSON FERRY ROAD

One of Hancock County's first roads, built in 1815, ran from Thompson Ferry Landing toward Hardinsburg in Breckinridge County. The land on this site later bought by George Emmick, who built on the riverfront here one of the oldest houses in Hancock County in 1854. *Presented by Mrs. Retha Emmick Newell.*

1915 ENCOUNTER AT BURNT MILL
(10 mi. E. of Providence, Jct. KY 630 & 120, Webster Co.)

On September 15, 1861, a short skirmish took place between Northern troops and community militia. Union soldiers under Col. Jas. F. Buckner and Capt. Wm. Buckner camped in Tirzah (Burnt Mill) Church. Capt. Al Fowler gathered Confederates and fought and captured the 25 soldiers. Area scene of activity by Johnson's Partisan Rangers. *Presented by the citizens of Webster County and Providence, Ky., for the Ky. Bicentennial.*

1916 CONVERGING OF INDIAN TRAILS
(Big Spring Park, E. Washington St., Princeton, Caldwell Co.)

Saline, Eddy, and Varmint traces met at Big Spring (Princeton) and developed into today's roads. First forged by buffalo, later used by Indians and pioneers. A fork of Saline crossed Ohio River at Cave-in-Rock; another at Golconda, Ill. Eddy Trace also known as Palmyra-Princeton Trail. Varmint Trace ran from Princeton to Cumberland River. *Presented by Caldwell Co., Ky. Bicentennial and the Ky. Bicentennial Commission.*

1917 FORT WRIGHT
(409 Kyles Ln., Municipal Building, Ft. Wright, Kenton Co.)

Near here stood Fort Wright, built in Sept. 1862 by Union troops to help defend Cincinnati area from advancing Confederate armies. Fort named for Maj. Gen. Horatio G. Wright, USA, who later was chief engineer for completion of the Washington Monument. The city of Fort Wright is named for both the fort and the engineer-general. *Presented by Citizens of Fort Wright.*

1918 HAWES FAMILY CEMETERY
(Yelvington, KY 662, Daviess Co.)

Richard Hawes (1772–1829) and wife Clary Walker Hawes (1776–1848) came here 1810 from Va. Their son Richard was Confederate governor of Ky. After husband's death, Clary was licensed to operate Hawesville and Cannelton ferry, 1831. Cemetery long maintained by Col. Benjamin Walker Hawes; he formed board of trustees for its future care. *Presented by Hawes Family Assoc.*

1919 CAMP WILDCAT
(Hazel Patch, 7 mi. NW of London, US 25, Laurel Co.)

Led by Gen. Felix K. Zollicoffer, 7,500 Confederates on October 21, 1861, attacked the entrenched camp of 5,000 Union men under Gen. Albin Schoepf. Union's natural defense advantage in the Rockcastle Hills stopped the Southern troops, who retreated to Tenn. This was major battle during 4 days of skirmishes, attacks, and heavy gunfire. Over. *Presented by Laurel County Bicentennial Commission and Forest Service, USDA.*
(Reverse)

UNION CIVIL WAR CAMP

The Camp Wildcat position was considered crucial for each side. Union forces camped two miles north of here to prevent Confederate attack into the Bluegrass region of Kentucky. Confederates wanted to prevent Union advance into eastern Tennessee, where many citizens remained loyal to the Union. *Presented by Laurel County Bicentennial Commission and Forest Service, USDA.*

1920 FELIX K. ZOLLICOFFER
(1 mi. S. of Nancy, KY 235, Pulaski Co.)

Brig. Gen. Felix K. Zollicoffer, CSA, died here, Jan. 19, 1862, in Battle of Logan's Crossroads (Mill Springs). This Tenn. native was veteran of Seminole War, editor of *Nashville Banner*, and 3-term U.S. congressman. In heavy rain and smoke of battle, Zollicoffer was killed approaching USA lines, which he mistook for own troops. Over. *Presented by Boy Scout Troop 79 of Somerset for the Kentucky Bicentennial.*
(Reverse)

"ZOLLIE TREE"

This large, white oak has been decorated annually in honor of Gen. Zollicoffer since 1902, when Dorotha Burton began tradition. Over 100 CSA soldiers are in mass grave at rear of park. Zollicoffer is buried in Nashville. Boy Scout Troop 79 Trail follows Confederate retreat to Cumberland River. Over. *Erected during 130th anniv. of the battle and the Ky. Bicentennial.*

1921 CALMES TOMB
(Paynes Mill Rd., off US 60, Versailles, Woodford Co.)

This stone mausoleum was built in family cemetery of "Caneland" plantation by Gen. Marquis Calmes, a friend of Lafayette during Amer. Revolution. Calmes (1755–1834), born in Va. of Huguenot ancestry, assisted in laying out Versailles and named it after French city. He and wife Priscilla Heale buried here. Tomb restored in July 1990. *Presented by Genealogical Society of Versailles.*

1922 ESTILL SEMINARY
(Estill Co. Middle School, Main St., Irvine, Estill Co.)

This site approved for Jefferson Seminary by act of Ky. General Assembly in February 1798. Name was changed to Estill Seminary, February 3, 1816. Trustees given authority to sell half of unclaimed lands, granted for educational purposes, to erect buildings and purchase library. Seminary was built in 1830 and used until 1897. *Presented by Estill County Schools.*
(Reverse)

COLLEGIATE INSTITUTE

On site of Seminary, the Estill Collegiate Institute established in 1906 through cooperation of Presby. Synod of Ky. and Estill Seminary trustees: B.F. Jacobs, W.W. Park, L.A. West, Thomas Williams, and Hugh Riddell. Present structure, 1948, was Estill Co. High School; it became middle school, 1971. *Presented by Estill County Schools to commemorate Ky. Bicentennial.*

1923 EARLY JEWISH CONGREGATIONS
(5101 Brownsboro Rd. at corner of Lime Kiln, Louisville, US 42, Jefferson Co.)

The Temple was created in 1976 by uniting Reform congregations Adath Israel and

Brith Sholom. Adath Israel was chartered
by Kentucky in 1842; it was the oldest Jewish congregation in Ky., 7th Reform in U.S.,
a founder of Union of American Hebrew
Congregations. Ritual of Isaac M. Wise,
founder of Reform Judaism, adopted in
1855. *Presented by Jean and Jacques Morris.*
(Reverse)

EARLY JEWISH CONGREGATIONS

Brith Sholom formed 1880 by German
Jews wishing a traditional service but tend-
ing toward reform. They joined UAHC,
1920. Jewish families moving farther east
led to the relocation of site and 1976 consolidation. This temple was dedicated 1980.
Cemetery is on Preston Highway. See over.
Presented by Jean and Jacques Morris.

1924 CAMPBELLSVILLE COLLEGE

(Entrance to campus, 200 W. College St., Campbellsville, Taylor Co.)

Founded as Russell Creek Academy by
Russell Creek Assoc. of Baptists in 1906.
C.R. Hoskins sold ten-acre site for $1,000.
On founding committee were J.L. Atkin-
son, J.R. Davis, George Durrett, James
Garnett, Jr., S.E. Kerr, W.R. Lyon, B.W.
Penick, Alexander Shively, W.T. Under-
wood, and H.C. Wood. *Presented by
Campbellsville College.*
(Reverse)

CAMPBELLSVILLE COLLEGE

Traveling central Kentucky by buggy, L.C.
Kelly, T.E. Ennis, H.S. Robinson, Abel
Harding, Ed Henderson, C.M. and J.R.
Durham raised funds needed to maintain
Russell Creek Academy. Institution became Campbellsville Junior College in
1924. Administration Building with class-
rooms and library burned in 1939. Rebuilt
and became senior college, 1960.

1925 MACKLIN HOUSE

(212 Washington St., Frankfort, Franklin Co.)

This townhouse, built ca. 1850, became
home of George B. Macklin, prominent
land owner and coal dealer. He came in
1867 from Forks of Elkhorn area. His coal
yard near L&N R.R bridge. Two-story brick
carriage house at rear, one of few in county,
built about same time. Blacksmith shop here
also. In Corner of Celebrities Hist. Dist. *Presented by John C. Ryan and Donald Duff.*

1926 FERNWOOD CEMETERY

(840 Madison St., Henderson, Henderson Co.)

Established 1849, cemetery contains graves
of some noted Kentuckians; among them
are Lazarus Powell and John Y. Brown.
Powell, Henderson's first governor (1851–
55), began state's first geological survey to
develop mineral and agricultural resources.
Brown elected to U.S. House of Rep. while
underage; later served 2 more terms. Supported new constitution and became gov.
1891.
(Reverse)

FERNWOOD CEMETERY

Buried here is Archibald Dixon, who
served in Ky. House of Rep. and Senate.
Lt. gov. 1844–48 under Wm. Owsley; appointed U.S. senator in 1852 to complete
term of the late Henry Clay. Teacher Mary
Towles Sasseen, who led her class in first
observance of Mother's Day, May 1887,
and promoted its recognition nationwide,
also buried here. Over. *Presented by
Henderson Jr. Historical Society.*

1927 BIBLE MISSION SCHOOL AND ORPHANAGE

(6 mi. W. of Albany, KY 1351, Clinton Co.)

John S. Keen, Methodist minister, began
school near here, 1891, for ministers and
teachers. After some 10 years as pres., Keen
sold school to W.H. Evans, who managed
orphans' home with school for a short time.
Closed by 1905, school had served hundreds of youth, including Robert Johnson.
His son Gov. Keen Johnson was named
after school's founder.
(Reverse)

BIBLE MISSION SCHOOL

Residents and students alike held the traditions of the school in high esteem. Two
became college presidents: Drs. A.B.
Mackey and T.W. Willingham. Others who
gave years of service to the community well
beyond the school era were Dr. R.E.
Gibson, physician and life-long resident,
and Rev. I.T. Stovall, minister and educator. *Presented by Friends of the Highway
Community.*

1928 AFRICAN-AMERICAN PHYSICIANS

(Lexington, 118 North Broadway, Fayette Co.)

Site of office building which housed prominent African-American physicians and pharmacy. Among the doctors who practiced here between 1909 and 1930 were Obed Cooley; Nathaniel J. Ridley; J.C. Coleman; John Hunter, first African-American surgeon at St. Joseph's Hospital; and Joseph Laine, who later founded a medical clinic in Louisville. *Presented by Professor Doris Wilkinson, Historical Sociologist at University of Ky.*

1929 BERT T. COMBS (1911–1991)
(Beech Creek Cem., near Manchester, KY 3432, Clay Co.)

Born in Clay Co., future gov. Combs practiced law in Manchester and Prestonsburg. A captain in World War II, he helped prepare evidence against Japanese war criminals. On Ky. Court of Appeals, 1951–55. Gov. of Ky., 1959–63. Federal Court of Appeals judge, 1967–70. A senior partner in Wyatt, Tarrant, & Combs, he won ruling that led to landmark school reform legislation, 1990.
(Reverse)
GOV. BERT T. COMBS (1959–1963)
Accomplishments during Combs's administration included highways connecting eastern and western Ky., expansion of state parks system, a statutory merit system for state employees, an end to segregation in public facilities, increased funding for teachers' salaries and state universities, 3% sales tax, and Ky. Educational Television. *Presented by Friends of Bert Combs & the K.J.H.S.*

1930 LINCOLN INSTITUTE CAMPUS
(Simpsonville, US 60 W, Shelby Co.)

Founded by Berea College trustees with Pres. Frost main fundraiser. This occurred after Day Law (1904) stopped coeducation of whites and blacks. In 1909, Berea board bought three farms totaling 444 acres for a school. Lincoln Institute opened to 85 black students on October 1, 1912. It stressed teacher training and industrial education. See over. *Presented by National Alumni Association.*
(Reverse)
LINCOLN INSTITUTE CAMPUS
Well known black leaders were financial agent James Bond and later Pres. Whitney M. Young, Sr. Institute designed by the New York firm of Tandy and Foster (black architects). In 1947, school became part of public education system. It opened as institute for gifted but disadvantaged youth, 1967. School officially closed in 1970. Over. *Presented by National Alumni Association.*

1931 McCUTCHEN MEADOWS
(Auburn, 12345 Bowling Green Rd., US 68/80, Logan Co.)

Earliest land grant to property is dated 1798 and signed by James Garrard, 2nd gov. of Ky. Issued to Elizabeth, widow of John McCutchen. Built by 1825, mansion originally had four rooms and wide central hall upstairs and down, with rear wing. Family owned home some 150 years. Burial ground on property. On National Reg. of Hist. Places. *Presented by Ken and Neda Knowles Preservation Society.*

1932 OGDEN MEMORIAL UNITED METHODIST CHURCH
(Princeton, 305 West Main, Caldwell Co.)

Congregation organized in 1818 as Methodist Episcopal Church at home of Richard Barnes, a tanner. First meeting house later built beside his home on S. Jefferson St. Became M.E. Church, South, 1845, when national church split over slavery. Renamed to honor Benjamin Ogden, first minister appointed to western Ky. and Tenn. by Bishop Asbury.
(Reverse)
OGDEN MEMORIAL UNITED METHODIST CHURCH
The first meeting house of Ogden Memorial was on South Jefferson Street. Several other evangelical denominations were organized there. The second building was erected in 1878 on South Seminary Street between Main and Washington. The present edifice, honoring Benjamin Ogden, erected 1928–29. *Presented by Mary McCamey Smith.*

1933 ROWAN COUNTY "WAR," 1884–1887
(Morehead, former C&O Passenger Depot, East First St., Rowan Co.)

Political tensions led to this three-year period of violence which resulted in some twenty deaths. Conflict between John Mar-

tin and Floyd Tolliver caused Tolliver's death. His brother Craig opposed Martin ally D.B. Logan and killed two of Logan's cousins. Tolliver group then seized virtual control of the county. See over. *Presented by Rowan County Fiscal Court.*
(Reverse)

ROWAN COUNTY "WAR," 1884–1887

Feud violence came to climax in summer of 1887, when Logan and Hiram Pigman led faction that surrounded Craig Tolliver and his men. Resulting shoot-out ended in deaths of Tolliver and three others. State militia was sent in three times to restore order, and a state report suggested that Rowan Co. be abolished. Over. *Presented by Rowan County Fiscal Court.*

1934 GEORGETOWN CEMETERY
(Georgetown, South Broadway, Scott Co.)

Incorporated 1850, with 31 acres purchased by 1860. Tombstones older than 1860 reflect reinterment from other graveyards. Buried here are Kentucky governors Joseph Desha and James F. Robinson, Confederate gov. George W. Johnson, equine artist Edward Troye, educator Thornton Johnson, Dr. Wm. Loftus Sutton, and reformer Anne Payne Coffman. *Presented by City of Georgetown & Cem. Board.*

1935 UNION STEAMBOAT CAPTURED
(Lewisport, 4th & Market Sts., Hancock Co.)

Pro-southern guerrillas led by Hawesville native Bill Davison and Isaac Coulter captured *Morning Star* here, Dec. 23, 1864. They killed three Union soldiers and robbed other passengers and crew of some $3,000 cash and jewelry. On Jan. 4, 1865, these same guerrillas burned the Daviess Co. courthouse at Owensboro. Records were saved. *Presented by City of Lewisport.*
(Reverse)

SITE OF FRONT STREET

Lewisport's first business district was along river on Front St. First permanent store built by Joseph C. Pell, 1841; his was only structure standing on Front St. after 1849 fire. Another early merchant was I.B. Hayden. In 1882, street began crumbling into river; only a footpath by 1920. Fourth became main business street instead. *Pre-*

sented by City of Lewisport.

1936 SPRING BAYOU BAPTIST CHURCH
(12 mi. W. of Paducah, McCracken Co.)

Organized Jan. 14, 1843 as Newton's Creek Church with fifteen charter members. Elder Henry Richardson was first pastor and served 1843–46. Church attained present name in 1847, after site chosen for first house of worship. Next church built 1853; third, 1870. Cemetery established ca. 1895. Present building dedicated Aug. 20, 1967. *Presented by Spring Bayou Baptist Church.*

1937 FIRST CHRISTIAN CHURCH
(Clinton, 201 N. Washington St., Hickman Co.)

Established 1876 on this site. First structure (frame) burned 1896; brick church built three years later. A 1951 fire caused damage, but complete repair achieved. This Kentucky Historical Landmark features a multi-spired roof, vaulted ceiling, curved pews, and original stained-glass windows with memorial pictures of donors. *Presented by Members and Friends.*

1938 NEW ZION
(4 mi. from Georgetown, KY 922, Scott Co.)

On Nov. 23, 1872, former slaves Calvin Hamilton and Primus Keene purchased 23 acres. They sold plots to other freedmen and formed black community of Briar Hill; it was later named New Zion. Keene sold land for community well, school, and church. Calvin Hamilton's home survives. Descendants of founders still live in New Zion. *Presented by Scott County Fiscal Court.*

1939 RITTE'S CORNER
(3634 DeCoursey, Covington, Kenton Co.)

Named for Henry Ritte's saloon at five-corner intersection, this area has been hub of Latonia commerce since 1880s, when original Latonia racetrack (1883–1939), one block away, started. The opening of a section of Covington and Lexington R.R. in 1854 initiated area as a rail crossroads. Electric street car service began in 1890s. Over. *Presented by the City of Covington.*
(Reverse)

RITTE'S CORNER

This five-street intersection provided a variety of shops, flats, saloons, restaurants, and banks. The Weber/Ritte Building at 3634 DeCoursey housed Weber's grocery/saloon by 1890, and Ritte's saloon from 1899 to 1927. Buildings at intersection comprise Ritte's Corner Historic District. *Presented by Gailen and Debra Bridges.*

1940 LT. PRESLEY N. O'BANNON, USMC
(On USS O'Bannon Destroyer, assigned to U.S. Navy's Atlantic Fleet)

First American to raise U.S. flag on foreign soil at Battle of Derne on shores of Tripoli, April 27, 1805. Led attack that overcame Barbary Coast pirates who were holding 180 American seamen for ransom. O'Bannon came to Logan County in 1807. Served in Kentucky House 1812, 17, 20–21, and in Senate 1824–26. Died in 1850. Remains moved to Frankfort, 1920. *Presented by Kentucky Friends.*

1941 MASON COUNTY SPY COMPANY
(Maysville, Limestone Landing, Mason Co.)

Company formed when Simon Kenton proposed to Gen. Charles Scott that a volunteer company of spies (scouts) be selected and trained to protect pioneer settlements. They were called out for short-term duty and became known for their daring successes against Indians. *Presented by estate of Col. Paul Warren Bennett, Vandalia, Mo., a great-great-grandson of Archibald Bennett.*
(Reverse)
MASON COUNTY SPY COMPANY
These scouts served for short-term duty, most from May 4 to Dec. 9, 1792, to protect early settlements.

Mercer Beason	John Dyal
Archibald Bennett	Matthew Hart
William Bennett	James Ireland
Henry Cochran	Ellis Palmer
Samuel Davis	Isaac Pennington
John Dowden	Cornelius Washburn

Presented by estate of Col. Paul W. Bennett.

1942 FIRST PRESBYTERIAN CHURCH
(Lancaster, 105 Danville St., Garrard Co.)

When founded in 1816 by Presbytery of Transylvania, it had 22 members. The first minister was James C. Barnes, who also served Paint Lick Church. Congregation worshiped in the Republican (Union) Church until 1846; second building on Buford and Stanford Streets. They built on the present site in 1879. Gov. Wm. O. Bradley was a member. *Presented by Members of First Presbyterian Church.*

1943 BETHLEHEM ACADEMY
(Bardstown, Bethlehem High School, 309 W. Stephen Foster Ave., US 31-E & 62, Nelson Co.)

Began 1819, when Bishop Flaget asked the Sisters of Charity of Nazareth to open elementary school in Bardstown area. Sisters Harriet Gardiner, Polly Beaven, and Nancy Lynch started school which Father David named Bethlehem. Served as elementary and high school for girls; moved to present site from 5th St., 1959. Became coed, 1970. *Presented by Bethlehem High School.*

1944 BRASHEAR'S STATION
(Shepherdsville, 2003 KY 44 East, Bullitt Co.)

An early station on the Wilderness Road between the Falls of the Ohio (Louisville) and Harrodsburg, Brashear's Station was a haven for pioneer hunters and travelers. It was built at mouth of Floyd's Fork near bank of Salt River, 1779. Founded by William Brashear, a famed woodsman from Maryland, who was killed by Indians, 1781. *Presented by Bullitt Co. Genealogical Society.*
(Reverse)
BRASHEAR'S STATION
Also known as Salt River Garrison or Froman's Station. Bullitt's Lick, major salt-producing area and hub of system of buffalo roads, was nearby. Early families who resided here for protection from the Indians included Froman, Ray, Briscoe, Crist, Collings, Overall, Pope, McGee, Hawkins, and Phelps. *Presented by Bullitt Co. Genealogical Society.*

1945 CALLOWAY NORMAL COLLEGE
(Kirksey, United Methodist Church, KY 299, Calloway Co.)

This institution of higher learning was established by 1899 under the leadership of Rainey T. Wells, later president of Murray State Teachers College. Land for college was deeded to trustees in 1899. Students

came from a wide area and boarded in private homes in Kirksey. The school operated as a teachers college until 1913. *Presented by Kirksey and Calloway Friends.*
(Reverse)

CALLOWAY NORMAL COLLEGE

After Calloway Normal College ceased operation in 1913, Kirksey High School occupied the property. It remained here until 1960, when county high schools were merged. The school then functioned as an elementary center until 1974, when these centers consolidated. The next year Kirksey United Methodist Church purchased property. Over. *Presented by Kirksey and Calloway Friends.*

1946 CAPT. HENRY RHOADS, JR. 1739–1814

(¾ mi. E. of Browder, KY 70, Muhlenberg Co.)

This house was built ca. 1792 by Henry Rhoads, Jr., a capt. in Rev. War under Gen. John Muhlenberg. Rhoads led settlers from Penn. to Green River area of Ky. in 1785. He laid out town of Rhoadsville, now called Calhoun. In 1798, as state legislator, he proposed name of Muhlenberg for new county. *Presented by Rhoads Descendants.*
(Reverse)

CAPT. HENRY RHOADS, JR.

Before moving to Ky., Henry Rhoads served as captain in Pennsylvania militia during Revolutionary War. He was a delegate to Pennsylvania state constitutional convention of 1776. As member of Kentucky state legislature, he suggested that newly formed county be named for his beloved commander, Gen. John Muhlenberg. He became this county's first state legislator (1798–1800).

1947 1869 "CUT-OFF"/BOWIE LAND

(Turnertown Rd. [KY 1170], on north side at Terrapin Cr., Simpson Co.)

In 1869 Ky. legislature changed original 1819 line dividing Simpson and Logan counties. Relocation of boundary brought new territory to Simpson County. This addition, extending from Tennessee to Warren County, Ky., included communities of Price's Mill, Middleton, Locust Grove, and some "Shaker Lands." *Presented*

in memory of James Bowie, born in this area (see other side).
(Reverse)

JAMES BOWIE BIRTH SITE

The adventurer-soldier of knife fame, Colonel James Bowie, who died 1836 at the Alamo in Texas, was born near this site in Logan, now Simpson Co., 1796. Family moved here, 1794, where his father Reason established mill, 1795; was issued a land warrant for 200 acres, 1796. Reason sold land, 1800; tract is in area later known as the "Cut-Off." *Presented in memory of James Bowie.*

1948 HANSON

(7250 Hanson Rd. at Kentucky Bank, Hanson, KY 40 & 260-E, Hopkins Co.)

This town, named for Henry B. Hanson, the civil engineer who planned it, was founded in 1869 and incorporated in 1873. Hanson became bustling tobacco center. "Hanson Twist" tobacco was shipped throughout the U.S. Four costly fires in 1889, 1894, 1905, and 1906, changed the town's history. *Presented by Citizens for Historic Preservation.*

1949 SECOND AFRICAN BAPTIST CHURCH

(First St. between Market and Main Streets, Louisville, Jefferson Co.)

Second African Baptist Church, now Green Street Baptist Church, was formally organized here, Sept. 29, 1844. As was usual in the years of slavery, the founding members had the sponsorship of a protection committee, appointed by First Baptist Church (now Walnut Street). The first pastor was Elder George Wells, 1844–1850. See over. *Presented by Green Street Baptist Church.*
(Reverse)

SECOND AFRICAN BAPTIST CHURCH

The church was more than a religious experience for African Americans. It was also a school, a social center, and a training ground in group cooperation. In 1848 the church relocated to Green Street (now Liberty) and took its current name in 1860. Church moved to its new edifice at 519 East Gray Street, September 29, 1930. Over. *Presented by Green Street Baptist Church.*

1950 CHARLES HANSFORD
(Calhoun Cem., Old Calhoun-Owensboro Rd., KY 81, McLean Co.)

A privateer in Virginia's Navy during the American Revolution, Hansford sailed off eastern coast of U.S., West Indies, and Spain. He was captured three times by the British. Only he and one other of 36 prisoners survived a three-month confinement on the prison ship *Jersey*, nicknamed "Hell Afloat." *Presented by Descendants of Charles Hansford.*
(Reverse)

CHARLES HANSFORD (1759–1850)
This Revolutionary War soldier enlisted in Virginia in 1775 and served six months; enlisted in 1777 and discharged in nine months. Charles Hansford then ran away and went to sea as a privateer. Buried NW of here on Mayo Hill, Scotts Bridge Road. *Presented by Descendants of Charles Hansford.*

1951 FIRST PRESBYTERIAN CHURCH
(200 E. Washington St., Glasgow, Barren Co.)

Congregation formed ca. 1802, when Isaac Robertson, a member, donated lot for log structure erected here. Rev. John Howe was first minister. Present Gothic Revival sanctuary built ca. 1853. Church's style of architecture features Tudor-arched window and door openings and brick pilasters. Site of town's oldest cemetery located behind church. *Presented by Church Memorial Committee.*

1952 NATIONAL REGISTER HISTORIC DISTRICT
(Morehead, University Boulevard, Rowan Co.)

Nine buildings erected from 1926–32 fitting in a "crescent moon" plan. Rader, Fields, Alllie Young Halls, 1926; Thompson Hall, 1927; Button Auditorium, 1928; President's Home, 1929; Breckinridge Training School and Camden Library, 1931; Senff Natatorium, 1932. Landscape plan: Olmstead Bros.; Collegiate Gothic design: Joseph & Joseph Architects.
(Reverse)

MOREHEAD STATE UNIVERSITY
Morehead Christian School founded in 1887 for United Christian Missionary Society of St. Louis by Mrs. Phebe Button and her son Dr. F. C. Button. Became easternmost State Normal School in 1922; changed to Morehead State Teachers College in 1930; and named Morehead State University in 1966. *Presented by MSU Foundation.*

1953 MILLER HALL 1898
(Lexington, U.K. Campus at Miller Hall, Fayette Co.)

Originally named Science Hall, this structure was one of the first UK classroom buildings. In 1940 it was renamed to honor Arthur McQuiston Miller (1861–1929), first Dean of Arts and Sciences, professor of geology, and first football coach at UK. Made of pressed brick trimmed with Bowling Green limestone, Miller Hall is a typical college building of its time. *Class of 1994.*

1954 PROVIDENCE KNOB BAPTIST CHURCH
(Rockfield, 210 Browning Road, Jct. US 68/80 and KY 1083, Warren Co.)

Oldest Missionary Baptist Church in Warren Assoc., it was organized in Sept. 1804 with nine members. Five churches in Bowling Green and Warren Co. have formed from the parent church, including First Baptist Church of Bowling Green, 1818. Two associations formed here: Gasper River–1812; Clear Fork–1860. Present building erected in 1852. *Presented by Providence Knob Baptist Church.*

1955 FRANKFORT UNION STATION
(Frankfort, Broadway & High Sts., Franklin Co.)

Built by Louisville & Nashville R.R., 1908, to replace depot located here by Lexington & Frankfort R.R. in 1850s. Present station was used by Chesapeake & Ohio, Louisville & Nashville, Frankfort & Cincinnati, and Kentucky Highlands. The last scheduled passenger train was C&O George Washington, April 30, 1971. *Presented by Ky. Assoc. of Highway Contractors.*
(Reverse)

EARLY TUNNEL IN KENTUCKY
Early transportation tunnel in Kentucky. It was hand bored by Lexington and Frankfort Railroad in 1849. First passenger train went through on February 23, 1850. Replaced incline, built 1835 just east of here, previously used by railroad to enter Frankfort. Incline built by Lexington & Ohio, the first railroad in Kentucky. *Presented by CSX Transportation.*

1956 AFRICAN AMERICAN ELKS
(Covington, 229 East 11th St., Kenton Co.)

Covington native Benjamin F. Howard (1860–1918) was co-founder, with Arthur J. Riggs of Shelbyville, of the first national African American Elks organization, called Improved Benevolent Protective Order of Elks of the World. Chartered in Ohio, 1899; Howard elected as first Grand Exalted Ruler. Covington's Ira Lodge No. 37 formed in early 1900s. *Presented by City of Covington and Kentucky African American Heritage Commission.*

1957 8TH OF AUGUST
(Paducah, Community Center, 505 S. 8th St., McCracken Co.)

Traditionally on August 8, African Americans assemble in Paducah to celebrate freedom and pay tribute to their roots. They gather annually for dances, ballgames, and picnics, as a family occasion and in a spirit of community remembrance. In some years people have come from as far away as St. Louis, Memphis, and Chicago. *Presented by Paducah-McCracken Co. Tourist Comm.*

1958 AFRICAN AMERICAN BUSINESS DISTRICT
(Danville, Constitution Sq., 2nd St. between Main & Walnut, Boyle Co.)

In this block a thriving African American business district stood for over 100 years. Restaurants, barber and beauty shops, medical and dental offices, and retail shops drew patrons from Boyle and nearby counties. Until razed by urban renewal in 1973, the district was a center of local African American social and economic life.
(Reverse)
DORIC LODGE NO. 18 (F. & A.M.-P.H.A.)
Danville's Doric Lodge No. 18 was founded 1888 as Boyle Association and moved to this site in 1920. For 50 years, the lodge was a cultural and social center of the African American community of Boyle County. Donations of $1,000 by each of ten members of the brotherhood secured a loan enabling construction of building in 1920. Over.

1959 EFFIE WALLER SMITH
(Pikeville, Hambley Blvd. at Police Dept., Pike Co.)

Born in Pike County, this poet was a daugh-

ter of former slaves, Frank and Sibbie Waller. All of their children attained a greater degree of education than usual at that time. They earned teaching certificates at Ky. State Normal School for Colored Persons (now Ky. State University) in Frankfort.
(Reverse)
EFFIE WALLER SMITH
In addition to being featured in major literary magazines, she published three poetry books: *Songs of the Months* (1904), *Rhymes from The Cumberland* (1909), and *Rosemary and Pansies* (1909). She married in 1909, was widowed in 1911, and moved to Wisconsin in 1918. Buried in Neenah, Wisconsin. Smith's last published poem, "Autumn's Winds," appeared in *Harper's Monthly*, 1917.

1960 ALICE ALLISON DUNNIGAN
1906-1983
(Russellville, at City Park, Logan Co.)

Born near Russellville, Logan Co., the granddaughter of slaves, Alice Dunnigan gained recognition as a journalist and civil rights leader. During an 18-year teaching career, she also wrote for African American newspapers and continued her education. Based in Washington, D.C., in 1940s, she reported on government at the highest levels.
(Reverse)
CIVIL RIGHTS ACTIVIST/AUTHOR
In 1948, Alice Dunnigan was first black reporter on campaign trail with a president—Truman. Under Presidents Kennedy and Johnson, she was member of President's Committee on Equal Opportunity. Author of: *A Black Woman's Experience—From Schoolhouse to White House* (1974) and *The Fascinating Story of Black Kentuckians: Their Heritage and Traditions* (1982). Over.

1961 LEXINGTON COLORED FAIR ASSOCIATION
(Lexington, 644 Georgetown St., Fayette Co.)

Started in 1869 by the Lexington Colored Agricultural and Mechanical Assoc., the annual fair promoted racial achievement and offered entertainment which attracted thousands from Ky. and beyond. When located on Georgetown Pike, the site had an exhi-

bition hall, amphitheatre, and racetrack.
(Reverse)
SUCCESSFUL ENTERPRISE
Though similar fairs were held statewide, Lexington's Colored Fair was most successful, lasting well into the 1930s. Fairs were as popular as Emancipation Day among the state's black citizens. Cash prizes were awarded winners in categories from livestock and racing to music and floral display. The fairs showed African American accomplishments since emancipation.

1962 ELISHA GREEN
RELIGIOUS LEADER
(Maysville, Forest Ave. at Bethel Baptist Church, Mason Co.)

Born into slavery in Bourbon County, Elisha Green grew up in Mason County at "Glen Alice" farm outside Maysville. He later purchased freedom for himself and part of his family. A spiritual leader, he helped form African American Baptist churches in Maysville and Paris, Ky., and preached to many congregations.
(Reverse)
ELISHA GREEN
RELIGIOUS LEADER
Believing freedmen needed to own land, Green and a white landowner founded African American community near Paris. Politically active, he was chosen a vice president of the Ky. Negro Republican Party at Lexington convention in 1867. He remained a dynamic force in Baptist churches in Maysville and Paris until his death in 1889. Over.

1963 COLORED ORPHAN INDUSTRIAL HOME
(Lexington, 644 Georgetown St., Fayette Co.)

Led by Mrs. E. Belle Mitchell Jackson, orphan home opened here 1894. Orphans and other black youth learned to read and write and acquired a trade; also refuge for elderly women. By 1909 home consisted of 18 acres and 2 brick houses. Burned in 1912. A new building dedicated 1913; serves as Robert H. Williams Cultural Center.

1964 CHARLES W. ANDERSON, JR.
1907–1960
(Louisville, 600 W. Jefferson St., in front of Hall of Justice, Jefferson Co.)

First African American elected to a southern state legislature in 20th century; six consecutive terms in Gen. Assembly, beginning in 1935. A Republican from Louisville, he sponsored repeal of Ky.'s public hanging law; funds for African Americans to attend graduate school outside Ky.; and employment of African Americans in government.
(Reverse)
CHARLES W. ANDERSON, JR.
Received Lincoln Institute Key (1940) for outstanding service to African Americans. Anderson served two terms as president of National Negro Bar Association, beginning in 1943. Assistant Commonwealth's Attorney for Jefferson Co., 1946. President Eisenhower appointed him to serve as an alternate U.S. Delegate to United Nations General Assembly in 1959. Over.

1965 CAMP NELSON REFUGEE CAMP
(Camp Nelson, New US 27 at Hall Rd., Jessamine Co.)

Established in 1863 to house families of African American soldiers, Camp Nelson became the chief center issuing emancipation papers to former slaves. Army's withdrawal from camp in 1866 exposed refugees to violence of white "regulators," who were opposed to presence of freed African Americans. See over.
(Reverse)
CONDITIONS AT REFUGEE CAMP
Many women and children died from disease and exposure to weather in make-shift camp. Brutal expulsion of refugees from camp in winter of 1864 was fatal to many. Only efforts by Rev. John G. Fee and other humanitarian workers improved conditions. A school, a hospital, and permanent housing later served up to 3,000 African Americans in their transition to freedom. Over.

1966 WBKY/WUKY
(McVey Hall, U.K. Campus, Lexington, Fayette Co.)

UK initiated radio broadcasting in 1929 in cooperation with WHAS radio in Louisville. Each weekday, live musical and educational programs were broadcast from the campus studios over WHAS. Later, WHAS and UK started radio "listening

centers" in eastern Ky. Battery-powered radios gave residents public access to educational programs. *Class of 1995.*
(Reverse)

WBKY/WUKY

In 1941, UK initiated radio broadcasting in Beattyville, Ky. WBKY broadcast educational programming for local residents. In 1944 UK established a radio station on the campus and WBKY began broadcasting from McVey Hall. Station call letters were changed from WBKY to WUKY in 1989. WBKY/WUKY is the oldest university-owned FM station in U.S. and Ky.'s first public radio station. *Class of 1995.*

1967 BEN LUCIEN BURMAN (1895–1984)
(Covington, Riverside Dr., Kenton Co.)

Born in Covington and inspired by the Ohio River, he became famed chronicler of life and people along America's rivers and in Kentucky's mountains. His 22 novels, fables, and works of nonfiction were widely translated. Burman's *Steamboat Round the Bend* (1933) became Will Rogers' last movie. See over. *Presented by Northern Kentucky Heritage League.*
(Reverse)

BEN LUCIEN BURMAN (1895–1984)

Hailed as "new Mark Twain" for his stories of river life, Burman also became "a second Aesop" with his "High Water at Catfish Bend" (1952) and six related fables of mythical animal folk. Awarded French Legion of Honor in 1946 for World War II reports from Africa. Roamed world as special writer for *Reader's Digest.* Over.

1968 SOLDIER'S RETREAT
(Nottingham Pkwy. & Seaton Springs, off Hurstbourne, Jefferson Co.)

Home of Colonel Richard C. Anderson 1750–1826, American Rev. patriot. Aide to Lafayette, wounded at siege of Trenton and Savannah, captured at Charleston, fought at Yorktown, where surrender of Lord Cornwallis to Washington in 1781 completed the Revolution. Married Elizabeth Clark, sister General George Rogers Clark. Second wife Sarah Marshall, cousin Chief Justice John Marshall. Over.
(Reverse)

SOLDIER'S RETREAT

Completed by Anderson in 1794, with massive walls of limestone over two feet thick, it was a refuge from possible Indian attack. Damaged by earthquake 1811 and lightning 1840, the homestead was later dismantled. Distinguished by 1983 listing on National Register Historic Places, Soldier's Retreat reconstructed by L. Leroy Highbaugh, Jr. *Presented by City of Hurstbourne.*

1969 CONGRESSMEN REPRESENTING FIRST DISTRICT WHICH INCLUDED JACKSON PURCHASE, 1819–1995
(2350 Jefferson St., Paducah, McCracken Co.)

In 1792, Kentucky separated from Virginia and became fifteenth state in the Union. It was not until 1818 that Indian lands west of Tennessee River were bought from the Chickasaws and named the Jackson Purchase.

Name	Party	Years
Alney McLean	Independent	1819–1821
Anthony New	Dem.-Rep.	1821–1823
Robert P. Henry	Dem.-Rep.	1823–1826
John F. Henry	Dem.-Rep.	1826–1827
Chittenden Lyon	Democrat	1827–1835
Linn Boyd	Democrat	1835–1837
John L. Murray	Democrat	1837–1839
Linn Boyd	Democrat	1839–1855

Presented by Paducah-McCracken County Convention and Visitors Bureau.
(Reverse)

CONGRESSMEN REPRESENTING FIRST DISTRICT WHICH INCLUDED JACKSON PURCHASE, 1819–1995

Name	Party	Years
Henry C. Burnett	Democrat	1855–1861
Samuel L. Casey	Republican	1862–1863
Lucian Anderson	Unionist	1863–1865
Lawrence Trimble	Democrat	1865–1871
Edward Crossland	Democrat	1871–1875
Andrew R. Boone	Democrat	1875–1879
Oscar Turner	Democrat	1879–1885
William J. Stone	Democrat	1885–1895
John K. Hendrick	Democrat	1895–1897
Charles K. Wheeler	Democrat	1897–1903
Ollie M. James	Democrat	1903–1913
Alben W. Barkley	Democrat	1913–1927
William V. Gregory	Democrat	1927–1936
Noble J. Gregory	Democrat	1937–1959
Frank Stubblefield	Democrat	1959–1974

Carroll Hubbard	Democrat	1975–1993
Tom Barlow	Democrat	1993–1995
Ed Whitfield	Republican	1995

Presented by Paducah-McCracken County Convention and Visitors Bureau.

1970 ANNA MAC CLARKE (1919–44)
(Courthouse lawn, Lawrenceburg, Anderson County)

This Lawrenceburg native was one of the first black women in Ky. to enlist during World War II. She joined Women's Army Auxiliary Corps in 1942, and was commissioned a 1st Lieutenant the next year in newly named Women's Army Corps. While stationed at Douglas Air Field, Arizona, she led fight to desegregate base theater. *Presented by Ky. African American Heritage Commission.*
(Reverse)
ANNA MAC CLARKE (1919–44)
A 1937 graduate of Lawrenceburg's Colored High School, Clarke earned B.A. from Ky. State College. After army enlistment, she became only African American in 15th Officer Training Class at Ft. Des Moines, Iowa. In 1943, she was first black WAAC assigned to duty with an all-white company as platoon commander (4th Co., 3rd Regt.). Buried Woodlawn Hills Cem., Stringtown.

1971 PARTISAN RANGERS
(Hanson, City Park, Sunset Rd., KY 260 W., Hopkins Co.)

Civil War Confederate irregular troops operated in western Ky. These Partisan Rangers, under Brig. Gen. Adam R. Johnson, fought skirmishes and disrupted Union communications and supply lines. Among Hopkins Countians serving were 2 brothers from Hanson—James Waller, who was killed, and J.S., who later urged reconciliation. *Presented by Citizens for Historic Preservation.*

1972 UNITED METHODIST TEMPLE
(Russellville, 395 S. Main St., Logan Co.)

Began 1808 as Methodist Society in home of Mr. and Mrs. Josiah Emmit with ten charter members. Bibb, Caldwell, Morton, and Barclay among first families. Early minister H. H. Kavanaugh became a noted bishop. First church was built ca. 1819 at site of Russellville Middle School. Present

church completed, 1854; A.M.E. Zion Church formed, 1872. The temple was remodeled in 1917.
(Reverse)
UNITED METHODIST TEMPLE
Church became known as a temple after a news story praised its windows during 1917 renovation. Its first pipe organ was provided by matching funds from Andrew Carnegie. Here, on Christian Heritage Day 1965, Logan Countians honored the memory of John Littlejohn and other circuit riders of all faiths. Over. *Presented by Rena Milliken.*

1973 GREENUP ASSOCIATION OF BAPTISTS
(Site of Palmyra Settlement, approx. 6 mi. from Greenup, KY 207, Greenup Co.)

In the log meeting house of Palmyra Baptist Church, once located near here, Greenup Assoc. was formed in 1841. John Young (1764–1855), early settler on Little Sandy River and Palmyra's pastor, enlisted two other churches from across Ohio River to form association. By 1991, its sesquicentennial year, original three churches had grown to fifty. *Presented by Greenup Assoc. of Baptist Churches.*

1974 "NEIGHBORHOOD HOUSE"
(Louisville, 428 S. First St., Jefferson Co.)

Begun in 1896 as first settlement house in Kentucky. The founders wanted to improve the lives of immigrants and urban residents by offering English and citizenship classes, job skills, public baths, kindergarten, and a playground. Mary Belknap donated Neighborhood House's first permanent site here, 1902. In 1996 this area park was renamed Settlement House Park.
(Reverse)
SETTLEMENT HOUSES
Before cities addressed issues such as child labor and housing, settlement houses were started by citizens to provide some relief. Neighborhood House and its sister agencies (Cabbage Patch, Louisville Central, Presbyterian Community Center, and Wesley House) still serve Louisville's urban families with cultural and educational services.

1975 JOHN SHARPE (1780–1856)
(8 mi. NE of Williamsburg off KY 26 on Jacks Ford Rd., Whitley Co.)

A veteran of the War of 1812, John Sharpe came to this area, then Knox Co., ca. 1817. After service on first Whitley Co. Court, he became first state representative in 1820. Great-grandson, Clifford M. Sharpe, served as state rep. from this district, 1970–1976. This land has been in family since 1822, when John Sharpe obtained a land grant. *Presented by Descendants of John Sharpe.*

1976 THE FILSON CLUB HISTORICAL SOCIETY
(Louisville, 1310 S. Third St., Jefferson Co.)

Founded in 1884 and named for John Filson (1753–88), Kentucky's first historian, this institution collects, preserves, and publishes historical material pertaining to Ky. and adjoining states. The collections of books, manuscripts, art, photographs, and artifacts are available to everyone. Over.
(Reverse)

THE FERGUSON RESIDENCE

At the time the most expensive home in Louisville, the residence was built for businessman Edwin Hite Ferguson (1852–1924) between 1902 and 1905 and is the finest example of residential Beaux Arts architecture in the city. In 1986 it became the headquarters for The Filson Club Historical Society.

1977 CLEANTH BROOKS (1906–94)
(Faculty Hall, Murray State University Campus, 16th St., Calloway Co.)

Murray native Cleanth Brooks became a major figure in the teaching and study of literature. With fellow Kentuckian Robert Penn Warren, he co-founded the *Southern Review* and directed attention to close reading of literature–the "New Criticism"–through the influential texts *Understanding Poetry* and *Understanding Fiction.*
(Reverse)

CLEANTH BROOKS (1906–94)

An acclaimed critic, Brooks wrote *Modern Poetry and the Tradition, The Well Wrought Urn,* and studies of William Faulkner's novels. A Rhodes Scholar 1929–32, educated at Vanderbilt and Tulane, he also received many honorary degrees. He taught at Loui-

siana State 1932–47 and at Yale 1947–75. *Presented by citizens of Murray and professional colleagues.*

1978 E.K. RAILWAY
(Argillite, KY 1 & 207, Greenup Co.)

Development of this area's rich coal, iron, and timber resources began 1867 when Eastern Kentucky Railway laid track from Ohio River to Argillite. But after years of operating losses, the railroad went into receivership in 1919, and the work of dismantling north end of track began in 1928. Total trackage was thirty-six miles. *Presented by E. K. Railway Historical Society and Greenup County Fiscal Court.*

1979 WHITE OAK POND CHURCH
(Richmond, 1238 Barnes Mill Rd., Madison Co.)

Original log church built here by 1790 became worship and community center for settlement of Milford, first county seat. Named for early minister J. R. Pond, church joined Tates Creek Baptist Assoc. in 1802. In the Civil War, J. R. Pond's nephew, Lt. Col. John Griffin Pond, fought for the Union, then later led forces against Ku Klux Klan. *Presented by C.Y.F. Youth in memory of Bill Whitaker, Jr.*
(Reverse)

WHITE OAK POND CHURCH

In 1827, county's first temperance society began here, where Nancy Irvine delivered first temperance talk for women in Kentucky and perhaps America. White Oak Pond and others joined Christian Church (Disciples of Christ) revival movement, 1830. In 1869, log church was disassembled and its hand-hewn timbers used to build present Greek Revival structure.

1980 SHAW'S STATION
(Leitchfield, Shaw's Station Rd., Grayson Co.)

Named for Benham (Bonum) Shaw, this pioneer settlement (today's Leitchfield) was located at the headwaters of Beaver Dam Creek. This station was a stop along the important trail which ran from settlements at Nashville, Tenn., northward to Louisville, Ky. Shaw was pioneer to Severns Valley, ca. 1779. A creek in present-day Elizabethtown also bears his name.

(Reverse)
BEAVER DAM CREEK BAPTIST CHURCH
Now known as First Baptist Church of Leitchfield, Beaver Dam Creek Baptist Church was constituted May 29, 1804; became member of Salem Assoc. Later joined Goshen Assoc. upon its formation in 1817. Pioneer Benham Shaw was deacon at Beaver Dam Creek Baptist Church. *Presented by First Baptist Church and Grayson County Tourism Commission.*

1981 FARMERSVILLE SCHOOL
(Farmersville, just off KY 139, 104 Enon Rd., Caldwell Co.)
First school in Farmersville began here in 1844, when Floyd Nash, age 24, commenced teaching "sixteen schollars" in a log structure at Donaldson Baptist Church. Classes held in various buildings until March 1943, when fire destroyed Farmersville School. Students then transferred to Fredonia. *Presented by Alumni of Farmersville School.*
(Reverse)
FARMERSVILLE SCHOOL
In 1838, William Asherst gave land to Donaldson Church; site later became permanent location for school. With Miss Ercel Egbert as the principal, Farmersville in 1922–23 became 4-year high school. Enrollment stood at 256 when fire in 1943 ended the Farmersville School, which had trained generations of community leaders. *Presented by Alumni of Farmersville School.*

1982 BERRYTOWN
(Berrytown, Haefer Ln. & LaGrange Rd., Jefferson Co.)
This eastern Jefferson County community began with five acres purchased in 1874 by Alfred Berry, a freedman. Other Berrytown founders were Wm. Butler, Sallie Carter, and Kidd Williams, all of whom bought land from Samuel L. Nock, a wealthy businessman. *Presented by Louisville and Jefferson County African American Heritage Committee, Inc.*
(Reverse)
BERRYTOWN
In the 1870s, Berrytown and Griffytown were created by freed African Americans. In 1915 Anchorage PTA got a train carrying the Liberty Bell to stop at neighboring

schools, including Berrytown and Griffytown. Until 1934, the Interurban Car System electric trolley transported residents into Louisville. *Presented by Louisville and Jefferson County African American Heritage Committee, Inc.*

1983 GRIFFYTOWN
(Griffytown, 401 Old Harrods Creek Rd., Jefferson Co.)
The Louisville and Frankfort Shortline railroad, which arrived in eastern Jefferson County through Hobbs Station (now Anchorage) in 1848, created a cluster of communities which would be known as Anchorage, Berrytown, and Griffytown. *Presented by Louisville and Jefferson County African American Heritage Committee, Inc.*
(Reverse)
GRIFFYTOWN
Local tradition holds that, in 1879, freedman Dan Griffith bought the cabin of early Middletown settler Minor White from his family. He moved the cabin to Old Harrod's Creek Road, founding the settlement known today as Griffytown (originally spelled Griffeytown). Cabin burned, 1956. *Presented by Louisville and Jefferson County African American Heritage Committee, Inc.*

1984 ALBERT B. "HAPPY" CHANDLER
(Park Field, Adkinson Park, off Elm St., Henderson, Henderson Co.)
This Henderson Co. native (1898–1991) was state sen. and lt. gov. before becoming governor in 1935 and 1955. U.S. sen., 1939–45. As baseball commissioner, he approved contract making Jackie Robinson first modern black major league player, 1947. Chandler elected to Baseball Hall of Fame, 1982. *Presented by Henderson World Series Association, Inc.*
(Reverse)
ALBERT BENJAMIN CHANDLER
This colorful orator and two-term governor was born near Corydon, Ky. As governor, Chandler was driving force behind establishment of Univ. of Ky. Medical Center, later named in his honor. Buried at Pisgah Presbyterian Church, Versailles. Park Field in Henderson was site of the 1996 Bambino World Series dedicated to "Happy" Chandler. *Presented by Henderson World Series Association, Inc.*

1985 SMOKETOWN
(Smoketown, Hancock St. & E. Broadway, Jefferson Co.)

This historically black community began to flourish following end of slavery in 1865, when thousands of African Americans moved to Louisville. Shotgun-type houses on closely spaced streets and alleys allowed both black and white landowners to profit from the dense settlement. Washington Spradling, Jr., a prominent African American, owned vast real estate in area.
(Reverse)

HISTORIC AREA
Many in Smoketown worked in tobacco warehouses as cutters, processors, and haulers. Community had one of city's first African American public schools, founded 1874. Smoketown is only post-Civil War neighborhood settled mainly by African Americans that remains in city of Louisville. *Presented by Louisville and Jefferson County African American Heritage Committee, Inc.*

1986 LABROT & GRAHAM DISTILLERY
(Versailles, 7855 McCracken Pike, Woodford Co.)

One of Kentucky's oldest working distilleries was built on Grassy Springs Branch of Glenn's Creek by Elijah Pepper about 1812. His son, Oscar Pepper, later hired Dr. James Crow as master distiller. Crow perfected the art of bourbon making by introducing scientific methods. The Labrot & Graham Distillery succeeded Old Pepper's in 1878. *Presented by Brown-Forman Corp.*

1987 LABROT & GRAHAM DISTILLERY
(Versailles, Jct. US 60 & Grassy Spring Road, Woodford Co.)

One of Kentucky's oldest working distilleries was built on Grassy Springs Branch of Glenn's Creek by Elijah Pepper about 1812. His son, Oscar Pepper, later hired Dr. James Crow as master distiller. Crow perfected the art of bourbon making by introducing scientific methods. The Labrot & Graham Distillery succeeded Old Pepper's in 1878. *Presented by Brown-Forman Corp.*

1988 PETERSBURG
(Petersburg/Newburg Community, Indian Trail & Petersburg Rd., Jefferson Co.)

Named Petersburg after freedman Peter Laws built log cabin in area after Civil War.

Oral tradition holds that freed slave Eliza Curtis Hundley Tevis farmed here from about 1820. She and her husband bought 40 acres at Indian Trail and (now) Petersburg Rd., 1851. As a land and slave owner, Tevis prospered and became a strong religious influence in the community. Over.
(Reverse)

NEWBURG
Newburg ("new town" in German) was settled in 1830s by four German immigrant families. Located near Poplar Level and Shepherdsville Roads, it became a coach stop to Louisville in 19th century. It had a post office, hotel, shops, and homes. Descendants of freed slaves remain in the area today. *Presented by Louisville and Jefferson County African American Heritage Committee, Inc.*

1989 SLAVERY LAWS IN OLD KENTUCKY
(Louisville, First St., between Market & Jefferson Sts., Jefferson Co.)

Ky.'s 1792 Constitution continued legalized enslavement of blacks in the new state; 1800 tax lists show 40,000 slaves. U.S. banned African slave trade in 1808 but selling of men, women and children in South continued. By 1830, blacks made up 24% of Ky. population. Kentucky Nonimportation Act of 1833 halted the transfer of blacks for resale. *Presented by Louisville and Jefferson County African American Heritage Committee, Inc.*
(Reverse)

SITE OF ARTERBURN BROTHERS SLAVE PENS
After Kentucky's Nonimportation Act repealed in 1849, Louisville slave markets expanded. The Arterburns advertised cash for farm hands and others. Iron-barred coops held people to be shipped south. Chained, they marched up Main Street to board boats in nearby Portland. Some died of shock or disease on the trip south.

1990 SLAVE TRADING IN LOUISVILLE
(Louisville, S.E. corner of 2nd & Main, Jefferson Co.)

By the 1850s, Kentucky was annually exporting between 2500 and 4000 of its slaves down river to the large plantations farther south. To prevent runaways, traders operating near the Ohio River kept slaves shackled together in pens when not being

displayed to buyers. Slave traders were often social outcasts avoided by all but fellow traders.
(Reverse)

GARRISON SLAVE PEN SITE

Matthew Garrison was a well known Kentucky slave speculator in the Deep South. A white abolitionist leader, Rev. Calvin Fairbank, wrote in 1851 that four slave markets, including Garrison's and Arterburn's, sold men, women, and children "like sheep." Slavery abolished by 13th Amendment, 1865. *Presented by Louisville and Jefferson County African American Heritage Committee, Inc.*

1991 FOUNDING OF MORGAN COUNTY

(West Liberty, Old Mill Park, Riverside Dr., US 460 & KY 7, Morgan Co.)

Edmund Wells (1777–1846) settled here (then Floyd Co.) about 1814, operating a mill, ferry, and tavern. First meeting of Morgan County Court held at his home March 10, 1823, as directed by Ky. legislature. He provided land for co. seat, West Liberty; built first jail and courthouse; and served as justice of peace, sheriff, and county's second state legislator.
(Reverse)

THE OLD MILL

Edmund Wells completed his grist mill here in 1816. Early roads connected Wells Mill (as first settlement was called) to Blaine in Lawrence County and other points in this county. The mill remained a central landmark beyond Wells' ownership (sold ca. 1838). *Presented by Morgan County Historical Society.*

1992 LOUISVILLE CEMETERY

(Eastern Pkwy. at Poplar Level Rd., property owned by Louisville Cem., Jefferson Co.)

Original 31 acres incorporated Mar. 23, 1886, by prominent black citizens Bishop W. H. Miles, H. C. Weeden, J. Meriwether, A. J. Bibb, W. P. Churchill, William H. Gibson, Sr., and Felix Johnson. Buried here are Dr. Robert B. Scott, cofounder of Louisville Red Cross Hospital; educator Atwood S. Wilson; blues guitarist Sylvester Weaver; and community activist Bessie Allen.

(Reverse)
WILLIAM WALKER, SR. (1860-1933)

Born a slave in Woodford County, jockey William "Uncle Bill" Walker won 1877 Kentucky Derby on Baden-Baden. Churchill Downs' leading rider between 1875 and 1878, he retired from saddle in 1896. An expert on Thoroughbred pedigree in America, Walker was instrumental in developing modern racehorse. *Presented by Louisville and Jefferson County African American Heritage Committee, Inc.*

1993 PELLVILLE

(Pellville, KY 144, near Jct. KY 2181, Hancock Co.)

Settlement of Pellville, originally called Bucksnort, began on the Hardinsburg-Owensboro Trail. The first post office established 1851 under name of Blackford, changed to Pellville 1868 in honor of Samuel P. Pell, state legislator (1855–1856) and Hancock County sheriff (1850–1864). Pellville incorporated February 25, 1870. *Presented by Hancock County Fiscal Court.*

1994 JAMES GUTHRIE (1792-1869)

(Louisville, 4th & Guthrie, Jefferson Co.)

This statesman and entrepreneur fostered Louisville's growth from small town in 1810 to nation's 10th largest city in 1850. Promoted building of Portland Canal and the first R.R. bridge over Ohio River. As president of the University of Louisville, he established its Medical College and Academic Dept. *Presented by Clan Guthrie–USA.*
(Reverse)
JAMES GUTHRIE (1792-1869)

Guthrie served in the state legislature, 1827–40. In 1849 he presided over the third Kentucky Constitutional Convention. Pres. Franklin Pierce named him Secretary of U.S. Treasury, 1853–57. As president of L & N Railroad, 1860 to 1868, he was instrumental in keeping Ky. in Union during Civil War. He was U.S. senator, 1865–68. *Presented by Clan Guthrie–USA.*

1995 JOSEPH ALEXANDER MATTHEWS (1902-1970)

(Benham, Main St., near Ky. Coal Mining Museum, KY 160, Harlan Co.)

Principal of the East Benham High School,

1934-60. Matthews taught math and coached ball teams. The students were children of employees of Wisconsin Steel Coal Company. Joseph Matthews and his wife Ruth were leaders in black community and bought food, clothes, and supplies for the needy. *Presented by Students, Faculty, and Friends and the Ky. African American Heritage Commission.*

1996 CITY OF AUDUBON PARK
(Main entrance to Audubon Park, 3100 Preston Highway, KY 61, Jefferson Co.)

The city was built on land granted to Col. William Preston in 1773 for service in French and Indian War. Its residential development (1912-45) proceeded from Audubon Country Club's incorporation, 1908. Credit is given to James L. Smyser of Audubon Realty Co. as "Father of Audubon Park" for his vision and promotion of this area. *Presented by City of Audubon Park.*
(Reverse)
A NATURAL GARDEN SPOT
To give Audubon Park the best features of both country and city life, N. Y. developer Clifford B. Harmon was hired. Naming of the park after naturalist John James Audubon reflected Back-to-Nature Movement in land use of early 20th century. Its shaded streets with planned green spaces, fresh air, and high ground made the park a place of permanent recreation.

1997 RUFF MEMORIAL WHEELMEN'S BENCH
(Wayside Park, Third St. & Southern Pkwy., Louisville, Jefferson Co.)
Erected 1897 by Ky. Div. of League of American Wheelmen to honor cycling pioneer A. D. Ruff (1827-96) of Owingsville, Ky. The League's oldest member, he had bicycled to Yellowstone National Park in 1893. Marble fountain and stone bench, known to generations of cyclists as "Wheelmen's Bench," designed by famed sculptor Enid Yandell.
(Reverse)
CYCLE CARNIVAL, 1897
On October 8, 1897, a parade of 10,000 cyclists passed here to celebrate a new cinder bicycling path along Southern Parkway.

Viewed by 50,000 spectators, parade began at Third and Broadway and ended at Iroquois Cycle Club. Many cyclists were in costume; ladies wore bloomers. Bugles and cannon fire marked the parade's progress. *Presented by The Louisville Bicycle Club – 1997.*

1998 HOME OF I. WILLIS COLE
(Louisville, 2217 West Muhammad Ali, Jefferson Co.)

Louisville pioneer in civil rights movement, Cole fought against segregation in public parks and on street cars. Ran for state senate on Lincoln Party ticket in 1922. Black votes provided necessary margin to get 19 bond issues passed which financed founding of Madison and Jackson Junior High Schools and Louisville Municipal College. *Presented by Louisville and Jefferson County African American Heritage Committee, Inc.*
(Reverse)
I. WILLIS COLE, 1887-1950
Militant editor and sole owner of *The Louisville Leader* and I. Willis Cole Publishing Co. (1917-1950). A race paper boasting, "We print your news, we employ your people, we champion your cause." Cole wielded power of the press to combat racism. A noted business and civic leader, devout churchman, and inductee of the National Negro Press Hall of Fame.

1999 BUENA VISTA
(Site of Todd summer home, US 421, Franklin Co.)

One-half mile south is site of two-story frame house best known as the summer residence of Robert S. Todd (1791-1849), father of first lady Mary Todd Lincoln. The large family took refuge here from the heat and cholera of summertime in Lexington. As a child, Mary Todd Lincoln spent many summers here. *Presented by Cliff and Joan Howard.*
(Reverse)
TODD HOUSE
Mary Todd Lincoln later brought her own sons on visits to her stepmother Elizabeth Humphreys. Sometimes the future president, Abraham Lincoln, was able to join them, traveling by rail to nearby Duckers Station. The house was razed in 1947. Only a remnant of stone spring house remains.

Over. *Presented by Todd and Lincoln Friends.*

2000 WILLIAM L. GRANT
(Covington, 824 Greenup St., Kenton Co.)

Wm. Grant (1820-82), Covington city clerk, councilman, and state rep., supported public education for black children. He deeded land on Seventh Street for elementary school, which opened 1880; renamed Lincoln School 1909. A black high school named in honor of William Grant opened in 1886. *Presented by City of Covington.*
(Reverse)

LINCOLN AND GRANT SCHOOLS

In 1931, this building constructed for black elementary and high schools to be known as Lincoln Grant and William Grant Schools. High school closed in 1965 and elementary in 1976. The original Seventh Street site occupied by the Board of Education; Northern Kentucky Community Center housed here beginning 1976. *Presented by Kenton County Fiscal Court.*

2001 WILLIAMSBURG/ORANGEBURG
(Orangeburg, Main St., KY 1234 & 1449, Mason Co.)

Established as Williamsburg, 1796. Named for John Williams, co-founder with Moses Bennett and Harry Parker. Village located on Stone Lick Creek, along Cabin Creek War Road, a main path into central Ky. for early pioneers. Name changed to Orangeburg in 1836, to honor a leading citizen, Providence Orange Pickering; town incorporated, 1860. *Presented by Mason County Fiscal Court.*

2002 CCC AT CUMBERLAND FALLS
(Corbin, Cumberland Falls, Whitley Co.)

Some 80,000 Kentuckians served in Civilian Conservation Corps. Three camps located in area (Companies 509, 563, and 1578). All helped develop Cumberland Falls State Park, blazing foot trails, drawing maps, and erecting cabins. Men also built DuPont Lodge; original log structure had 26 rooms, kitchen, and dining room. Lodge and cabins dedicated and given to Ky., 1934.
(Reverse)

CIVILIAN CONSERVATION CORPS

Roosevelt's New Deal included Civilian Conservation Corps (CCC). Begun in 1933, the Corps employed men throughout U.S. building roads and dams, and planting trees for flood control. Jobless boys ages 18-25 received 3 meals a day and usually $30.00 a month (most of which went to dependents). By 1941, 2 million youths had participated. *Presented by NACCCA, Kentucky Chapter 67.*

2003 FORKS OF ELKHORN BAPTIST CHURCH
(Ducker Station Rd. & US 421 South, Franklin Co.)

Constituted in June 1788, with Wm. Hickman its founder and first pastor. Land obtained and frame meeting house built, 1795, near present brick church, constructed 1945. A Virginian, Hickman visited Ky., 1776, and began preaching; returned to Ky. in 1784. Minister to Forks of Elkhorn almost 40 yrs. Reinterred Frankfort Cem., 1916. *Presented by church family of 1998.*

2004 THOMAS MERTON (1915-68)
(Louisville, 461 Fourth Ave., Jefferson Co.)

Trappist monk, poet, social critic, and spiritual writer. Born in Prades, France. After education at Cambridge and Columbia Univ., he entered Abbey of Gethsemani, Trappist, Ky., 1941; ordained as priest, 1949. His autobiography, *The Seven Storey Mountain* (1948), earned international acclaim. He is buried in abbey cemetery. *Presented by Thomas Merton Center Foundation.*
(Reverse)

A REVELATION

Merton had a sudden insight at this corner Mar. 18, 1958, that led him to redefine his monastic identity with greater involvement in social justice issues. He was "suddenly overwhelmed with the realization that I loved all these people...." He found them "walking around shining like the sun." *Conjectures of a Guilty Bystander. Presented by Thomas Merton Center Foundation.*

2005 JACOBS HALL
(Danville, School for the Deaf campus, S. Second St., Boyle Co.)

Kentucky School for the Deaf first opened 1823 in Danville, at 4th and Main Sts. In 1826, it moved to this campus. Jacobs Hall

is oldest surviving building, constructed 1855-57, of Italianate design by architect Thomas Lewinski. Its interior is marked by a main hall with curving staircase and four-story atrium open to the cupola. Exterior remains unchanged.
(Reverse)

JOHN A. JACOBS, SR. (1806-69)
KSD's first trained teacher, principal, third superintendent, 1825-1869. A Centre College student, he was sent in 1824 to Hartford, Conn., for training under T.H. Gallaudet and Laurent Clerc, pioneers of deaf education in America. He introduced Methodical Signs here and authored texts for deaf students.

2006 LOUIS D. BRANDEIS (1856-1941)
(Louisville, U of L, Belknap Campus, Wilson Wyatt Hall, off 3rd St., Jefferson Co.)

At this site rest cremated remains of U.S. Supreme Court Justice Louis Brandeis, who served on the Court from 1916-39. His support for the Law School, now named in his honor, is best shown by gift of his papers, which include more than 250,000 items. He is famous for cross-disciplinary "Brandeis brief" method of arguing socially significant cases. *U of L Bicentennial Committee.*
(Reverse)

LOUIS D. BRANDEIS (1856–1941)
Brandeis is also remembered for his early commitment to donated legal services, an area in which this school has been a leader. Brandeis was an opponent of the growing "bigness" of American institutions. He also wrote that "the right to be let alone" is fundamental. Remains of his wife, Alice Goldmark Brandeis, were placed here in 1945. *U of L Bicentennial Committee.*

2007 FOUNDING OF JEFFERSON SEMINARY
(Louisville, U of L, Belknap Campus, near Grawemeyer Hall, off 3rd St., Jefferson Co.)

April 3, 1798, is the university's symbolic founding date. On this date, eight Louisvillians pledged financial support for a new school. The 1798 benefactors were: William Croghan, Alexander S. Bullitt, James Meriwether, John Thruston, Henry Churchill, Richard Anderson, William Taylor, and John Thompson. *U of L Bicentennial Committee.*
(Reverse)

FOUNDING OF JEFFERSON SEMINARY
From this commitment to higher education came Jefferson Seminary, which evolved into University of Louisville. The Louisville Medical Institute opened 1837; merged in 1846 with Louisville College, an outgrowth of Jefferson Seminary. A law school was added, and the new entity named the University of Louisville in 1846. *U of L Bicentennial Committee.*

2008 CHARLES H. PARRISH, JR. (1899-1989)
(Louisville, U of L, Belknap Campus, Parrish Ct., Jefferson Co.)

In 1950-51 University of Louisville campus was integrated. One African American professor came from Louisville Municipal College, where only blacks had previously been enrolled. Charles H. Parrish, Jr., a noted sociologist and a lifelong civil rights activist, became the first black professor at a white southern school. *U of L Bicentennial Committee.*
(Reverse)

CHARLES H. PARRISH, JR.
In 1959 Parrish became first black department head at U of L, chairing the sociology department. He studied under the noted American sociologist George Herbert Meade at the University of Chicago. His work as an activist yielded friendships with many Civil Rights era luminaries. This place of gathering is named in his honor. *U of L Bicentennial Committee.*

2009 SCOVELL HALL
(Lexington, U of K, Scovell Hall, Fayette Co.)

Named for M.A. Scovell in 1913, this building was opened in 1905, with major additions in 1913 and 1937. Utilizing a colonial design, it was the largest building on campus for many years. Served until mid-1990s as a center of agricultural research, extension programs, and academic activities. *Class of 1998.*
(Reverse)

M.A. SCOVELL (1855-1912)
Melville Amasa Scovell, Ph.D., was named first director of the Experiment Station in

1885 and the first dean and director of the College of Agriculture in 1910. During his tenure, staff increased from 3 to 60, the number of departments grew from 2 to 11, and the agricultural farm expanded from 48.5 to 240 acres. *Class of 1998.*

2010 DANIEL R. MERRITT (1833-1907)
(Mayfield, Exchange Bank, S. 6th and E. Water Streets, KY 121, Graves Co.)

This Graves County businessman was founder and first president of Merit Clothing Co. (1899), located in brick building across Sixth St. Also organized Mayfield Exchange Bank, 1899. Was Confederate surgeon (1861-65) in 3rd and 7th Ky. Inf. Regts. Born in Todd Co., he had outstanding medical and business career. *Presented by Mrs. Ruth Merritt, Exchange Bank, and City of Mayfield.*

2011 SARAH BLANDING
(Lexington, U of K, Blanding Tower, Fayette Co.)

A 1923 U.K. graduate, Blanding (1898-1985) was President of Kappa Kappa Gamma sorority and Captain of the women's basketball team. After two years as Acting Dean, Blanding was named U.K. Dean of Women in 1925. She also taught political science. *Class of 1997.*
(Reverse)
SARAH BLANDING
Blanding left U.K. in 1941 to become Dean of the School of Home Economics at Cornell University. In 1946 she became Vassar College's first woman president, a position she held until 1964. In 1968 Blanding Tower was named in her honor. *Class of 1997.*

2012 GILLIS BUILDING 1889
(Lexington, U of K, between Gillis & Administration Buildings, Fayette Co.)

Erected in 1889 as U.K.'s first Agricultural Experiment Station; now second oldest building on the campus. Destroyed by fire in 1891, it was rebuilt on the same site. Named for Ezra Gillis (1867-1958) who joined the U.K. faculty in 1907 and served as Registrar from 1910 to 1937. *Class of 1996.*
(Reverse)
GILLIS BUILDING 1889

Home to the Chemistry Department (1905) and the College of Law (1925). In 1939 it became the Student Health Service and Infirmary, complete with 40 beds and medical services for students. Beginning in 1962 this structure housed offices of Admissions (1962-86) and Registrar (1962-91). *Class of 1996.*

2013 PFC WILLIAM B. BAUGH, USMC
(Hustonville, 1 mi. SW of McKinney at Area Reserve Squad, 3305 Highway 198, Lincoln Co.)

This Congressional Medal of Honor recipient born near here July 7, 1930. Baugh served with Co. G, 3rd Battalion, First Marines, First Marine Div. (Reinforced). Awarded honor posthumously for gallantry at risk of his life to spare others serious injury en route from Koto-ri to Hagaru-ri, Korea. *Presented by Ky. Marine Corps League, Ky. Chap. of First Marine Div. Assoc., and Ky. Council of Navy League.*
(Reverse)
MEDAL OF HONOR WINNER
Baugh was serving as a member of an Anti-Tank Assault Squad during a nighttime enemy attack on a motorized column, when a hostile grenade landed in his truck. He shouted a warning to other Marines in the vehicle and hurled himself upon the deadly missile, saving his comrades from injury or death. Gave supreme sacrifice Nov. 29, 1950. *Presented by Ky. Marine Corps League, Ky. Chap. of First Marine Div. Assoc., and Ky. Council of Navy League.*

2014 CLAY-BULLOCK HOUSE
(Covington, 528 Greenup St., Kenton Co.)

This two-story frame house was built in 1839 by John W. Clayton. The original exterior is of shingle siding, though the house has been subject to alterations in both 19th and 20th centuries. During the Civil War, Clayton's daughter, Mary C. Bullock, ran a private school here attended by Frederick Grant, son of Gen. Ulysses S. Grant. *Presented by City of Covington & Oakley Farris.*

2015 EARLY IRON WORKS
(Clay City, 4541 Main St., at Red River Museum, KY 15, Powell Co.)

Though there is evidence of iron production in area even earlier, land was bought for this purpose, 1805, by Robert Clark Jr. and Wm. Smith. Known as Clark & Smith's Iron Works, 1805-1808. A blast furnace called Red River Iron Works operated here from 1808 to 1830. Rebuilt as Estill Steam Furnace on another site; closed in 1869. *Presented by Red River Hist. Soc. with ISTEA Funds.*
(Reverse)

CLAY CITY TIMBER INDUSTRY

With Kentucky Union Railway Company's track laid in Powell Co. in 1886, the area's timber industry expanded. Red River Lumber Mills (1880) became largest steam-powered sawmill in Ky. In 1890, the steady run began at one of America's largest timber processing plants. A 1906 mill fire and deforestation of area's timber led to the end of "boom days" in Clay City.

2016 FRIENDSHIP BAPTIST CHURCH
(KY 323, approx. 4 mi. W. of KY 210, Taylor Co.)

One of Taylor Co.'s oldest churches was admitted to Russell Creek Assoc. in 1807 under name of Sand Lick Meeting House. On Sept. 17, 1815, pioneer missionary Luther Rice preached here and collected the first offering for foreign missions in the Russell Creek Assoc. The church name changed to Friendship Baptist by 1815. *Presented by Friendship Baptist Church.*
(Reverse)

SAND LICK MEETING HOUSE

In 1837 the two acres on which Sand Lick Meeting House stood were deeded to the church by Brig. Gen. Elias Barbee (1763-1843), one of its charter members. This site was across Friendship Rd. from current building. Gen. Barbee also served in Ky. House and Sen.; introduced bill to establish present Kentucky School for the Deaf in Danville. *Presented by Friendship Baptist Church.*

2017 RUSSELL NEIGHBORHOOD
(21ˢᵗ & Chestnut, SW corner, Louisville, Jefferson Co.)

Named, 1926, for Harvey C. Russell, Sr. (1883-1949), prominent African American educator. Boundaries extend from 9th to 31st, between Broadway and Market Sts.

For generations, Russell neighborhood was the center of African American business and professional and social life around Louisville. *Presented by African American Heritage Foundation.*
(Reverse)

RUSSELL NEIGHBORHOOD

By the 1830s, free blacks began buying property west of 9th St. African Americans began moving west of 21st St. after World War I. Predominantly black by the 1930s, Russell includes a large number of Victorian mansions, antebellum churches, Western Branch Library, businesses, and historic schools. *Presented by African American Heritage Foundation.*

2018 SAMUEL MAY HOUSE
(Prestonsburg, 117 N. Lake Dr., Old US 23 & US 460, Floyd Co.)

Built in 1817 by Samuel May, this is the oldest house in Prestonsburg. It was constructed of bricks manufactured at the site. The 350-acre farm, with its grist mill, was a recruitment and supply post for Confederates during Civil War. The house was restored in 1997 by the City of Prestonsburg and Friends of Samuel May House, Inc. *Presented by Burl Spurlock Family.*
(Reverse)

SAMUEL MAY (1783-1851)

Son of Revolutionary War veteran John May and Sarah Phillips May, Samuel settled in Prestonsburg around 1807. Commissioned to build county's first brick courthouse in 1818. Elected state senator in 1835, he proposed improving a critical road in eastern Ky., the Mt. Sterling-Pound Gap Rd. He died in California during gold rush. *Presented by E. Carter & P. Hughes Families.*

2019 LUSKA JOSEPH TWYMAN (1913-1988)
(Glasgow Public Square, Beulah Nunn Park, Barren Co.)

Born in Hiseville (Barren Co.). Graduate of Kentucky State Univ.; later member of Board of Regents. Also studied at Indiana Univ. and Peabody Coll. As principal of Ralph J. Bunche School, Twyman led its merger with Glasgow High School to achieve integration. On Kentucky Education Association Board of Directors. Buried, Bear Wallow Cem.

(Reverse)
LUSKA JOSEPH TWYMAN

Twyman was first African American elected to a full term as mayor of a Ky. city (Glasgow). Served 1968-1985. He was first black Kentuckian on U.S. Commission of Agriculture; served on Ky. Advisory Committee of the U.S. Commission on Civil Rights. He was in U.S. Army during WW II in Philippines, 1942-1946. *Presented by City of Glasgow.*

2020 LOUISVILLE MUNICIPAL COLLEGE
(Louisville, 7th & Ky. Sts., Jefferson Co.)

Located on original site of Simmons University and Bible College, a black institution. Opened on Feb. 9, 1931, as the segregated branch of University of Louisville in response to black political activism. It was third municipally supported college for blacks in the U.S., offering liberal arts and pre-professional programs. *Presented by Louisville & Jefferson County African American Heritage Committee, Inc.*
(Reverse)
LOUISVILLE MUNICIPAL COLLEGE

University of Louisville trustees voted to desegregate university in April 1950, closing Louisville Municipal College in 1951. One faculty member, Dr. Charles H. Parrish, Jr., son of president of Simmons University, joined U. of L. as first black faculty member of a white university in the south. *Presented by Louisville and Jefferson County African American Heritage Committee, Inc.*

2021 PAYNE-DESHA HOUSE
(Georgetown, 201 Quail Run Rd., Scott Co.)

Built ca. 1814-15 by Robert Payne, a veteran of Battle of the Thames in War of 1812. Former Kentucky Governor Joseph Desha bought the Federal-style stone house in 1841. In late 19th century, Italianate alterations to exterior included porches and roof brackets. Inside, original staircase, arched hallway, and hand-carved mantels remain. *Presented by Dr. and Mrs. Robert B. Shacklette, 1998.*
(Reverse)
JOSEPH DESHA (1768-1842)

A major general in War of 1812, Desha served in Ky. House of Representatives

(1797, 1799-1802), as state senator (1802-07), and in U.S. Congress (1807-19). His term as governor (1824-28) was marked by controversy. The Deshas retired to a Harrison County farm in 1828, then moved to this house 13 years later, where he died Oct. 11, 1842. *Presented by Dr. and Mrs. Robert B. Shacklette, 1998.*

2022 DESEGREGATION OF UK
(Lexington, U of K, Administration Circle, Fayette Co.)

In 1948 Lyman T. Johnson filed suit for admission to UK. In March 1949 Federal Judge H. Church Ford ruled in Johnson's favor, and that summer nearly 30 black students entered UK graduate and professional programs. Undergraduate classes desegregated in 1954. *Class of 1999.*
(Reverse)
LYMAN T. JOHNSON (1906-1997)

Educator and civil rights leader Lyman T. Johnson led the fight for the desegregation of UK. A Tennessee native, he was an educator in the Louisville Public Schools for forty years and served as president of the Louisville NAACP. UK awarded Johnson an honorary degree in 1979. *Class of 1999.*

2023 SKIRMISH AT SNOW'S POND
(Old Lexington Turnpike, halfway between Walton & Richwood, Boone Co.)

During 1862 Confederate invasion, rebel forces under General Basil W. Duke searched for approaches to Cincinnati. On September 25, 1862, over 500 attacked a federal camp here commanded by Brig. Gen. Quincy A. Gillmore. Many USA prisoners were marched to Falmouth and transported to Lexington, then the regional headquarters of CSA. *Presented by Jack Rouse.*

2024 ONEIDA BAPTIST INSTITUTE
(Oneida, 1 Mulberry St., Clay Co.)

The land for what became Oneida Baptist Institute was donated by Martha Coldiron Hogg and S.P. Hogg in September 1899. The school was founded by James Anderson Burns, December 20, 1899, as Mamre Baptist College to meet the social, educational, and spiritual needs of Clay County children. Mamre opened on Janaury 1,

1900. *Presented by Oneida Baptist Institute.*
(Reverse)
ONEIDA BAPTIST INSTITUTE
On October 29, 1904, the trustees changed the name to Oneida Baptist Institute. Five of the original trustees could not read or write. The first class of five boys graduated in May 1908. Henry B. Hensley (1843-1929), a one-time feudist, was baptized at age 66 and became a staunch supporter of the school. *Presented by Oneida Baptist Institute.*

2025 SITE OF WINNIE A. SCOTT HOSPITAL
(Frankfort, 228 E. 2nd St., Franklin Co.)
The Women's Club Hospital Company, with community support, established a hospital here on Dec. 26, 1915. It was named for Winnie A. Scott, a local teacher instrumental in its founding. The facility was the only Frankfort hospital serving African Americans until desegregation of King's Daughters Hospital in 1959. *Presented by Frankfort Civic Organizations and the Ky. African American Heritage Commission.*

2026 BRADLEY KINCAID (1895-1989)
(Point Leavell, approx. 4 mi. from Lancaster, KY 52-E, Garrard Co.)
"The Kentucky Mountain Boy," born at Point Leavell, Garrard County, was radio's pioneer singer of folk songs and ballads in the 1920s-40s. Kincaid began in 1926 at Chicago's WLS; later performed on WSM Grand Ole Opry (1944-50). He recorded over 200 songs and published 13 songbooks. Elected to Nashville Songwriters Hall of Fame, 1971. *Presented by the Kincaid Family.*

2027 EDWARD DUDLEY BROWN (1850-1906)
(Midway, Main St., Woodford Co.)
This well known African American horse owner, trainer, developer, and jockey was born into slavery, 1850. Raised as a stable boy near Midway, he was nicknamed "Brown Dick" after the record-setting racehorse of that name. Brown was associated with great horses such as Asteroid, Ducat, and Kingfisher. *Presented by City of Midway and the Ky. African American Heritage Commission.*

(Reverse)
NOTED HORSEMAN
"Brown Dick" worked with Kentucky Derby winners Baden Baden (1877), Ben Brush (1896), and Plaudit (1898). He died at a friend's house in Louisville, May 1906, of tuberculosis and was returned to Midway for burial. He was inducted into National Museum of Racing's Hall of Fame on August 8, 1984. *Presented by City of Midway and the Ky. African American Heritage Commission.*

2028 HIRAM LODGE #4 F. & A.M.
(Frankfort, 308 Ann St., Franklin Co.)
Chartered on December 11, 1799, by Virginia, as Hiram Lodge No. 57. It was renamed Hiram Lodge No. 4 on September 8, 1800, when the Grand Lodge of Kentucky was formed. The Ann Street lot was purchased on May 20, 1892; cornerstone laid April 1893; and dedicated on June 11, 1896. *Presented by Lodge of Free and Accepted Masons – Hiram #4.*
(Reverse)
HIRAM LODGE #4 F. & A.M.
Past members of Hiram Lodge #4 include Richard M. Johnson, U.S. vice president, 1837-41; Amos Kendall, U.S. postmaster general, 1835-40; Colonel John Allen, Grand Master, killed War of 1812; Judge George M. Bibb, Kentucky Court of Appeals, U.S. senator. *Presented by Lodge of Free and Accepted Masons – Hiram #4.*

2029 WILLIAM H. TOWNSEND (1890-1964)
(Lawrenceburg, Anderson Co. High School, US 127, Anderson Co.)
This renowned scholar, raconteur, and lawyer was born in Anderson Co. Educated first in a one-room school at Glensboro, he graduated from U.K. Law School in 1912. Among his books was *Lincoln and the Bluegrass* (1955). His talk on Cassius Clay, "The Lion of White Hall," now a taped classic. *Presented by Mary Genevieve and Joe Murphy.*
(Reverse)
WILLIAM H. TOWNSEND (1890-1964)
Townsend had the largest private collection of Lincolniana in U.S. Recognized as a leading expert on Abraham Lincoln, Townsend was a founder of the Ky. Civil

The Winnie A. Scott Hospital was the only one serving African Americans in Frankfort from 1915 until 1959. Kentucky Historical Society Collection.

War Round Table, 1953. He served as its first president until his death. Named posthumously to Fayette County Bar's Hall of Fame, 1996. *Presented by Mary Genevieve and Joe Murphy.*

2030 MEDAL OF HONOR WINNERS
(Richmond, Cem. Entrance, Main St., Madison Co.)

Pvt. William M. Harris and Pvt. Thomas W. Stivers were born in 1850 in Madison Co., Ky. Pvt. George D. Scott was born 1850 in Garrard Co., Ky. These three individuals joined Capt. Thomas B. Weir's Co. D, 7th U.S. Cavalry. They served in the Battle of Little Big Horn, Montana, under the command of General George Armstrong Custer.
(Reverse)

MEDAL OF HONOR WINNERS

At great risk, Privates Harris, Stivers, and Scott voluntarily took water to the wounded under fire of the enemy at the Battle of Little Big Horn. After discharge, they received Congressional Medal of Honor in 1878. Both Pvt. Harris and Pvt. Stivers are buried in Madison Co., Ky. Pvt. Scott's final resting place remains unknown.

2031 MELODYE PARK
(Frankfort, Todd St. & Lawrenceburg Rd., Franklin Co.)

Louis Horwitz, a Frankfort resident for forty years, bought land on the Kentucky River in 1935 where he built an extensive park named after his daughter. The nine-acre park was always open to visitors at no charge. For years it was Frankfort's only public park. *Presented by Kentucky Transportation Cabinet.*
(Reverse)

MELODYE PARK

Its features included fishponds, picnic tables, gardens, 4,000 roses, fountains, restrooms, boat docks, bathhouses, diving boards, and a man-made waterfall. Two Chinese pagodas were used for dancing, concerts, and movies. Music was piped through the park from the elaborate boathouse. The park was destroyed due to flooding in the 1950s.

2032 BERRYTOWN CEMETERY
(Cem. Entrance, Berrytown Rd., Jefferson Co.)

This cemetery became focal point for the Berrytown community, which began when Alfred Berry purchased five acres in 1874.

Berrytown Cem. was purchased on June 23, 1890, by United Brothers of Friendship Lodge #83. As trustees, Lodge members maintained cemetery and, in 1902, constructed its columns and entrance gate. *Presented by Jefferson Co. Commissioner Russ Maple.*
(Reverse)

BERRYTOWN CEMETERY

Berrytown Cemetery's more than 300 burials include the Berry family, other early settlers, and several military graves. Since 1984, Berrytown Cemetery has been owned and operated by a corporation formed by area residents and continues to exemplify the traditions of African American community building. *Presented by Jefferson Co. Commissioner Russ Maple.*

2033 FIRST LT. CARL H. DODD (1925-1996)
(Lily, Cumberland Memorial Gardens, Laurel Co.)

This Medal of Honor recipient was born in Harlan Co. Dodd served with Co. E, 5th Regimental Combat Team, U.S. Army. He was awarded the medal for heroic action in the Korean War for capture of Hill 256, a key terrain, with utter disregard for his safety, January 1951, near Subuk, Korea.
(Reverse)

MEDAL OF HONOR WINNER

President Harry S. Truman presented Carl H. Dodd with this award in May 1951. He achieved the rank of major before retiring from the U.S. Army on June 30, 1965. He lived in Laurel County the last 33 years of his life. Died on October 13, 1996. *Presented by VFW Post 3167, Williamsburg; VFW Post 3302, London; VFW District 11; DAV Chapter 158, Keavy; John C. Karr; and Walter Setzer.*

2034 LESLIE/LESLEY SETTLEMENT
(Mountain Pub Links, Lower John's Creek Rd., Pike Co.)

This early permanent settlement in the Big Sandy Valley was named for Rev. War veteran Wm. Robert Leslie (1729-1802). Leslie moved to this site at John's Creek ca. 1790. His son Robert joined him shortly before his father's death. William and Robert are buried in separate plots on original settlement site. *Presented by Leslie/Lesley Family Association.*

2035 SPOUT SPRING
(4 mi. E. of Benton, 1800 Foust-Sledd Rd., Marshall Co.)

In June 1842, nine justices met at James Clark's home near the spring on west side of old Benton-Paducah Rd. and organized first Marshall Co. Court. They were James Brien, Enos Faughn, Joel Gilbert, John McElrath, Robert Elliott, Wm. Rice, Absalom Smith, Joseph Staton, and James Stice. Fires at county clerk's office destroyed details of meeting. *Presented by Marshall County Genealogical and Historical Society.*

2036 MONETA J. SLEET, JR. (1926-1996)
(Owensboro, 714 W. 7th St., Daviess Co.)

Born in Owensboro, Sleet was a graduate of Ky. State College and New York Univ. Beginning in 1955, he worked as photojournalist for *Jet* and *Ebony* magazines for 41 yrs. During the 1950s-60s, his photos documented the African struggle for independence and the American civil rights movement. He inspired a generation of photographers. *Presented by City of Owensboro and* Messenger-Inquirer.
(Reverse)

PULITZER PRIZE WINNER

As friend of civil rights leader Martin Luther King, Jr., Sleet covered the Selma to Montgomery (Ala.) March and later King's Nobel Peace Prize ceremony. In 1969, he won Pulitzer Prize for photo of Coretta Scott King at Dr. King's funeral (first African American photographer to receive this award). His work has been part of numerous museum exhibitions.

2037 ROBERT H. BROOKS (1915-1941)
(Sadieville, 1/2 mi. from city limits, KY 32, Scott Co.)

Born Oct. 8, 1915, in Sadieville, this African American entered an "all white" National Guard unit before WW II began. As a private in Co. D, 192nd Tank Battalion, he was stationed in the Philippine Islands. Brooks was killed on Dec. 8, 1941, during the initial Japanese bombing of Clark Field, near Fort Stotsenburg.
(Reverse)

ROBERT H. BROOKS (1915-1941)

Brooks, at age 26, was officially declared the first U. S. Armored Forces casualty of

WW II. He is buried in the American-Manila Cemetery in the Philippine Islands. The main parade ground at Fort Knox was named Brooks Field in his honor on December 23, 1941. *Presented by City of Sadieville, Scott County Fiscal Court, and American Legion Scott Post No. 24.*

2038 HARROD'S CREEK
(Louisville, NE corner of Shirley Ave. & Salt River Rd., Jefferson Co.)

James Taylor (1885-1965) was chiefly responsible for the modern Harrods Creek community. Ambitious entrepreneur, Taylor purchased land from Mary Shirley Helm in 1919 and began to sell lots to other African Americans in 1923. The Taylor Subdivision became the nucleus for a thriving suburban African American community. *Presented by African American Heritage Foundation.*
(Reverse)

HARROD'S CREEK
African American community near Harrods Creek developed after Civil War when large estates were subdivided and African Americans settled in southern Oldham Co., along Harrods Cr., in Prospect, and in "The Neck" near Hoskins Rd. The Jacob School, built 1916 and named for former slave Jefferson Jacob, is a surviving landmark. *Presented by African American Heritage Foundation.*

2039 TOWN OF PATESVILLE
(Jct. KY 144 & 1700, Hancock Co.)

Crossroads was site of 19th-century town of Patesville. It was named for William Pate, who bought land and operated an inn about two miles east of here. A post office established, 1813. During Civil War, area was site of a gun battle pitting CSA guerrillas Sue Mundy, Bill Davison and Henry Magruder against John Clark's USA troops. *Presented by Hancock County Fiscal Court.*
(Reverse)

TOWN OF PATESVILLE
During its heyday in 1895, Patesville was a town of 250 people with a sawmill, three general stores, millinery, drugstore, blacksmith shop, undertaker's parlor, and hotel. *Presented by Hancock County Fiscal Court.*

2040 BASHFORD MANOR
(Louisville, 2040 Bashford Manor Ln., Jefferson Co.)

Designed for J. B. Wilder by Henry Whitestone, the residence was built in 1874. Wilder named Bashford Manor after an ancestral home in Maryland. In 1887 George J. Long purchased the farm and turned it into a nationally known racing stable. It was among Kentucky's top thoroughbred horse farms until the horses were sold in 1922. *Presented by The Kentucky Derby Museum.*
(Reverse)

BASHFORD MANOR
Three Kentucky Derby winners, Azra (1892), Manuel (1899), and Sir Huon (1906), were born here. The peacock blue and yellow silks were carried by two Derby winners, Azra and Sir Huon. Two Kentucky Oaks, a Preakness, and a Travers winner born on this farm. The barns razed in 1970; the mansion in 1973. Only original carriage house remains. *Presented by The Kentucky Derby Museum.*

2041 MOORE'S MILL
(3.5 mi. SE of Tompkinsville, KY 163, Monroe Co.)

Phillip Moore purchased a steam saw mill on Meshack Creek from S. A. Moore, 1874. Phillip's son Joel and 4 grandsons eventually moved mill here. In 1929 the expanded lumber mill was among first mills in area to operate at night with electric lights. Phillip's grandson, George Moore, owned mill from 1941 until his death in 1965. *Presented by the Moore Family.*
(Reverse)
(Metal photos of mill on reverse side)

2042 SAINT JOSEPH INFIRMARY
(Louisville, Eastern Pkwy., W. from Preston St., Jefferson Co.)

In 1836, the Sisters of Charity of Nazareth founded a hospital on Jefferson St. called St. Vincent Infirmary. When facility moved to Fourth St. in 1853, the name changed to St. Joseph Infirmary. To meet growing needs, a new 325-room facility opened here in 1926. Internationally renowned surgeon Dr. Irvin Abell Sr. based his practice at St. Joseph.
(Reverse)
ST. JOSEPH INFIRMARY

The School of Nursing, which graduated 1,540 nurses, operated here, 1926-1971. The facility was sold to Extendicare, 1970, and main building razed ten years later. Services moved to Audubon Medical Center on Poplar Level Rd. The surrounding St. Joseph Neighborhood is named after infirmary. *Presented by St. Joseph Neighborhood Association, CARITAS Medical Center, and the Sisters of Charity of Nazareth.*

2043 EMINENCE COLLEGE SITE
(1/4 mi. S. of Eminence, KY 55 North, Henry Co.)

Chartered as a high school by Kentucky Legislature in 1856. The school had as trustees Dr. D. Porter, S.T. Drane, Morris Thomas, Preston Thomas, James Drane, W.B. Wilson, and W.J. Mason. In 1861, the name Eminence College conferred on it. Men and women were equally represented at one of state's first coeducational boarding schools. *Presented by City of Eminence and Henry County Fiscal Court.*
(Reverse)
REV. W.S. GILTNER (1827–1921)
President of Eminence College from 1858-1893, W.S. Giltner trained at Bethany College, W. Va. He and his wife, Lizzie Rains Giltner, led the college, creating a commercial dept. (1880) and normal school for training teachers (1886). Reverend Giltner also preached at Eminence Christian Church. Enrollment peaked around 200; college closed in 1895.

2044 COLONEL GEORGE MORGAN CHINN, USMC
(Harrodsburg, Courthouse lawn, Main St., Mercer Co.)

This Mercer County native was one of nation's leading authorities on automatic weapons. He attended Millersburg Military Institute and Centre College. A Marine veteran of WW II and the Korean War, Chinn observed combat use of weapons and served as trouble shooter. His findings led to Navy-sponsored *The Machine Gun,* five volumes on evolution of automatic weapons.
(Reverse)
WEAPONS EXPERT
As consultant during Vietnam War, Chinn (1902–1987) helped develop grenade

launchers and related air and ground weapons which were also used in Persian Gulf War. He was awarded several weapons patents. In 1960 he became director of the Kentucky Historical Society and wrote works on Mercer County and pioneer Kentucky. *Presented by Marine Corps League of Kentucky.*

2045 NAMING OF THE CUMBERLAND RIVER
(Pine Mountain State Park, at Harbell Rd., 1 mi. S. of Pineville, US 25-E, Bell Co.)

Near this site where the creek enters the river, on April 17, 1750, Dr. Thomas Walker first viewed the river he named for the Duke of Cumberland. Known as the "Narrows," this area became a significant gateway for travelers on the Wilderness Road. *Presented by Bell County Fiscal Court.*

2046 SGT RONALD L. NIEWAHNER
(Villa Hills, Niewahner Dr. & Valley Trails Dr., Kenton Co.)

Born in Covington, SGT Niewahner (1948-1968) distinguished himself by heroic actions in Vietnam. As squad leader in Co. B, 1st Bn., 5th Inf., 25th Inf. Div., U.S. Army, he evacuated fallen comrade in bullet-swept area. Fatally wounded returning to rescue second soldier. Awarded Bronze Star, Silver Star, Gallantry Cross, and Purple Heart. *Presented by Villa Hills Historical Society.*

2047 PAWPAW TREE INCIDENT
(Near Buskirk, KY 1056, Pike Co.)

This episode is result of August 1882 election-day fight. Tolbert, a son of Randolph McCoy, exchanged heated words with Ellison Hatfield, which started a fight. Tolbert, Pharmer and Randolph McCoy Jr. stabbed Ellison to death. Later the three brothers were captured by Hatfield clan, tied to pawpaw trees, and shot in retaliation. *Presented by Pikeville-Pike County Tourism.*

2048 ROSENWALD SCHOOL
(1/2 mi. SE of Lebanon, 337 S. Harrison St., Marion Co.)

This Rosenwald School (1931–1961) is one of 158 schools built in Ky., 1917–1932. The building projects were initiated by the African American community and funded with aid of Julius Rosenwald and philanthropists to provide quality education to the African American community. This effort educated over 500,000 students in the South. *Presented by City of Lebanon and the Ky. African American Heritage Commission.*

2049 BOND-WASHINGTON SCHOOL
(1/2 mi. SE of Elizabethtown, Cemetery Park, Hardin Co.)

This site purchased in 1869 by the trustees of the African School of Elizabethtown. It was the location of District A School from 1888-1923, when East Side High School was built with aid from the local African American community and the Rosenwald fund. Renamed Bond-Washington Graded and High School, 1928. Served as high school until 1956; elementary school until 1959.
(Reverse)

JULIUS ROSENWALD FUND

Funded in 1917 by Booker T. Washington's Tuskegee Institute and Julius Rosenwald, a Jewish businessman, philanthropist, and president of Sears, Roebuck and Co. Fund provided for construction of 158 schools in Ky. between 1917 and 1932 to offer quality education to African Americans. This led to education of over 500,000 students. *Presented by City of Elizabethtown and the Ky. African American Heritage Commission.*

2050 WEST SIDE SCHOOL
(Harrodsburg, 200 Magnolia St., Mercer Co.)

This African American school was erected on this property in 1930, thanks to a donation from the Julius Rosenwald Fund. West Side was the only elementary and high school for African American children in Mercer County. It united the faculty, students, administration, and community in a common goal – education.
(Reverse)

WEST SIDE SCHOOL

Three principals served the school: Mrs. Maynette Elliott Sneed (1930-38), Miss Clara B. Clelland (1938-59), and Mr. Robert Jackson, Jr. (1959-61). In 1939, West Side beat Lexington Dunbar, 16-12, to win K.H.S.A.L. State Basketball Championship. Closed 1961 when local schools de-

segregated. *Presented by West Side School Reunion Com. and Ky. African American Heritage Commission.*

2051 LOUISVILLE BAR ASSOCIATION
(Louisville, Courthouse lawn, Jefferson Co.)

Roots traced to 1871, with meetings of lawyers advocating legal reform. Those efforts led to state law guaranteeing that a witness could not be barred from testifying on basis of race or color. Officially established on January 13, 1900, the LBA is Kentucky's oldest, continuously operating bar association. *Presented by Louisville Bar Association.*
(Reverse)

LOUISVILLE BAR ASSOCIATION

The LBA, with the Louisville Women's Club, was instrumental in establishing Louisville's Legal Aid Society in 1921, to provide legal aid for the poor. The LBA was also active in securing passage of the judicial article of 1975, which article barred non-lawyers from serving as judges and created a unified court system. *Presented by Louisville Bar Association.*

2052 JONESVILLE
(Bowling Green, Western Ky. Univ. Campus, Univ. Blvd. & US 68/80, Warren Co.)

This African American community was founded after the Civil War. It was bordered by Dogwood Dr., Russellville Road, and the railroad tracks. The community grew to include several hundred residents, an elementary school, businesses, and two churches. Frame and hand-hewn stone houses lined the streets of Jonesville. *Presented by Western Kentucky University.*
(Reverse)

JONESVILLE

The lives of most residents of this close African American community revolved around church, school and family activities. In the late 1950s Jonesville was one of two areas in Bowling Green designated for urban renewal. By 1968 the state had acquired the land and sold it to the university. *Presented by Western Kentucky University.*

2053 DR. CHARLES W. MATHERS 1856-1937
(Carlisle, Main St., Courthouse lawn, KY 36, Nicholas Co.)

This Nicholas Co. native served as county

judge; state representative, 1888 and 1890; and state senator, 1908. He was a medical doctor, extensive landowner, agriculturist, pres. of Farmers Bank of Carlisle, and a director of Exchange Bank of Millersburg. Dr. Mathers is buried in the Carlisle Cemetery. *Presented by Private Donations.*
(Reverse)
NICHOLAS COUNTY BENEFACTOR
Charles Mathers, philanthropist, anonymously paid tuition of orphan girls at Midway Orphan School and sent food and fuel to poor widows at Christmas. His trusts include the Mathers perpetual educational fund for needy children; a Nicholas County hospital fund; a school fund for Pike, Letcher, and Breathitt County children; and the Midway Female Orphans School Trust Fund.

2054 UNION COLLEGE
(Barbourville, 310 College St., Knox Co.)
Union College was incorporated in October 1879. The first degrees were conferred here June 8, 1893. Centennial Hall, formerly known as Classroom Building, was named to the National Register of Historic Places in 1975. Also named to the Register were Speed Hall in 1982 and Soldiers and Sailors Memorial Gymnasium in 1984.

2055 REV. WILLIAM H. SHEPPARD
(Louisville, Jct. Hancock & Jacob Sts., Jefferson Co.)
Born in Waynesboro, Virginia, in 1865, Sheppard attended Hampton and Stillman Institutes. Sent to the Belgian Congo in 1890, he served as missionary in Africa until 1910. Became a fellow of the Royal Geographic Society of London in 1893 for his explorations. Sheppard denounced the Belgian colonists' cruelty in the Congo. *Presented by Alderman George Unseld.*
(Reverse)
REV. WILLIAM H. SHEPPARD
Returning from Africa, Sheppard was pastor of Grace Presbyterian Church in Louisville from 1912 until his death in 1927. One of the city's most respected African American leaders, he was known for his work in the Smoketown community. Sheppard Park (1924) and Sheppard Square Housing Project (1942) named in

his honor. *Presented by Alderman George Unseld.*

2056 EASTERN KENTUCKY RAILWAY
(Webbville, at Fire Dept., KY 201, Lawrence Co.)
This site became the railhead of E.K. Railway when 1.77 miles of track was laid from Willard, 1889, completing 36 miles of track from Riverton. The extension from Willard to Webbville was made primarily to provide an outlet for forest products. The Blue Goose, a gasoline-powered car, made two daily rounds to Grayson. E.K. Railway ended in bankruptcy, 1933. *Presented by Eastern Ky. Railway Historical Society.*

2057 GOOD SHEPHERD CHURCH
(Frankfort, 310 Wapping St., Franklin Co.)
An active Catholic presence was established in Frankfort in 1808 with Reverend Angier as priest. In 1820s mass was offered at house on Broadway, opposite Capitol. In 1835 worship held in house near railroad tunnel; in 1837 Bishop Flaget of Bardstown purchased house for Catholics on corner of Broadway and High St. *Presented by Good Shepherd Church.*
(Reverse)
GOOD SHEPHERD CHURCH
By 1837 the Catholic community was formally called St. Patrick Mission. Ten years later there was an influx of German and Irish immigrants to Frankfort. A permanent pastor, Father J.M. Lancaster, was appointed in 1848. The property on Wapping Street was purchased in 1849. Congregation was renamed Good Shepherd with the dedication of the church in 1850.

2058 FERN CREEK HIGH SCHOOL
(Fern Creek, 9115 Fern Creek Road, [500 ft. off US 31E] Jefferson Co.)
Built on land purchased from S.A. Stivers; school opened with 25 pupils, Sept. 17, 1923. Established as alternative to distant Louisville schools, Fern Creek was a two-year school at first but later adopted a four-year program. The first four-year class graduated in 1927. The current building constructed, 1941. *Presented by Fern Creek Woman's Club and Community Organizations.*

2059 EDWARD BOONE (1740–80)
(870 See Rd., ¾ mi. N. of Jct. KY 537 & See Rd., Bourbon Co.)

Death site of Edward Boone, a brother of renowned Kentucky pioneer Daniel Boone. Edward was killed by Indians here Oct. 1780 at age 40 while hunting with Daniel. Boone Creek named for Edward. Daniel and Edward wed sisters, Rebecca and Martha Bryan, whose family built and settled Bryan Station near Lexington. *Presented by The Boone Society, Inc.*

2060 SUE BENNETT COLLEGE
(London, W. 5th [KY 1006 W] and College Streets, Laurel Co.)

Sue Bennett Memorial School, named for Madison Co. promoter, opened 1897 to educate mountain children. Funded by local people and the Methodists, school taught all grades. Commercial Dept. opened 1901; county high school, 1910-33. Normal school operated, 1900-1910, and became junior college, 1922. Name changed, 1930; closed 1997. *Presented by Friends of Sue Bennett.*
(Reverse)

SUE BENNETT COLLEGE

Educated more than 11,000 students, 1897-1997. School leaders: J. C. Lewis, 1897-1917; J.E. Savage, 1915-16; Ms. K.J. French, 1916-17; A.W. Mohn, 1917-22; K.C. East, 1922-42; H.V. McClure, 1939; Ms. J. Harrison, 1942-44; Ms. O. Sanders, 1944-58; L. Flynn, 1954; E.F. Hays, 1958-85; J.E. Patterson, 1985-88; Ms. J.K. Stivers, 1988-91; P.G. Bunnell, 1991-97; J. Cheek, 1997.

2061 THE FRANKFORT BARRACKS
(Frankfort, Shelby & New Sts., Franklin Co.)

The barracks, established in April 1871, and the command moved here in December of that year. Buildings were erected on Alexander Goldsmith Brawner's five acres known as Coleman's Spring lot. Post consisted of barracks, guardhouse, baking oven, and two one-story hospitals. *Presented by Franklin County Trust for Historic Preservation.*
(Reverse)

THE FRANKFORT BARRACKS

The purpose of the barracks was to provide a military presence and the protection of African Americans in the area. The post quartered members of the 4th and later the 16th U.S. Inf. Regiments. The Frankfort Barracks District was listed on the National Register of Historic Places in 1975. *Presented by Franklin County Trust for Historic Preservation.*

2062 SITE OF RANDOLPH MCCOY HOUSE
(4 ½ miles from Toler, KY 319, Pike Co.)

House was located on Blackberry Fork of Pond Creek. It burned Jan. 1, 1888, during a Hatfield raid. Two of Randolph's children, Alifair and Calvin, were killed in attack; their mother Sally was badly injured. Randolph and other children escaped. Site is part of Hatfield-McCoy Feud Historic Dist. *Presented by Pikeville-Pike County Tourism.*

2063 MCKINNEY'S FORT
(McKinney, 9 mi. SW of Stanford, ¼ mi. SE of McKinney Grade School on farm of Harold G. Chaney, Lincoln Co.)

Built by Archibald McKinney by 1792, this early trading post was an important stop on Cumberland Trace. The settlement began as four log cabins and a stockade. Early settlers are buried in a cemetery on a knoll visible due south of this marker. In 1874 name changed to McKinney Station. *Presented by McKinney Descendants and Community.*

2064 BETHLEHEM MISSIONARY BAPTIST CHURCH
(3 mi. north of Scottsville on Old US 31-E, Allen Co.)

Congregation founded 1801. Services held, uninterrupted, except for a Sunday in Nov. 1862, because of "Army passing down the pike and the house having sick soldiers in it." Called "Difficult" and located near Big Difficult Cr. whose name chosen because fords on creek were hard to predict. By 1810 permanent church built and renamed Bethlehem.
(Reverse)

BETHLEHEM CHURCH

Church constituted by Elders John Hightower, Alexander Devin, Joseph Logan and eight members: James and Margaret Atwood, Wm. and Dorcas Strait, Wm. and Mary Thos., Polly Richey and Thos. Spillman. Elder Joseph Logan was first pastor. Slaves were members, 1819. Church voted to erect new house of worship, 1847; present edifice built, 1910. *Presented by Bethlehem Missionary Baptist Church.*

2065 F. JULIUS FOHS (1884–1965)
(201 N. Walker, Marion, Crittenden Co.)

F. Julius Fohs was born in N.Y. but moved to Marion, Ky. in 1890. He graduated from Marion High School. Managed fluorspar mining operation, 1900-1904; served as assistant state geologist for Ky., 1905-12. Received honorary Doctor of Science degree from the Israel Institute of Technology for his assistance in the development of mineral resources, 1957.
(Reverse)

FOHS HALL

Julius Fohs had structure built and gave it to people of Marion, 1926. Located on lot where Fohs family lived. Fohs Hall, Inc., formed 1981 for perpetual preservation of Hall; to be used by citizens of Marion and Crittenden Co. as a community center and civic auditorium. It was listed on the National Register of Historic Places in 1982. *Presented by Fohs Hall, Inc.*

2066 HOG TRIAL
(McCarr, Next to Post Office, KY 319, Pike Co.)

In 1873 Randolph McCoy accused Floyd Hatfield of stealing his hog. A trial followed, presided over by Reverend Anderson Hatfield, justice of the peace. To be fair, the jury consisted of six Hatfields and six McCoys. One witness, William Staton, stated he had seen Floyd mark the hog's ear. This resulted in Floyd's acquittal. *Presented by Pikeville-Pike County Tourism.*
(Reverse)

ELECTION FIGHT

In August 1882 an election was held near Jerry Hatfield's house. A fight broke out between Tolbert McCoy and Elias Hatfield. Tolbert's brothers joined in the fight as did Ellison Hatfield, who was stabbed and shot. He later died in West Virginia. The McCoy brothers were captured and killed in the "pawpaw tree" incident. *Presented by Pikeville-Pike County Tourism.*

2067 McCOY CEMETERY
(4 1/2 mi. from Toler, KY 319, Pike Co.)

Among the graves in the McCoy Cemetery are those of Randolph McCoy's three sons –Tolbert, Pharmer, and Randolph Jr.–all killed by the Hatfields. Also buried here are Alifair and Calvin McCoy, who were killed by the Hatfields when cabin was burned. Cemetery is part of the Hatfield-McCoy Feud Historic District. *Presented by Pikeville-Pike County Tourism.*

2068 SITE OF KILLING OF ASA HARMON McCOY
(Entrance to Blackberry School, just off KY 1056, near Ransom, Pike Co.)

Asa Harmon McCoy, a Union soldier, was shot in 1865 by the Logan Wildcats. The Wildcats were led by Confederate "Devil Anse" Hatfield. Jim Vance was the suspected leader in the murder, although there was never a conviction. This was the first incident between the two families. *Presented by Pikeville-Pike County Tourism.*

2069 MAXWELL PLACE
(Lexington, University of Ky. Campus, Rose St., Fayette Co.)

Dennis Mulligan had Maxwell Place built in 1870-72 for his son, Judge James H. Mulligan and named for nearby Maxwell Springs. The property and Italianate home were purchased by UK in 1917 as the official president's residence. First occupied by President Frank L. McVey, it has served as home to every UK president since. *Class of 2000.*
(Reverse)

MAXWELL PLACE

Historically students lived at Maxwell Place, rooming in the attic or above the garage. Site of student events and host to visiting dignitaries, the home became a center of campus social life. Considered at one time for possible demolition, Maxwell Place was entered into the National Register of Historic Places in 1982. *Class of 2000.*

2070 BARKER HALL AND BUELL ARMORY
(Lexington, University of Ky. Campus, Administration Dr., Fayette Co.)

Dedicated in 1901 and known as Alumni Hall. The original structure was a central,

three-story building with a gymnasium and a drill hall on either side. Expanded in the 1930s with aid of WPA funds. The 19ᵗʰ-century bell from the Peter Taylor Methodist Chapel in Carrs (Lewis Co.) was installed in 1989. *Class of 2001.*
(Reverse)
Barker Hall and Buell Armory
Site of first UK basketball games. Utilized for physical education, student clubs, dance, and ROTC. Converted to an infirmary during 1918 flu epidemic. Named for UK's second president, Henry Stites Barker (1911-1917) and Union Civil War General and UK trustee Don Carlos Buell. *Class of 2001.*

2071 Southgate Street School
(Southgate St., Newport, Campbell Co.)

In 1870, the Newport City Council purchased property for a school for African Americans, and three years later a frame house constructed. Elizabeth Hudson was appointed first African American teacher at salary of $35 per month. Two major events of 1893 were school's first commencement and second floor addition. High school closed, 1921.
(Reverse)
Southgate Street School
In 1955, a desegregation program was submitted to the school board and the school was dissolved. All African American students through eleventh grade could then attend Newport schools. Twelfth-grade students continued at William Grant, and teachers went on to positions in other Newport schools. *Presented by Newport Lodge No. 120, O.E.S. Newport Chapter No. 105, and the Ky. African American Heritage Commission.*

Kentucky Historical Monument/Marker located at Soldiers' National Cemetery, Gettysburg, Pennsylvania.
Kentucky Honors Her Son, Abraham Lincoln, Who Delivered His Immortal Address at the Site Now Marked by the Soldiers' Monument
"Fourscore and seven years ago our fathers brought forth on this continent a new nation, conceived in liberty and dedicated to the proposition that all men are created equal.

"Now we are engaged in a great civil war, testing whether that nation or any nation so conceived and so dedicated can long endure. We are met on a great battlefield of that war. We have come to dedicate a portion of that field as a final resting place of those who here gave their lives that that nation might live. It is altogether fitting and proper that we should do this.

"But, in a larger sense, we cannot dedicate, we cannot consecrate, we cannot hallow this ground. The brave men, living and dead, who struggled here have consecrated it far above our poor power to add or detract. The world will little note nor long remember what we say here, but it can never forget what they did here. It is for us the living, rather, to be dedicated here to the unfinished work which they who fought here have thus far so nobly advanced. It is rather for us to be here dedicated to the great task remaining before us, that from these honored dead we take increased devotion to that cause for which they gave the last full measure of devotion; that we here highly resolve that these dead shall not have died in vain; that this nation, under God, shall have a new birth of freedom; and that government of the people, by the people, for the people, shall not perish from the earth."

Kentucky Historical Marker located at Shiloh, Tennessee.
Kentucky Troops in the Battle of Shiloh
As a border slave state that remained in the Union, Kentucky was sharply divided in its loyalty during the Civil War. The state provided many troops to both sides at Shiloh: Approximately 6,500 to the Federal forces; approximately 2,000 to the Confederate forces. Confederate Commanding General Albert Sidney Johnston, who was killed in action on April 6 at Shiloh, though a Texan by adoption, was a Kentuckian by birth, and he retained innumerable ties of blood and sentiment with his native state. Confederate Brigadier General John C. Breckinridge, who was a former Vice President of the United States, and who commanded the Confederate reserve corps at Shiloh, was from Kentucky.

Two sons of a distinguished United States Senator from Kentucky, Senator John J. Crittenden, were in opposing armies at Shiloh: Brigadier General Thomas L. Crittenden for the Union; Brigadier General George B. Crittenden for the Confederacy. Kentucky's "Confederate Governor," George W. Johnson, fought and died in the Southern ranks at Shiloh.

Five Kentucky Infantry regiments, plus the Kentucky cavalry squadron of Colonel John Hunt Morgan, the Kentucky cavalry company of Captain Philip Thompson, and the Kentucky artillery battery of Captain Robert Cobb, were in the Confederate forces at Shiloh. The 7th Kentucky Infantry served in the 2nd Brigade of the 2nd Division of Major General Leonidas Polk's 1st Corps; it was deployed initially at about 8:30 A.M. of April 6 as a supporting unit on the Confederate right; by 10:00 A.M. it was engaged at the Hornet's Nest. The 3rd, 4th, 6th, and 9th Kentucky Infantry regiments and Cobb's artillery battery served in Colonel Robert P. Trabue's 1st Brigade of Breckinridge's reserve corps. Detached from its parent corps early in the morning of April 6, the 1st Brigade entered the battle at 9:30 A.M. at the Crescent Field. Here the 3rd Kentucky Regiment was separated from the brigade by General Beauregard and ordered to another part of the battlefield. No further record remains of its location or action the first day. During the course of the fighting, the brigade was moved by stages across the front until late in the afternoon it rejoined Breckinridge's corps on the extreme Confederate right. At the close of the first day's combat the brigade was at the Indian mounds overlooking the Tennessee River. All of the Kentucky Confederate units experienced hard fighting and suffered heavy casualties during the day.

Only two Kentucky regiments, the 17th and 25th Infantry regiments, were present with the Federal Army (Army of the Tennessee) during the first day of the battle. Attached to the 3rd Brigade of Brigadier General Stephen H. Hurlbut's 4th Division, they were encamped in the northeast edge of Cloud Field (near the present marker) when the battle opened. Shifted from one hotly contested position to another during the first day of fighting, they had their severest action early in the afternoon at the Peach Orchard. Late in the day they were placed near the Pittsburg Landing road as a part of General Grant's final defensive perimeter.

The Army of the Ohio, which reinforced the Army of the Tennessee during the late afternoon and night of April 6 and the morning of April 7, contained ten regiments of Kentucky troops: the 5th Regiment of the 4th Brigade, 2nd Division; the 6th Regiment of the 19th Brigade, and the 1st, 2nd, and 20th Regiments of the 22nd Brigade, 4th Division; the 9th and 13th Regiments of the 11th Brigade, and the 11th and 26th Regiments of the 14th Brigade, 5th Division; and the 24th Regiment of the 21st Brigade, 6th Division. The initial unit of the Army of the Ohio to arrive at the scene of battle, the 4th Division, was commanded by Brigadier General William Nelson, a Kentuckian.

The Kentucky troops in both armies shared fully in the bitter fighting of April 7 as the strengthened and reanimated Federals pressed forward and as the outnumbered, exhausted, and demoralized Confederates gradually yielded the field. Morgan's Kentucky cavalry joined with Forrest's Tennessee cavalry and other detachments on April 8 to repel General Sherman's pursuit near Mickey's – the closing action of the battle of Shiloh.

Casualties among Kentucky troops at Shiloh: Union, 115 killed, 636 wounded, 29 missing; Confederate, 137 killed, 627 wounded, 45 missing.

For the full text of the inscription, the reader is referred to the corresponding number of the markers, not page numbers, in the numerical list.

Adair: 128, 604, 707, 806, 1139, 1599, 1782, 1813.

Allen: 730, 760, 1117, 1670, 1760, 2064.

Anderson: 572, 630, 812, 847, 1121, 1122, 1273, 1430, 1479, 1970, 2029.

Ballard: 46, 64, 757, 826, 1309, 1374.

Barren: 544, 609, 635, 687, 698, 1039, 1133, 1255, 1290, 1317, 1365, 1489, 1718, 1951, 2019.

Bath: 592, 862, 940, 993, 1050, 1193, 1226, 1342, 1528, 1542.

Bell: 54, 129, 198, 521, 683, 832, 1227, 1228, 1262, 1272, 1286, 1402, 1426, 1868, 2045.

Boone: 32, 550, 859, 999, 1194, 1253, 1387, 1640, 1646, 1765, 2023.

Bourbon: 51, 82, 93, 150, 178, 696, 753, 1141, 1246, 1283, 1462, 1493, 1566, 1596, 1722, 1824, 1855, 1886, 2059.

Boyd: 643, 772, 921, 1010, 1012, 1023, 1131, 1135, 1150, 1155, 1157, 1211, 1416, 1815.

Boyle: 23, 24, 36, 49, 58, 190, 192, 193, 194, 195, 197, 553, 754, 755, 756, 876, 923, 965, 1091, 1140, 1218, 1279, 1284, 1376, 1422, 1442, 1606, 1705, 1772, 1909, 1958, 2005.

Bracken: 94, 501, 750, 861, 996, 1213, 1502, 1565, 1614, 1842.

Breathitt: 841, 904, 961, 1289.

Breckinridge: 73, 134, 552, 557, 584, 850, 934, 1003, 1170.

Bullitt: 133, 890, 1022, 1136, 1162, 1296, 1324, 1413, 1415, 1944.

Butler: 569, 770, 822, 1172,

1265, 1467, 1769, 1781.

Caldwell: 142, 145, 579, 751, 834, 1278, 1453, 1630, 1902, 1903, 1908, 1916, 1932, 1981.

Calloway: 87, 147, 200, 825, 1263, 1373, 1427, 1770, 1945, 1977.

Campbell: 117, 121, 163, 507, 599, 889, 986, 990, 1059, 1151, 1351, 1386, 1395, 1434, 1506, 1642, 1706, 1730, 1776, 1867, 2071.

Carlisle: 563, 763.

Carroll: 216, 222, 634, 893, 911, 1094, 1184, 1291, 1361, 1725.

Carter: 209, 221, 637, 640, 642, 914, 1013, 1014, 1017, 1018, 1148, 1177, 1222, 1247.

Casey: 250, 684, 781, 888, 917, 1305, 1835.

Christian: 577, 618, 740, 851, 880, 882, 1041, 1042, 1045, 1179, 1224, 1268, 1269, 1313, 1501, 1625, 1690, 1759, 1910.

Clark: 116, 127, 137, 625, 679, 710, 731, 948, 951, 1047, 1048, 1068, 1217, 1274, 1318, 1319, 1358, 1399, 1894.

Clay: 531, 568, 723, 836, 908, 1293, 1382, 1397, 1929, 2024.

Clinton: 597, 780, 811, 1085, 1306, 1310, 1516, 1619, 1927.

Crittenden: 596, 615, 668, 1097, 1160, 1185, 1210, 1225, 1298, 1450, 1499, 1522, 1526, 2065.

Cumberland: 515, 583, 601, 885, 959, 1237, 1403.

Daviess: 590, 743, 744, 745, 883, 907, 1079, 1081, 1158, 1183, 1192, 1241, 1242, 1304, 1307, 1333, 1436, 1456, 1478, 1500, 1746, 1747, 1843, 1873, 1918, 2036.

Edmonson: 607, 797, 802, 910, 1385, 1396, 1669.

Elliott: 644, 711, 796.

Estill: 199, 555, 639, 810, 1054, 1055, 1056, 1219, 1507, 1922.

Fayette: 1, 2, 3, 4, 6, 9, 10, 11, 12, 14, 16, 17, 19, 20, 21, 65, 83, 125, 136, 139, 157, 166, 554, 741, 807, 864, 945, 952, 1001, 1033, 1110, 1163, 1215, 1280, 1404, 1406, 1437, 1440, 1445, 1447, 1459, 1466, 1470, 1480, 1483, 1549, 1550, 1551, 1552, 1553, 1554, 1555, 1556, 1557, 1558, 1595, 1613, 1635, 1636, 1687, 1714, 1742, 1773, 1780, 1783, 1784, 1806, 1809, 1826, 1864, 1875, 1876, 1888, 1928, 1953, 1961, 1963, 1966, 2009, 2011, 2012, 2022, 2069, 2070.

Fleming: 97, 173, 621, 789, 855, 950, 1388, 1438, 1559, 1568, 1569, 1736.

Floyd: 85, 151, 164, 172, 623, 690, 817, 905, 2018.

Franklin: 69, 103, 105, 106, 113, 123, 504, 522, 576, 595, 819, 1154, 1164, 1182, 1205, 1208, 1323, 1359, 1372, 1420, 1444, 1464, 1465, 1476, 1490, 1495, 1524, 1535, 1537, 1540, 1571, 1653, 1688, 1707, 1710, 1726, 1743, 1752, 1774, 1779, 1796, 1799, 1896, 1925, 1955, 1999, 2003, 2025, 2028, 2031, 2057, 2061.

Fulton: 131, 169, 652, 688, 973, 1169, 1209, 1408, 1410, 1563, 1587, 1859, 1860.

Gallatin: 720, 746, 747.

Garrard: 25, 699, 704, 713, 714, 1070, 1240, 1344, 1371, 1525, 1562, 1617, 1733, 1750, 1794, 1942, 2026.

Grant: 188, 722, 936, 942,

1560.

Graves: 180, 573, 654, 655, 732, 869, 1288, 1432, 1597, 1682, 1785, 2010.

Grayson: 212, 589, 768, 873, 906, 1592, 1602, 1634, 1741, 1828, 1980.

Green: 148, 165, 183, 603, 719, 844, 846, 1080, 1082, 1239, 1311.

Greenup: 31, 214, 520, 574, 784, 975, 976, 1008, 1009, 1011, 1015, 1016, 1019, 1020, 1076, 1130, 1132, 1142, 1143, 1147, 1149, 1156, 1178, 1529, 1585, 1808, 1814, 1973, 1978.

Hancock: 667, 762, 1678, 1738, 1756, 1789, 1856, 1914, 1935, 1993, 2039.

Hardin: 525, 606, 748, 833, 858, 932, 960, 1116, 1468, 1494, 1505, 1534, 1591, 1621, 1650, 1651, 1683, 1711, 1727, 1731, 1740, 1763, 1857, 1869, 1904, 1912, 2049.

Harlan: 570, 588, 775, 776, 785, 1803, 1995.

Harrison: 107, 109, 651, 673, 692, 1069, 1084, 1171, 1220, 1428, 1457, 1539.

Hart: 43, 119, 155, 204, 530, 656, 875, 879, 949, 1002, 1190, 1207, 1235, 1236, 1299, 1390, 1414, 1491, 1504.

Henderson: 66, 191, 527, 717, 870, 878, 1206, 1392, 1523, 1645, 1703, 1777, 1926, 1984.

Henry: 122, 549, 798, 805, 852, 2043.

Hickman: 60, 528, 891, 895, 1398, 1400, 1497, 1611, 1775, 1937.

Hopkins: 140, 580, 613, 849, 915, 1103, 1104, 1232, 1338, 1425, 1612, 1620, 1797, 1948, 1971.

Jackson: 697, 1145.

Jefferson: 22, 26, 88, 101, 111, 146, 174, 219, 532, 534, 535, 540, 541, 542, 548, 681, 835, 974, 983, 984, 991, 992, 1028, 1060, 1229,

1312, 1336, 1350, 1412, 1435, 1441, 1451, 1474, 1475, 1544, 1545, 1546, 1589, 1629, 1639, 1654, 1657, 1661, 1662, 1663, 1664, 1676, 1677, 1680, 1681, 1689, 1692, 1693, 1694, 1695, 1697, 1702, 1704, 1713, 1715, 1719, 1720, 1723, 1724, 1737, 1739, 1744, 1753, 1766, 1778, 1786, 1793, 1810, 1818, 1820, 1845, 1848, 1849, 1851, 1880, 1885, 1891, 1898, 1899, 1901, 1907, 1923, 1949, 1964, 1968, 1974, 1976, 1982, 1983, 1985, 1988, 1989, 1990, 1992, 1994, 1996, 1997, 1998, 2004, 2006, 2007, 2008, 2017, 2020, 2032, 2038, 2040, 2042, 2051, 2055, 2058.

Jessamine: 158, 201, 565, 675, 823, 894, 947, 1315, 1381, 1473, 1513, 1515, 1610, 1671, 1795, 1830, 1965.

Johnson: 556, 571, 608, 700, 735, 736, 903, 985, 1125, 1126, 1632.

Kenton: 50, 167, 519, 546, 1168, 1429, 1460, 1472, 1484, 1488, 1527, 1531, 1594, 1601, 1626, 1638, 1659, 1691, 1709, 1758, 1821, 1836, 1852, 1853, 1854, 1862, 1863, 1865, 1881, 1887, 1917, 1939, 1956, 1967, 2000, 2014, 2046.

Knott: 624, 653, 771, 791, 1119, 1152, 1512, 1532, 1543.

Knox: 72, 518, 782, 1600, 1811, 1884, 2054.

Larue: 120, 591, 749, 827, 1096, 1098, 1114, 1115, 1186, 1482, 1631.

Laurel: 53, 55, 102, 560, 661, 737, 843, 927, 1176, 1574, 1757, 1870, 1919, 2033, 2060.

Lawrence: 547, 632, 636, 886, 887, 1354, 1583, 1584, 2056.

Lee: 638, 792, 1805.

Leslie: 213, 558, 631.

Letcher: 510, 777, 809, 1188, 1197, 1294, 1700, 1732, 1804, 1906.

Lewis: 143, 205, 215, 778, 803, 1393, 1572, 1656.

Lincoln: 56, 95, 96, 152, 685, 774, 860, 955, 982, 1203, 1234, 1328, 1561, 1564, 1590, 2013, 2063.

Livingston: 663, 767, 801, 938, 1204, 1348, 1349, 1368, 1675.

Logan: 71, 74, 100, 170, 179, 203, 657, 658, 716, 871, 958, 969, 1071, 1137, 1138, 1252, 1260, 1261, 1314, 1334, 1345, 1455, 1514, 1623, 1761, 1791, 1931, 1960, 1972.

Lyon: 61, 130, 509, 779, 946, 1231, 1245, 1326, 1327, 1332, 1340, 1364, 1423, 1598, 1768.

McCracken: 169, 517, 575, 680, 793, 794, 795, 828, 829, 839, 840, 865, 866, 868, 899, 916, 918, 924, 939, 962, 963, 964, 966, 967, 968, 970, 977, 1006, 1025, 1027, 1029, 1030, 1031, 1032, 1035, 1036, 1037, 1043, 1044, 1052, 1053, 1057, 1058, 1061, 1062, 1065, 1072, 1090, 1105, 1106, 1107, 1108, 1111, 1112, 1134, 1146, 1161, 1174, 1175, 1180, 1214, 1276, 1277, 1287, 1352, 1377, 1421, 1431, 1452, 1469, 1518, 1698, 1721, 1754, 1936, 1957, 1969.

McCreary: 666, 702, 900, 1074, 1075, 1243, 1356, 1633.

McLean: 523, 664, 665, 830, 892, 1123, 1199, 1264, 1812, 1950.

Madison: 77, 79, 514, 533, 773, 1124, 1223, 1300, 1362, 1378, 1443, 1520, 1576, 1577, 1578, 1579, 1582, 1685, 1767, 1800, 1825, 1846, 1871, 1872, 1905, 1979, 2030.

Magoffin: 202, 566, 786, 901, 902, 1660.

Marion: 206, 207, 543, 585,

600, 670, 728, 867, 913, 1026, 1302, 1303, 1339, 1341, 1509, 1667, 1673, 2048.

Marshall: 169, 545, 874, 1405, 1538, 1647, 1648, 1749, 2035.

Martin: 726, 729, 814, 922, 1316.

Mason: 68, 81, 84, 91, 92, 124, 138, 144, 691, 694, 695, 738, 877, 1165, 1244, 1439, 1492, 1519, 1616, 1628, 1696, 1839, 1878, 1893, 1941, 1962, 2001.

Meade: 529, 536, 602, 766, 845, 1321, 1652, 1755.

Menifee: 189, 787, 1120.

Mercer: 141, 185, 539, 551, 627, 926, 928, 929, 1083, 1173, 1258, 1295, 1297, 1325, 1335, 1343, 1449, 1481, 1498, 1530, 1603, 1637, 1679, 1751, 1816, 1817, 1874, 1877, 2044, 2050.

Metcalfe: 678, 799, 1000, 1118, 1200, 1257, 1496, 1503, 1895.

Monroe: 524, 593, 721, 1093, 1347, 1391, 1394, 2041.

Montgomery: 112, 115, 153, 177, 586, 628, 629, 1216, 1331, 1655.

Morgan: 512, 648, 815, 1991.

Muhlenberg: 614, 761, 821, 1086, 1202, 1389, 1521, 1609, 1666, 1735, 1946.

Nelson: 168, 506, 674, 705, 820, 857, 896, 944, 956, 1021, 1077, 1078, 1101, 1102, 1113, 1281, 1282, 1285, 1433, 1471, 1586, 1604, 1668, 1686, 1771, 1827, 1883, 1897, 1943.

Nicholas: 162, 660, 708, 856, 897, 935, 1230, 1353, 1615, 1764, 2053.

Ohio: 581, 671, 1144, 1195, 1196, 1259, 1266, 1267, 1330, 1370, 1461, 1463, 1485, 1510, 1548, 1672, 1674, 1745, 1829, 1834, 1858.

Oldham: 182, 208, 650, 752, 909, 957, 1251.

Owen: 564, 725, 742, 831,

925, 943, 1181, 1575, 1608, 1658, 1790, 1819.

Owsley: 196, 561, 645, 813, 1627.

Pendleton: 34, 686, 937, 953, 1911.

Perry: 682, 703, 758, 759, 1249, 1346.

Pike: 52, 622, 727, 808, 884, 1533, 1728, 1866, 1913, 1959, 2034, 2047, 2062, 2066, 2067, 2068.

Powell: 132, 587, 790, 2015.

Pulaski: 677, 712, 863, 979, 980, 1007, 1212, 1607, 1684, 1807, 1920.

Robertson: 18, 693, 816, 1567.

Rockcastle: 676, 715, 1254, 1605, 1622, 1643, 1644.

Rowan: 567, 788, 972, 1034, 1933, 1952.

Russell: 724, 734, 838, 954, 1109, 1233, 1301, 1486, 1802.

Scott: 63, 135, 217, 218, 508, 610, 701, 718, 739, 1166, 1248, 1337, 1454, 1487, 1593, 1701, 1716, 1734, 1841, 1861, 1934, 1938, 2021, 2037.

Shelby: 28, 161, 709, 848, 971, 1088, 1089, 1128, 1129, 1238, 1320, 1379, 1409, 1419, 1889, 1930.

Simpson: 503, 562, 598, 611, 912, 978, 1271, 1369, 1850, 1947.

Spencer: 505, 594, 837, 1699, 1748, 1833.

Taylor: 89, 582, 605, 706, 995, 1383, 1448, 1536, 1729, 1924, 2016.

Todd: 57, 800, 824, 1073, 1355, 1384, 1879.

Trigg: 578, 619, 764, 872, 881, 994, 998, 1100, 1159, 1308, 1357, 1366, 1367, 1375, 1380, 1788, 1832, 1838, 1840, 1890, 1892.

Trimble: 765, 1099, 1822, 1823.

Union: 187, 211, 612, 616, 633, 842, 1092, 1250, 1329, 1424, 1547, 1588, 1717, 1762, 1787, 1844.

Warren: 67, 538, 662, 769, 981, 987, 997, 1024, 1049, 1051, 1063, 1127, 1187, 1191, 1201, 1360, 1401, 1417, 1418, 1458, 1573, 1665, 1792, 1831, 1882, 1954, 2052.

Washington: 526, 689, 853, 854, 930, 931, 933, 941, 1038, 1040, 1046, 1095, 1363, 1446, 1581, 1618.

Wayne: 75, 626, 804, 818, 988, 989, 1153, 1275, 1292, 1477.

Webster: 617, 783, 1004, 1508, 1915.

Whitley: 513, 672, 898, 919, 1067, 1517, 1801, 1837, 1975, 2002.

Wolfe: 175, 559, 646, 647, 920, 1256, 1712.

Woodford: 78, 86, 114, 516, 537, 649, 659, 733, 1005, 1087, 1167, 1221, 1322, 1511, 1541, 1580, 1624, 1641, 1649, 1708, 1798, 1847, 1900, 1921, 1986, 1987, 2027.

Subject Index

(Figures refer to marker numbers, not to page numbers.)

Abbey of Our Lady of Gethsemani, 168, 2004
Abbitt, George C., 1690
Abbott, John, 666
Abell, Irvin, Sr., 2042
Abell, John Barton, 1667
Abell, Joseph, 1115
Abell, Samuel IV, 1667
Able, Peter, 1078
Academies: Bethel, 1830; Bethlehem, 1943; Choctaw Indian, 135; Cincinnati Art Academy, 1854; Rittenhouse, 1487, 1841; Russell Creek, 1924
Academy Award nominations: *Doctor Dolittle*, 1881; *The Graduate*, 1881; *Last Picture Show*, 1881; *Oklahoma*, 1881; *Sting*, 1881; *Summer of '42*, 1881
Academy Awards: *Bad and the Beautiful*, 1881; *Ben-Hur*, 1881; Irene Dunne, 1899; *King Solomon's Mines*, 1881
Actors: Dorothy and Lillian Gish, 650; Ethel Barrymore, 1501, 1692; Helen Hayes, 1692; Irene Dunne, 1899; John Wilkes Booth, 1724; Marlene Dietrich, 1865; Mary Anderson, 1702; Mary Pickford, 650; Sarah Bernhardt, 1724; Una Merkel, 1865
Adair, John: 1325, 1372, 1536, 1883; county named for, 1139
Adair County: courthouse, 1599; naming of, 1139
Adairville. *See* Forts and stations: Dromgoole's Station
Adams, George, 1525
Adams, J. Wade, Jr., 1479
Adams, Jinney, 1525
Adams, John Quincy, 765
Adams, Samuel, 1121
Adams, Silas: 888; First Kentucky Cavalry, 684, 1486
Adams, William ("Uncle Billie"), 1660

Adams family, 928-929
Adamsville, 1660
Adath Israel (Louisville), 1923
Adena earthworks, 31, 1655
Admon, Benjamin, 1806
Adventures in Good Cooking (Hines), 1831
Adventures in Good Eating (Hines), 1831
Aetna Furnace, 949
Africa, 1877, 2055
African American: Alexander Walters, 1771; Alice Allison Dunnigan, 1960; Anna Mac Clarke, 1970; Arterburn Brothers Slave Pens, 1989; Arterburn Slave Market, 1990; Berrytown, 1982, 2032; Bond-Washington School, 2049; Burks Chapel A.M.E. Church (Paducah), 1518; Business District (Danville), 1958; Calvary Baptist, 1845; Camp Nelson Refugee Camp, 1965; Catholic High School (Louisville), 1793; Charles W. Anderson Jr., 1964; Charles H. Parrish Jr., 2008, 2020; Charles Young Birthplace, 124; Colored Orphan Industrial Home, 1963; Committee on Negro Affairs, 1815; Doric Lodge No. 18, 1958; Edward Dudley Brown, 2027; Effie Waller Smith, 1959; 8th of August (Paducah), 1957; Elisha Green, 1962; Elks, 1956; First Baptist Church (now Walnut Street), 1949; first black public school in Ky., 1898; Frankfort Barracks, 2061; Free-town Church (Monroe County), 1347; Garrett A. Morgan, 1493; Garrison Slave Pen Site, 1990; General Association of Colored Baptists, 1661; George W. Dupee, 1276, 1716; Green Street Baptist

Church, 1949; Griffytown, 1982; Harrod's Creek Community, 2038; I. Willis Cole, 1998; Jackie Robinson, 1762, 1900, 1984; Jackson Junior High School, 1998; Jacob Price, 1821; James Bond, 1662-1663; Jonesville, 2052; Joseph Alexander Matthews, 1995; Lincoln Institute, 1930; Kentucky State University, 1752; Knights of Pythias Temple, 1662; Lexington Colored Agricultural & Mechanical Association, 1961; Lexington Colored Fair Association, 1961; Lexington Dunbar, 2050; Louisville Cemetery, 1992; Louisville Municipal College, 1998, 2020; Louisville NAACP, 2022; Louisville Western Branch Library, 1545; Luska Joseph Twyman, 2019; Lyman T. Johnson, 2022; Madison Junior High School, 1998; manumission of slaves, 1514; Margaret Garner, 1863; Mary D. Hill School, 1898; Moneta J. Sleet Jr., 2036; Newburg, 1988; New Zion, 1938; Nonimportation Act (1833), 1989; Old Providence Church, 1068; Oliver Lewis, 1885; Patesville, 2039; Petersburg, 1988; physicians, 1928; Pleasant Green Baptist Church, 1806; Robert H. Brooks, 2037; Rosenwald School, 2048; St. John A.M.E. (Frankfort), 1495; Russell Neighborhood, 2017; Second African Baptist Church, 1949; Simmons University, 1661, 2020; Slavery Laws in Old Kentucky, 1989; Smoketown, 1985; Southgate Street School,

2071; Walnut Street Baptist Church, 1845; Washington Street Missionary Baptist Church (Paducah), 1276; West Kentucky Industrial College, 1469; West Side School, 2050; Whitney M. Young Jr., 1419; Rev. William H. Sheppard, 2055; Sheppard Park, 2055; Sheppard Square Housing Project, 2055; William L. Grant, 2000; Winnie A. Scott Hospital, 2025; Zion Baptist Church (Louisville), 1657

"Ah-wah-nee." *See* Station Camp

Airdrie: naming of, 1086

Airdrie Furnace, 1086

Airports: Bowman Field, 1676, 1731, 1901; Godman Field, 1731

Alabama: Selma to Montgomery march, 2036

Alamo: Battle of, 958, 964, 1335, 1947

Alanant-O-Wamiowee, 83, 84

Alaska: purchase of, 1576

Alexander, J. J., 943

Alexander, R. A., 1820

Alexander, Robert: Airdrie Furnace, 1086

Alexandria, 889

Alice Lloyd College, 653, 1532

Allen, Bessie, 1992

Allen, George D., 1351

Allen, Granville: first Union soldier killed in west Kentucky, 1172

Allen, James Lane, 1406, 1550, 1875

Allen, John (Bourbon County), 1774

Allen, John (Shelby County): 1128, 2028; county named for, 508, 760

Allen, "Phog," 1826

Allen, Thomas, 717

Allen, W. S., 1050

Allen, William, 1505

Allen County: naming of, 508, 760

Allensville Post Office, 1384

Allin, Ben C., 1297

All the King's Men (Warren), 1879

Almahurst Farm, 565

Alston, Philip, 1252

Altsheler, Joseph A.: birthplace of, 1002

Alumni Hall (University of Kentucky), 2070

Alvey, John, 1717

Alvey, Robert, 1717

A.M.E. Church: Burks Chapel (Paducah), 1518; St. John (Frankfort), 1495; Zion (Bardstown), 1771

Amanda Furnace, 1142, 1150

America (steamboat): burning of, 720

American Bar Association, 1852

American Legion: naming of, 1104

American Oil Well, Old, 1237

American (Know-Nothing) Party, 1886

American Printing House for the Blind, 1336

American Red Cross: 1398, 1478, 1775; first flood relief operation, 1032, 1065; founder of, 938; McCracken County Chapter, 1107

American Saddle Horse Association, 1629

Anchorage, 1982-1983

Anderson, Charles, 1332

Anderson, Charles W., Jr., 1964

Anderson, Dennis H., 1469

Anderson, Edward, 1754

Anderson, Elizabeth Clark, 1968

Anderson, J. Patton, 553

Anderson, Lucian, 1969

Anderson, Marian, 1692

Anderson, Mary, 1702

Anderson, Richard (Jefferson Co.), 2007

Anderson, Richard Clough: home of, 534, 1968

Anderson, Richard Clough, Jr.: county named for, 847

Anderson, Robert: birthplace of, 534

Anderson, Sarah Marshall, 1968

Anderson, Simeon: home of, 713

Anderson County: naming of, 847

Andrewartha, John, 1704

Andrews, Frank M., 1779

Andrews, James J.: home of, 173

Andrews, William M., 1545

Angier, Father Antoninus, 2057

Angles: home of Alben W. Barkley, 680

Annapolis, 878, 1273, 1479, 1564, 1612, 1769

Anthony, Susan B., 1800

Appalachia: 1728

Architects: A. L. Lassiter, 1754; Benjamin Latrobe, 121; B. J. McElfatrick, 1898; Clarke and Loomis, 1737; Cornelius Curtin, 1704; Frank Lloyd Wright, 1726; Frank M. Andrews, 1779; Gault Bros. of Lexington, 1847; Gideon Shryock, 945, 1406, 1524, 1677, 1697; Henry F. Hawes, 1746; Henry Whitestone, 1229, 2040; J. M. Colley, 1851; John B. Hutchings, 1746; Joseph & Joseph, 1952; McDonald and Dodd, 1545; McDonald Bros., 1599, 1835, 1866; Matthew Kennedy, 1549; Matthias Shryock, 945; Tandy & Foster, 1930; Thomas Lewinski, 1040, 1459, 2005; W. H. Redin, 1695; William Keely, 1639

Argillite Furnace, 975

Argus of Western America (Frankfort), 1799

Aristides (horse), 166, 1885

Armco Steel Corp., 214, 1012, 1149-1150

Armstrong, George A., 1129

Armstrong Hotel, 1129

Army: Air Corps Reserve Unit, 1676; Air Evacuation, School of, 1901; Air Force, U.S. Army, 1901; officers, 1479

Arnold, Josiah, 1735

Arnold, William: town named for, 942

Arnow, Harriette Simpson, 1807

Arsenal, State, 1490

Arterburns (slave dealers), 1989-1990

Arthur, Alexander: founder of Middlesborough, 832, 1227

Arthur, Gabriel, 697

Arthur, Nicholas, 1165

Artists: Charles Courtney Curran, 1485; Elizabeth Boott, 1854; Frank Duveneck, 1854; Gilbert White, 1779; John James Audubon, 1523; Leon Lippert, 1506; Louis Pickett, 1506; Matthew Harris Jouett, 78, 1541, 1888; Nicola Marschall, 681, 1686; Paul Sawyier, 675, 1780; Samuel W. Price, 1780; Theodore Brasch, 1506; Thomas Satterwhite Noble, 1780

Asbury, Bishop Francis, 10, 1278, 1574, 1725, 1830

Asbury College, 1830

Asbury Theological Seminary, 1830

Ashcraft, Jediah, 1115

Ashe, Rev. Christopher, 1724

Asher, Dillion, 723

Asherst, William, 1981

Ashland: Battle of, 9

Ashland: home of Henry Clay, 1, 139, 1211, 1876

Ashland: naming of town, 1211

Ashland Coal and Iron Railway Co., 1012

Ashland Furnace, 1012

A'Sturgus, Peter, 984

Atchison, David R.: president for a day, 1110

Atchison, Topeka and Santa Fe Railroad, 1110

Athiamiowee, 697

Atkins, Edward, 1754

Atkinson, Elisha, 1735

Atkinson, J. L., 1924

Atkinson, John Bond, 1338

Atomic Energy Plant (Paducah), 829, 840, 916, 918

Atwood, James, 2064

Atwood, Margaret, 2064

Audubon, John James, 66, 1321, 1523, 1645, 1652, 1763, 1996

Audubon, John Woodhouse, 1523

Audubon, Lucy, 1523

Audubon Country Club, 1996

Audubon Medical Center, 2042

Audubon Park, 1996

Audubon State Park, 1523

Augusta: College, 94, 750, 861; in Civil War, 501; public square, 1842

Austin, Stephen F., 1406, 1548

Authors: Abraham Flexner, 1654; Alice Hegan Rice, 1508, 1654; Amelia B. Welby, 1654; Annie Fellows Johnston, 1654; Ben Lucien Burman, 1967; Cale Young Rice, 1508, 1654; Charles Dickens, 535, 938; Clark McMeekin, 1654; Cleanth Brooks, 1977; Duncan Hines, 1831; Eleanor Mercein Kelly, 1654; Elizabeth Madox Roberts, 1046; Eugenia Dunlap Potts, 1344; Mrs. George Madden Martin, 1654; Gwen Davenport, 1654; Harriette Simpson Arnow, 1807; Henry Watterson, 1654; Irvin S. Cobb, 962; James Lane Allen, 1875; Janice Holt Giles, 1813; Jesse Stuart, 1808, 1814; Joe Creason, 1538, 1542; John Fox Jr., 1141; John Jacob Niles, 1654; John Mason Brown, 1654; Joseph Altsheler, 1002; Joseph Seaman Cotter, 1654; Laban Lacy Rice, 1508; Lewis Collins, 1488, 1492; Lucy Furman, 870; Madison Cawein, 1654; Richard Collins, 1488, 1492; Robert Emmett McDowell, 1654; Robert Penn Warren, 1879

Automobile: at Cumberland Falls, 1517

Aviation: Abram H. Bowman, 1676; Aero Club of America, 1564; Louis K. Godman, 1731; Matthew Sellers, 1222; Medals of Merit, 1564; Richard Caswell Saufley, 1564; Robert H. Gast, 1676

"Away in a Manger": composer of, 1202

Bacon Creek Bridge, 530

Badin, Father Stephen Theodore, 207, 1312, 1593, 1639

Bailey, P. J., 958

Bainbridge, John, 1446

Baird, John: pioneer Methodist, 1186

Baird's Town, 1668

Baker, Ben, 1837

Baker, Hazard Perry: Jefferson Davis's escort, 872

Baker, John H.: Belmont Furnace, 1136; Nolin Furnace, 1396; Salt River Furnace, 1162

Baker, Joshua: homesite, 1181

Baker Furnace, 1396

Baker Hill, 1049

Bakewell, Thomas, 1645

Ball, Robert, 165

Ballard, Bland W.: Blandville named for, 1374; county named for, 508, 826, 1374; grave of, 1088; massacre of family of, 1088

Ballard County: naming of, 826, 1374

Baltimore, 1699

Bank of Kentucky, 1883

Bank of Louisville, 88

Banta, Abraham, 852

Banta, Hendrick, 1848

Banta, Henry, 1481

Banta, John, 852

Banta, Samuel, 1481

Baptism: first in Kentucky, 1114

Baptist: Beaver Dam, 1330; Beaver Dam Creek, 1980; Cedar Creek (Jefferson County), 1891; Cedar Creek (Nelson County), 1078; Chenoweth Run, 1891; Cooperative Program, 1770; Georgetown College, 1487; Lottie Moon, 1705; Mamre Baptist College, 2024; Mercer County, 1530; Oneida Baptist Institute, 2024; Washington Baptist Church Cemetery, 1696; Beargrass (Jefferson County), 1544; Bethabara, 1873; Bethlehem Association, 1619; Bethlehem Missionary, 2064; Boone's Creek, 1773; Calvary (Louisville), 1845; Campbellsville, 1729; Clear Creek, 1624; Clear Fork, 1516, 1619; Clear Fork Association, 1954; Cooper's Run, 1596; Dawson, 1873; "Difficult," 2064; Donaldson (Farmersville), 1981; Donaldson Creek, 1788; Dripping Springs (Metcalfe County), 1118; Elijah Craig, 1841; Elisha Green, 1962; First Baptist (Bowling Green), 1954; First Baptist (Calvert City), 1405; First Baptist (Danville), 1705; First Baptist (Elizabethtown), 1621; First Baptist (Clinton Street, Frankfort), 1464; First Baptist (St. Clair Street, Frankfort), 1535; First Baptist (Fulton), 1587; First Baptist (Georgetown), 1716; First Baptist (Leitchfield), 1980; First Baptist, now Walnut Street (Louisville), 1949; First Baptist (Murray), 1770; First Baptist (Paducah), 1276; First Missionary Baptist (Hazard), 703; Forks of Dix River, 1617; Forks of Elkhorn, 2003; Friendship (Daviess County), 1873; Friendship (Taylor County), 2016; Gasper River Association, 1954; General Association of Colored Baptists, 1661; Georgetown College, 1487, 1841; Gilead, 1683; Green River Association, 1496; Green Street (Louisville), 1693, 1949; Greenup Association, 1973; Griers Creek, 1624; Hillsborough, 1624; Hopewell, 1873; Immanuel (Paducah), 1044; Indian Creek (Monroe County),

1394; in Lexington, 1552; Jacob Price, 1821; John Tanner, 999; Karn's Grove, 1873; Limestone (Washington), 1696; Long Run (Jefferson County), 101; Macedonia, 1873; Maple Grove, 1840; Maysville, 1962; Mount Union (Allen County), 1117; Mussel Shoals, 1575; New Bethel, 868; Newton's Creek, 1936; Old Church on the Dry Ridge, 1560; Old Hebron, 1521; Old Providence (Clark County), 1068; Old Union (Warren County), 1063; Palmyra, 1973; Paris, 1962; Petrey Memorial (Hazard), 703; Pitman Creek, 1729; Pleasant Green, 1806; Pleasant Grove, 827; Pleasant Hill (Taylor County), 1448; Portland Association, 1117; Providence Knob, 1954; Robinson Creek, 1729; Russell Creek Association, 2016; Salt River Church (Anderson County), 1430; Sand Lick Meeting House, 2016; Second African, 1949; Severns Valley, 1494, 1621; Shawnee Run, 1679; Shuttleworth Memorial (Campbellsville), 1729; Silas, 1596; South Fork 1114; Spring Bayou, 1936; Stockton Valley Association, 1619; Strawberry Association, 1496; Sugar Grove, 1873; Thomas Downs, 1834; Thomas Tinsley, 1530; Versailles, 1624; Walnut Street, 1845; Warren Cash, 1683; Washington Street Missionary (Paducah), 1276; West Union Baptist Association, 1611; William Downs, 1834; Zion (Louisville), 1657

Barbee, Daniel, 1536
Barbee, Elias, 1536, 2016
Barbee, John, 1536
Barbee, Joshua, 1376, 1536

Barbee, Thomas, 1536
Barbee, William, 1536
Barbourville: Civil War in, 518
Barclay family, 1972
Bard, David, 1668
Bard, William, 1668
Bardstown: 1363, 1433; Civil War in, 674, 1413; first school in, 1285; founding of, 1668
Bardstown-Louisville Turnpike, 1021-1022
Bardwell: Civil War in, 563
Barker, Henry Stites, 2070
Barker Hall (University of Kentucky), 2070
Barkley, Alben W.: 739-741, 1369, 1969; birthplace of, 573, 1214; church of, 1029; education of, 891; grave of, 1112; home of, 680, 829, 840, 916, 918; last words of, 1112; law office of, 1030; on Paducah, 1025
Barkley Dam and Lake, 1890
Barkley Field: Paducah, 829
Barlow, Edward, 628
Barlow, Tom, 1969
Barnes, Elias, Jr., 1871
Barnes, Elias, Sr., 1871
Barnes, H. I., 1581
Barnes, James, 1871
Barnes, James C., 1942
Barnes, Richard, 1932
Barnes, Sidney M., 555
Barnes, Stephen T., 598
Barnes, William F., 1581
Barnett, Alexander, 1463
Barnett, Cicero, 1266
Barnett, Hannah, 1463
Barnett, Joseph, 1144, 1463
Barnett, Rev. Joseph, 1078
Barney, Joshua, 1534
Barren County: CSA medalists, 1133; naming of, 1255
Barrett, John, 1266
Barry, William T., 1519
Barrymore, Ethel, 1501, 1692
Barton, Clara, 938, 1032, 1065, 1478
Baryshnikov, Mikhail, 1692
Baseball Hall of Fame, 1627, 1762, 1900, 1984
Bashford Manor, 2040
Baskett, Susannah, 1683
Bass, Myra Greeno: first Boy

Scout Troop, 1007
Bates, Humphrey, 1562
Bath County: naming of, 940
Bath Furnace, 1050
Battles. *See* names of Individual Battles
Bauer, Barbara, 1766
Bauer, John, 1766
Baugh, William B., 2013
Baughn, James R., 830
Baughn, Joseph F., 830
Bayou de Chine Church (Graves County), 1597
Beard, Daniel Carter ("Uncle Dan"), 50
Beard, William, 989
Beargrass Baptist Church (Jefferson County), 1544
Bear Wallow, 698; cemetery, 2019
Beason, Mercer, 1941
Beatty, Otho, 1707
Beattyville: 1805; named for, 702; radio broadcasting in, 1966
Beaty (Beatty), Martin, 702
Beauchamp, Anna, 1077
Beauchamp, Frances E., 1872
Beauchamp, Jereboam: execution of, 1077
Beauchamp-Sharp Tragedy, 1077
Beaumont College, 1173
Beaven, Sister Polly, 1943
Beaver Dam, 1330
Beaver Dam Furnace, 1120
Beck, James Burnie, 14
Beckham, J.C.W.: 1604, 1629, 1779, 1781; county named for, 1177
Beckham County: dissolution of, 1177
Beck House: residence of James Burnie Beck, 14
Bedford Springs and Hotel, 1823
Bedinger, George M.: home and grave of, 897
The Beeches: home of Annie Fellows Johnston, 208
Beech Grove, 863
Beechland (Jefferson County), 1744
Beechland (Spencer County), 1699
Belgian Congo, 2055

Belgium, 1887
Believers, The (Giles), 1813
Belknap, Mary, 1974
Belknap, William R., 541
Belknap Campus, University of Louisville, 541
Bell, John, 633
Bell, John L.: CSA medalist, 1183
Bell, Joshua Fry: county named for, 198
Bell, William: Tavern, 1039
Bell, William F., 1039
Bellarmine College, 1680
Bell County: naming of, 198
Bellefonte Furnace, 1020, 1149
Bellevue, 1351, 1506
Bell Mines, 633
Bell's Tavern, 1039
Belmont, August, 1215, 1635
Belmont Furnace, 1113, 1136
Belmont Stakes, 1215, 1635
Benard, Charlotte, 1512
Benedictine Sisters, 1887
Bennett, Archibald, 1941
Bennett, B. F., 1076
Bennett, Moses, 2001
Bennett, Pramley, 1076
Bennett, Sue, 2060
Bennett, Warfield Clay, Jr., 1479
Bennett, William, 1941
Bennett's Mill Covered Bridge, 1076
Bentley, Rev. D. S., 1495
Benton: Big Singing Day in, 1749
Benton, Allen H., 830
Benton Tribune, 1749
Berea College, 773, 861, 1663, 1767, 1930
Bergen, George, 852
Bernhardt, Sarah, 1724
Bernstadt Colonization Company, 843
Berry, Alfred, 1982, 2032
Berrytown, 1982, 2032
Bertram, Alvin, 1619
Bessemer, Sir Henry, 61, 946
Bessemer Process: Eddyville Furnace, 1326; Kelly Furnace, 61, 946; New Union Forge, 1332; Suwanee Furnace, 1327
Bethel Academy, 1830

Bethel College, 1269
Bethelridge, 1305
Bethlehem Academy (Hardin Co.), 1740
Bethlehem Academy (Nelson Co.), 857, 1943
Better Business Bureau, 1664
Bibb, A. J., 1992
Bibb, George M.: 123, 1281, 1888, 2028; home of, 883
Bibb, John B.: Bibb-Burnley House, 1205
Bibb, Richard, 1514
Bibb-Burnley House, 1205
Bibb family, 1972
Bibb lettuce, 1205
Big Boiling Springs. *See* Chalybeate Springs
Big Bone Lick, 32, 163, 859, 1253
"Big Cave." *See* Saltpeter Cave
Biggs, R. M., 914
Bigham, N. T., 1526
Big Hill. *See* Richmond: Battle of
Big Sandy: Civil War in, 85, 164, 608
Big Sandy Valley, 2034
Big Singing Day, 1749
"Big Spring, The": Harrodsburg, 1449, 1530, 1637, 1877
Bill Smothers Park, 744
Bingham, Barry, Sr., 1292
Bingham, Robert Worth, 1292
Bingham Cooperative Marketing Act, 1292
Bird, Henry: 150; British-Indian raid, 953; Ruddle's Station, 107
Birds of America (Audubon), 1321
Bird's War Road, 34
Birmingham, England, 1648
Birmingham, Kentucky, 1648
Birney, James G.: 754, 1442; home of, 36
Bishop, Rev. Robert, 894
Bishop, William, 632
Bishop, William Sutton: "Old Judge Priest," 839, 1025, 1029-1030
Bishops: Benedict Flaget, 857, 1312, 1639, 1827, 1897, 1943, 2057; C. H. Phillips,

1677; C. L. Russell, 1677; D. W. Clark, 1659; Edward Fenwick, 1593; Ferdinand Brossart, 1593; F.P. Kenrick, 1593; Francis Asbury, 10, 1278, 1574, 1725, 1830; G. A. Carroll, 1593; Guy Chatbrat, 1593; H. H. Kavanaugh, 1539, 1659; Martin John Spalding, 1639; U.V.W. Darlington, 1659

"Bivouac of the Dead" (O'Hara), 24

Black, James D., 1811

Black, Ziah, 1464

Blackacre State Natural Preserve, 1907

Blackburn, Rev. Gideon, 1045

Blackburn, Luke P., 131, 1466

Blackburn Correctional Complex, 1466

Blackford: first post office in Hancock Co, 1993

Black history: See African American

Black Horse Tavern, 1649

Black Patch War, 145

Blacksmith Shop, 1766

Blackstone Furnace. See Red River Iron Works

Blaine, James G., 754, 798

Blaine (Lawrence Co.), 1991

Blair, Robert A., 1517

Blake, Henry, and Company, 1132

Blakely, Charles, 1837

Blakely, William, 1118

Blanchard, Asa, 1784

Bland, Richard Parks, 1858

Blanding, Sarah, 2011

Blandville: naming of, 1374

Bledsoe, Jesse, 1101

Blind, School for, 1336

Bloch, Claude C., 1769

Bloody Monday riot, 1639

Blue, Thomas F., 1545

Blue Goose, 2056

Blue Licks: Battle of, 18, 217, 222, 729, 785, 800, 842, 917, 952, 1001, 1048, 1159, 1230, 1322, 1472, 1558, 1567, 1615, 1790

Blue Springs Farm: home of Richard M. Johnson, 135

Boggs, Robert, 1404

Boiling Spring Settlement, 1435, 1520

Bolles, William, 571

Bonaparte, Napoleon, 1534, 1779

Bond, James (financial agent), 1930

Bond, James (physician), 1662-1663

Bond-Washington School, 2049

Bone, John, 1735

Bon Harbor: founding of, 743

Bonner, Rev. M. J.: grave of, 1117

Books: A Black Woman's Experience–From Schoolhouse To White House (Dunnigan), 1960; All The King's Men (Warren), 1879; Bloody Ground (Day), 1736; Conjectures of a Guilty Bystander (Merton), 2004; Discovery, Settlement, and Present State of Kentucke (Filson), 1229; Flowering of the Cumberland (Arnow), 1807; Gulliver's Travels (Swift), 137; Guthrie's Arithmetic, 1539; Hell For Sartain (Fox), 775-777; History of Fayette County (Peter), 1480; History of Kentucky (Collins), 738, 1488, 1492; History of Morgan's Cavalry (Duke), 1861; Hunter's Horn (Arnow), 1807; Joe Creason's Kentucky, 1542; Lincoln and the Bluegrass (Townsend), 2029; "Little Colonel" series (Johnston), 208; Little Shepherd of Kingdom Come (Fox), 775-777, 1141; Man With a Bull-Tongue Plow (Stuart), 1808, 1814; Pioneer Life in Kentucky (Drake), 1628; Principal Diseases of the Interior of North America (Drake), 1628; Seedtime on the Cumberland (Arnow), 1807; Steamboat Round the Bend (Burman), 1967; The Believers (Giles), 1813; The Best Poetic Works of Cale Young Rice, 1508; The Dollmaker (Arnow), 1807; The Enduring Hills (Giles),

1813; The Fascinating Story of Black Kentuckians: Their Heritage and Traditions (Dunnigan), 1960; The Great Meadow (Roberts), 1046; The Seven Storey Mountain (Merton), 2004; The Thread That Runs So True (Stuart), 1800, 1814; Time of Man (Roberts), 1046; Trail of the Lonesome Pine (Fox), 775-777, 1141

Boone, Andrew R., 1969

Boone, Daniel: 148, 576, 825, 959, 988, 1168, 1230, 1274, 1280, 1371, 1426, 1435, 1443, 1472, 1524-1525, 1579, 1600, 1615, 1622, 1642, 1802; Boone Salt Works, 151; brother of, 952, 1773, 2059; cave, 1343; church of, 1068; county named for, 1253; Estill Springs, 555; Ft. Boonesborough, 1520; grave of, 113, 576; last home in Kentucky, 1230; Lower Blue Licks, 162; Lulbegrud Creek, 137; Pilot Knob, 132; pioneer station, 196, 848; reinterment of, 1322; 1775 exploration, 709; sister of, 721; station, 17, 196, 1790; station camp, 810; Twitty's Fort, 77; Warrior's Path, 697

Boone, Edward, 2059

Boone, Hannah: grave of, 721

Boone, Jemima: captured by Indians, 1048, 1181

Boone, Jesse, 1529

Boone, Mary: baptism of, 1068

Boone, Rebecca: 576, 1524; grave of, 113, 576

Boone, Samuel: 1773; baptism of, 1068; grave of, 952

Boone, Sarah, 1773

Boone, Squire: 1343, 1560, 1755, 1848; land of, 852; Lulbegrud Creek, 137; station, 28, 848, 991; station camp, 810

Boone, Squire, Jr.: baptism of, 1068

Boone, Thomas: death of, 952

Boone County: naming of, 1253

Boone Family Association, 1582

Boone Furnace, 1013

Boone Salt Springs, 151

Boonesborough: 113, 250, 848, 897, 1404, 1435, 1443, 1520, 1578-1579, 1782, 1802; founder of, 825; Captain John Holder, 856, 1048; settlement of, 576

Boone's Trace, 53, 1443, 1600, 1622

Booneville: 196; Civil War in, 561

Boone Way, 1644

Booth, John Wilkes, 1724

Boott, Elizabeth, 1854

Borglum, Gutzon, 1780

Borries, Fred "Buzz," Jr., 1479

Bosque Bonita: home of N. B. Buford, 649

Boston, Old (Nelson County), 1471

Boswell, Hart, 1701

Bottom, Squire H. P., 192

Bottom House, 192

Bourbon County: naming of, 1246

Bourbon Iron Works, 940, 993, 1193

Bourne, Benjamin, 1748

Bower, Jacob N., 1567

Bower Bridge Company: and restorations of covered bridges, 1439, 1559, 1566, 1571-1572

Bowie, James: birthplace of, 958, 1947; land, 1947

Bowie, Reason, 1947

Bowie Knife: designer of, 958

Bowling Green: Baker Hill, 1049; Civil War in, 1024, 1458; College Hill, 1051; College of Commerce, 1418; Confederate capital, 67; founder of, 981; Jonesville, 2052; naming of, 997; skirmish in, 671

Bowman, Abraham, 1783

Bowman, Abram H., 1676

Bowman, John: 926, 1472, 1909; Harrodsburg headquarters, 1083

Bowman Field: 1676; East,

1901

Boyd, Abraham, 1838

Boyd, Linn: 1969; county named for, 772, 1105; home of, 829, 1105

Boyd, Thomas, 1454

Boyd County: naming of, 772, 1105

Boyer, Levi, 909

Boyle, John: at Estill Springs, 555; county named for, 714, 1218; home of, 714; law practice of, 813

Boyle County: naming of, 714, 1218

Boy Scouts, 50, 1007, 1747

Bracken, Matthew, 122

Bracken, William: county named for, 861

Bracken County: naming of, 861; wine production in, 1213

Bradford, J. Taylor, 501

Bradford, John, 1864

Bradford, Joshua Taylor: birthplace of, 861

Bradley, William O.: 1684, 1942; home of, 699

Bradshaw, W. R., 1619

Brady, John Huston, 1479

Bragg, Braxton: 598, 683, 1121, 1296; at Bardstown, 674; Battle of Munfordville, 119; Battle of Perryville, 58, 193, 553; Big Hill Skirmish, 1124; in Bryantsville, 676; a Confederate Thrust, 519; Confederates here, 522; Crawford House, 193; Crawford Spring, 965; invasion of Kentucky, 749, 1255; retreat of, 704, 737

Bramlette, Thomas E.: 1301; birthplace, 1306

Brandeis, Alice Goldmark, 2006

Brandeis, Louis Dembitz: 1880, 2006; Law School, U. of L., 2006

Brandenburg: becomes county seat, 1652

Brandenburg, Solomon, 1652

Brandywine: Battle of, 81, 1496, 1608, 1683

Bran family: massacre of, 936

Branham, George C., 925

Brank, Ephraim M.: 1609; home of, 761

Brank, R. M.: duel, 611

Brank, Robert, 1562

Brasch, Theodore, 1506

Brashear, Robert S., 1346

Brashear, Walter (contractor), 1746

Brashear, Walter (physician), 1282

Brashear, William, 1944

Brasher, L. T., 1625

Brawner, Alexander Goldsmith, 2061

Breathitt, John: 1260, 1882; county named for, 961; home of, 658

Breathitt County: naming of, 961; World War I volunteers, 904

Breckinridge, Desha, 1876

Breckinridge, John: 1387, 1642, 1687; county named for, 1170

Breckinridge, John Cabell: 24, 136, 610, 754, 772, 1103, 1105, 1372, 1406, 1424, 1550, 1638, 1739; Beck House, 14; last home, 1742; U.S. vice president, 739-741

Breckinridge, Madeline McDowell, 1876

Breckinridge, Mary Cabell, 1687

Breckinridge, Mary Jane, 558

Breckinridge, Robert J., Jr., 188

Breckinridge, William Mattingly, 1479

Breckinridge County: naming of, 1170

"Breezin' Along With The Breeze" (song), 1836

Brent, George, 1276

Brent, Hugh, 1462

Brent, Thomas, 1462

Bretton Woods, New Hampshire, 1776

Bridger, Joseph, 1788

Bridgers, William, 1788

Bridges, Charity, 1840

Bridges (Bridgers, Bridger), Drury, 1788, 1840

Bridges, William, 1840

Bridges: Brooklyn, 1381, 1601; High, 1381; Roebling

Suspension at Covington, 1601. *See also* Covered Bridges

Bridgewater, James H., 549

Brien, James, 2035

Briensburg, 1648

Briggs, Mary, 1234

Bright, James, 1850

Briscoe family, 1944

Bristow, Benjamin Helm: birthplace of, 1355

Brith Sholom (Louisville), 1923

Broadenax, Henry P., 1741

Broadway Methodist Church (Paducah), 1029

Bronze Star, 2046

Brooklyn Bridge, 1381, 1601

Brooks, C. C., 1177

Brooks, Cleanth, 1977

Brooks, Robert H., 2037

Brossart, Bishop Ferdinand, 1593

Browder, Isham: grave of, 973

Browder, Kennedy and Company, 1373

Brown, Benjamin G.: home of, 123

Brown, Edward Dudley, 2027

Brown, Granville, 830

Brown, Jacob: town named for, 802

Brown, James (agriculturalist), 1848

Brown, James: first Kentucky secretary of state, 157; home of, 123

Brown, John: at Harper's Ferry, 1335

Brown, John (U. S. senator): 1372, 1653; home of, 123, 1653

Brown, John Marshall: one of designers of Wickland, 1604

Brown, John Mason, 1229, 1654

Brown, John Young, 1650, 1926

Brown, L. H., 1677

Brown, Margaretta, 1540, 1653

Brown, Orlando, Jr., 901

Brown, Patrick, 1114

Brown, Samuel, 1595

Brown, Thomas, 1115

Brown Hotel (Louisville), 1723

Brown Memorial C.M.E. Church, 1677

Brown-Pusey House, 1505

Brown's Run, Battle of, 1114

Brownsville: Civil War in, 607; naming of, 802

Bruce, Eli Metcalfe, 1638

Bruner, Otto, 843

Bryan, Daniel Boone, 1280

Bryan, James, 21

Bryan, Joseph, 21, 1280

Bryan, Martha, 2059

Bryan, Rebecca, 2059

Bryan, Samuel, 1642

Bryan, William, 21, 1280

Bryan, William Jennings, 1501, 1698, 1858

Bryantsville: Civil War in, 676

Buchanan, James, 211, 552, 1763

Buckner, Aylette Hartswell, 155, 1389-1390

Buckner, James F., 1915

Buckner, Philip, 1502, 1842

Buckner, Robert, 602

Buckner, Simon Bolivar: 1127, 1236, 1324; Battle of Perryville, 553; birthplace, 155; Civil War defense line, 538; skirmish at Bowling Green, 671

Buckner, S. B., Jr.: death of, 1236

Buckner, William, 1915

Buckner-Churchill Furnace, 1389

Buck Pond: home of Thomas Marshall, 114

Bucksnort (Pellville), 1993

Buell, Don Carlos: 649, 737, 863, 2070; Battle of Munfordville, 119; Battle of Perryville, 58, 195, 553, 674; headquarters of, 1040; home of, 1086; Rowlett's Station, 656

Buell Armory (University of Kentucky), 2070

Buena Vista: Battle of, 24, 964, 995; Furnace, 1010, 1135; Todd home at, 1999

"Buffalo Bill." *See* Cody, William

Buffalo Furnace, 976

Buffalo Road, 1307

Buffalo Trace, 217-218, 1519, 1567

Buford, Abraham: 517, 649; two successful raids, 654-655

Buford, John, 649

Buford, Napoleon Bonaparte, 649

Bullitt, Alexander Scott: 2007; county named for, 890, 983; home of, 983, 1474

Bullitt, Caroline, 1229

Bullitt, Priscilla, 983

Bullitt, Thomas, 133, 1435

Bullitt, Thomas W., 1229

Bullitt County: naming of, 890, 983

Bullitt's Lick, 133, 1944

Bullock, Edward: 165, 1284; founder of Perryville, 876

Bullock, Mary C., 2014

Bullock, Walter, 165

Bunnell, P. G., 2060

Buntline, Ned. *See* Judson, Edward Z. C.

Burbridge, Stephen G.: 109; at Mt. Sterling, 629; Civil War action, 569; Morgan Raiders' camp, 567; Morgan's Last Raid, 621-624, 691-695, 700

Burchard, Samuel D., 754

Burgin, Temple, 1679

Burgin: founding of, 1679

Burgin Christian Church, 1679

Burkesville: founding of, 959

Burks, Charles, 1509

Burks, George R., 1509

Burks, Moses, 1518

Burks, Samuel: founder of Burkesville, 959

Burley Tobacco Growers Association, 1292

Burlington, 1646

Burman, Ben Lucien, 1967

Burnett, Henry Cornelius: 67, 1969; home of, 764

Burns, James Anderson, 2024

Burns, Kenneth C. (Jethro), 1605

Burns, Robert: "Flow Gently, Sweet Afton," 1202

Burnside, Ambrose E.: town named for, 979-980

Burnside, Walter, 1562

Burnside: naming of, 979-980

Burnt Mill (Webster County), 1915
Burr, Aaron: 1652; in Frankfort, 1182; Kentucky land, 1154; trials of, 883, 1158
Burr, Jeff, 100
Burr, Theodore, 1569, 1585
Burris, Henry, 734
Burton, A. A., 699
Burton, Charles, 818
Burton, Dorotha, 1920
Bush, William, 1068
Business: oldest continuous in Kentucky, 1378
Buster, William Robards, 1479
Butchertown, 1713
Butler, Mann, 1654
Butler, Richard: county named for, 822
Butler, William (Jefferson County), 1982
Butler, William O.: birthplace of, 823; home of, 634
Butler County: Civil War in, 569; naming of, 822
Buttermilk Spring, 100
Button, F. C., 1952
Button, Phebe, 1952
Byrene, Rev. William, 1026
Cabin Creek, 143
Cabin Creek Covered Bridge, 1572
Cabins, 72, 723, 742
Caldwell, Andrew Jackson, 503
Caldwell, John: county named for, 834
Caldwell, William, 21
Caldwell County: Confederates from, 1630; county seat named, 1902; naming of, 834
Caldwell family, 1972
Caldwell Female Institute, 1705
Calhoun, Charity, 1788
Calhoun, James, 1446
Calhoun, John: town named for, 1123
Calhoun, John C., 1694
Calhoun: 1548, 1946; Civil War in, 665; naming of, 1123
Call, Richard, 1260
Callaway, Elizabeth: captured by Indians, 1048, 1181

Callaway, Frances: captured by Indians, 1048, 1181
Callaway, Mary, 1181
Callaway, Richard: buried, 1578; county named for, 825
Calloway, Charles, 1837
Calloway, Jack, 856
Calloway County: college in, 1427; first courthouse, 1263; naming of, 825
Calloway Normal College, 1945
Calmes, Marquis, 1921
Calvary Baptist Church (Louisville), 1845
Calvary Episcopal Church (Louisville), 1695
Calvary Settlement, 1667
Calvert, Potilla, 1405
Calvert City, 1405
Cameron, Rev. Archibald, 1285
Camp: Anderson, 1391; Beauregard, 180, 1597; Billy Williams, 1486; Bingham, 1292; Breckinridge, 1424, 1762; Charity, 506; Dennison, Ohio, 520, 637; Dick Robinson, 684, 1515, 1750; Knox, 1869; Marshall, 564; Morton, 540, 1629; Nelson, 1515, 1750, 1825; Nelson Covered Bridge, 1513; Nelson National Cemetery, 1610, 1825; Korean War, 1610; Prisoner of War (German), 1424; Refugee Camp, 1965; Spanish-American War, 1610; Taylor, 1663; Vietnam War, 1610; Wickliffe, 1631; Wildcat, 514, 684, 1622, 1919; World War I, 1610; World War II, 1610
Campbell, Rev. A. W., 1061
Campbell, Adam: town named for, 995
Campbell, Alexander, 19, 1477, 1511, 1590, 1636, 1679, 1710
Campbell, Andrew: town named for, 995
Campbell, Arthur: grave of, 129
Campbell, George, 1707

Campbell, James (judge): home of, 1061
Campbell, James (War of 1812), 129
Campbell, John (Revolutionary War): county named for, 889
Campbell, John (War of 1812), 129, 1017
Campbell, Rev. John P., 935
Campbell County: naming of, 889
Campbellsville: naming of, 995
Campbellsville Baptist Church, 1729
Campbellsville College, 1924
Camp Branch Furnace, 1143
Camp Ground Methodist Church, 1574
Canada, 1777
Canby, Edward Richard Sprigg, 1646
Candler, Wade, 1517
Cane Ridge Meeting House, 51
Cane Run Christian Church (Mercer County), 1679
Canewood: home of Nathaniel Gist and Charles Scott, 116
Caney Creek Community Center, 653, 1532
Caney Furnace, 1226
Caney Junior College, 653
Cannon, John W., 1756
Canton: N. B. Forrest in, 619
Cantrill, J. E., 1454
Capitals: Confederate, of Kentucky, 67; Kentucky, 105-106, 696, 1070, 1524, 1774; Nevada, 79; United States, 60
Capitols: Arkansas, 945; Kentucky, 945, 1524, 1779
Cardome: home of James F. Robinson, 718
Cardome Academy, 718, 1593
Cardwell, James, 1603
Carlin, William P., 553
Carlisle, John Griffin: county named for, 763; home of, 167
Carlisle: becomes seat of Nicholas County, 1615
Carlisle County: naming of, 763

Carlisle Passenger Depot, 1764
Carlow's Stone Wall, 1620
Carneal, Thomas, 1429
Carneal House, 1429
Carnegie, Andrew, 1654, 1972
Caroline Furnace, 1132
Carpenter, Adam, 1203
Carpenter, Conrad, 1203
Carpenter, George, Sr., 1203
Carpenter, John, 1203
Carr, Benjamin Franklin, 1587
Carr, John W., 1427
Carr Creek Center, 1152
Carrell, Bishop G. A., 1593
Carroll, Charles, 216
Carroll County: naming of, 216
Carrollton: founder of, 893; settlement, 10, 216, 1725. *See also* Port William
Carson, Christopher (Kit), 79, 1335
Carson City, Nevada, 79
Carter, Sallie, 1982
Carter, William Grayson: county named for, 1247
Carter Caves, 1247
Carter County: naming of, 1247
Cartwright, Rev. Peter: boyhood home, 1334
Cartwright, Samuel, 1339
Cary, Remos G., 830
Casey, Samuel, 211
Casey, Samuel L., 1969
Casey, William: 128, 250; county named for, 781, 806; home of, 806
Casey County: courthouse, 1835; naming of, 781, 806
Caseyville: Civil War in, 187, 616
Cash, Warren, 1683
Cassidy, Michael, 950, 1388
Castleman, John B., 1629
Casto, William T.: duel of, 996
Cathedral of the Assumption (Louisville), 1639
Catholic Church: 1100, 1667, 1682, 1740; Bishop Benedict Joseph Flaget, 1639, 1827, 1897, 2057; Cathedral of the Assumption (Louisville), 1639; Frank Duveneck, 1854; Good Shepherd

(Frankfort), 2057; Father Angier, 2057; Father J. M. Lancaster, 2057; first Louisville African American parish, 1303; high school for blacks, 1793; Holy Cross Church (Covington), 1887; Mother of God (Covington), 1460; Our Lady (Louisville), 1312; Sacred Heart Church (Campbell Co.), 1506; Sacred Heart Church (Union Co.), 1785; St. Augustine (Louisville), 1793; St. Charles (Carlisle County), 1785; St. Denis (Hickman County), 1785; St. Francis (Scott County), 1593; St. Francis de Sales (McCracken County), 1106; St. Jerome's (Graves County), 1682, 1785; St. Joseph's Cathedral (Nelson County), 1827; St. Mary's College, 1026; St. Patrick Mission (Franklin County), 2057; St. Peter Claver (Louisville), 1793; St. Rose Priory (Washington County), 941; St. Rose's (Washington County), 1682; St. Thomas (Nelson County), 857; Thomas Merton, 2004
Catholic pioneers, 913
Cattle, 205, 1184
Caudill, James: pioneer ancestor, 1197
Cave City, 1489
Caveland: home of Richard Hickman, 1318
Cave Spring: home of Captain Robert Boggs, 1404
Cave Spring: plantation of Isaac Hite, 1435
Cave Spring Tract: property of William Preston, 1557
Cawein, Madison, 1654
Cayce, Edgar, 1313
Cecil, Rev. Charles J., 1740
Cedar Bluff Female College, 1417
Cedar Creek Baptist Church (Nelson County), 1078
Cedar House, 1071
Cedars, The (Grayson County), 1602

Cemeteries: American (Manila), 2037; Barbourville, 1884; Berrytown, 2032; Birmingham, 1648; Camp Nelson National, 1825; Carlisle, 2053; Cave Hill, 1475, 1753, 1786; Cedar Creek Baptist Church (Jefferson County), 1891; CSA, 1905; Dils, 1728; East Broadway (Winchester), 1399; Elizabethtown, 1494; Elmwood, 1644; Evergreen, 1867; Fairview, 1831; Fernwood, 1926; Frankfort, 1882, 1896, 1910; Georgetown, 1934; German Reformed Presbyterian Church, 1028; Glasgow, 1317; Greenville, 1609; Highland (Kenton County), 1638, 1865; Horse Cave, 1091, 1207; Lexington, 679, 1550, 1809, 1875-1876; Lindsey (Harrison County), 1220; Longview (Bethel), 1542; Louisville (African American), 1992; Maple Grove (Nicholasville), 1473; Mapleview (Marion), 1499; Mother of God (Kenton County), 1854; Mt. Kenton (Paducah), 1112; Mystery (Bullitt County), 1415; Old Calvary/Holy Mary (Marion County), 1667; Paint Lick, 1562; Pioneer Burying Ground (Lexington), 1552; Pisgah (Woodford County), 1900; Pitman Church, 1729; Portland, 1778; Richmond, 1576; Robinson Church, 1729; Rosine, 1672; St. Louis (Louisville), 1785; Smith's Grove, 1573; South Fork (Larue County), 1114; Springfield, 930, 1046; The Old (Harrison County), 1428; Washington (Mason County), 1696; Winchester, 1047; Woodlawn Hills (Stringtown), 1970; Zachary Taylor National (Louisville), 1412
Center Furnace, 1357, 1366
Center of Kentucky, 867

Center of U. S. Population (1880), 1640
Center Street C.M.E. Church (Louisville), 1677
Centerville, 1097, 1204
Central Intelligence Agency (CIA), 1732
Central Park (Louisville), 1629
Central State Hospital, 1474
Centre College: 1564, 1606, 1705, 2005, 2044; first law dean, 728, 791; football coach, 1091, 1207; founding of, 923; Praying Colonels, 1091
Ceralvo, 1370
Cessna, Jonathan F., 1115
Cessna, William, 1115
Chabrat (Chatbrat), Bishop Guy Ignatius, 1312, 1593
Chalybeate Springs (Russell County), 1233; (Union County), 1588
Chambers, James: duel, 1101, 1281
Champ, William, 1525
Chandler, Albert Benjamin "Happy," 1819, 1900, 1984
Chandler Furnace. See Red River Iron Works
Chapel Hill Presbyterian Church, 1526
Chapman, Virgil Munday: birthplace of, 978
Charlotte Furnace. See Iron Hill Furnace
Chatbrat. See Chabrat
Chaumiere des Prairies, 158
Chautauqua Association: of Central Kentucky, 1341; Proctor Knott, 1341
Cheapside, 1553
Cheatham, Benjamin F., 553
Cheek, James E., 2060
Cheek, Joel, 1718
Chenault, D. W., 705
Chenault, William, 1229
Chenoweth, John T., 1204
Chenoweth, Richard, 992
Chenoweth Massacre, 992
Chenoweth Run, 1907
Cherokee Indians: 908, 922, 1074-1075, 1577; missionary to, 1045; Trail of Tears, 142, 1042, 1675
Cherokee Park, 1629

Cherry, Robert, 1214
Chestnut St. C.M.E. Church (Louisville), 1677
Chicago: Columbian World's Fair and Exposition in, 1394; International Show, 1470; WLS Radio, 2026
Chickasaw Park, 1663
Chickasaw Road, 1185
Chicken Bristle. See Savoyard
Child: first white born of American parents west of the Alleghenies, 574
China, 1705, 1727
Chinn, Christopher "Kit," 1295
Chinn, George M., 2044
Chinn, Jack, 1295
Chitwood, I. O., 1517
Choctaw Indian Academy, 135
Cholera: 1057, 1342, 1399, 1406, 1415, 1442, 1466, 1552, 1671, 1702, 1823, 1999; discovery of treatment for, 966, 1057, 1452
Christian, Anne, 974
Christian, William: county named for, 974, 1224; daughter of, 983; land grant of, 984
Christian Baptist School (Harrodsburg), 1173
Christian Church: 899, 1477; Big Spring (Woodford County), 1511; Burgin, 1679; Cane Run (Mercer County), 1679; Eminence, 2043; First Christian (Clinton), 1937; First Christian (Frankfort), 1710; First Christian (Fulton), 1587; founding of, 51; McCormack (Lincoln County), 1590; Main Street (Lexington), 19; Mt. Zion (Madison County), 1825; Old Concord (Nicholas County), 935; Oxford (Scott County), 1701; Quality (Butler County), 1467; South Elkhorn (Fayette County), 1636
Christian County: naming of, 974, 1224
Christian Heritage Day, 1972
Christmas Mishap: in Barren County, 544

Chuqualatague, Chief, 988
Churchill, Cadwallader, 1389-1390
Churchill, Henry (benefactor of Jefferson Seminary), 2007
Churchill, Henry (Louisville landowner), 1885
Churchill, John, 1885
Churchill, Thomas J., 1300, 1825
Churchill, W. P., 1992
Churchill Downs, 1885, 1992
Church Hill Grange House (Christian County), 1179
Church of the Ascension (Frankfort), 1537
Church of Christ: Grace United (Covington), 1531; Paducah, 1035
Church of Christ, Union, 1767
Church of England, 1582
"Church on the Twins." See New Liberty Baptist Church
Cincinnati: Art Academy, 1780, 1854; Daniel Drake in, 1628; defense of, 1917; first blockhouse, 842; Observatory, 1758
Cincinnati Times-Star, 1836
Civilian Conservation Corps, 1775, 2001
Civil rights: 1419, 1657, 1663, 1693, 1721, 1815, 1845, 1929, 1998, 2008, 2019, 2022, 2036
Civil War: 1486, 1490, 1498, 1513, 1524, 1540, 1560, 1562, 1576, 1621, 1638, 1691, 1697, 1724, 1728-1729, 1734, 1758, 1787, 1825, 1833, 1920, 2039; army base at Louisa, 643; Army of Six, 1103; Augusta in, 501; Bacon Creek Bridge, 530; Baker Hill, 1049; Barbourville in, 518; Bardstown in, 674; Bardwell in, 563; base at Smithland, 663; Basil W. Duke, 1861; Battle of "Ashland," 9; Battle of Cynthiana, 109, 567, 621-625, 646-648, 691-695, 700-701; Battle of Dutton's Hill, 712; Battle of Elizabethtown, 1116, 1296; Battle of Green

River Bridge, 89; Battle of Grubb's Crossroads, 830; Battle of Half Mountain, 556; Battle of Irvine, 1507; Battle of Ivy Mountain, 164; Battle of Lebanon, 600-601; Battle of London, 560; Battle of Middle Creek, 85, 172, 571, 643; Battle of Mill Springs, 75, 863, 1275; Battle of Mt. Sterling, 177, 567, 621-625, 628-629, 646-648, 691-695, 700, 841; Battle of Munfordville, 119, 698; Battle of Murfreesboro, 1333; Battle of Paducah, 1277, 1287; Battle of Panther Creek, 745; Battle of Perryville, 58, 192, 194-195, 539, 551, 553, 572, 627, 630, 649, 674, 676, 749, 1333, 1825; Battle of Richmond, 514, 683, 1124, 1825, 1905; Battle of Sacramento, 665; Battle of Tebb's Bend, 601, 706; Battle of Wildcat Mountain, 684; Bear Wallow, 698; Big Sandy in, 608; Black Measles epidemic, 1269; Boone Salt Springs, 151; Booneville in, 561; Bottom House, 192; Bowling Green in, 671, 1024; Brownsville in, 607; Bryantsville in, 676; Burnside in, 979-980; Butler County in, 569; Calhoun in, 665; Camp Beauregard, 180, 1597; Camp Charity, 506; Camp Dick Robinson, 684; Camp Morton, 1629; Camp Nelson, 1515; Camp Nelson National Cemetery, 1610; Camp Wickliffe, 1631; Camp Wildcat, 514, 1622, 1919; capture of Lexington, 567, 621-625, 628-629, 700-701; Caseyville in, 187; Casto-Metcalfe Duel, 996; Cave City in, 1489; Christmas mishap (Barren County), 554; Christopher (Kit) Carson in, 79; Clay-Bullock House, 2014; College Hill, 1051; Columbus in, 528; Confederate gover-

nor, 610; Confederate raids, 706-707; Confederate recruitment and supply post, 2018; Confederate state capital, 67; Confederate state convention, 74; CSA returns to Tennessee, 676; CSA starts retreat, 704; Confederate thrust, 519; Confederates in Frankfort, 522; courthouse a hospital, 756; courthouses burned during, 577-594, 596-597, 972; courthouse used as hospital, McCracken Co., 1377; Covington City Hall, 1862; Crawford House, 193; Crawford Spring, 965; Cumberland Ford, 1426; Cumberland Gap retreat, 637-638, 642, 644-648; death of a Morgan, 543; defense line, 538; Dorsey House, 195; Eddyville in, 509; Empire Furnace, 1357; Falmouth in, 686; Felix K. Zollicoffer, 1919; field hospital, 1825; First Kentucky Cavalry, 684; first Kentucky Federal death in, 1365; Forrest foraged, 598; Forrest reconnoitered, 612-618; Forrest's raid, 517; Fort Anderson, 828; Fort Heiman, 147; Fort Henry, 1364; Fort Jefferson site, 1309; Fort Mitchell, 546; Fort Southworth, 1810; Fort Webb, 1458; Fort Williams, 1290; Galt House, 535; Garfield Place, 172; generals, 603; Georgetown raided, 701; "Gibraltar of the West," 528; Goose Creek Salt Works, 531; Grant's Paducah Proclamation, 924; Grubb's Crossroads, 830, 1630; guerrilla Quantrill, 505; guerrilla raids on Clinton, 1400; gunsmith Ferd Hummel, 1062; Harrodsburg Springs in, 551; Henderson in, 527; Henry County in, 549; hospitals in, 542, 661, 756, 879, 1045, 1090, 1269, 1275,

1377, 1445, 1480, 1597, 1610, 1621, 1825, 1897, 1905; Independence Day–1863, 605; Indiana-Ohio raid, 1861; invasion (1862), 749; Iron Banks in, 60; James B. McCreary, 1846; Jamestown skirmishes, 724; Jefferson County in, 548; Jefferson Davis birthplace, 57; Jennie's Creek, 571; John Bell Hood home, 112; John Hunt Morgan, 1861; John Larue Helm, 1912; John Marshall Harlan, 1606; Johnston birthplace, 91; Jones Tavern, 1905; "Aunt Julia" Marcum, 672; Karrick-Parks House, 876; last skirmish in Kentucky, 1231; Lawrenceburg in, 630; Louisa in, 547; Louisville Legion, 1589; L & N Bridge, 1296; Louisville and Nashville Railroad, 1350, 1994; McLean County recruits, 830; Magoffin County in, 566; "Black Dave" Martin, in Shelbyville, 1089, 1379; masterful retreat, 520-521; Morgan at Midway, 516; Morgan's first raid, 524, 625-627, 673, 677, 685, 689, 696, 698, 701, 733, 1255; Morgan's headquarters, 602; Morgan's last raid, 567, 621-625, 691-695, 700, 841, 1331; "Morgan's Men Here," 627; Morgan's Ohio raid, 515, 525, 529, 679, 706-707; Morgan's second raid, 525, 705, 748, 1116, 1255; Morgan's third raid, 679, 689, 698, 706, 1331; Muldraugh's Hill, 705, 1296, 1324; Munfordville Presbyterian Church, 879; Nolin in, 748; Octagon Hall, 503; officers from Warren County, 1201; old mail stage route, 1816; Olympian Springs in, 1342; one of first skirmishes in Kentucky, 1600; Orphan Brigade, 1317; Paducah in, 829, 963, 1031; Paintsville in, 556, 566, 571, 608; Paris in, 696; Partisan Rangers (Hopkins Co.), 1971; Perryville prelude, 548; Pound Gap, 510; Prestonsburg in, 2018; Quicksand in, 841; raid in Fulton County, 1408; raiders enter Burkesville, 601; railroad wrecked in 1862, 652; Ranger leader blinded, 751; recruiting, 564; reprisals, 504, 722, 725; retreat from Cumberland Gap, 568; reunion, 221; Richmond–Prelude, 1300; robbery in Mt. Sterling, 1331; routes, 570, 689; Rowlett's Station in, 656; Russell House, 194; St. Joseph College, 1897; Salyersville in, 901; Sandy Hook in, 711; Albin Schoepf, 1919; Scott's raid, 513; Scottsville in, 730; secession abandoned, 732; Shaker Ferry Road, 1817; Shaker Landing, 1817; skirmish at Florence, 550; skirmish at Salem, 1204; skirmishes near Paducah, 545; sniper, 881; soldiers buried (Lexington Cemetery), 1550; Stage Coach Inn, 210; Stephen's Old Mill, 1356; "Sue Mundy," 536-537, 540; surprise attack, 523; terrorist, 780; two successful raids of, 645-655; Union camp site, 830; Union memorial, 215; Union supply base, 757; University of Louisville in, 541; Warfield in, 726; West Liberty in, 512; Williamstown raid, 188; Woodford County generals in, 649

Clark, Charles, 618-619

Clark, D. W., 1659

Clark, Elizabeth, 1968

Clark, Rev. Francis, 1772

Clark, George: station, 1140

Clark, George Rogers: 822, 1027, 1309, 1328, 1339, 1352, 1361, 1435, 1451, 1472, 1494, 1520, 1544, 1697, 1707, 1753, 1790, 1812,

1843, 1968; aide to, 1001; at Harrodsburg, 1083; Bird's war road, 34; county named for, 1217; Drennon Springs, 122; first blockhouse in Cincinnati, 842; Fort Jefferson, 64; home of, 835; Illinois Campaign, 690, 785, 800, 1065, 1217; land grant, 988, 1036; Ohio expeditions, 729, 817, 826, 834; Paducah, 575; Squire Boone's station, 28; surveyor for, 678; Wabash expedition, 931, 960, 1088; Wilderness Road, 219

Clark, James: home of governor, 127

Clark, James (Marshall Co.), 2035

Clark, James Beauchamp (Champ): birthplace of, 812

Clark, James E. (Christian Co.), 1625

Clark, Joab, 1625

Clark, John, 2039

Clark, M. Louis, 1885

Clark, Old Joe: 1605; ballad, 1382

Clark, Robert, Jr., 2015

Clark, William: 32, 803, 1451, 1595; founder of Paducah, 793, 829, 840, 865, 916, 918, 967, 1027, 1036, 1052, 1111, 1214, 1352

Clark County: hemp in, 1319; naming of, 1217

Clark Field (Philippines), 2037

Clark and Smith's Iron Works, 2015

Clarke, Anna Mac, 1970

Clarke, Beverly L., 1271

Clarke, George: pioneer educator, 1119

Clarke, Marcellus Jerome. See "Sue Mundy"

Clarkson, M. P., 768

Clark's War Road, 1361

Clay, Cassius M.: 1079, 1101, 1406, 1576, 1767, 1800, 1862, 2029; Berea College, 773; home of, 533

Clay, E. F., 556, 566

Clay, Green: county named for, 836

Clay, Henry: 136, 754, 911,

938, 948, 1101, 1193, 1342, 1406, 1429, 1444, 1459, 1511, 1535, 1539, 1550, 1666, 1694, 1763, 1799, 1876, 1882, 1886, 1926; Ashland, 1, 1211; Birney home, 36; cousin of, 836; father of, 1798; importation of shorthorn cattle, 1184; law office, 139; moderator of Campbell-Rice debate, 19; mother of, 1798; statue of in Richmond, Va., 710

Clay, Henry L., 814

Clay, James B. (son of Henry Clay), 1459

Clay, Rev. John, 1079, 1798

Clay, Laura, 1800

Clay, Rev. Porter, 1535

Clay, Robert Pepper, 1479

Clay, Thomas (Revolutionary War officer), 1079, 1304

Clay, Thomas (son of Henry Clay), 1459

Clay-Bullock House, 2014

Clay City, 2015

Clay County: naming of, 836

Clay Hill: home of James Sanders, 1448

Clayton, John W., 2014

Clay Villa: home of James B. Clay, 1459

Clear Creek Baptist Church (Woodford County), 1624

Clear Creek Furnace, 1050

Clear Fork Baptist Church (Clinton County), 1516, 1619

Clear Pond, 1647

Cleburne, Patrick R., 1300

Clelland, Clara B., 2050

Clemens, Jane Lampton. See Lampton, Jane

Clemens, John Marshall, 128

Clemens, Samuel Langhorne (Mark Twain), 128, 250, 781, 806, 1724, 1967

Clements, Earle C., 1844

Clerc, Laurent, 2005

Cleveland, Grover, 213, 609, 740, 763

Cliff Hagan Boys' Club, 1500

Clingman, Jacob, 1147

Clinton: "Athens" of west Kentucky, 1497; Civil War in, 1400

Clinton, DeWitt: county named for, 811
Clinton College, 1611
Clinton County: naming of, 811
Clinton Female Seminary: Academy, 1497
Clinton Furnace, 1155
Cloud, D. W., 958
Cloverport: early shipping point, 850
Cluke, Roy Stuart: 177, 679
Coal, 743, 1272, 1632, 1738, 1803-1805, 1925, 1978, 1995
Coal Oil: first, 557
Cobb, Gideon D., 1210
Cobb, Irvin S.: 795, 1452; birthplace of, 829, 840, 916, 918, 966, 1214; "Duke of Paducah," 795; grandfather of, 1057, 1452; grave of, 962; "Old Judge Priest," 839; on Paducah, 1025
Cobb, John Hiley, Jr., 1479
Cochran, Henry, 1941
Cochran, Melville, 986
Cockerham, H. D., 1657
Cody, William ("Buffalo Bill"), 938
Coffey, Benjamin F., 900
Coffin, Alice Virginia, 1715
Coffman, Anne Payne, 1934
Cohan, George M., 1692
Cohoon, John, 1892
Colbert, Alexander, 1309
Colbyville Tavern, 1358
Coldstream Farm, 166
Cold War, 1869
Cole, Alleniah, 1450
Cole, I. Willis, 1998
Cole, James, 1649
Cole, Richard, Jr., 1649
Coleman, J. C., 1928
Coleman, Robert, 1603
Coleman's Spring lot, 2061
College Hill, 1051
Colley, J. M., 1851
Collings family, 1944
Collins, Floyd, 1385
Collins, Lewis, 738, 1488, 1492
Collins, Richard H., 738, 1229, 1488, 1492
Colored Orphan Industrial Home, 1963

Colson, Rev. John Calvin: home of, 1228
Columbia: founder of, 1782; trustee of, 806
Columbus: 60; Civil War in, 528, 757; county seat at, 895; relocation of, 1398, 1775
Columbus-Belmont State Park, 1775
Colville Covered Bridge, 1566
Combs, Bert, 1837, 1929
Combs, Earle B., 1627
Combs, Elijah: founder of Hazard, 758
Combs, Ira, 759
Combs, John W., 1512
Combs, Josiah H., 1512
Combs, Mason, 759
Compromise on Kentucky/ Tennessee boundary, 1859-1860
Conestoga (gunboat), 880
Confederacy: artist of, 681
Confederate army: defense line, 863; surrender of, 872; uniform, 681; unknown dead, 727, 880; withdrawal from Kentucky, 737
Confederate Bivouac: Fulton County, 1410
Confederate cemetery (Oldham County), 182
Confederate financier, 1638
Confederate flag, 681, 1175, 1686
Confederate government of Kentucky, 764
Confederate governor of Kentucky, 67, 610, 1738
Confederate Medal of Honour winners: Albert M. Hathaway, 1183; Bayard Taylor Smith, 1133; Benjamin F. Parker, 1201; Enoch S. Jones, 1133; Ephraim R. Smith, 1133; George Walter Rogers, 1133; James Beverly Lewis, 1133; John L. Bell, 1183; Marcellus Smith Mathews, 1133; Mathias Garrett, 1183; Thomas W. Payne, 1133; William E. Kinman, 1201
Confederates: 2023, 2039;

Basil W. Duke, 1861; John Hunt Morgan, 1861; in Prestonsburg, 2018
Confederate state capital, 67
Confederate state convention, 74
Confederate States of America: cemetery, 182
Confederate thrust, 519
Congressional Medal of Honor. See Medal of Honor winners
Congressmen (Paducah), 1969
Conley, John, 1585
Conley, Michael, 830
Connelley, William Elsey: birthplace of, 985
Conner, John, 1560
Connolly, Rev. Henry, 1106
Connor, Harrison, 1226
Conrad, William, 1560
Consolidation Coal Company, 1804
Constitution: federal, 1223, 1242, 1244, 1722; Kentucky, 1522, 1650
Constitutional Convention (1792), 708-709, 844, 890, 933, 948, 983, 1070, 1079, 1139, 1171, 1238, 1240, 1409, 1474, 1722
Constitutional Convention (1799), 199, 781, 788, 806, 831, 836, 890, 983, 1079, 1170, 1181, 1502, 1618
Constitutional Convention (1849), 779, 1271, 1852, 1883
Constitutional Convention (1890–91), 728, 791, 1363, 1522, 1674, 1709, 1886
Cook, Clayton, 202
Cook, Rev. Valentine, 1761
Cool, Arnold, 1619
Cooley, Obed, 1928
Cooling Tower (Lawrence County), 887
Coomes, Jane, 1083
Coon Creek Girls, 1605
Cooperative Program (Baptist Church), 1770
Coovert, Isaac, 1603
Corban, Lewis, 1560
Cordia High School, 1543
Cornblossom, Princess: grave

of, 1074-1075

Corner in Celebrities (Frankfort), 123, 1925

Corn Island, 1352, 1753

Cornland: home of Joseph Hamilton Daveiss, 883

"Corn Stalk" Militia, 744, 837, 885, 1181

Cossitt, Rev. F. R., 1453

Cottage Furnace, 1056

Cotter, Joseph Seaman, 1654

Coulter, E. Merton, 985

Coulter, Isaac, 1935

Courier (Louisville), 1719, 1724

Courier-Journal (Louisville), 1002, 1292, 1538, 1542, 1718-1719, 1736

Courthouses: Adair County, 1599; Albany, burned, 597; Blandville, 1374; Boyle County's first, 756; Burkesville, burned, 583; burned during Civil War, 577-594, 596-597, 972; Cadiz, burned, 578; Calloway County, 1263; Campbellsville, burned, 582, 1729; Cedar House, 1071; early log, 49; Green County, 660; Greensburg, 165; Hardinsburg, 584; Harlan, burned, 588; Hartford, burned, 581; Hodgenville, burned, 591; Hopkinsville, burned, 577; Jefferson County, 945, 1697; Kentucky District, 49; Lebanon, burned, 585; Leitchfield, burned, 589; Livingston County, 1204; McCracken County, 1027, 1377; Madisonville, burned, 580; Marion, burned, 596; Meade County, 1652; Mt. Sterling, burned, 586; old log (Harrison County), 1539; Owensboro, burned, 590; Owingsville, burned, 592; Pike County, 1866; Princeton, burned, 579; Pulaski County, 1212; Rowan County, burned, 972; Scott County, 1454; Stanton, burned, 587; Taylorsville, burned, 594; Tompkinsville, burned, 593; Woodford County, 1847

Courtney, John, 1562

Court of Appeals, 1522

Courts, John, 875

Couture, Thomas, 1780

Covered Bridges: 1259; Bennett's Mill, 1076; Cabin Creek, 1572; Camp Nelson, 1513; Colville, 1566; Dover, 1439; East Fork, 1584; Goddard "White" Bridge, 1559; Hillsboro, 1569; Johnson Creek, 1567; Mt. Zion, 1581; Oldtown, 1585; Ringo's Mill, 1568; Sherburne, 1438; Switzer, 1571; Walcott (The White Bridge), 1565; Yatesville, 1583

Cove Spring. *See* McCall's Spring

Covington, Elijah M.: pioneer surveyor, 1191

Covington: bridge, 1601; African American Elks in, 1956; Diocese of, 1593; first city hall, 1862; founder of, 1429; school of industrial arts, 1527

Covington-Cincinnati Bridge Company, 1574, 1601

Cowan, John, 1083

Cowand, Ephriam, 1832

Cowgill, Rev. N. N., 1090

Cox, Austin P., 1850

Cox, Samuel, 1067

Cox and Peebles survey, 1859-1860, 1868

Crab Orchard Springs, 152

Craddock and Company, 1396

Craft, Archelous, 1700

Craig, Benjamin, 893

Craig, Elijah, 909, 1166, 1841

Craig, James, 1735

Craig, John, 1378, 1624

Craig, Rev. Lewis, 25, 893, 1617, 1636

Craighead, W. H., 1657

Cramer, Rev. Michael, 1594

Cravinston, George, 1748

Crawford, Rev. James: grave of, 1483

Crawford, Jane Todd: 183; library, 165

Crawford, William, 1409

Crawford House, 193

Crawford Spring, 193, 965

Creason, Joe, 1538, 1542

Creath, Jacob, Jr., 1636

Creath, Jacob, Sr., 1511, 1636

Creeks: Beargrass, 1848; Beaver Dam, 1980; Beechy Fork, 1788; Big Difficult, 2064; Big Twin, 1790; Blaine, 1583; Boone, 2059; Brashear's, 1748; Cabin, 1572; Caney, 1532; Clark's Run, 1279; Clear, 1624; Doe Run, 1755; Donaldson, 1892; Drake's, 1665; Eddy, 1902; Elkhorn (North), 1571; Elkhorn (South), 1557; Elkhorn (Town Branch), 1556; Fox, 1568; Gilbert's, 1636; Glenn's, 1986-1987; Harrod's, 2038; Hinkston, 1566; Holt's, 1614; John's, 2034; Johnson, 1567; Knob, 1482, 1834; Lecompte's Run, 218; Locust, 1566; Meshack, 2041; Panther, 1242; Pitman, 1729; Pond (Blackberry Fork), 2062; Robinson, 1729; Silver, 1685, 1871; Stone Lick, 2001; Sugar, 1617

Creel, Elijah, 1109

Creel, Elza, 1109

Creel, Enrique: 1109; home of, 1082

Creel, Reuben: home of, 1082; parents, 1109

Creelsboro: Civil War in, 1301; naming of, 1109

Crenshaw, King C., 1895

Crist family, 1944

Crittenden, George Bibb, 863, 1641

Crittenden, John J.: 660, 799, 1101, 1260, 1306, 1641, 1882, 1912; county named for, 1160; home of, 123, 657, 1154

Crittenden, Thomas L., 553, 665, 1641, 1796

Crittenden, Thomas S.: home of, 123

Crittenden Cabin, 1641

Crittenden Compromise, 657, 1160, 1641

Crittenden County: 1204; naming of, 1160

Crittenden Furnace, 1210
Crockett, Joseph, 838, 1757
Crockett, Robert, 1120
Croghan, George, 31
Croghan, Lucy Clark, 835
Croghan, William, 835, 2007
Cromie, J., 1739
Cropsey, A. J., 1301
Cross, William, 1619
Crossland, Edward, 1969
Crossland (horse), 649
Crow, James, 1986-1987
Crow, John, 1376
Cruft, Charles, 1300
Culbertson, John, 1017
Culver, John, 1142
Cumberland, Duke of, 903, 2045
Cumberland College, 1837
Cumberland County: establishment of, 959
Cumberland Falls: 1517; Moonbow, 1801; State Park, 2002
Cumberland Ford, 1426
Cumberland Gap, 520, 568, 1300, 1383, 1443, 1600, 1868, 1905
Cumberland Mountains, 1860
Cumberland Presbyterian Church, 1122, 1453
Cumberland Presbyterian College, 1453
Cumberland Trace: Green County, 1311; Lincoln County, 2063; Taylor County, 1383; Warren County, 981, 1665, 1792
Cummings, Thomas, 1354
Cummins, T. L., 1619
Curd, John, 1795
Curran, Charles Courtney, 1485
Curry family, 928-929
Curtin, Cornelius, 1704
Curtis, Charles, 1501
Custer, George Armstrong, 606, 1505, 2030
"Cut-Off," 1869 (Simpson Co.), 1947
Cynthiana: Battle of, 109, 567, 621-625, 646-648, 691-695, 700-701, 841; first newspaper in, 1539; naming of, 1428
Dailey, William, 1649

Dale, William C., 1894
Dallam, Frances, 1480
Daniel, James, 1838
Daniel, Walker, 49, 190, 1376
Daniel Boone National Forest, 1633
Danville: African American business district, 1958; early church in, 1442; early District Court sessions, 49; establishment of, 1376; political society, 755
Darlington, Carey Allen, 1450
Darlington, George W., 1156
Darlington, U. V. W., 1659
Darnall, Rev. Henry (Harry), 874
Darrow, Clarence, 1698
Darwin, Charles, 1698
Daughters' College, 1173
Daughters of the American Revolution: 1152, 1613; a founder of (Mary Desha), 807
Daveiss, Joseph Hamilton: 1285; county named for, 883, 1158; home of, 883
Davenport, Gwen, 1654
David, Father John Baptist: in Bardstown, 857, 1943
David, Rev. John Baptist Mary, 857, 896, 1702
Davie, George M., 1229
Davie, Montgomery, 1179
Davie, Winston Jones: 1179; home and grave of, 851
Daviess County: CSA medallists from, 1183; guerrillas in, 1935; naming of, 883, 1158; WW I servicemen from, 1456
Davis, Brinton, 1697
Davis, Garrett, 1886
Davis, J. C., 535, 1515
Davis, J. R., 1924
Davis, Jacob, 1123
Davis, James, 1052
Davis, Jane Cook, 57
Davis, Jeff C., 1515
Davis, Jefferson: 1201, 1690, 1724, 1744, 1849, 1861; birthplace, 57; capture of, 872; education of, 853-854, 941, 1406; residence of, 4; salute to Kentucky, 1073
Davis, Samuel, 57

Davis, Samuel (Mason Co.), 1941
Davis, W. P., 1659
Davison, Bill, 1935, 2039
Davison, William S.: home of, 1040
Dawson, Richard, 1838
Dawson Springs, 915
Day, J. Taylor, 175
Day, John F., 1736
Day Law (1904), 1663, 1930
Deaf, School for the, 197, 1536
Dean, Hazen A., 1747
Death Valley Scotty. See Scott, Walter E.
Deboe, W. J., 1499
Declaration of Independence: 1311, 1441, 1541; guardian of, 871
Deer Creek Furnace, 1450
Deering, Richard, 975, 1147
Delany's Ferry, 1774
de Longueil, Charles Lemoyne, 1253
Democrat (Louisville), 1719
Dempsey, Lewis, 1316
DeNardi, Rev. Charles, 1106, 1682
Denhardt, Henry H.: death of, 1129
Dennis, Alney, 1609
Denny, Alexander, 1525
Denny, George, 1562
Denny, J. W., 1707
Denny, James Beattie, 1479
Denton, Isaac, Sr., 1619
Denton, Joseph C., 1619
Derby Winners: Aristides, 166; Azra, 2040; Baden Baden, 2027; Ben Brush, 2027; Donerail, 1475; Manuel, 2040; George Smith, 1295; Leonatus, 1295; Plaudit, 2027; Sir Huon, 2040
Derne, Battle of, 1465
de Sales, Francis, 1593
Desha, Joseph, 807, 1878, 1934, 2021
Desha, Mary, 807
Devin, Alexander, 2064
Diamond: found in Kentucky, 734
Diaz, Porfirio, 1082
Dick, Alex, 838
Dickens, Charles, 535, 938,

1681
Dickinson, Charles, 100
Dietrich, Marlene, 1865
Dill, John, 1914
Dill, Lin, 1914
Distilleries: early Jefferson County, 1907; Labrot & Graham, 1986-1987; Maker's Mark, 1509; Old Pepper's, 1986-1987
Distinguished Flying Cross, 1727
Distinguished Service Medal, 1706
"Divine Elm" (Ft. Boonesborough), 1520, 1582
Dixie Highway, 1626
Dixon, Archibald, 1926
Dixon, Rev. Henry, 1126
Dobbs, Samuel C., 1664
Doctor's Creek, 553
Dodd, Carl H., 2033
Dodgers, Brooklyn (baseball team), 1762
Dodson, William, 1212, 1607
Dollmaker, The (Arnow), 1807
Dominicans, 853-854, 941, 1095
Donaldson, 1892
Donaldson Creek, 1892
Donelson, John, 1065
Doniphan, Alexander W., 877
Doolittle, J. H., 1727
Doric Lodge No. 18 (F.& A.M.-P.H.A.), 1958
Dorsey House (Perryville), 195
Doublehead, Chief, 1075
Douglas, Stephen A., 1650
Douglas Air Field, Arizona, 1970
Douglass, Jessamine: county named for, 947
Dover Covered Bridge, 1439
Dowden, John, 1941
Downs, John, 574
Downs, Lucy Virgin: grave of, 574
Downs, Thomas, 1834
Downs, Rev. William, 1834
Drake, Albritain, 1735
Drake, Daniel, 1627
Drake, Joseph: Long Hunter, 1187
Drane, James, 2043
Drane, S. T., 2043

Draper Manuscripts, 1782
Drennon, Jacob, 122
Drennon Springs, 122, 798
Dripping Springs Baptist Church (Metcalfe County), 1118
Dromgoole, James, 1252
Duckers Station, 1999
Dudley, Ambrose, 1596
Dudley, Benjamin W., 1447
Duels: Casto-Metcalfe, 996; Jackson-Dickinson, 100; noted dueling ground, 611; Rowan-Chambers, 1101, 1281
Duke, Basil W., 501, 686, 1229, 1861, 2023
Duke, Ben, 1693
Dukedom: Civil War in, 655
Duncan, Charles K., 1479
Duncan, Sanford, 611
Duncan, W. G., 1674
Duncan Tavern, 93
Dunhauser, T. D., 1835
Dunlap, George, 1344
Dunmore, Benjamin, 1495
Dunmore, John Murray, 1168, 1668, 1221
Dunmore's War, 709, 931, 960, 974, 1322, 1328, 1637
Dunne, Irene, 1899
Dunnigan, Alice Allison, 1960
Dupee, Rev. George W. ("Pappy"), 1276, 1716
Dupey, James, 1678
DuPont Lodge (Cumberland Falls), 2002
Durbin, Father Elisha, 1106, 1682, 1717, 1785
Durham, C. M., 1924
Durham, Hugh Murrey, 1479
Durham, J. R., 1924
Durham, John, 1772
Durrett, George, 1924
Durrett, Reuben T., 1229
Dutch Reformed Church, 141
Dutch settlers, 852, 1577, 1848, 1855
Dutton's Hill: Battle of, 712
Duveneck, Frank, 1460, 1854
Dyal, John, 1941
Eades, Thomas, 1824
Eades Tavern, 1824
Earle, John Baylis, 1338
Earlington, 1338
Earp, Wyatt, 938

Earthquakes, 688, 1968
Easley, Roy, 1837
East, K. C., 2060
Eastern Kentucky Railway, 1016-1017, 1178, 1978, 2056
Eastern Kentucky University, 1627
Eastern Star, Order of, 752, 1563
Eastern State Hospital, 1033
East Fork Covered Bridge, 1584
Eastin, Augustine, 1596
East Kentucky Power Cooperative, 1894
Easton, Harry, 964
Eaves, Sanders, 1123
Ebenezer Church (Jessamine County), 894
Eddy Trace, 1916
Eddyville, 130, 509, 1204, 1245, 1598
Eddyville Furnace, 1326
Edgar, William, 1414
Edgewood: home of Ben Hardin, 1101
Edison, Thomas: Butchertown House Museum, 1713
Edmonson, John: county named for, 508, 797
Edmonson County: naming of, 508, 797
Edmonton: founding of, 678
Edward, David, 1735
Edward VII: investor in first coal oil, 557
Edwards, John: 1372, 1722, 1774; home of, 1722
Edwards, Ninian: governor of Illinois, 1260
Egbert, Ercel, 1981
Eifort, Sebastian, 1013
Eighth Kentucky Infantry Volunteers, 555
Eighth of August celebration, 1957
Eisenhower, Dwight D., 1964
Electricity (Owen Co.), 1819; rural, 1894
Elenores: home of Elizabeth Madox Roberts, 1046
Elizabethtown: 1494, 1651; Battle of, 1116, 1296; Brown-Pusey House in, 1505; first brick house, 1534; naming of, 960, 1651

Elkin, Joshua, 1735
Ellerslie: home of Levi Todd, 1001
Elliott, John M.: 1688; county named for, 796
Elliott, Robert, 2035
Elliott, William, 1115
Elliott-Baker, Frank W. C., 1695
Elliott County: naming of, 796
Ellis, James, 1615
Ellis, James Tandy, 1291
Ellis, William, 25
Ellisville, 1615
Elmwood: home of William S. Davison, 1040
Elmwood: home of Captain John Lewis, 1623
Emerson, Ralph Waldo, 1681
Eminence Christian Church, 2043
Eminence College site, 2043
Emmick, George, 1914
Emmit, Mr. & Mrs. Josiah, 1972
Empire Furnace, 1357
Endicott, Moses, 1457
Enduring Hills, The (Giles), 1813
England: 1576, 1887; king and queen of, 1605; Royal Geographic Society, 2055
Engler, David, 1735
Ennis, T. E., 1924
Enterprise Furnace, 1147
Episcopal Church: 945; Calvary (Louisville), 1695; Christ (Louisville), 1724; Church of the Ascension (Frankfort), 1537; Grace (Hopkinsville), 1690; Grace (Paducah), 1090; St. Paul's (Campbell County), 1151; St. Paul's (Henderson), 1703; Trinity (Covington), 1527; Trinity (Danville), 1442; Trinity (Owensboro), 1500
Eschenbrenner, Rev. Daniel, 1146
Esculapia Springs, 778, 1656
Eskippakithiki, 1274
Eskridge, George, 1592
Eskridge Ferry Road, 1592
Essery, Jonathan, 1755
Estill, James: county named

for, 153, 1219, 1525
Estill's Defeat, 153, 1219, 1525
Estill Collegiate Institute, 1922
Estill County: naming of, 1219
Estill Seminary, 1922
Estill Springs, 555
Estill Steam Furnace: (Estill Co.), 1055; (Powell Co.), 2015
Eutaw Springs: Battle of, 1700
Evangelical Church: St. John's (Louisville), 1546
Evans, W. H., 1927
Evansville, Henderson, and Nashville Railroad, 1797
Eve, George, 1596
Everett, Mrs. M. O., 1712
Everett, Peter, 901
Evolution, theory of, 1698
Ewing, Baker, 1707
Ewing, Daniel, 1284
Ewing, Joshua, Sr., 1226
Ewing, Samuel R., 1478
Ewing, William, 1367
Exterminator (horse), 565
Fables: "High Water at Catfish Bend," 1967
Fairbank, Rev. Calvin, 1990
Fairfield: home of James Garrard, 82
Fairfield: home of John Bradford, 1864
Fairlawn, 1447
Fall, Philip S., 1710
Fallen Timbers: Battle of, 804, 826, 912, 1088, 1094, 1128
Fallon, Rev. John D., 1106
Falls 4-H Craft Center. See 4-H Craft Center
Falls of the Ohio, 219, 835, 1339, 1352, 1451, 1494, 1685, 1697, 1753, 1944
Falmouth: founder of, 1911; Civil War in, 686
Fancy Farm, 1682
Farmington, 174
Faughn, Enos, 2035
Faulkner, William, 1977
Fayette County: formation of, 1083, 1440
Fayette County Bar Hall of Fame, 2029
Federal Court of Appeals, 1929
Federal Hill: My Old Ken-

tucky Home, 788, 1102
Fee, Rev. John Gregg: 1767, 1965; Berea College, 773; birthplace of, 861
Feehan, Rev. Richard P., 1682
Feliciana (Graves County), 1432
Fenwick, Bishop Edward, 941, 1593
Ferguson, Champ: Civil War terrorist, 780
Ferguson, Edwin Hite, 1976
Fern Creek High School, 2058
Fernwood Cemetery, 790, 1926
Ferry: at Hawesville, 1918; at Shaker Landing, 1817; at Westport, 909; Delany's, 1774; first in Kentucky, 1578; Flynn's, 1298; in Grayson County, 1592; in Jessamine County, 1795; Thompson, 1914; Valley View, 1378
Feuds: Hatfield-McCoy, 1728, 1913, 2047, 2066; Rowan County, 1933
Feustel, Louis, 1635
Ficklin, Joseph, 4
Field, Benjamin, 1322
Field, Charles William, 649, 1322
Field, E. H., 1322
Field, Ezekiel, 1322
Field, John, 1322
Field, William, 1322
Fields, W. C., 1865
Fields, William Jason: home of, 640
Films: Anna and the King of Siam, 1899; Birth of a Nation, 650; Broken Blossoms, 650; Intolerance, 650; I Remember Mama, 1899; Orphans of the Storm, 650; Show Boat, 1899; Steamboat Round the Bend, 1967; Summer and Smoke, 1865
Filson, John: 1229, 1976; map of, 212, 984, 1283, 1435
Filson Club Historical Society, 1229, 1976
Fincastle County (Va.), 1557
Fink, Albert, 1697
Finley, John, 32, 697, 950, 1274; home of, 789

Finley, Rev. Robert, 935

First Baptist Church (Frankfort), 1464, 1535

First Baptist Church (Georgetown), 1716

First Baptist Church (Murray), 1770

First Baptist Church (Paducah), 868

First Christian Church (Clinton), 1937

First Christian Church (Frankfort), 1710

First Christian Church (Paducah), 899

First Kentucky Cavalry, 684, 724, 888, 1486

First Methodist Church (Frankfort), 1476

First Missionary Baptist Church (Hazard), 703

First Presbyterian Church (Ashland), 1416

First Presbyterian Church (Frankfort), 1540

First Presbyterian Church (Glasgow), 1951

First Presbyterian Church (Hopkinsville), 1045

First Presbyterian Church (Lancaster), 1942

First Presbyterian Church (Paducah), 1061

First United Methodist Church (Covington), 1659

Fisher, Adam, 1909

Fisher, Barnett, 1909

Fisher, Mary Magdalene Garr, 1909

Fisher, Stephen Albert, 1909

Fishing Creek. *See* Battle of Mill Springs

Fitch, Fred, 1054

Fitch, John: grave of, 944

Fitchburg: chartered, 1054

Flag: first American on foreign soil, 1261

Flaget, Bishop Benedict Joseph, 857, 1312, 1639, 1827, 1897, 1943, 2057

Flat Lick, 1600

Fleming, John: county named for, 950

Fleming, William, 1891

Fleming County: naming of, 950

Flemingsburg: naming of, 950

Fletcher, Rev. Custis, 1090

Flexner, Abraham, 1654

Floersh, Archbishop John A., 1680

Floods: of 1884, 1032, 1065; of 1927, 1775; of 1937, 1053, 1090, 1107-1108, 1585, 1601, 1890

Florence: Civil War skirmish at, 550

Flowering of the Cumberland (Arnow), 1807

"Flow Gently, Sweet Afton": composer of, 1202

Floyd, George Rogers Clark, 726

Floyd, John: 32, 49, 983, 1404, 1622, 1676, 1848; county named for, 817; grave of, 146; Long Run Massacre, 991; Royal Spring, 63; Station, 26, 817, 1060

Floyd County: "Little Floyd," 905; naming of, 817

Floyd's Fork, 548, 1944

Flynn, George, 1298

Flynn, Luther, 2060

Flynn's Ferry (Crittenden County), 1185, 1298

Foch, Ferdinand, 990

Fogle, McDowell, 1266

Fohs, F. Julius, 2065

Fohs Hall (Crittenden County), 2065

Foley, Red, 1605

Folk Music, 1512

Football: "Uncle" Charlie Moran, 1091

Forage Depot, 1486

Ford, H. Church, 2022

Forest Retreat: home of Thomas Metcalfe, 660

Forgy, James, 1467

Forks of Dix River Baptist Church (Garrard County), 1617

Forks of Elkhorn Baptist Church (Franklin County), 2003

Forrest, Nathan Bedford: 147, 1045; in Calhoun, 665; at Canton, 619; at Caseyville, 616; Civil War action, 545; Fort Anderson, 828; in Fulton County, 652; at Gold City, 598; in Graves County, 654-655; at Greenville, 614; headquarters, 880-881; at Hopkinsville, 618; at Madisonville, 613; at Marion, 615; at Morganfield, 612; in Paducah, 963, 1214, 1277, 1287; raid, 517, 1408; surprise attack, 523; in Trigg County, 881; Webster County, 617

Forscutt, C. F., 1701

Forsythe, Fred, 1295

Ft. Des Moines, Iowa, 1970

Fort Knox, 1857, 1869, 2037

Forts and stations: 34; Alston's Station, 1252; Anderson, 517, 828, 1287; Barnett's Station, 1144, 1463; Bishop, 547, 632; Boonesborough, 113, 576, 1520, 1577, 1579, 1802; Boone's Station, 17, 196, 952, 1790; Bowman's, 926; Brashear's Station, 1944; Bryan's Station, 21, 222, 250, 729, 952, 1280, 1575, 1624, 2059; "Burnt Station," 1586; Carpenter's Station, 250, 1203; Cartwright's Station, 1339; Casey's Station, 781, 806; Cassidy Station, 1388; Clark's Station, 1140; Clay, 9; Craig, 119, 1624; Crow's (John) Station, 49, 926, 1376; Donelson, 538, 540, 663, 1355; Dromgoole's Station, 1252; Duckers Station, 1999; Ellis Station, 1615; Fisher's Garrison, 1909; Fisher's Station, 926; Fleming's Station, 950; Floyd's Station, 26, 817, 1060; Ft. Thomas Army Post, 986; French and Indian War, 1849; Froman's Station, 1944; Gallup, 547; Glover's Station, 1311; Goodwin (Goodin), 1471; Gordon's Station, 926; Grant's Fort (Bourbon Co.), 1855; Grant's Station (Grant Co.), 942; Haggin's Station, 926; Harberson's Station, 876, 1284; Hardin's, 134; Harlan's Station,

785; Harman Station, 736; Harrod, 554, 670, 926, 1637, 1877; Hartford Station, 1144, 1195; Haycraft, Daniel, 1904; Heiman, 147; Henry, 538, 1364; Hill, 547; Holder's Station, 1048; Hynes Station, 1621; Indian Old Fields, 31; Jefferson, 64, 563, 757, 1309; Kaskaskia, 1352; Kenton's Station, 138, 1911; Kincheloe's Station, 1586; Knox, 1857, 2037; Leitch's Station, 117, 1741; Lexington, 1554; Licking Station, 202; Lindsay's Station, 218; Little, 57; Logan's Station, 56, 250, 709, 860, 1311, 1383, 1520, 1782; Low Dutch Station (Boyle County), 49; Low Dutch Station (New Holland), 1848; McAfee's Station, 928-929; McClelland's Station, 63; McFadin's Station, 981, 1665; McGary's Station, 926; McKinney's, 2063; McMurtry's Station, 926; Martin's Station, 150, 919, 953, 1753; Masterson's Station, 10; Maulding's, 1137; Mefford's, 92; Meigs, 836; Mitchel (Mitchell), 546, 1758; Modrel's, 1870; Morgan's Station, 115, 189; Morton, 540; Fort Paint Lick, 1525; Paint Lick Station, 1126; Phillip's Fort, 1096, 1098, 1114; Pitt, 1328; Pittman's Station, 1311, 1383; Polke's Station, 1586; Pottinger's Station, 1433; Rogers Station, 820, 1078; Rowlett's Station, 656, 1504; Ruddle's Station, 107, 953, 1753; Salt River Garrison, 1944; Sandusky Station, 670; Scott's Blockhouse, 1094; Shaw's, 1980; Simon Kenton's Station, 138; Smith's Station (Mercer Co.), 926; Smith's Station (Oldham Co.), 208; Southworth, 1810; Spring, 26; Squire Boone's Station, 28, 848, 991; Stockton's Sta-

tion, 97; Strode's Station, 97, 1047; Sturgus' Station, 984; Sumter, 533-534; Tanner's Station, 999; Three Forts, 1651; Todd's Station, 1783; Trigg's Station, 926, 1159; Twitty's (or Little Fort), 77; Tyler Station, 1088; Van Meter, 1494; Vienna, 1123; Webb, 1458; William, 974; Williams, 1290; Wood's Blockhouse, 53; Wright, 1917
Foster, Stephen Collins: at Augusta, 750; "My Old Kentucky Home," 1102
Foster, William, 1010, 1131
Founder's Shack (Pippa Passes), 1532
Fountains: in Fayette County, 864; in Shelbyville, 1379
Fountleroy, William, 958
4-H: first craft center in U.S., 666; first state camp, 1292; Sandhill (McCreary County), 1633
Fourth of July. See Independence Day
Fowler, Al, 1915
Fowler, Beman, 1838
Fox, Arthur, Sr., 1696
Fox, John, Jr.: 775-777, 1294, 1406; birthplace of, 1141
Frakes, Rev. Hiram M., 1286
France, 1576, 1887
Francisco, John, 1580
Frankfort: 1359, 2031; barracks, 2061; cemetery, 24, 675, 731, 784, 826, 1088, 1271, 1465, 1896, 1910, 1940, 2003; chosen as capital, 1774; Civil War in, 1490; Corner in Celebrities, 123, 1925; founding of, 105-106; Melodye Park, 2031; new capitol, 1779; old capitol, 1779; South Frankfort, 1707; Union Station, 1955; Wapping Street, 2057
Franklin, Benjamin, 1359
Franklin, Rev. H. Joseph, 1276
Franklin, James Gilbert, 1479
Franklin: becomes county seat, 912
Franklin County: naming of, 1359; settlement in, 1444

Franklin Lyceum, 1654
Frazer, George, 1555
Frazer, Joseph, 1555
Fredonia (Caldwell County), 1908
Freeman, John: grave of, 927
Freemasonry: Grand Consistory of Ky., 1739; poet laureate of, 752
Free Silver: 1857; Richard Parks Bland, 1858; William Jennings Bryan, 1858
Free-Town Church (Monroe County), 1347
Frémont, John C.: expedition of, 79, 1335
French, K. J., 2060
French-Indian War, 709, 974, 1578, 1680, 1849, 1996
French Legion of Honor, 1967
Froman family, 1944
Frontier Nursing Service, 558
Frost, William G., 1930
Fry, John, 917
Fugitives (agrarian writers), 1879
Fugitive Slave Law, 1863
Fulton, Robert: 944; county named for, 1169; partner of, 801
Fulton: founding of, 1587
Fulton County: naming of, 1169
Fulton Furnace, 1340
Funk, William M., 957
Funk Seminary, 957
Furman, Lucy: home of, 870
Futrell, Charity, 994
Futrell, Nathan, 994, 1892
Gaines, Abner, 1765
Gaines, John Pollard: 1765; homesite, 1194
Gaither, Emma Glass, 1690
Gaitskill Mound, 1655
Gallagher, Tom, 1517
Gallantry Cross, 2046
Gallatin, Albert: county named for, 747
Gallatin County: first court in, 1725; naming of, 747
Gallaudet, T. H., 2005
Gallaudet College, 1799
Gallup, George W., 556, 566, 643
Galt House, 535, 1515, 1664
Ganey, Mathew, 1735

Gano, John A., Sr., 1701
Gardiner, Sister Harriet, 1943
Gardner, Frances, 1717
Garfield, James A.: 52; Battle of Middle Creek, 85; Battle of Mill Springs, 863; Civil War Army Base, 643; Garfield Place, 172; Louisa in the Civil War, 547; Jennie's Creek, 571; Pound Gap, 510; war on the Big Sandy, 608
Garner, Margaret, 1863
Garnett, James, Jr., 1924
Garrard, James: 1372, 1931; county named for, 1240; grandson of, 570; structures associated with, 82, 1796
Garrard, John, 1078
Garrard, T. T., 570
Garrard County: first newspaper in, 1644; naming of, 1240
Garrett, Mathias: CSA medallist, 1183
Garris, Sikes, 1735
Garrison, Matthew, 1990
Gaseous Diffusion Plant (Paducah), 1180, 1214
Gaskins, Morris M., 1619
Gasper River Meeting House, 170
Gasper Society of United Believers in Christ's Second Appearance, 179, 1455
Gast, Robert H., 1676
Gatliff, Ancil, 1837
Gatliff, Captain Charles: grave of, 919
Gayle, John: home of, 742
"The General" (locomotive), 173
Genetic research, 1714
Genoa: home of Winston Jones Davie, 851
George II, 903
Georgetown: College, 718, 1487, 1535, 1716, 1841; raided, 701; Royal Spring, 63
Gerard Furnace, 1373
German Evangelical Unity Church, 1146
German Reformed Presbyterian Church Cemetery, 1028

Germans: colony in Trigg County, 1100; in Bracken County, 1213; in Frankfort, 2057; in Louisville, 1546, 1988; in northern Kentucky, 1506, 1531; in Paducah, 1146
Gershwin, George, 1692
Gethsemani, Abbey of, 168
Gettysburg, Battle of, p. 269
Ghent: naming of, 911
Gibbons, Joseph Howard, Jr., 1479
Gibbs, Julius, 1337
"Gibraltar of the West," 528
Gibson, R. E., 1927
Gibson, Randall Lee: home of, 659
Gibson, William H., Sr., 1992
Giddinge, George P., 1690
Gilbert, Charles Champion, 553
Gilbert, Jesse, 1647
Gilbert, Joel, 2035
Gilbert's Creek, 25, 1636
Gilbertsville, Old, 1647
Giles, Henry, 1813
Giles, Janice Holt, 1813
Gillespie, Haven, 1836
Gillis, Ezra, 2012
Gillis, John R., 1810
Gillmore, Quincy A., 712, 2023
Gilruth, Irwin, 1131
Giltner, H. L., 628-629
Giltner, Lizzie Rains, 2043
Giltner, Rev. W. S., 2043
Girty, Simon, 21
Gish, Dorothy and Lillian, 650
Gist, Christopher, 31-32, 510, 697, 1472
Gist, Nathaniel: home of, 116
Given, Henry F., 1349
Givens, George: homesite and grave, 1328
Glasgow: hospital founded in, 1503
Glasgow Normal Institute, 1418
Glen Lily: birthplace of S. B. Buckner, 155
Glen Willis: home of Willis Lee, 1444
Glenn, Andrew, 1735
Glensboro: one-room school

at, 2029
Globe Furnace, 1156
Goddard "White" Bridge, 1559
Godman, John W. I., 1666
Godman, Louis K., 1731
Godman Field: named for, 1731
Goebel, William, 1454, 1524, 1650, 1709, 1781, 1861, 1884
Goforth, William, 1628
Golden Pond, 1308
Gold rush (California), 2018
Golf, 1262
Gollaher, Austin: Lincoln's playmate, 827
Goode, James T., 830
Goode, John, 1838
Gooding, Michael, 553
Goodlett, John, 1267
Goodnight: Isaac Herschel, 1369; Memorial Library, 1369; Mrs. I. H., 1369
Good Shepherd Catholic Church (Frankfort), 2057
Goodwin, Samuel, 1471
Goose, Roscoe, 1475
Goose Creek Salt Works, 531
Gordon, Maurice K.: home of, 1104
Governors: Florida, 1260; Illinois, 746, 1260; Kentucky, 657-658, 1728, 1777, 1779, 1798; first, 157, 1551; first Republican, 699; from Logan County, 1260; Texas, 1260; West Virginia, 1728
Governor's Mansion, Old, 660, 799, 1208
Gower House, 938
Grace Episcopal Church (Hopkinsville), 1690
Grace Episcopal Church (Paducah), 1090
Grace Presbyterian Church (Louisville), 2055
Grace United Church of Christ (Covington), 1531
Graddy, Jesse, 1847
Graham, Christopher C., 1297, 1335
Graham, Mentor: "The Man Who Taught Lincoln," 719
Graham, Robert, 504
Graham Springs, 1297
Grand Ole Opry (WSM),

2026

Grand Rivers Coal, Iron and Railroad Company, 1368

Grand Rivers Furnace, 1368

Grange (Patrons of Husbandry), 779, 1179

Grant, Frederick, 2014

Grant, Hannah (Simpson), 1594

Grant, Jesse Root, 1594, 1656, 1659

Grant, John, 1642

Grant, Mary, 1594

Grant, Samuel, 942

Grant, Ulysses S.: 652, 1350, 1447, 1594, 1656, 1659, 1724, 1905, 2014; campaign against Smithland, 663; Civil War action, 514; demonstration–1862, 563; demonstration against Columbus, 757; at the Galt House, 535; Maysville Academy, 1616; in Paducah, 575, 828, 840, 916, 918, 924, 1065, 1175, 1214; son of, 2014

Grant, William L.: 2000; High School, 2000, 2071

Grant County: naming of, 942

Grant House, 1594

Grant's Lick, 1642, 1730

Grass Hills: home of Lewis Sanders, 1184

Graves, Benjamin Franklin: county named for, 869

Graves County: naming of, 508, 869

Grayson, Benjamin, 755

Grayson, William: county named for, 873

Grayson: railway to, 2056

Grayson County: earliest brick residence in, 1634; naming of, 873

Grayson Springs, 768

Grayson's Tavern, 755

Green, Elisha, 1962

Green, Willis, 906

Green County: courthouse, 660; naming of, 1239

Greene, Nathanael: 1375; county named for, 1239

Green Mill, 906

Green River, 1813

Green River Baptist Association, 1496

Green River Bridge: Battle of, 89

Green River Union Meeting House, 662

Greensburg: Civil War generals from, 603; courthouse, 165; origins, 1311

Green Springs Furnace, 1080

Green Street Baptist Church (Louisville), 1693, 1949

Greenup, Christopher, 834, 1325, 1372, 1751; circuit judge, 1144; county named for, 784

Greenup County: naming of, 784

Greenup Furnace. See Hunnewell Furnace

Greenup "Town Fathers," 1529

Greenville: cemetery, 1609; N. B. Forrest in, 614; Treaty of, 804

Greenville Institute, 1173

Greenville Springs, 1173

Gregory, Noble J., 1969

Gregory, William V., 1969

Gresham, James Bethel, 664; bridge named for, 1199

Greyhound (horse), 565

Grider, Benjamin C., 1201

Grider, J. H., 1201

Griffin, M. H., 1469

Griffith, Dan, 1983

Griffith, David Wark: grave of, 650

Griffith, Henry, 1123

Griffytown, 1982

Grimes family, 1656

Grist mills, 1509, 1568, 1712, 1748, 1782, 1828, 1892, 1911, 1991, 2018

Grubb's Crossroads: Battle of, 830, 1630

Grundy, Felix, 1101, 1285, 1618

Guadalcanal, 1322

Guerrant, E. O., 682

Guggenheim Museum, 1726

Gunpowder, 1595, 1623

Gunpowder Mill, 875

Gun Shop Site, 1265, 1335

Guthrie, James, 1883, 1994

Gwinn, A. W., 1659

Haeseley, Rev. Charles A., 1682

Hagan, Rev. Alfred, 1682

Haiti, 124

Haldeman, W. N., 1719

Half Mountain: Battle of, 556

Hall, Randolph: 1617

Hall, William: founder of Perryville, 876, 1284

Hamby, W. I., 915

Hamilton, Calvin, 1938

Hamilton, Milton, 1734

Hammon, John: 1575

Hampton, John: home of, 1688

Hancock, George, 1818

Hancock, Isaiah, 1735

Hancock, John: county named for, 762

Hancock, Rev. Walter A., 1682

Hancock County: early road in, 1914; naming of, 762

Hanging Rock: Battle of, 1700

Hanks, Nancy: 1591; marriage of, 526, 853, 885, 1038

Hanna, Ebenezer, 202

Hanna, John Harris, 1537, 1707

Hansford, Charles, 1950

Hanson, C. H., 561

Hanson, Charles S.: 600; home of, 951

Hanson, Henry B.: town named for, 1948

Hanson, Isaac S.: home of, 951

Hanson, Matilda Hickman, 951

Hanson, Richard H.: home of, 951

Hanson, Roger: home of, 951

Hanson, Samuel: home of, 951

Hanson Twist tobacco, 1948

Harberson, James, 876, 1284

Hardee, William J., 553

Hardin, Ben: grave of, 1363; home of, 1101

Hardin, John: county named for, 960; murder of, 931; Washington County claim, 853-854

Hardin, Mark, 819

Hardin, William (Indian Bill), 134

Hardin County: naming of,

960
Harding, Abel, 1924
Hardinsburg: founder of, 134
Hardy, James G., 1491
Hardy family, 969
Hardyville, 1491
Harlan, James: home of, 123
Harlan, John Marshall: 1786; birthplace, 1606; home of, 123, 1173
Harlan, Silas: county named for, 785
Harlan County: Medal of Honor, 2033; naming of, 785
Harman, Mathias, 690, 735-736
Harmon, Clifford B., 1996
Harmon, James, 1083
Harp, Micajah: killing of, 1004
Harp, Wiley, 1004
Harper, Adam, 537
Harper, John, 1735
Harper, Nathan, 1735
Harpers Ferry, 1335
Harper's Monthly, 1959
Harris, Field, 1322
Harris, William M., 2030
Harrison, Anna, 1428
Harrison, Benjamin: governor of Virginia, 917
Harrison, Benjamin: county named for, 1171
Harrison, Cynthiana, 1428
Harrison, Jeannetta, 2060
Harrison, Joseph, 1080
Harrison, Joseph Cabell, 1387
Harrison, Robert, 1428
Harrison, Sophia Rice, 1387
Harrison, William, 969
Harrison, William Henry: 714, 954, 1158, 1329, 1387, 1409, 1878; Wabash Campaign, 831, 837
Harrison Academy, 1428
Harrison County: naming of, 1171
Harrod, James, 1083, 1258, 1376, 1422, 1433, 1449, 1530, 1637, 1751, 1877
Harrodsburg: 136, 1038, 1449, 1520, 1751, 1877, 1944; early vital junction, 926; first District Court sessions, 49; founding of, 670,

1083, 1258
Harrodsburg Springs, 551
Harrod's Creek Community, 2038
"Harrod's Landing," 1751
Harrodstown. *See* Harrodsburg
Hart, George, 1083
Hart, Joel Tanner: birthplace of, 710, 731; Statue, "Woman Triumphant," 731, 1553
Hart, Josiah, 710
Hart, Judith, 710
Hart, Matthew, 1941
Hart, Nathaniel, 1577
Hart, Nathaniel G. T.: county named for, 43
Hart, Susannah, 1577
Hart County: formation of, 1236; naming of, 43, 508
Hartford: early merchant in, 1829; first covered bridge, 1259; first doctor in, 1267; naming of, 1195
Harvie, John: home of, 819
Haseltine, Herbert: Man o' War statue, 1215
Hastings, Thomas, 1692
Hatfield, Anderson, 1728, 2066
Hatfield, "Devil Anse," 2068
Hatfield, Elias, 2066
Hatfield, Ellison, 2047, 2066
Hatfield, Floyd, 2066
Hatfield, Jerry, 2066
Hatfield-McCoy Feud: 1728, 1913, 2047; election fight, 2066; historic district, 1728, 1866, 2062, 2067; Hog Trial, 2066
Hathaway, Albert M.: CSA medallist, 1183
Hawes, Benjamin Walker, 1918
Hawes, Clary Walker, 1918
Hawes, Henry F., 1746
Hawes, Richard (Daviess County), 1678, 1738, 1918
Hawes, Richard (Confederate governor of Ky.), 522, 1738, 1918
Hawes Family Cemetery, 1918
Hawesville, 1678, 1738
Hawesville Railroad Station,

1856
Hawkins, James, 893
Hawkins, P. B., 1201
Hawkins family, 1944
Hay, M. C., 1609
Haycraft, Daniel, 1904
Haycraft, Samuel, 960, 1534
Haycraft, Samuel, Sr., 932, 1651
Hayden, Basil, Sr., 913
Hayden, I. B., 1935
Hayes, Albert, 1052
Hayes, Helen, 1692
Hayes, Rutherford B., 1355, 1606
Hayfield: home of Charles Wilkins Short, 1818
Haynes, Henry D. (Homer), 1605
Hays, E. F., 2060
Hazard: founder of, 758; naming of, 1249
Hazard Baptist Institute, 703
Hazel, Caleb, 1482
Hazel Green Academy, 175
Hazel Patch, 53, 56
Head, Rev. Jesse: 526; homesite, 1038
Heale, Priscilla, 1921
Hebron Church (Anderson County), 1122
Helm, Ben Hardin: 1783; birthplace of, 1101; grave of, 833
Helm, Benjamin, 1534
Helm, Emilie Todd, 1101, 1783
Helm, John Larue: 1115, 1740, 1852, 1912; grave of, 833; wife of, 1101
Helm, Mary Shirley, 2038
Helm, Thomas, 960, 1651
Helm Cemetery, 833
Helm Place, 1783
Hematite Furnace, 1366
Hemp: Boyle County, 1279; Clark County, 1319; Fayette County, 1163; Franklin County, 1164; Jessamine County, 1315; Madison County, 1362; Mason County, 1165; Scott County, 1166; Shelby County, 1320; Woodford County, 1167
Hemp factory, 1809
Henderson, Alexander, 1562

Henderson, Ed, 1924
Henderson, Richard: 53, 56, 709, 1520, 1579, 1582; county named for, 1206
Henderson: Civil War in, 527; founding of, 66, 717
Henderson County: naming of, 1206
Henderson Settlement, 1286
Hendrick, John K., 1969
Henry, John F., 1969
Henry, Patrick: 122, 820, 926, 1084, 1309, 1337, 1386, 1528, 1541; county named for, 805; sister of, 974, 1573
Henry, Robert, 1562
Henry, Robert P., 1969
Henry Clay Furnace, 1390
Henry County: Civil War in, 549; naming of, 805
Henshall, James A., 651
Hensley, Henry B., 2024
Henson, Josiah: "Uncle Tom," 1241
Hermany, Charles, 1689
Herndon, William H.: birthplace of, 846
Hesler, Jacob, 1658
Heslerville (Hesler): early county seat at, 1658
Heth, Henry, 519, 546, 550, 673
Hewitt, R. C., 1580
Hickman, Paschal: county named for, 895
Hickman, Richard: home of, 1318
Hickman, William (Mercer Co.), 1530
Hickman, William (Franklin Co.), 2003
Hickman: county seat at, 1169
Hickman County: naming of, 508, 895
Hicks, Amanda, 1611
Hicks, Hubbard V., 830
Hicks, Stephen G., 828, 1031
Hiett, Hugh M., 509, 1204
Highbaugh, L. Leroy, Jr., 1968
High Bridge, 1381
Hightower, Rev. John (Warren Co.), 1063
Hightower, John (Allen Co.), 2064
Hill, Atkinson, 1078
Hill, John A., 1526

Hill, John Y., 1505, 1621
Hill, Michael, 1735
Hill, Richard, 1735
Hill, T. M., 1526
Hillman, Daniel, 1340, 1366, 1380, 1423
Hillman, Daniel, Iron Company, 1380
Hillsboro Covered Bridge, 1569
Hilton, M. T., 1211
Hinde, Thomas, 1386
Hindman, T. C., 607, 656
Hindman Settlement School, 771, 870, 1512
Hindoo Stakes, 1853
Hines, Duncan, 1831
Hines, Hardy, 1735
Hines, Thomas Henry: 798; birthplace of, 770; home of, 769
Hinkston, John, 107
Hinson, Jack: Civil War sniper, 881
Hinton, James, 1123
Hiram Lodge: #4 F. & A.M., 2028; No. 57, 2028
Hiseville, 2019
History of Kentucky: Lewis and Richard H. Collins, 738
Hite, Isaac: home of, 670, 1435, 1474
Hiter, William L., 1349
Hobbs, Elizabeth, 1682
Hobson, Atwood G.: 1201; home of, 1127
Hobson, E. H., 603, 751
Hobson, William E., 1127, 1201
Hockensmith, George, 1571
Hockersmith, L. D., 1425
Hockersmith House, The, 1425
Hodgen, Robert, 1096
Hodgenville: establishment of, 1096
Hogg, Martha Coldiron, 2024
Hogg, S. P., 2024
Holder, John, 856, 1048
Holderman, Jacob, 949, 1080
Hollister, H., 976
Holman, Richard, 1603
Holman, Rev. William, 1476
Holmes, Andrew, 1182, 1653, 1774
Holmes, Daniel Henry, 1691

Holmes, Daniel Henry, Jr., 1691
Holmes, Oliver Wendell, 1681
Holmes, Oliver Wendell, Jr., 1880
Holt, Joseph: birthplace and grave of, 552
Holy Cross Church (Covington), 1887
Homer and Jethro, 1605
"Honey" (song), 1836
Hood, Andrew, 690, 1529
Hood, John Bell: birthplace of, 862, 940; home of, 112
Hood, Thomas, 1529
Hoover, Herbert, 1839
Hopewell. See Paris
Hopewell Furnace, 1143, 1348-1349
Hopewell Presbyterian Church (Paris), 1855
Hopkins, Samuel: 744; city and county named for, 717, 849
Hopkins, William, 1735
Hopkins County: naming of, 717, 849
Hopkinsville: cemetery, 880; First Presbyterian Church, 1045; N. B. Forrest in, 618, 880; naming of, 717; Peace Park, 1041; Pioneer Graveyard, 1268
Horse Hollow Cabin, 1477
Horse racing, 6, 982, 1083, 1820, 1853, 1992, 2027, 2040
Horses: American Flag, 1635; Aristides, 166, 1885; Asteroid, 2027; Azra, 2040; Baden-Baden, 1992, 2027; Bateau, 1635; Battleship, 1635; Ben Brush, 2027; Black Gold, 1853; Blockade, 1635; Broadway Jones, 1853; Brown Dick, 2027; Clyde Van Dusen, 1853; Consuelo II, 1295; Crossland, 649; Crusader, 1635; Donerail, 1475; Ducat, 2027; Edith Cavell, 1635; Epinard, 1853; Equipoise, 1853; Exterminator, 565; Fair Play, 1635; Florence Nightingale, 1635; Gallant Knight, 1853; George

Smith, 1295; Greyhound, 565; Handy Mandy, 1853; Holystone, 1635; Inquirer, 649; Kingfisher, 2027; Leonatus, 1295, 1853; Longfellow, 1295; Mahubah, 1635; Maid at Arms, 1635; Man o' War, 1215, 1635, 1853; Manuel, 2040; Nellie Gray, 649; Out of Reach, 1295; Peter Volo, 565; Phaeton, 1295; Plaudit, 2027; Rock Sand, 1635; Scapa Flow, 1635; Semper Felix, 1295; Sir Barton, 1635; Sir Huon, 2040; Upset, 1635, 1853; Versailles, 649; War Admiral, 1215, 1635; Wing Commander, 1470; Zev, 1853
Horsfall, William H., 1867
Horton, Elijah, 504
Horwitz, Louis, 2031
Hoskins, C. R., 1924
Hospitals: Extendicare (Louisville), 2042; King's Daughters (Frankfort), 2025; St. Joseph Infirmary (Louisville), 2042; St. Joseph's (Lexington), 1928; St. Vincent (Louisville), 2042; tuberculosis, 1503, 1815; Winnie A. Scott (Frankfort), 2025
Hotels: Armstrong, 1129; Bedford, 1823; Beula Villa, 1895; Brown, 1723; Jacksonian, 1760; Latham, 1501; Seelbach, 1723
Houk, L. C., 560
House of History: Washington County, 1446
House on the Hill: Thomas Marshall home, 81
Houston, Joe, 850
Houston, Sam, 964, 1843; duel, 611
Howard, Benjamin F., 1956
Howard, C. C., 1503
Howard, William, 1347
Howe, J. H., 1739
Howe, Rev. John, 1951
Howe, Samuel G., 1336
Howe, William, 1583
Howell, John: land of, 1461
Hoy, Jones, 856

Hubbard, Carroll, 1969
Hucaby, Isaac, 1619
Hudson, Elizabeth, 2071
Hudson, H., 1739
Hudson, Samuel A., 830
Hudson, William H., 1599
Hudspeth, William, 912
Huggans, George M., 1598
Hughs, John M., 730, 1290
Huguenot (ancestry), 662, 1209, 1921
Huling, Marcus, 702
Hull, William, 507-508
Hummel, Ferd: gunsmith, 1062
Humphrey, Alex P., 1229
Humphrey, John T., 1825
Humphreys, Elizabeth, 1999
Hunley, Benjamin, 1495
Hunnewell Furnace, 1017
Hunt, Charity, 1521
Hunt, Daniel, 1521
Hunt, John, 1521, 1735
Hunt, Thomas, 504
Hunter, Jacob, 1790
Hunter, John, 1928
Hunter's Horn (Arnow), 1807
Hunt-Morgan House (Lexington), 1714
Hunt Settlement, 1521
Hurricane Furnace, 1225, 1450
Huston, George, 1787
Hutcherson, C. B., 1365
Hutcheson, John, 1296
Hutchings, E. T., 1692
Hutchings, John B., 1746
Hyden: Frontier Nursing Service, 558
Hynes, Andrew, 960, 1651
Hynes, John, 1174
Illinois Central Railroad, 794, 1134, 1647, 1711
Immanuel Baptist Church (Paducah), 1044
Imobersteg, Karl, 843
Imperial Hotel (Tokyo), 1726
Improved Benevolent Order of Elks of the World, 1956
Independence Day: first celebration, 201; of 1863, 605
Indian Creek Baptist Church (Harrison County), 1457
Indian Creek Church (Monroe County), 1394
Indian Old Fields, 31, 1274

Indians: 817, 825, 1067, 1168, 1299, 1520, 1574-1575, 1578, 1614, 1637, 1696, 1848, 1878, 1941, 2059; Abraham Lincoln, 101; Adena, 1655; ambush, 1299; Barnett's Station, 1463; Battle of Blue Licks, 18, 217, 222, 729, 785, 800, 842, 917, 952, 1001, 1048, 1159, 1230; Big Bone Lick, 32; Bird's War Road, 34; Boone's Cave, 1343; British-Indian Raid, 953; Bryan's Station, 21; Cabin Creek, 143; camp, 1600; Cartwright's Station, 1339; Chanoah Marker, 31; Chenoweth Massacre, 992; Cherokees, 922, 1577, 1675; Chickasaws, 169, 793, 829, 1006, 1309, 1892, 1969; Chief Paduke, 793; Chief Red Bird, 908; Chief Thunder, 1525; Choctaw Indian Academy, 135; Clark's Campaigns of 1780 and 1782, 1435; William Crawford, 1409; Cumberland Ford, 1426; discovery of the Ohio River, 22; early vital junction, 926; Estill Springs, 555; Estill's Defeat, 153; Floyd's Station, 1060; Fort Hartford, 1195; Fort William, 974; Gaitskill Mound, 1655; Goodwin (Goodin) Fort, 1471; Hancock Taylor, 1685; Harberson's Station, 876; Hart County, 43; Hazel Patch, 53, 56; Jackson Purchase, 169; Jenny Wiley, 735; John Floyd's Grave, 146; John Hardin, 931; John Holder, 1048; Kincheloe's Station, 1586; John Knight, 1409; last raid in Kentucky, 189; last recorded raid in Hart Co. area, 1414; Leestown, 103; Lexington, 136; Long Run Massacre, 991; McNitt's Defeat, 102; Martin's Station, 150, 919, 953, 1753; Massacre, 1309; Maulding's Fort, 1137;

Modoc, 1646; Morgan's Station, 115; Moses Stepp, 922; mounds, 921; Murder Branch Massacre, 189; Ohio River, 1614; Old Fields, 31, 1274; Old Threshing Rock, 1293; one of last massacres in Kentucky, 936; Phillips Fort, 1098; pioneer hero-heroine, 919; Pioneer Route, 1185; Pioneer Ward, 729; Price's Meadow, 988; Remember the Raisin!, 508; Richards home site, 842; Ruddle's Station, 107, 953, 1753; Scott's Blockhouse, 1094; Shawnees, 1253, 1274, 1472; Spring Fort, 26; Squire Boone's Station, 28; Station Camp, 810; Tanner's Station, 999; Three Forts, 1651; Tick Creek Massacre, 1088; Trail of Tears, 142, 1042, 1097; trails, 1916; treaty (1786), 822; Treaty of Greenville, 804; Twitty's (Little Fort), 77; Van Meter Fort, 1494; Walker Daniel, 190; Warrior's Path, 697

Industrial School of Reform and House of Refuge (Louisville), 541

Industry: Grayson County, 906; pioneer, 838

Influenza epidemic (1918), 2070

Ingles (Inglis), Mary: 32, 163, 859; captivity, 1253

Inherit the Wind (play), 1698

Inman, James, 1123

Inns: Doe Run (Meade County), 1755; Haycraft (Radcliff), 1904; Old Crow (Boyle County), 1376; Old Stone (Shelby Co.), 1889; Stagecoach Stop (Warren Co.), 1573; Young's (Hardin County), 1763

Inquirer (horse), 649

Instone, John, 1205

International Federation of Business and Professional Women, 1473

International Joint Commission, 1777

International Monetary Fund and Bank, 1776

Inventors: Edward Rumsey, 1264; Edward West, 1556; Garrett A. Morgan, 1493; John Fitch, 944; John T. Thompson, 1270; Nathan Bowman Stubblefield, 87; Robert Fulton, 801, 944, 1169; Thomas Edison, 1713

Ira Combs Memorial Church (Perry County), 759

Ireland, James, 1941

Irish immigrants: in Frankfort, 2057

Iron Banks, 60

Iron Hill Furnace, 1014

Iron Horse Memorial, 794

Iron industry, 975-976, 993, 998, 1008-1020, 1023, 1050, 1054-1056, 1080, 1086, 1113, 1120, 1130-1132, 1135-1136, 1142-1143, 1147-1150, 1155-1157, 1162, 1193, 1210-1211, 1225-1227, 1247, 1326-1327, 1332, 1337, 1340, 1348-1349, 1354, 1357, 1364, 1366-1368, 1373, 1380, 1389-1390, 1395-1396, 1402, 1421, 1423, 1434, 1450, 1598, 1978, 2015

Iroquois Park, 1629

Irvin, J. C., 1585

Irvine, Nancy, 1979

Irvine, William: town named for, 199

Irvine: naming of, 199; Battle of, 1507

Irving, Washington, 1548, 1681

Irwin, John, 1113

Island: establishment of, 1812

Israel Institute of Technology, 2065

Ivy Mountain: Battle of, 164

Ivy Point, 901

Iwo Jima hero, 855

Jackson, Andrew: 634, 761, 823, 835, 930, 1125, 1210, 1519, 1681, 1760, 1763, 1799; Carneal House, 1429; Colbyville Tavern, 1358; county named for, 1145; duel, 100; Jackson Purchase, 169, 1006; Liberty Hall, 1653; Old Munford

Inn, 204; Sanders Tavern, 1448; town named for, 961

Jackson, Andrew, Jr.: Hurricane Furnace, 1225

Jackson, Beckley: stage stop, 1797

Jackson, E. Belle Mitchell, 1963

Jackson, James S., 607, 649; grave of, 882

Jackson, John H., 1752

Jackson, Robert, Jr., 2050

Jackson, Thomas J., 1620

Jackson: naming of, 961

Jackson County: naming of, 1145

Jackson-Dickinson duel, 100

Jackson Furnace. *See* Hurricane Furnace

Jackson Hall (Kentucky State University), 1752

Jacksonian Hotel, 1760

Jackson Purchase, 169, 200, 967, 1006, 1111, 1169, 1263, 1785, 1969

Jacob, Jefferson, 2038

Jacobs, B. F., 1922

Jacobs, John A., Sr., 2005

Jacobs, Thomas, 1702

Jacobs Hall (Kentucky School for the Deaf), 2005

James, Frank, 1649

James, Jesse: 1649; bank robbed by, 969

James, Ollie M.: 1499, 1969; birthplace of, 668; buried, 1499

James, Zerelda (Cole), 1649

Jamestown: Civil War in, 724; establishment of, 954

Jansen, Rev. Herman W., 1106

January, Ephraim, 894

January, Samuel, 1428

Japan: Paleliu Island, 1672

Jarrett, Dinah, 1518

Jarrett, Emily, 1175

Jarvis, Edward, 1735

Jefferson, Lucy. *See* Lewis, Lucy Jefferson

Jefferson, Thomas: 32, 801, 803, 926, 1170, 1309, 1451, 1528, 1595, 1653, 1680, 1687, 1697; county named for, 1441; Farmington, 174; home of, 989; Jack Jouett Home, 78, 1541; sister of,

767

Jefferson County: Civil War in, 548; courthouse, 945, 1697; creation of, 1083, 1441; defense against Indians, 974; naming of, 1697

Jefferson Seminary (Estill County), 1922

Jefferson Seminary (Jefferson County), 2007

Jeffries, Robert, 1748

Jenkins, George C., 1804

Jennie's Creek, 571

Jennings, Samuel C., 1678

Jeptha's Knob, 161

Jersey (ship), 1950

Jessamine County: naming of, 947

Jesse, Matt Gay, 1005

Jessee, George M., 549

Jews: early congregations, 1923; in Paducah, 1058; Louis Dembitz Brandeis, 1880

Jim and I Furnace, 1326

Job Corps Training Center (Union County), 1424

Johnson, Adam R.: 89, 527, 830, 1630, 1915, 1971; Army of Six, 1103; blinded, 751

Johnson, Andrew: 764, 1629, 1638; impeachment trial, 1059, 1151

Johnson, Ben: birthplace of, 1686

Johnson, Felix, 1992

Johnson, George W.: 67, 1934; Confederate governor, 610

Johnson, John T., 1710

Johnson, Keen, 1768, 1927

Johnson, Lyman T., 2022

Johnson, Lyndon B., 1844, 1960

Johnson, Mattie H., 1768

Johnson, Nancy, 1686

Johnson, Richard M.: 1406; county named for, 1125; home of, 135; Morgan Row, 185; U.S. vice president, 739, 2028

Johnson, Rev. Robert, 1768, 1927

Johnson, Thornton, 1934

Johnson, W. A. E., 1659

Johnson, William, 1686

Johnson County: naming of, 1125

Johnson Creek Covered Bridge, 1567

Johnston, Abigail H., 1696

Johnston, Albert Sidney: 24, 1406, 1696; birthplace of, 91; Civil War defense line, 538; mother of, 1696

Johnston, Annie Fellows: 208, 1654; home, The Beeches, 208

Johnston, Robert, 1283

Johnston's Inn, 1283

Joliet, Sieur Louis, 46

Jones, Enoch S.: CSA medalist, 1133

Jones, George L., 830

Jones, H. W., 1693

Jones, John Paul, 1534

Jones, Joshua, 989; pioneer surveyor, 1153

Jones, Rev. Laban, 1122

Jones, Ora C., 1619

Jonesville, 2052

Joseph & Joseph Architects, 1952

Jouett, John "Jack": 1707, 1888; buried, 1528; home, 78, 1541

Jouett, Matthew Harris, 78, 1541, 1888

Jouett, Sally S., 1707

Jouett, Thomasine, 1707

Jouett, William R., 1707

Journal (Louisville), 1719, 1724

Journalists: Alice Allison Dunnigan, 1960; Amos Kendall, 1799; Arthur Krock, 1718; Desha Breckinridge, 1876; Henry Watterson, 1719

"Judge Priest." *See* Bishop, William Sutton

Judson, Edward Z. C.: Ned Buntline, 938

K.H.S.A.L. State Basketball Championship, 2050

Kalakaua: King of Hawaii, 1447

Kallendar, Robert, 31

Kappa Kappa Gamma sorority, 2011

Karrick, James V., 876

Karrick-Parks House, 876

Kaskaskia, 1352, 1520, 1843

Kavanaugh, Bishop H. H.,

1476, 1539, 1659, 1972

Kavanaugh, Rhoda C., 1273, 1479

Kavanaugh School, 1273; alumni of, 1479

Keely, William, 1639

Keen, John S., 1927

Keenan, Adam, 1539

Keene, John, 2

Keene, Primus, 1938

Keeneland, 2

Keene Springs Hotel, 1671

Keith, Mary, 81

Kelly, Eleanor Mercein, 1654

Kelly, James, 1674

Kelly, L. C., 1924

Kelly, William, 61, 946, 1326-1327, 1332, 1598

Kelly Furnace, 61

Kelsey: town established, 1908

Kemper, Ira, 1819

Kendall, Amos, 1799, 2028

Kennedy, John, 1649

Kennedy, John F., 1680, 1960

Kennedy, Matthew, 1549

Kennedy, Peter, 1471

Kennedy, Thomas: 1429, 1562, 1774; homesite, 1070

Kennedy Center, 1899

Kennedy family, 936

Kenrick, Bishop F. P., 1593

Kenton, Eldrige, 1893

Kenton, Simon: 928-929, 1339, 1472, 1555, 1614, 1696, 1941; county named for, 1168; frontier scout, 1181; Iron Furnace named for, 1015; Limestone, 68; station, 138

Kenton, W. T., 1893

Kenton, William G., 1893

Kenton County: naming of, 1168

Kenton Furnace (Campbell Co.), 1434

Kenton Furnace (Greenup Co.), 1015

Kenton Iron Company, 1434

Kentucky
- Academy, 86
- Athletic Hall of Fame, 1475, 1627
- bicentennial, 1920
- Bluegrass region, 1919
- center of, 867

- Civil War Round Table, founder of, 2029
- Commission on Interracial Cooperation, 1663
- constitution (1792), 125, 708-709, 844, 890, 933, 948, 983, 1070, 1079, 1139, 1171, 1989
- constitutional convention (1799), 199, 781, 788, 806, 831, 836, 890, 983, 1079, 1170, 1181, 1618
- constitutional convention (1849), 779, 1363, 1883, 1886, 1994
- constitutional convention (1890-91), 728, 791, 1674, 1926
- County (Virginia), 1083, 1440-1441, 1472, 1697, 1753
- Court of Appeals, 1929, 1878, 1884
- Dam, 1647, 1648
- Derby: 166, 1064, 1295, 1475, 1635, 1885, 2040; Baden-Baden, 1992; William "Uncle Bill" Walker, 1992
- Division of League of American Wheelmen, 1997
- Education Association Board of Directors, 2019
- Educational Television, 1929
- Equal Rights Association, 1800, 1876
- Female Orphan School, 1087
- first state constitution of, 1474
- *Gazette*, 1864
- General Assembly, 157, 1922
- Geological Survey, 1480, 1910, 1926
- Historical Society: 1329, 1524; director, 2044; first president, 788; Highway Marker Program: father of, 1420
- Kentucky-Tennessee Boundary, 1859-1860, 1868
- Lake, 147, 1648
- last execution by hanging, 1862
- Life Museum (Waveland),

1280
- Military Institute, 649, 1474
- National Guard, 2037
- Negro Republican Party, 1962
- Normal and Theological Institute, 1661
- Oaks, 2040
- Poet Laureate (Stuart), 1808, 1814
- Railway Museum, 1720
- Resolutions (1798), 1170
- River, 1443, 1774, 1805, 1817, 2031
- School for the Blind, 1336
- School for the Deaf, 1536, 2005, 2016
- School of Medicine, 542
- State College, 1419, 1469, 1970, 2036
- state government: in Lexington, 1551; in Louisville, 522
- State Penitentiary, 1466, 1874, 1910, 1959
- state park system, 1815, 1844, 1929
- State University, 1752, 2019
- Thoroughbred Breeders Association, 1475
- Union Railway Company, 2015
- Village. *See* Blackburn Correctional Complex
- Women's Christian Temperance Union, 1872
"Kentucky Riflemen," 1589
Kerr, Rev. and Mrs. John R., 197
Kerr, S. E., 1924
Kimmel, Husband E., 878
Kimmel, Manning M., 878
Kincaid, Bradley, 2026
Kincheloe, Peter, 1735
Kincheloe, William, 1586
King, A. D. Williams, 1657
King, Amon B., 964
King, Coretta Scott, 2036
King, Rev. D. E., 1276, 1657
King, John Edwards, 1403
King, Rev. Martin Luther, Jr.: 1657, 1693, 2036; Nobel Peace prize ceremony, 2036
Kingdom Come, 1294
King's Daughters Hospital

(Frankfort), 2025
King's Mountain, Battle of, 797, 1575
Kinman, William E.: CSA medallist, 1201
Kinniconick: tanyard at, 1656
Kirby Smith, E.: 630, 1300, 1600, 1646, 1825; Battle of Perryville, 553; Big Hill Skirmish, 1124; Civil War action, 514; Confederates here, 522; day of Perryville, 572; following Perryville, 676, 704; headquarters, 518; in Anderson County, 1121; invasion of Kentucky, 683
Kitson, Henry H., 1043
Kiwanis Trail, 1517
Knight, James, 565
Knight, John, 1409
Knight, John Richard, 1479
Knights of Pythias Temple, 1662
Knob Creek Farm, 120, 827, 1482, 1834
Knott, J. Proctor: 1629, 1673; birthplace of, 728; county named for, 728, 791; father of, 1673; home of, 1341
Knott, Joseph P., 1673
Knott, Thomas P., 1673
Knox, Henry: 1869; county named for, 782
Knox, James, 635, 709
Knox, Sarah, 1849
Knox County: naming of, 782
Korean War: 1322, 1424, 1610, 1643, 1869, 2013, 2033, 2044; Charles Moran, 1207; Darwin K. Kyle, 1906
Kouns, Jacob, 1157
Kouns, John C., 1157
Krock, Arthur, 1718
Kuhr, Rev. Ferdinand, 1460
Ku Klux Klan, 606, 1979
Kuttawa, 1332
Kyle, Darwin K., 1906
Kyle, Dominie Thomas, 141
Labrot & Graham Distillery, 1986-1987
Lafayette, Marquis de, 2, 534, 938, 1429, 1440, 1653, 1798, 1888, 1921, 1968
Lafferty, Thornton, 504
Laffoon, Ruby, 1232

Laine, Joseph, 1928
Lair, John, 1605
Lake Erie: Battle of, 1196, 1249, 1284
Lampton, Jane: home of, 128
Lampton Brothers, 1018
Lancaster, Father J. M., 2057
Lancaster Academy, 1371
Landers, Charles, 1738
Landing Run, 1751
Lane, W. A., 1050
Larkin, George E., Jr., 1727
LaRue, Squire, 1115
Larue County: naming of, 1115; officials in, 1115
La Salle, Robert Cavelier, Sieur de, 22, 46
Lassiter, A.L., 1754
Latham, John C., 880, 1041, 1501, 1690
Latonia, 1853, 1887, 1939
Latonia Derby: Broadway Jones, 1853; Gallant Knight, 1853; Handy Mandy, 1853; Upset, 1853
Latrobe, Benjamin Henry: James Taylor Home, 121; Owings House, 1193
Laura Furnace, 998
Laurel County: 2033; naming of, 1176
Laurel Furnace, 1019
Laurel Seminary, 661
Lawless, O. G., 1619
Lawrence, James: county named for, 886
Lawrenceburg: in Civil War, 572, 630
Lawrence County: naming of, 886
Laws, Peter, 1988
Leader (Lexington), 1736
League of American Wheelmen, Ky. Div. of, 1997
League of Nations, 1719
Lebanon: Battle of, 600-601, 951, 1413, 1486; settlement of, 867
LeClerc, Gilbert, 1299
Lecompte, Charles: Lindsay's Fort, 218; Stamping Ground, 217
Lee, George Russell, 1479
Lee, Hancock: Leestown, 103, 1444; Ohio Company of Virginia, 20

Lee, Henry, 1774
Lee, Mother Ann, 1481
Lee, John, 1649
Lee, Reuben, 1716
Lee, Robert E.: 1335; county named for, 792
Lee, Willis: Leestown, 103
Lee, Willis A., Jr., 1444
Lee County: naming of, 792
Leedom, S. V., 1390
Leer, Jacob, 753
Leestown: founder of, 1444; settlement, 103, 1774
Legerwood's Bend, 1774
Legislature, first, 157
Leitch, David, 117, 1730, 1741
Leitchfield Landmarks, 1741
Lemon, James R., 1749
Lemoyne de Longueil, Charles, 32
Leonatus (horse), 1295
Leprosy, 1452
Leslie, Preston H.: birthplace of, 1085; county named for, 213; home of, 609
Leslie, Robert, 2034
Leslie, William Robert, 2034
Leslie County: naming of, 213, 1085
Leslie/Lesley Settlement, 2034
Letcher, Robert P.: 1325; county named for, 714, 809; home of, 123, 714
Letcher County: coal in, 1804; naming of, 714, 809
Level Woods Methodist Church (Larue County), 1186
Lewinski, Thomas, 1040, 1459, 2005
Lewis, Catherine Washington, 1623
Lewis, Charles L., 767
Lewis, Daniel, 1914
Lewis, Fielding, 1623
Lewis, George (Mason County), 68
Lewis, George (Russell County), 838
Lewis, J. C., 2060
Lewis, James Beverly: CSA medallist, 1133
Lewis, John (Hancock County), 1789
Lewis, John (Logan County),

1623
Lewis, Joseph H., 1290, 1317, 1365
Lewis, Lucy Jefferson: home of, 767
Lewis, Mary Ann, 1623
Lewis, Meriwether: 1352, 1451, 1595; county named for, 803
Lewis, Oliver, 1885
Lewis, Thomas, 1558
Lewis, William, 1349
Lewis and Clark Expedition, 803, 840, 916, 918, 1451, 1595
Lewis County: naming of, 803, Union monument in, 215
Lewis Manor, 1558
Lewisport, 1789, 1935
Lexington: 1556, 1613, 1905; blockhouse and fort, 1554; capture of, 567, 621-625, 628-629, 691-695, 700-701; Cemetery, 543, 659, 679, 807, 809, 1550, 1809, 1875; Colored Agricultural and Mechanical Association, 1961; Colored Fair Association, 1961; Colored Orphan Industrial Home, 1963; courthouses, 1553; Dunbar School, 2050; Herald, 1876; Leader, 1736; library, 1551; Main Street Christian Church, 19; naming of, 554, 1001; oldest house in, 1437; Pioneer Burying Ground, 1552; settlement, 136, 554, 1774
Lexington, Versailles and Midway Road Company, 1649
Lexington Light Infantry, 43
Lexington and Ohio Railroad, 69, 1580
Lexington Rifles, 506, 1235
Lexington Rifles Infantry, 1809
Liberia, 124, 1514
Liberty. See Westport
Liberty Hall, 1653
Liberty Station, 1361
Library: first in Frankfort, 1537; first in Lexington, 1551; Louisville Free Pub-

lic, 1654; Louisville Polytechnic, 1723; Louisville
Western Branch, 1545, 2017
Licking Furnace, 1395
Lillard Spring. *See* McCall's
Spring
Lilly, Percy Anthony, Jr., 1479
Limestone: settlement of, 68.
See also Maysville
Lincoln, Abraham: 718, 1306,
1325, 1334, 1446, 1482,
1515, 1591, 1704, 1711, 1724,
1834, 1910, 1912, 1914,
1999, 2029; assassination
of, 552; family of, 853-854;
Farmington, 174; father of,
885; first law case, 667;
Helm Cemetery, 833;
home of, 120; law partner,
846; Lincoln Family Trail,
73; Lincoln Homestead,
526; mentor of, 719; only
political speech in Ken-
tucky, 1329; parents of,
1038; playmate of, 827;
president, 649, 1082, 1109,
1606, 1750, 1910, 1912,
1914; Todd House, 11, 1999;
travels in Kentucky, 858,
932, 1003, 1681
Lincoln, Abraham (grandfather of the president), 101,
250, 853-854
Lincoln, Benjamin: county
named for, 774
Lincoln, Mary Todd, 11-12;
Buena Vista, 1999; grand-
father of, 1001, 1783; Helm
Cemetery, 833; home of,
945; Lexington, 136; sister
of, 1101; Todd House, 11-12
Lincoln, Nancy Hanks, 526,
853, 885, 1038, 1591
Lincoln, Sarah, 1482
Lincoln, Thomas: 73, 885,
932, 1468, 1591, 1834, 1914;
family travels in Ky. and
Ind., 73, 858; Lincoln
Homestead, 526; marriage
of, 853, 1038; state park,
526
Lincoln County: history of,
860, 1083; naming of, 774
Lincoln family: travels in Ky.
and Ind., 73, 858
Lincoln-Haycraft Memorial

Bridge, 932
Lincoln Heritage House, 1468
Lincoln Institute, 1663, 1930,
1964
Lincoln Party, 1998
Lind, Jenny, 1505, 1763
Linden Grove Cemetery
(Covington), 167
Lindsay, Anthony: grave of,
218
Lindsay, Elizabeth, 1613
Lindsay, Joseph, 1558
Lindsey, Daniel W., 1743
Lindsey, David: grave of,
1220
Lindsey, Isaac, 1254
Lindsey Cemetery, 1220
Line Island Furnace, 1367
Lingenfelter, John L., 722, 725
Lingenfelter, William P., 722,
725
Linkumpinch: noted dueling
ground, 611
"Lion of White Hall" (Cassius
M. Clay), 533
Lippert, Leon, 1506
Lisle, Daniel, 165
Little, John W., 830
Little Big Horn: Battle of,
(Montana), 2030
"Little Colonel," 208
"Little Floyd," 905
Littlejohn, John, 871, 1972
Little Mountain, Battle of, 153,
1525
Littlepage, John, 1735
Little Sandy River, 1973
Little Shepherd of Kingdom Come
(Fox), 775-777, 1294
Little Shepherd Trail, 775-777
Little Yellow Banks. *See* Lewis-
port
Livermore Bridge, 892
Livingston, Robert R.: county
named for, 801
Livingston County: county
seats of, 1204; naming of,
801
Lloyd, Alice, 653, 1532, 1543
Locust Grove: George Rogers
Clark home, 835, 1753
Lodge, Henry Cabot, 1680
Lodging for a Night (Hines),
1831
Logan, Benjamin: 53, 56, 709,
860, 1472, 1575, 1622, 1790;

county named for, 1138; sis-
ter of, 1234
Logan, D. B., 1933
Logan, Emmett, 1665
Logan, John: 157; home of,
1561
Logan, Joseph, 2064
Logan, Marvel Mills: birth-
place of, 910
Logan County: Genealogical
Society, 1791; jail, 1791;
Kentucky governors from,
1260; naming of, 1138;
Shaker colony in, 179
Logan's Cross Roads. *See*
Battle of Mill Springs
Logan Wildcats, 2068
Logwood, T. H., 1410
London: Battle of, 560
Long, Eli, 649
Long, George J., 2040
Long, John, 504
Long, Nimrod, 969
Longfellow, Henry Wads-
worth, 1344
Long Hunters, 148, 635, 709,
988, 1187, 1426, 1600
Long Run Baptist Church, 101
Long Run Massacre, 991,
1088
Longsworth and Company:
Timber Tunnel, 900
Lookout Mountain hero, 639
Looney, Absalom, 1868
Loretto, Sisters of, 206-207
Lotts Creek Community
School, 1543
Loughborough, Preston, 1707
Loughborough, Thomas, 1707
Louis Philippe: 940, 1182,
1193
Louis XIV, 46
Louis XVI, 1697
Louisa: Civil War in, 547, 643,
726
Louisa River: naming of, 903
Louisville: 1723, 1774, 2027;
airport, 1676; Bar Associa-
tion, 2051; Better Business
Bureau, 1664; Cemetery
(African American), 1992;
City Hall, 1704; College,
2007; *Courier-Journal,* 1718-
1719, 1736; founder of, 835,
1697; Fourth Street, 1723-
1724; Free Public Library,

1654; Grays, 1589; Guards, 1589; *Herald*, 1718; Jefferson Seminary, 2007; Jockey Club, 1885; Kentucky state government in, 522; *Leader*, 1998; Legal Aid Society, 2051; Legion, 1589, 1629; Medical College, 1737; Medical Institute, 1628, 2007; Memorial Auditorium, 1692; movie houses in, 1723; Municipal College, 1998, 2008, 2020; named for, 1697; NAACP, 2022; oldest existing school, 1702; park system, 1629; Red Cross Hospital, 1992; steamboats at, 1681; *Times*, 1665, 1718; Water Co., 1689; Western Branch Library, 1545, 2017; whipping post in, 1704; Women's Club, 2051

Louisville and Jefferson County Air Board, 1676

Louisville and Nashville Railroad: 716, 1101, 1116, 1296, 1338, 1350, 1573, 1644, 1746, 1764, 1856, 1883, 1912, 1955, 1994; bridge, 1925

Love, Elizabeth, 1653

Love, Thomas: Love House, 1182

Lovelace, Isaac, 970

Low Dutch (New Holland) Station, 1848

Lowe, William, 1625

Lower Blue Licks: Salt Lick, 162

Lowry, Stephen, 205

Loyal Land Company, 72, 898, 1176

Lulbegrud Creek, 137

Lunatic Asylum. *See* Eastern State Hospital

Lusby's Mill, 564, 722

Luther, Martin: "Away in a Manger," 1202

Lynch, Sister Nancy, 1943

Lynch: company-owned town at, 1803

Lyndon: founding of, 1474

Lynn, Rev. Benjamin, 1114

Lyon, Chittenden: 1969; county named for, 1245

Lyon, Hylan B., 509; courthouse burned by, 577-583, 589

Lyon, Matthew, 1245; grave of, 130

Lyon, W. R., 1924

Lyon County: naming of, 1245

Lyth, Rev. John, 1083, 1582

Lyttle, David Yancey, 1397

McAboy, Paradise Lost, 1696

Macadamized road, 144

Macauley Theater, 1724

McAfee, George, 928-929, 1121, 1603

McAfee, James, 928-929, 1121

McAfee, Robert, 555, 928-929, 1121, 1498

McAfee, Samuel, 928-929, 1121, 1603, 1751

McAfee, William, 928-929

McAfee brothers: at Big Bone Lick, 32

McAfee Company, 103, 1498

McBride, James, 222

McCabe family, 1649

McCall, Thomas, 1122

McCall, William, 1837

McCall's Spring, 1121-1122

McClernand, J. S., 563

McCloskey, Bishop George, 907

McCloskey, Bishop William, 1680, 1682

McClure, H. V., 2060

McClure family, 936

McConnell, William: 136, 205, 554, 1555, 1557; Lindsay's Fort, 218; Stamping Ground, 217

McCook, Alexander McDowell, 553

McCook, Edward Moody, 194

McCool's Creek Settlement. *See* Ghent

McCord, J. E., 1625

McCord, W. E., 1625

McCorkle, James, 1680

McCormack, Daniel, 1590

McCormack Christian Church (Lincoln County), 1590

McCoun, James, Jr., 1121

McCoun family, 928-929

McCoy, Alifair, 1866, 1913

McCoy, Asa Harmon: site of killing, 2068

McCoy, Calvin, 1866

McCoy, James, 1147

McCoy, Martha: grave of, 1728

McCoy, Pharmer, 1866, 2047, 2067

McCoy, Randolph: 2047, 2066-2067; Alifair (daughter of), 2062, 2067; Calvin (son of), 2062, 2067; grave of, 1728; Sally (wife of), 2062; site of house, 2062

McCoy, Randolph, Jr., 1866, 2047, 2067

McCoy, Roseanna: grave of, 1728

McCoy, Sam: grave of, 1728

McCoy, Sarah: grave of, 1728

McCoy, Tolbert, 1866, 2047, 2066-2067

McCoy, William, Sr., 1316

McCoy Cemetery, 2067

McCracken, Virgil: county named for, 508, 840, 916, 918

McCracken County: courthouse, 1377; naming of, 508, 840, 916, 918

McCreary, James B.: 851, 1846; county named for, 1243

McCreary County: naming of, 1243

McCreery, Charles: pioneer surgeon, 1267

McCreery, Thomas Clay: 1079, 1304

McCullough, A., 1018

McCullough, Samuel D., 1437

McCutchen, Elizabeth, 1931

McCutchen, John, 1931

McCutchen Meadows, 1931

McDonald, Henry P., 1695

McDonald Brothers: architects, 1599, 1835

McDougal, John, 1115

McDowell, Ephraim: 23, 1442, 1876; Jane Todd Crawford, 165, 183

McDowell, James E., 1142

McDowell, Robert Emmett, 1654

McDowell, Samuel, 49

McElfatrick, B. J., 1898

McElrath, John, 2035
McElroy, Hugh: home of, 1040
McElroy, J. W., 1819
McElroy, James, 867
McElroy, Rhodam Yarrott, 1479
McElroy, Samuel, 867
McFadin, Andrew, 981, 1665
McGary, Daniel, 1104
McGary, Hugh, 1751
McGee, John, 1603
McGee family, 928-929, 1944
McGinty, Ann, 1083
McGrath, H. P., 1885
McGrath, Thomas C., 1089
McGrathiana: noted horse farm, 166
McGready, Rev. James: Gasper River Meeting House, 170; Red River Meeting House, 71
McGuffey, William Holmes, 178
Machen, Willis B.: home of, 779
McHenry, Henry D., 1510, 1674
McHenry, Jennie Taylor, 1510
McHenry, John H., 569, 1172
McHenry: naming of, 1674
Machine Gun, The (Chinn), 2044
Mack, Albert, 1662
MacKay, Hugh Trent, 1479
McKee, Andrew Irwin, 1479
McKee, Logan, 1479
McKee, Samuel: home of, 714
Mackey, A. B., 1927
Mackey, Albert G., 1739
McKinney, Archibald, 2063
McKinney, John, 1553, 1755
McLean, Alney: 1969; county named for, 1123
McLean, Ephraim, 1735
McLean, Frank, 1123
McLean, John: home of, 947; Supreme Court service, 1484
McLean County: Civil War recruits, 830; first officers, 1123; naming of, 1123
Macklin, George B., 1925
Macklin House, 1925
McMahon, John, 1735
McMeekin, Clark, 1654

McMillan, Rev. Gideon, 1442
McMurtry, Joseph, 1148
McNary, T. L., 1903
McNeill, Archibald, 1279
McNitt's Defeat, 102
McReynolds, James Clark: birthplace of, 824
McShane, Edward, 1457
McTyre, Alfred, 1671
McVey, Frank L., 2069
Madison, Dolly, 1242, 1323
Madison, Gabriel, 1195, 1829
Madison, George, 1372, 1874, 1896
Madison, James: 871, 948; county named for, 1223; Kentucky land, 1242; town named for, 1104
Madison, Susannah Henry, 1573
Madison County: hemp in, 1362; naming of, 1223
Madisonville: Civil War in, 1103; naming of, 1104; Nathan B. Forrest in, 613
Madrid Bend, 1169, 1859
Magazines: *Ebony*, 2036; *Jet*, 2036; *Reader's Digest*, 1967
Magoffin, Beriah: 718, 1325, 1335; county named for, 786
Magoffin County: Civil War in, 556; naming of, 786
Magruder, Henry, 2039
Mahan, James P., 1837
Mahan, Thomas B., 1837
Main Street Christian Church (Lexington), 19
Makemson (McKemson), Andrew, 1220
Makemson (McKemson), John: grave of, 1220
Makemson Mill and Distillery, 1220
Maker's Mark Distillery, 1509
Malcolm (Malcom), Howard, 1487, 1716
Mammoth Cave: 910, 1039; first survey of, 1191
Mammoth Furnace, 1364
Mamre Baptist College, 2024
Mann, Dudley, 1539
Manning, William S., 1479
Man o' War (horse): 1635, 1853; life history, 1215; statue, 1215

Mansfield: home of Henry Watterson, 1719
Mansfield: home of Thomas Clay, 1459
Manson, Mahlon D., 1300
Mantle Rock, 1675
Man with a Bull-Tongue Plow (Stuart), 1808, 1814
Maple Grove Baptist Church (Trigg County), 1840
Marcum, "Aunt Julia," 672
Maret, James, 1644
Marines, 1465, 1672, 1940, 2013, 2044
Marion, Francis, 1467; county named for, 867
Marion: N. B. Forrest in, 615
Marion County: naming of, 867
Markham, Charles H.: Illinois Central Railroad, 1134
Marks, Albert Smith: birthplace of, 1333
Marsh, Olive V., 1152
Marschall, Nicola, 681, 1686
Marshall, Humphrey (Federalist), 1372, 1444
Marshall, Humphrey (Civil War): 85, 564, 570, 863; Jennie's Creek, 571; War on the Big Sandy, 608
Marshall, John: 1968; county named for, 874; father of, 81, 114
Marshall, Mary Keith, 81
Marshall, Rev. Robert, 935
Marshall, Sarah, 1968
Marshall, Thomas: homes of, 81, 114
Marshall College, 812
Marshall County: Civil War in, 545; court, 2035; naming of, 874
Martin, Albert, 1347
Martin, David "Black Dave," 1089, 1379
Martin, Mrs. George Madden, 1654
Martin, Hugh, 1735
Martin, John, 1933
Martin, John P.: county named for, 814
Martin, R. M., 629
Martin, Samuel, 1290
Martin County: first county

seat, 726; naming of, 814
Marvin College, 891
Mason, George: 1081; county named for, 1244
Mason, George W., 1081
Mason, J. T., 1120
Mason, Margaretta, 1653
Mason, W. J., 2043
Mason County: naming of, 1244; Spy Company, 1941
Masonheimer, J. H., 1089
Masonic: College, 752, 957; Home, 1644; Lodges, 1620, 2028
Masterson, "Bat," 938
Masterson, Richard, 10, 1725
Masterson, Sarah, 10, 1725
Matheny, Daniel, 753
Mathers, Charles W., 2053
Mathews, Marcellus Smith: CSA medallist, 1133
Mathis, Frederick B., 1833
Mathis, H. C., 1469
Matthews, Rev. G. H., 1518
Matthews, Joseph Alexander, 1995
Matthews, Ruth, 1995
Matthews, Thomas J.: survey by, 1868
Maulding, James, 1137
Maulding, Morton, 1137
Maulding, Wesley, 1071
Maupin, George Washington, 1794
Maxwell, Thomas, 1562
Maxwell House Coffee Company, 1718
Maxwell Place (University of Kentucky), 2069
Maxwell Springs, 2069
May, Andrew Jackson, 164, 512
May, John (Floyd Co.), 2018
May, John: 49; Maysville named for, 68; pioneer teacher, 928-929
May, Samuel, 2018
May, Sarah Phillips, 2018
Mayfield: Civil War in, 654, 732, 1277; Exchange Bank, 2010; *Messenger*, 1749; Presbytery, 1597
Mayo, John C. C., 1632, 1804
Mayo State Vocational School, 1632
May's Lick, 1628

Maysville: *Eagle*, 1492; naming of, 68
Maysville Academy, 1616
Maysville and Washington Turnpike Company, 144
Maysville Road, 144
Meade, David: home of, 158
Meade, George Herbert, 2008
Meade, James: county named for, 508, 845
Meade County: Civil War in, 766; naming of, 508, 845
Meagher, John, 1707
Means, Thomas W., 1135
Medal of Honor winners: Carl H. Dodd, 2033; Darwin K. Kyle, 1906; David M. Smith, 1643; George D. Scott, 2030; Samuel Woodfill, 990; Thomas W. Stivers, 2030; Wesley Phelps, 1672; William M. Harris, 2030; Willie Sandlin, 631; William B. Baugh, 2013; William H. Horsfall, 1867
Medaris, R. C., 1837
Mefford George, 92
Melmont: home of John Edwards King, 1403
Melodye Park, 2031
Melville, Herman, 1681
Mendel, Gregor Johann, 1714
Menefee, Richard H.: birthplace of, 940; county named for, 787
Menifee County: naming of, 787
Mental hospital: second in United States, 1033
Mercer, Hugh: county named for, 1258
Mercer County: creation of, 1083; Legerwood's Bend, 1774; naming of, 1258
Merit Clothing Co., 2010
Meriwether, James, 2007
Meriwether, Jesse, 1992
Merkel, Una, 1865
Merrimac: builder of, 1037
Merritt, Daniel R., 2010
Merton, Thomas, 1680, 2004
Messenger (Mayfield), 1749
Metcalf, Rev. John: founder of Nicholasville, 947
Metcalfe, Leonidas: 514; Big

Hill Skirmish, 1124; duel, 996
Metcalfe, Thomas: 1208, 1798; county named for, 799; Greensburg courthouse, 165; home of, 123, 660; son of, 996
Metcalfe County: naming of, 799
Methodist: Alvan Drew School, 1712; Augusta College, 94; Charles Wallace, 1745; circuit riders, 871, 1186, 1334; early church leader, 973; first society, 1772; Francis Asbury, 10, 1278, 1574, 1725, 1830; Francis Clark, 1772; Henderson Settlement, 1286; Marvin College, 891; Sue Bennett Memorial fund, 2060; Valentine Cook, 1761
Methodist Church: Broadway Methodist Church (Paducah), 1029; Brown Memorial C.M.E. Church (Louisville), 1677; Camp Ground (Laurel County), 1574; Center St. C.M.E. Church (Louisville), 1677; Chestnut St. C.M.E. Church (Louisville), 1677; Christian Heritage Day, 1972; first conference in Kentucky (Lexington), 10, 1476; First Methodist Church (Frankfort), 1476; First United Methodist Church (Covington), 1659; Fourth St. Church (Louisville), 1694; John S. Keen, 1927; Kirksey United Methodist Church (Calloway County), 1945; Level Woods (Larue County), 1186; Louisville Convention (Louisville), 1694; Mayo Memorial (Paintsville), 1632; Methodist Episcopal (Louisville), 1694; Methodist Society, 1972; Ogden Memorial United Methodist Church (Princeton), 1932; Peter Taylor Methodist Chapel (Lewis Co.), 2070; Sehon Methodist Church (Louisville),

1695; Third General C.M.E. Conference (Louisville), 1677; unification of, 814; United Methodist (Louisville), 1694; United Methodist Temple (Russellville), 1972

Methodist Episcopal Church: and sectional crisis, 1694

Mexican War: 634, 649, 741, 823, 866, 925, 939, 964, 986, 1082, 1109, 1194, 1322, 1412, 1589, 1758, 1809, 1871; Covington City Hall, 1862; Doniphan's Expedition, 877; Newport Barracks, 599; Zachary Taylor, 995, 1849

Meyers, Mrs. A. R., 1107

Meyzeek, Albert, 1662

Middle Creek: Battle of, 85, 172, 571, 643

Middlesboro: Alexander Arthur in, 1227; founding of, 832; Golf Club, 1262; oldest house, 1228

Midway: 1580, 2027; John Hunt Morgan in, 516; Junior College, 1087

Midway (Fredonia), 1908

Midway Female Orphans School Trust Fund, 2053

Midway Orphan School, 2053

Midwifery: Frontier Nursing Service, 558

Mile posts, 1021-1022

Miles, Bishop W. H., 1992

Milford (Madison County), 1223, 1757, 1979

Military History Museum, 1490

Miller, Abraham, 1115

Miller, Arthur McQuiston, 1953

Miller, Christopher, 1828

Miller, George, 1778

Miller, J. O., 1331

Miller, Jacob, Jr., 1828

Miller, John, 1223

Miller, Mary M., 1778

Miller, Mordecai, 1113

Miller, Nicholas, 1828

Miller, William (Garrard County), 1525, 1562

Miller, William (Nelson County), 1113

Miller Hall (University of Kentucky), 1953

Millersburg Military Institute, 2044

Millerstown, 1828

Mill Hole Farm, 1669

Mills, Benjamin: early gun shop site, 1335

Mills: Audubon's, 1645; Barnes, 1871; Burks', 1509; grist mills, 1494, 1509, 1645, 1991, 2018; Moore's, 2041; paper, 838; Red River Lumber, 2015; saw mills, 1645

Mills' Point. See Hickman

Mill Springs: Battle of, 75, 863, 1275, 1920

Mineral Springs. See Individual Names

Minimum Foundation Act, 1310

Minnegerode, James G., 1695

Miss Bristow's Boarding and Day School, 1484

Mississippi River, 1775, 1778, 1859

Mitchell, Lucius L., 830

Mitchell (Mitchel), Ormsby MacKnight, 538, 1049, 1758

Mitchell, Robert Byington, 553

Mitchell, Western, 830

Mize, William O., 175

Modrel, Robert, 1870

Mohn, A. W., 2060

Monmouth: Battle of, 81, 1461, 1683

Monroe, James: 835, 847, 1653, 1681; county named for, 1093

Monroe County: naming of, 1093

Monterey: naming of, 925. See also Williamsburg

Montgomery, Richard: county named for, 1216

Montgomery County: naming of, 1216

Monticello: naming of, 989; surveying of, 1153

Monticello-Burnside Stage, 818

Montour, Andrew, 31

Montreal Royals (baseball farm club), 1762

Moon, Lottie, 1705

Moonbow Inn, 1801

Moonlight Schools, 1034

Moore, George (Monroe Co.), 2041

Moore, George (Warren Co.), 997

Moore, Joel, 2041

Moore, O. H., 89, 605

Moore, Phillip, 2041

Moore, Robert: founder of Bowling Green, 981, 997

Moore, S. A., 2041

Moore, Thomas: grave of, 1220

Moore, William: grave of, 1220

Moran, Charles: Korean War hero, 1207

Moran, "Uncle" Charlie, 1091, 1207

Morehead, Charles S.: 1260, 1910; home of, 123, 819

Morehead, James T., 1260, 1641, 1882

Morehead State University, 1427, 1952

Morgan, Abigail, 1314

Morgan, Calvin, 543

Morgan, Charles, 1642

Morgan, Daniel: 931, 1314, 1547; county named for, 815; family cemetery, 1314; Morganfield named for, 1250, 1547

Morgan, Mrs. Daniel, 1314

Morgan, Garrett A., 1493

Morgan, George, 1295

Morgan, George Washington: 520-521, 560-561, 568, 711, 1600; masterful retreat of, 568, 637-638, 642, 644-648

Morgan, John Hunt: 540, 568, 585, 674, 711, 769, 798, 1296, 1350, 1355, 1406, 1425, 1489, 1531, 1550, 1686, 1714, 1809, 1861; Bacon Creek Bridge, 530; Battle of Cynthiana, 109; Battle of Green River Bridge, 89; Battles, June 8-9, 1864, 628-629; brother of, 543; 1862 raid in Lawrenceburg, 630; first raid, 524, 625-627, 630,

673, 677, 685, 689, 698, 701, 733, 1255; friend to, 943; headquarters, 602; home of, 3; Independence Day, 1863, 605; induction into CSA, 1235; last raid, 567, 621-625, 628, 646-648, 691-695, 700, 841, 1331; Lexington Rifles Infantry, 506, 1809; at Midway, 516; Ohio raid, 515, 529, 679, 706-707, 1413; at Paris, 696; second raid, 525, 705, 748, 1116, 1255; Stony Castle, 1084; surrender of, 601, 684; third raid, 679, 689, 698, 706
Morgan, Squire Joseph, 185
Morgan, Thomas: death of, 543
Morgan, Thomas Hunt, 1714
Morgan County: founding of, 1991; naming of, 815
Morganfield: first bank in, 1787; naming of, 1250, 1547; Nathan B. Forrest in, 612
Morgan House: home of John Hunt Morgan, 3
Morgan Row, 185
Morgan Springs, 1547
Morgan's Raiders: and Sue Mundy, 536-537; at Burkesville, 601; at Camp Morton, 1629; at Glasgow, 544; at Grayson, 637; at Lebanon, 600; at Midway, 516; at Mt. Sterling, 1331; at Pound Gap, 510; camp, 567, 766; harassment by, 520-521, 568, 637-638, 642, 644-645; in Augusta, 501; naming of, 1235; pursuit of, 561; reunions of, 555; threat of, 527
Morris, Emmanuel, 1718
Morris, Henrietta, 1718
Morris, Rev. Joshua, 1078
Morris, Rob: "Poet Laureate of Freemasonry," 752, 1563
Morris, Robert, 549
Morrison, James, 1406
Morrison Hall: designer of, 945, 1406
Morrow, Edwin P.: 1427, 1837; home of, 1684
Morse, Samuel F. B., 1799

Morton, D. W. "Mush," 1612
Morton family, 1972
Mosley, George W., 830
Moss, Edwin S., 1837
Mother of God Church (Covington), 1460
Mother's Day, 191, 1926
Mottley, E. L., 1201
Mt. Gilead Methodist Society, 753
Mt. Horeb Presbyterian Church (Lexington), 1687
Mt. Lebanon: earliest Governor's Mansion, 82
Mounts, Ellison, 1866, 1913
Mt. Saint Joseph Motherhouse and Academy, 907
Mount Savage Furnace, 914
Mt. Sterling: Battle of, 177, 567, 621-625, 628-629, 646-648, 691-695, 700, 841
Mt. Sterling-Pound Gap Road, 2018
Mt. Union Church (Allen County), 1117
Mt. Zion Christian Church (Madison County), 1300, 1825, 1905
Mt. Zion Covered Bridge (Washington County), 1581
Mt. Zion Presbyterian Church (Lexington), 16
Muddiman, E. C., 1701
Mud Lick Springs. See Olympian Springs
Muhlenberg, John Peter Gabriel: county named for, 821, 1946
Muhlenberg County: naming of, 821, 1946
Mulberry Hill General Baptist Church. See Mt. Union Church
Muldraugh's Hill: in Civil War, 705, 1296, 1324, 1448
Mulkey, Philip, 721
Mulligan, Dennis, 2069
Mulligan, James H., 2069
"Mundy, Sue." See "Sue Mundy"
Munford, Thomas, 204
Munfordville: Battle of, 119, 698; Civil War in, 698, 879
Munfordville Presbyterian Church, 879
Munich, Germany, 1854

Munsell, Luke, 1850
Murder Branch Massacre, 189
Murdoch, Harvey Short, 682
Murphy, D. X., 1702
Murray, A. L., 1565
Murray, Ed: home of, 1037
Murray, Eli H., 523
Murray, Henry H., 1444
Murray, John L., 1969
Murray, William, 1707
Murray: becomes county seat, 1263
Murray State University, 1427
Murrell, J. L., 1659
Murrell, Samuel, 1573
Museums: Duncan Tavern, 93; Edison, 1713; Guggenheim, 1726; Kentucky Historical Society, 1490, 1524; Kentucky Railway, 1720; Ohio County Historical Society, 1829; Shaker, 203
Mussel Shoals Baptist Church (Owen County), 1575
Muter, George, 49
Myers, Jacob, 993
"My Old Kentucky Home" (song), 1102. See also Federal Hill
NAACP, 1721, 1771, 2022
Nally, James D., 830
Nally, James P. (Jimmy), 1588
Nally, Thomas A., 830
Nally Spa, 1588
"Narrows," 2045
Nash, Floyd, 1981
Nashville Banner, 1920
Nashville, Tennessee: Songwriters Hall of Fame, 2026
Natchez (steamboat), 1092, 1756
Nation, Carry A., 1733
National American Woman Suffrage Association, 1800, 1876
National Federation of Business and Professional Women's Clubs: founder of, 1473
National Historic Landmark, 1653, 1689
National Museum of Racing Hall of Fame, 2027
National Negro Bar Association, 1964
National Negro Press Hall of

Fame, 1998
National Post Road, 1519
National Racing Association, 1820
National Register of Historic Places, 1553, 1559, 1565-1569, 1571-1572, 1581, 1583-1585, 1590, 1599, 1601, 1621, 1639, 1655, 1662, 1669, 1677, 1686, 1688, 1695, 1697, 1699, 1702-1704, 1720, 1723, 1726, 1733-1734, 1737, 1745, 1749, 1752, 1754-1755, 1764-1765, 1822, 1824, 1830, 1835, 1866, 1887, 1904, 1931, 1939, 1952, 1968, 2054, 2061, 2065, 2069
National Urban League, 1419
Native Americans. See Indians
Naval Officers, 1479
Navy, 2044; Saufley Field, 1564
Nazareth College, 896
Neal, Benjamin, 1735
Neal, Ezekiel, 1895
Neeley, Alexander, 137
Neighborhood House (Louisville): 1974; Cabbage Patch, 1974; Louisville Central, 1974; Presbyterian Community Center, 1974; Wesley House, 1974
Nellie Gray (horse), 649
Nelson, Thomas: county named for, 956
Nelson, William: 1300, 1515, 1631, 1825; assassination of, 535; Battle of Ivy Mountain, 164; Camp Dick Robinson, 1750; West Liberty—Civil War, 512
Nelson County: naming of, 956
Nelson Furnace, 1113
Nerinckx, Father Charles, 206-207, 768, 913
Nevitt, John C., 1115
New, Anthony, 1969
New Bethel First Baptist Church (Paducah), 868
Newburg, 1988
New Capitol, 1524, 1779
New Hampshire Furnace, 1130
New Liberty Baptist Church,

742
New Liberty, Old, 742
New Madrid earthquake, 688
Newman, Eugene W.: birthplace of, 1000
Newman, William Henry: railroad manager, 1257
New Orleans: 103, 1685, 1699, 1817; Battle of, 634, 761, 933, 1139, 1145
New Orleans (steamboat), 1065, 1681
New Orleans and Jackson Railroad, 939, 1043
New Orleans and Ohio Railroad, 1134
Newport: City Council, 2071; county seat at, 889; early doctor in, 1386; in War of 1812, 507
Newport Barracks, 599
New Providence Presbyterian Church (Mercer County), 928-929, 1498
Newspapers: Argus of Western America, 1799; Benton Tribune, 1749; Cincinnati Times-Star, 1836; Danville Review, 1488, 1492; Frankfort Yeoman, 24; Guardian of Liberty, 1539; Kentucky Gazette, 1864; Lexington Herald, 1876; Lexington Leader, 1736; Louisville Courier, 1719, 1724; Louisville Courier-Journal, 1538, 1542, 1718-1719, 1736; Louisville Democrat, 1719; Louisville Herald, 1718; Louisville Journal, 1719, 1724; Louisville Leader, 1998; Louisville Times, 24, 1665, 1718; Mayfield Messenger, 1749; Maysville Eagle, 738, 1492; Nashville Banner, 1920; New York Times, 1718, 1836; Ohio County News, 1266; Owen News, 742
Newton, Abraham, 1735
New Union Forge, 1332
New York University, 2036
New York Yankees, 1627
New Zion, 1938
Nicholas, George: 983, 1184; county named for, 708; grave of, 125; town named for, 947

Nicholas County: naming of, 708; passenger depot in, 1764
Nicholasville: naming of, 947
Nichols, Keziah, 1288
Nichols, Rev. P. A., 1518
Niewahner, Ronald L., 2046
"Night Riders," 145, 1041, 1786
Niles, John Jacob, 1654
Nixon, Richard M., 1419
Nobel Prize: 1714; Peace Prize ceremony, 2036
Noble, Thomas Satterwhite, 1780
Nock, Samuel L., 1982
Noel, Silas M., 1535
Nolin: Civil War in, 748
Nolin Furnace, 1396
Nonimportation (of Slaves) Act, 1989
Northern Kentucky Community Center, 2000
Northern Kentucky University, 1730
Northup, Jay H., 1354
Norton, Rev. John N., 1537
Norton Furnace, 1023
No-Tillage Farming, 1759
Nunn, C. S., 1522
Nunn, T. J., 1522
Nunnery, C. A., 1659
Oak Hill: home of Potilla Calvert, 1405
Oakland Furnace, 1157
Oates, Jesse, 1735
O'Bannon, Presley N.: 1465, 1940; home of, 1261
Oberhulsman, Rev. William, 1106
O'Brien, Cecily, 1717
Octagon Hall, 503
Offutt, Horatio, 1649
Offutt-Cole Tavern, 1649
Ogden, Rev. Benjamin, 1278, 1932
Ogden, Robert, 1360
Ogden College, 1360, 1769
Ogden Memorial United Methodist Church (Princeton), 1932
O'Hara, Theodore, 24
Ohio and Licking Rivers: confluence of, 1472
Ohio Company of Virginia, 20, 1472

Ohio County: first public building, 1196; naming of, 1144

Ohio County Historical Society, 1829

Ohio County News, 1266

Ohio River: 1144, 1298, 1307, 1330, 1361, 1675, 1973, 1967, 1994; boat tragedy, 720; discovery, 22; exploration, 222; falls, 219; flood of 1884, 1032; flood of 1937, 1053, 1107-1108, 1601; Roebling Suspension Bridge, 1601; slave escape (Covington), 1863

Ohio Valley Flood (1937), 1107-1108, 1890

Oil Wells, 702, 1237, 1760

Old American, 1237

Old Capitol, 1779. 1781. *See* Old State House

Old Church on the Dry Ridge, The, 1560

Old Concord Church (Nicholas County), 935

Old Concord College, 742

Old Court/New Court struggle, 127, 813, 1878

Old Crow Inn, 1376

Oldham, William: county named for, 1251

Oldham County: naming of, 1251; Prospect, 2038; "The Neck," 2038

Old Morrison, 1406

Old Mud Meeting House, 141

Old Mulkey Church (Monroe County), 721

Old Munford Inn, 204

Old Providence Church (Clark County), 1068

Old Sandy Valley Seminary, 729

Old State House, 103, 945, 1524, 1535, 1781

Old State Road, 1905

Old Stone Inn, 1889

Oldtown Covered Bridge, 1585

Old Trinity Centre, 1500

Old Union Church (Warren County), 1063

Old Walnut Log Tavern, 1652

Olive Landing Furnace, 1367

Olmstead Bros., 1952

Olympian Springs, 1342, 1358

Oneida Baptist Institute, 2024

Orangeburg, 2001

Order of the Eastern Star, 752, 1563

Oregon: early shipping port, 1751

Oregon Territory, 1194

Orphanages: Bible Mission School and Orphanage, 1927; first in Louisville, 1702; St. Thomas, 1680; St. Vincent, 1680

Orr, Samuel, 1838

Osenton, Jennie Scott, 574

Ottenheim: German-Swiss settlement, 955

Ottenheimer, Joseph, 955

Our Lady Church (Louisville), 1312

Ovariotomy, first, 183

Overall family, 1944

Overby, Captain S. M., 1231

Owen, Abraham: county named for, 831

Owen County: naming of, 831; recruitment camps in, 564

Owen News, 742

Owensboro: 1436, 1500, 1747, 2036; first permanent settlement in, 744

Owen's Island, 1352

Owenton, 1658

Owings, John Cockey, 993, 1668

Owings, Thomas Deye: Estill Steam Furnace, 1055; home of, 1193; town named for, 940

Owingsville: 1997; naming of, 940, 1193

Owsley, William: 1926; county named for, 713, 813, 1422; home of, 713, 1422; judge, 24

Owsley County: naming of, 713, 813

Oxford: Christian Church (Scott County), 1701; historic district, 1701

Oxmoor: home of Alexander S. Bullitt, 983, 1474

Ozeoro Furnace, 1349

P.E.O.(professional group for women), 1715

Pactolus Furnace, 1148

Paderewski, Ignace, 1692

Paducah: Alben W. Barkley on, 1025; Barkley Field, 829; Battle of, 545, 963, 1031, 1277, 1287; boundary, 865; Broadway Methodist Church, 1029; Church of Christ, 1035; city hall, 1214; Civil War in, 517, 924, 963, 1031, 1175; Clara Barton in, 1032; Clark land grant, 1352; Community College, 1721; Confederate Flag of Welcome, 1175; county seat moved to, 1377; "Duke of Paducah," 795; Eighth of August celebration, 1957; First Christian Church in, 899; first frame house in, 1052; first log cabin in, 1052; First Presbyterian Church, 1061; first public well in, 1174; flood wall, 1053, 1108; founding of, 829, 840, 916; Furnace, 1421; Gaseous Diffusion Plant, 1180; gunsmith Ferd Hummel, 1062; harbor, 1161; historic riverfront, 1065; history of, 840, 1214; Immanuel Baptist Church, 1044; in Mexican War, 964; in Texas Revolution, 964; Iron Company, 1421; Irvin S. Cobb on, 1025; Marine Ways, 977; naming of, 793, 916, 918, 1111; 1937 flood in, 1053, 1107-1108; pictorial, 968; railroad shops, 794, 1134; Ride Round the Rivers, 1161; St. Francis de Sales Church, 1106; St. Paul Lutheran Church, 1072; site of, 1036; skirmishes near, 545; Temple Israel, 1058; Unity Church, 1146; visitors to, 575

Paduke, Chief: grave of, 967; Paducah named for, 793, 829, 840, 865, 916, 918, 1111, 1214

Page, Thomas, 1707

Painted Stone. *See* Squire Boone's Station

Paint Lick, 1525

Paint Lick Presbyterian Church, 1562, 1942
Paintsville: Civil War in, 556, 566, 571, 608; founding of, 1126
Palladio, Andrea, 1429
Palmer, Ellis, 1941
Palmyra-Princeton Trail, 1916
Panama-Pacific Exposition (San Francisco), 1854
Panther Creek: Battle of, 745
Paper Mill, Early, 838
Paris: Civil War in, 696; county seat at, 1246; first post office in, 1824
Park, W. W., 1922
Parker, Benjamin F.: CSA medallist, 1201
Parker, Harry, 2001
Parker, Nathan, 1823
Parker, Mr. and Mrs. Noah, 1823
Parks, Floyd, 1837
Parrish, C. H., 1845
Parrish, Charles H., Jr., 2008, 2020
Parrish, James, 1087
Partisan Rangers, 751, 830, 1630, 1915, 1971
Pate, Samuel, 667
Pate, William, 2039
Patesville: town named for, 2039
Patrick, Reuben: grave of, 902
Patterson, J. E., 2060
Patterson, Robert, 136, 205, 554, 1613
Patterson, Sam, 1233
Paull, Archibald, 1020, 1142
Pawpaw Tree Incident, 2047
Paxton, Thomas, 595
Paxton, W. F., 1107
Payne, Robert, 2021
Payne, Thomas W.: CSA medallist, 1133
Payne-Desha House, 2021
Peace Park (Hopkinsville), 1041
Pearl Harbor: 1612; attack on, 878, 1769
Peck, George C., 1354
Peebles, Benjamin, 1850
Peebles, John, 1682
Pegram, John, 712
Pekin. See Paducah
Peking Opera, 1692

Pell, Joseph C., 1935
Pell, Samuel P., 1993
Pellville, 1993
Pemberton, Malcolm Wood, 1479
Pendleton, Edmund: county named for, 937
Pendleton County: naming of, 937
Penick, B. W., 1924
Penney, J. C., 1430
Penney, John, 1430
Pennington, Isaac, 1941
Pennsylvania Furnace, 1016
Pepper, Elijah, 1986-1987
Pepper, Oscar, 1986-1987
Pere Marquette. See Marquette, Jacques
Perkins, F. D., 1770
Perry, C. S., 1659
Perry, David, 205
Perry, Oliver Hazard: Battle of Lake Erie, 1196; town and county named for, 758, 876, 1249, 1284
Perry County: naming of, 758, 1249
Perryville: 1284; Battle of, 58, 192-195, 539, 548, 551, 553, 572, 627, 630, 649, 674, 676, 683, 685, 689, 704, 737, 749, 756, 876, 882, 965, 1040, 1124, 1333, 1610; naming of, 876
Perryville Prelude, 548
Pershing, John J., 664, 990, 1199
Persian Gulf War, 2044
Peter, Robert: writings, 1480
Peters, John, 1017
Petersburg (Boone Co.), 999
Petersburg (Jefferson Co.): named for, 1988
Petersburg (Woodford Co.), 1774
Peter Taylor Methodist Church (Lewis Co.), 2070
Peter Volo (horse), 565
Petrey, Rev. Asbel S.: Mountain Missionary, 703
Petrey Memorial Church (Perry County), 703
Pettis, Rev. W. M., 1090
Pettit, Katherine: Hindman Settlement School, 771
Pewee Valley, 208

Peyton, Samuel O., 581
Phelps, Celia (Stapp), 1802
Phelps, John, 1802
Phelps, John Quincy, 1802
Phelps, Shadrach, 1802
Phelps, Wesley, 1672
Philippine Islands, 2037
Phillips, Bishop C. H., 1677
Phillips, Lena Madesin: birthplace of, 1473
Phillips, Philip, 1098
Piatt, Robert, 1646
Piatt's Landing, 1646
Pickering, Providence Orange, 2001
Picket, Louis, 1506
Pickford, Mary, 650
Pierce, Franklin, 211, 1883, 1994
Pigeon Roost: early post office at, 1510
Pigman, Hiram, 1933
Pike, Zebulon M.: county named for, 808
Pike County: courthouse/jail in, 1866; "Little Floyd," 905; naming of, 808
Pikes Peak: naming of, 808
Pikeville College, 884
Pikeville Collegiate Institute, 1533
Pilot Knob, 132
Pine Grove Furnace, 1011
Pinkerton, Lewis L., 1087
Pinkerton High School, 1087
Pioneer Furnace, 1354
Pirtle, Henry, 1704
Pirtle, James S., 1229
Piscator (J. A. Henshall), 651
Pisgah Church (Woodford County), 86
Pitt, Joseph, 1735
Pittsburg (Laurel County), 1757
Plato, Samuel, 1693
Platt, W. H., 1695
Pleasant Hill, 1481, 1816-1817. See also Shakertown
Pleasant Retreat: William Owsley home, 713
Poage, Edwin P., 1142
Poage, George, 1155
Poage, Hugh A., 1155
Poage, James, 1416
Poage, John H., 1142
Poage, Robert C., 1142

Poage, Thomas H., 1155
Poage, William L., 1142, 1155
Poage's Landing. *See* Ashland
Poague, George, 1020
Poe, Edgar Allan, 1077
Poets: Cale Young Rice, 1508; Daniel Henry Holmes, Jr., 1691; Effie Waller Smith, 1959; Jennie Taylor McHenry ("Rosine"), 1510; Madison Cawein, 1654; Rob Morris, 1563; Theodore O'Hara, 24
Point Isabel. *See* Burnside
Point Leavell (Garrard Co.), 2026
Polk, James K., 938, 1110
Polk, Leonidas K.: 676; Battle of Perryville, 553; Bear Wallow, 698; "Gibraltar of the West," 528; headquarters, 1101; prayer of, 539; retreat of, 704
Polke, Charles, 1586
Pollard Inn, 798
Pond, J. R., 1979
Pond, John Griffin, 1979
Pope, John: 853-854, 1285; home of, 930
Pope, L. M., 1625
Pope, Worden, 542
Pore, James, 1052
Pore, William, 1052
Porter, D., 2043
Portland, 1312, 1989
Portland Canal, 1994
Port William, 10, 216, 893, 1725. *See also* Carrollton
Postlethwait, G. L., 1671
Post office: at Donaldson, 1892; in Hancock County, 1993; at Hodgenville, 1096; at Patesville, 2039; at Pigeon Roost, 1510; at Stony Castle, 1084
Potter College, 1417
Pottinger, Samuel, 1433
Potts, Eugenia Dunlap, 1344
Pound Gap, 510
Powell, Lazarus W.: county named for, 790; grave of, 1926
Powell County: naming of, 790
Power Plant (Clark Co.), 1894
Powers, Caleb, 1884

Powers, Francis Gary, 1732
Poynter, Juliet J., 971
Poynter, W. T., 971
Poynter, Mrs. W. T., 971
Prange, Charles F., 830
Prange, Charles W. D., 830
Prater, Archibald, 202
Prather, Henry, 1673
Preakness, 1215, 1635, 1820, 2040
Prehistoric Site: Edmonson County, 1669
Prentice, George D., 542, 1719
Prentice School, 542
Prentis, James, 1789
Prentis, John, 1789
Presbyterian: 894, 1708, 1726; Child Welfare Agency, 682; founders of Lebanon, 867; Synod of Kentucky, 1922
Presbyterian Church: 884, 1437, 1533, 1609, 1708; Bayou de Chine (Graves County), 1597; Boyd County, 1416; Chapel Hill (Crittenden County), 1526; earliest west of Alleghenies (Danville), 754, 844; First (Frankfort), 1540; First (Glasgow), 1951; First (Hopkinsville), 1045; First (Lancaster), 1942; First (Lexington), 945; First (Paducah), 1061; Gasper River Meeting House (Logan County), 170; Grace (Louisville), 2055; Hopewell, 1855; Morris Fork (Breathitt County), 1289; Mt. Horeb (Fayette County), 1687; Mt. Zion (Fayette County), 16; New Providence (Mercer County), 928-929, 1498, 1603; Old Concord (Nicholas County), 935; Old Greenville Cemetery (Muhlenberg County), 1609; Paint Lick (Garrard County), 1562, 1942; Pisgah (Woodford County), 86; Red River Meeting House (Logan County), 71; Richwood, 1387; Stanford (Lincoln County), 1234; Upper Benson (Franklin County), 595;

Walnut Hill (Fayette County), 1483; Westminster (Paducah), 1431
Presbytery: Springfield, 51; Transylvania, 1855, 1942
Presentation Academy, 1702
Presley, Malvin, 830
Preston, John, 690, 1126
Preston, William (Civil War general), 67, 1101
Preston, William (surveyor), 1557, 1680, 1685, 1996
Preston Park Seminary, 1680
Prestonsburg: capture of, 512; city of, 2018; founding of, 690, 905; oldest house, 2018
Price, Benjamin: station of, 988
Price, Jacob, 1821
Price, John, 947
Price, Samuel W., 1780
Price, William, 201
Price's Meadow, 988
Priestley, James, 1285
Prince, William, 1902
Princess Furnace, 1135
Princeton: 1902; educational institution in, 1903
Princeton (Big Spring), 1916
Prisoner of War Camp (German), 1424
Proctor, George M., 1039
Proctor, Joseph, 810
Prohibition, 1509, 1719, 1733, 1872
Prospect, 2038
Provine, John, 1562
Puerto Rico, 1629
Pulaski, Count Casimir: 1607; county named for, 1212
Pulaski County: naming of, 1212, 1607
Pulitzer Prize, 1718-1719, 1808, 1814, 1879, 2036
Purple Heart, 855, 2046
Pusey, Robert Brown, 1505
Pythians, 1662
Quachita River, 1778
Quality: founding of, 1467
Quantrill, William, 505, 537
Quicksand: Civil War in, 841
Quigley, Quintus Quincy, 680
Quills, Harry, 1806
Quirk, Thomas: A Christmas Mishap, 544

Raccoon Furnace, 1009
Race Course: circular, 982; first, 6; Latonia (Kenton County), 1853; Woodlawn (Louisville), 1820. *See* also Churchill Downs, Keeneland
Rachmaninoff, Sergei, 1692
Radio: 1605, 1966; inventor of, 87
Rahner, Karl, 1680
Railroads: 1709, 1720, 1723; Cincinnati Southern, 1381, 1679; Covington and Lexington, 1939; Eastern Kentucky Railway, 1178, 2056; Evansville, Henderson, and Nashville, 1797; Illinois Central, 1134, 1711, 1746; Iron Horse Memorial, 794; Kentucky Union Railway Company, 2015; Lexington and Danville, 1381; Lexington and Maysville, 1764; Lexington and Ohio, 69, 1580, 1955; Louisville, Henderson and St. Louis, 1746, 1856; Louisville, St. Louis, and Texas, 1856; Louisville and Nashville, 1272, 1296, 1573, 1720, 1746, 1764, 1856, 1883, 1955; Louisville, St. Louis, and Texas, 1856; Portage, 987; Southern, 1381; wrecked in 1862, 652
Raisin River: Battle of, 43, 507-508, 634, 760, 797, 823, 826, 840, 845, 869, 895, 912, 916, 918, 1088, 1128
Rand, Jacob W., 1616
Randolph, Alifair, 2062
Randolph, Calvin, 2062
Randolph, Sally, 2062
Rankin, Rev. Adam, 16, 894, 1090, 1437
Rankin, Rev. John, 935
Rannels, Rev. Samuel, 935
Ransdell, Lister, 1819
Rawlins, John, 1594
Ray, G. W., 1497
Ray, James, 1673
Ray, John, 1673
Ray, Lloyd, 1673
Rayburn, French, 1367
Raywick: early settlers of, 1673
Read, William B., 1115
Red Bird, Chief, 908
Red Bird River Community Hospital, 723
Redin, W. H., 1695
Redman, James, 1115
Red River, 1778
Red River Iron Works (Estill Co.), 1054
Red River Iron Works (Powell Co.), 2015
Red River Lumber Mills, 2015
Red River Meeting House, 71
Reed, Lewis, 1115
Reed, Phillip, 1186
Reed, Stanley F., 1839
Reelfoot Lake, 688
Reese, Esco, 838
Reiter, John B., 1887
Render, George, 1674
Renfro Valley, 1605
Republican State Convention (1860), 1862
Republican (Union) Church, 1942
Reservoir Hill. *See* College Hill
Resolutions of 1798, 1170
Resorts. *See* Individual Names
Revere, Paul, 1784
Revival of 1800, 71, 170, 662, 1334
Revolutionary War, 136, 140, 150, 554, 565, 678, 708-709, 717, 721, 729, 762, 774, 782, 784-785, 789, 797, 800, 804, 815, 820-822, 849, 853, 873, 894, 897, 917, 931, 942, 944, 947-948, 950, 953-954, 956, 960, 973, 981, 994, 1070, 1079, 1094, 1171, 1190, 1203, 1212, 1216-1217, 1220-1221, 1224, 1238-1239, 1248, 1250-1251, 1258, 1275, 1280, 1283, 1314, 1322, 1328, 1337, 1352, 1371, 1375, 1388, 1403-1404, 1409, 1433, 1444, 1457, 1461, 1467, 1472, 1494, 1496, 1502, 1514, 1521, 1528, 1536, 1541, 1547-1548, 1558, 1562, 1575, 1578, 1592, 1603, 1607-1608, 1615, 1617, 1623-1624, 1653, 1665, 1667, 1683, 1699-1700, 1707, 1717, 1735, 1783, 1788, 1790, 1795, 1802, 1812, 1842-1843, 1849, 1869, 1871, 1892, 1896, 1902, 1909, 1911, 1921, 1946, 1950, 1968, 2018, 2034
Reynolds, Richard D., 1735
Rhoades, Solomon, 1123
Rhoads, Henry, Jr., 1735, 1946
Rhoadsville, 1123, 1946
Rice, Alice Hegan, 1508, 1654
Rice, Cale Young, 1508, 1654
Rice, Rev. David: 754, 1234, 1387, 1562; home of, 844
Rice, Laban Lacy, 1508
Rice, Luther, 2016
Rice, Nathan L., 19
Rice, William, 2035
Rice, William B., 1735
"Rice's School." *See* Transylvania Seminary
Richards, Lewis: home site, 842
Richardson, Henry, 1936
Richardson, Thomas G., 1616
Richeson, W. W., 1616
Richey, Polly, 2064
Richmond: 1223; Battle of, 683, 1124, 1300, 1825, 1905
Richwood Presbyterian Church, 1387
Rickenbacker, Eddie, 1501
Rickey, Branch, 1762
Riddell, Hugh, 1922
Riddle, Samuel D.: 1215, 1635; Faraway Farm, 1635
Ridley, Nathaniel J., 1928
Ridgely, Frederick, 1282, 1806
Riffe, Christopher, 250
Riffe, George, 1584
Riffe, John, 1584
Riggs, Arthur J., 1956
Riley, Amos, 1241
Riley, Lafayette, 830
Riley, William, 1301
Riney, Mancil G., 1711
Riney, Sylvester, 1711
Riney, Zachariah, 1482, 1711
Rineyville, 1711
Ringos Mill Covered Bridge, 1568
Rislerville, 1361
Ritchie, Jean, 1837
Ritte, Henry, 1939

Rittenhouse Academy, 1487, 1841
Ritte's Corner: 1939; historic district, 1939
Ritte's saloon, 1939
Rivers: Barren, 1665; Cumberland, 702, 1916, 1920, 2045; Green, 1813; Kentucky, 138, 1513, 1515, 1524, 1636, 1685, 1805, 1817, 2031; Licking, 1519; Little Beech Fork, 1581; Little Sandy, 1584-1585, 1973; Mississippi, 1699, 1756, 1859; Muddy, 1761; Nolin, 1828; Ohio, 1519, 1601, 1614, 1646, 1675; Rockcastle, 1622; Rough, 1592; Salt, 1498, 1748, 1944
Riverton, 2056
Roads, William L., 830
Roads: Alanant-O-Wamiowee, 83-84; Athiamiowee, 697; Bird's War Road, 34; Boone Trace, 53; Cabin Creek War, 2001; "Chickasaw Road," 1185; Cumberland Trace, 981; Eddy Trace, 1916; first macadamized, 1519; former buffalo trace, 218; Lincoln Family Trail, 73; Louisville-Nashville Turnpike, 1904; Maysville Road, 144; Mt. Sterling-Pound Gap Road, 2018; National Post Road, 1519; Old Mail Stage Route, 1816; Palmyra-Princeton Trail, 1916; Route for Horses and Cattle, 205; Saline Trace, 1916; Scuttle Hole Gap Road, 1188; Skaggs Trace, 53; Smith's Wagon Road, 1519; "Varmintrace," 142, 1916; Warrior's Trace, 83-84, 697; War Road, 810; Wilderness Road, 54-55, 113, 219, 576, 927, 981-982, 1311, 1339, 1383, 1426, 1600, 1622, 2045
Robbers' Roost Cave, 1074
Robert E. Lee (steamboat): race with *Natchez*, 1092, 1756
Roberts, A. J., 1659
Roberts, Elizabeth Madox, 1046
Roberts, Lucy Flournoy: gravesite, 1209
Robertson, Felix H., 659
Robertson, George: 816; county named for, 714, 816; home of, 714; student of, 1271
Robertson, Isaac, 1951
Robertson, Jerome Bonaparte: birthplace of, 659
Robertson, Mark L. T., 830
Robertson County: naming of, 714, 816
Roberts Spring, 1414
Robinson, H. S., 1924
Robinson, Jackie, 1762, 1900, 1984
Robinson, James F.: 1934; home of, 718
Robinson, Richard M., 1750
Robinson, Rev. Stuart, 1540
Rockcastle County: naming of, 1254
Rockcastle Hills, 1919
Rockefeller, John D., 1837
Rocky Hill: home of Lucy Jefferson Lewis, 767
Rodgers, William, 1204
Rodman, Hugh, 123
Rodman, Jesse, 1115
Roebling, John A., 1381, 1601
Roebling Suspension Bridge, 1601
Rogers, Benjamin Lone, 1602
Rogers, Edmund, 678
Rogers, Fleming P., 1889
Rogers, George Walter: CSA medallist, 1133
Rogers, James, 820, 1078
Rogers, John, 1604
Rogers, Rev. John, 935
Rogers, Jonathan, 1078
Rogers, Matthew, 1078
Rogers, Will, 1967
Rogers, William, 1078
Rogers' Gap, 1300
Rogers Springs, 1602
Roland, Chester Clayton, 1819
Roll, Michael, 1735
Roll, Oliver, 1674
Roosevelt, Franklin D., 1112, 1723, 1839, 2002
Roosevelt, Mrs. Franklin D., 1605
Roosevelt, Nicholas, 1065
Roosevelt, Theodore, 699, 1720, 1723
Rose Hill: home of George Frazer, 1555
Rose Hill Academy, 1005
Rosenthal, Joe, 855
Rosenwald, Julius: 2048; fund, 2048-2050; school, 2048
Rosine: cemetery in, 1672; founding of, 1510
Ross, Samuel, 1078
ROTC, 2070
Rousseau, Lovell H., 553
Routt, John, 1617
Rowan, John: 1101, 1281, 1285, 1536; boyhood home of, 1123; county named for, 788; duel, 1101; Federal Hill, 1102
Rowan-Chambers duel, 1101, 1281
Rowan County: courthouse burned, 972; naming of, 788; "war," 1933
Royal Geographic Society of London, 2055
Royal Spring, 63
Rubinstein, Artur, 1692
Ruddell (Ruddle), Abram, 1462
Ruddell (Ruddle), Isaac, 107, 1462
Ruddell's (Ruddle's) Mills, 1462
Ruff, A. D., 1997
Ruff Memorial (Wheelmen's Bench), 1997
Rumsey, Edward, 1264
Rumsey, James: town named for, 1264
Rumsey: naming of, 1264
Runner, William Taylor, 1401
Rupp, Adolph F., 1826
Rural Electric Cooperative Corporation (RECC), 1392, 1819
Rural Free Delivery (RFD): first in Kentucky, 1384
Russell, Bishop C. L., 1677
Russell, Msgr. Edward, 1682
Russell, Harvey C., Sr., 1469, 2017
Russell, William: county named for, 954

Russell County: naming of, 954

Russell Creek Association of Baptists, 1924

Russell House, 194

Russell Neighborhood (Louisville), 2017

Russellville Convention, 67, 74, 764

Russia: purchase of Alaska from, 1576; U-2 Spy incident, 1732

Rust, Marion, 1398, 1775

Rutledge, Wiley B.: birthplace of, 934

Sacramento: Battle of, 618, 665

Sadieville, 2037

Sadowski (Sandusky), Anthony, 670

Sadowski (Sandusky), Jacob, 670

Sadowski (Sandusky), James, 670

St. Albans Raid, 532

St. Asaph's. See Forts and stations: Logan's

St. Augustine's Church (Grayson County), 768

St. Bernard Coal Company: founded Earlington, 1338

St. Catharine of Sienna School (Washington County), 1095

St. Charles Church (Carlisle County), 1785

St. Clair, Arthur, 574, 822, 837, 1251

St. Denis Church (Hickman County), 1785

St. Francis Church (Scott County), 1593

St. Francis de Sales (Paducah), 1106

St. Jerome's Church (Graves County), 1682, 1785

St. John's Evangelical Church (Louisville), 1546

St. Joseph Infirmary (Jefferson Co.): 2042; neighborhood, 2042; School of Nursing, 2042

St. Joseph's Cathedral (Nelson County), 857, 1827

St. Joseph's College (Nelson County), 790, 857, 1897

St. Joseph's Hospital (Lexington), 1928

St. Joseph's Parish (Trigg County), 1100

St. Magdalen Academy. See St. Catharine of Sienna School

St. Mary's College (Marion County), 1026

St. Paul's Episcopal Church (Henderson), 1703

St. Paul's Episcopal Church (Newport), 1151

St. Paul's Lutheran Church (Louisville), 1072

St. Rose Priory (Washington County): founding of, 941

St. Thomas: Farm (Nelson County), 857; Orphanage (Louisville), 1680; Orphanage (Nelson County), 857; Plantation (Nelson County), 896; Seminary (Nelson County), 857; School (Washington County), 941

St. Vincent: Academy (Union County), 1717; Infirmary (Jefferson Co.), 2042; Orphanage (Louisville), 1680

St. Vincent de Paul Society (Marion County), 1302

Salem (now Bardstown), 1668

Salem (Livingston Co.), 1097, 1204

Salem Academy, 1285

Saline (steamboat), 1778

Saline Trace, 1185, 1298, 1916

Salt Lick, 1525, 1579, 1642

Saltpeter caves, 209, 715, 1247

Salt River: 1498, 1748, 1944; Church, 1430; Furnace, 1162

Salt wells, 702, 1642, 1895

Salt Works: Boone Salt Springs, 151; Bullitt's Lick, 133, 974, 1944; Goose Creek, 531; Grant's, 942; Lower Blue Licks, 162; Mary Ingles, 163; Perry County, 1346; Young's, 151

Salyersville: 1660; Civil War in, 901

Sampson, Flem D., 1316, 1884

Sand Cave, 1385

Sanders: Carroll County, 1361

Sanders, Henry, Jr., 1448

Sanders, James, 1448

Sanders, Lewis: home of, 1184, 1198

Sanders, Oscie, 2060

Sanders, Samuel, 911

Sanders, W. P., 1507

Sanders, "Wash," 1361

Sanders Tavern, 1448

Sandford, Alfred: home of, 1484

Sandford, Thomas, 1484

Sandhill 4-H Conservation Camp, 1633

Sandlin, Willie, 631

Sandusky (Sadowski), Anthony, 670

Sandusky (Sadowski), Jacob, 670

Sandusky (Sadowski), James, 670

Sandusky Station, 670, 1776

Sandy Furnace, 1131

Sandy Hook: Civil War in, 711

Sanford, Thomas, 1484

Sanford Duncan Inn, 611

Sansburgy, Mother Angela, 1095

"Santa Claus Is Comin' To Town" (song), 1836

Sassafras Tree (Owensboro), 1192

Sasseen, Mary Towles, 1926

Satterwhite, J. H., 1819

Saufley, Richard Caswell, 1564

Saufley Field, U.S. Navy, 1564

Saunders, John Bartlett, 1452

Saunders, Reuben: 1452; birthplace of, 1057; home of, 966

Savage, J. E., 2060

Savoyard (Eugene W. Newman), 1000

Sawyier, Paul, 675, 1780

Schacht, Rev. Ivo, 1106

Schenk, Paul, 843

Schlundt, Rev. Theodore S., 1546

Schmitt, Johann, 1460

Schoepf, Albin Francisco, 553, 863, 1919

Scholarship Fund: Rural Kentucky Medical, 1503

School for the Deaf, 197, 1536, 2016

School of Medicine: Fayette County, 1445

Schools: Alvan Drew, 1712;

Asbury College, 1830; Asbury Theological Seminary, 1830; Bethel Academy, 1830; Bethlehem Academy, 1740; Bible Mission School and Orphanage, 1927; Bond-Washington, 2049; Breckinridge Training School, 1952; Butler High, 1903; Caldwell County High School, 1903; Caldwell Middle School, 1903; California Institute of Technology, 1714; Calloway Normal College, 1945; Catholic High (Louisville), 1793; Central Colored, 1898; Clinton College, 1611; Clinton High School, 1611; Columbia University, 1714; Cottey College, 1715; Covington High, 1691; Cumberland College, 1837; Dixon School, 1890; Du-Pont Manual Boys School, 1851; early schoolhouse (Campbell Co.), 1730; East Benham High School, 1995; East Side High, 2049; Farmersville High, 1981; Female High School, 1851; Fern Creek High, 2058; Funk Seminary, 957; Georgetown College, 1487, 1535, 1716; Glasgow High School, 2019; Gosney School (Campbell County), 1730; Hampton Institute, 2055; Holmes High, 1691; Iowa Wesleyan, 1715; Israel Institute of Technology, 2065; Jackson, 1998; Jacob School, 2038; Jefferson Seminary, 2007; John's Hill (Campbell County), 1730; Kentucky State Normal School for Colored Persons, 1959; Kentucky State College, 1970, 2036; Kentucky State University, 1959; Kirksey High School, 1945; land grants for, 800; Lexington Dunbar, 2050; Lincoln Grant, 2000; Lincoln Institute, 1930; Louisville Girls High School, 1851;

Louisville Municipal College, 1998, 2020; Lower Donaldson, 1890; Maple Grove, 1840; Madison, 1998; Mamre Baptist College, 2024; Marion High, 2065; Mary D. Hill, 1898; Moonlight, 1034; Morehead Christian School, 1952; Morehead State Teachers College, 1952; Morehead State University, 1952; Murray State Teachers College, 1945; New York University, 2036; Northern Kentucky University, 1730; Oneida Baptist Institute, 2024; Paducah Community College, 1721; Presentation Academy, 1702; Princeton College, 1903; Princeton Collegiate Institute, 1903; Princeton High, 1903; reform legislation, 1929; Ralph J. Bunche, 2019; Rosenwald, 2048; Russell Creek Academy, 1924; Russellville Middle School, 1972; St. John's (Campbell County), 1730; St. Joseph College, 857, 1897; St. Joseph Prep School, 1897; St. Mary's College, 1026; St. Vincent's, 1717; Science Hill School, 971; Simmons University Bible College, 1661, 2020; Southgate Street School, 2071; State College of Kentucky, 1714; Stillman Institute, 2055; Sue Bennett College, 2060; Sue Bennett Memorial, 2060; Tuskegee Institute, 2049; Union College, 1811, 2054; University of Kentucky, 1714, 1721, 1730, 1900; University of Louisville, 541, 1661, 1737, 1994, 2020; Upper Donaldson, 1832; West Side, 2050; William Grant, 2000, 2071
Schultz, G. A., 734
Scopes, John T.: 1698; "Monkey Trial," 1698
Scott, Charles: 1372, 1670, 1726, 1941; blockhouse, 1094; county named for,

1248; home, 116
Scott, Dessie: Children's Home, 1712
Scott, George D., 2030
Scott, Joel, 1524
Scott, John S.: Battle of London, 560; Civil War action, 514, 1300, 1507; Scott's Raid, 513
Scott, Joseph, 1154
Scott, Marshall, 1115
Scott, Robert B., 1992
Scott, Walter E.: Death Valley Scotty, 1069
Scott, William, 1838
Scott, Winfield: aide-de-camp to, 1194
Scott, Winnie A., 2025
Scott County: courthouse in, 1454; naming of, 1248
Scottish Rite Temple (Louisville), 1739
Scottsville: Civil War in, 730; naming of, 1670
Scovell Hall (University of Kentucky), 2009
Scovell, Melville Amasa, 2009
Scowden, Theodore R., 1689
Sculptors: Enid Yandell, 1997; Gutzon Borglum, 1780; Herbert Haseltine, 1215; Joel T. Hart, 710, 731, 1553; Lorado Taft, 793
Scuttle Hole Gap Road, 1188
Sears, Roebuck and Co., 2049
Seaton, Samuel, 1130
Second Cavalry Regiment, Ky. Volunteers, CSA, 1235
Seedtime on the Cumberland (Arnow), 1807
Seelbach Hotel, 1723
Sellers, Matthew: aviation pioneer, 1222
Seminaries: Estill, 1922; Jefferson, 1922
Settle, Felix, 687
Settle, Sister Mary, 1481
Settle, Simon, 687
Settle, William, 687
Settle, Willis, 687
Settlement House Park, 1974
Settles Rifles, 687
Seven Storey Mountain (Merton), 2004
Seventy-Six Falls: birthplace of Ed Warinner, 1310

Severns Valley Baptist Church,
1621
Shakers: 179, 627, 852, 1455,
1481, 1816-1817; museum,
203; tavern, 716
Shakertown, 1481, 1816-1817.
See also Pleasant Hill
Shaler, Charles, 1381
Shaler, Nathaniel Southgate,
32
Shandy Hall (Princeton), 1902
Shanklin, Elliott West, 1479
Shannoah: Shawnee village,
31
Shannon, Rev. Samuel, 595,
935
Sharp, Solomon P.: murder of,
1077
Sharpe, Clifford M., 1975
Sharpe, John, 1975
Shaw, Benham (Bonum), 1980
Shawnee Indians: 31, 810,
859, 899, 1253, 1274, 1472;
early camp, 555
Shawnee Park, 1629
Shelby, Evan, 1558
Shelby, Isaac: 157, 507, 761,
1114, 1153, 1318, 1371-1372,
1403, 1472, 1577, 1641,
1730, 1896; county named
for, 1238; home of, 95; in-
augurated, 1551; Jackson
Purchase, 169, 1006
Shelby, Susannah Hart, 95,
1577
Shelby County: hemp in,
1320; naming of, 1238
Shelbyville Blockhouse, 1089
Shelbyville Fountain, 1379
Shepherdsville: occupation of,
1296
Sheppard, Rev. William H.:
Sheppard Park, 2055;
Sheppard Square Housing
Project, 2055
Sherburne Covered Bridge,
1438
Sheridan, Philip H., 553
Sherman, William T.: 535,
603, 829, 1324, 1350, 1594
Shiloh: Battle of, 91, 610, 1355,
p. 269
Shinkle, Amos, 1574, 1601,
1659
Shipbuilding, 977
Shively, Alexander, 1924

Short, Charles Wilkins, 1818
Short, William A., 830
Shreve Brothers: steam fur-
nace, 1008
Shryock, Cincinnatus, 945
Shryock, Gideon: 945, 1406,
1524, 1697; Bank of Louis-
ville, 88; Center St. C.M.E.
Church, 1677; Old State
House, 1524
Shryock, Matthias, 945
Sickel, Rev. B., 1072
Silas Baptist Church (Bourbon
County), 1596
Siler, Eugene, 1837
Siler, John W., 1837
Silk industry, 1212
Silkwood, Solomon, 1104
Sill, J. W., 572, 630
"Silver Dick" (Richard Parks
Bland), 1858
Silver Mine: John Swift's, 559
Silversmiths: Asa Blanchard,
1784; D. H. Spears, 1446;
Paul Revere, 1784
Silver Star, 2046
Simmons, William J., 1661
Simmons University, 1661,
2020
Simms, W. E., 67
Simpson, Anderson, 722, 725
Simpson, John: town and
county named for, 508, 912,
1128
Simpson County: boundary
disputed in, 1850; naming
of, 508, 912, 1128
Simpsonville: naming of, 1128
Singleton, Mason, 1671
Sinks of Beaver Creek Baptist
Church. *See* Dripping
Springs Baptist Church
Sir Barton (horse), 1635
Sisters of Charity of Nazareth:
857, 896, 1702, 1717, 1793,
1943, 2042; founders, 1702
Sisters of Loretto, 206-207,
1740
Skaggs, Henry: Long Hunter,
635, 1187, 1622
Skaggs Trace, 53, 1622
Skiles, Jacob, 1792
Skirvin, Joel, 722, 725
Slaughter, Gabriel, 1115,
1325, 1761, 1874, 1896
Slaughter, James, 1078

Slaughter, Presley, 1838
Slavery: 897; Petticoat Aboli-
tionist, 1099; slave escape,
1863; slave markets, 1989-
1990; *Uncle Tom's Cabin*
(Stowe), 1070
Slavin, John, 1562
Sleet, M. J., 1469
Sleet, Moneta J., Jr., 2036
Sleeth, Jack B., 575
Slone, Alice, 1543
Sloo, James C., 1348
Smallpox: vaccination against,
1595
Smeathers, William, 744,
1307, 1548
Smith, Absalom, 2035
Smith, Bayard Taylor: CSA
medallist, 1133
Smith, Bishop Benjamin
Bosworth, 1527, 1537, 1690,
1703
Smith, C. M.: duel, 611
Smith, Charles, Sr., 1596
Smith, Charles F., 828
Smith, Charles Shaler, 1381
Smith, David, 1174
Smith, David M., 1643
Smith, Effie Waller, 1959
Smith, Ephraim R.: CSA
medallist, 1133
Smith, Frank, 1479
Smith, Green Clay, 1837
Smith, H. S., 1116
Smith, Henry S., 208
Smith, Horace: first Boy Scout
Troop, 1007
Smith, James, 1544
Smith, James P., 1754
Smith, John: early postmaster,
1084
Smith, John "Raccoon," 1477,
1636, 1701
Smith, Lee Potter, 1214
Smith, Preston, 1300
Smith, R. A.: monument, 119
Smith, Robert, 32
Smith, Thomas: 1173; Beau-
mont College, 1173
Smith, William (Powell Co.),
2015
Smithey, Thomas, 1603
Smithland: 1204; Civil War
base in, 663; Edward Z. C.
Judson in, 938
Smith's Wagon Road, 1519,

1615

Smoketown, 1985, 2055

Smoky Mountains, 1675

Smothers, Bill, 744, 1307, 1548

Smuthers, William, 1299

Smyser, James L., 1996

Sneed, Maynette Elliott, 2050

Snow's Pond: skirmish at, 550, 2023

Society of Cincinnati: organizer of, 782

Soldier's Retreat: Anderson family home, 534, 847, 1968

Somerset, 1212, 1607, 1870

Sons of the American Revolution, 1420

Sousa, John Philip, 1501

Sousley, Franklin Runyon, 855

South Elkhorn Christian Church (Fayette County), 1636

Southern Exposition (1883), 1713

Southern Harmony: hymn singing, 1749

Southern Hotel (N.Y.C.), 1638

Southern Normal School and Business College, 1418

South Fork Baptist Church (Larue County), 1114

Southgate, William W., 1429

Southgate Street School, 2071

South Union (Logan County), 203

Spalding, Benedict, 867, 1667

Spalding, Mother Catherine, 896, 1639, 1702

Spalding, Bishop John Lancaster, 1303

Spalding, Martin John, 1302, 1639, 1897

Spalding Hall (Bardstown), 1897

Spanish-American War, 775-777, 1589, 1610, 1684, 1769, 1779

Sparks, Henry, 1608

Spears, Abram, 1462

Spears, D. H., 1446

Speed, James, 1704, 1724

Speed, John: home of, 174

Speed, Joshua, 174

Speed, Thomas, 1229

Spence, Brent: 1776; church of, 1151

Spencer, Spear: county named for, 837

Spencer County: naming of, 837

Spencer House, 1833

Spillman, Thomas, 2064

Spilman, Rev. Jonathan E., 1202

Spink, Angela, 1717

Sportsman's Hill: home of William Whitley, 96, 982

Spotswood, Alexander, 212

Spout Spring, 2035

Spradling, Washington, Jr., 1985

Spriggs, Joseph, 1011

Springfield: founder of, 853-854, 1446

Spring Hill: home of Hubbard Taylor, 948

Springs: 32, 940, 1602; Bedford, 1823; "The Big Spring," 1449, 1530, 1637; Blue Hole (Lexington), 1555; Chalybeate, 1233, 1588; Crab Orchard, 152; Crawford, 193, 965; Dawson, 915; Esculapia, 778, 1656; Estill, 555; Graham, 1297; Grayson, 768; Harrodsburg, 551; Keene, 1671; Maxwell, 2069; Morgan, 1547; Nally Spa, 1588; Olympian, 1342, 1358; Rogers, 1602; Scottsville Public, 1670; Spout, 2035; sulphur and fresh water, 1579, 1588; Swango, 920; Tar, 934

Spurlock, Hugh L., 1894

Stacker, Charles, 1364

Stacker, John, 1326, 1364

Stacker, Samuel, 1326, 1367

Stacker Furnace, 1367

Stagecoach: first in Kentucky, 1342

Stagecoach stops: Boone County, 1765; Caldwell County, 1908; Garrard County, 1750; Hopkins County, 1797; Scott County, 1337; Warren County, 1573

Stage line: Lexington-Cincin-

nati, 1765; Monticello-Burnside, 818

Stage route, 1816, 1833

Stamping Ground, 217

Stanbery, Henry: 1151; homesite, 1059

Stancliff, Charles, 1697

Standley, Mary, 1375

Stanford: named county seat, 860

Stanley, Augustus Owsley, 1777, 1811

Stanton, S. S., 1391

Star Furnace, 1018

Starkweather, John C., 553

Station Camp, 810

Stations. See Forts and stations

Staton, Joseph, 2035

Staton, William, 2066

Steamboats: at Monterey, 925; at Beattyville, 1805; John W. Cannon, 1756; John Fitch, 944; Robert Fulton, 801, 944, 1169; James Rumsey, 1264; Edward West, 1556; inventor of, 944, 1264; *Alice Dean*, 529, 602; *America*, 720; *Clermont*, 944, 1169; *John B. McCombs*, 529; *Josh V. Throop*, 1032; *Lucy Wing*, 1264; *Mary M. Miller*, 1778; *Morning Star*, 1935; *Natchez*, 1092, 1756; *New Orleans*, 1065, 1681; *Robert E. Lee*, 1092, 1756; *Saline*, 1778; *United States*, 720

Steel: 214, 1598, 1803; Kelly Furnace, 61, 946; sheet rolling mill, 214

Steele, Richard, 26

Steele, Theophilus, 188

Steele, William, 1868

Stephens, William, Sr.: early gunsmith, 1265

Stephen's Mill: McCreary County, 1356

Stepp, Moses: grave of, 922

Sterett, John, 1678

Steuben, Friedrich Wilhelm Ludolf von, 140

Steuben's Lick, 140

Stevenson, Adlai Ewing: U.S. vice president, 739-741

Stevenson, John H., 1626

Stevenson, John White, 609,

1085, 1527, 1852
Stevens School for Retarded Children, 542
Stewart, Cora Wilson: Moonlight Schools, 1034
Stewart, James, 997
Stice, James, 2035
Stirman, William Doswell, 1478
Stirman's Folly, 1478
Stivers, J.K., 2060
Stivers, S.A., 2058
Stivers, Thomas W., 2030
Stockdale, Fletcher, 1260
Stockton, George, 97, 950
Stockton, Rev. Robert: home of, 1496
Stogner, Alexander, 830
Stone, Barton W., 51, 935, 1477, 1636
Stone, Columbus, 1599
Stone, Edward Durell, 1214
Stone, May: Hindman Settlement School, 771
Stone, Stephen, 1115
Stone, William J., 1969
Stoneman, George, 1594
Stoner, Michael, 988, 1435
Stony Castle, 1084
Stovall, Rev. I. T., 1927
Stowe, Harriet Beecher, 1070, 1241
Strait, Dorcas, 2064
Strait, William, 2064
Stratton, Seriah, 1529
Stratton, Solomon, 690
Stratton, Tandy R.: "Little Floyd," 905
Stratton Settlement, 690, 905
Strawberry Baptist Association, 1496
Street, Frank T., 1392
Strode, John, 1047
Stuart, Gilbert, 1888
Stuart, Jesse, 1808, 1814
Stuart, John, 137, 1343
Stubblefield, Frank, 1969
Stubblefield, Nathan Bowman: birthplace, 87
Stultz, Ronald Francis, 1479
Submachine gun, 1706
Submarine: Wahoo, 1612
Submarine cable: first successful, 575
Sue Bennett College, 2060
"Sue Mundy": at Patesville,

2039; captured, 536; execution of, 540; grave of, 562; raid of, 537
Sunday school: first west of Alleghenies, 1653
Surgery, 1267, 1282
Suribachi: flag raising at, 855
Surtees, Robert L., 1881
Sutton, William Loftus, 1934
Suwanee Furnace, 1327
Swan, John, 1494
Swango, Green Berry, 175
Swango Springs, 920
Swift, John: Silver Mine, 559
Swift's Iron and Steel Works, 1395
Swiss Colony, 843, 955
Switzer Covered Bridge, 1571
"Sycamore Hollow," 1579
Sycamore Shoals: Treaty of, 1075
Sypert, L. A., 1231
Tackett, J. L., 1819
Taft, Lorado, 793
Taft, William Howard, 1082, 1684
Talbert, Henry, 1457
Tanner, Alfred, 1123
Tanner, John, 1773
Tanner, Rev. John, 999
Tanyards: Lewis County, 1656
Taos, New Mexico, 79
Tar Springs, 934
Taul, Micah, 989
Taverns: Black Horse, 1649; Colbyville, 1358; Cuckoo, 1528; Eades, 1824; Frankfort, 1688; Hart Boswell, 1701; Keene Springs, 1671; Merritt Jones/Wayside, 1905; Offutt-Cole, 1649; Old Walnut Log, 1652; Sanders, 1448; Watkins, 1798
Taylor, Rev. Caleb Jarvis, 753
Taylor, Colby, 1358
Taylor, H. Boyce, 1770
Taylor, H. D., 1370
Taylor, Hancock: 103, 1649; grave of, 1685
Taylor, Hubbard: home of, 948
Taylor, James (Jefferson County): 2038; Taylor Subdivision, 2038
Taylor, James (War of 1812

general): 1351; church of, 1151; home of, 121
Taylor, James A., 830
Taylor, John, 999, 1624, 1773
Taylor, John H., 830
Taylor, Philip W., 1748
Taylor, Richard (Confederate general), 1646
Taylor, Richard (father of Zachary), 1849
Taylor, Richard (pioneer): Taylorsville named for, 1748
Taylor, Sarah Knox, 1724, 1744, 1849
Taylor, William (Anderson Co.), 1430
Taylor, William (Jefferson Co.), 2007
Taylor, William (Kenton Co.), 1709
Taylor, William B., 830
Taylor, William Sylvester, 661, 1650, 1709, 1781
Taylor, Zachary: 835, 938, 1110, 1154, 1194, 1653, 1744; burial site, 1412; county named for, 995; home of, 111, 1849
Taylor County: naming of, 995
Taylorsville, 1748
Teater, Earl, 1470
Tebb's Bend: Battle of, 601, 706
Tecumseh, 250, 1181
Temperance movement, 1979. See also Prohibition
Temple Israel (Paducah), 1058
Templin, Rev. Terah, 1097
Tennessee Rolling Mills, 1380, 1423
Tennessee Valley Authority, 1107-1108, 1647-1648, 1768
Terrell (Terrill), Edward, 505, 1129
Terry, A. H., 1594
Terry, B. F., 1504
Tetterton, Thomas, 1735
Tevis, Eliza Curtis Hundley, 1988
Tevis, Julia A., 971
Texas: annexation of, 772, 829, 1105
Texas Revolution, 964
Thames: Battle of, 96, 185,

250, 507, 982, 1067, 1125, 1139, 1168, 1403, 1472, 1641, 1878, 2021

Thanksgiving: first in Kentucky, 809, 1325

"That Lucky Old Sun" (song), 1836

Thien, Wenceslaus, 1460

35th Regiment Ky. Volunteer Mounted Infantry, 830

Thomas, Elisha, 1481

Thomas, George H., 553, 863, 986, 1515

Thomas, Hardin, 1468

Thomas, Jack, 1634

Thomas, James, 1371

Thomas, James, Sr., 1375, 1892

Thomas, John C., 1829

Thomas, Mary, 2064

Thomas, Morris, 2043

Thomas, Preston, 2043

Thomas, William, 2064

Thompkins, Henry, 1847

Thompkins, James, 1847

Thompson, Rev. Albert J., 1106, 1682

Thompson, Col. Albert P., 828, 963

Thompson, Catlett W., 1895

Thompson, Ed Porter, 1200

Thompson, Hugh, 1914

Thompson, James, 1371

Thompson, John (Jefferson Co.), 2007

Thompson, John (Washington Co.), 1446

Thompson, John T., 1706

Thomson, Rev. A. J., 1526

Thread That Runs So True, The (Stuart), 1808, 1814

Three Forks, 1651

Three Springs, 1792

Threshing Rock, Old, 1293

Thruston, Algernon S., 1843

Thruston, Charles Mynn, 1843

Thruston, John, 1818, 2007

Thunder, Chief, 1525

Tick Creek Massacre, 1088

Tiffany's, 1820

Tilghman, Lloyd: 866; home of, 939; statue, 1043

Timberlake, C. L., 1469

Timberlake, Joseph, 1190

Timberlake, William Thornton,

1626

Timber Tunnel, 900

Tinsley, Rev. Thomas, 1530

Tinsley, Wilburn, 1266

Tippecanoe: Battle of, 826, 831, 845, 883, 954, 1158, 1285

Titus, John B., 214

Tobacco, 145, 861, 1786, 1795, 1948, 1985

Tobin, Lawrence: home of, 819

Tocqueville, Alexis de, 1681

Todd, Emilie, 833, 1101, 1783

Todd, John: 1435, 1554; county named for, 800

Todd, Levi: 1483; home of, 1001; Station, 1783

Todd, Mary. See Lincoln, Mary Todd

Todd, Robert, 1774

Todd, Robert S.: 833, 1999; father of Mary Todd Lincoln, 1999

Todd, Thomas S.: home of, 123, 1323

Todd County: naming of, 800

Todd House: home of Mary Todd Lincoln, 11

Tollgate: first in Kentucky, 723

Tollgate House: Nicholas County, 1353; Woodford County, 1649

Tolliver, Craig, 1933

Tolliver, Floyd, 1933

Tombstones, Rare, 710

Tomlinson, Joseph S., 750

"Tommygun": inventor of, 1706

Tompkins, Daniel: town named for, 1093

Tompkinsville: naming of, 1093

Tornadoes, 1652, 1689-1690

Townsend, William H., 1783, 2029

Town Spring (Somerset), 1607

Trabue, Daniel, 1782

Trail of Tears, 142, 1042, 1097, 1675

Transylvania: 1406, 1520; Company, 66, 113, 717, 849, 1206, 1443, 1577; Convention, 1435; Medical Hall, 1445; Medical School, 1447, 1480, 1595, 1628; Pavilion,

1549; Seminary, 844, 928-929, 974, 1624; University, 4, 65, 86, 125, 790, 816, 945, 1001, 1110, 1202, 1406, 1480, 1613, 1708, 1809, 1864, 1875, 1888, 1910

Trappist-Cistercians, 168

Trappists, 913, 2004

Traveler's Rest: home of Isaac Shelby, 95

Traveling (Travelling) Church, 25, 893, 1617, 1636

Travers Stakes, 1215, 2040

Travis, Merle, 1605

Treasurer, United States, 211

Tree: famous tree in Monroe County, 1394; magnificent pin oak (Lewis County), 1393; sassafras (Owensboro), 1192

Triangular Jog (Simpson County), 1850

Tribune (Benton), 1749

"Tribute to a Dog": oration by George Graham Vest, 1436

Trigg, Stephen: county named for, 1159

Trigg County: court, 1838; creation of, 1892; early schoolhouse in, 1840; naming of, 1159

Trigg Furnace, 1380

Trimble, David, 975, 1009

Trimble, John, 975

Trimble, Lawrence, 1969

Trimble, Robert: 1824; county named for, 765

Trimble County: jail in, 1822; naming of, 765

Trinity Episcopal Church (Boyle County), 1442

Trinity Episcopal Church (Kenton County), 1527

Trinity Episcopal Church (Owensboro), 1500

Triplett, Mrs., 1495

Triplett, Philip, 883

Triplett, Robert: first coal by rail, 743

Triplett, Robert S., 1436

Tripoli: Battle of Derne, 1465, 1940

Troutman, John, 1078

Troye, Edward, 1934

True American, 533

Truman, Harry S., 1112, 1768,

1856, 1960, 2033
Tuberculosis, 1503, 1815, 1876
Tubman, Emily T., 1710
Tullis, Bishop E. L., 1476
Turner, Oscar, 1969
Twain, Mark. *See* Clemens, Samuel Langhorne
28th Infantry Regiment: organizer of, 940
Twitty, William, 77
Twyman, Isham R., 1115
Twyman, Luska Joseph, 2019
Tyler, Edward, 1907
Tyler, Edward III, 1907
Tyler, John, 1787
Tyler, Moses, 1891, 1907
Tyler, Robert (Jefferson County), 1907
Tyler, Robert (Shelby County), 1088
Tyler, Will, 100
Tyler, William, 1907
Tyler Settlement (Jefferson County), 1907
"U-2 Incident," 1732
"Uncle Rambo" (James Tandy Ellis character), 1291
"Uncle Tom": Josiah Henson, 1241
Uncle Tom's Cabin (Stowe), 1070, 1241
Underground Railroad, 121, 1099
Underwood, W. T., 1924
Underwood Furnace, 1348
Union Agricultural and Mechanical Fair, 742
Union army: Camp Nelson National Cemetery, 1610, 1825; Camp Dick Robinson, 1750; Camp Nelson, 1515; Civil War Drilling Camp, 1631
Union Church of Christ (Berea), 1767
Union City, Tennessee: federal garrison captured, 1408
Union College: 1811; Centennial Hall, 2054; Classroom Building, 2054; Soldiers and Sailors Memorial Gymnasium, 2054; Speed Hall, 2054
Union County: naming of, 1250
Union Memorial, 215

Union Station (Owensboro), 1746
United Society of Believers in Christ's Second Appearance, 1481
United States (steamboat), 720
United States: Army, 2046; Constitution, 1499; Corps of Engineers, 1108, 1890; flag, 1465; Military Academy, 124, 1479, 1646, 1706; Naval Academy, 1479, 1564, 1612; Steel Corporation, 1777, 1803; Supreme Court, 1839; Philippines, 2019; Co. E, 5th Regimental Combat Team, 2033
Unity Church-The United Church of Christ, 1146
Universalist Church, Consolation, 1625
University of Kentucky: admissions, 2012; Agricultural Experiment Station, 2012; basketball, 2070; Henry Stites Barker, 2070; Blanding Tower, 2011; Dean of Women (Sarah Blanding), 2011; Don Carlos Buell, 2070; Chemistry Department, 2012; College of Agriculture, 2009; College of Law, 2012, 2029; Experiment Station, 2009; extension center in northern Kentucky, 1730; Gillis Building, 2012; John T. Scopes, 1698; Lyman T. Johnson, 2022; Maxwell Place, 2069; Medical Center, 1900, 1984; Miller Hall, 1953; radio broadcasting by, 1966; registrar, 2012; Scovell Hall, 2009; Thomas Hunt Morgan, 1714; Student Health Services Infirmary, 2012
University of Louisville: 541, 1629, 1661, 2007-2008; Academic Department, 1994; Law School, 1880, 2006; Medical College, 1994; Medical Department, 1737; Louisville Municipal College, 2020
Unsell, Abraham, Jr., 1735

Unsell, Frederick, 1735
Unsell, Henry, 1735
Upper Benson Church (Franklin County), 595
Upper Blue Licks, 143, 856, 1048
Upper Donaldson School, 1832
Upset (horse), 1635
Ursuline College, 1680
Vacation Guide (Hines), 1831
Vallandingham's barn: Civil War recruiting camp, 564
Valley Forge, Pennsylvania, 140, 1608, 1683
Valley View Ferry, 1378
Vance, Jim, 2068
VanderMeer, Nola, 1289
VanderMeer, Samuel, 1289
Van Meter, Jacob, Sr.: grave of, 1494
Van Wyck, S. M., 615
"Varmintrace," 142
Varmint Trace, 1916
Vassar College, 2011
Vaucluse: Jacob Yoder home, 1699
Vaughn, Larkin, 550
Venable, John W., 1690
Versailles: naming of, 1221, 1921
Versailles (horse), 649
Versailles Peace Conference, 1718
Vest, George Graham: 1436; home, 123, 1743
Vest-Lindsey House, 1743
Vice presidents born in Kentucky, 680, 739-741, 1742
Vietnam War, 1589, 1869, 2044, 2046
Vincennes, 1843
Vinson, Frederick M.: birthplace of, 636
Virgin, Brice, 574
Virgin, Jeremiah, 574
Virgin, Lucy, 574
Virginia General Assembly, 103, 554, 1668
Virginia-Monitor engagement, 1037
Volk, Rev. Paul Joseph, 907
Wadesboro, 200, 1263
Wadlington, Ferdinand, 1838
Wainscott, George, 722, 725
Wait, Cyrenius: first raw silk

produced by, 1212
Walcott Covered Bridge (The White Bridge), 1565
Walker, George, 1372
Walker, John W., 1794
Walker, Lizzie, 1824
Walker, Solomon, 1806
Walker, Thomas: 1126, 1850, 2045; expeditions of, 697, 898, 903, 1126, 1176, 1254; first cabin in Kentucky, 72, 898; grandson, Joshua Fry Bell, 198; Perryville founder, 1284
Walker, William, Sr., 1992
Walker foxhounds, 1794
Wallace, Caleb: law office, 1708
Wallace, Charles: home of, 1745
Wallace, Lew, 546, 829, 938
Waller, Edward, 68
Waller, Frank, 1959
Waller, James, 1971
Waller, John, 68
Waller, J. S., 1971
Waller, Sibbie, 1959
Wallsend Mine, 1272
Walnut Hill Presbyterian Church (Fayette County), 1483
Walters, Alexander, 1771
Walters, John: Indian fighter grave, 1114
Walton, Matthew: 853-854, 1446; home of, 933
War Admiral (horse), 1215, 1635
Ward, Charles, 1696
Ward, David L. (Carter County), 1148
Ward, David L. (Jefferson County), 1818
Ward, James (Martin County), 729
Ward, James (Mason County), 1696
Ward, John (Frankfort): church founder, 1464
Ward, John (Lexington): cholera victim, 1399
Ward, Junius R., 1734
Ward, Sallie, 1734
Ward, William, 1143
Ward, William B.: grave of, 729

Ward, William T., 603, 1082, 1109
Ward Hall: home of Junius R. Ward, 1734
Warfield, John, 726
Warfield: Civil War in, 726
War Fork Creek, 697
Waring, John, 1015
Waring, Thomas, 1529
Warinner, Ed P.: birthplace of, 1310
War of 1812: 599, 714-715, 802, 808-809, 869, 871, 875, 995, 1067, 1114, 1194, 1205, 1238, 1328, 1342, 1409, 1412, 1516, 1534, 1548, 1595, 1609, 1619, 1626, 1652, 1888, 1896, 1975, 2028; Battle of Fort Meigs, 836; Battle of Lake Erie, 1196, 1249, 1284; Battle of New Orleans, 993; Battle of River Raisin, 43, 507-508, 760, 797, 840, 845, 869, 895, 912, 916, 918, 1088; Battle of the Thames, 1125, 1168, 1403, 1472, 1641, 1878, 2021; Battle of Tippecanoe, 831, 1285; Christopher Riffe, 250; George Madison, 1896; Isaac Shelby, 1318; James Taylor, 1351; Leestown, 103, 1595, 1619; Matthew H. Jouett, 1888; Newport in, 507; Newport Barracks, 599; Saltpeter Cave, 209; Sportsman's Hill, 96
Warren, Joseph: county named for, 987
Warren, Robert Penn, 1879, 1977
Warren County: Civil War officers from, 1201; naming of, 987
Warrington, 1838
Warrior's Path, 84, 697, 1274, 1600
Warwick, 1751
Washburn, Cornelius, 1941
Washington, Booker T., 2049
Washington, George: 114, 140, 574, 717, 774, 1239, 1314, 1388, 1404, 1534, 1623, 1653, 1683; aide-de-camp, 873; bodyguard, 1190,

1608; county named for, 853-854; land, 212; oath administered to, 801
Washington, Lucy Payne, 1323
Washington, Kentucky, 144
Washington County: 4-H camp in, 1292; naming of, 853-854
"Washington Guards," 1589
Washington Historic District, 1696
Washington Street Missionary Baptist Church (Paducah), 1276
Waters, Philemon, 1339
Wathen, Henry Hudson, 1667
Watkins, Elizabeth, 1798
Watkins, Henry, 1798
Watkins Tavern, 1798
Watson, John C., 123
Watson, Ruth E., 1152
Watson, Thomas Tennessee, 1326, 1340, 1357, 1423
Watterson, Henry: 1654, 1665, 1719, 1724; home of, 1719
Watts Furnaces, 1227, 1402
Watts Steel and Iron Syndicate, Ltd., 1227, 1402
Waveland: Joseph Bryan home, 1280
Wayne, Anthony: 837, 912, 1782, 1828, 1878; Battle of Fallen Timbers, 912, 1088, 1128; county named for, 804
Wayne County: naming of, 804
WBKY/WUKY Radio, 1966
Weapons, Automatic, 1706, 2044
Weaver, Sylvester, 1992
Webb, Rev. Charles, 1457
Webb, Lewis, 1735
Webber, Frederick, 1739
Webbville, 2056
Weber/Ritte Building (Covington), 1939
Webster, Daniel: 1429, 1694; county named for, 783; in Frankfort, 1154
Webster, Delia: petticoat abolitionist, 1099, 1822
Webster County: N. B. Forrest in, 617; naming of, 783
Weeden, H. C., 1992

Weir, James, 1609
Weir, Thomas B., 2030
Welby, Amelia B., 1654
Well, Sulphur (Metcalfe Co.), 1895
Wells, Edmund, 1991
Wells, George, 1693, 1949
Wells, Rainey T., 1427, 1945
Wells, T. N., 1611
Wells Mill (settlement), 1991
Welsh, Rev. James, 935
Wentworth, W. A., 1420
Wernwag, Lewis V., 1513
Wesley, Silas, 1305
West, Edward, 1556
West, Isaac, 1275
West, L. A., 1922
Western Baptist Theological Institute, 1484
Western Kentucky University, 1360, 1417-1418, 2052
Western Military Academy, 122
Western Military Asylum, 551
Western Military Institute, 798
West Kentucky Industrial College, 1469
West Liberty, 512,1991
West-Metcalfe House, 1275
Westminster United Presbyterian Church (Paducah), 1431
Weston: town incorporated, 1298
West Point, 649, 862, 866, 939, 986, 1273, 1479, 1646, 1706, 1758
Westport, 909
West Side School (Harrodsburg), 2050
Westwood: home of John Edwards, 1722
Wharton, John A. 553
WHAS Radio, 1966
Wheeler, Charles K., 1030, 1969
Wheeler, Joseph, 749
Wheelmen's Bench (Ruff Memorial), 1997
Whelan, Father Charles Maurice, 913
Whiskey Rebellion, 815
Whitaker, Aquilla, 1544
Whitaker, John, 1544
White, Gilbert, 1779
White, Leonard, 1348

White, Minor, 1983
White, William: duel, 611
White, Rev. Willis, 1611
White Hall: home of Cassius M. Clay, 533, 1485
Whitehaven: home of Edward Anderson, 1754
Whitehouse, Henry, 2040
White Oak Springs, 1577
Whitestone, Henry, 1229, 1704
Whitfield, Ed, 1969
Whiting, Ruggles, 949
Whitley, William: 1140, 1622; county and town named for, 982, 1067; home of, 96, 982
Whitley County: naming of, 982, 1067
Whitman, Walt, 1681
W-Hollow (Greenup County), 1808, 1814
Wickland: home of three governors, 1604
Wickliffe, Arrington, 1735
Wickliffe, Charles A.: 1604, 1631; grandson of, 1604; son of, 1604
Wickliffe, Moses, 1666
Wickliffe, Nancy, 1673
Wickliffe, Robert C.: governor of Louisiana, 1604
Wickliffe: becomes county seat, 1374
Wildcat Mountain: Battle of, 684
Wilder, J. B., 2040
Wilder, John T., 119
Wilderness Revival, 1530
Wilderness Road, 54-55, 113, 219, 576, 723, 927, 981-982, 1234, 1311, 1339, 1383, 1426, 1600, 1622, 1757, 1944, 2045
Wiley, Jenny, 735
Wilkins, Charles, 949, 1080
Wilkinson, James, 105-106, 1205, 1652; Love House, 1182
Willard, Frances E., 1872
Willard: railroad at, 2056
Willett, Mother Aloysius, 907
Willett, Samuel, 1682
William Grant School (Newport), 2071
Williams, Cratis, 1837

Williams, David J., 1578
Williams, James: town named for, 925
Williams, John (Magoffin Co.), 202
Williams, John (Mason Co.), 2001
Williams, Kidd, 1982
Williams, Mason H. P., 1688
Williams, Samuel, 1674
Williams, Thomas (Estill County), 1922
Williams, Thomas (Mason County), 138
Williamsburg (Mason County), 2001
Williamsburg (Owen County), 925. See also Monterey
Williamsburg (Whitley County): Institute, 1837; naming of, 1067
Williams Rapid Fire Gun, 902
Williamstown: naming of, 942; raid, 188
Willich, August, 656, 1504
Willingham, T. W., 1927
Willis, Britton, 1735
Willis, Simeon, 1815
Willkie, Wendell, 1763
Willson, Augustus E., 1779, 1786
Wilmington: 840, 916, 918, 970; courthouse, 1027
Wilson, Atwood S., 1992
Wilson, Caroline Bullitt, 1229
Wilson, F. S., 1671
Wilson, Hugh, 1457
Wilson, John C.: Lookout Mountain hero, 639
Wilson, Mary Towles Sasseen, 191
Wilson, Rev. Robert, 1416, 1696
Wilson, Rev. Robert T., 1106
Wilson, Rev. S. T., 1095
Wilson, Father Thomas, 941
Wilson, Thomas Edward, 1229
Wilson, Tom, 1214
Wilson, W. B., 2043
Wilson, Woodrow, 668, 1880
Wine: produced in Bracken County, 1213
Wing, Charles, 1609
Wing, Nancy, 1609
Wing Commander (horse),

1470

Winlock, Joseph, 1409

Winn, Matt, 1885

Winnfield Cottage, 1646

Wisconsin Steel Coal Company, 1995

Wise, Isaac M., 1923

Witcher, V. A., 726

Withers, James, 572

Withers, William T., 1447

Witherspoon, J. F., 1331

Witherspoon College, 682

Withrow, J. T., 1009

WLS Radio, 2026

Wolfe, James, 1386

Wolfe, Nathaniel: county named for, 1256

Wolfe County: naming of, 1256

Wolford, Frank L.: 888, 1486, 1489; birthplace of, 604; First Kentucky Cavalry, 684

Wolfram, Anna E., 1351

Womack, W. A., 1585

Woman suffrage, 1800, 1872, 1876

Women's Army Corps, 1970

Women's Christian Temperance Union, 1872

Women's Club Hospital Company, 2025

Wood, Alvin, 1474

Wood, Bartholomew, 1268

Wood, H. C., 1924

Wood, William (Clinton County), 1516

Wood, William (Mason County), 1696

Woodfill, Samuel, 990

Woodford, William: county named for, 1221

Woodford County: Civil War generals born in, 649, 659; courthouse, 1847; Delany's Ferry, 1774; Historical Society, 1649; naming of, 1221; Petersburg, 1774

Woodlawn: home of Philip Buckner, 1502

Woodlawn Race Course, 1820

Woodlawn Vase, 1820

Woods, James, 1562

Woods, Samuel, 1562

Woodyard, Thomas Washington, 1479

Wooldridge, D. M., 1625

Wooldridge, Edmund Tyler, 1479

Wooldridge, Henry, 1288

Wooldridge Monuments, 1288

Woolfolk, George, 1036

Works Progress Administration, 1377, 2070

World Series, 1627

World's Fair and Exposition (1893-94), 1394

World War I: 631, 668, 1291, 1322, 1382, 1401, 1456, 1493, 1589, 1610, 1676, 1692, 1719, 1769, 1803, 1844, 1856, 1929; Breathitt County Volunteers, 904; Camp Taylor, 1663; Director of Arsenals, 1706; first American killed in, 664, 1199; Samuel Woodfill, 990

World War II: 1236, 1269, 1419, 1424, 1589, 1610, 1612, 1672, 1731, 1762, 1769, 1869, 1967, 1970, 2019, 2037, 2044; first U. S. Armored Forces casualty, 2037; Bowman Field–East, 1901; destroyer named for Richard Caswell Saufley, 1564; Doolittle's Raid, 1727; Guadalcanal, 1322; Iwo Jima hero, 855; Kentucky hemp in, 1163-1164, 1279, 1315, 1319-1320, 1362

Worthington, J. W., 1659

Worthington, William, 1735, 1812

Worthley, Sam, 1054

Wright, Frank Lloyd, 1726

Wright, Horatio G., 1917

Wright, James, 1376

Wright, W. H., 1662

Writers. See Individual Names

Wroe, Susannah, 1722

WSM Radio, 2026

Wurts, George, 1016, 1019

Wurts, Samuel, 1016, 1019

Wyandot Indians: and Estill's Defeat, 153, 1219; at Upper Blue Licks, 856; language of, 985

Xaverian Brothers, 1897

YMCA, 1662-1663

YWCA, 1473

Yandell, Enid, 1997

Yates, Richard, 746

Yates, W. R., 1659

Yatesville Covered Bridge, 1583

Yellow Banks. See Owensboro

Yellow Fever Epidemic, 131

Yellow House: early site of school for deaf, 197

Yellowstone National Park, 1997

Yocum, Isaiah, 1833

Yocum, Kate, 1833

Yoder, Jacob: home of, 1699; grave of, 1699

"You Go To My Head" (song), 1836

Young, Bennett H., 532

Young, Charles: birthplace of, 124

Young, Dan, 1131

Young, Harry, 1759

Young, James, 1763

Young, John (Boyd County), 1131

Young, John (Greenup County), 1973

Young, Laurence, 1759

Young, Paul Everett, Sr., 1345

Young, Whitney M., Jr., 1419

Young, Whitney M., Sr., 1419, 1930

Young, William, 1735

Young Ladies School, Harrodsburg, 1173

Youngland: home of Bennett H. Young, 532

Young Memorial Park (Logan County), 1345

Young's Inn, 1763

Young's Salt Works, 151

Zedwitz, Baron von, 1676

Zeigler, Rev. Jesse R.: home of, 1726

Zimmerman, Andrew, 702

Zimmerman, Matthew, 1735

Zion Baptist Church (Louisville), 1657

Zollicoffer, Felix: 75, 863, 1275, 1301, 1600, 1920; Camp Wildcat, 1919; Civil War actions, 518

"Zollie Tree," 1920